Public Speaking and Civic Engagement

Second Edition

J. Michael Hogan
Penn State University

Patricia Hayes Andrews
Indiana University

James R. Andrews
Indiana University

Glen Williams
Southeast Missouri State University

Allyn & Bacon
Boston Columbus Indianapolis New York San Francisco Upper Saddle River
Amsterdam Cape Town Dubai London Madrid Milan Munich Paris Montréal Toronto
Delhi Mexico City São Paulo Sydney Hong Kong Seoul Singapore Taipei Tokyo

Editor-in-Chief, Communication: Karon Bowers
Editorial Assistants: Stephanie Chaisson and Megan Sweeney
Development Manager: David Kear
Assistant Editor: Corey Kahn
Associate Development Editor: Angela Pickard
Media Producer: Megan Higginbotham
Marketing Manager: Blair Tuckman
Project Manager: Anne Ricigliano
Project Coordination, Text Design, and Electronic Page Makeup: Elm Street Publishing Services
Composition: Integra Software Services Pvt. Ltd.
Cover Design Manager: Anne Nieglos
Cover Designer: Ilze Lemesis
Cover Photo: Ellen M. Banner
Photo Researcher: Pearson Image Management System/Sheila Norman
Image Permission Coordinator: Annette Linder
Manufacturing Manager: Mary Ann Gloriande
Printer and Binder: Quebecor World/Taunton
Cover Printer: Lehigh-Phoenix Color/Hagerstown

Library of Congress Cataloging-in-Publication Data

Public speaking and civic engagement / J. Michael Hogan ... [et al.].—2nd ed.
p. cm.
Includes bibliographical references and index.
ISBN-13: 978-0-205-74479-4 (alk. paper)
ISBN-10: 0-205-74479-6 (alk. paper)
1. Public speaking. 2. Persuasion (Rhetoric) I. Hogan, J. Michael
PN4129.15.P832 2010
808.5'1—dc22 2010009669

Allyn & Bacon
is an imprint of

PEARSON

www.pearsonhighered.com

1 2 3 4 5 6 7 8 9 10—QWT—13 12 11 10

ISBN-13: 978-0-205-74479-4
ISBN-10: 0-205-74479-6

BRIEF CONTENTS

CONTENTS

PREFACE

A lot has happened since the first edition of *Public Speaking and Civic Engagement.* In 2008, Mitt Romney became the first Mormon to compete seriously for the Republican presidential nomination, while Hillary Clinton nearly became the first woman to head a major party's presidential ticket. In November, of course, we witnessed a historic event: the election of the first African-American president of the United States. The past few years also have brought new problems and challenges, including an escalating war in Afghanistan and the worst economic downturn since the Great Depression. Meanwhile, we continue to debate health care reform, educational policy, environmental protection, immigration, and countless other difficult issues. As citizens in a democracy, we have a responsibility to participate in these discussions, and that means *communicating* with others—sharing our insights and ideas, listening to those whose opinions differ from our own, and deliberating with our fellow citizens. This book can help you become a better communicator *and* a better citizen. It will help you understand your rights and responsibilities as a citizen in a democracy.

OUR APPROACH AND THEMES

Three convictions continue to guide our approach to *Public Speaking and Civic Engagement*:

- We believe that public speaking is not just a valuable personal skill but an important part of engaged citizenship in a democracy. You will deliver many speeches in your life, but the most important will be those you deliver as a citizen.
- We approach public speaking as a collaborative partnership between the speaker and the audience. No speaker can succeed alone—the audience is crucial to the planning, delivery, and outcome of the speech.
- We view public speaking as more than a set of performance skills. Truly successful speakers have ideas or information worth communicating. They think critically and reason soundly, and they are not just effective speakers, but also careful and critical listeners, engaged citizens, and ethical human beings.

The Speaker as Citizen

Preparing a classroom speech should be no different from planning a speech for a business conference or a town hall meeting. The classroom is a public space, and your fellow students are citizens. You should treat a speech to your classmates as seriously as you would a speech to any other group of co-workers or citizens.

In treating public speaking as a type of civic engagement, this book encourages you to develop an ethic of active participation. It urges you to read widely and reflectively, and it holds you responsible for becoming well informed about your topic. As you begin to seek out opportunities to speak in public, you will learn to listen critically yet also to respond in a spirit of mutual respect and cooperation. You will learn to speak persuasively, but you also will be encouraged to join *with* your fellow citizens in a spirit of inquiry and common cause. As you work with others to find solutions to our common problems, you will come to understand what it means to deliberate "in good faith."

The emphasis on civic engagement makes this book different from many public speaking books. Some books treat public speaking as a tool of personal success—a skill that you need to "beat the competition" or climb the ladder of success. We approach public speaking as something more than that. Emphasizing ethical and civic concerns, we view public speaking as an essential tool of democratic citizenship. Protected by the First Amendment to our Constitution, our right to free speech distinguishes us from citizens in totalitarian states and empowers us to govern ourselves. In this book, speech is treated as a means for defining our purposes and identity as a nation, discussing the choices we face, and resolving the differences and disagreements among us. Even ceremonial speeches are treated as important expressions of our democratic culture and traditions. Your course in public speaking will contribute to your personal and professional success. But the best reason to study public speaking is that it will help you become a better citizen. By becoming a better speaker, you will be better prepared to participate in civic life.

The Speaker-Audience Partnership

This book does not treat the audience as something to be changed or manipulated, but rather as an active partner in the communicative process. From the earliest stages of planning a speech to the question-and-answer period that may follow, your listeners will be important to your success. You need to consider your listeners' needs and interests in tandem with your own. You need to ask these questions: What are my listeners' priorities and concerns? How can I persuasively advance my own ideas while still respecting their values and beliefs? Am I open to being influenced by my audience even as I try to persuade them? What can I do to promote a genuine spirit of democratic deliberation in which my audience and I have a shared interest in finding common ground?

When considering your audience, it is important to recognize that our society is now more diverse than ever before. Your audience may consist of people of all genders, races, and religions. It may even include people from other parts of the world. At the very least, your audience will have widely varying interests and values and hold differing political or religious opinions. Respecting this diversity is crucial to connecting with your audience. In this book, we recognize the challenges of communicating in an increasingly diverse society, yet we also stress the need for people to come together in a spirit of dialogue and collaboration. If we hope to find solutions to our common problems, we need to communicate effectively and work together to realize our shared goals.

Respecting the speaker-listener partnership is more than a practical necessity; it is an ethical obligation. Ethical speakers keep in touch with the audience's needs, concerns, and welfare, even as they pursue their own purposes in speaking. In *Public Speaking and Civic Engagement*, we treat the speaker-listener partnership as both a practical necessity and an ethical responsibility.

The Citizen-Critic

By studying public speaking, you will become not only a better speaker, but also a more careful and engaged listener—one who pays close attention when other people speak and thinks carefully about what they are saying. In our mass-mediated society, we can point to any number of speakers who try to fool the public with a "slick" delivery or deceptive, even manipulative speeches. As a student of public speaking, you will learn to recognize and resist the techniques of these demagogues and propagandists. You will learn to be a more critical consumer in the "marketplace of ideas."

Our democracy rests on the assumption that ordinary citizens are smart enough to govern themselves. Yet it is not always easy to distinguish between sound, well-reasoned arguments and speeches carefully designed to distract or mislead us. Part of your responsibility as a citizen is to learn *how* to distinguish between good and bad arguments, between speeches that contribute something valuable to public discussion and those that serve only the selfish interests of the speaker. By studying public speaking, you will learn to listen carefully and think critically about the speeches you hear. You will learn how to evaluate the quality of a speaker's evidence and reasoning. You will study ethical principles that have been part of the study of speech for centuries, and you will become familiar with famous speeches in history that both promoted and violated those principles. In short, you will become a "citizen-critic"—a careful and informed listener who holds all who speak in public to high intellectual and ethical standards.

WHAT'S NEW IN THE SECOND EDITION?

The second edition of *Public Speaking and Civic Engagement* includes a number of new features and updates, and the book as a whole has been rewritten in a more concise, more accessible style. Although the basic principles of effective speaking remain the same, we have revised and expanded our coverage of a number of important topics, including communication apprehension and critical listening. We also have updated our examples, statistics, and other types of information throughout the book, and we have included more material from actual student speeches. At the same time, we cut less useful or outdated material and eliminated some redundancies in the first edition. The result is a shorter, more concise book, yet one still packed with practical guidance and the latest information about the political, cultural, and technological developments that affect public speaking.

Although the basic structure of the book remains the same, users of the first edition will notice a number of changes and additions in each chapter. These include the following:

CHAPTER 1:

- A more concise discussion of the challenges of democratic citizenship, with updated information about civic participation in the United States, including recent signs of civic renewal.
- New examples from the 2008 presidential election, the Bernard Madoff scandal, and other recent events.
- An updated discussion of the classical tradition, including a new reference to Isocrates,

who stressed the civic purposes of public speaking.
- New annotations for the sample speech by Granny D, focusing on the unique rhetorical qualities of the speech.

Chapter 2:

- A streamlined and updated discussion of the ethical responsibilities of democratic citizenship, including the latest information on how young people define what it means to be a "good citizen."
- New examples and new information about the political attitudes and behaviors of young people.
- A new annotated speech by Secretary of State Hillary Clinton, delivered at the National Prayer Breakfast in Washington, D.C.

Chapter 3:

- A new *Focus on Civic Engagement* about a student speakers bureau at a small college in Wisconsin.
- An expanded section on factors that contribute to communication apprehension, along with a new personal report of communication apprehension for students to complete.
- A new *Highlighting Organization* feature outlining a speech about Internet voting.
- A new *Focus on Civic Engagement* about a young man who confronted his own racial prejudices.

Chapter 4:

- A new section on listening as a multistep process.
- A new *Highlighting Listening and Leadership* feature with statements from both experts and prominent business and political leaders on the importance of listening.
- An extensive revision of the material on stereotyping, including a new feature about *Highlighting Stereotypes in the Media*.

Chapter 5:

- An expanded discussion of the importance of race and ethnicity in audience analysis.
- A new *Focus on Civic Engagement* about searching for common ground.
- A new *Focus on Civic Engagement* featuring President Obama on the importance of public service.
- A new annotated speech by Barack Obama: his controversial 2009 commencement address at the University of Notre Dame.

Chapter 6:

- More emphasis on brainstorming topics of public concern.
- A revised discussion of how to conduct a self-inventory to discover topics for informative and persuasive speeches.
- A new discussion of speaking about highly emotional topics.

Chapter 7:

- Updated coverage of note-taking during research, including electronic means of managing notes.
- A reorganized discussion of research methods, placing more emphasis on electronic databases and other online sources.
- A new discussion of gathering information via online networking.
- Expanded coverage of citing sources of quoted and paraphrased materials in speeches.

Chapter 8:

- An expanded section on critical thinking.
- A new *Highlighting Specific Examples* feature about why America still needs local newspapers.
- A new *Highlighting Examples and Statistics* feature showing how statistics can be brought to life by a striking example.
- A new annotated speech by Dr. Robert Stone, a physician and health care reform advocate.

CHAPTER 9:

- New student examples to illustrate various organizational patterns and techniques for beginning and ending speeches.
- A new *Focus on Civic Engagement* illustrating the narrative organizational pattern with a personal story.
- An expanded discussion of the guidelines for organizing the main ideas of a speech, including new student examples.
- A revised discussion of "transitions as connectives," including advice on how to use rhetorical questions as transitional devices.
- New examples of introductory and concluding devices from speeches by former President Bill Clinton and J. K. Rowling, among others.

CHAPTER 10:

- An expanded discussion of bibliographic formats, including a new illustration of the MLA format.
- An updated *Focus on Civic Engagement* featuring a formal outline for a speech about job training for the poor.
- A new annotated formal outline, including a complete bibliography, from an actual student speech about autism.

CHAPTER 11:

- An extended discussion of the differences between written and oral style.
- A new discussion of language and influence with additional source citations.
- A new *Highlighting Language* feature with passages from John McCain's acceptance speech at the 2008 Republican National Convention.

CHAPTER 12:

- A new *Highlighting the Importance of a Good Voice* feature about vocal delivery, recounting Demosthenes' legendary efforts to improve his speaking voice.
- New material comparing different methods of delivery and new advice on how to handle the question-and-answer period following your speech.

CHAPTER 13:

- A new *Highlighting Visual Literacy* feature on how to think critically about images and the way they are used.
- Streamlined coverage providing a comprehensive yet concise overview of what speakers and listeners need to understand about visual support for ideas.
- Updated examples to reflect more recent events, including an illustration of how a graph with homicide rates may be misleading.
- New and updated examples of various types of presentational aids, reflecting the state of the art in new technologies.

CHAPTER 14:

- A revised and reorganized section on organizing the informative speech.
- A revised discussion of the chronological pattern of organization, illustrated with a new student speech about the women's suffrage movement.
- A new extended example of the categorical organizational pattern, featuring a student speech about a local nonprofit agency.
- A revised, more concise section about helping listeners learn.

CHAPTER 15:

- New examples of public controversies, including an extended example from the recent debate over the use of "enhanced interrogation techniques" in the War on Terror.
- New examples of ethos or credibility issues, including an analysis of former Illinois governor Rod Blagojevich's attempts to rebuild his ethos after his arrest on federal corruption charges.
- A new *Highlighting Credibility* feature with excerpts from Republican presidential candidate Mike Huckabee's speech to the 2008 Republican National Convention.

Chapter 16:

- Updated examples to illustrate the components of a complete argument, the various forms of reasoning, and the fallacies or errors of reasoning.
- A new annotated student speech about climate change.

Chapter 17:

- A clearer, more concise discussion of the differences between ceremonial and other types of speeches.
- Updated examples of the kinds of events and "everyday heroes" that inspire ceremonial speaking, including the example of "Sully" Sullenberger, the pilot who landed his crippled airliner on the Hudson River in January 2009.

Chapter 18:

- A new *Focus on Civic Engagement* about *The Exchange: A Marketplace of Student Ideas*, a program at the National Constitution Center that teaches high school students how to deliberate over controversial issues.
- An expanded discussion of town hall meetings, including reflections on the raucous town hall meetings on health care in the summer of 2009.
- A new section on leadership in group discussions and deliberation.
- A new *Highlighting the Written Record* feature about keeping written records of group meetings and deliberations.

SPECIAL FEATURES

Public Speaking and Civic Engagement offers a number of distinguishing features designed to make the book an engaging teaching and learning tool.

A Unique Approach

A strong introductory chapter establishes the unique framework of the book by highlighting the connections between public speaking and democratic citizenship. From the start, you will be encouraged to think of public speaking not just as a tool of personal success, but also as a way to serve others in a democratic society. A stand-alone chapter on ethics follows, reinforcing the theme that public speaking entails certain responsibilities beyond your personal interests: the responsibility to become well informed on your topic, for example, and to respect those who sincerely disagree with your views. The book includes chapters on all the topics typically addressed in a public speaking textbook, including communication apprehension, audience analysis, organization, and style. Yet throughout the book, the focus on civic engagement is sustained by an emphasis on the ethics as well as the techniques of public speaking and by historical and contemporary examples of both responsible and irresponsible speakers.

Among the unique chapters of the book are those discussing the various *types* of public speaking. Distinguishing persuasive from informative speaking in terms of the situations that "invite" persuasion, the book defines *public controversy* and discusses a speaker's *burden of proof* in various situations. It also discusses different ways to prove your claims and to make reasonable arguments based on sound evidence and reasoning. At the same time, it sustains a strong emphasis on the ethics of persuasion, distinguishing between responsible persuasion and the manipulative and deceptive techniques of the propagandist or demagogue. The book also offers the first serious treatment of ceremonial speaking as a mode of civic engagement and community building, and its chapter on communicating in groups focuses on town hall meetings and other deliberative forums. In these chapters and throughout the book, the emphasis is not only on how to prepare an effective speech, but also on the importance of being a committed and responsible speaker. That is what makes this book unique: it combines sound instruction in the techniques of public speaking with a sustained emphasis on the ethics of speech and the importance of public speaking and civic engagement in our democratic society.

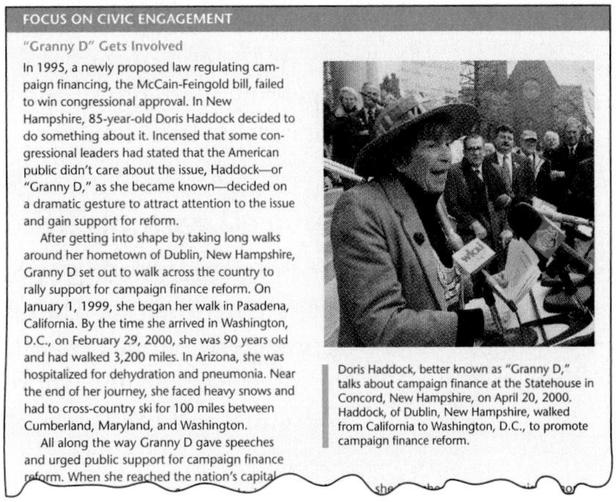
FOCUS ON CIVIC ENGAGEMENT

"Granny D" Gets Involved

In 1995, a newly proposed law regulating campaign financing, the McCain-Feingold bill, failed to win congressional approval. In New Hampshire, 85-year-old Doris Haddock decided to do something about it. Incensed that some congressional leaders had stated that the American public didn't care about the issue, Haddock—or "Granny D," as she became known—decided on a dramatic gesture to attract attention to the issue and gain support for reform.

After getting into shape by taking long walks around her hometown of Dublin, New Hampshire, Granny D set out to walk across the country to rally support for campaign finance reform. On January 1, 1999, she began her walk in Pasadena, California. By the time she arrived in Washington, D.C., on February 29, 2000, she was 90 years old and had walked 3,200 miles. In Arizona, she was hospitalized for dehydration and pneumonia. Near the end of her journey, she faced heavy snows and had to cross-country ski for 100 miles between Cumberland, Maryland, and Washington.

All along the way Granny D gave speeches and urged public support for campaign finance reform. When she reached the nation's capital

Doris Haddock, better known as "Granny D," talks about campaign finance at the Statehouse in Concord, New Hampshire, on April 20, 2000. Haddock, of Dublin, New Hampshire, walked from California to Washington, D.C., to promote campaign finance reform.

Focus on Civic Engagement

Most chapters include boxed special features showcasing real-world examples of politicians, celebrities, students, and ordinary citizens who have made a difference by speaking out or otherwise getting involved in the civic life of their community or their nation. These stories about real people—young and old, famous and not-so-famous—are designed both to illustrate course concepts and to inspire students to get involved themselves.

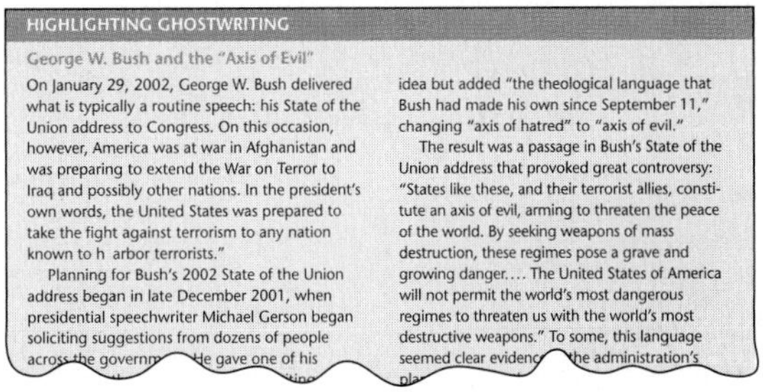
HIGHLIGHTING GHOSTWRITING

George W. Bush and the "Axis of Evil"

On January 29, 2002, George W. Bush delivered what is typically a routine speech: his State of the Union address to Congress. On this occasion, however, America was at war in Afghanistan and was preparing to extend the War on Terror to Iraq and possibly other nations. In the president's own words, the United States was prepared to take the fight against terrorism to any nation known to h arbor terrorists."

Planning for Bush's 2002 State of the Union address began in late December 2001, when presidential speechwriter Michael Gerson began soliciting suggestions from dozens of people across the govern... He gave one of his

idea but added "the theological language that Bush had made his own since September 11," changing "axis of hatred" to "axis of evil."

The result was a passage in Bush's State of the Union address that provoked great controversy: "States like these, and their terrorist allies, constitute an axis of evil, arming to threaten the peace of the world. By seeking weapons of mass destruction, these regimes pose a grave and growing danger.... The United States of America will not permit the world's most dangerous regimes to threaten us with the world's most destructive weapons." To some, this language seemed clear evidenc... the administration's

Highlighting Key Concepts

Extended examples of key concepts such as ethos, advocacy, visual literacy, critical listening, fallacies, ethics, and cultural diversity are illustrated through special "highlighting" features throughout the book.

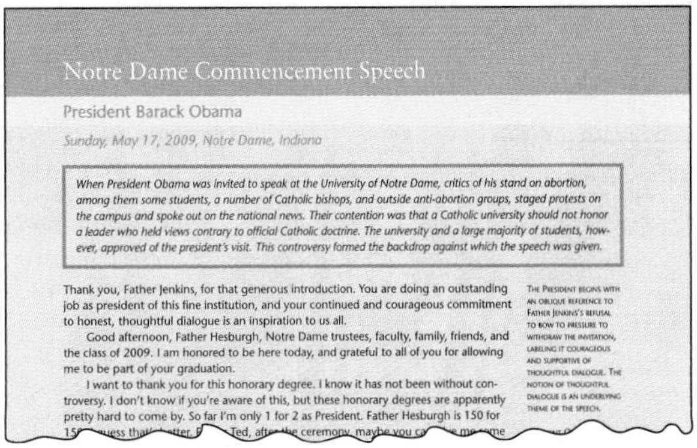
Notre Dame Commencement Speech

President Barack Obama

Sunday, May 17, 2009, Notre Dame, Indiana

When President Obama was invited to speak at the University of Notre Dame, critics of his stand on abortion, among them some students, a number of Catholic bishops, and outside anti-abortion groups, staged protests on the campus and spoke out on the national news. Their contention was that a Catholic university should not honor a leader who held views contrary to official Catholic doctrine. The university and a large majority of students, however, approved of the president's visit. This controversy formed the backdrop against which the speech was given.

Thank you, Father Jenkins, for that generous introduction. You are doing an outstanding job as president of this fine institution, and your continued and courageous commitment to honest, thoughtful dialogue is an inspiration to us all.

Good afternoon, Father Hesburgh, Notre Dame trustees, faculty, family, friends, and the class of 2009. I am honored to be here today, and grateful to all of you for allowing me to be part of your graduation.

I want to thank you for this honorary degree. I know it has not been without controversy. I don't know if you're aware of this, but these honorary degrees are apparently pretty hard to come by. So far I'm only 1 for 2 as President. Father Hesburgh is 150 for

THE PRESIDENT BEGINS WITH AN OBLIQUE REFERENCE TO FATHER JENKINS'S REFUSAL TO BOW TO PRESSURE TO WITHDRAW THE INVITATION, LABELING IT COURAGEOUS AND SUPPORTIVE OF THOUGHTFUL DIALOGUE. THE NOTION OF THOUGHTFUL DIALOGUE IS AN UNDERLYING THEME OF THE SPEECH.

Annotated Speeches

Nearly half of the book's chapters conclude with an annotated speech that offers critical commentary and analysis. Each speech deals with a substantive issue and provides a real-world illustration of civic engagement. The speakers include political figures, celebrities, students, and ordinary citizens, and the speeches cover a range of issues such as global climate change, health care reform, and the role of religion in politics.

Pedagogical Features in Each Chapter

Within the text, we provide a variety of pedagogical features that clarify and reinforce the material or summarize key points. Specifically, each chapter contains:

- A *Chapter Survey* to overview key topics addressed in the chapter.
- *Learning Objectives* to give students learning goals against which they can measure their personal progress.
- *Previews* to give readers a map of the material in each section of the chapter.
- *Real-world examples* to illustrate, highlight, and clarify principles discussed.
- A *Summary* to reiterate the chapter's core concepts.
- *Questions for Review and Reflection* to help students review the ideas presented in each chapter and to assist them in test preparation.

At the end of the book, a Glossary defines key terms and technical language appearing throughout the book. Another useful pedagogical tool, Questions for Application and Analysis, can be found in the Instructor's Resource Manual.

Service-Learning Resources

For those interested in approaching the course from a service-learning perspective, the Instructor's Manual includes a sample syllabus for a service-learning approach to public speaking. The manual also suggests activities and assignments for a service-learning approach to the course and provides a list of organizations, Web sites, and other resources on service learning.

RESOURCES IN PRINT AND ONLINE

Name of Supplement	Available in Print	Available Online	Instructor or Student Supplement	Description
Instructor's Resource Manual and Test Bank (ISBN: 0205717489)		✓	Instructor Supplement	Prepared by author Glen Williams of Southeast Missouri State University, with Bob Clubbs, this **Instructor's Manual** addresses such key topics as what it means to be a teacher, the defining qualities of effective teaching, course and lesson planning, teaching methods, testing and evaluation, the role of feedback, classroom management, and professional development. The Instructor's Manual also provides a chapter-by-chapter guide to the textbook and provides time-tested activities, sample syllabi, and class assignments. In addition, the **Test Bank** portion of the manual, also written by Glen Williams, contains numerous multiple choice and essay questions. The Test Bank provides questions that engage the entire cognitive domain, from the basics of recall and comprehension to application, analysis, and evaluation. This variety allows each instructor to create exams of varying types and differing degrees of difficulty. The multiple choice, short answer, and essay questions are rated on a scale of 1 to 3, making question selection easy. Answers for each question are given along with the page number where they can be found within the book. Available for download at www.pearsonhighered.com/irc (access code required).
MyTest (ISBN: 0205717586)		✓	Instructor Supplement	This flexible, online test-generating software includes all of the Test Bank questions, allowing instructors to create their own personalized exams, edit the existing test questions, and even add new questions. Other special features of this program include random generation of test questions, creation of alternate versions of the same test, scrambling of question sequence, and test preview before printing. Available online at www.pearsonmytest.com (access code required).
Supervisor's Manual (ISBN: 0205027695)		✓	Instructor Supplement	The Supervisor's Manual, written by the authors and designed to work in tandem with the Instructor's Manual and the Teacher Training Video, provides a variety of resources useful to instructor training programs, including a guide to the video, discussion prompts, and an orientation schedule. It also includes useful information about the role of the course director, leadership styles, constructing and administering exams, and other matters of special interest to course supervisors and program heads. Available for download at www.pearsonhighered.com/irc (access code required).
Teacher Training Video (ISBN: 0205546455)	✓		Instructor Supplement	This video, introduced by author Jim Andrews, contains fourteen different discussion prompts, or "triggers," on an array of teaching challenges, including how to deal with challenges to authority and grade complaints, how to offer feedback, how to stimulate classroom discussion, and how to deal with communication apprehension. The Supervisor's Manual provides an extensive guide to the video, including ideas for responding to the discussion prompts during teacher training programs. See your Pearson representative for details; some restrictions apply.

(continued)

RESOURCES IN PRINT AND ONLINE (*continued*)

Name of Supplement	Available in Print	Available Online	Instructor or Student Supplement	Description
PowerPoint™ Presentation Package (ISBN: 0205717497)		✓	Instructor Supplement	This text-specific package, prepared by Michael Simmons and Glen Williams of Southeast Missouri State University, provides a collection of lecture outlines and graphic images keyed to every chapter in the book. Available for download at www.pearsonhighered.com/irc (access code required).
Study Card for Public Speaking (ISBN: 0205441262)	✓		Student Supplement	Colorful, affordable, and packed with useful information, Pearson Allyn & Bacon's Study Cards make studying easier, more efficient, and more enjoyable. Course information is distilled down to the basics, helping students quickly master the fundamentals, review a subject for understanding, or prepare for an exam. Because they're laminated for durability, these Study Cards can be kept for years to come and students can pull them out whenever they need a quick review. Available for purchase.
Pearson A&B Public Speak-ing Study Site (Open access)		✓	Student Supplement	This open-access Web site features public speaking study materials for students, including a complete set of practice tests, relevant Web links, and learning objectives for all major topics in the public speaking course. These topics have also been correlated to the table of contents for your book. Available at www.abpublicspeaking.com.
The Public Speaking and Civic Engagement Blog		✓	Instructor and Student Supplement	Created by the authors, this site is updated periodically with news and information useful to teachers and students of public speaking. The site includes tips for teaching from the textbook and for using the supplemental materials. Instructors and students can also post comments, offer their own ideas, or simply get in touch with the authors of the book. Available at www.personal.psu.edu/jmh32/blogs/civicengagement
Civic Engagement Speeches DVD (ISBN: 0205618014)	✓		Instructor Supplement	This DVD features a unique blend of speeches and presentations, including nonprofit leaders speaking as advocates for their agencies, citizens speaking out at a public hearing, panelists responding to audience questions, professionals and concerned citizens speaking to inform and persuade, and students speaking on topics related to civic engagement. Many of these speeches also are featured in the MySpeechKit that accompanies this text (see below). Please contact your Pearson representative for details; some restrictions apply.
MySpeechKit		✓	Instructor and Student Supplement	MySpeechKit is an interactive and instructive online solution for public speaking. Designed to be used as a supplement to a traditional lecture course, MySpeechKit includes book-specific learning objectives, chapter summaries, flash cards, and practice tests, as well as Web links, an outlining wizard, media clips, and interactive activities to aid student learning and comprehension. New to MySpeechKit is Pearson's MediaShare, a video upload tool that allows students to upload speeches for their instructor and classmates to watch (whether face-to-face or online) and provide online feedback and comments. MediaShare also includes a completely customizable grading rubric for instructors, which allows grades to be imported into most Learning Management Systems. Structured much like a social networking site, MediaShare can help promote a sense of community among students. Also included in MySpeechKit is Pearson's MySearchLab™, a valu-able tool to help students conduct online research. **Access to MySpeechKit can be packaged with your text** and is also available for purchase at www.myspeechkit.com (access code required).

ACKNOWLEDGMENTS

We are indebted to many individuals who provided encouragement, support, and inspiration as we began this project and who helped make the first edition a success. We extend our special thanks to the undergraduates at Indiana University, Southeast Missouri State University, and Penn State University, whose enthusiasm for our approach to public speaking was unwavering, and to the graduate students at these schools, whose passion for critical pedagogy and civic engagement led to provocative discussions and, in some cases, to exciting new ideas.

We also wish to thank a number of friends, current or former students, and colleagues who contributed to either the first or the second edition of the book. Some have served as reviewers, others have supplied ideas or materials used in the book, and all have given us encouragement and inspiration. These include the following:

Rukhsana Ahmed, Ohio University
Kevin J. Ayotte, California State University, Fresno
Diane M. Badzinski, Bethel College
Kristin M. Barton, Dalton State College
Sean Beppler, Syracuse University
Jennifer A. Bieselin, Florida Gulf Coast University
Lynn Borich, Missouri State University
LeAnn M. Brazeal, Kansas State University
Kristine Bruss, University of Kansas
Nanci M. Burk, Glendale Community College
Martín Carcasson, Colorado State University
Ellen R. Cohn, University of Pittsburgh
Linda Czuba Brigance, State University of New York at Fredonia
Donnette Dennis-Austin, Broward Community College
Cynthia Duquette Smith, Indiana University
Michael Eaves, Valdosta State University
Lyn J. Freymiller, Penn State University
Grace Giorgio, University of Illinois
John Gore, Ivy Tech State College
Kathryn Gromowski, Penn State University
Debra Hawhee, Penn State University
Gary Hiebsch, College of the Ozarks
Patricia S. Hill, University of Akron
Mark E. Huglen, University of Minnesota, Crookston
Daisy L. Johnson, Heartland Community College
Hillary Jones, Penn State University
Una Kimokeo-Goes, Penn State University
Stephen A. King, Delta State University
Rick Lindner, Georgia Perimeter College
Steve E. Martin, Ripon College
Rick Maxson, Drury University
Richard McGrath, Central College
Sara Ann Mehltretter, Penn State University
Lisa M. Orick-Martinez, Central New Mexico Community College
Dean A. Pape, Ripon College
Shawn J. Parry-Giles, University of Maryland
Barry C. Poyner, Truman State University
Claire H. Procopio, Baton Rouge Community College
Kimberly Rosenfeld, Cerritos College
Jody M. Roy, Ripon College
Claudia Ruediger, Southeast Missouri State University
Shawn Spano, San Jose State University
Sanda Tomuletiu, Duquesne University
Mary E. Triece, University of Akron
Esin C. Turk, Mississippi Valley State University
Jill Weber, Hollins University
Katerina Katsarka Whitley, Appalachian State University
Alaina M. Winters, Heartland Community College

We also are grateful for those who were our inspiration and mentors: the late Gayle Compton, Donald Zacharias, Lloyd Bitzer, Stephen E. Lucas, the late J. Jeffery Auer, and the late Robert G. Gunderson—all gifted and caring teachers and engaged citizens of their communities. Through actions and words, they taught us about the importance of communication and what it means to be a good citizen in a democracy.

Finally, we want to thank the staff at Pearson/Allyn & Bacon, especially Karon Bowers, our editor-in-chief, who has supported our project, listened to our concerns, challenged our thinking, and made suggestions that improved our work. Others who played an instrumental role in this second edition are development manager David Kear, development editors Corey Kahn and Stephen Hull, supplements editor Angela Pickard, editorial assistant Stephanie Chaisson, and Kristin Jobe of Elm Street Publishing Services.

In 1952, William Norwood Brigance, a professor of speech at Wabash College, published his ground-breaking text, *Speech: Its Techniques and Disciplines in a Free Society*. In it, he wrote:

Democracy and the system of speechmaking were born together. Since that early day we have never had a successful democracy unless a large part, a very large part, of its citizens were effective, intelligent, and responsible speakers. Today, as twenty-three centuries ago, a system of speechmaking is imperative for preserving democracy.

Brigance's philosophy inspired our writing of *Public Speaking and Civic Engagement*, and it is to his memory that we again dedicate this book.

Mike Hogan
Patty Andrews
Jim Andrews
Glen Williams

CHAPTER

1

Public Speaking and Democratic Citizenship

CHAPTER SURVEY

Public Speaking and Civic Engagement

The Rhetorical Tradition

Communication Challenges of the Twenty-first Century

The Responsible Citizen-Speaker

CHAPTER OBJECTIVES

After studying this chapter, you should be able to

1. Discuss some of the challenges facing our democratic system.
2. Describe how the rhetorical tradition relates to civic engagement.
3. Identify some of the challenges of speaking and listening in the modern age.
4. Describe some of the legal and ethical obligations of the responsible citizen-speaker.

What does it mean to be a citizen in a democracy? For some, it means voting in elections, donating money to political candidates, or making "statements" about their political views by displaying bumper stickers or yard signs. For others, citizenship means getting involved in their local community, perhaps raising money for a worthy cause or joining with neighbors to clean up a local park. Whatever citizenship means to you, it involves sharing ideas with others and talking about important issues and controversies. In other words, being a citizen means *communicating* with others. Throughout history, the ability to communicate effectively has been not only the mark of great leaders, but also an important skill for ordinary citizens.

This book is dedicated to helping you become a better speaker—*and* a better citizen. It offers practical advice about preparing and delivering speeches in a variety of public settings. Beyond that, it discusses the responsibilities of citizenship, including your ethical obligations to your fellow citizens and to your community. In the process, we will introduce you to a number of people—both famous and not so famous—who have made a difference by "speaking out." We also will teach you how to recognize and resist the techniques of demagogues and propagandists—those who use the power of speech to manipulate and deceive others. When you complete your course in public speaking, you will have the confidence and skills necessary to participate fully in civic life. More than that, you will understand what it means to be a "good citizen."

PUBLIC SPEAKING AND CIVIC ENGAGEMENT

Preview. *As you read this, you may be a full-time student, a business major, or a student who hasn't yet decided on a major. You are many other things as well. You are a daughter or a son; you may be a single parent, a United Methodist, a part-time employee, a tennis player, a movie buff, a sports fan, or a camp counselor. We all play many different roles in life, but we all have one thing in common: we are citizens in a democracy. Our country's future depends on how well we perform that role. As citizens, we have a responsibility to become involved in the civic life of our communities. Public speaking is among the most important skills of citizenship, and your effectiveness as a speaker can make a real difference in your own life and in the life of your community.*

Did the 2008 presidential election mark a turning point in American history? In one sense, it clearly did: Americans elected the first African-American president in our nation's history. But did all the excitement over this historic election, especially among young people, mean that Americans had rediscovered what it means to be "good citizens"? As Robert D. Putnam argued in his best-selling book *Bowling Alone: The Collapse and Revival of American Community*, the last four decades of the twentieth century witnessed troubling declines in voter turnout, newspaper readership, and participation in voluntary and civic associations. According to Putnam, our social and community bonds have been disintegrating, and this unraveling of our civic culture poses a serious threat to our democratic way of life.[1] Now, however, there appear to be signs of a rebirth in **civic engagement**. We still face enormous challenges, but we have reason to hope that we may be able to work together to meet those challenges.

The Challenges of Democratic Citizenship

First, the bad news. Over the past half century, barely half of all eligible Americans have bothered to vote in presidential elections,[2] and the United States continues to trail most of the world's democracies in voter turnout.[3] Over the years, young people have been especially apathetic about voting. After the 26th Amendment lowered the voting age from 21 to 18 in 1971, turnout among Americans aged 18–24 steadily declined, from about 50 percent in 1972 to only 32 percent in the 1996 election and 36.5 percent in 2000.[4] Other indicators of civic engagement likewise have declined, including the number of people who pay attention to the news, attend public meetings, or work for political causes.[5] According to surveys by the Roper organization, there have been significant declines in the number of people signing petitions, writing letters to their elected representatives or local newspapers, giving speeches at meetings and political rallies, or writing articles for a magazine or newspaper. By the mid-1990s, 32 million fewer Americans were involved in these sorts of activities than was the case just two decades earlier.[6]

Americans now donate *more* money to political and civic causes today than ever before, and the *Encyclopedia of Associations* reports that the number of nonprofit organizations in America doubled from 1968 to 1997, increasing from 10,299 organizations to 22,901.[7] Yet these statistics only seem to confirm that we have become a nation of *spectators* rather than *participants* in public life. For many Americans, "getting involved" means writing a check to a political cause or to some special interest group. In effect, we are paying others to do our politics *for* us! Unfortunately, those paid professionals sometimes degrade the quality of our public discussions. When paid professionals dominate our politics, slogans and sound bites replace the voices of ordinary people. Principled leadership gives way to appeals shaped by polling and focus groups, and slick public relations campaigns displace the give-and-take of public debate. In political campaigns, what former president Bill Clinton once called the "politics of personal destruction" prevails, while in our legislative assemblies negotiation and compromise has given way to ideological combat and gridlock. Scholars and politicians alike have lamented this loss of civility and substance in our nation's political talk. But the real losers are the citizens, whose voices have been drowned out by the voices of more strident activists.[8]

Yet there are hopeful signs of a rebirth of civic engagement in America. Ironically, that rebirth began following the terrorist attacks of September 11, 2001, as many Americans came together in common cause, contributing to relief and charity efforts or even volunteering for military service. As Putnam observed, the 9/11 attacks at least "interrupted" the downward trend in "political consciousness and engagement," increasing the public's interest in political affairs to levels "not seen in at least three decades."[9] This spike in political awareness was also evident in the 2004 elections, as Americans voted at the highest rate since 1968. According to some estimates, about 15 million *more* Americans voted in 2004 than in the 2000 presidential election, including a significant increase in the number of young voters.[10] And finally, of course, voter turnout was up again in the 2008 presidential election, hitting a 40-year high as a record 131 million Americans turned out to vote. That represented 61.6 percent of the nation's eligible voters, according to George Mason University political scientist Michael McDonald—a level of civic

A crowd of young people participate in a "Vote or Die" rally at Miami Dade Community College. The rally reflected the increased participation of young voters in the presidential elections of 2004 and 2008.

engagement not seen since the 1960s.[11] Still more evidence of a revival in civic engagement has come in a recent survey of incoming college freshmen that revealed the highest level of political interest since the survey began in 1966,[12] along with another study that concluded that young people have embraced new "norms of engaged citizenship" that have redefined what it means to be a "good citizen."[13]

Some of the credit for these positive signs must go to the many schools, charitable foundations, and civic groups that have launched new initiatives to promote participatory democracy. After documenting the problem in *Bowling Alone*, for example, Robert Putnam founded the Saguaro Seminar, which is an ongoing initiative of the John F. Kennedy School of Government at Harvard University concerned with developing "far-reaching, actionable ideas to significantly increase Americans' connectedness to one another and to community institutions."[14] At the University of Texas, the Annette Strauss Institute for Civic Participation has a similar mission: "(1) to conduct cutting-edge research on how civic participation, community understanding, and communication are undermined or sustained, and (2) to develop new programs for increasing democratic understanding among citizens."[15] Another initiative, Project Pericles, provides funding to colleges across the nation to improve their community-service efforts and to "make civic engagement a part of the curriculum in every department."[16] And at the more than 1,100 colleges and universities affiliated with Campus Compact, millions of students have been involved over the past 20 years in a variety of civic and community-service projects.[17]

New technologies also hold promise of reinvigorating grassroots democracy in America. During the 2008 elections, for example, Barack Obama used social networking tools such as Facebook and text messaging to engage new voters, while John McCain reached younger voters by advertising on YouTube. A variety of other politicians and political activists have also used the Internet to organize and mobilize like-minded citizens. In addition to social networking sites, weblogs (or *blogs*) have become an important forum for political news and debate, and there are indications that at least some young people are turning to the Web more frequently for political news and information.[18]

Still, we cannot count on new technologies to solve all our problems. Although the Internet has great potential, it also has been used by extremist groups to spread their messages of hate, and a few Internet users seem to have withdrawn into a virtual world of political fantasies and bizarre conspiracy theories. Other Internet users visit only sites that echo views they already hold, and too few of us seek out information that may challenge our thinking. It is important to remember that when television was first invented, it too was touted as a magical new tool of civic engagement—a technology that would reinvigorate our democracy. Instead, it became what former FCC chairman Newton N. Minow famously described as a "vast wasteland," dominated by mindless entertainment programming rather than news and political information.[19] If new technologies are to benefit our democracy, we must *learn* to use them wisely. We must learn to be critical consumers of information we find on the Internet and in other media, and we must learn to use those technologies to benefit society. In the information age, **Internet literacy**—the ability to distinguish between good and bad information on the information superhighway—will become a critical skill for every citizen.

The Engaged Citizen

So what does it mean to be a "good citizen"? And what can *you* do to help revitalize our democracy? We've already suggested part of the answer: *get involved*, whether that means voting in the next presidential election, speaking out at a local town hall meeting, or volunteering to help others in your community. This book will not only remind you why it's important to get involved, but also help you develop some of the skills you need to really make a difference. It also will help you understand what it means to communicate *responsibly* in a democracy. The good citizen is not just an effective communicator but one with a strong code of ethics and a commitment to serving others.

Many people engage in civic activities to build their résumés—it looks good on a college or job application to be "involved" in one's community. But civic involvement is more than simply a way to advance your career. It is also a commitment to a cause or activity that helps make your community a better place. Wherever you get involved—in your school, at your place of work, in your town, or in a broader national or even international arena—you contribute to the *common* good. The benefits of getting involved are shared benefits. Everyone is better off when you support a worthy cause. *Somebody* has to take the lead in making our communities better places to live. Why not you?

Even busy college students can make a big difference. At Penn State University, for example, the largest student-run charitable organization in the world raises money to fight childhood cancer with an annual dance marathon. "Thon," as it is popularly called, involves hundreds of students in a variety of activities, from planning the event to the care and feeding of the dancers

Participants in the 2009 Penn State Interfraternity/Panhellenic Dance Marathon hold up signs bearing the grand total of money raised by that year's "Thon": $7,490,133.87.

themselves. Thon even has a communications committee for "Penn State students with a passion for spreading the word." To date, this group of involved students has raised more than $52 million to combat pediatric cancer. In 2009 alone, Thon raised nearly $7.5 million.[20]

Even a small handful of students can make a difference. At Indiana University, for example, a group of students in a service-learning course worked at a day shelter for the homeless and realized that dental care was a serious problem for many of the poor people in the community. After presenting a Community Action Symposium to their classmates, the students wrote to large companies asking for donations of dental hygiene products. One company responded: the John O. Butler Company of Chicago donated 450 toothbrushes and two cases of toothpaste to residents of the shelter.

The good citizen not only helps others, but also strives to be well informed and thoughtful. In a democracy, you have a right to your opinion. Yet, recognizing the difference between an informed opinion and one grounded in ignorance or prejudice, the good citizen forms an opinion only after careful investigation and thoughtful evaluation of the evidence. In other words, the good citizen bases his or her opinions on a careful survey of the facts, the testimony of credible experts, or firsthand experience. The good citizen does not simply claim the "right" to an opinion, but rather *earns* that right by developing an *informed* opinion. If you choose to participate in civic affairs, you have an obligation to first develop the knowledge and skills you need to "speak out" responsibly. The study of public speaking dates back to ancient times, and that knowledge has been handed down to us in what scholars call the *rhetorical tradition*.

THE RHETORICAL TRADITION

Preview. *Rhetoric is an ancient discipline concerned with the techniques and ethics of speech. There are three traditions of scholarship and teaching in rhetoric that focus on the knowledge and skills necessary for democratic citizenship:*

- *the tradition of rhetorical theory that dates back to ancient Greece and Rome*
- *the tradition of rhetorical criticism, which emphasizes the critical analysis of public discourse in all its various forms*
- *the tradition of historical studies in public address, which focuses on the lessons we may learn from the speakers, speeches, social movements, and persuasive campaigns of the past*

The scholarly traditions of rhetorical theory and criticism have something important to contribute to our understanding of public speaking and civic engagement. In recognizing rhetoric as one of the oldest scholarly traditions, we realize that the ability to communicate in public has long been considered an important part of democratic citizenship. By learning to speak in public, and by developing our skills at evaluating the speeches of others, we develop what may be called **civic literacy**.

Speaking Responsibly

The study of speech dates back to ancient times, with some of the great Greek and Roman thinkers, including Aristotle and Cicero, counted among the earliest rhetorical theorists. In the classical tradition, personal ethics and **civic virtue**, or devotion to one's community and the common good, were the cornerstones of rhetorical education. For example, Isocrates, a Greek orator and teacher of rhetoric who lived from 436 to 338 BC, viewed the study of rhetoric not only as preparation for life and leadership in Athenian politics, but as a tool for creating unity out of diversity and defining that larger "public good." For Isocrates, rhetoric was more than a collection of techniques for persuading an audience. It was a source of the communal values and the moral standards that made democratic civilization itself possible.[21] Similarly, the Roman rhetorician Quintilian described the ideal orator as "a good man skilled in speaking"—with the emphasis on the "good man."[22] Quintilian's ideal orator was more than an effective platform speaker. He was, first and foremost, a good citizen—a civic leader, a lover of wisdom and truth, a sincere advocate of worthy causes, and a servant of the community. For both Isocrates and Quintilian, responsible orators promoted the best interests of the whole community, not just their own selfish interests.

We must acknowledge the greater challenges of public speaking in the United States today. Unlike the ancients, we live in a diverse, multicultural society, and we must take account of changing social values, new information technologies, and the realities of the consumer age. But that does not mean we cannot still strive to be "good citizens"—that is, people who assume the responsibilities of leadership, tell the truth, believe sincerely in our causes, and serve our communities. In the modern world, it is more important than ever that we rise above our own personal interests and promote some larger public

"Don't worry too much about math, science, or history — just make sure you get good marks in *rhetoric.*"

Source: Reprinted by permission from www.cartoonstock.com.

good. If we hope to resolve the difficult problems of the twenty-first century, we must learn to deliberate *together* and find common ground.

The classical rhetorical tradition still has something important to teach us: that public speaking in a democratic society must be grounded in a strong code of ethics and a commitment to the public good. The classical tradition suggests an approach to public speaking that emphasizes not the techniques of manipulation, but rather the character and civic virtues of the speaker and the shared interests of speakers and listeners. Now more than ever, citizens must learn how to deliberate with their fellow citizens. That requires that we embrace the ideals of Isocrates and the virtues of Quintilian's ideal orator and *demand* that all who speak in public do so responsibly. And that is where the second tradition of scholarship and teaching in rhetoric comes in—the tradition of rhetorical criticism.

Thinking Critically

Today, citizens must be more than skilled speakers. They also must have the skills necessary to critically evaluate the messages of others. In the economic marketplace, we have consumer watchdogs who warn us against false advertising and defective products. But in the "marketplace of ideas," we must learn to protect ourselves against those who may seek to manipulate or deceive us. We must learn how to recognize and resist illogical arguments, misleading or irrelevant evidence, and appeals to our emotions that short-circuit our thinking.

During presidential campaigns, newspapers and television news programs occasionally evaluate the truth and accuracy of political campaign commercials. Similarly, editorial columnists sometimes evaluate major political speeches, such as the president's annual State of the Union address. At colleges and universities, professional rhetorical critics publish detailed evaluations of major speeches and debates, and some comment on important speeches in the popular media. The interested citizen may consult all of these sources in deciding whether to accept or reject the claims in a political ad or speech. But often we must render judgments on the spot, without the benefit of research or time for reflection. In the day-to-day world of democratic life, we all must be **citizen-critics,**[23] ready and able to make our own judgments about who deserves to be believed—and why.

By studying public speaking, you are not only developing your ability to communicate effectively but also learning how to recognize misleading arguments, faulty reasoning, or inadequate evidence in other people's speeches. Demagogues, or speakers who employ "highly suspect means in pursuit of equally suspect ends,"[24] abound in our media-saturated world. So it is important that we, as citizens, recognize and resist their attempts to mislead us. Should we believe that speaker who insists that the U.S. government was actually behind the 9/11 terrorist attacks? What about that politician who claims he knew nothing about those illegal campaign contributions? And what about that preacher who insists that all "good Christians" must vote for a particular candidate? Studying the principles and methods of public speaking can help you decide how to respond to such appeals. It can help you distinguish between a reasonable argument and an attempt to deceive or mislead.

Obviously, it is not possible that everything you read or hear is true, especially when so many messages are contradictory. Consider, for example, the debate over a national sales tax. Proponents argue that this tax would simplify the tax structure and impose exactly the same burden on all citizens. Those opposed to such a tax insist that it is grossly unfair, placing the greatest burden on those who can least afford to pay. How would you go about sorting out the competing claims of advocates on both sides of this debate? How would you evaluate all the contradictory testimony, statistics, and other forms of evidence? In short, whom should you believe? Students of public speaking learn to take nothing at face value. Becoming a citizen-critic means learning how to investigate claims, weigh evidence, and come to reasoned conclusions based on a careful examination of the arguments on all sides of an issue.

In a democracy, citizens must know not only how to communicate well but how to critically evaluate the speaking of others. It is not enough that we speak responsibly; we also must demand that *all* who speak in public live up to high ethical standards. Critical listening and thinking are no less central to the rhetorical tradition than the skills of preparing and delivering a speech. If democratic deliberation is to lead to sound collective judgments, we all must learn to be more critical consumers of public discourse.

Lessons of the Past

Finally, a healthy democracy requires a common store of historical and political knowledge. It requires appreciation for the well-crafted argument and the eloquent speech, as well as an understanding of the American rhetorical tradition and our unique history as a deliberative democracy. In short, it requires some measure of historical and civic *literacy.* Unfortunately, as Bruce Cole, former chairman of the National Endowment for the Humanities, has noted, Americans have forgotten much of their own country's history, and that historical "amnesia" clouds our vision of the future. "We cannot see clearly ahead if we are blind to history," Cole argues, for "a nation that does not know why it exists, or what it stands for, cannot be expected to long endure." Urging more study of our history and political traditions, Cole concludes: "We must recover from the amnesia that shrouds our history in darkness, our principles in confusion, and our future in uncertainty."[25]

One of the best ways to learn about our past is by studying the great speakers and speeches of American history. The most basic principles of our government were forged by speakers who assumed the responsibilities of leadership and put the public good ahead of their own personal opinions and interests. During the Constitutional Convention, for example, Benjamin Franklin admitted that he had reservations about the proposed U.S. Constitution. Nevertheless, he consented to ratification "because I expect no better, and because I am not sure that it is not the best. The opinions I have had of its errors I sacrifice to the common good."[26] Similarly, Abraham Lincoln is remembered as a great president in part because of his lofty, magnanimous speeches in the closing days of the Civil War. Putting that terrible tragedy in perspective and beginning a process of national healing, Lincoln used his second inaugural address to urge "malice toward none" and "charity for all." Pledging to "bind up the nation's wounds," Lincoln pointed the way to "a just and lasting peace among ourselves and among all nations."[27]

Many of the issues and controversies debated in the early years of our republic are still with us today. Past debates shape the way we think about our own times. The great controversy over slavery and the rights of freed slaves after the Civil War echo in today's debates over racial discrimination and affirmative action. In the nineteenth century, Susan B. Anthony's demand for women's suffrage laid the groundwork for today's debates over women's rights and gender equality. Debate over the Pure Food and Drug Act of 1906 foreshadowed today's arguments over genetically engineered foods, food additives, and labeling requirements. We may think we live in an unprecedented age of scientific and technological progress, yet many of the challenges we face today have roots deep in our past.

By studying the great speakers and speeches of the past, we learn not only about the origins of contemporary controversies but about the principles of public advocacy and democratic deliberation. By examining the speeches of the great African-American abolitionist Frederick Douglass, for example, we can learn how appeals to "higher law" can motivate us to live up to our national ideals. By studying the inaugural addresses and fireside chats of Franklin Roosevelt, we can witness the power of speech to boost morale and promote sacrifice for the common good. By reflecting on how our ancestors debated controversies over America's role in the world or our economic and social policies, we can learn how to disagree while still working together toward common goals. American history is, in large measure, a history of people who made a difference by "speaking out."

FOCUS ON CIVIC ENGAGEMENT

Voices of Democracy: The U.S. Oratory Project

In an online educational resource funded by the National Endowment for the Humanities, *Voices of Democracy: The U.S. Oratory Project*, teachers and students can study great speeches and debates from throughout U.S. history. In addition to authenticated texts of each speech featured, the Web site includes biographical and historical information, critical interpretations of each speech, and teaching/learning materials that explore each speech's historical significance and contemporary relevance. By visiting the site, you will be able to learn about important moments in U.S. history when "speaking out" really made a difference. You also may learn more about the principles of effective and ethical public speaking. *Voices of Democracy* is free and open to the public at http://www.voicesofdemocracy.umd.edu/.

By studying those voices, we can both learn about our past and find inspiration and guidance for meeting today's challenges.

America has always had its share of propagandists and demagogues. Yet we can learn from them, too, as the rhetorical theorist Kenneth Burke suggested in a study of Adolf Hitler. By studying the rhetoric of Hitler, Burke wrote, we can "discover what kind of 'medicine' this medicine-man ... concocted," so that we know "what to guard against" in our own country.[28] How do leaders of religious cults persuade their followers to sacrifice everything, even their lives, for some imagined reward in the hereafter? How have groups like the Ku Klux Klan manipulated hatred and bigotry to promote their racist agendas? How have political demagogues like Joseph McCarthy exploited people's fears to increase their own personal power? And, more recently, how did Bernard Madoff and others persuade so many smart and successful people to risk their life savings in fraudulent investment schemes?[29] By studying such scam artists, we can learn to guard against demagoguery and deception in the future.

Today, we continue to witness the power of public speaking to inspire and unify—or to polarize and divide. Speaking at the National Cathedral only three days after the 9/11 attacks, President George W. Bush sought to comfort a grieving nation, to honor the heroic first responders, and to urge the nation to embrace its "responsibility to history." Quoting Franklin Delano Roosevelt, the president celebrated what FDR called the "warm courage of national unity" and assured us that America would prevail against the "enemies of freedom."[30] Yet just two years later, actor Tim Robbins complained of a "chill wind" in America and accused Bush of silencing debate over the war in Iraq with a rhetoric of "fear and hatred."[31] And today some even argue that George W. Bush and other administration officials ought to be prosecuted for war crimes during the War on Terror.[32]

The American news media, of course, thrive on political conflict. Rarely do we hear from speakers who propose compromise or voice respect for their political opponents. Political talk shows also seem to encourage people to take extreme positions, to shout at one another, or to call each other names. In a now-legendary TV moment, comedian Jon Stewart, appearing on CNN's *Crossfire* in 2004, complained that such shows only "hurt America" by substituting "partisan hackery" for real debate. Reminding hosts Tucker Carlson and Paul Begala of their "responsibility to public discourse," Stewart concluded: "You're doing theater, when you should be doing debate."[33] Shortly after the show aired, the president of CNN, Jonathan Klein, canceled *Crossfire*, stating that he agreed "wholeheartedly" with Stewart's assessment.[34]

We all should join Jon Stewart in denouncing those speakers who hurt our democracy. As citizen-critics, we need to speak out against those who engage in reckless or divisive political speech. We need to hold all who speak in public to a higher standard. For self-government to succeed, we need more than a shared understanding of our history and traditions. We also need a shared commitment to what political commentator E. J. Dionne has called "serious speech"—speech motivated by the search for "truth"; speech designed not just to defeat political adversaries but to aid citizens in their common search for understanding; speech that *engages* citizens in a continuous and ongoing effort to balance worthy but competing values, to mediate conflicts, to resolve disputes, and to solve problems.[35] The American rhetorical tradition is rich in such speech, so we have much to learn by studying the speakers, speeches, and debates of the past. By studying past speeches, we can learn much about the ideas that have shaped our nation's history and gain a better appreciation for "serious speech."

COMMUNICATION CHALLENGES OF THE TWENTY-FIRST CENTURY

Preview. *Communication is an integral part of our lives, occurring in a wide variety of settings. Public speaking has always been crucial in the conduct of human affairs and has a direct bearing on our own successes—in personal relationships, at school and work, in our community, and in various groups to which we belong. In the contemporary world, speakers face new challenges as new media and more diverse audiences have changed how we speak in public.*

When you speak in public, you assume a leadership role. Perhaps you will be asked to report to your dorm on the results of a new recycling program. Or you may someday urge fellow members of a service organization to help raise funds for a local children's hospital. As a citizen, you may find yourself addressing a town hall meeting on tax relief or aid for education. At some point in your life, you may even become a national or international leader, addressing some great issue such as the global economy or human cloning. Whatever the setting, your success as a citizen—and as a leader—will depend on your ability to communicate effectively.

Sometimes you are motivated to speak out for ordinary though personally important reasons: Think of the time, for example, that you sought to persuade your friends to support some cause important to you. Or perhaps you have found yourself stifled by a domineering member of a group project at school—and finally felt the need to speak up. In a job interview, you may be asked, "What are your strengths and weaknesses?" Or, as part of your job, you may be called on to address a group of co-workers, clients, or customers. Whatever you do in life, you will at some point need to voice your needs, desires, beliefs, or opinions. We communicate—and we react to communication by others—every day, no matter what our role or station in life.

Speaking in public, of course, presents a special challenge. It arouses more anxiety than other speaking situations, but we must overcome those anxieties if we hope to share our ideas with others. As citizens in a democracy, we must develop the confidence to voice our opinions. If we are afraid to speak out, we have no say in the decisions that affect our lives.

The Importance of Public Speaking

Throughout your life, public speaking will be important to your personal success. The ability to express yourself clearly and effectively will help you now, as a student, as well as later in life, as a professional and a citizen. As a student, you will learn principles in your public speaking class that can help you write better essays and term papers. Furthermore, more and more colleges and universities are requiring oral presentations in courses as diverse as marketing, biology, history, and foreign languages. Some colleges and universities are even requiring students to demonstrate proficiency in oral communication before they graduate.[36]

Good communication skills also have become increasingly important in the workplace. Surveys reveal that most of us experience problems at work arising from poor communication. Many employees wish that their co-workers could communicate more effectively.[37] Employers and professional groups increasingly emphasize the importance of effective communication, and many now offer courses or training workshops to bolster communication skills.[38] Although administrators, board directors, and chief executive officers have always given speeches, employees at all levels are called on to speak in today's workplace. Organizations of all types have downsized, eliminating many middle managers.[39] As this happens, managerial work is carried out by employees throughout the organization. A team leader may be called on to present the group's ideas to those higher up in the organization. Successful professionals, whether they work in business, health care, education, law, or government, will inevitably be required to speak in public.

Effective public speaking is more than an important job skill, however. Many of the great leaders in history have felt a responsibility, even a special *calling*, to "speak out." In the early nineteenth century, for example, abolitionist Angelina Grimké stood up to hostile mobs as she traveled about the country speaking out against slavery. In September 1919, President Woodrow Wilson also risked his health to take his case for the League of Nations to the people on a grueling 8,000-mile, 22-day whistle-stop tour.[40] In the 1930s, Franklin Delano Roosevelt called on his oratorical skills to give hope and inspiration to millions of Americans dispirited by the Great Depression, and Winston Churchill did the same for the British people during the darkest days of World War II. In the 1960s, Martin Luther King Jr.'s powerful voice became the driving force behind a civil rights movement that dramatically transformed America, and today King's legacy continues to live on in powerful memories of his most famous speech, "I Have a Dream."

Today, the ability—and the inspiration—to "speak out" remains the hallmark of effective leadership. Yet you do not have to be a famous politician or the leader of a great social movement to make a difference. In the mid-1990s, Doris Haddock, an 85-year-old great-grandmother from New Hampshire, took it upon herself to do something about the corruption of the American political process by big money. Testing both her public speaking skills and her physical endurance, "Granny D" took her case for campaign finance reform on the road, speaking to thousands of her fellow citizens as she, quite literally, walked across America.

So what *are* the communication skills that we need as students, workers, and citizens? They include not only the ability to speak in front of an audience but the ability to perform well in interviews and group discussions. They also include the analytical and critical-thinking skills needed to evaluate the messages of others. As a student, you may be asked to lead a class discussion one day—for 20 percent

FOCUS ON CIVIC ENGAGEMENT

"Granny D" Gets Involved

Doris Haddock, better known as "Granny D," talks about campaign finance at the Statehouse in Concord, New Hampshire, on April 20, 2000. Haddock, of Dublin, New Hampshire, walked from California to Washington, D.C., to promote campaign finance reform.

In 1995, a newly proposed law regulating campaign financing, the McCain-Feingold bill, failed to win congressional approval. In New Hampshire, 85-year-old Doris Haddock decided to do something about it. Incensed that some congressional leaders had stated that the American public didn't care about the issue, Haddock—or "Granny D," as she became known—decided on a dramatic gesture to attract attention to the issue and gain support for reform.

After getting into shape by taking long walks around her hometown of Dublin, New Hampshire, Granny D set out to walk across the country to rally support for campaign finance reform. On January 1, 1999, she began her walk in Pasadena, California. By the time she arrived in Washington, D.C., on February 29, 2000, she was 90 years old and had walked 3,200 miles. In Arizona, she was hospitalized for dehydration and pneumonia. Near the end of her journey, she faced heavy snows and had to cross-country ski for 100 miles between Cumberland, Maryland, and Washington.

All along the way Granny D gave speeches and urged public support for campaign finance reform. When she reached the nation's capital, she was met by more than 2,000 people, including representatives of various reform groups and several members of Congress. Many of these supporters walked the final miles with her.

Granny D is widely credited with helping to push the final bill into law. Al Gore, in adopting a finance reform plank in his campaign platform during the 2000 presidential election, credited Senator John McCain, former senator Bill Bradley, and Granny D.

Granny D passed away on March 9, 2010 at the age of 100. In her final years, she remained politically active. In 2003, she launched a drive to register more working women to vote, and in 2004, she ran for the U.S. Senate herself. She may not have defeated New Hampshire's incumbent Senator, but she did win a respectable 34 percent of the vote.

The text of a speech given by Doris Haddock to the freshman class of Franklin Pierce College follows this chapter. Its theme is the importance of involvement in civic affairs.

Source: Reprinted by permission from Doris "Granny D" Haddock. Copyright © 2003.

of your grade. As a worker, you may find yourself addressing your fellow employees, reporting to your boss, or interviewing prospective clients. As a citizen, you may one day appear before the local school board to oppose cutbacks in extracurricular programs. Whatever the situation, the ability to speak effectively is an important skill that you will need throughout your life. The ability to speak well is more than just a job skill; it is an essential part of being a "good citizen." The good citizen not only votes, but "speaks out" on issues of concern to the community and the nation.

Public speaking creates opportunities for you to share your knowledge, life experiences, and ideas with others, and it allows you to get feedback on your ideas. Whenever you speak in public, you will grow from the experience, developing more confidence and respect for differing points of view. This textbook will help you communicate more effectively and become a more critical consumer of other people's messages. At the same time, it will highlight your ethical obligations as a speaker and the challenges you will face when you stand up to speak.

Speaking and Listening Today

Speakers today face different challenges from speakers in the past. Many speeches today are broadcast over radio, television, or the Internet, reaching millions of listeners. In addition, the audiences we address are far more diverse than those addressed by our parents or grandparents. In the nineteenth century, many considered it scandalous to address what was then called a **promiscuous audience**—an audience composed of both men and women! Today, we routinely address audiences that include a wide diversity of people from different races and ethnic groups, socioeconomic backgrounds, and religious and moral traditions. On the Internet we can even speak to global audiences. Obviously, times have changed, and a one-size-fits-all speech will no longer do.

Electronic media have extended the reach of speakers, but they also have posed new challenges and problems. They have even changed the way we speak, rendering the passionate, arm-waving style of an earlier era obsolete. Most of today's speakers use a more conversational style, a style that one rhetorical scholar has labeled "effeminate." According to Kathleen Hall Jamieson, this **effeminate style**—a style that emphasizes storytelling, self-revelation, and emotional appeals—is a natural response to the intimacy of television. On television, we see speakers close up, as if they are sitting in our own living rooms. We would be shocked to hear them yell and pound on a podium as they spoke to us. On television, the more successful speakers are those who have a relaxed, conversational style, tell good stories, and communicate with us on a personal level. On television, the best speakers are those who seem to talk *with* us, not *at* us.[41]

Former president Ronald Reagan—known as the Great Communicator—was a master of the effeminate style. On TV, Reagan communicated warmth and personal charisma, smiling and nodding his head, telling stories, and generally talking with his TV audiences as if they were having a casual conversation. His personal anecdotes were legendary, and he used self-deprecating humor to good effect. To millions of Americans, Reagan seemed like an ordinary American—just "one of us."

Another former president, Bill Clinton, likewise connected personally with voters via television. After a disastrous debut speech at the Democratic National Convention in 1988, Clinton restrained his tendency toward long-winded policy speeches and instead took a lesson from Reagan: talk *with*, not *at* your audience. With his voice full of emotion, Clinton convinced many who were struggling economically that he could "feel their pain," and he reassured black Americans of his commitment to racial justice. Unlike some politicians, Clinton never looked wooden or stiff when speaking on television. To the contrary, he looked relaxed and confident, communicating sincerity as he spoke.

Of course, we must always be on guard against politicians who may deceive or manipulate us with a polished speaking style. As citizen-critics, we need to recognize that politicians carefully cultivate their TV images and that sometimes we can be distracted from the real issues at hand. We also must guard against being sidetracked by irrelevant concerns blown out of proportion by media coverage. During the 2008 presidential campaign, for example, the news media focused on a variety of "issues" that had little to do with the qualifications or policies of the candidates, such as Barack Obama's skills as a bowler or vice presidential candidate Sarah Palin's clothes. Journalists also seem obsessed with entertainment celebrities, checking in with the likes of Chuck Norris and Paris Hilton for their perspectives on the election. After the final presidential debate, the media even created a new celebrity by reporting on an ordinary voter mentioned by John McCain during the debate: Samuel Joseph Wurzelbacher, better known as Joe the Plumber. By introducing Joe the Plumber, McCain hoped to focus attention on the differences between his economic plan and that of Barack Obama. Instead, the story took on a life of its own, exposing every detail of Joe's life, including how much money he made and his qualifications as a plumber.

This example points to the challenge politicians face trying to get their message across in today's mediated environment. The news business is highly competitive, and journalists tend to prefer the striking or dramatic story that can be simply told. "If it bleeds, it leads," as the old saying goes. This is especially true of television news, where the desire for compelling visuals often overrides more important concerns. On television news, complex issues are rarely discussed in depth. Speakers talk in slogans and sound bites, oversimplifying complex issues and reducing them to simplistic, black-and-white terms. In a speech during the 2008 presidential campaign, for example, Barack Obama challenged John McCain's claim that he was a "maverick" with an old colloquial saying: "You can put lipstick on a pig, but it's still a pig." Despite the fact that Obama and McCain had both used the phrase previously, some interpreted Obama's statement as a personal attack on McCain's running mate, Alaska governor Sarah Palin.[42]

As citizens, we are challenged to go beyond the sound bites and media spin to evaluate messages critically. We need to look beyond mere appearances—and even beyond what respected journalists or political commentators tell us. As citizens, we are called on to make our own judgments, and we should take responsibility for educating ourselves about important issues. To be a good citizen is to be an *informed* and *critical* consumer of public communication. It means making an effort to understand the motives of speakers, evaluating their evidence and reasoning, and suspending judgment until we are fully informed. It means being fair-minded and respectful toward those who disagree, and it means being sensitive to the advantages some advocates have because they have more resources or greater media access.

Another major challenge faced by speakers today is the growing diversity of audiences. We live in a world where men and women of all ages, races, religions, and educational backgrounds must come together to resolve problems. During the 1980s, immigrants accounted for more than one-third of U.S. population growth, and our increasing cultural diversity can now be seen in all regions of the country.[43] An overwhelming 92 percent of Americans recognize that the United States is now made up of many different cultures.[44]

Whether you make a speech in your classroom or to a community group, your audience will undoubtedly be more diverse than it would have been even a decade ago. You can't assume that all of your listeners will be like you, sharing the same values, beliefs, and experiences. Not all listeners will view fraternities and sororities the same way you do. Not all listeners will trust the police to protect them. Not all listeners will agree that the measure of success in life is how much money one makes. And not all listeners will define the term *family values* the same way. Indeed, some listeners may completely reject your most cherished principles and values.

Does that mean we can no longer discuss important issues and find common ground in our diverse, multicultural society? Let's hope not! The growing diversity of American society makes it more important than ever that we learn how to communicate both effectively and responsibly. We may be a more diverse nation today, but we still have common problems and shared dreams and aspirations. If we hope to sustain America's great experiment in democratic government, we must learn to resolve our competing interests and work together for the common good.

THE RESPONSIBLE CITIZEN-SPEAKER

Preview. *In a democracy, every speaker should be committed to communicating responsibly. Responsible speakers examine their own motives. They insist on accuracy and are concerned with the ways in which they acquire and present information. They see human communication as respectful dialogue and strive to live up to the legal and ethical standards of the larger community.*

As a speaker, you hope to influence your audience. Like any speaker, you hope your audience will respond positively to your ideas and proposals. Yet that does not mean you should be willing to say *anything* to "win the day." Nor does it mean that you should shamelessly pander to your audience. You want to be an *effective* public speaker, but you also want to communicate *responsibly.* But what does that mean—to communicate "responsibly"? What are the *responsibilities* that go along with the *right* of free speech in America?

Characteristics of the Responsible Citizen-Speaker

First, communicating responsibly means speaking honestly and truthfully, with a genuine concern for the well-being of your listeners. Responsible speakers also examine their own motives, and they do not slant the truth just to "win" an argument. Responsible speakers are committed to respectful dialogue; they honor the right of their listeners to raise questions, suggest alternatives, or even disagree. Responsible speakers carefully research their topics and present their findings accurately. Responsible speakers adapt to their audience's interests and needs, but they do not pander. They may compromise on some issues, but they do not abandon their core beliefs in order to win their audience's approval.

Public speaking is an ancient art, because citizens in democracies have always had a need to *learn* the habits and practices of **public deliberation**. Deliberation is what democracy is all about; it is the mechanism through which citizens come together to talk about their common problems and to make collective decisions. For our democracy to work, however, we must agree on some *rules* of deliberation. Some of those rules are actually written into law; others are more informal social norms.

Legal and Ethical Issues in Public Speaking

Imagine having to speak to an audience you know to be opposed to your ideas. How far will you go to win their agreement? Or imagine you are making a sales presentation to a group of potential customers. Are you willing to say *anything* in order to "close the deal"? Would you knowingly resort to misleading statements or attack the competition in order to make that sale?

All who speak in public must wrestle with these sorts of questions, and in recent years the lines between acceptable and unacceptable speech have become even more blurred. The news media nowadays seem most interested in voices from the extremes of the political spectrum: Ann Coulter on the right, for example, or Michael Moore on the left. Some public figures, such as Howard Stern, even push the boundaries of decency and good taste. Still others, such as white supremacist Matthew Hale, openly preach hate and advocate violence. So where do we draw the line? What are the limits of free speech in America? And who has the power to define the rules of acceptable speech? We have laws against slander and libel, of course, and the Supreme Court has ruled that speech that threatens public safety is outside the protections of the First Amendment. Yet controversies remain. To what extent, for example, should the Federal Communications Commission (FCC) be able to regulate what we see on television or hear on the radio? Should a city government be allowed to close an art exhibit that it deems pornographic? Do "pro-life" activists have a First Amendment right to advocate violence against doctors who perform abortions? All of these questions point to difficult dilemmas for our free society.

Generally, we all recognize that there must be limits to free speech. By law, for example, we do *not* have a First Amendment right to slander or threaten others, nor do we have a right to incite mob violence. Beyond these legal limitations, however, there are few clear guidelines for acceptable speech. As a result, all public speakers must make choices. As a public advocate, will you resort to

Citizens have a right to free speech in America, even the right to protest. But along with those rights come a responsibility to respect certain legal and ethical standards.

name-calling or exaggerated fear appeals in order to win an argument? Will you attempt to prevail by labeling your opponents "ignorant" or "radical," or by trying to scare your audience into agreeing with your position? Or will you show respect for your listeners by grounding your speech in the best available information, supporting it with sound evidence and reasoning, and acknowledging the legitimacy of opposing points of view?

Issues that matter to people should be explored in depth, not clouded by language that dismisses rather than engages the arguments of the opposition. In the heat of political battle, some speakers may be tempted to exaggerate their case, to state mere opinions as fact, or to make promises they cannot keep. Those who resort to such methods may sometimes carry the day, but in the long run they likely will be denounced by their fellow citizens and discredited in history. You may think that it doesn't matter much what you talk about in your public speaking classroom, but the classroom *is* a public forum. What you say in the classroom does matter, and communicating responsibly *is* part of your assignment.

In the next chapter, we will discuss at greater length the ethics of public speaking, considering in more detail the relationship between ethical and effective communication and reflecting on some of the key ethical issues in public speaking—such as plagiarism. As you prepare for your first public speaking assignment, don't forget: the truly successful citizen-speaker is both an effective advocate for his or her ideas *and* a good citizen.

SUMMARY

- The engaged citizen "gets involved," strives to be well informed and thoughtful, and speaks out on matters of civic concern.
- The tradition of scholarship and teaching in rhetoric emphasizes the knowledge and skills necessary for democratic citizenship.
  - Theories of rhetoric dating back to ancient Greece and Rome have stressed the ethics of public speaking and civic virtue.
  - Rhetorical criticism teaches us to be citizen-critics—that is, to carefully evaluate the arguments and evidence we hear in speeches or in the mass media.
  - By studying the great speakers and speeches of the past, we can learn about American history and about the principles and traditions of democratic deliberation.
- In our increasingly diverse, mass-mediated society, the ability to communicate effectively has become more important than ever.
  - Public speaking skills are crucial to success in school, in the workplace, and in your role as a citizen.
  - Electronic media have created new challenges for speakers and changed the character of our public discourse.
  - The growing diversity of our society challenges speakers to understand and adapt to cultural differences.
- The responsible citizen-speaker is committed to honesty, respects his or her audience and the process of deliberation, and understands the legal and ethical constraints on free speech in a democratic society.

QUESTIONS FOR REVIEW AND REFLECTION

1. How is public speaking related to "civic engagement"? Offer some concrete examples.
2. What evidence suggests that Americans have become less politically involved or community spirited? Do you believe that Americans are less engaged than in the past? Alternatively, can you think of ways that citizens have become *more* civically engaged in recent years?
3. On your campus, what activities, clubs, or other special opportunities invite students to participate in civic affairs? Offer at least three examples.
4. How is the rhetorical tradition relevant to concerns with civic engagement? What kinds of knowledge and skills can be learned from the rhetorical tradition?
5. What are the communication skills that are most important in the twenty-first century? Is public speaking more or less important today than it was, say, 100 years ago?
6. In what ways has public speaking been important historically? Other than those listed in the book, offer at least one example of a public speaker who has had a significant impact on his or her community, state, nation, or the world.
7. How have mass media (and television, in particular) altered the way we deliver speeches? What makes a speaker effective on television?
8. What are the characteristics of the responsible citizen-speaker? What are some of the legal and ethical constraints on speakers in a democracy?

ENDNOTES

1. Robert D. Putnam, *Bowling Alone: The Collapse and Revival of American Community* (New York: Simon & Schuster, 2000).
2. See Infoplease, "National Voter Turnout in Federal Elections: 1960–2008," www.infoplease.com/ipa/A0781453.html (accessed March 25, 2009).
3. Center for Voting and Democracy, "International Voter Turnout, 1991–2000," www.fairvote.org/turnout/intturnout.htm (accessed March 25, 2009).
4. Center for Voting and Democracy, "Youth (Non-)Voters," www.fairvote.org/turnout/youth_voters.htm (accessed May 13, 2005).
5. Putnam, *Bowling Alone*, 31–47. Declining attention to the news is particularly evident among young people. See David T. Z. Mindich, *Tuned Out: Why Americans under 40 Don't Follow the News* (New York: Oxford University Press, 2005), esp. 18–33.
6. Putnam, *Bowling Alone*, 43–45.
7. Ibid., 49.
8. See James Davidson Hunter, *Culture Wars: The Struggle to Define America* (New York: Basic Books, 1991), 135–70.
9. Robert Putnam, "Bowling Together," *American Prospect*, February 11, 2002, 20–22.
10. According to the Center for Information and Research on Civic Learning and Engagement (CIRCLE), turnout among voters between ages 18 and 24 increased by about 5.8 percent in 2004, rising to 42.3 percent from just 36.5 percent in the 2000 election." See Center for Information and Research on Civic Learning and Engagement, "Youth Voting in the 2004 Election," Fact Sheet, November 8, 2004 (updated January 25, 2005), www.civicyouth.org/PopUps/FactSheets/FS-PresElection04.pdf (accessed May 13, 2005).
11. "Turnout in Presidential Elections Hit 40-Year High," *Politico*, December 15, 2008, www.politico.com/news/stories/1208/16576.html (accessed March 13, 2009).
12. Eric Hoover, "Freshman's Views: Politics, Admissions, and Marijuana," *Chronicle of Higher Education*, January 30, 2009, A18.
13. Russell J. Dalton, *The Good Citizen: How a Younger Generation Is Reshaping American Politics* (Washington, DC: CQ Press, 2008).
14. "The Saguaro Seminar: Civic Engagement in America," www.hks.harvard.edu/saguaro/ (accessed March 25, 2009).
15. "Our Purpose," *The Strauss Report: A Publication of the Annette Strauss Institute for Civic Participation*, 2005–2006 edition, n.p.
16. Jeffrey R. Young, "Persuading Students to Care: Eugene Lang's Program Aims to Prod Colleges into Encouraging Civic Involvement," *Chronicle of Higher Education*, April 11, 2003, A47.
17. See Campus Compact, "About Us," www.compact.org/about/ (accessed March 25, 2009).
18. A study done at UCLA found that more than 55 percent of Internet users aged 18–34 obtain news online in a typical week, and a Nielsen/NetRatings study showed that traffic to the 26 most popular sites in 2003 grew by 70 percent from May 2002 to October 2003. Pew Charitable Trusts, "State of the News Media 2004 Fact Sheet," March 2004, www.pewtrusts.org/news_room_detail.aspx?id=22562 (accessed March 25, 2009).
19. "Minow's Speech to the National Association of Broadcasters," May 9, 1961, www.historychannel.com/speeches/archive/speech_194.html (accessed August 15, 2005).
20. "THON: Penn State IFC/Panhellenic Dance Marathon," www.thon.org (accessed March 21, 2009).
21. See Takis Poulakos, *Speaking for the Polis: Isocrates' Rhetorical Education* (Columbia: University of South Carolina Press, 1997).
22. Quintilian, *Institutes of Oratory*, trans. J. S. Watson (London: G. Bell & Sons, 1913), 2: 391.
23. See Rosa A. Eberly, *Citizen Critics: Literary Public Spheres* (Urbana: University of Illinois Press, 2000).
24. Stephen R. Goldzwig, "A Social Movement Perspective on Demagoguery: Achieving Symbolic Realignment," *Communication Studies* 40 (1989): 202–28. For Aristotle's classical definition, see William A. Dunning, "The Politics of Aristotle," *Political Science Quarterly* 15 (1900): 273–307.
25. Bruce Cole, "Our American Amnesia," *Wall Street Journal*, June 11, 2002, www.wethepeople.gov/newsroom/wsjarticle.html (accessed March 25, 2009).
26. Benjamin Franklin, "On the Constitution," in *A Choice of Worlds: The Practice and Criticism of Public Discourse*, ed. James R. Andrews (New York: Harper & Row, 1973), 100.

27. Abraham Lincoln, "Second Inaugural Address," in *American Voices: Significant Speeches in American History, 1640–1945*, ed. James R. Andrews and David Zarefsky (New York: Longman, 1989), 294–96.
28. Kenneth Burke, *The Philosophy of Literary Form* (Baton Rouge: Louisiana State University Press, 1941), 191.
29. See Robert Frank, Amir Efrati, Aaron Lucchetti, and Chad Bray, "Madoff Jailed after Admitting Epic Scam," *Wall Street Journal*, March 13, 2009, A1.
30. George W. Bush, "Remarks at the National Day of Prayer and Remembrance Service," September 14, 2001, *The American Presidency Project*, www.presidency.ucsb.edu/ws/index.php?pid=63645 (accessed March 28, 2009).
31. Tim Robbins, "'A Chill Wind Is Blowing': Transcript of the Speech Given by Actor Tim Robbins to the National Press Club in Washington, D.C., on April 15, 2003," www.commondreams.org/views03/0416–01.htm (accessed March 25, 2009).
32. Rev. Lennox Yearwood, "War during Lifetime," *The Huffington Post*, March 21, 2009, www.huffingtonpost.com/rev-lennox-yearwood/war-during-lifetime_b_177429.html (accessed March 21, 2009).
33. Cable News Network, *Crossfire*, October 15, 2004.
34. Bill Carter, "CNN Will Cancel 'Crossfire' and Cut Ties to Commentator," *New York Times*, January 6, 2005, C5.
35. E. J. Dionne Jr., *They Only Look Dead: Why Progressives Will Dominate the Next Political Era* (New York: Touchstone Books, 1997), 261.
36. See "Integrity in the Curriculum: A Report to the Academic Community," Association of American Colleges, Washington, D.C., 1985; see also the National Communication Association's *Spectra* (March 1995): 9, for a summary of a Department of Education study identifying the communication skills that faculty, employers, and policy makers believe are critical for college graduates.
37. David A. Whetten and Kim S. Cameron, *Developing Management Skills*, 6th ed. (Englewood Cliffs, NJ: Prentice Hall, 2005); Dan B. Curtis, Jerry L. Winsor, and Ronald D. Stephens, "National Preferences in Business and Communication Education," *Communication Education* 38 (1989): 6–15.
38. See, for example, "Speak for Success" and "Advanced Presentations Workshop," published for the American Bar Association (Boston: Speech Improvement Company, n.d.). Many self-help books also offer advice on how to improve one's communication skills.
39. David L. Bradford and Allan R. Cohen, *Power Up: Transforming Organizations through Shared Leadership* (New York: Wiley, 1998); Peter F. Drucker, "The Coming of the New Organization," *Harvard Business Review* 66 (1988): 45–53.
40. See J. Michael Hogan, *Woodrow Wilson's Western Tour: Rhetoric, Public Opinion, and the League of Nations* (College Station: Texas A&M University Press, 2006).
41. Kathleen Hall Jamieson, *Eloquence in an Electronic Age* (New York: Oxford University Press, 1988), 67–89.
42. See "'Lipstick on a Pig': Attack on Palin or Common Line?" *CNNPolitics.com*, September 10, 2008, www.cnn.com/2008/POLITICS/09/10/campaign.lipstick/ (accessed March 25, 2009).
43. Sally J. Walton, *Cultural Diversity in the Workplace* (New York: Irwin Professional, 1994).
44. Pew Hispanic Center/Kaiser Family Foundation, *The 2004 National Survey of Latinos: Politics and Civic Participation*, July 2004, 73.

Speech to Franklin Pierce College Freshmen

Doris "Granny D" Haddock

*After becoming famous for her cross-country walk in support of campaign finance reform in 1999–2000, Doris "Granny D" Haddock published a memoir (*You're Never Too Old to Raise a Little Hell*), led voter registration campaigns, and delivered dozens of speeches at political rallies and on college campuses. In this speech, she offered the incoming freshmen at Franklin Pierce College some advice on life, the world around them, and their obligations as citizens in a democracy.*

September 5, 2003

To the Freshman Class at Franklin Pierce College, New Hampshire

Thank you.

It is a great pleasure to grow old and to be asked to dispense advice and to not have to follow it oneself. In that department, let me urge you to go to bed early, get up at dawn, keep well ahead of your studies, stay well behind your credit limit, refrain from smoking and drinking and wild living. I give you that advice, not because I have ever followed it myself, but because life's pleasures are all the more delicious if an old lady has told you to do otherwise.

GRANNY D OPENS ON A HUMOROUS NOTE, ESTABLISHING HER ETHOS AS A REBEL.

The fact is, life is a feast of great pleasures and we are rude to our Creator if we do not partake of the beauty and fun and pleasure of this life. So I do hope you will take care of yourself and that you will mind your schedules to the extent that you will not always be behind and worried and stressed and missing out on the joy all around you. The captain of a well-run ship can afford the time to enjoy the breeze and the view. Be that to your own life, starting with college. It is a challenge, I know, but if you keep at it, you will get the hang of living well in this life.

HERE SHE USES THE METAPHOR OF A "WELL-RUN SHIP" TO EMPHASIZE HER POINT.

You will see that some of the students around you are forever behind and worried, and others seem on top of it and have a smile. Your choice, indeed. The moment of truth is when you are tempted away from your resolve. Will you be a person of strong character? Here is the test of it: a person of character stays true to a task, long after the passing of the mood in which that resolution was made. Watch for that: your conscious overview of your daily life can guide you toward improvements that will strengthen your hold on life and its happiness. Let me warn you more specifically that problems like depression and chronic procrastination are always a good excuse for a visit to the health center, where you can get very useful help. The brain is no less fixable an organ than the stomach, and we do get our aches and pains and should go for help sooner rather than later.

IN THIS PARAGRAPH, SHE DISPLAYS HER CONCERN FOR THE WELL-BEING OF HER AUDIENCE.

Now, that is all boilerplate advice. Let me tell you something more interesting. You come into college with the expectation of learning many new things—of becoming an expert in many areas. But there is one area where you are already the expert, and where the professors and the other old birds are not. Young people bring something special and, if you are not fully aware of this superior quality, you might waste it unknowingly.

HERE SHE FLATTERS HER AUDIENCE, NOTING THAT YOUNG PEOPLE HAVE "SOMETHING SPECIAL," A FRESH "VIEW OF THE WORLD."

I am not speaking of your athletic or more personal areas of strength and stamina, though I am sure you are very impressive to watch in action. I am speaking of your view of the world, which in many ways is superior to the view seen by older eyes.

Trust your sensibilities toward justice and fairness and toward the environment and peace. Understand that your value judgments in these areas are better because they have not been beaten down or crusted over. Information overload can make us insensitive. While your eyes are wide open—and so also your heart—trust what you see. Do not hang back from involvement in addressing the problems of the world, waiting to become an expert. You are expert enough. You are our annual re-supply of new eyes and fresh hearts to give our sorry species its best hope for improvement and survival. Take your part in the great dramas and the great struggles now still in their opening acts in this world. It is the part where you storm on stage with a confused but mischievous look and the audience cheers you madly. Don't wait to know the part too well, or the moment will pass without you.

In a theatrical metaphor, Granny D urges her listeners to "storm on stage" and play their role in the "great dramas" of life.

What is your passion? There is a place for you in that passion. Or are you drifting, looking for your passion? Let your curiosity lead you to it. Trust the force of that curiosity—it is a lighted way for you, and just for you. Be brave when your curiosity takes you to places you would rather not go—it knows what it is doing and it has served you well for much longer than you can possibly imagine.

Again calling them to service, she urges the students to find their "passion" in life.

Look around every now and then and wonder what all this life is about. Whom is served by all this life? Whom does life serve? Life serves life, and we are happiest and at our best when we let our full life force—indeed our divine life force—rise within us as we engage our lives in service to the world, to the life around us. We are happiest when we are serving life and adding to its health and bounty. We are simply made that way—made for cooperation and joining of every kind.

"Service to the world, to the life around us" is her theme in this paragraph as well.

This is an extraordinary time you have chosen to come. What an amazing world! The young woman college student in Iran, wearing her Levi's under her burka, is your sister and your friend. The farmer in Central America who is trying to get a fair price for his coffee beans so that he can build a better house for his children is your uncle and a man you deeply respect. The Navajo woman who is fighting for the right to stay on land that has been her family's for generations is your grandmother, and she needs your help.

Here she reflects on the "extraordinary times" in which we live, a common theme in commencement addresses.

It is not too much. It is all quite beautiful. Cast your heart into this world right now, for your eyes and your heart are open and your senses of justice and fairness and your sense of the right thing to do by the planet that sustains us are fully matured and at their perfect moment to give hope and progress to the world. Don't save yourselves for later; spend yourselves today in love, and your investment will come back to you a hundredfold if you survive.

Employing a figure of speech called synecdoche, Granny tells the students to "cast your heart into this world." She also uses a banking metaphor, promising them that their "investment" in love will come back "a hundredfold."

Most of the social progress of the past hundred years has come from college students demanding a better world.

A good friend of mine was flying across the U.S. this past week and his seatmates were a young man and woman from Iran. The man was a naturalized U.S. citizen. The young woman had come here more recently. She told my friend how she had grown up under the artillery barrages of the Iran-Iraq War. She described how the Iranians saw that war: that the Americans had built up the Shah's army to be among the strongest in the region, but that when he was toppled by the Ayatollah, the U.S. then armed Saddam Hussein in Iraq and encouraged him to take down the Iranian army a few notches. It was in that game that she found herself as a child target of artillery. My friend asked her if she did not resent Americans for that time in her young life. She said that she tried not to hold Americans responsible for the actions of their government, as she hoped she wouldn't be held responsible for the actions of the Iranian government. She said that Americans seemed so kind and so unaware of what was being done in their names around the world, and she said she thought it must be like being the children in a family where the daddy is a monster—their lives are comfortable, but they know there is something wrong. They do not ask too many questions because they love their way of life. She said that she did not like to tell Americans about all that she knew, because it was kind of a shame to wake them up to all this when their lives were so cluelessly blissful—her words.

HERE THE SPEECH ASSUMES A SHARPER POLITICAL EDGE, AS SHE TELLS THE STORY OF A YOUNG IRANIAN WOMAN WHO SUFFERED BECAUSE OF U.S. SUPPORT FOR SADDAM HUSSEIN DURING THE IRAN-IRAQ WAR OF THE 1980S.

Well, she was wrong on many counts. As citizens of a democratic republic, we are indeed responsible for what our nation does in our name. And it is no discourtesy to help us be the awakened citizens we must be.

America is a great country and we love it. We love this planet, too. And you young people here today are the bright eyes that must be the open and awake eyes, though still full of joy and honor, love and mischief, duty and courage to serve life in a time when life is challenged by its old foes: fear and hate and ignorance.

Be you a great brotherhood and sisterhood of love and action. Arrange your personal lives so that you have the time and resources to take your part on this great stage. And smile the smile of the peaceful warrior whose weapons are love and light, and ever more love and more light.

CONCLUDING WITH A CALL TO ACTION, GRANNY URGES THE STUDENTS TO GET INVOLVED, PLAYING THEIR PART ON THE "GREAT STAGE" OF CIVIC LIFE AND BECOMING "PEACEFUL WARRIORS" WIELDING THE "WEAPONS" OF "LOVE AND LIGHT."

Thank you and good luck in this great scholastic and political year.

If it gets too crazy, come down to my porch in Dublin and we'll talk it over—if I'm not away on some adventure of my own. Call first.

Thank you very much.

Source: Used by permission of Doris "Granny D" Haddock.

CHAPTER

2

The Ethical Public Speaker

CHAPTER SURVEY

The Responsibilities of Citizenship

The Ethics of Public Speaking

Deliberation and Demagoguery in the Media Age

CHAPTER OBJECTIVES

After studying this chapter, you should be able to

1. Explain what it means to be an engaged citizen.
2. Describe various ways to become involved in civic affairs.
3. Identify some important ethical issues in public speaking.
4. Define *plagiarism* and *ghostwriting.*
5. Explain what it means to deliberate in good faith.
6. Define *demagoguery* and describe some of the characteristics of the demagogue.

Following World War I, a young artillery officer named William Norwood Brigance returned from the battlefields of France to teach high school speech and history. In 1922, he began a 38-year career teaching speech and coaching debate at Wabash College, a small liberal arts college in Crawfordsville, Indiana. Brigance earned his doctoral degree while on sabbatical from Wabash in 1929–30—the first Ph.D. in speech ever granted by the University of Iowa. By that time, he already had published more than a dozen scholarly articles and two books, all written when he had time off from teaching in the summers.

Brigance's career at Wabash spanned some of the most turbulent times in our nation's history. The 1930s, of course, brought the Great Depression, which left millions of Americans broke and out of work. Then came Adolf Hitler, World War II, and the horrors of the Nazi concentration camps. Throughout the 1950s and 1960s, the Cold War kept Americans on edge, with a whole generation of Americans growing up under the shadow of the atomic bomb. Brigance, like many Americans of his day, worried about America's future. Yet he also had faith in the American people.

Brigance's teaching and scholarship emphasized the need for every citizen in a democracy to be an "effective, intelligent, and responsible" speaker. A "system of speechmaking" was "imperative for preserving democracy," he wrote, for in the modern world there were only two kinds of people: "Those who in disagreements and crises want to *shoot* it out, and those who have learned to *talk* it out." If America hoped to remain a "government by talk," it needed *leaders* who spoke "effectively, intelligently, and responsibly," and it needed "popular intelligence," or a citizenry trained both to speak and to "listen and judge." In troubling times, Brigance concluded, the people needed to understand the challenges they faced and consider "both sides of every public question." Those were the "conditions" essential to the "survival of democracy" itself.[1]

Brigance was too old to fight in World War II, but he still reflected the values of what former *NBC Nightly News* anchor Tom Brokaw called America's "greatest generation."[2] Like many in his day, he talked less about the *rights* than about the *responsibilities* of citizenship, reminding his fellow Americans of their duties as citizens. According to Brigance, nobody was *born* with the right to state their opinions in public. One had to *earn* that right by becoming well informed and respecting the rules and traditions of democratic deliberation in America. As Brigance explained:

> We are beset by choices and temptations. We are haunted by shadows of fear. We listen to speakers, then, because we hope they will throw light on our problems, temptations, and fears. We listen because we hope they will give us new information, new ideas, or will simply water and cultivate old ideas. We listen because we want to be given encouragement, to renew our faith, to strengthen our determination.

According to Brigance, we had a right to hear speeches "worth listening to," and those who failed to deliver deserved to be "put out of business."[3]

Today, speech "worth listening to" seems harder to come by. Our public debates are often overheated, polarized, and unproductive, and speakers often seem more interested in scoring political points than in solving problems. Some even fear that, as a nation, we have lost that sense of *duty* and *service* that characterized

Brigance's generation. Yet many Americans, including many young people, still get involved in politics or public service. As citizens in a democracy, they recognize that we have an *ethical* responsibility to speak out on matters of public importance and to participate in civic life.

THE RESPONSIBILITIES OF CITIZENSHIP

Preview. *Citizenship entails responsibilities as well as rights, most notably the responsibility to get involved. There are many different ways to participate in civic life, and more and more young people today are involved in political and volunteer activities.*

We began this book with an important question: What does it mean to be a citizen in a democracy? For some, as we noted, citizenship means paying one's taxes or voting in elections. For others, it means volunteering to help the less fortunate or donating money to a worthy cause. However you define it, citizenship involves an *ethical* commitment to working with others to make our communities better.

The Engaged Citizen

By "getting involved" in your community, you *can* make a difference. In Foxborough, Massachusetts, a local resident named Phillip Henderson organized a group of neighbors to fight plans by a fast-food chain to build a new franchise on an environmentally sensitive site. Henderson's group, the Quality of Life Committee, fought for seven years to stop the development. They finally prevailed, and the disputed land is now part of a 19-acre protected wetland and wildlife preserve.[4] In Washington State, Pete Knutson, the owner of a small family fishing operation, organized an unlikely alliance of working-class fishermen, middle-class environmentalists, and Native Americans to protect salmon fisheries in the Pacific Northwest. Standing up against powerful special interests, Knutson's alliance pushed for cleaner streams, enforcement of the Endangered Species Act, and an increased flow of water over regional dams to help boost salmon runs. When the special interests pushed for new regulations that would have put small family fishing operations out of business, Knutson and his supporters defeated the effort in a statewide referendum.[5]

"Getting involved" is not just something older Americans do. All across America, college and even high school students have been making a difference by participating in civic or service activities. In one survey, two-thirds of the respondents between ages 18 and 30 said that they had volunteered their time, joined a civic or service organization, or advocated some public cause in the past three years.[6] In 2002, the Center for Information and Research on Civic Learning and Engagement (CIRCLE) found that more than 40 percent of young people surveyed had participated in a charitable event, and more than half had boycotted some product "because of the conditions under which it was made."[7] In its most recent survey, CIRCLE again found young people "involved in many forms of political and civic activity," including voting, grassroots organizing, or volunteer work. More than 70 percent of the young people surveyed said they "followed what's going on" in government and public affairs, and more than a third said they had volunteered or participated in "political discussions."[8]

Some college students even give up their spring breaks to help others. According to Break Away, a nonprofit group that organizes "alternative" spring breaks, nearly 65,000 students from across the country spent their spring vacations in 2009 building homes, tutoring migrant farm workers or inner-city kids, working with homeless people, or participating in other sorts of volunteer or community service. In 2002, some 300 students from James Madison University participated in 30 different spring break service programs, such as trail and campground projects in national parks and working with at-risk youth in Washington, D.C. Each spring dozens of students from the University of Southern California travel to a Navajo reservation in Utah to paint houses; other USC students have built furniture for a new school in Guatemala or planted trees on Isla Mujeres, near Cancún, Mexico. During spring break 2005, some 80 students from Slippery Rock University ran youth programs in inner-city Baltimore, tutored high school dropouts in Denver, or helped rebuild homes destroyed by hurricanes in Florida. "It's just a really great way to spend your spring break," said Laura Creamer, a 21-year-old English major at Agnes Scott College, who was among the 10,000 students taking part in Habitat for Humanity's spring break program. "It's a really great experience to help someone out who's less fortunate."[9]

FOCUS ON CIVIC ENGAGEMENT

Students against Breast Cancer

What motivates young people to get involved? For Erica Pamenta and Sarah Costello, it was knowing somebody who was diagnosed with breast cancer. Erica, a biology major at Rutgers University, sought a way to participate in the fight against breast cancer after her best friend's mother was diagnosed with the disease. Sarah, a political science major at Ramapo College, also became concerned about breast cancer while still in high school—after her own mother was diagnosed with the disease.

Even as busy college students, Erica and Sarah have continued their fight against breast cancer. At Rutgers, Erica organized a Relay for Life to benefit the American Cancer Society (ACS), while Sarah worked to establish a student chapter of the ACS's Cancer Action Network. The two students go to different schools, but they are partners in a common cause: raising money for the Susan G. Komen foundation, which for more than 20 years has been a leader in the fight against breast cancer.

"Cancer is not a pleasant topic and many people do not want to talk about it," Erica observed while taking a break from her busy schedule. According to Sarah, the hardest thing about mobilizing other students is getting their attention in the first place: "You need to create an interest, a passion, for high school or college students to become involved." Both students developed their public speaking skills through participation in high school forensics, and both have found those skills invaluable as they spread the word about breast cancer—a disease that kills an estimated 40,000 women annually in the United States alone and is the second-leading cause of cancer deaths among women worldwide.

For more information, visit the Susan G. Komen foundation at http://www.komen.org/. Also see "Imaginis: The Breast Health Resource," http://imaginis.com/breasthealth/statistics.asp (accessed May 16, 2009).

Thousands of people, including many breast cancer survivors, participate in education and fund-raising events organized by the Susan G. Komen Race for the Cure.

By volunteering to help others, you can have an immediate, tangible impact. Perhaps that explains why so many young people prefer community service over more "traditional" political activities, such as circulating petitions or supporting political candidates. According to CIRCLE, many of today's college students are "turned off" by the "spin" and "polarized debate" of traditional politics, and they seek more "open and authentic" ways to participate in civic affairs. In comparison to Generation X, today's so-called Millennials are more politically active and aware, yet many of them are tired of the "competitive and confrontational atmosphere" of electoral politics and are finding new ways to "get involved."[10] In short, today's young people are redefining what it means to be a "good citizen"—indeed, they are redefining politics itself—by participating in a "wider repertoire of activities that give them direct voice in the decisions affecting their lives."[11]

Getting Involved in Politics

Perhaps you are among those who view politics as too negative or less effective than volunteer work or community service. But if you really hope to make a difference, you can't ignore politics. Many of the problems we face today are, in the final analysis, *political* problems. Why do we have homeless citizens? Partly because we have not made affordable housing a high political priority. Why do we need volunteers to build trails or to help clean up our national parks? Again, the answer involves politics: our elected officials have chosen *not* to spend taxpayer dollars to fund such projects. In the 2008 presidential election, 51 percent of eligible voters under age 30 showed up at the polls, suggesting that most young people recognize that politics *do* matter.[12] Moreover, politics can take many forms, such as supporting candidates, donating money to a cause, grass-roots organizing, and protests or boycotts. However you define politics, you *can* make a difference.

Getting involved in politics does *not* mean that you must be loud or combative, like some of the political activists and commentators we see on TV. As political scientist Morris P. Fiorina has suggested, members of the so-called political class tend to be more aggressive than the rest of us: "They are completely certain of their views; they are right and their opponents are wrong." Moreover, some of those activists and commentators view all who disagree not just as misguided or misinformed, but as "corrupt, stupid, evil, or all three."[13] Most Americans are not so sure of themselves, and they take moderate, middle-of-the-road positions even on such "hot-button" issues as abortion or gun control. For most of us, politics is not about scoring points or defeating some enemy; it is about finding solutions to difficult problems.

All this is not to say that we should ignore or silence those who feel passionate about politics. Devoted political activists—even those whom sociologist Eric Hoffer once called "true believers"[14]—have played an important role in American history, giving voice to the powerless and calling attention to injustices long ignored. Many of the most important social and political reforms in U.S. history—the abolition of slavery, women's suffrage, and environmental protection, to name just a few—were brought about by passionate activists who, at one time, were considered too radical. Indeed, our nation's founders were radicals, as were many later activists we now consider heroic, including abolitionist Wendell Phillips, women's suffrage activist Susan B. Anthony, and civil rights leader Martin Luther King Jr.

Still, the loud, passionate voices of a few should never be allowed to drown out the quieter, more moderate voices of the majority. Nor should we *have* to shout or make a scene in order to be heard. As Fiorina concludes, the "less intense and less extreme" voices in American politics should be given *at least* as much weight as those of the passionate activists. Not only would that "lower the decibel level of American politics," it would focus attention on more "mainstream concerns."[15]

Whatever your political views, you have the right to speak out. At the same time, you have an *ethical* obligation to respect the right of others to be heard. You also have an obligation to speak honestly, to know what you're talking about, and to remain open to changing your mind when confronted with compelling arguments. Good citizens keep up with current events and pride themselves on having informed opinions. They take advantage of opportunities to learn more about the issues, and they carefully weigh all the arguments before forming their own opinions. They may feel strongly about their views, but they respect the opinions of others. Good citizens—people of goodwill—can and will disagree, sometimes passionately. But they remain committed to free and open debate and to resolving their differences through democratic processes.

Perhaps by speaking out you will someday influence the decision of your local school board or city council. Or by discussing political issues with your neighbors, maybe you will help change public opinion or influence the outcome of an election.

As a citizen in a democracy, you have an ethical obligation to become informed about news and events before voicing your opinions.

Whatever the results of your participation, it is important—both to you and our democracy—that you get involved. Before you do, however, you should understand your *ethical* responsibilities as a speaker. Those responsibilities, like the study of speech itself, date back to the earliest democracies of the ancient world.

THE ETHICS OF PUBLIC SPEAKING

Preview. *You must keep your ethical responsibilities as a public speaker in mind at every stage of the speech-making process, from your decision to speak out in the first place to the choices you make as you research, prepare, and deliver your speech. Not only must your goals be ethical, but you have a responsibility to speak honestly and to take responsibility for what you say.*

At the time of our nation's founding, the classical rhetorical tradition—with its emphasis on moral character and **civic virtue**—was the foundation of our educational and political culture. "To the revolutionary generation," as historian Gordon Wood has explained, "rhetoric lay at the heart of an eighteenth-century liberal education," and the ability to speak effectively was "regarded as a necessary mark of a gentleman and an indispensable skill for a statesman, especially for a statesman in a republic."[16] Since that time, we have lost touch with the classical tradition, and demagoguery—deceptive or manipulative speech—has become more commonplace in our civic life. Today we have no formal "code of conduct" for those who speak in public, yet the ethical principles of the classical tradition can still provide guidance. Like the ancient rhetoricians, we can still demand truth from those who speak in public, and we can insist on sound evidence and reasoning. Today, as in ancient times, we can insist that all who speak in public be honest and accountable for what they say.

Ends and Means in Public Speaking

Perhaps it goes without saying that ethical public speakers do not pursue unethical goals. We may all agree, for example, that Adolf Hitler was wrong to advocate genocide, whatever his rationale. Yet questions of ethics are rarely that clear-cut. For one thing, speakers often face *ethical dilemmas*, or situations in which they must choose between the lesser of two evils. In addition, *circumstances* sometimes affect the ethics of public speaking, complicating the speaker's choices by clouding the ethical issues involved.

Many speakers face ethical dilemmas arising out of their professional obligations. Lawyers, for example, may find themselves assigned to defend clients who they believe are guilty. What are their ethical obligations in that situation? They are professionally committed to defending their clients. Yet they are also ethically bound to tell the truth. Similarly, people in advertising or public relations often face ethical dilemmas when asked to represent products or companies that they do not personally endorse. What would *you* do if asked to develop an advertising campaign for a product that you considered harmful to the environment or dangerous to consumers? As a public relations consultant, would you work for a company that you felt exploited its workers?

Sometimes the ethics of your goals as a speaker may depend, at least in part, on the circumstances. Ordinarily, for example, we may consider it unethical to advocate violence or war. Yet most cultures recognize a right of self-defense, and some religions have a "just war" doctrine that specifies the circumstances under which war may be morally justified.[17] Within the Catholic Church, for example, war is considered morally legitimate only when the cause is just, all other means of resolving the conflict have been exhausted, and the resort to arms does not threaten to do even greater harm than whatever provoked it. If these and other conditions have been met, Catholics can, in good conscience, support going to war. Yet it is always debatable whether these conditions have been met, which is why Catholics may still disagree over whether a particular war is just. The same is true of most other ethical guidelines. Changing circumstances—and, in some cases, ambiguities in the ethical code itself—always leave room for debate.

If the ethical implications of your goals as a speaker are debatable, that is all the more reason to give them careful thought.

- Are your purposes consistent with prevailing social norms or the religious beliefs of your audience?
- By speaking out, would you be violating your own personal ethics?

- Are you willing to stick to your own ethical principles at the risk of offending your audience?
- What, exactly, are the ethical standards of your community or the larger culture?

These are important questions, and they ought to be asked every time you speak in public. Yet it is not enough to have ethical *goals*. Ethical issues arise at every stage of the speech-making process, and you must take them into account every step of the way.

Honesty and Accountability

Your most basic ethical obligation as a public speaker is to tell the truth and take responsibility for what you say. You also have an ethical obligation to give credit where credit is due for ideas or language that you borrow from others. No doubt you recognize that principle from your other classes; you probably have been taught the definition of plagiarism and told to cite your sources. Yet honesty and accountability in public speaking are more than just academic requirements. They suggest a broader commitment to intellectual honesty and social responsibility—a commitment that we should demand of *all* who speak in public.

PLAGIARISM In a survey of 4,500 high school students in 2002, some 75 percent admitted to cheating in school, with more than half admitting to plagiarizing work they found on the Internet. Even more troubling, some did not see anything wrong with cheating. "What's important is getting ahead," said one student at George Mason High School in Falls Church, Virginia. "In the real world, that's what's going to be going on."[18] Unfortunately, cheating already has become a way of life for this student, and she no doubt will continue to cheat—at least until she gets caught. Other students do not cheat intentionally, instead committing plagiarism "accidentally." Cheating results not only from the attitude that "getting ahead" is more important than honesty but from simple carelessness or confusion over what constitutes academic dishonesty.

So what exactly *is* plagiarism? According to Northwestern University's "Principles Regarding Academic Integrity," **plagiarism** may be defined as "submitting material that in part or whole is not entirely one's own work without attributing those same portions to their correct source."[19] At first glance, this definition makes plagiarism a simple matter: you should never "borrow" all or even part of your speech from somebody else—at least not without acknowledging your sources. Yet the issue is complicated by gray areas in our definitions of plagiarism, as well as by confusion over when and how to cite your sources in an *oral* presentation. Thus, it is important that you have a clear understanding not only of what constitutes plagiarism, but also of how to avoid inadvertent plagiarism when preparing and delivering a speech.

Students sometimes take shortcuts in their speech class that constitute obvious and deliberate plagiarism. You are obviously guilty of plagiarism if you take your whole speech from a file at your fraternity house, for example, or if you buy your speech from an Internet site that sells ready-made papers and speeches. You are also guilty of plagiarism if you "cut and paste" all or part of your speech from Internet sources. But what if you "borrow" just a few quotations from that same source? Or what if you just paraphrase an article you read, borrowing some information and ideas but putting them into your own words? Does that constitute plagiarism? Here is where misunderstanding the rules may result in accidental plagiarism.

In a term paper, of course, you use quotation marks or indented block quotes to indicate passages that you took verbatim from others. But how do you indicate quoted material in a speech? Some people *say* "quote" and "unquote" to signify that they are quoting, but that can become annoying if overused. A better way is to use phrasing, structural strategies, and/or vocal inflections to indicate quoted material. Notice, for example, how the following passage is structured to signal where the quoted passage begins and ends: "Theodore Roosevelt stated his approach to American foreign policy in simple terms when he said: 'Speak softly but carry a big stick.' In saying this, Roosevelt actually took a middle ground between the imperialists and the isolationists of his day."

In a speech, of course, you can't cite your sources in parentheses, footnotes, or endnotes. So how *do* you "footnote" a speech? The answer is simple: you must cite your sources *in the text of the speech itself*. Even if your instructor requires that you turn in a list of sources for your speech, you should get into the habit of citing your sources orally and saying something to establish their credibility. In a speech opposing the use of military drones in the war on terrorism, for example, you might say, "We should stop using drones to strike targets in Pakistan. In an editorial in the *New York Times* last May, David Kilcullen, a counterinsurgency adviser to General Petraeus, and Andrew McDonald Exum, a former army officer who served in Iraq and Afghanistan, concluded that 'Drone attacks in Pakistan are doing more harm than good.'" You need not mention the exact date and page number of the editorial; that information will be in your bibliography. But as we will discuss further in Chapter 15, your *ethos* or credibility as a speaker depends in part on how the audience perceives the credibility of your sources. Speakers who cite well-qualified sources impress us with their research; those who cite questionable sources or no sources at all damage their own ethos.

Paraphrasing refers to putting the ideas or insights of others into your own words. When paraphrasing, you should strive for language that differs significantly from the original. Yet that still doesn't excuse you from giving credit for ideas or insights that are not your own. You need not document your own unique insights or conclusions, nor do you need to cite sources for what can be considered common knowledge or generally accepted facts. Yet how do you know when you have a genuinely original idea? And what constitutes common knowledge? Here is a useful rule of thumb: when in doubt, cite your sources.

If you find yourself tempted to take your speech off the Internet, remember that new technologies not only have made it easier to cheat; they also have made it easier to *catch* cheaters. Many teachers now use Internet search engines, or Web sites such as Turnitin.com, in their fight against plagiarism. At Turnitin.com, papers are checked against several massive databases, including more than 10 billion Web sites; more than 70 million student papers already submitted to the site; and more than 10,000 major newspapers, magazines, and scholarly journals. Turnitin even checks papers against an electronic library of thousands of books, including many literary classics. Within seconds, Turnitin.com returns an "Originality Report" highlighting possible instances of plagiarism and linking those passages to their sources. Although Turnitin.com is used mostly by teachers to detect and deter plagiarism, students also can use the site to learn more about how to paraphrase and cite their sources properly.[20]

Plagiarism can cost you much more than a good grade on your speech. At Penn State University, for example, penalties for plagiarism range from warnings, grade penalties, or academic probation to expulsion from the university. In the fall of 2000, Penn State even adopted a new XF grade to indicate failure of a course because of academic dishonesty. In 2001–02, there were 268 cases of alleged academic dishonesty at Penn State, up from just 51 the year before. Out of those students, five ended up with an XF grade on their permanent records. About half of those accused of academic misconduct failed the assignment in question, and about 30 percent received an F in the course.[21] Other schools also have toughened up their penalties for plagiarism. Some have even rescinded degrees or expelled students from honorary societies like Phi Beta Kappa after discovering later that the students had plagiarized academic work.[22]

Beyond the classroom, plagiarism can have serious, real-world consequences. In 1988, for example, Vice President Joseph R. Biden, then a U.S. senator from Delaware, was forced to withdraw from the race for the Democratic presidential nomination when an opposing campaign released a videotape showing him repeating passages taken directly from a speech by British Labour Party leader Neil Kinnock.[23] More recently, Nevada's Republican governor Jim Gibbons, when he was a congressman, delivered a hard-hitting attack on liberals at a Lincoln Day dinner in Elko, Nevada, including this stinging shot at the music and film industries: "I say we [tell] those liberal, tree-hugging, Birkenstock-wearing, hippie, tie-dyed liberals to go make their movies and music and whine somewhere else." Unfortunately for Gibbons, it soon came out that he had stolen almost his entire speech from a copyrighted address delivered in 2003 by Alabama state auditor Beth Chapman. "Not only is it a bad speech," commented one Democratic party leader, "it's a bad, stolen speech."[24]

Among those whose reputations have been damaged by accusations of plagiarism are such well-known figures as the Reverend Martin Luther King Jr. and historians Stephen Ambrose and Doris Kearns Goodwin. In these cases, the plagiarism may have been unintentional, but the accusations nevertheless proved embarrassing. At other times, the plagiarism is obviously deliberate, as in the case of a young *New York Times* reporter named Jayson Blair. Blair's blatant use of stolen and fabricated stories led to his own resignation and to the resignations of two high-ranking editors at the *Times*.[25] Plagiarism is *not* just something that you worry about in college. In the "real world," the penalties for plagiarism are severe, and the consequences can be devastating.

GHOSTWRITING Presenting somebody else's words or ideas as your own is not always unethical. Since ancient times, ghostwriters, or professional speechwriters, have helped others write their speeches. Today **ghostwriting** is considered an inevitable (if not fully understood) part of our political and corporate culture. Many political and business leaders are simply too busy to write their own speeches. The president of the United States employs a whole team of researchers and speechwriters. Generally, we do not consider this unethical, so long as the speaker takes full responsibility for his or her words.

The earliest ghostwriters actually helped make democracy possible. Assisting citizens as they prepared speeches for the deliberative and legal assemblies of the Greek city-state, the first ghostwriters also *taught* the art of public speaking. Subsequently, ghostwriting "proliferated through the ages," and today almost every speech by a major political, business, or academic leader is "written by someone else."[26] America's first president, George Washington, had a speechwriter: Alexander Hamilton. So, too, have many other presidents, including some whom we consider among our greatest orators: Franklin Delano Roosevelt, for example, and John F. Kennedy.[27] Even the Great Communicator, Ronald Reagan, employed not only a ghostwriter but a whole team of researchers and writers to help prepare his speeches. One of those writers, Peggy Noonan, wrote many of Reagan's most famous lines.[28] Still, we remember those famous words as the words of Ronald Reagan.

When does ghostwriting become unethical? According to Craig R. Smith, a speechwriter for both President Gerald Ford and Chrysler Corporation's Lee Iacocca, ghostwriting becomes unethical when the use of a speechwriter is "hidden from the audience." According to Smith, if "someone who uses a ghostwriter denies it," then he or she is "lying and acting unethically." Beyond that, Smith holds ghostwriters to the same ethical standards to which he would hold any writer or speaker: if their speeches are "purposefully deceptive," then they are unethical. Comparing ghostwriters to lawyers, Smith denies that it is unethical for ghostwriters to "write against their personal convictions." Just as lawyers sometimes defend people who they know are guilty, a speechwriter may defend an idea simply to ensure that it gets "fair play in the marketplace of ideas." Smith has never done that himself, but for practical, not ethical reasons: "I personally don't do it because I don't write as effectively when I'm writing about an idea I don't believe in."[29]

Today, ghostwriters rarely hide their role in the speech-making process. To the contrary, some presidential speechwriters have become celebrities in their own right, writing best-selling memoirs or achieving fame in politics, journalism, or even popular entertainment. Among the former presidential speechwriters who have become well-known celebrities are William Safire, Patrick Buchanan, television personality Ben Stein, and former presidential press secretary Tony Snow. Some still question the ethics of speechwriters profiting from inside accounts or going directly from the White House into journalism. Generally, however, we respect speechwriters who are honest about what they do.

The role of research and new technologies in speechwriting raises additional ethical concerns. With polling and focus groups, speechwriting teams can now create what one scholar has described as "quantitatively safe" speeches,[30] or speeches scientifically designed to offend nobody. Through research, ghostwriters also can test which arguments or evidence the public will find convincing or determine which emotional appeals will best move the public. Famous for such research, former Clinton adviser Dick Morris has described a process called *triangulation*, in which polling data was used to position Clinton in the most politically advantageous positions.[31] Morris denies that he was a spin doctor who

HIGHLIGHTING GHOSTWRITING

George W. Bush and the "Axis of Evil"

On January 29, 2002, George W. Bush delivered what is typically a routine speech: his State of the Union address to Congress. On this occasion, however, America was at war in Afghanistan and was preparing to extend the War on Terror to Iraq and possibly other nations. In the president's own words, the United States was prepared to take the fight against terrorism to any nation known to "harbor terrorists."

Planning for Bush's 2002 State of the Union address began in late December 2001, when presidential speechwriter Michael Gerson began soliciting suggestions from dozens of people across the government. He gave one of his assistants in the presidential speechwriting office, David Frum, a difficult task: develop justifications for expanding the War on Terror. As Frum recalls in his memoir, *The Right Man*, he began by rereading a speech that he had last read on September 11, 2001: Franklin Roosevelt's War Address after the Japanese attack on Pearl Harbor in 1941. He began to see parallels between the Axis powers in World War II—Japan, Nazi Germany, and Italy—and the terrorist states that now threatened America. The result was a memo to Gerson in which Frum labeled Iraq, Iran, and North Korea a new "axis of hatred." As Frum recalls, he expected his "radical" memo to be ignored. Instead, Gerson not only embraced the idea but added "the theological language that Bush had made his own since September 11," changing "axis of hatred" to "axis of evil."

The result was a passage in Bush's State of the Union address that provoked great controversy: "States like these, and their terrorist allies, constitute an axis of evil, arming to threaten the peace of the world. By seeking weapons of mass destruction, these regimes pose a grave and growing danger. . . . The United States of America will not permit the world's most dangerous regimes to threaten us with the world's most destructive weapons." To some, this language seemed clear evidence of the administration's plans to invade other countries, and a little more than a year later the United States did, in fact, invade Iraq.

George Bush did not invent the phrase *axis of evil*, but by uttering those words in his State of the Union address, he made them his own. Moreover, he took full responsibility for the language even before he delivered the speech. As Frum writes: "Bush read the speech closely. He edited it in his own bold hand. He understood all its implications. He backed them with all the power of his presidency."

Source: David Frum, *The Right Man: The Surprise Presidency of George W. Bush* (New York: Random House, 2003), 224–45.

distorted the truth or manipulated public opinion. But the use of polling to craft presidential messages raises new concerns that, rather than leading or educating, politicians merely pander to public opinion.[32]

Political ghostwriters are quick to defend their craft as a noble and worthy profession. Some college students even aspire to careers as professional speechwriters. What is the best preparation for such a career? According to Noonan, "communications majors" do *not* make the best speechwriters, but by that she means journalism or mass communications majors who neglect the study of history, literature, and other liberal arts.[33] Ghostwriter Craig R. Smith clarifies Noonan's point, suggesting that aspiring speechwriters *should* major in rhetoric or *speech* communication, in which they study not only the practical arts of argumentation and style but the history of great speeches, critical theory and methods, and the liberal arts. According to Smith, the "rhetorically trained ghost" puts out "a much better product" than one without such training. By studying rhetoric, students learn how to clearly "state the case and prove it."[34]

As you study the American rhetorical tradition, you'll learn that public speaking is *not* just about "winning" debates. It is also about leadership, public service, and respect for our traditions of free speech and democratic deliberation. The great speakers in history are not those who have successfully manipulated public opinion. To the contrary, we most remember those who have educated and inspired their audiences, such as Abraham Lincoln and Franklin D. Roosevelt. To be sure, unethical demagogues have sometimes risen to power in American politics. In the long run, however, history honors those who use the power of public speaking not to deceive or manipulate but to serve the public good.

President Bush delivering his 2002 State of the Union address, in which he labeled North Korea, Iraq, and Iran an "axis of evil" and warned that their pursuit of weapons of mass destruction posed a "grave and growing danger."

DELIBERATION AND DEMAGOGUERY IN THE MEDIA AGE

Preview. *Those who speak in public need not be objective, or free of all personal opinions and biases, but they do have an obligation to be well informed and fully prepared. In most respects, the rules of ethical speech have not changed since ancient times, although unethical speech, or demagoguery, has assumed new forms in the modern world.*

As the late U.S. senator Daniel Patrick Moynihan used to say, we are all entitled to our own opinions, but not to our own facts.[35] What Moynihan meant, of course, is that we should never twist the truth or invent facts just to win an argument. As public speakers, we have an ethical obligation to speak honestly and to make the necessary effort to gather reliable information about our topic. We also have an obligation to remain open to other points of view and to respect those who disagree with our opinions. Democratic deliberation is not about winning and losing. It is about joining with other citizens in a search for solutions to our common problems.

Deliberating in Good Faith

Perhaps you've heard the expression **deliberating "in good faith."** What does that mean? Does it mean that we must always strive to be objective? The answer is no. Nobody is completely objective. We all have personal experiences, religious beliefs, political biases, and social values that influence our opinions. As a speaker, nobody expects you to erase your past, nor do audiences demand that you deny your own beliefs and values, however controversial they may be. To the contrary, democratic deliberation is all about airing those differing opinions. It is about reconciling our disagreements through discussion and debate. Your fellow citizens do not expect you to be perfectly objective, but they do expect you to make good arguments in support of your opinions. That means providing sound reasoning and evidence to back up your views. It also means being open-minded enough to consider other people's views and perhaps even to change your opinion when confronted with compelling evidence.

In many situations, you will be *expected* to take sides on a controversial issue. If, for example, you plan to speak on the health care crisis in America, your audience will expect you to criticize existing policies and advocate some alternative system for providing health care in America. Yet that does not mean that you will simply announce your proposal and wait for your audience to shout its approval. You must provide *reasons* for your opinion and *evidence* to back it up. Nor does taking a stand on a controversial issue mean that once you deliver your speech, you should close your mind to the possibility of changing your own opinion. Ethical speakers avoid allowing their existing opinions to blind them to new information, and they remain open to persuasion by advocates with different points of view. Once you have carefully researched your topic, you may be confident that your conclusions are thoughtful and fair. Yet down the road, you may need to reevaluate your opinion in light of new information or changing circumstances.

As a public speaker in a democratic society, you have an ethical obligation to be well informed and fully prepared. Speaking in public is not like casual conversation, in which you just "bounce a few ideas" off a friend. It is a *formal presentation*, often in a setting where people have gathered to discuss issues crucial to their own lives and communities. In such a setting, you owe it to your listeners to investigate your topic carefully and to provide information that is relevant, reliable, and up-to-date. More than that, you should organize and deliver that information in the most effective manner possible. Being fully prepared means more than developing an informed opinion—although that is a crucial first step. It also means carefully organizing your ideas, choosing the right language to express them, and supplying solid evidence to back up them up.

When you speak in public, you ask your fellow citizens not only for their time and attention, but also for their trust. You therefore have an *ethical* obligation to contribute something useful to their deliberations—to deliver a speech "worth listening to," as Brigance put it. Perhaps you can contribute some fact that others have overlooked. Or maybe you have a unique way of looking at a problem or some new ideas for solving that problem. Whatever your contribution, you should investigate your topic thoroughly, consider all sides of the issue, and make sure that you have your facts straight. As Moynihan reminded us, you have a right to your own opinion, but not to your own facts.

Demagoguery and the Ethics of Emotional Appeal

As Charles Lomas observed in *The Agitator in American Society*, **demagoguery** is a word that is loosely thrown around in American politics and is "difficult to define."[36] To the Greeks who invented the word, a "demagogue was simply a leader of the people." Yet even in ancient Greece the term implied deceit and manipulation, with Euripides describing the demagogue as "a man of loose tongue, intemperate, trusting to tumult, leading the populace to mischief with empty words."[37]

Today, we use the term *demagogue* to describe speakers who deceive or manipulate their audiences, usually by provoking strong emotional responses. In a widely cited study, for example, historian Reinhard Luthin defined the demagogue as a "mob-master" who, with "considerable histrionic variety and always noisily," seeks to "whip up and intensify the emotions, the prejudices and the passions, of the voting public." According to Luthin, the demagogue stirs up emotions but rarely offers much in the way of "public service and constructive thinking."[38]

Demagogues typically appeal to the darker emotions, such as fear, anger, or hatred. During the Great Depression, for example, Huey P. Long, a U.S. senator from Louisiana, exploited the fears and hopelessness of many Americans by offering a quick fix to America's economic woes: a vague, utopian plan to "share the wealth." Similarly, Senator Joseph McCarthy became a household name in the 1950s by exploiting fears of communism and the uncertainties of the cold war era. McCarthy accused high-ranking government officials and even U.S. military leaders of disloyalty, but these reckless accusations later proved unfounded. But for a time he whipped the entire country into an anticommunist frenzy.

Of course, not all appeals to emotions are, in and of themselves, unethical. Emotions play an important role in all aspects of our lives. As speakers, we must recognize that people get excited, upset, or angry about issues that concern them. Emotions are also a powerful motivator. If you want your audience to *do* something, you simply cannot ignore the role of emotions in human behavior. Many speakers use emotional appeals to move people to do good—donate time or money to a charitable cause, for example, or fight for better schools in their community. Actor Michael Douglas uses emotional appeals to persuade us to help children affected by the AIDS epidemic in Africa. The Red Cross uses emotional appeals to solicit aid for victims of hurricanes and other natural disasters. The Veterans of Foreign Wars appeal to our emotions when they call on us to "support our troops." Appeals to emotions take many forms, and they are not *all* demagogic. If your goals are ethical and you are honest in what you say, there is nothing inherently wrong with appealing to emotions.

Senator Huey P. Long's flamboyant speaking style mesmerized audiences, yet many considered him a demagogue because of his emotional appeals and his utopian plan to "share the wealth." Long was assassinated at age 42 by the son-in-law of a political rival.

Yet emotional appeals should never *substitute* for sound, well-supported arguments, and as speakers we need to give careful thought to when—and under what circumstances—emotional appeals may be appropriate. In addition, we need to recognize that *some* forms of emotional appeal are, almost by definition, unethical. Name-calling, for example, is a kind of emotional appeal that is always unacceptable. By calling people derogatory names rather than responding to their arguments, you demean, degrade, or even dehumanize others. In the hands of the demagogue, name-calling is *designed* to do just that—to short-circuit the reasoning process by demeaning those with different points of view. Thus, the demagogue may characterize all feminists as "man-haters" or all evangelical Christians as religious "fanatics." This sort of name-calling (what the Greek rhetoricians called *ad hominem*) is not only intellectually dishonest; it silences others and undermines democratic debate.

Finally, scholars have identified a number of specific rhetorical techniques typically employed by the demagogue. According to J. Justin Gustainis, demagogues not only employ excessive emotional appeals and name-calling, they focus attention on their own personalities rather than the issues, oversimplify complex matters, and make logically unsound arguments. Like emotional appeals, none of these tactics is *necessarily* demagogic. Political candidates, for example, may emphasize their personal qualifications for office, and speakers sometimes oversimplify complex issues for uninformed or uneducated audiences. Demagogues, however, *habitually* use such tactics, and they do so to promote their own selfish interests, not the public good. In other words, demagogues deceive and manipulate others to promote *themselves*, and in the process they rarely show "concern for the truth."[39]

However offensive they may be, even demagogues enjoy the protections of the First Amendment. Direct incitements to violence go beyond the bounds of free speech, but even the most offensive forms of name-calling and stereotyping are generally considered protected speech under our Constitution. In recent years, a number of colleges and universities have tried to ban so-called **hate speech** on campus, but these speech codes rarely stand up in court. Nor do libel and slander laws offer much protection against even the most vicious personal attacks on public figures. Perhaps that helps explain why there is so much "mudslinging" during our political campaigns. Inevitably, some will exploit our right to free speech to say unfair or even offensive things about others.

In an era of rapid technological and social change, the ethics of public speaking have become even more complicated. Hate speech has found a new home on the Internet, where its sources can remain anonymous and not be held accountable. Meanwhile, our society grows more diverse every day, complicating our efforts to identify shared ethical standards. Yet the basic principles of ethical speech—honesty, accountability, good faith, and commitment to the larger "public good"—remain as relevant today as they were more than 2,000 years ago. It is up to us—each and every one of us—to speak out against demagoguery and contribute something positive and constructive to the public dialogue. As William Norwood Brigance put it, we should all insist on speech "worth listening to"—speech that serves our democracy by helping us make good choices.

HIGHLIGHTING ETHICAL COMMUNICATION

In 1999, the leading professional organization for scholars and teachers of communication, the National Communication Association, adopted the following Credo for Ethical Communication:

1. We advocate truthfulness, accuracy, honesty, and reason as essential to the integrity of communication.
2. We endorse freedom of expression, diversity of perspective, and tolerance of dissent to achieve the informed and responsible decision making fundamental to a civil society.
3. We strive to understand and respect other communicators before evaluating and responding to their messages.
4. We promote access to communication resources and opportunities as necessary to fulfill human potential and contribute to the well-being of families, communities, and society.
5. We promote communication climates of caring and mutual understanding that respect the unique needs and characteristics of individual communicators.
6. We condemn communication that degrades individuals and humanity through distortion, intimidation, coercion, and violence, and through the expression of intolerance and hatred.
7. We are committed to the courageous expression of personal convictions in pursuit of fairness and justice.
8. We advocate sharing information, opinions, and feelings when facing significant choices while also respecting privacy and confidentiality.
9. We accept responsibility for the short- and long-term consequences for our own communication and expect the same of others.

Source: Reprinted by permission from the National Communication Association. www.natcom.org.

SUMMARY

- Democratic citizenship entails responsibilities as well as rights, including the responsibility to "get involved."
  - For some, getting involved may mean supporting political candidates.
  - For others, it may mean volunteering to help others or "speaking out" on the issues.
- Civic engagement involves *communicating* with others, so it is important that citizens in a democracy learn *how* to communicate both effectively and ethically.
- Your ethical responsibilities as a public speaker should be kept in mind at every stage of the speech-making process.
  - The ethical speaker pursues worthy goals.
  - The ethical speaker is honest and accountable, avoiding plagiarism and taking full responsibility for words spoken in public.
- The basic rules of ethical speech have not changed since ancient times, although demagoguery has assumed new forms and the ethical issues relating to speech have been complicated by technological and social change.
  - The ethical speaker deliberates "in good faith" and is well informed and fully prepared.

- The ethical speaker avoids the techniques of the demagogue and never substitutes appeals to the emotions for sound, well-supported arguments.
- The ethical speaker uses the power of speech to enlighten and inspire his or her fellow citizens and to serve the public good.

QUESTIONS FOR REVIEW AND REFLECTION

1. What, in your opinion, are the most important responsibilities of citizenship in a democracy? What does it mean to "get involved" as a citizen, and what sorts of involvement are most satisfying or effective?
2. What are the most important ethical concerns surrounding public speaking in a democracy? What does it mean to speak "ethically"? How, if at all, have the ethical considerations in public speaking changed over time?
3. How would you define the term *plagiarism*, and what are the differences between deliberate and "accidental" plagiarism?
4. What ethical concerns, if any, are raised by the practice of ghostwriting? Is ghostwriting always unethical, or is it unethical only under certain circumstances? How might we distinguish ethical from unethical ghostwriting?
5. What does it mean to deliberate in "good faith"? Does deliberating in good faith mean being completely objective? Can you be passionate about your political views and still deliberate in good faith?
6. Define *demagoguery*. How does demagoguery relate to the use of emotional appeals? Is it always demagogic to appeal to your audience's emotions? How, if at all, would you distinguish between ethical and unethical emotional appeals? Beyond emotional appeals, what other techniques in public speaking are associated with demagoguery?

ENDNOTES

1. William Norwood Brigance, *Speech: Its Techniques and Disciplines in a Free Society*, 2nd ed. (New York: Appleton-Century-Crofts, 1961), 1, 4–5.
2. Tom Brokaw, *The Greatest Generation* (New York: Random House, 1998).
3. William Norwood Brigance, *Speech Communication*, 2nd ed. (New York: Appleton-Century-Crofts, 1955), 2–3.
4. Judith Forman, "Grass-Roots Activism Is Thriving; Causes Differ, but Aim Is Better Communities," *Boston Globe*, November 1, 2001, 1.
5. Paul Rogat Loeb, *Soul of a Citizen: Living with Conviction in a Cynical Time* (New York: St. Martin's Press, 1999), 4–6, 199–200.
6. Peter D. Hart and Mario A. Brossard, "A Generation to Be Proud Of," *Brookings Review* 20 (Fall 2002): 36–37.
7. Michael Olander, "How Young People Express Their Political Views," Center for Information and Research on Civic Learning and Engagement, Fact Sheet, July 2003, www.civicyouth.org/PopUps/FactSheets/FS_How_Young_Express_Views.pdf (accessed May 14, 2009).
8. Mark Hugo Lopez, Peter Levine, Deborah Both, Abby Keisa, Emily Kirby, and Karlo Marcelo, *The 2006 Civic and Political Health of the Nation: A Detailed Look at How Youth Participate in Politics and Communities* (College Park, MD: Center for Information and Research on Civic Learning and Engagement, 2006), 3, 9.
9. See Elham Khatami, "Spring Breakers Skip Cancun for Volunteer Work," *CNN.com*, March 4, 2009, www.cnn.com/2009/TRAVEL/getaways/03/04/alternative.spring.break.travel/index.html (accessed May 12, 2009); Eleni Berger, "Students Look beyond the Beach for Spring Break," *CNN.com*,

March 12, 2003, www.cnn.com/2003/TRAVEL/02/27/spring.service/ (accessed May 12, 2009); James Madison University, Office of Public Affairs, "Students Battle Hunger, Poverty in Alternative Spring Break," news release, web.jmu.edu/mediarel/PubAffairs-asp/PR-thisRelease.asp?AutoID=347 (accessed May 12, 2009); Jane Engle, "For This Party over Spring Break, Bring Your Own Hammer," *LATimes.com*, February 20, 2005, www.latimes.com/travel/la-tr-insider20feb20,1,2302870.column (accessed May 12, 2009); and Karl E. Schwab, "80 SRU Students to Spend Spring Break Offering Community Service across U.S.," *SRU News*, www.sru.edu/pages/10651.asp (accessed May 12, 2009).

10. Abby Kiesa, Alexander P. Orlowski, Peter Levine, Deborah Both, Emily Hoban Kirby, Mark Hugo Lopez, and Karlos Barrios Marcelo, *Millennials Talk Politics: A Study of College Student Political Engagement* (College Park, MD: Center for Information and Research on Civic Learning and Engagement, 2007).
11. Russell J. Dalton, *The Good Citizen: How a Younger Generation Is Reshaping American Politics* (Washington, DC: CQ Press, 2008), 29.
12. Megan Eckstein, "Youth Vote in 2008 Election Ranked among the Highest Ever, Data Show," *Chronicle of Higher Education*, April 29, 2009, chronicle.com/news/article/?id=6396 (accessed May 12, 2009).
13. Morris P. Fiorina, *Culture War? The Myth of a Divided America* (New York: Pearson, 2005), 102.
14. Eric Hoffer, *The True Believer* (New York: Harper & Brothers, 1951).
15. Fiorina, *Culture War?*, 111.
16. Gordon S. Wood, "The Democratization of the American Mind," in *Leadership in the American Revolution* (Washington, DC: Library of Congress, 1974), 70.
17. See Alexander Moseley, "Just War Theory," *The Internet Encyclopedia of Philosophy*, www.utm.edu/research/iep/j/justwar.htm (accessed May 16, 2009).
18. Kathy Slobogin, "Survey: Many Students Say Cheating Is OK," *CNN.com*, April 5, 2002, archives.cnn.com/2002/fyi/teachers.ednews/04/05/highschool.cheating/index.html (accessed May 13, 2009).
19. "How to Avoid Plagiarism," www.northwestern.edu/uacc/plagiar.html (accessed May 13, 2009).
20. See the home page for Turnitin.com, www.turnitin.com/static/index.html (accessed May 13, 2009).
21. Jeremy R. Cooke, "More Cheaters Found, XF Grade on the Rise," *Daily Collegian Online*, January 20, 2003, www.collegian.psu.edu/archive/2003/01/01-20-03tdc/ 01-20-03dnews-02.asp (accessed May 13, 2009).
22. See Ronald B. Standler, "Plagiarism in Colleges in U.S.," www.rbs2.com/plag.htm (accessed May 13, 2009).
23. See Jim Geraghty, "Biden His Time," *National Review*, January 22, 2003, www.nationalreview.com/comment/comment-geraghty012203.asp (accessed May 13, 2009).
24. Erin Neff, "Gibbons' Speech Plagiarism: 15 Paragraphs Came from Copyrighted Talk by Alabama Woman," *Las Vegas Review-Journal*, March 4, 2005, www.reviewjournal.com/lvrj_home/2005/Mar-04-Fri-2005/news/25992087.html (accessed May 13, 2009).
25. "Reporter Says He 'Never Meant to Hurt Anyone,'" *CNN.com*, March 1, 2004, www.cnn.com/2003/US/Northeast/06/06/nytimes.blair/index.html?iref=newssearch (accessed May 13, 2009).
26. Lois Einhorn, "Ghostwriting: Two Famous Ghosts Speak on Its Nature and Its Ethical Implications," in *Ethical Dimensions of Political Communication*, ed. Robert E. Denton Jr. (New York: Praeger, 1991), 115.
27. Kennedy's speechwriter, Theodore C. Sorensen, not only wrote speeches but served as one of Kennedy's closest and most trusted advisers. Sorensen later wrote a best-selling biography of the 35th president. See Theodore C. Sorensen, *Kennedy* (New York: Harper & Row, 1965).
28. See Peggy Noonan, *What I Saw at the Revolution: A Political Life in the Reagan Era* (New York: Ivy Books, 1990).
29. Einhorn, "Ghostwriting," 127–30.
30. See Wynton C. Hall, "The Invention of 'Quantifiably Safe Rhetoric': Richard Wirthlin and Ronald Reagan's Instrumental Use of Public Opinion Research in Presidential Discourse," *Western Journal of Communication* 66 (2002): 319–46.
31. Dick Morris, *Behind the Oval Office: Getting Reelected against All Odds* (Los Angeles: Renaissance Books, 1999).

32. For a review of the literature and a discussion of the debate surrounding these issues, see J. Michael Hogan et al., "Report of the National Task Force on the Presidency and Public Opinion," in *The Prospect of Presidential Rhetoric*, ed. James Arnt Aune and Martin J. Medhurst (College Station: Texas A&M University Press, 2007), 293–316.
33. Noonan, *What I Saw at the Revolution*, 73.
34. Einhorn, "Ghostwriting," 135–40.
35. Qtd. in Fiorina, *Culture War?*, ix.
36. Charles W. Lomas, *The Agitator in American Society* (Englewood Cliffs, NJ: Prentice Hall, 1968), 18.
37. Qtd. in T. Harry Williams, *Huey Long* (New York: Knopf, 1969), 411.
38. Reinhard H. Luthin, "Some Demagogues in American History," *American Historical Review* 57 (1951): 22, 45.
39. J. Justin Gustainis, "Demagoguery and Political Rhetoric: A Review of the Literature," *Rhetoric Society Quarterly* 20 (1990): 155–61.

Speech to the 58th National Prayer Breakfast, February 4, 2010

Secretary of State Hillary Clinton

The National Prayer Breakfast is an annual event in Washington, D.C. where prominent people—from Mother Teresa, to former British Prime Minister Tony Blair, to the humanitarian rock star Bono—are invited to reflect upon the role of religious faith in their life and work. Every president since Dwight Eisenhower has attended the event, and it now attracts some 3,500 participants from more than 100 countries. Hosted by The Fellowship Foundation, a group of conservative Christians within Congress, the event provoked controversy in 2010 after reports linked the sponsoring group to efforts to pass anti-gay legislation in Uganda. Ignoring calls to boycott the event, Clinton instead used the breakfast as an opportunity to denounce intolerance and violence in the name of religion and to go on record as strongly opposed to such discriminatory legislation.

Thank you. Thank you very much. I have to begin by saying I'm not Bono. (Laughter.) Those of you who were here when he was, I apologize beforehand. (Laughter.) But it is a great pleasure to be with you and to be here with President and Mrs. Obama, to be with Vice President Biden, with Chairman Mullen, with certainly our host today, my former colleagues and friends, Senators Isakson and Amy Klobuchar. And to be with so many distinguished guests and visitors who have come from all over our country and indeed from all over the world.

CLINTON OPENS ON A LIGHT NOTE, ESTABLISHING COMMON GROUND BY RECALLING THE ROCK STAR BONO'S HUMOROUS KEYNOTE ADDRESS THE PREVIOUS YEAR. SHE BUILDS HER OWN CREDIBILITY BY MENTIONING HER LONG ASSOCIATION WITH THE EVENT.

I have attended this prayer breakfast every year since 1993, and I have always found it to be a gathering that inspires and motivates me. Now today, our minds are still filled with the images of the tragedy of Haiti, where faith is being tested daily in food lines and makeshift hospitals, in tent cities where there are not only so many suffering people, but so many vanished dreams.

When I think about the horrible catastrophe that has struck Haiti, I am both saddened but also spurred. This is a moment that has already been embraced by people of faith from everywhere. I thank Prime Minister Zapatero for his country's response and commitment. Because in the days since the earthquake, we have seen the world and the world's faithful spring into action on behalf of those suffering. President Obama has put our country on the leading edge of making sure that we do all we can to help alleviate not only the immediate suffering, but to assist in the rebuilding and recovery. So many countries have answered the call, and so many churches, synagogues, mosques, and temples have brought their own people together. And even modern technology through Facebook and telethons and text messages and Twitter, there's been an overwhelming global response. But of course, there's so much more to be done.

TURNING QUICKLY TO WORLD EVENTS, CLINTON DESCRIBES THE U.S. RESPONSE TO THE EARTHQUAKE IN HAITI AND THE IMPORTANT ROLE OF RELIGIOUS GROUPS IN THE RELIEF EFFORTS.

When I think about being here with all of you today, there are so many subjects to talk about. You've already heard, both in prayer and in scripture reading and in Prime Minister Zapatero's remarks, a number of messages. But let me be both personal and speak from my unique perspective now as Secretary of State. I've been here as a First Lady. I've been here as a senator, and now I am here as a Secretary of State. I have heard heartfelt descriptions of personal faith journeys. I've heard impassioned pleas for feeding the hungry and helping the poor, caring for the sick. I've heard speeches about promoting understanding among people of different faiths. I've met hundreds of visitors from countries across the globe. I've seen the leaders of my own country come here amidst the crises of the time and, for at

ADOPTING A PERSONAL TONE, CLINTON RECALLS BEING INSPIRED BY PREVIOUS NATIONAL PRAYER BREAKFASTS. IN THE PROCESS, SHE CRITIQUES THE "SMALLNESS, IRRELEVANCY, AND EVEN MEANNESS" OF OUR "POLITICAL CULTURE" AND RECALLS HOW HER OWN PERSONAL FAITH HAS BEEN STRENGTHENED BY HER CONNECTIONS least a morning, put away political and ideological differences. And I've watched and I've listened to three presidents, each a man of faith, speak from their hearts, both sharing their own feelings about being in a position that has almost intolerably impossible burdens to bear, and appealing often, either explicitly or implicitly, for an end to the increasing smallness, irrelevancy, even meanness, of our own political culture. My own heart has been touched and occasionally pierced by the words I've heard, and often my spirit has been lifted by the musicians and the singers who have shared their gifts in praising the Lord with us. And during difficult and painful times, my faith has been strengthened by the personal connections that I have experienced with people who, by the calculus of politics, were on the opposite side of me on the basis of issues or partisanship.

TO PEOPLE WHO, POLITICALLY, WERE ON THE "OPPOSITE SIDE."

After my very first prayer breakfast, a bipartisan group of women asked me to join them for lunch and told me that they were forming a prayer group. And these prayer partners prayed for me. They prayed for me during some very challenging times. They came to see me in the White House. They kept in touch with me and some still do today. And they gave me a handmade book with messages, quotes, and scripture, to sustain me. And of all the thousands of gifts that I received in the White House, I have a special affection for this one. Because in addition to the tangible gift of the book, it contained 12 intangible gifts, 12 gifts of discernment, peace, compassion, faith, fellowship, vision, forgiveness, grace, wisdom, love, joy, and courage. And I have had many occasions to pull out that book and to look at it and to try, Chairman Mullen, to figure out how to close the gap of what I am feeling and doing with what I know I should be feeling and doing. As a person of faith, it is a constant struggle, particularly in the political arena, to close that gap that each of us faces.

SUGGESTING THE NEED FOR MORE CIVILITY AND COOPERATION AMONG PEOPLE OF DIFFERING VIEWS, SHE TELLS THE STORY OF A BIPARTISAN GROUP OF WOMEN WHO FORMED A PRAYER GROUP AT THE FIRST PRAYER BREAKFAST SHE ATTENDED AND LATER SUPPORTED HER THROUGH SOME "VERY CHALLENGING TIMES."

In February of 1994, the speaker here was Mother Teresa. She gave, as everyone who remembers that occasion will certainly recall, a strong address against abortion. And then she asked to see me. And I thought, "Oh, dear." (Laughter.) And after the breakfast, we went behind that curtain and we sat on folding chairs, and I remember being struck by how small she was and how powerful her hands were, despite her size, and that she was wearing sandals in February in Washington. (Laughter.)

CLINTON CONTINUES TO INVOKE MEMORIES OF PREVIOUS PRAYER BREAKFASTS BY RECALLING HER MEETING WITH MOTHER TERESA, IN 1994. AT THAT MEETING, CLINTON AND MOTHER TERESA FOUND COMMON GROUND ON THE DIVISIVE ISSUE OF ABORTION BY AGREEING TO WORK TOGETHER TO PROMOTE ADOPTION.

We began to talk, and she told me that she knew that we had a shared conviction about adoption being vastly better as a choice for unplanned or unwanted babies. And she asked me—or more properly, she directed me—to work with her to create a home for such babies here in Washington. I know that we often picture, as we're growing up, God as a man with a white beard. But that day, I felt like I had been ordered, and that the message was coming not just through this diminutive woman but from someplace far beyond.

So I started to work. And it took a while because we had to cut through all the red tape. We had to get all the approvals. I thought it would be easier than it turned out to be. She proved herself to be the most relentless lobbyist I've ever encountered. (Laughter.) She could not get a job in your White House, Mr. President. (Laughter.) She never let up. She called me from India, she called me from Vietnam, she wrote me letters, and it was always: "When's the house gonna open? How much more can be done quickly?"

Finally, the moment came: June, 1995, and the Mother Teresa Home for Infant Children opened. She flew in from Kolkata to attend the opening, and like a happy child, she gripped my arm and led me around, looking at the bassinets and the pretty painted colors on the wall, and just beaming about what this meant for children and their futures.

A few years later, I attended her funeral in Kolkata, where I saw presidents and prime ministers, royalty and street beggars, pay her homage. And after the service, her successor, Sister Nirmala, the leader of the Missionaries of Charity, invited me to come to the Mother House. I was deeply touched. When I arrived, I realized I was one of only a very few outsiders. And I was directed into a whitewashed room where the casket had already arrived. And we stood around with the nuns, with the candles on the walls flickering, and prayed for this extraordinary woman. And then Sister Nirmala asked me to offer a prayer. I felt both inadequate and deeply honored, just as I do today. And in the tradition of prayer breakfast speakers, let me share a few matters that reflect how I came on my own faith journey, and how I think about the responsibilities that President Obama and his Administration and our government face today.

As Amy said, I grew up in the Methodist Church. On both sides of my father's family, the Rodhams and the Joneses, they came from mining towns. And they claimed, going back many years, to have actually been converted by John and Charles Wesley. And, of course, Methodists were methodical. It was a particularly good religion for me. (Laughter.) And part of it is a commitment to living out your faith. We believe that faith without works may not be dead, but it's hard to discern from time to time.

TURNING TO HER OWN PERSONAL "FAITH JOURNEY," CLINTON DESCRIBES HERSELF AS A METHODIST, A FOLLOWER OF THE TEACHING OF JOHN WESLEY. IN THE PROCESS, SHE BUILDS HER OWN CREDIBILITY AS ONE WHOSE MISSION IN LIFE IS TO "DO GOOD."

And of course, John Wesley had this simple rule which I carry around with me as I travel: Do all the good you can by all the means you can in all the ways you can in all the places you can at all the times you can to all the people you can, as long as ever you can. That's a tall order. And of course, one of the interpretive problems with it is, who defines good? What are we actually called to do, and how do we stay humble enough, obedient enough, to ask ourselves, am I really doing what I'm called to do?

It was a good rule to be raised by and it was certainly a good rule for my mother and father to discipline us by. And I think it's a good rule to live by, with the appropriate dose of humility. Our world is an imperfect one filled with imperfect people, so we constantly struggle to meet our own spiritual goals. But John Wesley's teachings, and the teachings of my church, particularly during my childhood and teenage years, gave me the impetus to believe that I did have a responsibility. It meant not sitting on the sidelines, but being in the arena. And it meant constantly working to try to fulfill the lessons that I absorbed as a child. It's not easy. We're here today because we're all seekers, and we can all look around our own lives and the lives of those whom we know and see everyone falling so short.

And then of course, as we look around the world, there are so many problems and challenges that people of faith are attempting to address or should be. We can recite those places where human beings are mired in the past—their hatreds, their differences—where governments refuse to speak to other governments, where the progress of entire nations is undermined because isolation and insularity seem less risky than cooperation and

CONSIDERING THE ROLE OF "PEOPLE OF FAITH" IN WORLD AFFAIRS, CLINTON LAMENTS THAT RELIGION TOO OFTEN DIVIDES RATHER THAN UNIFIES. SHE CITES collaboration, where all too often it is religion that is the force that drives and sustains division rather than being the healing balm. These patterns persist despite the overwhelming evidence that more good will come from suspending old animosities and preconceptions from engaging others in dialogue, from remembering the cardinal rules found in all of the world's major religions.

NORTHERN IRELAND AS PROOF THAT IT IS POSSIBLE TO OVERCOME EVEN THE MOST DEEPLY ENTRENCHED RELIGIOUS DIFFERENCES.

Last October, I visited Belfast once again, 11 years after the signing of the Good Friday Agreement, a place where being a Protestant or a Catholic determined where you lived, often where you worked, whether you were a friend or an enemy, a threat or a target. Yet over time, as the body count grew, the bonds of common humanity became more powerful than the differences fueled by ancient wrongs. So bullets have been traded for ballots.

As we meet this morning, both communities are attempting to hammer out a final agreement on the yet unresolved issues between them. And they are discovering anew what the Scripture urges us: "Let us not become weary in doing good, for at the proper time we will reap a harvest if we don't give up." Even in places where God's presence and promise seems fleeting and unfulfilled or completely absent, the power of one person's faith and the determination to act can help lead a nation out of darkness.

Some of you may have seen the film Pray the Devil Back to Hell. It is the story of a Liberian woman who was tired of the conflict and the killing and the fear that had gripped her country for years. So she went to her church and she prayed for an end to the civil war. And she organized other women at her church, and then at other churches, then at the mosques. Soon thousands of women became a mass movement, rising up and praying for a peace, and working to bring it about that finally, finally ended the conflict.

TURNING TO ANOTHER TROUBLED PART OF THE WORLD, CLINTON IDENTIFIES TWO AFRICAN COUNTRIES WHICH HAVE SUFFERED GREATLY FROM VIOLENCE AND WARFARE: LIBERIA AND CONGO. IN BOTH, SHE SUGGESTS, PEOPLE OF FAITH—PARTICULARLY WOMEN—HAVE LED EFFORTS TO STOP THE VIOLENCE AND RESTORE PEACE AND HOPE.

And yet the devil must have left Liberia and taken up residence in Congo. When I was in the Democratic Republic of Congo this summer, the contrasts were so overwhelmingly tragic—a country the size of Western Europe, rich in minerals and natural resources, where 5.4 million people have been killed in the most deadly conflict since World War II, where 1,100 women and girls are raped every month, where the life expectancy is 46 and dropping, where poverty, starvation, and all of the ills that stalk the human race are in abundance.

When I traveled to Goma, I saw in a single day the best and the worst of humanity. I met with women who had been savaged and brutalized physically and emotionally, victims of gender and sexual-based violence in a place where law, custom, and even faith did little to protect them. But I also saw courageous women who, by faith, went back into the bush to find those who, like them, had been violently attacked. I saw the doctors and the nurses who were helping to heal the wounds, and I saw so many who were there because their faith led them to it.

As we look at the world today and we reflect on the overwhelming response of outpouring of generosity to what happened in Haiti, I'm reminded of the story of Elijah. After he goes to Mount Horeb, we read that he faced "a great wind, so strong that it was splitting mountains and breaking rocks in pieces before the Lord, but the Lord was not in the wind; and after the wind an earthquake, but the Lord was not in the earthquake; and after the earthquake a fire, but the Lord was not in the fire; and after the fire a sound of sheer silence—a still small voice." It was then that Elijah heard the voice of the Lord. It is often when we are only quiet enough to listen that we do as well. It's something we can do at any time, without a disaster or a catastrophe provoking it. It shouldn't take that.

Clinton demonstrates her command of biblical texts by relating the story of Elijah. She then expounds upon the ethical commands common to all religions: care for the poor and suffering, the Golden Rule, and love for one's neighbors.

But the teachings of every religion call us to care for the poor, tell us to visit the orphans and widows, to be generous and charitable, to alleviate suffering. All religions have their version of the Golden Rule and direct us to love our neighbor and welcome the stranger and visit the prisoner. But how often in the midst of our own lives do we respond to that? All of these holy texts, all of this religious wisdom from these very different faiths call on us to act out of love.

In politics, we sometimes talk about message discipline—making sure everyone uses the same set of talking points. Well, whoever was in charge of message discipline on these issues for every religion certainly knew what they were doing. Regardless of our differences, we all got the same talking points and the same marching orders. So the charge is a personal one. Yet across the world, we see organized religion standing in the way of faith, perverting love, undermining that message.

Sometimes it's easier to see that far away than here at home. But religion, cloaked in naked power lust, is used to justify horrific violence, attacks on homes, markets, schools, volleyball games, churches, mosques, synagogues, temples. From Iraq to Pakistan and Afghanistan to Nigeria and the Middle East, religion is used a club to deny the human rights of girls and women, from the Gulf to Africa to Asia, and to discriminate, even advocating the execution of gays and lesbians. Religion is used to enshrine in law intolerance of free expression and peaceful protest. Iran is now detaining and executing people under a new crime—waging war against God. It seems to be a rather dramatic identity crisis.

Turning to the dark side of faith-based politics, Clinton laments how religion is sometimes used to justify oppression and violence. Speaking on behalf of the Obama administration, she pledges to fight against human rights abuses perpetrated "in the name of religion." In the process, she indirectly criticizes the Fellowship Foundation for its alleged support of anti-gay legislation in Uganda.

So in the Obama Administration, we are working to bridge religious divides. We're taking on violations of human rights perpetrated in the name of religion. And we invite members of Congress and clergy and active citizens like all of you here to join us. Of course we're supporting the peace processes from Northern Ireland to the Middle East, and of course we are following up on the President's historic speech at Cairo with outreach efforts to Muslims and promoting interfaith dialogue, and of course we're condemning the repression in Iran.

But we are also standing up for girls and women, who too often in the name of religion, are denied their basic human rights. And we are standing up for gays and lesbians who deserve to be treated as full human beings. (Applause.) And we are also making it clear to countries and leaders that these are priorities of the United States. Every time I travel, I raise the plight of girls and women, and make it clear that we expect to see changes. And I recently called President Museveni, whom I have known through the prayer breakfast, and expressed the strongest concerns about a law being considered in the parliament of Uganda.

We are committed, not only to reaching out and speaking up about the perversion of religion, and in particularly the use of it to promote and justify terrorism, but also seeking to find common ground. We are working with Muslim nations to come up with an appropriate way of demonstrating criticism of religious intolerance without stepping over into the area of freedom of religion or non-religion and expression. So there is much to be done, and there is a lot of challenging opportunities for each of us as we leave this prayer breakfast, this 58th prayer breakfast.

In 1975, my husband and I, who had gotten married in October, and we were both teaching at the University of Arkansas Law School in beautiful Fayetteville, Arkansas—we got married on a Saturday and we went back to work on a Monday. So around Christmastime, we decided that we should go somewhere and celebrate, take a honeymoon. And my late father said, "Well, that's a great idea. We'll come, too." (Laughter.)

Transitioning into her conclusion with another personal story, Clinton recalls her honeymoon and a subsequent trip to Haiti. This connects back to her introduction, where she first mentioned Haiti, and signals that she is about to conclude. It also reinforces her credibility as a Secretary of State who truly empathizes with the Haitians and is committed to helping them long after the news cameras leave. Invoking religious language and imagery, she concludes with a prayer, reinforcing her theme that we must bridge our religious and political differences if we hope to be a "greater force for good on behalf of all creation."

And indeed, Bill and I and my entire family—(laughter)—went to Acapulco. We had a great time, but it wasn't exactly a honeymoon. So when we got back, Bill was talking to one of his friends who was then working in Haiti, and his friend said, "Well, why don't you come see me? This is the most interesting country. Come and take some time." So indeed, we did. So we were there over the New Year's holidays. And I remember visiting the Cathedral in Port-au-Prince, in the midst, at that time, so much fear from the regime of the Duvaliers, and so much poverty, there was this cathedral that had stood there and served as a beacon of hope and faith.

After the earthquake, I was looking at some of our pictures from the disaster, and I saw the total destruction of the cathedral. It was just a heart-rending moment. And yet I also saw men and women helping one another, digging through the rubble, dancing and singing in the makeshift communities that they were building up. And I thought again that as the scripture reminds us, "Though the mountains be shaken and the hills be removed, yet my unfailing love for you will not be shaken nor my covenant of peace be removed."

As the memory of this crisis fades, as the news cameras move on to the next very dramatic incident, let us pray that we can sustain the force and the feeling that we find in our hearts and in our faith in the aftermath of such tragedies. Let us pray that we will all continue to be our brothers' and sisters' keepers. Let us pray that amid our differences, we can continue to see the power of faith not only to make us whole as individuals, to provide personal salvation, but to make us a greater whole and a greater force for good on behalf of all creation.

So let us do all the good we can, by all the means we can, in all the ways we can, in all the places we can, to all the people we can, as long as ever we can.

God bless you. (Applause.)

Source: From Hillary Rodham Clinton, "Keynote Address at the 58th National Prayer Breakfast, February 4, 2010." Published 2010 by U.S. Department of State.

CHAPTER

3

Preparing to Speak with Commitment and Confidence

CHAPTER SURVEY

CHAPTER OBJECTIVES

After studying this chapter, you should be able to

1. Understand the meaning and importance of transactional communication.
2. Be able to explain the nature and significance of the speaker-listener partnership.
3. Know the key principles involved in preparing yourself to speak.
4. Understand how to deal with communication apprehension while preparing yourself to speak with confidence.

CIVIC ENGAGEMENT AND PUBLIC SPEAKING

Preview. *Communication models stress that the aim of communication is to get a response from an audience. As a form of civic engagement, however, public speaking is audience centered and assumes an equal, collaborative partnership between the speaker and listeners. For a speech to be truly successful, the audience as well as the speaker should derive some benefit from the exchange.*

Some view communication as a one-way street. If the speaker gets what he or she is after, according to this view, the speech is effective. But that's only part of the picture. In a democratic society, the true value of a speech must be judged by the outcome for all parties involved in the communication process: the speaker *and* the listeners. In addition, a speech should be judged by its larger contributions to society. Does it contribute something useful to public discussion? Does it help the community resolve important controversies, or does it motivate members of the community to do good things?

To communicate effectively, you must respect your listeners' needs, sensitivities, and rights. You must know something about their predispositions, tastes, prejudices, capabilities, and knowledge. If you hope to get a response from your listeners, you need to consider what characteristics they share as a group and what qualities individual members bring to the public speaking situation. Seeing public speaking as a mutually beneficial experience for both speaker and listener means that taking advantage of an audience—getting them to do something that is harmful to them, buy something that is useless, or act in some destructive

FOCUS ON CIVIC ENGAGEMENT

The Ripon College Speakers Bureau

Ripon College, a small liberal arts school in Wisconsin, has a long and distinguished tradition of teaching speech and debate. In 2006, however, two faculty members at the college, Jody Roy and Steve Martin, decided that public speaking should be about more than speaking to other students in a classroom or competing for a trophy at a speech or debate contest. They envisioned students becoming engaged citizens and leaders in their communities, as emphasized in the classical and neoclassical rhetorical traditions. The result was the formation of the Ripon College Speakers Bureau, a co-curricular program that creates partnerships between student speakers and local and national nonprofit groups.

Since its inception in 2006, the Speakers Bureau has helped students at Ripon College put into practice what they learn in the classroom. Advocating on behalf of these local and national partners, the students have benefited both themselves and their communities. Currently, Ripon students serve as advocates for Students Against Violence Everywhere, a national nonprofit association promoting conflict management skills and good citizenship, as well as the Huntington's Disease Society of America, which promotes awareness of this devastating degenerative brain disorder. Ripon students also have assisted a number of local partners, including the Green Lake Area Animal Shelter and the Ripon Public Library.

The Speakers Bureau trains participating students and then sends them into the community, often to speak to middle school or high school students. Alyssa Paulsen, for example, has spoken way—should never be your goal. Public speaking is a way of promoting the public good, and as such, it must occur within an ethical framework.

The Speaker-Listener Partnership in a Democratic Society

More than 40 years ago, communication scholar David Berlo, in his groundbreaking book *The Process of Communication*, argued that all communication, including public speaking, should be viewed as a process.[1] Later, Gerald Miller described that process as "transactional," or as an exchange between the "sender" and the "receiver."[2] In this model, communication is seen as a process in which speakers and listeners continuously exchange messages and negotiate meanings. As communications scholars Steve Duck and David McMahon put it, **transactional communication** is the process of constructing "shared messages or understandings between two or more individuals."[3] In other words, the speaker should make adjustments based on the messages that come back from the audience. As we will explain in Chapter 4, listeners are not passive; they send information about their reactions to the speaker. Together, the speaker and the listener create a relationship in which they share meanings and negotiate shared interpretations.

In Figure 3.1 you can see the elements of a transactional model and how this differs from the idea of simply sending out a message to an audience. The speaker **encodes** a message; that is, the speaker takes his or her ideas and puts them in a form to be sent though a channel (the speech). The listener **decodes** the messages—that is, interprets the verbal and nonverbal aspects of the message so as to give

to high school students in Sheboygan, Wisconsin, about how to discourage bullying and harassment. Sarah Hopkins spoke to 280 low-income middle-school students in Racine, Wisconsin, encouraging them to follow their dreams of attending college. Ryan Greene speaks to both college students and adult prison inmates about the causes and harms of domestic violence. And Shawn Karsten, who lost his father to suicide, shares his highly personal narrative with young people struggling with their own family tragedies. Since participating in the Speakers Bureau, Shawn has become a professional speaker, traveling around the country telling his story of life with a famous but tragically alcoholic father. Speaking to audiences at leadership conferences, at-risk youth programs, school assemblies, educational conferences, and addiction and grief-management programs, Shawn's most popular speeches include "From Pain to Purpose," which recounts how he found peace by reaching out to help others, and "This is What It Feels Like to be Your Kid," which is targeted at adults in alcohol and addiction recovery programs.

More and more students are getting involved with the Speakers Bureau at Ripon College, yet it has become so popular with its partner organizations that it has trouble filling all its requests for student speakers!

Sources: Ripon College, "Bookings, Flight Schedules, and Network News Interviews: Speakers Bureau Scrambles to Keep Up with Demand," *The Proof: Department of Communication Newsletter* (Winter 2009), 5; Students Against Violence Everywhere, www.nationalsave.org/ (accessed July 9, 2009); "Shawn Karsten: Transformed by Tragedy—Speaking to Survive," www.shawnkarsten.com (accessed July 9, 2009).

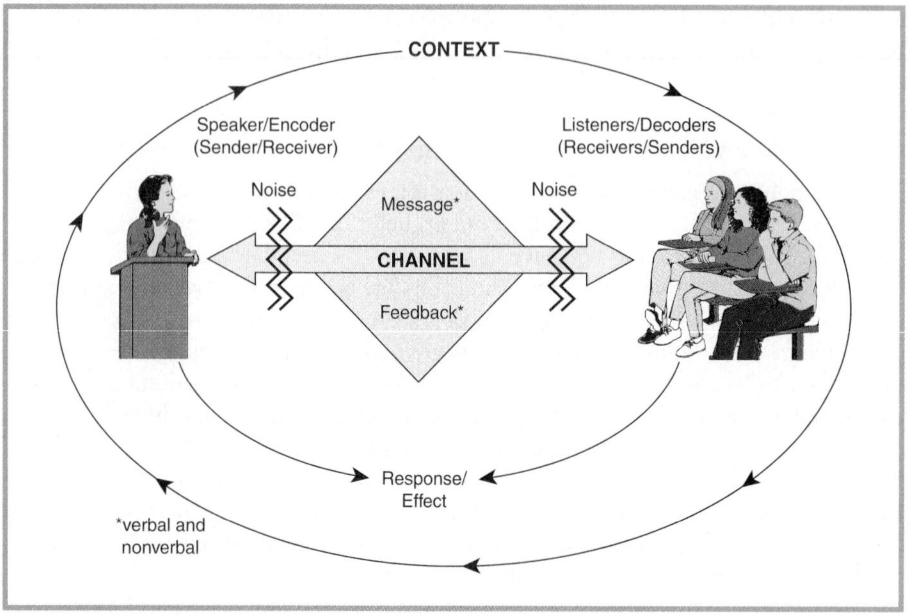

FIGURE 3.1
A Transactional Model of Communication.

them meaning—and sends back verbal and nonverbal messages to the speaker. As these messages go back and forth, there is the possibility of interference, or "noise." All this occurs within a situation or context that also influences the way messages are sent and received.

This view of communication fits well within a broader perspective on public speaking as civic engagement. When you speak in a democratic society, your goal should never be to manipulate your audience just to get your way. Rather, you should join *with* your fellow citizens in deliberating over the best solutions to our common problems. This process—this exchange—presents a variety of challenges. Sometimes messages flow smoothly. At other times, **noise** may distort or interrupt the message flow. A hot, stuffy room will offer a greater challenge to a speaker than a comfortable setting. A **captive audience** is more likely to be preoccupied with other matters than is an audience who has come specifically to hear a speaker. A speaker may create noise himself or herself: too many handouts that distract listeners, or random gestures and boring delivery. Any kind of interference, such as a squeaky microphone or hostile attitudes, constitutes noise in the system. Furthermore, all of us filter messages through our own beliefs and values. We understand, believe, or act based partly on our own experiences, the values we hold, our age or sex, or our cultural practices. These factors will be discussed in detail in Chapter 5, where we consider audience analysis and **adaptation**. For now, just remember that the situation in which you speak and the backgrounds and interests of the listeners can influence the way your message is received. A good speaker will anticipate the nature and extent of these influences.

Speeches always take place in a context. If you were a student at Tulane University or the University of New Orleans, the economic impact of hurricanes would be inherently more interesting to you than it would be to a student at the University of Wisconsin. If a fellow student was attacked at night while walking across campus, the issue of safety would undoubtedly concern you and other students in your audience. If environmental activists have tried to stop logging in a nearby state forest by spiking trees or sabotaging equipment, you may expect students on your campus to have some understanding of radical environmentalism. In short, *where* and *when* you speak can make a big difference. A speech must be designed not only for a specific audience, but also for a particular historical, political, or social context.

Viewing public speaking as a process is important. Both speakers and listeners must be involved in the communication process, and both also have some larger responsibilities to the community. Speakers have an obligation to address serious matters of public concern, and listeners have the responsibility to listen attentively and to critically yet fairly evaluate the speaker's ideas and proposals. If the speaker has been successful, both the speaker and the listeners will benefit. As rhetorical scholar William Norwood Brigance once observed, we may have a right to free speech, but we also have a responsibility to deliver "*useful goods to the listener.*"[4]

Public speaking, in short, connects the speaker to the audience in an ongoing, collaborative partnership. It is not just something that you do *to* an audience, but rather something that depends on the active participation *of* the audience in the communication process.

PREPARING YOURSELF TO SPEAK

Preview. *The overview of the basic principles of public speaking that follows will be developed in detail throughout the rest of this book. These principles will guide you in selecting a topic, establishing credibility, analyzing the audience, gathering relevant materials, constructing reasonable arguments, delivering the speech, and determining the audience response.*

This book is designed to help you acquire the skills you need to speak in public. But first, you must have some *reason* to speak. In your public speaking class, you may speak because you've been given an assignment to do so. In life outside the classroom, however, the need to speak goes deeper than that: it is part of your responsibilities as a citizen in a democracy. Our history is filled with examples of people who felt the need to speak out, including some who risked their lives by doing it. William Lloyd Garrison, the fiery nineteenth-century abolitionist, for example, spent much of his life speaking out against slavery, often facing hostile mobs and threats against his life. More than 30 years before the Civil War, Garrison described his determination to end slavery in the first issue of his famous abolitionist periodical, the *Liberator*: "I am in earnest—I will not equivocate—I will not excuse—I will not retreat a single inch; and I will be heard!"[5] Few of us are as passionately involved with a cause as William Lloyd Garrison. But as citizens in a democracy, we all have the right and the responsibility to speak out on matters of public concern.

Once you have made the decision to speak, you may think that the next step is to write the speech itself. But what about preparing *yourself* to speak? This is not just a trick of words. It is important to think about what *you* need to do to get ready to speak. Preparing yourself to speak means, first, deciding to speak in public, then learning about the principles of effective and ethical public speaking.

Know Yourself

You are your most important asset as a public speaker. Your own beliefs, abilities, knowledge, and potential are the foundation on which any speech is built. Yet few people have speeches in their heads just waiting to be delivered. Getting ready to give a speech is hard work; it involves study, research, reflection, and a desire to contribute to public discussion. It begins with what you know and care about. In Chapter 6 we examine ways to develop significant topics. The key word here is *significant*. Your speeches ought to be about things that matter, things that are important on your campus or in your community, things that affect you and your audience locally, nationally, or globally.

Many students initially think they don't have anything to talk about. But you should start with what is important to you—such as the knowledge you gain as a student of literature or history, or as a prospective teacher, lawyer, computer specialist, or manager. What problems do you and your friends face as you try to get an education? What does the future hold for you and your audience in a world filled with both opportunities and serious dangers? When you turn your attention to such questions, you begin to generate ideas for issues that you can address in your speeches.

Although you may first canvass your own interests and concerns in deciding what to talk about, you also need to think about another dimension of yourself: your credibility. Perhaps you've heard the expression, "If you could only see yourself as others see you." As a speaker, you need to do just that—try to see yourself as others do. We use the word *ethos*, a concept developed more than 2,000 years ago by the philosopher-rhetorician Aristotle, to describe how an audience perceives your character, intelligence, and motives as a speaker.

Some speakers have a well-established **ethos** related to their expertise or experiences. When Dwight Eisenhower ran for president in 1952 and promised to bring the Korean conflict to an end, people believed him because he had led the Allied armies that defeated Nazi Germany in World War II. During the 2008 primary election, Barack Obama valued Senator Ted Kennedy's endorsement because the senator had strong ethos among many Democratic voters. These advantages of reputation, however, are not afforded to most of us. What you do to prepare for your speech and what you do during the speech itself will most affect how your audience perceives you. Being well prepared lets the audience know that you take them and your topic seriously, and are in command of the facts. Being able to communicate directly and easily with your audience reassures them that you can be trusted. In short, in preparing yourself to speak, you must consider how you will be perceived and what you might do to improve your own ethos.

Know Your Audience

Speeches are delivered to specific audiences, and you must consider that audience's needs, interests, beliefs, and knowledge. Your knowledge of yourself must be supplemented by knowledge about those who will be listening to what you have to say.

Knowing your audience makes it possible to adapt to their special needs or interests. If you wished to critique plans to reform Social Security, for example, you might emphasize different points, depending on the age of the audience. If talking to people about to retire, you might emphasize the immediate impact of the reform proposal on benefit payments. If, on the other hand, you are talking to an audience of college students, you might emphasize instead the long-term solvency of the system—whether Social Security will still be there for them when they retire in 40 or 50 years. This doesn't mean you would ignore the impact of the plan on age groups not represented in your audience, but only that the emphasis would change as you adapt to your listeners. Further, the United States encompasses people from many different cultures, not all of whom have the same priorities, values, or experiences.

It would be foolish to assume that everyone belonging to a particular demographic group, such as older people or college students, will react in exactly the same way to a particular message. But it is possible to make limited generalizations about listeners based on their group characteristics. We'll take this up in detail in Chapter 5, but the point here is simply that you must consider carefully the characteristics of the audience and take them into account when you speak.

Adapting to your audience does not mean pandering to what your listeners may *want* to hear. In the 1950s, for example, a Republican senator from Wisconsin, Joseph McCarthy, made vicious, unsubstantiated personal attacks on politicians, government officials, and other public figures, accusing them of Communist sympathies. In the anticommunist climate of the time, criticizing McCarthy's crusade was considered dangerous, possibly leading to the destruction of one's own career and personal life. It was in this atmosphere of fear that Senator Margaret Chase Smith of Maine rose in the Senate to introduce "A Declaration of Conscience." "I speak," she began, "as a Republican. I speak

Senator Margaret Chase Smith of Maine reminded her audience of basic values as she stood up against character assassination and reckless charges made by Senator Joseph McCarthy and his followers.

as a woman. I speak as a United States senator. I speak as an American." In spite of the risk of political backlash, she asserted that "those of us who shout the loudest about Americanism in making character assassinations are all too frequently those who, by our own words and acts, ignore some of the basic principles of Americanism: the right to criticize; the right to hold unpopular beliefs; the right to protest; the right of independent thought." The "exercise of these rights," she went on to say, "should not cost one single American citizen his reputation or his right to a livelihood nor should he be in danger of losing his reputation or livelihood merely because he happens to know someone who holds unpopular beliefs."[6] Senator Smith did not succeed in silencing Senator McCarthy and his supporters; it would be four more years before the Senate formally censured McCarthy for his campaign of character assassination. But in making her case, Smith reminded her audience of basic values that they shared and offered hope to those who objected to McCarthy's irresponsible accusations.

As a speaker, you never set out to deliberately alienate your audience. In speaking your mind, however, you will sometimes tell an audience something they don't want to hear. It is important, of course, that controversial ideas be presented respectfully and supported with convincing arguments and strong evidence. When you are presenting unpopular ideas, your persuasive challenge becomes greater.

FIGURE 3.2

Collecting Information about Your Audience

SOME GUIDING QUESTIONS

1. Does the audience expect me to address a particular aspect of a topic?
2. What is the audience composition?
   a. audience size
   b. age (range and distribution)
   c. sex (mixed or largely same sex)
   d. race/ethnicity
   e. values (religious, political, economic, etc.)
3. What is the speaking environment like?
   a. size and arrangement of room
   b. availability of podium, blackboard, flip chart, microphone
   c. degree of formality
   d. location of building (do I need to get a map?)
   e. parking issues?
4. Are there any time constraints?
5. Will questions follow the speech?
6. What is the anticipated length of the entire meeting? When should I arrive?
7. Can I arrive early or check out the setting ahead of time?

Know the Situation

The setting for a speech can significantly influence how your audience responds to you. You may be speaking in a comfortable or an uncomfortable physical setting. Or you may be close to your audience or separated from them by an orchestra pit. You may be speaking directly to them or using a microphone. You may be talking to them first thing in the morning or right after lunch. Your audience may be there because they are interested in what you have to say or because their attendance is required. It is to your advantage to know in advance something about the setting in which you will be speaking so that you can anticipate potential problems and capitalize on any advantages that the setting may afford.

Shortly after his election in 1912, President Woodrow Wilson dramatically illustrated the importance of a speech's setting. What we now refer to as the State of the Union address was, at the time, called the "annual message." Since Thomas Jefferson's day, this message had been written out by the president, then sent to Congress, where it was read aloud by a clerk. It rarely generated much excitement. Wilson decided to break with precedent and appear in person before a joint session of Congress to deliver his annual message. Although some deplored the break with tradition, Wilson's speech captured national attention and generated so much excitement that every president since has followed his example.[7]

In addition to the setting, the **temporal context** of your speech will influence how it is received. Consider how much the events of September 11, 2001, changed the context for George W. Bush's speeches. After the terrorist attacks, political disagreements suddenly seemed petty, and some even thought it disrespectful or unpatriotic to criticize the commander in chief. President Bush's speeches, at least for a time, received more respectful attention and less partisan criticism. By 2008, however, the context had changed and both the Republican and Democratic candidates for president criticized Bush's policies. With the president's approval ratings dropping below 30 percent and the economy in a slump, Bush became a "lame duck" president and the target of more criticism.

On a smaller scale, you face the challenge of recognizing and adapting to what is going on in your listeners' world. Imagine, for example, that you are giving a class presentation on the role of government in student aid. The student newspaper has just published a story detailing proposed cuts in student aid programs. It is likely that your audience will be aware of this turn of events and will be listening for what you have to say about it. Before you speak, you need to be aware of what is happening in your audience's immediate world that is relevant to your topic.

Aim for Audience Response

Think about the model of communication we presented earlier in the chapter. When you speak, your goal is to bring about some specific response from your audience. This principle is fundamental to everything else you will learn about public speaking, although it does *not* mean that you will resort to any means necessary to get that response. Still, knowing specifically what you want the audience to believe or do will help you determine what ideas to include in your speech. Do you want your audience simply to understand a concept or to take a specific action? For example, if you were giving an informative speech about solar energy, you could explain how it works and the types of equipment needed. If, however, you wished to give a persuasive speech, you might spend less time on such background information and focus more on the need to reduce our dependence on foreign oil and the environmental advantages of solar energy.

One of the first things you should do in preparing yourself to speak is to determine your specific purpose as precisely as possible because it will affect all your other choices. That choice should be realistic, yet that does not mean you should never think big or take a long-range view. Elizabeth Cady Stanton, who organized the first women's rights convention in Seneca Falls, New York, in 1848, advocated that women should have the same rights as men, including the right to vote. It would be another 70 years before women could vote in national elections, but Stanton at least raised the issue in 1848 and started a national debate over women's rights.[8] There may be times when you will realize that your views are not widely accepted and that it is unrealistic to think you can change people's minds overnight. In such situations, you might aim for a more modest response—to get your listeners to admit that there is some problem that needs to be addressed, or to get them at least thinking about an issue that concerns you.

Gather Relevant Materials

As you begin to work on your chosen speech topic, you will most likely have some information already in your head. You may be building on your knowledge of the stock market, the frustrations with the educational system that led your family to choose homeschooling, or your experiences when volunteering at a shelter for battered women. But even with this kind of experience or knowledge, you will have to learn a great deal more to become a credible speaker. Once you have decided on the specific topic of your speech, you will still need to explore other sources of information and find supporting material to back up your ideas. It is especially important to realize that in the process of learning more about your topic, you may even change your position. As you do research, you may find that some of your preconceptions are wrong. As a public speaker you should always be open to the possibility that your own views may change.

Gathering pertinent information may begin with reading about an issue in a general news magazine, such as *Time* or *Newsweek*. These will give you a broad overview and offer multiple perspectives. You also might search for materials on the World Wide Web, although you need to be careful when using information from the Web. Because it is relatively easy to post material, many Web sites present highly biased or even totally false information, rumors, or unsubstantiated gossip. Even the names of Web sites can be misleading. If, for example, you were to come upon http://www.martinlutherking.org/, you might think you had found a good source of biographical information about the famous civil rights leader. In fact, that site is hosted by Stormfront, a white supremacist hate group. The Southern Poverty Law Center has described this site as "the first major hate site on the Internet ... created by former Alabama Klan leader

Don Black in 1995."[9] Unless you know an online source to be highly reliable (a government bureau, the *New York Times*, or a professional journal, for example), it is best to confirm information through other sources. Of course, you can always find reliable articles, books, and government publications in your campus or local public library. You may also want to interview experts, depending on the subject of your speech. Experts can be quoted as sources, and often they can direct you to additional resources. Whatever sources you use, they must be authoritative, reliable, and correctly cited, as we will discuss further in Chapters 7 and 8.

All speakers, no matter how knowledgeable, can benefit from learning more about their topic. Any topic of importance calls for research, and the process of research does not stop as you construct your argument. You must be well informed and, armed with knowledge, begin to form the ideas that will help you accomplish your purpose before you begin to craft your specific arguments.

Construct a Reasonable Argument

When you have decided what you hope to accomplish in your speech, you will need to set about framing ideas and finding material that supports those ideas and builds a reasonable argument. You should seek information that will connect your topic with your audience's feelings, needs, and emotions—what is often referred to as *pathos*—and that makes logical sense. Remember that public speaking is a process: your purpose may change as you gather more information. As you learn more, however, what you hope to accomplish will become clearer.

Consider the following example of how to develop an argument. You are about to cast a vote in a presidential election for the first time. As you try to sort out the issues and where the candidates stand, you realize that a lot of things going on in the campaign do not really encourage you to think for yourself. You would like to look at the issues and decide which person and/or party would exert the best leadership. There are a lot of irrelevant appeals for your vote, however, and a lot of misinformation has been disseminated. You may wonder, for example, why the endorsement of a candidate by a rock star or a country music singer should matter. You see the media paying a lot of attention to personal accusations and to who is ahead in the latest polls. Much of what the candidates say about education or jobs is ignored by the media. You see 15- or 30-second ads that offer slogans and assertions with nothing to back them up. Acting on arguments based exclusively on the advice of celebrities, rejecting a candidate because of unsubstantiated attacks, or voting for a candidate because most people seem to like him or her would not be reasonable actions to take. Moreover, this state of affairs seems to you to trivialize the electoral process.

As you mull this over, you determine that you want to talk about presidential campaigns and, more specifically, about media coverage and advertising in presidential campaigns. Finally, you shape this into a specific purpose—specifically describing the response you want from your audience: *I want my audience to look more critically at the political information presented to them during presidential campaigns.* You then ask yourself, Why do I believe this is so?

Why should my audience agree with me? By answering these questions, you begin to form main ideas—ideas that will be convincing—such as the following:

- Relying on the advice of others can be a mistake.
- Campaign ads may be technically true but still very misleading.
- Campaign news focuses on polls and other aspects of the "horse race" rather than on the issues.

As you then set about studying the topic, these ideas may be modified or new ones may emerge. As you conduct research, you will find specific data or relevant information that will help you make these ideas more convincing to your audience—that is, you collect supporting material. You may support your first idea, for example, by doing any of the following:

- Describing the lack of credentials and expertise among well-known celebrities who have been politically active.
- Quoting from real political experts on the content and effects of political ads and news coverage.
- Uncovering for your audience the sponsors of campaign material that is hostile to one candidate or the other and explain those sponsors' stake in the election.

This process helps you build your argument. As you begin to find relevant material, this material helps you refine your ideas and provides data to make those ideas more convincing to your audience. Consulting several different kinds of sources and always looking for differing perspectives will help you build the strongest, most compelling argument possible.

Give Your Message Structure

Well-organized speeches make it easy for the audience to follow the speaker's argument. They help the audience remember what has been said, and they give clear and convincing reasons for responding as the speaker wishes. If your audience perceives that you are disorganized—if they cannot follow your ideas—they will have trouble accepting your information and arguments and may doubt your credibility.

For an audience to follow your ideas, your speech must have structure. Your ideas must relate to one another logically. Taken together, they must present a coherent case in support of your argument. In an introduction, you will need to plan ways to relate your topic to an audience, gain their attention and interest, and establish your own credibility. Usually you would include a preview and state your thesis. The body of your speech, built around main ideas supported with evidence, needs to be planned carefully. You can help listeners move with you smoothly from one idea to the next by devising strong transitions between your ideas and selecting places where it makes sense to summarize what has already been said. Finally, your conclusion, as the last word to the audience, will repeat the thesis of your speech, summarize your main ideas, and leave listeners with a memorable quotation or anecdote or challenge them to act.

The speech must form a pattern that is clear to your audience. Using a meaningful pattern of organization helps the audience take mental notes as you speak and remember what you have said. Your organizational pattern also makes clear to them how everything in the speech fits together, points to the desired response, and contributes to your ethos as a speaker. The many patterns available to you will be discussed in more detail in Chapter 9, but an example of a short speech that illustrates a simple organizational structure appears in the *Highlighting Organization* feature on pp. 66–67. You will see that it has the characteristics of a well-structured speech: a clear purpose, a short introduction that points out the importance of the topic and attempts to enhance the speaker's ethos, clear transitions, well-developed main ideas designed to help the speaker achieve his purpose, and a conclusion that raises thought-provoking questions.

Speak Directly with Your Audience

The language you use and the way you use it can have a great impact on your audience and the way it responds to your speech. By choosing language suitable to the audience and the occasion, and by developing a conversational and direct speaking style, you will promote understanding and belief on the part of the audience. Suitable language is language that is precise, clear, interesting, and appropriate to both the audience and the situation in which you speak. Beginning speakers sometimes believe that public speaking always demands formal language, with the result that their speeches sound stiff. Perhaps you've heard a friend describe a particular event or personal experience in an animated and natural way, then recount the same story in a stiff, awkward way in a formal speech.

It helps to think of public speaking as an enlarged conversation with friends. Speaking to an audience is not the same as a casual conversation. After all, you plan a speech in advance, and it is more carefully organized than casual remarks. In a speech, you also should avoid language that is *too* informal, including the "fillers" we sometimes use in casual conversation—the "likes" and "you knows" that clutter everyday speech. Yet the same conversational style that you use in conversing with friends may be perfectly appropriate in most public speaking situations. In addition, many of the personal experiences and stories you talk about with your friends may well work in your speech, depending on the topic.

Of course, all situations do not call for the same style of delivery. Some formal occasions may call for manuscript speaking, in which you read a carefully prepared speech to an audience. At other times you may be asked to speak on the spur of the moment, with little or no time for preparation; this is called **impromptu speaking**. On rare occasions, you may be expected to memorize your whole speech. Most often, however, you will be speaking **extemporaneously**—that is, with careful preparation but with minimal notes and a less formal, more direct, and audience-centered delivery.

HIGHLIGHTING ORGANIZATION

Specific Purpose

I want my audience to agree that obstacles to a uniform system of Internet voting should be eliminated.

Thesis Statement

Internet voting is hampered in the United States by varying state regulations and practices.

Introduction

Last October I decided to vote early. I went to a satellite voting station set up in Briscoe Quad. When I got there the lines were very long and moving slowly. Since I had only about an hour between classes, I decided not to wait. A few days later, after my last class, I went downtown to the clerk's office, but the line there was so long that I was told that the office would close before anyone joining the line then would get in. I tried again the next day, and after about two hours, I did get in and cast my vote. This was pretty frustrating. What's even worse is that a good friend of mine had a similar experience and finally just gave up—he never did get to vote. I believe that voting is so important, and such a privilege in a world where many don't have that opportunity, that inconvenience is not a good excuse to give up. But I also know that college students have classes to go to, papers to write, tests to take, and, for many of us, part-time jobs to go to. Time is something we can't waste. Today I want to offer a solution to this problem by considering Internet voting. We'll look at possible technical problems, consider its successes, and see how it could be instituted.

Transition

It is a great thing that so many students, despite the time involved, got out to vote, but voting does not have to be so hard. Let's consider a more efficient way.

Body

I. Internet voting has potential technical problems that are solvable.

The speaker supported this idea by presenting possible objections to voting, including security and privacy concerns and possible fraud. He further developed the idea by pointing out that the same problems occur with voting machines and explained technical solutions that have been offered.

No matter how much work you put into preparing yourself to speak, what the audience finally sees and hears will determine their response. The best delivery does not call attention to itself; you don't want the audience to pay more attention to *how* you talk than to *what* you have to say. Good delivery, in most of the contexts in which you will speak, should be conversational and relaxed. If the delivery is good, listeners can hear and understand what you say and will not find themselves distracted by mannerisms, inappropriate language, or an overly dramatic presentation.

The overview of principles we have been discussing in this section will help you become an effective speaker and an engaged citizen. Although they will be developed in more detail in the rest of this book, they can serve as the foundation on which you can begin now to prepare yourself to speak.

One other important factor needs to be considered at the outset. The prospect of getting up in front of an audience can make anyone nervous. The degree of nervousness varies from person to person, but feeling apprehensive is normal. This is something all speakers face. In the next section we offer some practical advice on how to deal with that nervousness.

Transition

Even though there are suggested solutions to potential problems, how do we know that Internet voting works in the real world?

II. Internet voting has been tried successfully, and can be done simply and efficiently.

The speaker developed this idea first with information from the Pew Foundation regarding the seven states in the United States that permit military and overseas voters to use e-mail to cast absentee ballots. He also gave examples of the use of Internet voting in Democratic primaries in Michigan and Arizona. He then offered an extended example, pointing out that Estonia, a world leader in e-government innovations, devised a plan whereby voters with a national ID and a private PIN issued by the government could vote as easily and safely as using a bank teller machine.

Transition

If online voting works, why don't we have it?

III. Online voting in the United States will come about only if a national policy is adopted.

The speaker developed this idea by pointing out that every state has control of its own voting procedures, and past practices and political cultures lead to a jumble of conflicting laws and regulations. An extended example of Internet voting in Arizona shows how complicated it can be when the state tries to preserve the traditional official role of the counties in vote collecting and counting.

Conclusion

So we can see that voting via the Internet has potential problems that can be overcome. It has worked in the past in limited circumstances in the United States, and it's worked very well in countries such as Estonia. Implementing online voting here would take a national effort to override the tangle of voting laws in the various states. But it can be done. If we really believe that voting is the duty of every citizen, if our generation really wants to have an impact on policies in this country, then the challenge for us is to put pressure on our representatives to establish a fair, efficient and safe method of voting. Given the way technology has advanced in recent years, Internet voting is inevitable—the sooner the better for all of us.

SPEAKING WITH CONFIDENCE

Preview. *Everyone experiences communication apprehension. In order to deal with it, you will need to understand what communication apprehension is and the factors that contribute to it, discover ways to manage it, and realize how it can actually benefit you.*

No one was more universally admired than our nation's first president, George Washington. Yet this heroic figure was extremely nervous when delivering his first inaugural address. One senator who attended the ceremony observed that this "great man was agitated and embarrassed more than ever he was by the leveled cannon or pointed musket."[10] His successor, the second president of the United States, was also terrified about delivering his inaugural address. After a sleepless night, John Adams felt ill and was afraid he might faint during his speech. He was so scared that he told his wife, Abigail, that he was "in great doubt whether to say anything" at all "besides repeating the oath."[11]

Understanding and managing communication apprehension will help you speak with confidence.

Understanding Communication Apprehension

When even national heroes suffer from **communication apprehension**, it is not surprising that the rest of us become nervous when asked to speak in public. In one famous survey, it was discovered that people are more afraid of public speaking than they are of dying.[12] Comedian Jerry Seinfeld joked about this finding:

> According to most studies, people's number one fear is public speaking. Number two is death. Death is number two. Does that seem right? That means to the average person, if you have to go to a funeral, you're better off in the casket than doing the eulogy.[13]

For many people, however, fear of speaking is no laughing matter. Doctors at Duke University Medical Center actually consider public speaking sufficiently stressful that they include it on a list of "mental stress tests." Physicians use these tests in identifying those most at risk for future heart problems.[14]

Communication scholar James McCroskey, who has studied communication apprehension for more than 30 years, defines it as "an individual's level of fear or anxiety associated with either real or anticipated communication with another person or persons."[15] Not only can it become a significant barrier to your personal success, but it can rob you of your voice as a citizen.[16] Indeed, if you are afraid to speak out, you *have* no voice in our democratic system.

Factors That Contribute to Communication Apprehension Most speakers who have experienced communication apprehension would prefer to feel more confident when they speak. Often they don't really understand what it is they fear or why they feel anxious in some speaking situations but remain calm and confident in others. Understanding the underlying causes of communication apprehension is the first step in learning to manage it effectively.

Sometimes speakers feel apprehensive about speaking in public because they know they are ill-prepared. Perhaps their ideas are poorly documented or their thoughts disorganized, or they may have failed to practice aloud with their notes. Unlike other communication apprehension triggers, poor preparation is a legitimate cause for concern.

Other factors that contribute to communication apprehension vary from person to person. We know, for example, that some speakers are generally apprehensive across speaking situations, suffering from **trait anxiety**.[17] Whenever they

FIGURE 3.3

ASSESSING YOUR COMMUNICATION APPREHENSION

Communication scholar James McCroskey developed the following instrument to help people identify their level of communication apprehension. Answer the statements, then calculate your overall score and your subscores for each of the four communication contexts.

Personal Report of Communication Apprehension (PRCA-24)

DIRECTIONS: This instrument is composed of twenty-four statements concerning feelings about communicating with other people. Please indicate the degree to which each statement applies to you by marking whether you **strongly agree (1-SA), agree (2-A), undecided (3-U), disagree (4-D), or strongly disagree (5-SD)**. Work quickly; record your first impression.

1. I dislike participating in group discussions.

   1 - SA 2 - A 3 - U 4 - D 5 - SD

2. Generally, I am comfortable while participating in group discussions.

   1 - SA 2 - A 3 - U 4 - D 5 - SD

3. I am tense and nervous while participating in group discussions.

   1 - SA 2 - A 3 - U 4 - D 5 - SD

4. I like to get involved in group discussions.

   1 - SA 2 - A 3 - U 4 - D 5 - SD

5. Engaging in a group discussion with new people makes me tense and nervous.

   1 - SA 2 - A 3 - U 4 - D 5 - SD

6. I am calm and relaxed while participating in group discussions.

   1 - SA 2 - A 3 - U 4 - D 5 - SD

7. Generally, I am nervous when I have to participate in a meeting.

   1 - SA 2 - A 3 - U 4 - D 5 - SD

8. Usually I am calm and relaxed while participating in meetings.

   1 - SA 2 - A 3 - U 4 - D 5 - SD

9. I am very calm and relaxed when I am called upon to express an opinion at a meeting.

   1 - SA 2 - A 3 - U 4 - D 5 - SD

10. I am afraid to express myself at meetings.

    1 - SA 2 - A 3 - U 4 - D 5 - SD

(*continues*)

FIGURE 3.3 (*continued*)

11. Communicating at meetings usually makes me uncomfortable.

    1 - SA 2 - A 3 - U 4 - D 5 - SD

12. I am very relaxed when answering questions at a meeting.

    1 - SA 2 - A 3 - U 4 - D 5 - SD

13. While participating in a conversation with a new acquaintance, I feel very nervous.

    1 - SA 2 - A 3 - U 4 - D 5 - SD

14. I have no fear of speaking up in conversations.

    1 - SA 2 - A 3 - U 4 - D 5 - SD

15. Ordinarily I am very tense and nervous in conversations.

    1 - SA 2 - A 3 - U 4 - D 5 - SD

16. Ordinarily I am very calm and relaxed in conversations.

    1 - SA 2 - A 3 - U 4 - D 5 - SD

17. While conversing with a new acquaintance, I feel very relaxed.

    1 - SA 2 - A 3 - U 4 - D 5 - SD

18. I'm afraid to speak up in conversations.

    1 - SA 2 - A 3 - U 4 - D 5 - SD

19. I have no fear of giving a speech.

    1 - SA 2 - A 3 - U 4 - D 5 - SD

20. Certain parts of my body feel very tense and rigid while giving a speech.

    1 - SA 2 - A 3 - U 4 - D 5 - SD

21. I feel relaxed while giving a speech.

    1 - SA 2 - A 3 - U 4 - D 5 - SD

22. My thoughts become confused and jumbled when I am giving a speech.

    1 - SA 2 - A 3 - U 4 - D 5 - SD

23. I face the prospect of giving a speech with confidence.

    1 - SA 2 - A 3 - U 4 - D 5 - SD

24. While giving a speech, I get so nervous I forget facts I really know.

    1 - SA 2 - A 3 - U 4 - D 5 - SD

FIGURE 3.3 (*continued*)

SCORING: Compute subscores for four communication contexts–group discussions, meetings, interpersonal conversations, and public speaking–and an overall communication apprehension. To compute your scores merely add or subtract your scores for each item as indicated below.

Sub scores	Scoring Formula
Group discussion	18 + scores for items 2, 4, and 6; – scores for items 1, 3, and 5
Meetings	18 + scores for items 8, 9, and 12; – scores for items 7, 10, and 11
Interpersonal conversations	18 + scores for items 14, 16, and 17; – scores for items 13, 15, and 18
Public speaking	18 + scores for items 19, 21, and 23; – scores for items 20, 22, and 24

Scores on the four contexts (groups, meetings, interpersonal conversations, and public speaking) can range from a low of 6 to a high of 30. Any score above 18 indicates some degree of apprehension.

To determine your overall CA score, add together all four sub scores

Your score should range between 24 and 120. If your score is below 24 or above 120, you have made a mistake in computing the score.

Scores between **83 and 120** indicate a high level of communication apprehension.

Scores between **55 and 83** indicate a moderate level of communication apprehension.

Scores between **24 and 55** indicate a low level of communication apprehension.

Source: McCroskey, *An Introduction to Rhetorical Communication, Personal Report of Communication Apprehension (PRCA-24)*, © 1982 by Pearson Education, Inc. Reproduced by permission of Pearson Education, Inc.

are asked to share their thoughts in a meeting, introduce a speaker, or deliver a short report, their hearts race. Speakers with trait anxiety try to avoid speaking in public whenever possible.

Other speakers have unrealistic self-expectations, hoping for perfection when they deliver a speech.[18] If they make the slightest mistake, they feel like a failure. They are their own harshest judges. At the other extreme, some speakers may fear evaluation by others. They may perceive that listeners will judge them critically and be quick to note flaws in their performance.[19] Of course, evaluation is a given in any public speaking classroom because instructors grade student speeches, and everyone wants to perform well.

Speakers may also experience **state anxiety** in which a particular set of circumstances triggers feelings of communication apprehension. They may, for example, see a particular audience or speech setting as threatening. When confronted with giving a speech in a large auditorium for the first time, for example, an otherwise calm and confident speaker may feel anxious. Or, a speaker may possess lower status than the audience. Professional contexts can really highlight this anxiety trigger. Speakers may also feel apprehensive if they anticipate a hostile or negative response from listeners, especially if the topic they are addressing is emotionally charged for all (for example, gay marriage, abortion, or gun control).[20]

Even though we know that most of us experience communication apprehension at some time in our lives, some speakers feel isolated when they experience it. In classroom settings, for example, a student speaker may perceive classmates as confident while *they* feel panicked.[21] Finally, when any speaker becomes apprehensive, he or she may experience an array of physiological reactions, including a dry mouth, sweaty palms, or cold hands. Overreacting to these can aggravate anxiety, even though these reactions usually subside once the speaker becomes involved in talking about a topic that really matters.

Most of us experience only mild to moderate communication apprehension, but for some, speaking anxiety can be quite severe—so severe, in fact, that they may avoid speaking at all.[22] Fortunately, we can all learn to better manage our fears of public speaking.

Managing Communication Apprehension

All of us experience communication apprehension in some degree and have to find ways to overcome it. Even great leaders have to find ways of conquering their fear of speaking, no matter how momentous the occasion or how high the stakes. In 1859, for example, Abraham Lincoln faced the biggest challenge of his young political career when he was invited to speak at the Cooper Union in New York City, a traditional proving ground for presidential candidates. Self-educated and with a "rough and tumble" style,[23] Lincoln was hardly known as a great orator. Yet now his whole future—indeed, the future of the nation—rested on this single speech. A successful speech would make him a leading candidate for president; a poorly received speech could doom his career. As his law partner, William H. Herndon, recalled, "No former effort in the line of speech-making had cost so much time and thought as this one."[24] In the end, that effort paid off. After putting off the sponsors long enough to carefully research and prepare his remarks, Lincoln delivered a tremendously successful speech—a speech that Harold Holtzer aptly characterized in the subtitle of his book *Lincoln at Cooper Union: The Speech That Made Abraham Lincoln President.*

How did Lincoln do it? Part of the answer, of course, lies in the extra time he took to research and prepare his speech. But just as important was his firm conviction that he was *right* in taking the position he took: that the Republican Party should oppose the further spread of slavery in America. In other words, Lincoln was thoroughly prepared and firmly *believed* in what he said, and those are the most critical factors in dealing with communication apprehension. This leads to the two most fundamental principles in combating communication apprehension: addressing substantive issues to which you are committed and being well prepared.

ADDRESS SUBSTANTIVE ISSUES TO WHICH YOU ARE COMMITTED A genuine commitment to your topic can help you overcome the anxiety you may have about speaking in public. You are more likely to speak with confidence if you are addressing a topic that really matters to you and your audience. As part of a community forum on health care, for example, an emergency room doctor might speak out on the critical importance of finding ways to care for the uninsured—perhaps arguing that universal health insurance would ensure that everyone who needed health care would get it, thereby creating a more humane society. A student whose roommate has been attacked outside the school library might make an impassioned plea to a group of campus administrators, asking them to fund more lighting, police patrols, and campus escort services. Because of the commitment of these speakers to their topics, any communication apprehension they might have felt at the start of their speeches would likely fade as they focused on their arguments and the importance of persuading their audiences.

Be Well Prepared There is no better psychological defense for dealing with communication apprehension than honestly being able to say to yourself that you *are* well prepared. You have selected a topic of interest and value to you as well as your audience. You have done your homework, perhaps even conducting an audience survey. You have devoted significant time and effort to gathering information and to broadening your understanding of the subject. You have carefully organized your speech into a clear, coherent, and unified whole. You have practiced by going over your speech—aloud—several times, timing yourself and fine-tuning your ideas. You have asked friends for **feedback**. You feel confident that there is little more you could have done to prepare for your speech.

Reminding yourself of your careful preparation can be reassuring and even liberating as you grapple with feelings of anxiety. Your delivery will reflect your careful preparation, and the audience will sense that you have worked hard out of respect for their time and attention. Also remember that your audience *shares* responsibility for the success of your speech. You have a right to expect that. Just as you have prepared well and met your responsibilities as a speaker, your audience, too, has a responsibility to listen carefully and constructively to what you have to say.

The best way to reduce speech anxiety is to address topics that genuinely concern you and to be well prepared for your presentation. In addition, you may

FOCUS ON CIVIC ENGAGEMENT

Speaking with Conviction

In 1993 a young man named Quay Hanna graduated from college, got on a bus, and traveled throughout the country. He had grown up in a small town where there was little diversity but a lot of suspicion of those who were different. Racism seemed to him to be just a reflection of reality. As is explained on his Web site, "Nine weeks, thirty-seven states, and twelve-thousand miles later, he got more than an incredible journey and hundreds of stories to tell. As he traveled he was forced to confront his own racist and prejudiced beliefs, making him realize that he had more to offer the world than his lifelong hatred of others."

So Quay set out to talk about his transformation from a self-proclaimed "redneck" to a passionate advocate for racial understanding. Speaking with conviction and passion to thousands of young people throughout the United States, Quay has helped his listeners examine their own prejudices and beliefs. Professor Jody Roy of Ripon College, who has done extensive research on hatred and prejudice, writes that "Quay's conviction, his complete commitment to his topic, is a critical part of his exceptional success."

Source: www.quayhanna.com/

employ a variety of other strategies for managing communication apprehension. As you give more speeches, you will no doubt find strategies that work especially well for you. For now, however, let's examine some of the specific strategies that experienced speakers have found helpful for dealing with communication apprehension.[25]

DEVELOP A POSITIVE ATTITUDE What do you think of when you imagine yourself making a speech? Do you picture yourself stumbling over your own words, dropping your note cards, or freezing as you attempt to respond to a listener's question? Research has clearly shown that people with high speech anxiety tend to have more negative thoughts before the delivery of a speech than people who are comfortable speaking.[26] It stands to reason, then, that developing more positive thoughts may help in managing or reducing anxiety.

When you dread making a speech, when you think of it as a burden or something that you "have to do" for a class or for your job, you are more likely to develop severe communication apprehension. What if you learned to view it differently: as an opportunity to change minds, to share what you know, or to make a real difference in the community where you live? In other words, you should start telling yourself: "I want to give a speech because what I have to say may help my audience." The principle here is simple: speakers who anticipate success rather than failure suffer less apprehension about speaking.

PRACTICE YOUR SPEECH Ideally, you should practice over a period of a few days, not a few hours. It is always a mistake to put off rehearsing your speech until the last minute. Prepare your speech well in advance and give yourself ample time to practice. You may be able to get a friend or a few friends to listen to your speech. Practicing early and often is the key here. No one can tell you exactly how many times to practice or what techniques may work best for you. As you give more speeches over time, you will learn what approach works best for you.

ANTICIPATE THE SPEECH SITUATION There are times in life when it is nice to be surprised, but before or during the delivery of a public speech is not one of them. As we have said before, effective speakers know their audiences. Gathering information about your audience and the speaking situation *before* you speak helps you focus on the audience right from the start. Whenever someone invites you to make a speech, try to obtain as much information as you can. If you are addressing a community group that holds regular meetings, ask permission to attend one of those meetings, to get a feel for the room and the typical audience, and to note how they interact. If the organization has a Web site, you will also want to visit that, and you can ask the person who invited you to speak to respond to a few questions before the speech. Figure 3.2 provides some basic questions that you may want to ask about your audience and the speech situation.

PRACTICE ACTIVE LISTENING Active listening can be a powerful tool for managing communication apprehension.[27] Rarely do you make a speech under circumstances in which you arrive, immediately stand up and talk, then quickly depart. More likely, your speech will be part of a longer program, meeting, or banquet, and others will speak before you. Listening closely to those speakers will draw your attention away from your own anxieties and may even give you ideas about last-minute changes to your own speech. In your speech class, you will be listening to other speakers before and after you make your speech. Instead of fretting over your notes, strive to listen carefully to those who speak before you. You may learn something, and hopefully you also will find yourself a bit more relaxed when it is your turn to speak. In addition, you may be able to refer to something in an earlier speech that complements your own speech in some way.

EXERCISE FOR RELAXATION If you feel tense and nervous before you speak, you can do some simple physical exercises to relax. One excellent way to relax is by breathing deeply. **Deep breathing** allows you to take in a large quantity of air, giving you a good supply of oxygen and the potential for enhanced vocal control. You will also want to breathe deeply before you speak and to continue breathing deeply and regularly while you are delivering your speech for better vocal support and ongoing relaxation.

Isometric exercise, which involves tensing and then relaxing specific muscles, can also be a useful relaxation technique. Try clenching and unclenching your fists, pressing your legs firmly together and then relaxing them, or squeezing the palms of your hands together as if you were trying to flatten a piece of clay. Alternatively, you can push your leg, arm, or foot against some immovable object, such as a wall, a table, or even the podium. After you have pressed firmly, release the muscle, relaxing it as completely as possible. These isometric exercises are subtle—you can do them without being noticed, even in the middle of your speech. They can also be used before and after the speech.

Finally, performing **aerobic exercise** before your speech can help reduce communication apprehension. Aerobic exercise, such as walking, jogging, running, or swimming, is not only good for your cardiovascular system and general well-being, it also helps reduce tension and brings communication apprehension into a manageable range.

ACKNOWLEDGE THE POTENTIAL BENEFITS OF MODERATE COMMUNICATION APPREHENSION
Some people have serious problems with speech anxiety and are virtually incapacitated by their fear of speaking.[28] Most of us, however, can learn to manage our speech anxiety, and experienced speakers even find ways to channel their nervous energy in positive directions. They are able to do this, in part, because they have developed specific techniques that work for them. Some speakers, for example, begin their speaking day with meditation, prayer, a two-mile run, or a quiet walk. Everyone will benefit from getting a good night's rest and eating a light, nutritious meal before making a speech. Wearing comfortable clothes that make you feel good about yourself also will contribute to a positive mental attitude. What is important is to learn what helps *you* most in managing your feelings of anxiety.

In most speaking situations, however, a little anxiety can be a *good* thing, because that little spurt of adrenaline can energize your mind and body, keep you alert, and perhaps even contribute to a more dynamic delivery. As you gain experience as a public speaker, you will become more comfortable and confident standing up before an audience, and eventually you may even come to anticipate and welcome that adrenaline rush that we all feel when we speak in public.

MAINTAIN A SENSE OF PERSPECTIVE No matter how well you prepare for any speech, bad things can happen. The microphone may fail. The person who introduces you may mispronounce your name. You may get something under your contact lens or drop one of your note cards. By preparing well you can reduce the likelihood that something will go wrong, but you will never have complete control over the situation. Do not be intimidated by that fact. The unpredictability is what makes public speaking both challenging and interesting.

You need to maintain a sense of perspective. Prepare well, do your best, be flexible, and pay attention to **feedback** from your listeners. Even if, in your judgment, your entire speech goes badly—that is, *you* feel disappointed in your performance—you should view it as a learning experience. Concentrate on what you learned. Get ready to have another go at it. No matter how brilliantly or poorly you think you performed, it is important that you view each speech as a chance for personal growth. If you are truly committed to speaking out, you will have other opportunities to speak on the subject.

By employing any or all of these strategies for managing communication apprehension, you *can* become a more poised and confident speaker.

SUMMARY

- A speech is successful only if it benefits both speaker and audience.
- You must have a collaborative approach to preparing and presenting your speech.
- Basic principles for preparing yourself to speak:
  - examining your own knowledge, ability, beliefs, and potential (*know yourself*)
  - discovering the audience's needs, interests, beliefs, and knowledge (*know your audience*)
  - understanding how the setting and other outside factors may influence the speech (*know the situation*)
  - devising a clear purpose that reflects the desired response (*aim for audience response*)
  - exploring potential sources of information (*discover relevant material*)
  - using language and delivering the speech in a manner suitable to the audience and the occasion (*speak directly with your audience*)
  - practicing a well-prepared presentation frequently enough to give yourself oral command of the speech (*develop confidence through practice*)
- Understanding what communication apprehension is, the factors that contribute to it, and how to manage it will help you gain confidence. Communication apprehension is a normal reaction to speaking in public.
- Poor preparation, inappropriate self-expectations, fear of evaluation, excessive self-focusing, concern about the audience, and failure to understand the body's physiological reactions may all contribute to communication apprehension.

- Commitment to your topic and thorough preparation are fundamental to building your confidence.
- A positive attitude, practice, anticipating the situation, listening actively, exercise, acknowledging the benefits of apprehension, and maintaining a sense of perspective will also help you overcome apprehension.

QUESTIONS FOR REVIEW AND REFLECTION

1. Explain the significance of the speaker-listener partnership. Offer one example of how the speaker and listener are mutually interdependent.
2. Explain your understanding of a transactional communication model. What are the main components? Why are they important?
3. What are the most important things you will do to prepare yourself to speak responsibly and ethically?
4. In your view, are any of these elements more important than others? Why or why not?
5. As you learn to give speeches, what do you imagine will be your greatest challenge? How might you begin to grapple with it?
6. What is meant by communication apprehension?
7. This book suggests that commitment and preparation are the most significant factors in reducing communication apprehension. Do you agree or disagree? Explain.
8. The book lists several factors that may contribute to a speaker's communication apprehension. Which of these have you experienced? Elaborate.
9. What are some of the most useful strategies for managing communication apprehension? How have they worked for you in the past?

ENDNOTES

1. The process perspective is widely referred to as the "transactional perspective." David K. Berlo, *The Process of Communication* (New York: Holt, Rinehart & Winston, 1960).
2. Raymond G. Smith, *Speech Communication: Theory and Models* (New York: Harper & Row, 1970), 14.
3. Steve Duck and David McMahon, *The Basics of Communication: A Relational Perspective* (Thousand Oaks, CA: Sage, 2009), 9.
4. William Norwood Brigance, *Speech: Its Techniques and Disciplines in a Free Society*, 2nd ed. (New York: Appleton-Century-Crofts, 1961), 20.
5. Cited by James Brewer Stewart, *Wendell Phillips: Liberty's Hero* (Baton Rouge: Louisiana State University Press, 1986), 46.
6. Margaret Chase Smith, "A Declaration of Conscience," Washington, DC, June 1, 1950, http://gos.sbc.edu/s/chasesmith.html (accessed August 29, 2005).
7. Robert Alexander Kraig, *Woodrow Wilson and the Lost World of the Oratorical Statesman* (College Station: Texas A&M University Press, 2004), 131–33.
8. See Karlyn Kohrs Campbell, *Man Cannot Speak for Her: A Critical Study of Early Feminist Rhetoric*, 2 vols. (New York: Praeger, 1989), 51–58.
9. T. K. Kim, "Electronic Storm: Stormfront Grows a Thriving Neo-Nazi Community, 2005," www.splcenter.org/intel/intelreport/article.jsp?aid=551 (accessed August 20, 2005).
10. James Thomas Flexner, *George Washington and the New Nation: 1783–1793* (Boston: Little, Brown, 1969), 188.
11. Letter to Abigail Adams, March 17, 1797, in *John Adams: A Biography in His Own Words*, ed. James Bishop Peabody (New York: Harper & Row, 1973), 359.
12. "What Are Americans Afraid Of?" *Bruskin Report* 53 (July 1973): 8.

13. Jerry Seinfeld, *SeinLanguage* (New York: Bantam Books, 1993), 120.
14. "Mental Stress Test Indicator of Future Cardiac Problems," *Bloomington (IN) Herald-Times*, June 5, 1996, A6.
15. James C. McCroskey, "Oral Communication Apprehension: A Summary of Recent Theory and Research," *Human Communication Research* 4 (1977): 78–79.
16. A great deal of research during the past three decades has focused on communication apprehension. See, for example, Ralph R. Behnke and Chris R. Sawyer, "Milestones of Anticipatory Public Speaking Anxiety," *Communication Education* 48 (1999): 165–72; Ralph R. Behnke and Chris R. Sawyer, "Public Speaking Anxiety as a Function of Sensitization and Habituation Processes," *Communication Education* 53 (2004): 164–73; Amy M. Bippus and John A. Daly, "What Do People Think Causes Stage Fright? Naive Attributions about the Reasons for Public Speaking Anxiety," *Communication Education* 48 (1999): 63–72; and Rebecca B. Rubin, Alan M. Rubin, and Felecia F. Jordan, "Effects of Instruction on Communication Apprehension and Communication Competence," *Communication Education* 46 (1997): 104–14.
17. See Virginia P. Richmond and James C. McCroskey, *Communication: Apprehension, Avoidance, and Effectiveness*, 5th ed. (Boston: Allyn & Bacon, 2000), for an extended discussion of the nature, types, and causes of communication apprehension.
18. Marion Woodman, *Addiction to Perfection* (Toronto: Inner City Books, 1982).
19. James C. McCroskey, "The Communication Apprehension Perspective," in *Avoiding Communication Shyness, Reticence, and Communication Apprehension*, ed. John D. Daily and James McCroskey (Beverly Hills, CA: Sage, 1984), 13–84.
20. Joe Ayres, "Situational Factors and Audience Anxiety," *Communication Education* 29 (1990): 283–91.
21. Michael J. Beatty, "Situational and Predispositional Correlates of Public Speaking Anxiety," *Communication Education* 37 (1988): 28–39.
22. James C. McCroskey and Virginia P. Richmond, "The Impact of Communication Apprehension on Individuals in Organizations," *Communication Quarterly* 27 (1979): 55–61.
23. Waldo W. Braden, *Abraham Lincoln: Public Speaker* (Baton Rouge: Louisiana State University Press, 1988), 3.
24. Harold Holtzer, *Lincoln at Cooper Union: The Speech That Made Abraham Lincoln President* (New York: Simon & Schuster, 2004), 28.
25. See Joe Ayres, "Speech Preparation Processes and Speech Apprehension," *Communication Education* 45 (October 1996): 228–35, for an interesting study on how the nature of speaking preparation is vital to the quality of the speech as delivered.
26. Joe Ayres and Tim Hopf, *Coping with Speech Anxiety* (Norwood, NJ: Ablex, 1993), 5–21.
27. In the interpersonal communication and interviewing literature, *active listening* refers to a listening approach in which the listener participates in the conversation by summarizing, paraphrasing, and occasionally interrupting the speaker with clarifying, supportive questions. We are using the term in a different way here.
28. James McCroskey, *An Introduction to Rhetorical Communication*, 7th ed. (Boston: Allyn & Bacon, 1997), 39–61.

CHAPTER

4

The Listener as Engaged Citizen

CHAPTER SURVEY

The Importance of Effective Listening

Understanding Barriers to Good Listening

Guidelines for Improving Listening

CHAPTER OBJECTIVES

After studying this chapter, you should be able to

1. Describe the importance of effective listening.
2. Embrace your responsibility to listen critically yet respectfully.
3. Identify the major barriers to effective listening.
4. Implement strategies for listening more effectively.

Listening is an important communication skill—in the classroom, in professional life, and in our communities. Listening well—attentively, respectfully, and critically—is not only an essential part of effective communication but an important responsibility of citizenship in a democracy. As we listen closely to others, we become better-informed and more discerning consumers of information and ideas. We also become more likely to make judicious decisions about whom to vote for, what causes to invest in, and what courses of action to pursue.

Studies show that we typically spend about 70 percent of our waking hours in some form of communication. Whether talking on the telephone or participating in meetings, we spend most of our time exchanging ideas and information.[1] Much of this communication involves listening. Research shows, for example, that the average employee spends 40 percent of his or her time listening.[2] Recognizing how attentive we're expected to be, author Stephen Covey argues that effective listening is one of the "seven habits of highly effective people."[3] We value those who are good listeners, and we'll be valued if we are good listeners ourselves.

Regardless of your chosen occupation, listening will be important. The wise doctor listens carefully to patients' concerns before diagnosing their illnesses. Investment counselors listen to clients' financial goals before suggesting an investment strategy. Assembly-line workers and construction workers must listen to explanations of safety regulations if they hope to remain accident-free. Leaders also benefit from listening well. In fact, members of the Academy of Certified Managers rated "active listening" as the number one skill for managerial success.[4] In another survey, 170 businesspeople were asked to describe the communication skills that they considered most important; listening was ranked first.[5] Across diverse occupations and situations, good listening is crucial.

Yet effective listening can be a challenge. Listening expert Ralph Nichols estimates that the average white-collar worker listens at about a 25 percent efficiency level.[6] This figure is supported by research showing that immediately following a ten-minute presentation, a typical audience member recalls only about 50 percent of the information presented. After 48 hours, the recall level drops to 25 percent. In addition, poor listeners often *overestimate* how effectively they listen, assuming that poor listening is someone else's problem.[7]

Of course, statistics on listening can be misleading. Sometimes we may listen carefully because we know we are going to be evaluated on how much we can remember. Or a speaker's information may be especially relevant or important to us. On other occasions, we may barely pay attention because we do not agree with the speaker or because we are distracted by other thoughts. Whatever the circumstances, we can all benefit from becoming better listeners.

THE IMPORTANCE OF EFFECTIVE LISTENING

Preview. *Listening may serve varied purposes—such as enjoyment or the critical assessment of ideas. When we listen well, we experience an array of positive outcomes, including more knowledge and awareness of the world around us, a clearer sense of ourselves, improved interpersonal relationships, and enhanced public speaking skills. In addition, our* *willingness to listen is crucial to our role as engaged citizens in a deliberative democracy. As citizens, we have an obligation to listen to our fellow citizens and to give their views respectful consideration.*

Diverse Purposes for Listening

Depending on our goals, we may approach listening differently in differing situations.[8] Sometimes we may **listen for appreciation**, as when we listen to good music. We do not expect to be analytical or critical; we are simply listening for enjoyment. On other occasions, we may engage in **empathic listening**, or listening to show our support and understanding for the feelings of another person. By doing so, we may hope to strengthen our relationships with other people or demonstrate that we care. By making everybody feel valued, empathic listening may also build greater cohesiveness within civic and professional groups, as we will discuss at greater length in Chapter 18.

As citizens, we are most likely to engage in informational or critical listening. In **informational listening**, we seek to take in information accurately and expand our knowledge about a subject. We want to understand and remember what we are hearing. In **critical listening**, we aim to *analyze* and *evaluate* the speaker's message. In both kinds of listening, we make judgments about the relevance, accuracy, timeliness, and validity of the message. In many instances, informational listening serves as the foundation for critical listening; what we learn from listening can help us evaluate other messages we encounter.

Understanding the Listening Process

Regardless of our goals as listeners, whether we are listening for information or analysis, we need to recognize that listening is a multi-step process with several components.

- *Hearing.* The first step in the listening process is hearing what the speaker has said. This is the physiological part of listening. Hearing can be challenging if the speaker talks too softly or rapidly, or if there are competing sounds. At a recent Race for the Cure rally, listeners strained to hear speakers who were trying to project their voices over the outdoor sounds of dogs barking, children laughing, and cars whizzing past the park. Because they could not hear, listeners were unable to process and react to the speakers' remarks.
- *Focusing.* Once we hear a message, our next task is focusing. When we focus on a speaker's message, we are able to filter out competing messages, concentrate on the message at hand, and begin to grapple with its meaning. It's usually easier for us to focus when we respect the speaker and view the message as important. For the cancer survivors and their friends and relatives attending the Race for the Cure rally, their personal involvement motivated them to focus on each speaker's testimony in spite of challenges presented by the listening environment.
- *Understanding.* The next stage of the listening process is understanding. Sometimes we hear and are able to focus on a speaker's message. Yet we do

not *really* comprehend the speaker's meaning—perhaps because the message is unclear, or because we have gaps in our experience and knowledge. When we cannot understand or we misinterpret a speaker's message, we fail as listeners.

- *Responding.* Once we understand the speaker's message, we will respond in some way. We may agree or disagree, remain neutral or indifferent, or become passionate about a cause. Our responses may be nonverbal, as we smile and nod our heads, scowl and look away, or stand and applaud. If we have the chance, we may also respond verbally by asking questions, complimenting the speaker, or offering our own perspective or experiences.
- *Remembering.* What will we remember of the speaker's comments—a few hours later, or even the next day? We know that speakers strive to be moving and memorable. Yet as listeners, we often forget—not only details, but also main ideas and key information. We can help ourselves remember by taking notes, by relating the speaker's ideas to what we already know, and by discussing the topic with others.

Positive Outcomes of Effective Listening

There are plenty of good reasons for becoming a better listener. Whether in the classroom, the workplace, or the community, we can all benefit from enhanced listening skills. Indeed, our society as a whole benefits when respectful, careful listening becomes a shared goal.[9] Here are just a few of the reasons we should all work to become better listeners:

- *Listening carefully helps us become better informed.* Many of our ideas come from listening to others. Whether we are participating in a group discussion, watching the news, or listening to a formal speech, we can learn information that will help us make more informed decisions. Students who are good listeners usually perform better in their classes. Citizens who are good listeners become better-informed voters and tend to participate more actively in civic life.
- *Listening to others is part of our responsibility as citizens in a democratic society.* When we listen closely to others' arguments, we show respect for their views and can respond more thoughtfully and intelligently. By listening carefully as others share their ideas, we also communicate a desire for dialogue and collaboration. By listening respectfully and attentively while others are speaking, we demonstrate our faith in the democratic process and our conviction that the views of every citizen deserve a respectful hearing.
- *Listening gives us a clearer sense of who we are and what we value.* Listening allows us to compare and contrast our own beliefs and values with those of our fellow citizens. By listening to others, we get a better sense of who we are and how our views compare to those of others. If we find that our views are out of the mainstream, we may want to ask, "What influences or life experiences have shaped my unique perspective on this issue?" or "Why might others have developed a different point of view?"
- *Good listening helps us develop and sustain better interpersonal relationships.* Listening to others shows that we care about them. Furthermore, good listening is often reciprocated. When we show that we care by listening carefully to the

problems, perspectives, and ideas of others, they are more likely to give our views full and fair consideration.

- *By becoming better listeners, we can become better speakers.* By carefully observing how others communicate, we can learn to communicate more effectively ourselves. Moreover, listening carefully helps us better understand our audiences when we speak. By listening to what our audience members say about themselves—by interacting with them before or after a speech—we can gather information that will help us frame our own ideas and arguments.

In short, effective listening is both a practical necessity and an ethical responsibility for citizens in a democracy.

Preparing for Critical Listening: Our Responsibility as Citizens

If we are to listen effectively, we must possess sufficient information and knowledge to comprehend and assess the ideas of others. If we plan to attend a community forum on affordable housing, for example, we should know something about the topic in advance. How expensive is housing in our community? How does our community compare with surrounding communities? If our housing has become unaffordable, what may account for that? What options do we have for creating more affordable housing? Who needs to be involved in addressing the problem?

HIGHLIGHTING LISTENING AND LEADERSHIP

Listening has been linked to effective leadership in the business and professional world, as well as in the public arena.

- Leadership experts, such as Ronald Heifetz of Harvard University, point out that the foundation of good listening is "curiosity and empathy." Excellent listeners are able to look *beyond* the speaker's verbal and nonverbal messages and uncover the underlying argument beneath the disagreement or conflict.
- Former Chrysler CEO, Lee Iaccoca (credited with saving Chrysler from bankruptcy in the 1980s), emphasizes the strong link between motivating employees to give their best efforts and listening to their ideas, questions, and concerns. Even if the "system" labels someone as "average or mediocre," they may truly excel simply because someone has "listened to [their] problems and helped [them] solve them."
- As Hillary Clinton prepared to run for the U.S. Senate in New York in 2000, she embarked on a "listening tour" which enabled her to obtain firsthand feedback from everyday Americans as well as local government officials as they talked with her about "their concerns and aspirations for the families and communities."
- When Senator John Kerry succeeded in his 2004 bid for the Democratic presidential nomination, a *USA Today* correspondent attributed his success to his "communication skills" and his willingness to listen "patiently to voters for hours on end" as they bombarded him with their questions and concerns.
- In 2009 President Obama traveled to London for the first time during his presidency. He expressed a balanced commitment to advancing ideas and listening thoughtfully and responsively. He had come, he said, "to listen and not to lecture."

Sources: From Andrew D. Wolvin, "Listening Leadership: Hillary Clinton's Listening Tour," *International Journal of Listening 19*. Copyright © 2005 by *International Journal of Listening*; From Barack Obama, Joint Press Availability with President Barack Obama and Prime Minister Gordon Brown, April 1, 2009. Published 2009 by The White House, Office of the Press Secretary.

FOCUS ON CIVIC ENGAGEMENT

National Issues Forums: The Role of Listening in Democratic Deliberations

The National Issues Forums (NIF) is a network of educational institutions, civic groups, churches, and other organizations that convene gatherings where citizens can talk about public issues. They emphasize deliberation, not debate, using a structured approach that stresses "listening carefully to the views of others and talking through the conflicts that arise when people disagree." These forums occur throughout the country and focus on timely and critical topics, such as health care, immigration, and terrorism. The results are shared with local, state, and federal officials.

Former Florida legislator Scott Clemens emphasizes the real benefit of having lawmakers attend a forum where they listen more than they speak. He points out that legislators don't have to play the role of "experts." Instead, they "have the chance to listen . . . to really focus on what people are saying."

To read more about NIF, see Chapter 18.

Source: National Issues Forums Institute, "News," www.nifi.org/news. See in particular Bruce Feustel, "Connecting Citizens with Legislators" (accessed March 3, 2009).[10]

These are only a few of the questions that the thoughtful citizen might ask even *before* attending the presentation.

In your public speaking classroom, you may not know much about some of the topics your classmates will address. Even so, you should make an effort to be as well informed as possible. Get into the habit of regularly consulting reputable news sources—on the Internet, in newspapers and magazines, and on television. Make an effort to talk about important public issues with your classmates, family, and friends. By becoming more knowledgeable about a wide array of local, state, national, and international issues, you can become a better listener and a more informed citizen.

As we become better informed, we are better able to distinguish fact from opinion, assess the quality of a speaker's ideas and arguments, and pose thoughtful questions. Listeners who are uninformed have difficulty distinguishing sound and useful information from that which is irrelevant, invalid, or unreliable. Sometimes poorly prepared listeners may not be able to grasp a speaker's arguments at all.

Clearly, there are both personal and social benefits to good listening. When speakers *and* listeners are well informed, democratic deliberation works better and the prospects for constructive problem solving are enhanced.

UNDERSTANDING BARRIERS TO GOOD LISTENING

Preview. *Most of us underestimate the effort it takes to listen effectively. We want to listen well but often fail to recognize the barriers we will need to overcome if we hope to become better listeners. Most of these barriers are grounded in our attitudes toward listening, as well as in certain deficiencies in our listening behaviors. As we learn to identify and understand the barriers that impede our ability to listen effectively, we recognize that good listening is an acquired skill.*

Passivity Syndrome

Many of us are vaguely aware of the statistics on poor listening and simply assume that they do not apply to us. We think listening is easy, at least for us! After all, we have been listening since we were born, and as students we listen for many hours every day. Perhaps we feel that we already know all there is to know about listening. Or maybe we feel that the primary responsibility for good listening rests with the speakers. As long as we show up, we believe that we have done our part, and it is up to speakers to *make* us want to listen. If they fail, too bad for them!

This line of reasoning—known as the **passivity syndrome**—is rooted in a view of public speaking as a one-way street. In this view, the speaker acts and the listener reacts; the speaker controls the communication process, while the listener remains passive. At a conscious level, few of us want to admit that as listeners, we are overly compliant, easily manipulated, or uninvolved in the communication process. Yet that is precisely what happens if we allow ourselves to be passive listeners. If we listen passively, we give up control.

The principle that *should* influence our approach to listening is simple: *listening is an active process.*[11] Anyone can make us hear just by turning up the volume. But no one can make us *listen.* We have to *want* to listen, and we have to be willing to work at it. Speakers can encourage us to listen by presenting their ideas effectively. But if they do not—if their performance is disappointing in some way—that does not let us off the hook. No speaker is perfect; they all need our goodwill and understanding. When we attend a public talk, we hope to learn, to grow, to be stimulated, or perhaps to discover new strategies for solving a community problem. If we come away empty-handed, we must share some of the blame. If we hope to derive some benefit from listening, we must do our part. We must get actively involved in the communication process by listening more carefully.

Mental Games

Listening is more difficult when a speaker challenges our existing beliefs or values. We prefer listening to speakers whose thinking is consistent with our own.[12] If a speaker challenges our worldview, we may try to avoid listening altogether, or we may be jarred into defensiveness. It can be difficult to listen to a speaker who argues that Walmart exploits its female employees if you are a male who has worked for Walmart for ten years and been promoted three times. It can be painful to listen to a speaker discuss the dangers of smoking if you happen to be a smoker. Or perhaps you feel so passionately about the issue of gay marriage that you immediately turn off anybody who disagrees with your views.

Sometimes we try simply to escape from distressing communication. We have seen members of our family turn off the TV in disgust when a politician they dislike begins to speak. Others may utter disrespectful comments or otherwise "talk over" a speaker they do not want to hear. When attending a live speaking event, we rarely encounter such avoidance behaviors. Few listeners get up and walk out during a speech. Even so, it is always possible to turn off a speaker mentally. We may *pretend to listen* to a speaker without really listening at all. Instead, we may fantasize, reflect on our day, or think about our plans for later that evening.

When we do this, we are not only being disrespectful to the speaker, but we're also robbing ourselves of an opportunity to learn something new.

When we become defensive about something we hear, we typically engage in **mental argument**, silently refuting the ideas of a speaker. This may be preferable to pretending to listen, but mental argument is not the same as listening. As we concentrate on refuting the speaker's ideas, we often lose the thread of the argument. When the speech is finished, we may not recall the speaker's whole argument because we were too busy coming up with our own reservations and counterarguments. It is hardly surprising, then, that during question-and-answer periods, those who oppose the speaker's position often ask questions that reveal that they were not listening closely to the speech.

As effective and ethical listeners, we should allow the speaker to state his or her whole case before we jump to conclusions. We should give every speaker a fair and honest hearing before raising whatever objections we may have. It is perfectly acceptable to disagree with points made by the speaker, but during the speech itself, you may just note those points and continue listening. After you have listened to the speaker's whole argument, you are in a better position to respond to those ideas with which you disagree.

Unfortunately, too many public advocates today simply refuse to listen to others. On political talk shows, for example, we frequently see speakers interrupt or shout down those who disagree with their views, apparently thinking this is how you "win" a debate. Although these sorts of "debates" may be entertaining to some, they are hardly models of effective and constructive listening. If democratic deliberation is to lead to sound collective decisions, we need to listen to one another without becoming combative or defensive. Genuine listening means listening actively with an open mind and respect for those who may disagree.[13]

When speakers are combative or confrontational, trying to score points instead of listening to others, they undermine democratic deliberation.

Short Attention Span

How long can you listen to someone speak without starting to fidget or finding that your mind is wandering? Can you easily listen to your professor's 45-minute lecture and remain focused and attentive throughout? If you can, you have an excellent attention span.

Modern technology has significantly changed the way we listen and what we listen to. In the age of television and the Internet, we can hardly imagine listening to a series of seven political debates, each lasting three hours. Yet that is exactly what happened during the famous Lincoln-Douglas debates in 1858; the people of Illinois flocked to hear two candidates for the Senate engage in a "sustained public discussion" of the issues.[14] Used to long speeches, sermons, and lectures, Americans of the nineteenth century were happy to listen to Daniel Webster speak for hours when commemorating the landing of the Pilgrims or debating the great issues of the day on the floor of the Senate.[15] The most famous preacher of that era, Henry Ward Beecher, would entertain huge crowds for hours with his provocative and entertaining lectures.[16]

Today, our attention spans are simply not as long as they used to be. We now demand shorter messages, sometimes losing interest after only a few minutes. Some experts advise teachers to break their lectures into small chunks, with no chunk lasting longer than fifteen minutes.[17] According to these experts, television has contributed to our shorter attention spans by breaking every ten or twelve minutes for commercials or station identification.[18] Not only television but newspapers, video games, text messaging, tweets, and social networking sites have conditioned us to expect our information in short bits or "sound bites." In the classroom, teachers may accommodate our shorter attention spans by stopping for discussion, showing video clips, or staging a group exercise. During a public speech, however, we would be surprised if a speaker were to stop in the middle of the talk to ask *us* questions or to break us into small groups for discussion.

As listeners, we have a responsibility to work at overcoming our own short attention spans. We need to accept that we will sometimes be asked to listen to talks that run 30 minutes or more, and we need to work at remaining attentive in such situations. If we find ourselves fading in and out during a speaker's presentation, we need to catch ourselves, refocus our attention, and practice some of the techniques of active listening discussed later in this chapter. Good listening does not just happen. We must make an effort to overcome our short attention spans and become better listeners.

Stereotyping

In the early twenty-first century, we thankfully have left behind many sexual, cultural, racial, religious, and ethnic stereotypes. Even so, not all stereotypes have disappeared. Although racial and gender stereotypes have been discredited in recent years, even well-meaning people sometimes still stereotype older people, people with disabilities, or people from particular ethnic groups or geographical regions. Moreover, racism and sexism may have taken on new, more subtle forms, and some scholars believe they continue to be deeply embedded in our society.[19]

As early as 1922, journalist Walter Lippmann likened stereotypes to "pictures in the head," or mental reproductions of reality, and from there, the term gradually came to mean generalizations—or, quite often, overgeneralizations—about the members of a group.[20] The *American Heritage Dictionary* defines *stereotype* as "a conventional, formulaic, and oversimplified conception or image."[21] When **stereotyping**, we observe a few members of a particular category (African-American males, Asians, older women, homosexuals, and so forth) and draw conclusions about all others belonging to that same group. The difference between making a generalization about a group of individuals and stereotyping them is that, in stereotyping, we leave no room for individual differences. We believe that every individual will fit the same mental mold we have created for the group.

Stereotyping represents a problem in many realms of life. Scholars have linked stereotyping to prejudice and discrimination, as well as to lower self-esteem, adverse health outcomes, and impaired performance among the targets of racial and sexist stereotyping.[22] Stereotypes may be based on direct experience, family members' expressed views and attitudes, or various media portrayals, but whatever their source they can unfairly categorize and stigmatize people.

HIGHLIGHTING STEREOTYPES IN THE MEDIA

One of the main places that children and adults learn stereotypes is the mass media. Many studies have found that advertisements, television programs, movies, and other media are saturated with racial and gender stereotypes, as well as stereotypes about age, occupation, education, class, geographical location, or sexual orientation.

The sheer volume of advertising suggests that many people are exposed to stereotypes on a daily basis, and they may profoundly influence how people perceive and relate to one another. One study found that male interviewers who had watched sexist television commercials later judged a female job applicant as less competent, remembered less biographical information about her, and remembered more about her physical appearance than did interviewers who had not watched these kinds of commercials.

Beyond advertising, other media-based stereotypes wield considerable influence. For instance, research has shown the following:

- White television viewers who watch a stereotyped comic portrayal of black people are later more likely to judge a black defendant guilty of an assault.
- Males who view movie scenes objectifying women are later more likely to believe that a date rape victim experienced pleasure and "got what she wanted."
- People who watch a music video objectifying women later rate a woman as more sexual and submissive when she returns a man's advances.
- Heterosexual men who look at attractive women in magazine erotica later rate their romantic partners as less attractive.

These studies and many more document the negative influences of media stereotypes on social perception and behavior.

Source: Scott Plous, "The Psychology of Prejudice, Stereotyping, and Discrimination: An Overview," in *Understanding Prejudice and Discrimination*, ed. S. Plous (New York: McGraw-Hill, 2003), 3–48.

Stereotyping can greatly interfere with our ability to listen effectively. When we are preoccupied with a speaker's gender, race, age, or other characteristic, we are focusing on dimensions that may have little or nothing to do with his or her message. We are not focusing fully on the information and ideas being communicated. For example, suppose you were listening to a speech that addressed the problem of the **glass ceiling**, an invisible barrier of prejudices and discrimination that allegedly hampers women's ability to rise to the top of business and professional organizations. Would you listen to that speech carefully and with an open mind if you already had stereotyped the speaker as a radical feminist?

In examining our tendency to stereotype speakers, it may be useful to think about how you would feel if others stereotyped you. Consider making a list of your personal qualities, organizational memberships, and other characteristics. What sorts of stereotypes may be associated with those traits? More important, in what ways do you believe you *differ* from those stereotypes? Suppose, for example, that you are a white male, a former Boy Scout, a Baptist, and a lifelong resident of Alabama. Does that mean you fit the stereotype of a "southern redneck"? Of course not. Perhaps you drive a Smart car, not a pickup truck, and you may even be a liberal Democrat. Even if it were true that *most* people with all those characteristics are conservative or prefer pickups to Smart cars, *you* are unique and you undoubtedly resent being stereotyped.

Dr. Martin Luther King Jr. overcame many distractions when he delivered his famous "I Have a Dream" speech.

Stereotypes are inevitably misleading. Everybody is unique, and nobody perfectly fits the stereotypes that may be applied to them. In all communication situations—and public speaking is no exception—we need to respect each person's individuality and resist falling for stereotypes.

Distractions

Sometimes we fail to listen effectively because of distractions in our surroundings. We may even use distractions as excuses for our own failure to listen. We sit in the last row and then complain about the speaker's voice not carrying very well. Or perhaps we sit by an open window and find ourselves distracted by a lawn mower, the shouts of children, or the beauty of the view. We tell ourselves that we had every intention of listening carefully but fell prey to distractions.

There are times, of course, when listening to a speech can be challenging. Distractions are often real as well as imagined. In most instances, however, we can overcome those distractions if we really want to. When Dr. Martin Luther King Jr. delivered his famous "I Have a Dream" speech in August 1963, the distractions were many.

Standing in front of the Lincoln Memorial, King addressed tens of thousands of listeners, in sweltering heat, some so far away that they could barely see the speaker. And yet, somehow, everyone listened with rapt attention and departed with a renewed commitment to fighting for civil rights. Few speeches are so historic, but if we are determined and motivated to listen, we can overcome almost any distraction.

In addition to the surrounding environment, speakers themselves sometimes present distractions. Most public speakers are "on display" before they make their speeches. Seated at a luncheon table or on a speaker's platform, they can be viewed before speaking to the audience. Thus there is plenty of time for listeners to look at them and form early and often misguided impressions. What would you conclude about a speaker who wore sandals and casual attire at an event where everyone else was dressed formally? How might a speaker's weight, build, or personal attractiveness influence the way you react? To some extent, your reaction may depend on the topic and situation. If a speaker is addressing the problem of obesity in America, his or her weight may seem relevant to the speech rather than a distraction. If the topic is adult literacy, however, the speaker's physical appearance should be irrelevant.

The point is that we should not be distracted by a speaker's physical appearance. And we certainly should never allow a speaker's appearance to determine our ultimate judgment of a speech. Some listeners may be impressed by a speaker who appears in an Armani suit; they may be disposed to suspend their critical faculties and believe what he says simply because he *looks* successful. If we allow ourselves to be distracted by first impressions, we have failed to fulfill our responsibilities as listeners. We should recognize the first impression for what it is—a *first* impression—and not allow it to determine our reactions to a speech.[23]

Nonverbal communication is important and cannot be ignored, of course, but what we observe with the eyes is only the beginning. We are there to listen to the speaker's complete presentation. Only then—on the basis of all that we have heard and observed—can we formulate a reasonable reaction to the speaker and the speech.

Finally, we need to recognize that visual images can sometimes distract us from listening closely. In some cases, visual images may function as powerful influences on our ideas and behaviors without our even being aware of their impact. The colors used in some images, for example, can elicit feelings or establish moods—and may influence the way we feel about what the speaker is saying.[24] In some cases, as communication scholar Kathleen Hall Jamieson has argued, visual images can even *substitute* for persuasive political arguments.[25] As discerning audience members, we must critically evaluate visual messages by asking ourselves how what we are *seeing* may influence our thoughts, feelings, and beliefs. We will return to the subject of visual images later in this book (Chapter 13).

Let us now lay out the tactics, most of which we have alluded to in the preceding pages, that should form our listening strategy. Effective listening provides the foundation for critical and constructive thinking and offers a powerful tool for anyone who wishes to participate fully in civic life. Good listening is essential if citizens are going to exchange information and ideas and work together to solve problems through democratic deliberation.

GUIDELINES FOR IMPROVING LISTENING

Preview. *Effective listening requires considerable effort. As we work to improve our listening skills, we need to consider our existing attitudes and predispositions. We also need to reflect on what we can do to enhance our listening effectiveness. Above all, we must remind ourselves of our ethical responsibility to take listening seriously; to listen to others attentively, critically, and constructively; and to approach listening as an active and ongoing process.*

In an ideal world, all speakers would be well prepared, articulate, and knowledgeable. They would strive to engage us intellectually and emotionally. They would deliver their presentations with passion and conviction and present clear and forceful arguments. They would attempt to minimize distractions in the speaking environment. They would structure their remarks logically and emphasize main ideas through their delivery, language, and strategic use of presentational aids. They would listen carefully when their listeners asked questions after the speech, and they would respond thoughtfully and respectfully to each question.

Unfortunately, not all speakers live up to this ideal. As a result, we need to assume our own responsibilities as listeners and make an effort to compensate for any shortcomings on the part of the speaker. The guidelines that follow will assist you in listening more effectively. Some suggest specific behaviors you might employ; others focus more on the expectations and attitudes you have as a listener.

Remember Your Responsibilities as a Listener

Because good listening requires some effort, it is easy to become lazy and minimize its importance. So we need to remind ourselves often of how much we can learn, how we can benefit, by becoming better listeners. If you catch your mind wandering while listening to a speech, remind yourself that every speech has the potential to broaden your knowledge, teach you something important, or give you insight into people or issues you also may address someday.

The U.S. Constitution protects the right to free speech, but the rights and responsibilities of citizenship extend to listening as well as speaking. If democracy is to work, those who ultimately make the decisions—the citizens themselves—must be critical, well-informed listeners. Effective listening is a must for all who aspire to be responsible and engaged citizens.

Come Prepared to Listen and Offer Feedback

Before you attend a speech or community forum, read as widely as you can on the topic. Formulate some tentative questions. Give some thought to your existing views and any potential biases you may have toward the speaker or topic. Commit yourself to listening with an open mind. Recognize the effort it will take to listen carefully and promise yourself that you will make that effort.

Following many speeches, you will have the opportunity to ask questions and offer feedback to the speaker. Knowing that you will have an opportunity to respond to a speaker may help you focus your attention and listen carefully and critically. You will want to ask intelligent, appropriately challenging questions and offer comments relevant to the substance of the speech.

In the classroom, your instructor may ask that you regularly offer feedback to your classmates after they speak. You may be invited to comment on the overall strengths of the speech or on specific areas that need improvement, such as the speaker's organization or use of supporting material. Whatever sort of feedback you give—general or specific, oral or written—be sure to say something positive and constructive about your classmates' speeches. Your goal should be to help boost their confidence and improve their speaking skills, not "show them up" or "tear them down."

Understand Your Identity as a Listener

Who we are colors how we listen to and interact with speakers. Your background, your personal characteristics, and the roles you play in life all contribute to certain predispositions and biases that will influence how you listen. No one can totally eliminate bias, but you can, through self-analysis, discover some of the forces at work in your own listening behaviors. Only by understanding yourself—what you bring to a speaking situation and who you are in relation to it—will you be able to listen in a critical yet fair-minded way.

Listen with a Purpose

The speaker has a purpose in getting up to talk. As audience members we, too, should have a purpose, whether that purpose is to learn, to evaluate, or to prepare for our own speech before the same audience. Do you want simply to gather information from a speech? Or do you hope to better understand an opposing point of view? Are you interested in relating the topic to your life or in preparing to speak out yourself on the topic the speaker is addressing?

Your purposes may evolve as you listen. You may begin by thinking you just want information about a problem, such as global warming. But as you listen, you may decide that you want to get involved—to do something to address the problem. By listening purposefully, you can respond to the message on your own terms while still maintaining a healthy respect for the speaker's position and purpose.

Understand the Setting and Intended Audience

As we pointed out earlier, the setting of a speech imposes certain restrictions and expectations on a speaker. A political candidate who buys 30 seconds of radio time is limited in what he or she can say. A speaker at an outdoor rally works under different constraints than one in a lecture hall. When you listen, be aware of how the particular setting may be affecting the speaker's efforts. If the speaker is given little time to speak, for instance, you may be less critical if his or her main points are not fully developed. If the speaker had no time to prepare, you may forgive minor errors or an unpolished style. The circumstances under which the speaker prepared and delivered the speech should always be taken into account.

Sometimes a speaker's words are aimed at more than one audience. For example, at a large state university, a series of racially motivated incidents resulted in several protest demonstrations and rallies on campus. At these rallies, students spoke to an audience of their peers—their immediate audience. However, these students also knew that members of the press were present. Through the press, the speakers hoped to send powerful persuasive messages to a wider audience on campus and in the community. The types of appeals speakers make, or the types of arguments they advance, may be puzzling to listeners who do not reflect enough on the target audience.

Consider the Speaker's Purpose

Understanding what the speaker hopes to accomplish by speaking helps prepare us to listen effectively. Speakers do not always make their purpose clear, and some may even intend to mislead the audience. If a speech is poorly structured, it may not be easy to identify the speaker's goal or purpose. Knowing something about the setting, the speaker, and the general nature of the topic may help us identify the speaker's goal. Once we think we discern the basic purpose of the speech, we are in a better position to make judgments about the quality of the ideas and information that follow.

Examine the Impact of the Speaker's Ethos

Often when we listen to a speech, we have some initial perceptions of the speaker's credibility. If we are not careful or honest with ourselves, we may find ourselves overly influenced by *who* the person is rather than *what* he or she says in the speech.

If, for example, you do not like the speaker, then face up to that fact. You may be tempted to fool yourself into believing that your personal opinion of the speaker has nothing to do with your assessment of his or her ideas or proposals. But the real reason may be that you just do not *want* to believe anything this speaker has to say. If the matter is not of vital importance, it may not matter whether your judgment is biased by your opinion of the speaker. But suppose it is a serious matter that could affect your health or the well-being of your community. Separating your personal views of the speaker from your assessment of his or her message *can* be vital.

Practice Critical Listening as an Active Process

All these guidelines point to the hard work that must go into preparing yourself to listen effectively. Here are some more specific and practical tactics that you can use to become a more active and engaged listener.

COMMUNICATE NONVERBALLY Use **nonverbal communication** to show the speaker that you are actively listening. When you look at the speaker or lean forward as he or she talks, you show your interest in the speech. You also may smile or nod your head in agreement to show the speaker that you are interested, are engaged, or even endorse his or her point of view. Through your facial expressions, you can show interest, agreement, confusion, or concern.[26]

As we have stressed throughout the book, effective communication demands thoughtful, responsible, and active participation by all those involved in the process. When you are an audience member, you have a *responsibility* to offer feedback.

After the speech, you can ask questions and make comments, but during the speech, most of your feedback will be nonverbal. Based on your nonverbal feedback, the speaker can begin to process your concerns, clarify points of confusion, or anticipate issues or objections that you may raise after the speech. In this way, you, as a listener, can show that you are an active partner in the communication process.

Take Notes as You Listen Effective note taking can help you follow the speech and record critical information and ideas for later use.[27] Because note taking requires some action on your part, it also can help keep you engaged in active listening.[28] In taking notes, you may want to jot down a basic outline of the speech, as well as specific questions you will want to ask after the speech. You also may make note of any statistics, facts, or particular examples that you want to remember.

Note taking consumes time, so it can slow down our thinking and help synchronize our listening with the tempo of the speaker.[29] Finally, note taking helps us remember. Our notes can help us ask better questions after the speech and provide us with some recorded information to ponder and possibly use in the future. Some researchers argue that it is not until *after* a speech is over that we typically process most of the ideas and information we gathered while listening. A good set of notes can help in this process of analysis and reflection.[30] See the *Highlighting Note Taking* feature for advice on the note-taking process.

Minimize Distractions Do all you can to stay focused on the speech. Note taking will help. Arriving early enough to get a good seat will help, too.

HIGHLIGHTING NOTE TAKING

Suggested Strategies

- *Write down the ideas and key points that are most important.* You cannot write down everything the speaker says. Focus instead on jotting down the thesis and main ideas.
- *Use keywords to record main ideas.* Attempting to write down every word is inefficient and likely impossible. Routinely omit articles (*the, a, an*), many prepositions, and some verbs. Just make sure you retain the *sense* of the idea being communicated.
- *Abbreviate and use symbols whenever possible.* Some of these may be unique to you. So long as you understand them, you will be fine. For example, in taking notes on a speech on civic engagement, you may simply write *CE* in place of *civic engagement. CA* may be used to designate *communication apprehension.* More common symbols may include *w* (for *with*), *w/o* (for *without*), = (for *equal*), > (for *more than*), or < (for *less than*).
- *Organize your notes as a rough outline of the speech.* Once you have identified major headings, you can also record substantiating material. Leave room in the left-hand margin and between items in your notes so that you can add things as the speaker presents them. Do not concern yourself with following a formal outlining format. Nearly any format will work, so long as you are able to distinguish main ideas from supporting (subordinate) material.
- *Use your notes to help you evaluate the speech.* Your notes serve two purposes: recording the speaker's ideas and assessing their quality. If you feel a main idea is unsubstantiated, you may write "weak" in brackets next to the recorded idea. If you think of a specific question or concern, jot that down as well.

Beyond that, put distractions—whether they come from the speaker or from the environment—in perspective. Remind yourself that your purpose is *not* to offer a critique of the speaker's gestures or hairstyle, nor to do an acoustical analysis of the room. Rather, you are there to listen to the ideas and information advanced by the speaker and to react as intelligently and thoughtfully as you can.

Remember, too, that the visual aspects of a speaker's presentation may influence the way you react. Good listeners will not allow visual images to distract them from the substance of the speaker's message. The ability to think critically about visual images, or so-called **visual literacy**, is an increasingly important skill in the modern world.[31] (We discuss visual literacy in Chapter 13.)

THINK CRITICALLY WHILE SUSPENDING JUDGMENT As you identify main ideas, pay attention to the evidence used by the speaker to support them. Did the speaker cite credible sources of information? Were the statistics used clear and meaningful in helping you grasp the magnitude of the problem? To what extent did the speaker rely on personal experiences and opinions? If the speaker leaned heavily on personal knowledge, were you convinced that his or her personal experiences were sufficient proof?

You will also want to consider the quality of the speaker's reasoning. Did the speaker seem to jump to any conclusions too quickly, or with too little evidence? Did he draw any analogies or comparisons that did not make sense? Did she attack someone personally instead of responding to his arguments? Were you urged to do something simply because a lot of other people are doing it? There may be plenty of good reasons for doing as the speaker suggests, but you need to focus on the reasoning in the speech itself. Can it withstand critical scrutiny? In taking notes, jot down important evidence and arguments that you want to remember, and make note of any information or conclusions that you doubt or have questions about.

As a good critical thinker, you need to be reflective—about your own ideas and those of others. When a speaker advances a claim, you will want to ask, "What is he basing this on?" "Why should I believe what she is saying?" You will also want to distinguish fact from opinion and unstated assumptions from explicit claims. If you are well versed on the speaker's topic (and if you are well read in general), you will be better able to think critically about how problems are framed and whether proposed solutions appear sound.

You should suspend final judgment of a speech until the speaker is finished. As you listen, you will, of course, make some tentative judgments. You will, for example, assess and reassess your perceptions of the speaker's ethos throughout the speech. As a responsible listener, however, you should strive for some measure of open-mindedness. Give the speaker a fair and reasonable chance.

Whatever your ultimate reaction to the speech, it should come at the *end* of the speaker's presentation. Better yet, wait until you have heard the speaker's responses to questions from the audience to decide what you think of the speech. Sometimes speakers will clarify and illuminate their main ideas as they address listener concerns. The point here is simple: we owe it to every speaker to suspend judgment until we have heard everything he or she has to say. A good critical listener is interested in hearing the most complete version of the speaker's arguments and ideas before rendering a judgment.

SUMMARY

- Effective listening is an important communication skill. In virtually any context—whether professional, personal, or community life—listening well is highly valued. Yet as we know from research, most of us often do not listen carefully.
- We listen for a variety of purposes, some of which require little effort.
  - Sometimes we listen merely for pleasure or to provide a "sympathetic ear" to a friend or co-worker.
  - Other times, we may seek information or need to critically evaluate the ideas of others. In those situations, it is important that we listen carefully and actively evaluate the information that we hear.
- Listening is a multi-step process that involves hearing the speaker's message, focusing our attention, understanding what has been communicated, responding both verbally and nonverbally, and remembering important ideas, arguments and information.
- There are many excellent reasons for striving to improve our listening skills.
  - By becoming better listeners, we can improve our interpersonal relationships and become better speakers ourselves.
  - We also can learn a great deal from listening well, both about the world and about ourselves.
  - As citizens in a democracy, we need to listen carefully to others as we participate in public deliberations. By listening actively and respectfully to our fellow citizens, we can improve the quality of discussion and debate in our democratic society and, hopefully, make better collective decisions.
- Unfortunately, there are many barriers to effective listening.
  - Some listeners take a passive approach to listening, assuming that it is the speaker's job to keep them interested.
  - Other listeners may try to avoid information that they do not want to hear, or perhaps they become defensive when a speaker disagrees with their existing opinions.
  - Short attention spans contribute to poor listening, and stereotypes can still get in the way of effective listening.
  - A variety of physical and mental distractions can prevent us from listening effectively. Perhaps we are distracted by the speaker's appearance or mannerisms, or by other visual images he or she presents during the talk. Whatever the distraction, it detracts from our ability to really "hear" what is said.
- With genuine desire and effort, all of us can learn to become better, more engaged listeners.
  - Remember your responsibilities as a listener, especially in a democratic society, and come prepared to listen and offer feedback without allowing your own personal biases to get in the way.
  - Recognize your purpose and identity as a listener and how your role and background may color your perceptions of the speech.
  - Try to understand the speaker's purposes and how the setting or intended audience may have affected the speaker and the speech.

- Actively and critically *engage* the speaker, giving nonverbal feedback and perhaps taking notes while evaluating the ideas and evidence presented in the speech itself.

QUESTIONS FOR REVIEW AND REFLECTION

1. Why is listening effectively so important?
2. How would you describe the listening effectiveness of most people?
3. List the steps in the listening process, explaining each one and offering an example.
4. Describe several different reasons for listening. Give an example of each.
5. How is effective listening related to good citizenship in a democratic society?
6. What positive outcomes are associated with listening effectively?
7. Describe your understanding of critical listening as an *active* process.
8. Name at least five problems that audience members often experience when listening to a public speech. Give an example of each.
9. Describe at least five ways that audience members can improve their listening skills. Why is each potentially valuable?
10. In your past experiences as a listener (in your classroom, profession, or community), what have been your greatest listening challenges? Provide examples of each. What have you done to address these challenges?

ENDNOTES

1. See, as examples, Deborah Borisoff and M. Purdy, ed., *Listening in Everyday Life: A Personal and Professional Approach*, 2nd ed. (Lanham, MD: University Press of America, 1997); Ralph G. Nichols and L. A. Stephens, "Listening to People," *Harvard Business Review* 60 (1990): 95–102; and David A. Whetten and Kim S. Cameron, *Developing Management Skills*, 6th ed. (Englewood Cliffs, NJ: Prentice Hall, 2005).
2. Madelyn Burley-Allen, "Listen Up," *HR Magazine* (2001): 115–20.
3. Stephen Covey, *The Seven Habits of Highly Effective People* (New York: Golden Books, 1997).
4. Samuel L. Becker and L. R. Ekdom, "The Forgotten Basic Skill: Oral Communication," *Association for Communication Bulletin* 33 (1980): 12–15. In addition, an excellent source of information about all aspects of listening is the Web site of the International Listening Association, www.listen.org.
5. Vincent DiSalvo et al., "Communication Skills Needed by Persons in Business Organizations," *Communication Education* 25 (1976): 269–75.
6. Ralph G. Nichols, "Listening Is a 10-Part Skill," *Nation's Business* 75 (1987): 40; Andrew D. Wolvin and Carolyn Gwynn Coakley, *Listening*, 5th ed. (Dubuque, IA: Brown & Benchmark, 1996).
7. Ralph G. Nichols, *Are You Listening?* (New York: McGraw-Hill, 1957), 1–17; Judi Brownell, *Listening: Attitudes, Principles, and Skills*, 3rd ed. (Boston: Allyn & Bacon, 2006).
8. The International Listening Association defines *listening* as "the process of receiving, constructing meaning from, and responding to spoken and/or nonverbal messages."
9. See, for example, Kay Lindahl, *The Sacred Art of Listening* (Woodstock, VT: Skylight Paths, 2002).
10. Periodically, the NIF publishes reports to communicate the outcomes of forums held across the nation about a particular issue. These publications can be accessed online at www.nifi.org/reports/issues. Sample report titles include "Examining Health Care: What's the Public Prescription?," "Terrorism: What Do We Do Now?," "Protecting Our Rights: What Goes on the Internet," "The National Piggybank: Does Our Retirement System Need Fixing?," "Mission Uncertain: Reassessing America's Global Role," and "The Troubled American Family: Which Way Out of the Storm?"
11. Carl Rogers and Richard E. Farson, "Active Listening," in *Organizational Communication*, 2nd ed., ed. Stewart D. Ferguson and Sherry Ferguson (New Brunswick, NJ: Transaction, 1988), 319–34.

12. Joseph A. DeVito, *The Interpersonal Communication Book*, 10th ed. (Boston: Allyn & Bacon, 2003), 64.
13. For an extended discussion of these ideas, see Susan Bickford, *Listening, Conflict, and Citizenship: Dissonance Democracy* (Ithaca, NY: Cornell University Press, 1996).
14. David Zarefsky, *Lincoln, Douglas, and Slavery: In the Crucible of Public Debate* (Chicago: University of Chicago Press, 1990), x.
15. See Robert Remini, *Daniel Webster: The Man and His Time* (New York: Norton, 1997), esp. chap. 9, "The Plymouth Oration," 178–87, and chap. 18, "The Webster-Hayne Debate," 312–31.
16. Debby Applegate, *The Most Famous Man in America: The Biography of Henry Ward Beecher* (New York: Doubleday, 2006), esp. 215–19.
17. Joan Middendorf and Alan Kalish, "The Change-Up in Lectures," *National Teaching and Learning Forum* 5 (1996): 1–4.
18. Peter J. Frederick, "The Lively Lecture: 8 Variations," *College Teaching* 34 (1986): 43–50; A. H. Johnstone and F. Percival, "Attention Breaks in Lectures," *Education in Chemistry* 13 (1976): 49–50.
19. See, for example, Patricia Hill Collins, *Black Feminist Thought: Knowledge, Consciousness, and the Politics of Empowerment*, 2nd ed. (New York: Routledge, 2000); and bell hooks, *Black Looks: Race and Representation* (Boston: South End Press, 1992).
20. Walter Lippmann, *Public Opinion* (New York: Harcourt, Brace, 1922), 75–89.
21. *The American Heritage College Dictionary*, 3rd ed., s.v. "Stereotype."
22. See, for example, Jon Hurwitz and Mark Peffley, "Public Perceptions of Race and Crime: The Role of Racial Stereotypes," *American Journal of Political Science* 41 (1997): 375–401; Debra L. Oswald and Richard D. Harvey, "Hostile Environments, Stereotype Threat, and Math Performance among Undergraduate Women," *Current Psychology* 19 (2000): 338–56; and Shani H. Peterson et al., "Images of Sexual Stereotypes in Rap Videos and the Health of African American Female Adolescents," *Journal of Women's Health* 16 (2007): 1157–64.
23. We know, for example, that interviewers form early impressions of job applicants, rarely changing their judgments after the first five minutes. See Robert W. Eder and Michael M. Harris, ed., *The Employment Interview Handbook* (Thousand Oaks, CA: Sage, 1999); and Charles B. Stewart and William B. Cash, *Interviewing: Principles and Practices*, 10th ed. (New York: McGraw-Hill, 2003).
24. Paul Martin Lester, *Visual Communication: Images with Messages* (Belmont, CA: Wadsworth Thomson Learning, 2000).
25. Kathleen H. Jamieson, *Eloquence in an Electronic Age* (New York: Oxford University Press, 1988), 114–17.
26. Carol A. Carrier, "Note-Taking Research: Implications for the Classroom," *Journal of Instructional Development* 6 (1983): 19–25; J. L. Fisher and M. B. Harris, "Effect of Note Taking and Review on Recall," *Journal of Educational Psychology* 65 (1973): 321–25.
27. Burley-Allen, "Listen Up," 119–20; "Train Yourself in the Art of Listening," *Positive Leadership* (July 1998): 10.
28. See K. Bosworth and J. Hamilton, ed., *Critical Thinking and Collaborative Learning: Underlying Processes and Effective Techniques* (San Francisco: Jossey-Bass, 1994); Rosabeth Moss Kanter, "Thinking across Boundaries," *Harvard Business Review* 68 (1990), editor's foreword; and S. Holly Stocking et al., *More Quick Hits: Successful Strategies by Award-Winning Teachers* (Bloomington: Indiana University Press, 1998), esp. "Fostering Critical and Creative Thinking," 40–57.
29. Research has shown that the average speaker talks at a rate of 125 words per minute, while listeners' minds race along at speeds of 400–500 words a minute. See Patricia Hayes Andrews and John E. Baird Jr., *Communication for Business and the Professions*, 8th ed. (Long Grove, IL: Waveland Press, 2005), 238–42; and Wolvin and Coakley, *Listening*, 12–15.
30. For recent insights on note taking, see Rick Reis, "Tomorrow's Professor Message #163: More Effective Note-Taking Strategies," Stanford Center for Teaching and Learning, cgi.stanford.edu/~dept-ctl/cgi-bin/tomprof/posting.php (accessed May 20, 2009); and Rick Reis, "Tomorrow's Professor Message #172: Teaching Students to Take Better Notes," Stanford Center for Teaching and Learning, cgi.standofr.edu/~dept-ctl/cgi-bin/tomprof/posting.php (accessed May 21, 2009).
31. B. A. Chauvin, "Visual or Media Literacy?" *Journal of Media Literacy* 23 (2003): 119–28.

CHAPTER

5

Diverse Audiences in a Democratic Society

CHAPTER SURVEY

Understanding Diverse Audiences

Identifying Individual Listener Needs and Values

Identifying Communal Needs and Values

Gathering Information for Audience Adaptation

Ongoing Strategies for Audience Adaptation

CHAPTER OBJECTIVES

After studying this chapter, you should be able to

1. Explain the role and significance of audience analysis in public speaking.
2. Describe the diverse audience characteristics you need to consider as you prepare to deliver a speech.
3. Identify individual and communal needs and values.
4. Gather information about an audience, including conducting an audience survey.
5. Implement strategies for adapting to audiences.

Audiences come together to hear about matters of importance, although they may have different reasons for being concerned about an issue. A new interstate highway may not come anywhere near a person's property, but that person may still be concerned about the possible impact of the highway on the environment or the economy. Others, such as real estate developers or construction workers, might have their own reasons for being interested in the issue. Some audience members may come to hear a speech simply to learn more about an issue; others who show up already have strong views. Sometimes an audience is even *required* to listen to a speech, as in your public speaking class or in a job training program, for example.

As a responsible speaker and listener, you try to recognize your own biases and understand how they can affect your judgment. At the same time, you need to think about how the characteristics and biases of your audience may affect *their* reactions to your speech. Before you speak, you will want to gather all the information you can about your audience so you can adapt what you have to say to your listeners.

UNDERSTANDING DIVERSE AUDIENCES

Preview. *As a responsible speaker, you must think carefully about your listeners. You and the members of your audience form a partnership, and you need to frame and deliver your message with the characteristics of your audience in mind.*

Many factors go into making people who they are. These factors can influence the way people see events and how important they consider an issue, which in turn can mold their values, determine how attentive they will be to a speech, or suggest whether they will accept or reject change. Table 5.1 lists some audience **demographics** that every speaker must consider. These audience characteristics often shape listeners' values and beliefs. If you know a lot about your listeners, you will be in a better position to determine what might be relevant to them, to appeal to their interests and concerns, and to recognize how their assumptions and perspectives might differ from your own. Understanding demographics, along with the individual and community values that grow out of them, will form the basis of the strategies you will use to adapt to your audience.

TABLE 5.1

AUDIENCE DEMOGRAPHICS

- Age
- Gender
- Race and ethnicity
- Intercultural factors
- Religion
- Geographic/cultural environment
- Education
- Occupation or profession
- Economic status

The demographics of an audience may suggest certain *tendencies*, but you can never really predict human behavior. Advertisers study demographics carefully and try to promote their products in publications, on TV shows, and on Web sites that will reach a particular **target audience**. Yet not all teenage girls read *Seventeen*, and those who do will not all respond to an ad in the same way. Nor will every member of AARP (formerly the American Association of Retired Persons) be interested in long-term care insurance. As we pointed out in Chapter 4, we cannot assume that all people within a particular demographic group are the same. Yet advertisers know better than to run ads for denture cleaners on MTV or ads for Rollerblades on a show with older viewers. It would be foolish to disregard the tendencies of certain groups to share characteristics that may influence how they respond to your message.

Age and Values

The age of audience members will influence the way they receive messages. Some may argue that age is mostly a state of mind rather than a physical fact. Even so, our age influences the sorts of experiences we have had and the issues that most concern us.

Being "young" or "old" means, in part, living through different times. Although two people of exactly the same age can have widely divergent experiences, they also share certain experiences and memories that influence the way they perceive the world. Today's students may look back on World War II or the turbulent 1960s as ancient history. Their views have been shaped by the terrorist attacks of September 11, 2001, not by the Japanese attack on Pearl Harbor or the antiwar protests of the Vietnam era. By 2025, another generation of college students will come of age with no memory of planes crashing into the World Trade Center or the devastation of the recent earthquake in Haiti. The point, of course, is that the shared experience of a generation affects its outlook. That is just one reason that you, as a speaker, must consider the age of your audience.

Audience members who are over age 40 are more likely to be married, have children, and own homes than are audience members who are under age 20. Each generation will have danced to different music, watched different movies, admired different political leaders, and used different technologies during their formative years. As a result, different issues have different degrees of **saliency**, or personal relevance, for people of different ages. In debates over Social Security, for example, older people tend to be more suspicious of changes in the program, while younger people are more likely to support reform, probably because they think those reforms might benefit them in the long run.[1] To take another example, college students may have wondered whether the economic stimulus package passed in 2009 would improve their prospects for a job after graduation, whereas older Americans were probably more worried about its effects on their retirement accounts.

Shared experiences, social mores, and personal concerns related to age all have an impact on one's values. Recent research demonstrates, for example, that a generation that has lived through hard economic times is more likely to value security and stability than a generation that has experienced few threats to their material well-being. Generally, older groups who value stability will tend to be more resistant to change, whereas younger people are usually more adventuresome and

HIGHLIGHTING AGE AND VALUES

Dr. Bristow Speaks to the AMA

Well, without going so far as to even hint that any of us in this room today are "elderly," let me say that your support is critical. If you agree with me and America's physicians that the program now being considered by Congress is best for patients, best for the generations to follow, and, yes, best for doctors, too, then speak out.

If I've done my job of "selling it here," then help us sell it everywhere. Write. Call. FAX. Send e-mail. Whenever it's possible, actually visit your Senators and Representatives. Let them know you support the AMA's plan to transform Medicare. Tell them you want it for today, sure. But tell them that—even more important—you want it for tomorrow. For your children's sake. For your grandchildren's sake . . .

I'm reminded of something I saw last night when I was driving home—here at Rossmoor. I turned a corner and my headlights shined [*sic*] on three deer. A stag, a doe, and a fawn.

You know what their first instinct was? No. They didn't run. That was their second act. The first thing that the stag and the doe did was turn so that their bodies shielded the fawn from the approaching harm. And that's what every older generation does. We shield our young from harm. We protect the generation we're leaving behind. It's an instinct as primal as food and shelter and warmth.

And that's what is being asked of us today. We are like those deer. . . . We are harvesting the accumulated wisdom and knowledge of a lifetime and sharing it with those who have it in their power to enact change to help the generations to come. To protect the generations to come. It is our time.

willing to take risks. Likewise, older people are more likely to value tradition and conformity than are younger people.[2]

In the *Highlighting Age and Values* feature above, note how Lonnie Bristow, a former president of the American Medical Association, urged an older audience to accept the AMA's plan to reform Medicare—not so much because it would benefit them, but for their grandchildren's sake.

Gender Roles and Stereotypes

Although anatomy defines our sex—whether we are male or female—**gender identity** is more complex. Differences and similarities in the way men and women behave, what they value, and what they believe are shaped in large measure by social norms and expectations that vary across cultures and change over time. There was a time in the nineteenth century, for example, when it was considered scandalous or even unnatural for a woman to speak in public or for a man to take care of children. In the twenty-first century, however, behaviors that society assigns to men and women are much more flexible, at least in Western societies. Although in some parts of the world there are still strict rules about what men and women should wear, how they should relate to each other, and even whether they should appear together in public, women in our culture have more freedom of choice. Still, it is important to remember that gender, along with many of the demographics discussed here, is **socially constructed**, which is to say that different cultures have different ideas about what roles, behaviors, or even modes of dress are appropriate for men and women.

As men and women challenge prescribed gender roles and attitudes toward sexuality change, listeners will respond differently to gender-related issues. One can no longer assume that only women will want to hear a speech about fashion or that only men are interested in sports. Jokes that portray women as vain, silly, or nagging are not only in bad taste but offensive, and references to men as insensitive, arrogant, and unfeeling seem outdated.[3]

Even though gender roles are more flexible now than in the past, the gender composition of your audience remains an important concern. Your listeners' gender still has an impact on their outlook and experiences. For example, single women and widows have more difficulty obtaining credit than do men. Furthermore, men's and women's tastes and interests still differ, and our popular culture still reflects those differences. Movie producers target some films at female audiences (so-called chick flicks, for example) and others at males (war movies, for example). Listeners' sexual orientations also lead to different experiences and perspectives. Women and men with longtime same-sex partners, for example, still face greater barriers in adopting children and in obtaining housing than do male-female married couples.

As with age, gender may influence how salient a particular topic may be. Certain health concerns are obviously of more concern to women, such as breast cancer, whereas men may be more concerned about prostate cancer. More women still tend to be caregivers than men and are thus likely to be more attentive to topics related to that subject. Thoughtful speakers give serious attention to how the issues they address or the plans they advocate may affect men and women differently.

Although all of this may be true, we need to constantly remind ourselves that no demographic category—whether age, race, or gender identity—automatically predetermines an individual listener's responses, interests, or life experiences. *Stereotypes*, or common assumptions about people of a particular group, often prove misguided. It is sometimes assumed, for example, that gays tend to work in certain industries, such as fashion or interior design. Yet a survey of more than 4,000 gay men and lesbians conducted by Overlooked Opinions, a Chicago market-research firm, reported that 40 percent more homosexuals are employed in the finance and insurance industries than in the entertainment and arts industries, and 10 times as many homosexuals are in the computer industry as in the fashion industry. There are also more homosexuals working in science and engineering than in social services.[4]

In addition, we should not assume that because an issue is sometimes labeled a "women's issue" that male listeners will not care about it. A *good* speaker should be able to persuade an audience of women *and* men to participate in a breast cancer walk. Similarly, a *good* speaker should strive to persuade both men and women to care about the problem of sexual assault on campus, perhaps even to take part in a "Take Back the Night" march.

Although the distinction between generalizing and stereotyping is sometimes hard to make, stereotyping is harmful. The feminist movement of the late twentieth century should have taught us all one truth: that men and women may have concerns and experiences unique to their sex, but they also have aspirations, attitudes, and aptitudes that are common to all people. The advocate

Men and women, and people of different ages and races, can be brought together to fight for common causes, as in this American Cancer Society Rally for Life.

who hopes to inspire, engage, and motivate listeners must be sensitive to both differences and commonalities across genders.

Race and Ethnicity

At one time, Americans were thought to be a relatively homogeneous people. The myth was that we arrived as immigrants, then emerged from the "melting pot" of U.S. culture with a distinctively American character. Today, there still may be certain ways of looking at things that are especially or even uniquely American. In recent years, however, we have come to realize that the melting-pot concept can be misleading. Within our broader culture are a variety of subcultures that continue to differ. Although people who fall within these various groupings may share characteristics with the general U.S. culture, they also differ in ways that could affect their responses to your speech.

The color of one's skin is biologically determined based on genetic factors. The constellation of characteristics said to make up "race," however, are not determined by biological, genetic, or inherited factors, but are also the product of politics, social definitions, and personal preferences.[5] People may define themselves as members of a particular race and see the world through African-American, Asian-American, or Caucasian eyes.[6] It is important to understand how these racial identities may influence your listeners.

Over time, we have come to realize that just as each race has its own identity, each also has its own perceptions and problems. Recognizing these racial differences is not racism. **Racism**, or the belief in the superiority or inferiority of particular races, leads to prejudice, antagonism, fear, and oppression. It denies the essential humanity of those who are different and thus severely limits the potential for communicating successfully. Racism is often about power, as dominant groups use racial differences to justify subordinating others. Historically, European colonial powers used race to justify dominating Africans and Asians politically and economically, and the "ethnic cleansing" that we have witnessed in certain parts of the world likewise reflects efforts to keep certain groups or tribes in subordinate positions.

Those who appreciate the distinctions between people of different races are better equipped to talk effectively with diverse audiences. Speakers must understand that people of color and white Americans have different histories and cultural experiences. Communication between different races can be extremely complicated and, too often, fraught with distrust.[7] Some Americans, for example, may view affirmative action programs as reverse discrimination, while others consider such programs necessary to level the playing field. By the same token, some African Americans may be skeptical that the local police are really there to "serve and protect" them, either because they've had a bad experience with the police or because they believe that racism is systemic in America.

Despite these challenges, successful communication across races can and does occur every day.[8] For that to happen, however, speakers must be sensitive to the racial makeup of their audiences and reflect on how race may influence an audience's beliefs and attitudes on a particular issue.

The forebears of most Americans came from someplace else. With the exception of Native Americans, whose ancestors migrated to the North American continent in prehistoric times, most Americans can trace their ancestors to people who emigrated from other countries beginning in the seventeenth century, and new immigrants are still arriving today. Depending partly on when they arrived, partly on their habits and tastes, and partly on where they settled, the outlook of these immigrants has been colored by their own national history, customs, and experiences. Because some listeners identify strongly with their ethnic heritage, you need to realize that they may be particularly sensitive to issues that involve their country of origin or their ethnic group. An Irish American, for example, may be especially interested in the history of religious conflicts in Northern Ireland, while an immigrant from Mexico may worry more about the drug-related violence that has plagued that country in recent years.

A culture's particular viewpoints and values can influence even its transplanted citizens and their descendants. For example, different ethnic groups may have different expectations regarding care for their parents in their old age. As a study by AARP concluded, older Americans of Asian and Latino descent still expect their children to take care of them, whereas parents of European heritage are more likely to view living with their children as a sign of failure. European-Americans are more likely to expect a combination of family care and community services as they age.[9]

One of the most significant problems plaguing the world today is **ethnocentrism**, the belief that one's own ethnic heritage is superior to all others. The results of such feelings can range from discrimination and exclusion ("We don't associate with *those* people") to the outright warfare that has torn apart countries in the Balkans and that still plagues parts of Africa and the Middle East. It is important that speakers respect differences in customs, practices, and beliefs grounded in ethnic origins and take them into account when speaking to ethnically diverse audiences.

Cultural Differences

Beyond racial and ethnic differences, those who grew up in cultures outside the United States may hold values and exhibit behaviors that differ from those of other Americans. Scholars may not agree on the causes of those differences, yet most agree that the differences are real. Some of the most recent studies have implications for the ways people communicate with each other, how they judge speaker credibility, and how they react to arguments opposed to their own views. In a recent study, for example, student subjects were asked to analyze a conflict between mothers and daughters. "American subjects quickly came down in favor of one side or the other. Chinese subjects were more likely to see merit in both sides, commenting, for example, 'Both the mothers and the daughters have failed to understand each other.'"[10] There are many other examples. While many Americans often seem in a hurry, viewing time as something not to be wasted, people from other cultures may prefer to move more slowly, spending time getting to know one another instead of "getting right down to business." Whereas Americans tend to be individualistic and value their privacy, more group-oriented cultures associate privacy with loneliness and isolation. Americans also tend to be future-oriented, while more traditional societies tend to view the past more positively. In cultures that value subtlety and indirection, Americans may seem blunt and insensitive when they are just trying to be open and direct.[11] These are just a few of the intercultural differences that may affect how we communicate.[12]

Cultural differences, both within American subcultures and across international lines, affect all of our efforts to communicate—in the classroom and in the community—and we need to make strenuous and sincere efforts to bridge cultural divides and emphasize what we all have in common. It can be hard work to communicate effectively across cultural lines, but the effort is necessary if we hope to work together in our increasingly interdependent world.

Religion

Your listeners' religious beliefs—or lack of religious beliefs—can also influence how they evaluate and respond to your speech. On some issues, religious leaders have taken a clear political stand. Not all Catholics are opposed to legalized abortion, for example, but many do embrace their church's official opposition to abortion. Similarly, Jews tend to be strong advocates of U.S. support for Israel, and most Quakers are pacifists who oppose all war.

Religion can also influence your audience's general attitude toward political controversies. Some religions stress obedience and conformity, whereas others emphasize individualism and challenging state authority. Some religions stress personal salvation and rarely take strong stands on controversial political or social issues; others insist that all such issues are of concern to the church. Church teachings can make a difference in the way people respond to a speech. Fundamentalists, for example, may be more open to messages that emphasize tradition, whereas those with more liberal religious views may respond more to calls for social reform.[13]

Conventional wisdom once advised public speakers to avoid talking about religion. Some instructors even advise students not to choose religious speech topics because they are too personal or potentially explosive. Yet religious differences are reflected in many of the most important social and political controversies of our time, and we cannot simply ignore the role of religion in public life. If you *do* talk about a religious issue, it is important to recognize that not everybody in your audience may share your assumptions about what is "true" and what religious sources are "authoritative." Indeed, your audience may hold fundamentally different religious beliefs. That does not mean we cannot communicate across religious differences. In our time, many bitter divisions over social issues, such as abortion, stem cell research, and gay marriage, grow from varying interpretations of religious doctrines and moral principles. That should not make it impossible, however, for those on different sides of religious controversies to talk with each other and find common ground. Early in 2004, for example, Senator Hillary Clinton spoke to an abortion rights group and expressed the need to recognize and respect their differences. This effort to engage an issue of civic importance in a cooperative way is illustrated in the report on her speech in the *Focus on Civic Engagement* feature below.

Geographical Environment

Where a listener lives can make a difference in how he or she reacts to a speech. Even though people may come from the same part of the country, their outlooks can differ depending on the kind of community in which they live. Newark, New Jersey, is not the same as Franklin, New Jersey; Chicago, Illinois, is not the same as Peoria, Illinois; and Dallas, Texas, is not to be confused with College Station, Texas.

People who have grown up in rural areas may develop different habits and lifestyles from those who grow up in the city. Muggings, commuting on unreliable

FOCUS ON CIVIC ENGAGEMENT

Seeking Common Ground

Senator Hillary Rodham Clinton said on Monday that the opposing sides in the divisive debate over abortion should find "common ground" to prevent unwanted pregnancies and ultimately reduce abortions, which she called a "sad, even tragic choice to many, many women."

In a speech to about 1,000 abortion rights supporters near the New York State Capitol, Mrs. Clinton firmly restated her support for the Supreme Court's ruling in *Roe v. Wade,* which legalized abortion nationwide in 1973. But then she quickly shifted gears, offering warm words to opponents of legalized abortion and praising the influence of "religious and moral values" on delaying teenage girls from becoming sexually active. "There is an opportunity for people of good faith to find common ground in this debate—we should be able to agree that we want every child born in this country to be wanted, cherished and loved," Mrs. Clinton said. . . .

Mrs. Clinton called on abortion rights advocates and anti-abortion campaigners to form a broad alliance to support sexual education—including abstinence counseling, family planning, and morning-after emergency contraception for victims of sexual assault as ways to reduce unintended pregnancies.

trains, or moving at a frantic pace may be unimaginable to the rural resident, whereas the city dweller imagines that rural life would be dreadfully boring. Each also has a different set of problems and concerns. To the urbanite, the following may be the most important questions: How do we reduce crime? How do we improve mass transit? How do we create more affordable housing? By contrast, the resident of a farming community may be more interested in these questions: How do we save the family farm? How can we reduce property taxes? And what can be done to stabilize the prices paid to farmers for their produce?

Over time, different sections of the country have developed unique ways of looking at things. Easterners, westerners, southerners, southwesterners, and midwesterners have different ethnic mixes in their populations, different industries, different religious views, and different approaches to social and political problems. Westerners, for example, often boast of their rugged individualism; New Yorkers value their cultural and artistic sophistication; and many Sunbelt communities are proud of their climates and reputations as safe, comfortable places for older citizens to live.

Education

Education provides us with specific knowledge, ways to solve problems rationally, awareness of the choices open to us, and ways of evaluating the best choices to make. To be truly engaged, you must be informed on issues of civic concern. Being an informed citizen is fundamental to being an effective speaker.

The educational level of listeners—their acquired knowledge—influences how they react to messages. You may be giving a speech on emergency preparedness to a junior high school assembly and a speech on the same topic to a college group. Yet what each group expects from your speech will differ, based on what they already know about the topic and their different experiences. Even first- and second-year college students differ in their levels of sophistication and knowledge, and both groups differ in these respects from college seniors.

How well audience members have been educated will determine not only whether they are familiar with your speech topic but whether they can intelligently evaluate the message. One speaker may claim that a proposed health care plan would fail to meet the needs of low-income families. Another may claim that voting for a particular candidate will improve your economic situation. Educated listeners should be in a good position to evaluate such claims. They should have specific facts at their disposal and already know something about the topic.

Suppose, for example, that you hear someone argue that force must be used in response to a foreign-policy crisis. And suppose they back up that claim by comparing the current situation with the situation Americans faced in the 1940s when confronted by Nazi Germany. If, as an educated person, you take the time to think, you will not just automatically accept the comparison because you know Nazism was evil. You will ask questions about the legitimacy of the comparison. You will demand that the speaker *prove* to you that the situation before World War II was really similar to the present situation.

As you judge a speaker's argument, you should apply principles you have learned and the knowledge you have acquired to render an *informed* judgment.

If you find the speaker unconvincing, or if you cannot fully test the argument by your own knowledge and experience, you should suspend judgment. You should wait and see—listen to other arguments, read more material, and assemble more facts—before you reach a judgment. That is what it means to have an *educated response* to a speech.

Occupation or Profession

Your job or profession can make a difference in the attitudes you hold and the ways in which you grasp specific information. When people hear a message they sometimes ask themselves, "How is this going to affect me?" When discussing how to improve our schools, for example, a travel agent may be uneasy about a proposal to keep schools open all year because that may mean canceled vacations and less business. People who work at the school or who provide transportation for students, on the other hand, may be all for the idea.

The occupations we hold make us feel differently about the world around us. Teachers, doctors, construction workers, dancers, postal clerks, and lawyers all deal with specific sets of problems. The constant practice of these problem-solving skills is what establishes people as experts. When experts listen to a speech, they bring a whole set of competencies and attitudes with them to the speaking situation. An engineer, for example, will respond to technological information as a specialist, and the speaker must be aware of this. Professional experience also will affect responses to issues. Recently, an insurance company covering a large number of university employees informed its clients that anesthesiologists at the

Sharing common occupations may cause listeners to see issues in a way especially related to their professional problems and interests.

local hospital had withdrawn from the plan. Policyholders were asked to consider a medical center 50 miles away for elective surgery. Many policyholders initially saw this as a greedy move on the part of the doctors. A clinical psychologist with a private practice, however, noted that most health care providers were also unhappy with the insurance company. She sympathized with the anesthesiologists. In this case, health care providers viewed this issue from a perspective strongly influenced by their professions.

Finally, one's job or profession may affect one's perspective on what are the most important or relevant issues relating to a specific topic. Take the problem of health care, for example. Most people seem to agree that everyone should have some kind of coverage. Yet as Barack Obama learned when he tried to bring together the various stakeholders in the health care debate, those stakeholders have specific concerns that are sometimes difficult to reconcile. Large corporations want a plan that relieves them of the high cost of health care benefits, and small-business owners worry that providing health care benefits to just a few employees would be too costly. Insurance companies are concerned about losing business if the government assumes more responsibility for health care, and physicians object to plans that give insurance companies the power to decide which medical procedures may be appropriate. Consumers worry about having to pay higher premiums and absorb higher deductibles. If a speaker fails to anticipate and prepare for responses stemming from these different occupational perspectives, even a good idea may be impossible to sell.

Economic Status

The income of listeners may influence their response. Again, the extent to which this factor is important and the precise ways in which it may affect listener responses depend on the speaker's subject and purpose. The topic of a message may naturally interest some income groups and not others. A speech on tax shelters, for example, may have limited appeal to low-income listeners. By the same token, those with high incomes may not be interested in a speech on need-based tuition assistance.

How groups think their income level compares with that of others may have profound effects on the communication process. People in the middle-income group, for example, may see themselves as overburdened with taxes and yet excluded from the benefits of social welfare. Such people may look on social welfare programs with the jaundiced eye of those expected to foot the bill.

Professional persuaders, such as advertisers, go to great lengths to target their messages to particular income groups. They carefully choose a mailing list (such as American Express cardholders) that will put their material in the hands of those who can afford to buy their product. They carefully choose the magazines they advertise in, the time slots for their television ads, and the radio stations that air their ads. They are concerned with many factors besides income, but it is crucial that they reach people who can afford to buy their products.

The financial resources available to listeners may determine their response to any idea or proposals involving money. A student urging other students to volunteer for a service project, for example, may need to consider whether his listeners could afford to work without pay for the summer, or whether they could afford only to participate in the project a few hours a week. The wise speaker tries to anticipate how listeners' income may influence their response to his or her message.

In addition to the specific characteristics that distinguish listeners, it is also important to remember that all of us—no matter who we are or what we do—have fundamental human needs that have to be met and common values that we all embrace.

IDENTIFYING INDIVIDUAL LISTENER NEEDS AND VALUES

Preview. *Like all people, audience members have fundamental needs. Maslow's hierarchy provides an excellent conceptual framework for understanding those shared needs—physical well-being, safety and security, love and belonging, esteem, and self-actualization.*

So far we have considered the ways that audience members may differ and how you need to acknowledge those differences in analyzing your audience. Yet whatever differences listeners may bring to the speech situation, they still share certain universal human needs.

In a groundbreaking work, psychologist Abraham H. Maslow described basic human needs in terms that help us understand and develop tactics for listener involvement.[14] As illustrated in Figure 5.1, Maslow presented the needs in a hierarchy, noting that some needs are more basic than others.

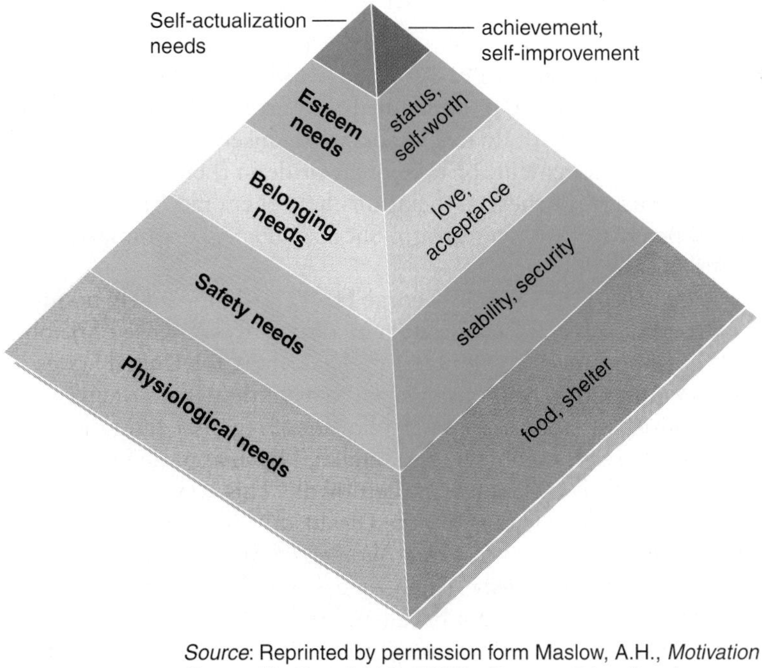

Source: Reprinted by permission form Maslow, A.H., *Motivation and Personality*. Copyright © 1987 by Pearson Education, Inc.

FIGURE 5.1
Maslow's Hierarchy.

Satisfying Basic Physiological Needs

People have physiological needs. Basic to all human life is the need to be physically secure. We all need food and drink, clothing, shelter, and sexual gratification if we want to feel comfortable and avoid the discomforts of pain, sickness, injury, and so on.

Most of the audiences you will talk with, however, have had their basic needs met. Freed from the preoccupation of satisfying those needs, most listeners will be more successfully engaged by appealing to their "higher" needs.

Ensuring Listeners' Personal Safety

We all desire a secure world. We all want to be protected from dangerous, surprising, or unfamiliar situations that threaten our safety. In any organized society, we have many people and groups—police, firefighters, military personnel—dedicated to ensuring our safety. We have government agencies, such as the Food and Drug Administration, that protect us from being poisoned. Despite all these efforts, of course, bridges still do collapse sometimes, and tainted foods still do escape detection on occasion and sicken or even kill people. Thus, we all still worry about our safety, and those concerns may influence how we respond to a speaker. The wise speaker will consider what ways, if any, listeners may find her proposal threatening or how it may make them feel safer.

Reinforcing Feelings of Love and a Sense of Belonging

Once safety needs are satisfied, people begin to think of other needs, such as belonging needs, or the need to be loved by others. There is a distinct human need to be accepted, wanted, or welcomed into groups. People join clubs, maintain close family or ethnic ties, associate themselves strongly with a church or religious movement, or take great pride in their patriotic feelings toward their country. All these associations help them meet their need to be accepted and be part of a larger group. Successful speakers understand and often engage this need.

In his 1988 acceptance speech, George H. W. Bush, the newly nominated Republican candidate for president, attempted to convey a sense of belonging as he stressed the importance of volunteerism. Describing the United States as "a nation of communities, of thousands and tens of thousands of ethnic, religious, social, business, labor union, neighborhood, regional and other organizations, all of them varied, voluntary, and unique," Bush appealed to individuals who might not have felt important on their own: "This is America: the Knights of Columbus, the Grange, Hadassah, the Disabled American Veterans, the Order of Ahepa, the Business and Professional Women of America, the union hall, the Bible study group, LULAC, Holy Name—a brilliant diversity spread like stars, like a thousand points of light in a broad and peaceful sky."[15]

Listeners are likely to be more emotionally involved when they believe that a speaker is advocating a proposal that will be of direct benefit to those whom they love, reduce their feelings of isolation, or contribute to their sense of belonging.

Helping Listeners Feel Appreciated by Others

In addition to a sense of belonging, people want to feel that they have some worth and importance. People like to feel that they control their destiny, that they are not constantly under the thumb of other people, and that others recognize them as being good or important human beings. This need is frequently the basis of advertising that would have us believe that driving a particular type of car or wearing some fashionable style of shoes will help us acquire status. These kinds of appeals to status are aimed more at achieving the communicator's sales goals than genuinely benefiting the listener. On the other hand, a student describing her experiences as a volunteer helping to rebuild homes destroyed by Hurricane Katrina may legitimately emphasize all the expressions of gratitude from those she helped. Those expressions of gratitude demonstrate how important the volunteer's work was and reveal what her listeners may hope to gain by volunteering for similar missions: the sense that they will be making important contributions that others will greatly appreciate.

Helping Listeners Realize Their Own Potential

When people know that others respect them, they can begin to think about self-fulfillment. These **self-actualization needs** reflect that we all want to realize our own potential. Not everyone has the same goals or the same ambitions. For some, the highest ambition in life may be great material wealth; for others, realizing one's own potential may mean making a difference in the lives of his or her fellow citizens. At a town hall meeting in France in April 2009, as noted in the *Focus on Civic Engagement* on the following page, President Obama made the case for realizing one's own potential by serving others.

Most people strive to better themselves throughout life yet never achieve everything they had hoped for. Nevertheless, the speaker who realizes that people *want* to realize their highest potential can appeal to that desire. In advocating more support for the arts and humanities, for example, a student might stress the importance of a broad liberal education for one's "emotional intelligence," or the intelligence one needs for healthy everyday living and good relationships with others. By promoting "emotional intelligence," she might conclude, studying outside one's own professional field can lead to a richer and more satisfying life.[16]

Identifying Audience Values

When you analyze an audience by cataloging listener characteristics and identifying their needs, you are doing so, in part, to uncover audience **values**. You are looking for areas of agreement as well as potential conflict, and you will want to think about how listeners' values may shape the way you approach your speech. For certain audiences, patriotic values may be extremely important; for others, the desire to get ahead or to advance their education may take precedence.

All of us possess a network of interlocking values, some of which conflict with others. For example, Americans tend to admire individualism, yet we also

FOCUS ON CIVIC ENGAGEMENT

President Obama on Public Service

. . . I truly believe that there's nothing more noble than public service. Now, that doesn't mean that you have to run for President. (Applause.) You know, you might work for Doctors Without Borders, or you might . . . be somebody working for the United Nations, or you might be the mayor of Strasbourg. Right? (Applause.) . . .

But the point is that what I found at a very young age was that if you only think about yourself—how much money can I make, what can I buy, how nice is my house, what kind of fancy car do I have—that over the long term I think you get bored. (Applause.) I think . . . if you're only thinking about yourself, your life becomes diminished; and that the way to live a full life is to think about, what can I do for others? How can I be a part of this larger project of making a better world?

Now, that could be something as simple as . . . the joy of taking care of your family and watching your children grow and succeed. But I think especially for the young people here, I hope you also consider other ways that you can serve, because the world has so many challenges right now, there's so many opportunities to make a difference, and it would be a tragedy if all of you who are so talented and energetic, if you let that go to waste; if you just stood back and watched the world pass you by.

Better to jump in, get involved. And it does mean that sometimes you'll get criticized and sometimes you'll fail and sometimes you'll be disappointed, but you'll have a great adventure, and at the end of your life hopefully you'll be able to look back and say, I made a difference.

Source: From "Remarks by President Obama at Strasbourg Town Hall." Published 2009 by The White House, Office of the press Secretary.

recognize the need for teamwork.[17] We may profess the golden rule—do unto others as we would have them do unto us—while also valuing a competitive spirit. We hear of the "work ethic," the "business ethic," and the "Puritan ethic," all of which denote different sets of values at work in our society. Your challenge as a speaker will be to identify the values most relevant to the issue you are discussing.

Once you have considered your audience's values, you should reflect on how those values translate into specific **attitudes** and **beliefs**. For instance, you may determine that both you and your listeners value integrity and social responsibility. Yet in an election year, you may discover that your listeners distrust the political candidate you are supporting. Whereas you see the candidate as honest, experienced, and trustworthy, your listeners may see her as unqualified or dishonest or untrustworthy. In this case, you would not try to change listener values (which you share). Instead you would try to convince them that they have misjudged your candidate. Perhaps they believe that your candidate's background has not prepared her adequately for the office she seeks. Or maybe they do not like your candidate's record on environmental protection, which is a real priority for them. Whatever the nature of their objections, you need to understand those objections before you can adapt your speech to your audience. Perhaps you can establish common ground by emphasizing the values you share. Then you can try to change their beliefs and attitudes toward your candidate.

IDENTIFYING COMMUNAL NEEDS AND VALUES

Preview. *Listeners are usually members of a variety of communities. The groups and organizations your listeners belong to and identify with will have an impact on their response to your speeches.*

What group affiliation is uppermost in the minds of your listeners? A single listener may belong to the American Baptist Church, the Democratic Party, the Parent-Teacher Organization, the American Bar Association, and the executive board of the United Way. These affiliations will almost certainly influence how your listeners respond to a speech.

The Saliency of Key Group Memberships

Some memberships may be more important than others. When you attend a meeting of a particular group (a fraternity, a political club, the Boys and Girls Club, or the Future Farmers of America), the reasons for being in that organization may be important to you at that moment. You hear and respond to messages as a member of that group. At other times, and in other contexts, the goals of that group may seem less relevant.

No single group membership is foremost in all our decisions. Whether we are Democrats or Republicans will hardly matter as we decide which toothpaste to buy. However, there are times when a particular group membership may be so important that all other concerns pale in comparison.[18] Some devout Catholics and evangelical Christians, for example, vote against any candidate who favors legal abortions, whereas devout members of the National Rifle Association (NRA) may care only about a candidate's stand on gun control. These single-issue voters may completely ignore their disagreement with a candidate's positions on the economy, foreign affairs, or the environment; all that matters is their position on that one highly controversial issue. Democratic theory suggests that we should consider a variety of issues and the qualifications of candidates as well in deciding how to vote. But as a speaker, we must realize that our listeners' salient group memberships can greatly influence their opinions.

Complicating the speaker's task is the fact that important issues sometimes force us to consider multiple group associations. Consider, for example, the issue of poverty. The latest statistics from the Census Bureau show how poverty relates to gender and age: poverty affects children under age 18 more than any other age group, and women typically have principal responsibility for children. Poverty is also a matter of race and ethnicity: 24.7 percent of blacks and 21.9 percent of Latinos live below the poverty line, whereas non-Latino whites represent only 8.6 percent of the poor population.[19] Furthermore, although the number of people living in poverty has decreased slightly in recent years, the number of people in *extreme* poverty (those with incomes at less than half the poverty level) has increased.[20] When you consider the effects that poverty can have on the cost of social programs, health care, and educational opportunities, one can easily imagine that this issue affects everybody. Yet, a good speaker still reflects on how poverty disproportionately affects certain groups and adapts his or her remarks accordingly.

Membership in groups that are important to listeners will influence how they react to messages that are salient to those groups.

A further complication arises when our audience identifies with two groups whose goals conflict. In Florida, for example, the National Rifle Association supported a bill that would have made it a felony for an employer to prohibit employees from bringing guns to work. The bill was strongly opposed by the Chamber of Commerce, a leading association of businesspeople. A legislator who had received high ratings from both the chamber and the NRA admitted that "it's very awkward for me."[21] In such situations, a speaker needs to take the listeners' conflicting opinions into account, but in the end it may prove impossible to reconcile such incompatible goals.

It should be clear by now that it is important to design your speech for the specific audience you will address. As a good citizen, you hope to achieve your purposes as a speaker, but you also hope to serve the larger public interest and contribute something positive to your community. To connect your message with your listeners, you begin by analyzing the situation and the audience. In order to adapt your message to your audience, you need to gather as much information about your listeners as you can.

GATHERING INFORMATION FOR AUDIENCE ADAPTATION

Preview. *There are different ways of collecting information about your audience. Information can be gathered by conducting research on the Internet, through interviewing, or with an audience survey. You should continuously assess your audience before, during, and after your speech.*

Gathering information about your audience is extremely important. As we have emphasized throughout this chapter, you need to adapt your message to your specific listeners if you hope to achieve your goals as a speaker, and your listeners also will get more out of your speech if it is designed specifically to address their interests and needs. But how do you go about getting the information you need to adapt your speech to a particular audience?

Internet Research

You can learn much about an organization or group you will be addressing by conducting research on the Internet. Suppose you represent a group that wants to promote discussion of an important issue on campus, such as recent increases in tuition costs, how proposed immigration laws may affect international students, or new regulations on off-campus housing. If you wanted to find ways to engage other students, perhaps you might search your university's Web site for student organizations that may be interested in hosting a forum on such topics, or perhaps your university's student government could take up the issue. If you were to conduct such a search at Indiana University, for example, you might begin at the Union Board home page, where you would find contact persons for the Debates and Issues Committee, which organizes public forums, and the Lectures Committee, which engages outside speakers with special expertise.[22] Or, at the Pennsylvania State University, you might visit the Web site or even the Facebook page of the Student Programming Association (SPA), which promotes "outreach and collaboration" among a wide variety of student organizations, including a Distinguished Lecture Series and other public forums.[23]

Interviewing for Information

A good way to begin gathering information about an audience is to interview the person who asked you to speak. Usually this contact person is a member of the group or organization that you will address and can tell you much about the audience. Your goal is to find out as much as you can about the audience—their experiences, level of knowledge, values, and interests, and the particular speaking situation.[24] Regardless of the specific topic, here are some of the questions you may want to ask:

- How many listeners will likely be present when I speak?
- How diverse is the audience in terms of age, sex, and other characteristics?
- Could you describe the room where I'll be speaking?
- How knowledgeable is the audience about my topic?
- What relevant experiences might audience members have had?
- How likely are they to be open to the sort of information I'm discussing or the proposal I'm making?
- Are there likely to be great differences of opinion or experience within the audience?
- How much time is available for my presentation?
- Will there be a question-and-answer period after the speech?

Of course, you will want to adapt this basic interviewing format to the specific situation.

You also may consider attending a meeting of the group that you will address to learn for yourself about their concerns, interests, and values. This strategy is practical only if you have the time and the opportunity. Your contact person should prove helpful in arranging this.

Administering an Audience Survey

With the permission of the group you will be addressing, you may also construct and administer an *audience survey*, which allows you to pursue questions about your listeners' characteristics, knowledge, and opinions in greater depth. This approach to gathering information is sometimes used in public speaking classes, in which some instructors encourage students to design and administer a brief questionnaire so that they can learn more about their fellow students. Even though you may not be able to administer such a survey in other settings, the survey suggests the kind of information that you should attempt to find out about any audience before you speak.

Although survey construction can be fairly complicated, you can learn to design a basic questionnaire that will serve as a valuable analytical tool.[25] Following are some principles to follow as you design your audience survey:

- *Use the survey to collect relevant demographic information about the audience.* For some topics, for instance, you may want to know the age or major of your audience. For others, you may want to know about their political affiliation or religion.
- *Allow your listeners to remain anonymous as they complete the survey.* They are more likely to respond with candor if they do not have to identify themselves.
- *Use different kinds of questions to gather the kind of information you need.*[26] Some questions may ask audience members to check the appropriate answer from among several choices. Others may ask them to write a few sentences.
- *Limit your audience survey to a few good questions that can be answered in a short period of time.* This way, respondents will be more willing to participate and are more likely to provide you with accurate and better-developed responses. If listeners take the questionnaire home, they will be more inclined to complete and return the survey if it is not too long and complicated. Better yet, get them to complete the survey on the spot, if at all possible.
- *Be sure to use the results of the survey as you craft your speech and adapt your message to your audience.* Administering an audience survey is not just an academic exercise. It is one of the most direct means available of finding out about your audience's knowledge, opinions, and values.

When you conduct an audience survey, you may choose to probe listener attitudes regarding a specific topic, or you may survey their beliefs and values more generally.

Devising Good Questions for an Audience Survey

Whether you are interviewing for information or constructing an audience questionnaire, you should include both closed and open questions (see Chapter 7). Closed questions yield limited information, whereas open questions may be hard to tabulate and are more time-consuming to complete. The key is balance.[27]

There is no magic formula for constructing an audience survey, but here are some tips to guide you:

- *Begin the survey with closed, fixed-choice questions relevant to your topic to collect basic demographic and other factual information.* For example:

  What is your class standing?
  Freshman ______ Sophomore ______ Junior ______ Senior ______
  Are you registered to vote?
  Yes ______ No ______ Not sure ______
  If you are registered to vote, are you registered as a(n):
  Democrat ______ Republican ______ Independent ______ Other ______
  Do you drive or would you consider driving an SUV?
  Yes ______ No ______ Maybe ______
  Do you like to walk?
  Frequently ______ Sometimes ______ Not much ______

  Through these kinds of questions, you can collect "bottom-line" information quickly. However, the responses give you no insight into how strongly listeners identify with the choices they make. For example, one person may be registered as an Independent but consistently vote for candidates from one party.

- *Use scale questions to acquire more precise information from respondents or to understand how firmly committed they are to their opinions and beliefs.* For example:

  How many news broadcasts do you typically watch or listen to each week?
  Seven or more ______ Five or six ______ Three or four ______
  One or two ______ None ______

  Indicate the extent to which you agree or disagree with the following statements:
  I believe that a flat tax of 15 percent for everybody would be the fairest tax.
  Strongly agree ______ Somewhat agree ______ Somewhat disagree ______
  Strongly disagree ______ Not sure ______
  I read a newspaper or newsmagazine, print or online.
  All the time ______ Most of the time ______ Rarely ______
  Never ______ Not sure ______

Scale questions allow you to gather more precise information and to measure degrees of commitment.

- *You will also want to include some open questions on your survey to provide greater depth of response.* For instance:

  How do you feel about the proposal to make this campus pedestrian-only by the year 2012?

  In your view, why do so few U.S. citizens vote in the presidential elections?

Through open questions, you give the audience the freedom to respond as they choose. By examining their responses, you may grow to better understand *why* they believe as they do and how they justify their actions and opinions. At the same time, you may find that some listeners will give you irrelevant information and some will simply refuse to write out a response. When used in combination with other questions, however, open questions should enrich your survey's results.

- *Finally, avoid leading or* ***loaded questions***. Make sure you phrase your questions with neutrality and **objectivity** so that you do not lead respondents to a particular answer. If you were giving a speech about drinking on campus, you might ask this question on your audience survey: "Describe your drinking

TABLE 5.2

SAMPLE AUDIENCE SURVEY ON VEGETARIANISM

1. Please check the categories that most accurately describe you:
   Sex: Male ______ Female ______
   Major: Liberal arts ______ Business ______ Health care professions ______
   Music ______ Engineering ______ Other ______
2. How would you define vegetarianism?
3. Are you a vegetarian?
   Yes ______ No ______
4. Do you have a close friend or relative who is a vegetarian?
   Yes ______ No ______ Not sure ______
5. Do you agree or disagree with the following statement?
   Vegetarians can enjoy a nutritious and flavorful diet.
   Strongly agree ______ Somewhat agree ______ Undecided ______
   Somewhat disagree ______ Strongly disagree ______
6. If you are a vegetarian, please explain your reasons for becoming one.
7. In your view, what are the main reasons that people choose to become vegetarians?

habits." A leading version of the same question might read, "Describe the last time you drank excessively." The second version assumes that the respondent does in fact drink excessively. By contrast, the first version invites the respondent to describe an array of behaviors ranging from complete abstinence to extreme drinking. All survey questions should be written in the most neutral way possible.[28]

Table 5.2 is an example of an audience survey used by one public speaking student who was interested in giving a persuasive speech on vegetarianism. She initially planned to try to get her audience to agree with her that vegetarianism was both ethically and morally preferable to eating meat.

After studying the following results of her survey, she decided to change her basic approach.

1. Definitions of vegetarianism varied widely among audience members. About one-third believed that a person is a vegetarian if he or she does not eat red meat. Two class members believed that vegetarians do not eat any animal products (such as milk or eggs). The speaker knew that she would have to take some time early in the speech to clarify her definition of vegetarianism.
2. Only 2 students (other than the speaker herself) out of a class of 24 students were vegetarians. In addition, six other students, or 25 percent of the class, said that they had a vegetarian friend or relative. The speaker realized that she could not count on much direct experience among the audience.
3. The reasons the two students gave for becoming vegetarians were primarily related to their own health rather than moral objections to consuming meat.
4. Sixty percent of the class did not believe that vegetarians could enjoy a healthy, flavorful diet.
5. Students tended to view vegetarians as having taken a rather extreme approach to a healthy diet. Some cited dangers. Out of the class, two or three seemed hostile toward vegetarians—one calling them "kooks" and another referring to them as "granola." In general, men were more negative than women. Nearly 70 percent of the women discussed animal rights as one reason for vegetarianism. Students' majors seemed unrelated to their responses.

The speaker's own commitment to vegetarianism grew from a deep ethical conviction regarding animal rights. Based on the survey results, however, she felt that converting this particular audience to her point of view would be unrealistic, given their initial views and the short time available for persuading them. Instead, she decided to make them aware of the problems (for both animals and humans) associated with factory farms (with a specific focus on poultry farms). She would acknowledge inhumane killing, but she would go beyond that to discuss the dangerous working conditions and the low pay of the workforce, along with the unsanitary conditions under which the chickens are bred, fed, and killed—making them unsafe for consumers. As a result of her survey, then, she had devised a more modest but potentially attainable goal: her specific purpose was to get her audience to purchase only free-range chickens—for the welfare of the workers, the animals, and the consumers.

Had the speaker not conducted the audience survey and had she given her original speech, she surely would have been doomed to failure. As it was, her speech was extremely well received, and five or six students said that they were going to purchase only free-range chickens in the future.

The audience survey is an extremely helpful tool that enables a speaker to gather the kind of information he or she needs to adapt a message to the concerns, experiences, and priorities of an audience.

Thus, through various avenues—using the resources available to you through the Internet, the community, your contact person, and the group itself—you should be able to craft your speech with a clear sense of your audience.

ONGOING STRATEGIES FOR AUDIENCE ADAPTATION

Preview. *Sometimes we assume that audience analysis is done only before the day of the speech. Of course, much analysis will be done in advance. But a resourceful speaker can continue to assess and adapt to the audience immediately before, during, and even after a speech.*

Many speeches are delivered at conferences, public meetings, and other ongoing events. When you arrive at a conference or meeting room and begin to interact with the audience before your speech, you may learn a good deal about their interests and priorities. If you wish to be heard during the time allotted for public input at a city council meeting, attend one beforehand or, if possible, watch a few meetings on your local community-access channel. Get to the meeting early and observe the audience. You may discover that the audience looks a little different from what you had imagined. They may be younger, they may sound more conservative, or they may express interests you had not anticipated in advance. Based on what you learn immediately before the speech, you may choose to make minor adjustments in your presentation.

It is even possible to adapt to your audience while you are speaking. To some extent, all effective speakers do this. If they sense that the audience is bored, they may cut some material and move on to the next point. They may use more humor if the audience seems to enjoy it, or they may move closer to listeners and speak more informally if they sense that the podium is creating a barrier. Finally, based on your perceptions of how much you are "on target" with your planned remarks, you may choose to shorten your speech so that you can devote more time to the audience's questions after the speech.

Audience analysis and adaptation is an ongoing process. From the moment you learn you are to make a speech until the moment you stop interacting with listeners, you can continue to learn more about them and adjust your strategy, style, and responses. And from this experience, you may reflect on what you have learned, how your speech was received, and what you would like to change if you were to give it again. This kind of reflective analysis will help you deliver better speeches in the future.

SUMMARY

- In analyzing an audience, you seek to learn all that you can about listener values, beliefs, and attitudes.
- A speaker-listener partnership with mutual benefits is central to the success of any public speaking venture.
- Consider the listeners' diversity while remaining mindful of the needs and values they likely share.
- Audiences are rarely homogeneous; avoid overgeneralizing or stereotyping listeners.
- In analyzing your audience, consider such diverse factors as the following:
  - age
  - gender
  - race and ethnicity
  - intercultural factors
  - religion
  - education
  - occupation
  - geographic/cultural environment
  - economic status
- Recognize that there are some universal human needs that all listeners share: basic physiological needs, as well as the need for safety and security, love and belonging, esteem, and self-actualization.
- Consider the communal needs and values of audiences related to the groups with which they identify and the relevance of these associations to your topic.
- Gather specific information about your listeners by exploring the Internet, interviewing relevant people, observing the audience in their natural environment, or conducting an audience survey.
- Because audience adaptation is an ongoing process, you can make adjustments immediately before and even during the speech, as you assess, watch, listen, and reflect on the communication experience.

QUESTIONS FOR REVIEW AND REFLECTION

1. What is your understanding of the meaning of *audience adaptation*?
2. What are some key situational factors you will want to consider as you analyze your audience and anticipate the speaking situation? Consider the topic you plan to use for your next speech. Which of these situational factors may be especially important?
3. What are the major stereotypes associated with the following groups: football players, sorority members, accountants, lawyers, and college professors? For each category, offer at least one example of someone you know who violates the stereotype.
4. What are the major audience characteristics you ought to consider when planning a speech? Why is each important?

5. Think of a topic that you believe may be a good one to use in your public speaking class based on your interests and your perceptions of your fellow classmates' interests and values. How could this topic be adapted to a significantly older audience?
6. In your view, are there any topics that would be of greater interest to women than to men? How about the opposite? How might you broaden the appeal of a topic that you associate with either sex?
7. How might the location or geography of your hometown affect the kinds of issues that people who live there consider important?
8. What are some topics that are of interest to you as a college student? Now imagine that you are pursuing the occupation of your choice in the future (attorney, teacher, salesperson, or computer analyst, for example). What sorts of topics would likely interest you as a member of that occupational group?
9. The following are some possible speech topics:
   a. gun control
   b. exercising for fitness
   c. finding the career that's right for you
   d. how to excel as a first-year college student
   e. the health care crisis
   f. alternative energy sources
   g. pain management
   h. becoming a volunteer for the local humane society

   Of the needs described in Maslow's hierarchy, which ones would you probably want to consider in speaking about each of these topics? Why would those needs be especially important?
10. Besides conducting a survey, what are some other audience-adaptation methods you can use before, during, and after you make a speech?

ENDNOTES

1. See The Pew Charitable Trust, "Public Divided on Alaska Drilling, as Well as Social Security," www.pewtrusts.org/news_room_detail.aspx?id=23134 (accessed April 16, 2009).
2. Shalom Schwartz, "Human Values," European Social Survey Education Net (2009), http://essedunet.nsd.uib.no/cms/topics/1/ (accessed April 10, 2009).
3. See A. Cann and W. D. Siegfried, "Sex Stereotypes and the Leadership Role," *Sex Roles* 17 (1987): 401–08.
4. T. A. Stewart, "Gay in Corporate America," *Fortune*, December 6, 1991, 43–56.
5. Richard D. Alba, *Ethnic Identity: The Transformation of White America* (New Haven, CT: Yale University Press, 1990).
6. According to the findings of the Human Genome Project on Race, "DNA studies do not indicate that separate classifiable subspecies (races) exist within modern humans. While different genes for physical traits such as skin and hair color can be identified between individuals, no consistent patterns of genes across the human genome exist to distinguish one race from another. There also is no genetic basis for divisions of human ethnicity. People who have lived in the same geographic region for many generations may have some alleles in common, but no allele will be found in all members of one population and in no members of any other."
7. See L. Barna, "Stumbling Blocks in Intercultural Communication," in *Intercultural Communication: A Reader*, ed. L. Samovar and R. Porter (Belmont, CA: Wadsworth, 1988), 322–30. Barna has found that individuals are often so steeped in their own culture that they do not recognize how it influences their thinking, views, beliefs, norms, and values, and they assume that others think, perceive, and value things similarly.
8. To help all communicators better understand and communicate with one another, researchers have studied how people in racially mixed groups interact. See, for example, Melanie Booth-Butterfield and Felecia Jordan, "Communication Adaptation among Racially Homogeneous and Heterogeneous

Groups," *Southern Communication Journal* 54 (1989): 253–72.

9. Sheel Pandya, "Racial and Ethnic Differences among Older Adults in Long Term Care Service Use," AARP Public Policy Institute, June 2005, www.aarp.org/research/longtermcare/trends/fs119_ltc.html (accessed February 15, 2006).
10. Erica Goode, "How Culture Molds Habits of Thought," *New York Times*, August 8, 2000, D1, D4.
11. Ohio State University Extension Fact Sheet: Family and Consumer Sciences, "Working with Diverse Cultures," n.d., http://ohioline.osu.edu/bc-fact/0014.html (accessed April 16, 2009).
12. Myron W. Lustig and Jolene Koester, *Intercultural Competence*, New York: Harper Collins, 1993: 104. Note several value differences between those of different cultures. For instance, they point out that "the fast, hectic pace of European Americans, governed by clocks, appointments, and schedules, has become so commonly accepted that it is almost a cliché. The pace of life in cultures such as India, Kenya, and Argentina and among African Americans is less hectic, more relaxed, and more comfortably paced"
13. Arnold D. Hunt, Marie T. Crotty, and Robert B. Crotty, eds., *Ethics of World Religions*, rev. ed. (San Diego: Greenhaven Press, 1991).
14. Abraham H. Maslow, *Motivation and Personality* (New York: Harper & Row, 1954).
15. George Bush, "Acceptance of the Republican Nomination for President," in *Contemporary American Voices*, ed. James R. Andrews and David Zarefsky (New York: Longman, 1992), 389.
16. Daniel Goleman, *Emotional Intelligence* (New York: Bantam Books, 1995).
17. James R. Andrews, "Reflections of the National Character in American Rhetoric," *Quarterly Journal of Speech* 57 (October 1971): 316–24.
18. George Cheney, "On the Various and Changing Meanings of Organizational Membership: A Field Study of Organizational Identification," *Communication Monographs* 50 (1983): 342–62; George Cheney and Phillip K. Tompkins, "Coming to Terms with Organizational Identification and Commitment," *Central States Speech Journal* 38 (1987): 1–15.
19. "Poverty: 2004 Highlights," U.S. Census Bureau, August 30, 2005, www.census.gov/hhes/www/poverty/poverty04/pov04hi.html (accessed January 5, 2006).
20. "Why Are People Homeless?" National Coalition for the Homeless, September 2002, www.nationalhomeless.org/publications/facts.html (accessed February 12, 2006).
21. Barbara Liston, "Caught in a Gunfight," *Time*, February 20, 2006, 17.
22. "Contacts," Indiana Memorial Union, http://imu.indiana.edu/board/contacts.shtml (accessed March 6, 2010).
23. "Student Programming Association," Penn State University, www.spa.psu.edu/index.html (accessed April 13, 2009).
24. There are many excellent books on interviewing. See, for example, Jeanne Tessier Barone and Jo Young Switzer, *Interviewing Art and Skill* (Boston: Allyn & Bacon, 1995); Arnold B. Kanter, *The Complete Book of Interviewing: Everything You Need to Know from Both Sides of the Table* (New York: Times Books, 1995); and Charles J. Stewart and William B. Cash Jr., *Interviewing: Principles and Practices*, 11th ed. (Boston: McGraw-Hill, 2006).
25. Priscilla Salant, *How to Conduct Your Own Survey* (New York: Wiley, 1994).
26. Jeane M. Converse and Stanley Presser, *Survey Questions: Handcrafting the Standardized Questionnaire* (Newbury Park, CA: Sage, 1986); see also Floyd J. Fowler Jr., *Survey Research Methods* (Newbury Park, CA: Sage, 1993), for an excellent discussion of how to construct survey questions.
27. Stanley L. Payne, *The Art of Asking Questions* (Princeton, NJ: Princeton University Press, 1980). Also see Robert W. Eder and Michael M. Harris, ed., *The Employment Interview Handbook* (Thousand Oaks, CA: Sage, 1999). Although this book is focused on the employment interview, it contains an excellent section on questioning as related to structured and unstructured interviews (pp. 143–216).
28. For additional information about survey construction, see Paul Rosenfeld, Jack E. Edwards, and Marie D. Thomas, "Improving Organizational Surveys," *American Behavioral Scientist* 36 (1993): 414–26; and Sam G. McFarland, "Effects of Question Order on Survey Responses," *Public Opinion Quarterly* 45 (1981): 208–15.

Notre Dame Commencement Speech

President Barack Obama

Sunday, May 17, 2009, Notre Dame, Indiana

> *When President Obama was invited to speak at the University of Notre Dame, critics of his stand on abortion, among them some students, a number of Catholic bishops, and outside anti-abortion groups, staged protests on the campus and spoke out on the national news. Their contention was that a Catholic university should not honor a leader who held views contrary to official Catholic doctrine. The university and a large majority of students, however, approved of the president's visit. This controversy formed the backdrop against which the speech was given.*

Thank you, Father Jenkins, for that generous introduction. You are doing an outstanding job as president of this fine institution, and your continued and courageous commitment to honest, thoughtful dialogue is an inspiration to us all.

THE PRESIDENT BEGINS WITH AN OBLIQUE REFERENCE TO FATHER JENKINS'S REFUSAL TO BOW TO PRESSURE TO WITHDRAW THE INVITATION, LABELING IT COURAGEOUS AND SUPPORTIVE OF THOUGHTFUL DIALOGUE. THE NOTION OF THOUGHTFUL DIALOGUE IS AN UNDERLYING THEME OF THE SPEECH.

Good afternoon, Father Hesburgh, Notre Dame trustees, faculty, family, friends, and the class of 2009. I am honored to be here today, and grateful to all of you for allowing me to be part of your graduation.

I want to thank you for this honorary degree. I know it has not been without controversy. I don't know if you're aware of this, but these honorary degrees are apparently pretty hard to come by. So far I'm only 1 for 2 as President. Father Hesburgh is 150 for 150. I guess that's better. Father Ted, after the ceremony, maybe you can give me some pointers on how to boost my average.

PRESIDENT OBAMA THEN ATTEMPTS TO ESTABLISH RAPPORT WITH THE AUDIENCE THROUGH REFERENCES TO FATHER HESBURGH, THE UNIVERSITY'S FORMER LONGTIME PRESIDENT. HE ALSO USES HUMOR TO RELATE TO LOCAL EVENTS WITH WHICH THE STUDENT AUDIENCE WILL BE FAMILIAR.

I also want to congratulate the class of 2009 for all your accomplishments. And since this is Notre Dame, I mean both in the classroom and in the competitive arena. We all know about this university's proud and storied football team, but I also hear that Notre Dame holds the largest outdoor 5-on-5 basketball tournament in the world—Bookstore Basketball.

Now this excites me. I want to congratulate the winners of this year's tournament, a team by the name of "Hallelujah Holla Back." Well done. Though I have to say, I am personally disappointed that the "Barack O'Ballers" didn't pull it out. Next year, if you need a 6′2″ forward with a decent jumper, you know where I live.

Every one of you should be proud of what you have achieved at this institution. One hundred and sixty three classes of Notre Dame graduates have sat where you are today. Some were here during years that simply rolled into the next without much notice or fanfare—periods of relative peace and prosperity that required little by way of sacrifice or struggle.

You, however, are not getting off that easy. Your class has come of age at a moment of great consequence for our nation and the world—a rare inflection point in history where the size and scope of the challenges before us require that we remake our world to renew its promise; that we align our deepest values and commitments to the demands of a new age. It is a privilege and a responsibility afforded to few generations—and a task that you are now called to fulfill.

This is the generation that must find a path back to prosperity and decide how we respond to a global economy that left millions behind even before this crisis hit—an economy where greed and short-term thinking were too often rewarded at the expense of fairness, and diligence, and an honest day's work.

We must decide how to save God's creation from a changing climate that threatens to destroy it. We must seek peace at a time when there are those who will stop at nothing to do us harm, and when weapons in the hands of a few can destroy the many. And we must find a way to reconcile our ever-shrinking world with its ever-growing diversity—diversity of thought, of culture, and of belief.

In short, we must find a way to live together as one human family.

It is this last challenge that I'd like to talk about today. For the major threats we face in the 21st century—whether it's global recession or violent extremism; the spread of nuclear weapons or pandemic disease—do not discriminate. They do not recognize borders. They do not see color. They do not target specific ethnic groups.

The president describes the many challenges facing the graduates. He suggests that they all are connected to his fundamental premise: finding common ground is essential to resolving disputes.

Moreover, no one person, or religion, or nation can meet these challenges alone. Our very survival has never required greater cooperation and understanding among all people from all places than at this moment in history.

Unfortunately, finding that common ground—recognizing that our fates are tied up, as Dr. King said, in a "single garment of destiny"—is not easy. Part of the problem, of course, lies in the imperfections of man—our selfishness, our pride, our stubbornness, our acquisitiveness, our insecurities, our egos; all the cruelties large and small that those of us in the Christian tradition understand to be rooted in original sin. We too often seek advantage over others. We cling to outworn prejudice and fear those who are unfamiliar. Too many of us view life only through the lens of immediate self-interest and crass materialism; in which the world is necessarily a zero-sum game. The strong too often dominate the weak, and too many of those with wealth and with power find all manner of justification for their own privilege in the face of poverty and injustice. And so, for all our technology and scientific advances, we see around the globe violence and want and strife that would seem sadly familiar to those in ancient times.

We know these things; and hopefully one of the benefits of the wonderful education you have received is that you have had time to consider these wrongs in the world, and grown determined, each in your own way, to right them. And yet, one of the vexing things for those of us interested in promoting greater understanding and cooperation among people is the discovery that even bringing together persons of goodwill, men and women of principle and purpose, can be difficult.

The soldier and the lawyer may both love this country with equal passion, and yet reach very different conclusions on the specific steps needed to protect us from harm. The gay activist and the evangelical pastor may both deplore the ravages of HIV/AIDS, but find themselves unable to bridge the cultural divide that might unite their efforts. Those who speak out against stem cell research may be rooted in admirable conviction about the sacredness of life, but so are the parents of a child with juvenile diabetes who are convinced that their son's or daughter's hardships can be relieved.

Here the president offers examples of common ground that may be found between opposing sides of a question.

The question, then, is how do we work through these conflicts? Is it possible for us to join hands in common effort? As citizens of a vibrant and varied democracy, how do we engage in vigorous debate? How does each of us remain firm in our principles, and fight for what we consider right, without demonizing those with just as strongly held convictions on the other side?

Nowhere do these questions come up more powerfully than on the issue of abortion.

As I considered the controversy surrounding my visit here, I was reminded of an encounter I had during my Senate campaign, one that I describe in a book I wrote called *The Audacity of Hope.* A few days after I won the Democratic nomination, I received an e-mail from a doctor who told me that while he voted for me in the primary, he had a serious concern that might prevent him from voting for me in the general election. He described himself as a Christian who was strongly pro-life, but that's not what was preventing him from voting for me.

HAVING LAID THE GROUNDWORK FOR HIS ARGUMENT, PRESIDENT OBAMA FACES THE DIVISIVE ISSUE THAT HAS COME TO THE FORE WITH HIS PRESENCE AT NOTRE DAME'S COMMENCEMENT.

What bothered the doctor was an entry that my campaign staff had posted on my website—an entry that said I would fight "right-wing ideologues who want to take away a woman's right to choose." The doctor said that he had assumed I was a reasonable person, but that if I truly believed that every pro-life individual was simply an ideologue who wanted to inflict suffering on women, then I was not very reasonable. He wrote, "I do not ask at this point that you oppose abortion, only that you speak about this issue in fair-minded words."

Fair-minded words.

After I read the doctor's letter, I wrote back to him and thanked him. I didn't change my position, but I did tell my staff to change the words on my website. And I said a prayer that night that I might extend the same presumption of good faith to others that the doctor had extended to me. Because when we do that—when we open our hearts and our minds to those who may not think like we do or believe what we do—that's when we discover at least the possibility of common ground.

THIS PERSONAL EXAMPLE IS AN EFFECTIVE WAY TO DEMONSTRATE THE SPEAKER'S OWN WILLINGNESS TO SEEK COMMON GROUND. HE FOLLOWS IT WITH MORE SPECIFIC EXAMPLES OF HOW BOTH SIDES IN THE ABORTION DEBATE MAY SEEK COMMON GOALS AND RESPECT CONFLICTING OPINIONS THAT THEY CANNOT ACCEPT.

That's when we begin to say, "Maybe we won't agree on abortion, but we can still agree that this is a heart-wrenching decision for any woman to make, with both moral and spiritual dimensions.

"So let's work together to reduce the number of women seeking abortions by reducing unintended pregnancies, and making adoption more available, and providing care and support for women who do carry their child to term. Let's honor the conscience of those who disagree with abortion, and draft a sensible conscience clause, and make sure that all of our health care policies are grounded in clear ethics and sound science, as well as respect for the equality of women."

Understand—I do not suggest that the debate surrounding abortion can or should go away. No matter how much we may want to fudge it—indeed, while we know that the views of most Americans on the subject are complex and even contradictory—the fact is that at some level, the views of the two camps are irreconcilable. Each side will continue to make its case to the public with passion and conviction. But surely we can do so without reducing those with differing views to caricature.

Open hearts. Open minds. Fair-minded words.

It's a way of life that has always been the Notre Dame tradition. Father Hesburgh has long spoken of this institution as both a lighthouse and a crossroads. The lighthouse that stands apart, shining with the wisdom of the Catholic tradition, while the crossroads is where ". . . differences of culture and religion and conviction can co-exist with friendship, civility, hospitality, and especially love." And I want to join him and Father Jenkins in saying how inspired I am by the maturity and responsibility with which this class has approached the debate surrounding today's ceremony.

This tradition of cooperation and understanding is one that I learned in my own life many years ago—also with the help of the Catholic Church.

I was not raised in a particularly religious household, but my mother instilled in me a sense of service and empathy that eventually led me to become a community organizer after I graduated college. A group of Catholic churches in Chicago helped fund an organization known as the Developing Communities Project, and we worked to lift up South Side neighborhoods that had been devastated when the local steel plant closed.

It was quite an eclectic crew. Catholic and Protestant churches. Jewish and African-American organizers. Working-class black and white and Hispanic residents. All of us with different experiences. All of us with different beliefs. But all of us learned to work side by side because all of us saw in these neighborhoods other human beings who needed our help—to find jobs and improve schools. We were bound together in the service of others.

And something else happened during the time I spent in those neighborhoods. Perhaps because the church folks I worked with were so welcoming and understanding; perhaps because they invited me to their services and sang with me from their hymnals; perhaps because I witnessed all of the good works their faith inspired them to perform, I found myself drawn—not just to work with the church, but to be in the church. It was through this service that I was brought to Christ.

At the time, Cardinal Joseph Bernardin was the Archbishop of Chicago. For those of you too young to have known him, he was a kind and good and wise man. A saintly man. I can still remember him speaking at one of the first organizing meetings I attended on the South Side. He stood as both a lighthouse and a crossroads—unafraid to speak his mind on moral issues ranging from poverty, AIDS, and abortion to the death penalty and nuclear war. And yet, he was congenial and gentle in his persuasion, always trying to bring people together; always trying to find common ground. Just before he died, a reporter asked Cardinal Bernardin about this approach to his ministry. And he said, "You can't really get on with preaching the Gospel until you've touched minds and hearts."

THE USE OF NOTRE DAME'S FORMER PRESIDENT, FATHER HESBURGH, A REVERED FIGURE, AND CARDINAL BERNARDIN, BOTH CREDIBLE SOURCES FOR THIS AUDIENCE, PROMOTES IDENTIFICATION AND ADDS TO THE PRESIDENT'S OWN CREDIBILITY. THE PERSONAL EXAMPLE OF OBAMA'S WORK WITH SEVERAL FAITH COMMUNITIES, INCLUDING CATHOLICS, FURTHER STRENGTHENS HIS ETHOS.

My heart and mind were touched by the words and deeds of the men and women I worked alongside with in Chicago. And I'd like to think that we touched the hearts and minds of the neighborhood families whose lives we helped change. For this, I believe, is our highest calling.

You are about to enter the next phase of your life at a time of great uncertainty. You will be called upon to help restore a free market that is also fair to all who are willing to work; to seek new sources of energy that can save our planet; to give future generations the same chance that you had to receive an extraordinary education. And whether as a person drawn to public service, or someone who simply insists on being an active citizen, you will be exposed to more opinions and ideas broadcast through more means of communications than have ever existed before. You will hear talking heads scream on cable, read blogs that claim definitive knowledge, and watch politicians pretend to know what they're talking about. Occasionally, you may also have the great fortune of seeing important issues debated by well-intentioned, brilliant minds. In fact, I suspect that many of you will be among those bright stars.

In commenting on the lack of civil discourse that often prevails over contentious issues, the President compliments his audience as those who will engage in well-intentioned debate in the future. He follows this by connecting faith with the need to be open minded.

In this world of competing claims about what is right and what is true, have confidence in the values with which you've been raised and educated. Be unafraid to speak your mind when those values are at stake. Hold firm to your faith and allow it to guide you on your journey. Stand as a lighthouse.

But remember too that the ultimate irony of faith is that it necessarily admits doubt. It is the belief in things not seen. It is beyond our capacity as human beings to know with certainty what God has planned for us or what He asks of us, and those of us who believe must trust that His wisdom is greater than our own.

This doubt should not push us away from our faith. But it should humble us. It should temper our passions, and cause us to be wary of self-righteousness. It should compel us to remain open, and curious, and eager to continue the moral and spiritual debate that began for so many of you within the walls of Notre Dame. And within our vast democracy, this doubt should remind us to persuade through reason, through an appeal whenever we can to universal rather than parochial principles, and most of all through an abiding example of good works, charity, kindness, and service that moves hearts and minds.

The President offers another appeal to common ground through the shared belief in the Golden Rule and the shared commitment of all religions to service.

For if there is one law that we can be most certain of, it is the law that binds people of all faiths and no faith together. It is no coincidence that it exists in Christianity and Judaism; in Islam and Hinduism; in Buddhism and humanism. It is, of course, the Golden Rule—the call to treat one another as we wish to be treated. The call to love. To serve. To do what we can to make a difference in the lives of those with whom we share the same brief moment on this Earth.

So many of you at Notre Dame—by the last count, upwards of 80 percent—have lived this law of love through the service you've performed at schools and hospitals; international relief agencies and local charities. That is incredibly impressive, and a powerful testament to this institution. Now you must carry the tradition forward. Make it a way of life. Because when you serve, it doesn't just improve your community, it makes you a part of your community. It breaks down walls. It fosters cooperation. And when that happens—when people set aside their differences to work in common effort toward a common good; when they struggle together, and sacrifice together, and learn from one another—all things are possible.

After all, I stand here today, as President and as an African-American, on the 55th anniversary of the day that the Supreme Court handed down the decision in *Brown v. the Board of Education. Brown* was of course the first major step in dismantling the "separate but equal" doctrine, but it would take a number of years and a nationwide movement to fully realize the dream of civil rights for all of God's children. There were freedom rides and lunch counters and billy clubs, and there was also a Civil Rights Commission appointed by President Eisenhower. It was the twelve resolutions recommended by this commission that would ultimately become law in the Civil Rights Act of 1964.

There were six members of the commission. It included five whites and one African-American; Democrats and Republicans; two Southern governors, the dean of a Southern law school, a Midwestern university president, and your own Father Ted Hesburgh, President of Notre Dame. They worked for two years, and at times, President Eisenhower had to intervene personally since no hotel or restaurant in the South would serve the black and white members of the commission together. Finally, when they reached an impasse in Louisiana, Father Ted flew them all to Notre Dame's retreat in Land O'Lakes, Wisconsin, where they eventually overcame their differences and hammered out a final deal.

Years later, President Eisenhower asked Father Ted how on Earth he was able to broker an agreement between men of such different backgrounds and beliefs. And Father Ted simply said that during their first dinner in Wisconsin, they discovered that they were all fishermen. And so he quickly readied a boat for a twilight trip out on the lake. They fished, and they talked, and they changed the course of history.

I will not pretend that the challenges we face will be easy, or that the answers will come quickly, or that all our differences and divisions will fade happily away. Life is not that simple. It never has been.

But as you leave here today, remember the lessons of Cardinal Bernardin, of Father Hesburgh, of movements for change both large and small. Remember that each of us, endowed with the dignity possessed by all children of God, has the grace to recognize ourselves in one another; to understand that we all seek the same love of family and the same fulfillment of a life well-lived. Remember that in the end, we are all fishermen.

If nothing else, that knowledge should give us faith that through our collective labor, and God's providence, and our willingness to shoulder each other's burdens, America will continue on its precious journey towards that more perfect union. Congratulations on your graduation, may God bless you, and may God bless the United States of America.

THE DISCUSSION OF FATHER HESBURGH'S WORK WITH CIVIL RIGHTS BOTH RESONATES WITH NOTRE DAME AND OFFERS A SPECIFIC EXAMPLE OF HOW PEOPLE WITH DIFFERENT POINTS OF VIEW, WORKING IN GOOD FAITH, CAN COME TOGETHER.

THE CONCLUSION OFFERS A CHALLENGE TO THE AUDIENCE, REMINDS THEM OF THE SUPPORT HE TAKES FROM TWO HIGHLY CREDIBLE FIGURES, AND ALLUDES TO THE BIBLICAL REFERENCE TO JESUS'S DISCIPLES AS FISHERS OF MEN.

Source: From "Remarks by the President Obama in Commencement Address at the University of Notre Dame." Published 2009 by The White House, Office of the Press Secretary.

CHAPTER

6

Developing Significant Topics

CHAPTER SURVEY

Finding a Suitable Topic

Narrowing the Topic

Ethical Obligations in Selecting a Topic

General Purposes

Crafting and Testing Specific Purposes

Constructing a Thesis Statement

CHAPTER OBJECTIVES

After studying this chapter, you should be able to

1. Generate significant speech topics.
2. Revise and narrow your topic.
3. Determine how ethical considerations affect your choice of a topic.
4. Understand what is meant by a general purpose.
5. Distinguish among the goals of informative, persuasive, and ceremonial speeches.
6. Devise a good specific purpose for your speech.
7. Write a clear thesis statement.

After giving a poor speech, a student came to talk to his instructor and told this story. Two weeks before he was scheduled to give a five- to seven-minute informative speech, David had not yet chosen a topic. He admitted that he was clueless. As he sat in his political science class, he had a bright idea. His professor was explaining how a president is elected in the United States. David had taken several pages of notes and read two chapters on the subject. That seemed to him to be a lot of information. Why not, David thought, just summarize his notes and develop a short speech? He felt great relief as he decided to speak about presidential elections.

Although David's choice of a speech topic may seem sensible, it was not. Randomly choosing a topic can prove disastrous. In David's case, the choice was inspired by convenience rather than the demands of the situation. For one thing, his topic was too broad to be covered in the available time. His information was also too technical for his listeners. In short, David had problems because he failed to take into account his audience's knowledge and interests. This "boiled-down" version of a lecture was not appropriate for his public speaking assignment.

To make matters worse, David had not taken the time to come up with a clear focus for his speech. He thought only about his general purpose—talking about presidential elections—instead of the specific ideas he wanted his audience to understand. Beginning with his own interests, coupled with important issues of the day, David should have asked himself, "What do I care about that would be significant and interesting to this audience?" Many worthy topics might have emerged from this kind of reflection. David might have chosen to speak about political action committees, campaign finance reform, or the evolution of the national party conventions. These topics might have grown out of what David already knew something about, but they also could have been fashioned to connect with the interests and needs of the audience. Naturally, David would have to do additional research to address these topics intelligently. He also would need to think more specifically about how he hoped to influence the audience's behavior and thinking. In short, David still needed to go through the process of refining and narrowing his topic.

FINDING A SUITABLE TOPIC

Preview. *As you start thinking about a topic, first focus your attention on what you know and care about. Taking an inventory of your personal concerns and their relationship to community issues, your intellectual and educational interests, your career goals, and your leisure activities will help you come up with good speech topics. These interests represent a starting point for considering matters of significant public concern that you are motivated to learn more about.*

Deciding what to talk about may or may not be one of your initial concerns as a speaker. In some situations, the topic of your speech will be predetermined. You may be invited to talk because of your expertise or experience, and the invitation determines the topic. If, for example, you have been especially active in an environmental group, you may be asked to speak at a service club about environmental problems in your community. Or perhaps the student association at your school distributes funds to campus organizations, and you have been chosen to speak as an advocate for your group. Sometimes the situation determines the topic, as when you attend a public meeting to speak for or against a specific proposal. Many times, however, you will be asked to determine your own topic. Your public speaking class is one such situation. In most cases, you will be assigned only a *type* of speech and you will choose the topic. Your task, then, will be to find the right topic—one that is important, fits with your interests, meets the needs of the situation, and positively impacts your listeners.

Early in your public speaking class, you may be assigned a specific topic that does not require much preparation or specialized knowledge, just to help you get comfortable speaking before a group. You may be asked to give a short speech describing a person you admire, for example, or a speech introducing yourself or a classmate. Normally, however, you will have to choose your own topic, whether speaking in or outside your class. In most cases, neither circumstances nor setting nor audience demands will determine your specific topic. It will be up to you to choose the best topic.

Brainstorming Topics of Public Concern

Keeping up with the news is one way to identify potential speech topics. Reading widely about the issues that affect your community, the nation, and the world can help you not only identify topics of public significance, but also begin to form your own opinions and arguments.

Suppose, for example, that you read an article in *Newsweek* about the controversy surrounding alternative fuel sources. At the outset, you may have given little thought to this controversy, but you begin to see it as an important issue and a good topic for a speech. As you read further, you become interested in whether ethanol is really a good alternative fuel source. You notice contradictory opinions. On the one hand, you read that ethanol burns cleaner than fossil fuels. At the same time, you learn that the process of *making* ethanol consumes almost as much energy as it produces. You begin to wonder whether ethanol could be produced more efficiently, as some experts suggest, or whether we ought to be looking for other ways to reduce our dependence on foreign oil. As you gain more knowledge of the subject, you not only decide that this is a good topic for your speech but also begin to form your own opinions on the issue. You'll want to choose wisely; choosing a topic that you are interested in and know will be worthwhile for your listeners will help you do your best work.[1]

However extensive your initial knowledge of the topic, you should always be willing to do additional research, consulting reference works, good newspapers (such as the *New York Times* or the *Wall Street Journal*), periodicals, books, and other library resources. Many of these resources are now available online.

HIGHLIGHTING SOURCES FOR IDENTIFYING TOPICS OF PUBLIC CONCERN

Using a Library Research Guide

At Southeast Missouri University, public speaking students are asked to consult the *Kent Library Research Guide,* a guide that suggests resources and research strategies for developing public presentations.

- The *Guide* provides suggestions on where and how to look for journal articles, local and national newspapers, editorials, statistics, Web resources, and other guides.
- It points to valuable resources for selecting current, controversial, or classically debated topics, including the following:
  - CQ Researcher—provides a print service with comprehensive weekly reports on various topics
  - Facts.com—offers subscription access to Facts on File
  - Newseum.org—allows the reader to read the front pages of newspapers from all over the world
  - White House News and Policies—offers a policies and initiatives column with topics arranged by group
  - World Headlines—allows the reader to follow the links of various news outlets
- Other resources focus on opinion pieces, Web directories, and video sources.

Source: To access this guide, go to http://library.semo.edu/learn/guides/publicspeaking.html. Ask your own librarian if your university has a comparable guide.

In *Highlighting Sources for Identifying Topics of Public Concern*, we describe one university's online guide to library resources. Your own college or university may have a similar online guide that can help you identify and research topics of public concern.

What Matters to You?

Another good way to identify possible topics is by thinking about your own interests and experiences. The fundamental question is, "What do I already know and care about?" This does not mean, "What can I already give a speech about?" Do not try to find a ready-made speech in your head or limit yourself to topics on which you are already an expert. That kind of thinking could lead you to imagine that you can just give a speech "off the top of your head." In fact, giving a good speech takes a lot of work, and part of that work is learning more about your topic. Research is essential to support your personal knowledge, opinions, and experiences, but research also may lead you to change your initial topic or your opinions about that topic.

Conducting a Self-Inventory

By doing a **self-inventory**—taking a thoughtful look at what you really know and care about—you can come up with a list of potential topics. Think about issues that affect you and your community. Or do an inventory of your intellectual and educational interests, your career goals, and your leisure activities and interests. By doing a self-inventory, you can begin to generate possible topics that are both meaningful to you and significant issues for your audience.

Begin by **brainstorming**—writing down anything that comes to your mind under a particular category. At first, don't worry about whether the topic would be interesting to your audience, whether you will be able to get enough material, or anything else. Just put down all the possibilities that come to you. When you have come up with a number of ideas, you can then evaluate each topic, considering whether it may be a good topic for your speech.

PERSONAL CONCERNS AND COMMUNITY ISSUES The best place to begin your search for a topic is with issues and questions that are important to you *and* important to your community. Here are two major questions to start you thinking of topics in this category.

- **What Is Going On in My Life That Bothers or Concerns Me?**

All of us know of things that we would like to change. We have all been upset by certain people or events, and we all have values and ideals that we wish others would embrace. Begin a list of things that frustrate or upset you—things that you would like to see changed—and then consider the possible speech topics you might generate from such a list.

One student began her self-inventory of personal concerns by reflecting on the difficulty she and her friends were having completing their degree requirements in four years. That suggested a speech arguing that the college ought to offer more courses during the summer, or perhaps a proposal to change the college's degree requirements. She also considered ways that the university might help students better balance work, study, and classes, leading to a proposal that the university offer workshops or support groups for students. She often worried about proposed cutbacks in student loans, suggesting a speech opposing such cuts or advocating more state support for students. Finally, she recalled that spring break was coming up soon, and she began to wonder if there was a better way to spend that time than lying on a beach. This led her to explore opportunities for getting involved in volunteer work over the break, such as through Habitat for Humanity's Collegiate Challenge.

- **What Is Happening Outside My Immediate World That Is Unfair, Unjust, or in Need of Reform?**

What good things going on in the world deserve more support? As you read newspapers and newsmagazines, watch television news programs, and search the Internet, write down issues that capture your interest. Ask yourself what kinds of news stories concern you the most, and consider what topics may arise out of those concerns. Perhaps a story about a tragic death on campus will lead you to speak about the dangers of binge drinking. Or maybe a story about Congress passing a new "Bill of Rights" for credit card holders got you thinking about how easy it is for college students to get credit cards and go into debt. As you follow the news about the war on terrorism, you may decide to talk about the recent controversy over the use of so-called enhanced interrogation techniques on suspected terrorists. As you hear news about the development of nuclear weapons in Iran or North Korea, you may reflect on nuclear proliferation treaties and how well they work. The possibilities are limitless. Pay attention to what is happening in your community, your country, and the world and you will generate a long and varied list of possible speech topics.

INTELLECTUAL AND EDUCATIONAL INTERESTS Your self-inventory can prod you to consider important topics that you would like to know more about. When considering your intellectual and educational interests, you may ask yourself these questions:

- **What Do I Like to Read?**

One student listed the books she had most enjoyed reading in the past year and asked herself what they had in common. Two books that she particularly liked, *Three Cups of Tea* and *A Thousand Splendid Suns*, dealt with cultural values in the Muslim world and how values are learned or imposed. This led her to consider a speech topic dealing with different cultural values, and then to a possible topic: the differences between Islamic values and traditional Western values. She was still a long way from a specific topic, but she had taken the first step.

- **What Interesting Things Have I Learned from Television or Movies?**

Another student began by considering the television programs and movies he most enjoyed and came up with a list of sitcoms, dramas, reality shows, and nature films. As he thought about the significant issues that might emerge from the shows he watched, all sorts of possible topics arose. A fan of *Saturday Night Live*, he began to consider the influence of late-night comedy on politics. Thinking about his favorite TV reality program, *The Apprentice*, led him to consider a speech on business ethics. The movie *The Soloist* suggested a speech on homelessness and mental illness. His problem was not to find a topic, but to select and develop one of the many topics that his brainstorming generated.

- **What Specific Courses, or Issues Covered in My Courses, Have Particularly Interested Me?**

Courses in your major field of study can also be a source of topics. Here are some examples of topics generated by students from their majors: a physics major spoke on the benefits of space exploration; an English major chose to talk about the way in which literary works shape our view of the world; a psychology major explained how cognitive dissonance is experienced and its consequences in making important decisions; a business major decided to examine the tensions between the profit motive and ethics in large corporations. In each case, the topic grew from something the student had learned about in a course, and all addressed important issues.

CAREER GOALS Students usually have an ultimate career goal in mind; many may already be pursuing a career. The major question to start with here is, "What do I hope to do with my life?" Follow up on this question by brainstorming possible issues associated with that profession. One student who planned to be a lawyer brainstormed by asking these questions: Do lawyers have an obligation to work with any client who can afford to hire them? What if you think a potential client

Concern for problems, whether in the world, the country, or your community will generate significant topics for speeches. These students from Taylor University, helping to rebuild homes in New Orleans, would have many compelling experiences on which to build a speech.

is guilty? Is it right to approach a potential client who has suffered a tragic loss? What do you do if your personal interests conflict with a client's best interests? What can be done about the widespread mistrust of lawyers? As he considered these questions, he soon realized that they all raised important questions about the ethical code that lawyers follow.

Other careers may suggest additional topics. A future teacher may speak about how the success of democracy depends on well-educated citizens. A future engineer may address the dangers of our deteriorating infrastructure. If you plan to be an accountant, perhaps you would speak on the need for tax reform. A future research chemist may speak about generic drugs and how they affect consumers. If you hope to become a marketing analyst, you may choose to address how wise consumers make choices among similar products. A future television producer may speak about how viewers can influence network programming. Giving a speech related to your future career has the added bonus of providing you with information you can use in the future. By thinking about your prospective career, you may not only discover a good speech topic but also learn more about the career you are considering.

LEISURE ACTIVITIES AND INTERESTS Things you do for pleasure or enjoyment may be a source of speech topics. Yet a word of caution is in order: speeches that some audiences may find useful or interesting may seem ordinary or trivial to others. For example, you may have experience teaching children how to string their own tennis rackets, but your college classmates would not likely respond well to a speech titled "How to String a Tennis Racket." Playing bridge, dancing, or watching football may be enjoyable for you, but do they suggest speech topics that your audience would consider substantive and important? Probably not.

Nevertheless, a sports enthusiast *could* come up with some significant topics. Among the hotly debated issues in the sports world today are the use of performance-enhancing drugs, the obligations of colleges and universities to support women's athletics, and the enormous salaries paid to some professional athletes. Similarly, a movie buff may decide to talk about how films help shape the rules of social interaction in our culture, or the ways in which our history is manipulated in films to promote particular political beliefs or social values. Someone who sees a lot of movies also may address the topic of censorship or the controversy over how movies and other forms of entertainment are rated.

Conducting a self-inventory that surveys your intellectual and educational interests, career goals, personal and social concerns, and favorite leisure activities and interests will serve as a starting point as you search for your own topics. Of course, the broad topics you generate through brainstorming may need to be narrowed and focused. A consideration of the situation and the audience will help you do this.

NARROWING THE TOPIC

Preview. *The potential speech topics that emerge from brainstorming are just that—potential topics. Once you have chosen a topic, you can then narrow and refine your choice by considering how the situation, time constraints, and audience will influence your speech.*

Any topic must be appropriate for the audience and the occasion. It must stretch listeners' present understanding or perception of your topic or add to their knowledge. As you refine the purpose of your speech, conduct research, develop arguments and supporting material, and organize your ideas, you will probably find that you need to fine-tune your topic. The first step is to consider your audience carefully and to decide more precisely what you hope to accomplish. In the previous chapter we discussed audience analysis and adaptation. For now, let us review two guidelines that will help you focus and refine your topic.

Consider the Situation

- Does the topic I am considering relate to recent events that may be of concern to my listeners?
- Would I be able to convince my listeners to care as much about my potential topic as I do?
- Do I have sufficient time to cover the topic adequately?

Consider the Audience

- What does my audience already know?
- What common experiences has my audience had?
- What do my listeners and I have in common?
- How diverse is my audience?

Let us consider how to apply the guidelines in specific cases through an example.

Ruiz, a meteorology major, was interested in how weather systems developed. For him, situational factors proved decisive in narrowing his topic. When he asked himself if his audience would be familiar with any immediate events relevant to his topic, he thought of all the recent news stories about the devastation caused by hurricanes. Then he asked himself if this topic would be of serious concern to his audience. Although they had all heard about hurricanes, they did not live in an area that had been affected by such storms. He wondered how he might encourage his listeners to be more concerned about weather disasters and therefore support investing in improved methods of weather forecasting. If his audience could understand how disasters caused by weather have consequences for *everyone*, he reasoned, they would find his speech more interesting and convincing. He also asked himself how much he could say in seven minutes, the time allotted for his speech. This kind of thinking helped him focus on how weather disasters, even in a distant part of the country, could affect his audience. This is how he began his speech:

> Everyone is aware of the devastating effects of Hurricane Katrina in 2005. That storm cost many lives, destroyed people's homes and businesses, and forced homeless victims to move to other parts of the country. We have all heard about the millions of dollars spent by the government to help people rebuild. We may even have relatives or friends from the affected areas. Schools and universities in our own state took in students and people opened their homes to strangers displaced by the storm. Rebuilding still goes on today, years after the event. From a purely humanitarian point of view, that is probably sufficient for us to support efforts to improve weather forecasting in America.
>
> But there are also other, less dramatic ways that weather-related disasters directly impact us. After you watched scenes of that hurricane hit the Gulf Coast, did you notice that the price of gasoline went up? The same thing happens to the price of bread and breakfast cereals when rivers in the wheat-producing states flood following heavy winter snows. It happens all the time: Florida has a deep freeze in December, and in early January your orange juice costs fifty cents more. There's a drought in California, and all of a sudden iceberg lettuce costs twice as much. As Mark Twain once quipped, "Everybody talks about the weather, but nobody does anything about it." Yet today we have the scientific and technological knowledge to do a much better job predicting the weather, if only we are willing to commit the necessary resources to that effort. Specifically, we need to invest more in weather prediction technologies and early-warning systems that have the potential to save lives and property.

This student had gone from selecting possible topics though a self-inventory to narrowing the possibilities by considering his own interests. He then focused his speech on a topic that mattered to his audience and that concerned the welfare of the broader community.

Considerations of situation and audience are just as important to speakers outside the classroom. A public health official, for example, may be asked to speak to a community group about swine flu. Just as the student speaker did, this speaker needs to consider the situation. Is there a real threat of a pandemic?

Has there been a lot of coverage of the issue in the local media? Are flu shots available? He also needs to ask questions about the audience. Do his listeners have much medical knowledge? Is there serious concern among the group that the flu will be widespread? Is the group made up of people who are more susceptible to the flu? Does the audience include parents who may be worried about their children? Based on such considerations, he may decide to narrow the topic to explain exactly what swine flu is and how it is transmitted. Or he may wish to explain the symptoms of the flu, how to avoid contracting it, and what to do if one exhibits the symptoms. He may, instead, wish to assure his audience that there is no need to panic and focus on the reasons the flu is *not* likely to affect them. So, from the topic of swine flu, this speaker may narrow the topic in a number of ways to better suit the situation and audience.

ETHICAL OBLIGATIONS IN SELECTING A TOPIC

Preview. *As you choose a topic, you should consider your ethical obligations to the audience. You should commit to becoming knowledgeable about your topic through careful research. Although you may have strong feelings about your topic, you also should strive to be fair-minded. And you will want to exercise good judgment in considering the audience's standards of taste.*

Ethics may be described as a set of behavioral standards. Some would argue that ethics are universal and unchanging, but others may argue that they are relative to a particular culture or situation. In either case, such standards represent a behavioral code, and a person who lives by that code is considered ethical. If your listeners sense that you are ethical, they will find your speech more convincing.[2]

As a speaker, you will draw on your own ethical code in choosing a topic, as well as in deciding how to approach that topic. Ethical considerations cannot be taken up after you have finished your work, nor can they be dealt with and dismissed early on. A good speaker integrates ethical concerns into every aspect of his or her speech.[3]

Although we may not always agree on what is ethical, there are some ethical considerations you should take into account as you choose a topic—namely, your responsibility for accuracy, fair-mindedness, good taste, and sound judgment.

Accuracy

When searching for a topic, you would not reject a possibility because you did not know enough to speak about it without any preparation. As we pointed out earlier, you should not expect to have a ready-made speech in your head. A major part of preparing to speak is learning more about your topic. You may not be an expert in a particular field, but you owe it to your audience to know as much as possible about your topic. What does this have to do with ethics?

Without careful research, you cannot come to a sound conclusion yourself. Speaking to influence people carries with it the ethical obligation to know what you are talking about and to believe in what you say. If you are not knowledgeable, you may inadvertently misinform, mislead, or even harm your audience. Suppose, for example, that you wanted to speak about the problem of obesity in America. If you were to give a speech based on just one article about dieting, you might suggest practices that would hurt rather than help your listeners. The article may have been outdated, it may not have covered all the potential objections to the diet, it may have asserted as fact matters that are not yet scientifically verified, or it may have come from a biased source. Even if you are not trying to persuade an audience, you still have an ethical obligation to strive for accuracy. Any speech that contains information that is misleading or untrue is considered unethical.

Just as important as the quantity and quality of your information is the credibility of your sources. Would you want to try an amazing marshmallow diet touted by a supermarket tabloid? Or would you feel more comfortable taking advice based on a study reported in the *New England Journal of Medicine*? When you are giving a speech, you are the information resource for your audience. Citing reputable sources will make you a more credible and ethical speaker.

Urging people to take actions or to modify their behavior in ways that could have negative consequences is clearly unethical. The consequences need not be physical, such as endangering one's health. Misinformation or poorly developed ideas can also lead to bad decisions on economic, social, or political matters that affect people's lives.

Objectivity versus Subjectivity

We rarely, if ever, achieve the ideal of perfect objectivity. None of us can be entirely neutral toward topics we know or care about. We cannot help having subjective reactions based on our experiences and the values we have learned. We have religious feelings, political biases, or expectations for social behavior that are a part of us whether we consciously recognize them or not. As a speaker, you cannot erase your past and approach any topic as if it had no relationship to your life. On the contrary, potential topics grow from such life experiences. Nor does an audience really expect such complete objectivity. What an audience *does* expect, however, is fair-mindedness—a willingness to suspend your own biases and to remain open to competing ideas.

Because you will select significant topics of public concern or from your particular areas of interest or expertise, you will likely have preexisting opinions, biases, or strong feelings about those topics. However, an ethical speaker approaches topic selection in a fair-minded way. You may be in favor of the comprehensive health care plan proposed by the president, or you may prefer a plan that helps consumers obtain affordable health care through private insurance companies. Whatever position you take, you have the ethical obligation to be open to the possibility that your research may lead you to modify your initial point of view. Ethical speakers remain open to changing their minds and do not avoid or screen out information that may challenge their initial opinions. Once you have thoroughly researched your topic and come to a thoughtful and fair conclusion, you can be more confident in taking a strong, well-reasoned stand on an issue.

Taste and Judgment

Generally, you should avoid topics that audiences may find embarrassing or offensive. Putting listeners in such a position may be considered unethical. An audience-centered perspective is crucial here. *You* may find certain topics appealing, amusing, or of great importance. Thinking about how your audience will react to your topic, however, may put it in a different light.

Imagine a student in your public speaking class giving a speech that tried to convert you to his or her religion. Although the student has the right to hold particular beliefs, your classroom is likely made up of people whose beliefs differ and who may be offended by a speaker trying to convert them. The likelihood of offense increases when the audience is a captive one: listeners in a classroom have no choice but to hear that speech; they cannot simply get up and leave. Attempting to force one's beliefs on a captive audience will likely be viewed as a tasteless demonstration of poor judgment on the part of the speaker. Moreover, trying to change deeply held beliefs is not a practical goal in a single speech. In a public speaking class, you need to be wary of trying to radically change your listeners' views, especially on issues that arouse great passion or deeply divide your audience.

This does not mean that you should avoid controversial topics. Most issues of significant public concern stir up strong feelings and spirited debate: being engaged will inevitably lead you to advocate positions that are contested. What is important is that you be sensitive to contrary opinions and aware of the limits imposed by those opinions. A speech simply explaining the beliefs of a particular religion may be appropriate—as long as you do not try to convert your listeners. In any case, different audiences may view the same topic in different ways. As an ethical speaker, you must consider each audience separately and try to understand its members' particular tastes and dispositions toward your topic.

Once you have selected a topic, you still need to hone in on the general and specific purposes of your speech.

GENERAL PURPOSES

Preview. *Public speaking is always purposeful—that is, a speaker always aims to get responses from listeners. Sometimes the principal kind of response you want from an audience is understanding, so you give an informative speech. At other times, you want to influence the way listeners feel, what they believe, or how they act. In those cases, you give a persuasive speech. Finally, you may give a ceremonial speech when you want to reinforce values and engage in community building.*

Just as speakers contemplate the situation, their own interests, and those of the audience in selecting a topic, they use those same considerations to formulate their general and specific purposes. As you refine your topic, you try to translate it into a specific statement of the audience response you desire. Successful public communication rests on having a clear purpose. The first step in determining your purpose is to consider the general response you want from your audience.

Sometimes you want your audience to simply understand some concept or process; on other occasions you may hope to change their minds or motivate them to act.

In most classroom speeches, your **general purpose** will likely be part of the assignment. At work or when you speak in the community, however, your general purpose may not be determined in advance and you will need to make choices based on the situation and the audience. Let us now consider the three general purposes that will account for most of the speeches you give.

Informative Purposes

When we talk about informing people, we naturally think about giving them new information. But as a speaker, what do you want *from* your audience when you give an informative speech? You want *understanding*; you give an informative speech to gain understanding from your listeners.

This is not just playing with words; an important concept is involved. Have you ever been in a class where the instructor gave a lecture with a lot of information that you did not understand? Or have you gotten directions from someone, but then found that you still could not reach your destination? Have you ever been given instructions on how to do a job, only to find that you still could not complete the task? If anything like this has happened to you, you have experienced the difference between just getting information and gaining understanding. In all of these cases, the person attempting to communicate with you failed to help you understand.

When you give an informative speech, your goal is to help your listeners understand something they did not understand before. After you have finished speaking, listeners will not just have *heard* something new; they will have *learned* something new. This focus on learning will lead you to avoid topics that are controversial, searching instead for topics that add to the listeners' knowledge. We discuss informative speaking in more detail in Chapter 14.

Persuasive Purposes

Persuasion surrounds us; it intrudes on almost every aspect of our lives. We are urged to give our time to worthy causes, to donate money to charity, to vote for particular politicians, or to protest a decision by the local school board. We are asked to embrace new beliefs or values, to accept new ideas, and to defer to the opinions of others. Like informative messages, persuasive messages aim to get something from us: agreement, empathy, or maybe even some change in our behavior. Persuasive speakers do not just want us to understand their point of view; they want to influence our beliefs, values, and actions.

Persuasion is more than telling listeners what they ought to do or believe. It is more than simply giving an audience facts or statistics. It is more than simply stating your opinion. It is more than asking, recommending, or demanding. We often hear advertisers, politicians, telemarketers, or salespeople give many reasons why we should accept their arguments. But we do not always do what they would like us to do. We are not always persuaded.

Persuasion requires that we give our audience good reasons for accepting our claims. As a speaker, you want listeners to feel more strongly about an issue, to agree with you, or to take some definite action. We discuss the goals of persuasive speaking in more detail in Chapters 15 and 16.

Ceremonial Purposes

Many speaking occasions offer the opportunity for community building. We may be called on to honor someone, celebrate an event of shared significance, or pay tribute to someone we have loved or lost. Ceremonial speaking uplifts us, comforts us, and reinforces our sense of community with others.[4]

In ceremonial speeches, we articulate and reinforce shared values. We ask questions such as these: What has brought us together? What defines us as a community? Which of our accomplishments give us the most pride? What are the principles *we* cherish? In some ceremonial speeches, we may honor our heroes—those who personify or illuminate our shared values. By holding them high, praising their accomplishments, and remembering how they lived their lives, we are reminding ourselves of the values we cherish. On other occasions, we may be presenting an award, honoring graduates, or trying to motivate our listeners to serve their communities. In doing so, we offer encouragement and inspiration to our listeners. We suggest how hard work, determination, and the desire to succeed will ultimately pay off. In the United States, we may celebrate values associated with our founders or some national holiday. In other cultures, different values may be celebrated.[5] But the general purpose of ceremonial speaking remains the same: to reaffirm and strengthen the shared values that define our communities and our cultures.

Ceremonial speeches may be given by anyone—political leaders, community leaders, citizens, or students speaking in a classroom. U.S. presidents give a variety of ceremonial speeches, such as inaugural addresses, commemorative speeches on national holidays, and commencement addresses. Sometimes they are even called on to comfort the nation in times of tragedy. Thus, for example, Ronald Reagan delivered a famous eulogy to the astronauts killed when the space shuttle *Challenger* exploded shortly after takeoff in 1986, referring to them as "seven heroes . . . who were daring and brave and [who] had that special grace."[6] More often, presidents are asked to mark special occasions or national holidays. On Memorial Day 2009, for example, President Barack Obama delivered a speech calling on all Americans to "pause in national unity" at three P.M., "ring a bell," and offer a "prayer" and a silent "thank you" to all who had died defending America. He then asked his listeners to "commit to give something back to this nation—something lasting—in their memory" and to "affirm in our own lives and advance around the world" those values that Memorial Day represents: those "enduring ideals of justice, equality, and opportunity for which they and so many generations of Americans have given that last full measure of devotion."[7]

In your speech class, you may not be called on to eulogize national heroes or memorialize those who have died in battle. But you may be asked to deliver a ceremonial speech marking a special occasion or paying tribute to an important

In his commencement speech at Notre Dame, President Obama sought to blunt criticism by emphasizing common values.

person in your own life. One word of caution: be careful about choosing ceremonial topics that strongly affect you emotionally. Eulogizing a close friend or relative who has died recently, for example, can be difficult for some people.

We will discuss ceremonial speaking in greater detail in Chapter 17.

Your general purpose, then, points you in the direction you want to go. The next step is to refine that general purpose into a specific purpose statement that spells out precisely the response you want from your audience.

CRAFTING AND TESTING SPECIFIC PURPOSES

Preview. *Specific purpose statements describe the response you want from your audience. They are shaped by your goals as a speaker, the situation in which you speak, and the potential benefits to the audience. You can test your specific purpose by making sure that it aims for a specific response from the audience, reflects the realities of the situation, and is clear and ethical.*

Although speakers may hope to accomplish many things in a speech, the **specific purpose** is the ultimate response that the speaker hopes to achieve. Crafting the specific purpose statement carefully is a vital step in clearly focusing the speech.

Purpose and Response

Successful speakers think carefully about the response they desire from their audience and never allow themselves to be vague or unclear about their specific purpose. Imagine, for example, a speaker who said, "My purpose is to talk about energy conservation." Such a statement identifies no specific purpose. It says something vague about the speaker's topic, but it does not specify an audience response. Furthermore, "energy conservation" is so broad that it says little about the speaker's specific goals. With the purpose stated this broadly, the speaker would have had a difficult time choosing what to include and what not to include in the speech. If you want to give an informative speech, you should state specifically what you want your audience to understand. Returning to our example, you might say *I want my audience to understand ways in which each one of them can conserve energy in their daily lives*. If, on the other hand, you wished to give a **persuasive speech**, you might take a specific position on any number of controversies surrounding the best *ways* to conserve energy. You might, for example, state your purpose this way: *I want my audience to agree* *that the government should invest more in the development of solar and wind power.* Or you might decide to address a different controversy: *I want my audience to agree that the best way to end our dependence on fossil fuels is to build more nuclear power plants.* These potential purposes both relate to the topic of energy conservation, yet each represents a different specific purpose.

Purpose and the Situation

The specific purpose of your speech should also be shaped by the demands of the situation. Suppose you wanted to give a speech in class about crime on campus. On a rural or suburban campus, you might decide that your audience is likely unaware of the extent of crime on campus or how it might affect them. In that case, you might decide on this specific purpose: *I want my audience to understand the nature and extent of crime on our campus.* On an urban campus, where students may be more likely to have been victims of crime, a better specific purpose may be this one: *I want my audience to understand how they can reduce their chances of being a victim of crime.* Of course, your civic concerns and responsibilities extend beyond your immediate environment, and so you may on some occasions take a broader perspective on your topic. To return to our example, your specific purpose in that case might be something like this: *I want my audience to understand how "white collar" crime affects us all.* Or perhaps you might decide on this specific purpose: *I want my audience to understand how the state of the economy relates to the nation's crime rate.* Whatever your specific purpose, it should reflect careful consideration of the situation in which you'll speak and your audience.

Purpose and Audience Benefits

In devising a specific purpose, you need to consider how you want listeners to respond and what you have to offer your listeners. The benefits to the audience should be apparent in the speech. Too often speakers ignore this basic principle. A speaker at a large university, for example, addressed a crowd gathered to protest proposed fee increases at the university. The listeners had come because they wanted to know how they could help stop the increases. The speaker, however, delivered a long, angry speech about student apathy and implied that such ignorant, unresponsive people deserved what they got at the hands of an unsympathetic legislature. Clearly, this speaker should have taken a different approach. His audience was already motivated to act, so he might have focused on the actions they could take to put pressure on lawmakers. His tirade about student apathy instead irritated and alienated an audience that was not apathetic at all. In fact, they had been looking forward to an enthusiastic show of unity and determination.

When you go to the grocery store, it helps to have a clear goal: you plan to buy food, and you probably have a list of specific items. You don't go to the store "just to shop." Shopping is a means to an end. In the same way, giving a speech is not just "talking about something." It, too, is a means to an end. When you speak, you want a specific reaction from your audience, and you hope to provide some benefit to them as well. So, instead of "talking about," say, immigration, you should develop a specific purpose that identifies both the response you desire and the benefits for the audience: *I want my audience to agree that a guest worker program remains the best plan for controlling illegal immigration while allowing deserving immigrants a chance to become U.S. citizens.*

Testing Specific Purposes

Because your specific purpose is the foundation of your speech, we have devoted a great deal of space in this chapter to describing how to develop it. Let us consider some quick ways to test the specific purposes you develop. Basically, there are four questions you can ask yourself to determine whether you have a sound specific purpose statement.

A Good Specific Purpose Asks for an Audience Response Does your purpose statement call for a response from the audience? Here are some ideas that are *not* good specific purposes because they suggest no audience response:

- What to do about Darfur, Sudan?
- The humanitarian crisis in Sudan
- Stability in the Sudan
- Our responsibility in Africa

These may be topics or titles, but they do not designate the response you want from the audience. A better specific purpose statement might be *I want my audience to support U.N. intervention to enforce the Comprehensive Peace Agreement for Darfur signed under the auspices of the African Union in 2006.*

A Good Specific Purpose Is Realistic Does your specific purpose reflect the realities of the situation? Among the factors you should consider in crafting a realistic specific purpose are the amount of time you have to give a speech, the probability that your listeners can actually respond the way you want them to, whether the speech's goals have some reasonable expectation of success, and what kind of impact the setting or occasion may have on the outcome of the speech.

Consider the following specific purpose: *I want my audience to understand how Congress works.* This is an absurdly broad topic that could well be the subject of an entire course in political science. What can you accomplish in a short speech? If you are giving an informative speech, you may craft a more focused, achievable purpose in the time available to you, such as *I want my audience to understand how conference committees resolve differences between House and Senate versions of a bill.* If you are giving a persuasive speech, its purpose could be *I want my audience to agree that lobbyists have too much influence over congressional legislation.* Or, to take another example, suppose you were to offer as a specific purpose *I want my audience to agree with me that all federal elections should be publicly funded.* This is a correctly stated specific purpose, but you need to consider whether such a policy is feasible and realistic in the current political climate. The practicality of your purpose is an important consideration. To take another example, if you are going to ask your audience to give 20 hours a week to volunteering for a good cause, you must ask yourself whether full-time students, some of whom already have jobs, could realistically volunteer so much time.

A Good Specific Purpose Is Clear Is your specific purpose clear? An audience can be confused by a speech that grows out of a vague purpose. Communication is almost always unsuccessful when speakers are unclear about what they want to accomplish.

I want my audience to agree with me about health care is not a clear statement of purpose. Although it sounds like a purpose statement, it shows that the speaker does not know precisely *what* he or she wants the audience to believe or do. If you want to persuade your audience to agree about the need for health care reform, you should state your support for a specific health care policy: *I want my audience to support the Obama administration's plan for health care reform.*

A Good Specific Purpose Is Ethical So far, in discussing specific purposes, we have been concerned with issues of response, clarity, and realism. These are all important considerations, but they could all be fulfilled and still the purpose could be unethical.

As we pointed out previously, ethical speakers pursue goals that are in the best interests of their listeners and their society. The following specific purpose, for example, is clearly not ethical: *I want my audience to understand how they can avoid paying taxes by hiding their cash in offshore accounts.* Cheating on your income tax not only is socially irresponsible, it is also illegal. Yet even if something *is* legal, we sometimes still face ethical questions, questions about right and wrong.[8] Suppose a speaker in your class wanted to give a speech with this purpose: *I want my audience to understand how to purchase term papers over the Internet.* You would not be sent to jail for buying your term papers online, but you would be guilty of academic dishonesty. This speaker would be advocating something that violates both the ethical norms and the specific regulations of every college and university in the country. Nor would it be ethical for a speaker to promote a fad diet that is seriously questioned by health professionals and may actually cause harm. Again, to knowingly advocate such a diet would be unethical.

Of course, ethical boundaries are not always clear. Conflicts of interest often occur in public debates over controversial issues. Take, for example, the issue of capping medical malpractice awards. On the one hand, we realize that large malpractice awards raise the cost of insurance for doctors and the cost of health care for everyone. On the other hand, we sympathize with the victim of malpractice who may have lost a limb or even his or her life because of the carelessness of a doctor. What is the ethical position to take in this controversy? Both sides in this controversy can make the case that they are advocating the more ethical policy and that their interests are the same as the public's interest.

Like other aspects of public speaking, our specific purposes often have ethical implications. As speakers, we need to think about who we are, who our listeners are, and what we have to gain or lose. As speakers, we have an ethical obligation to ask how our audience may benefit or be hurt or misled by the information that we are sharing with them or the actions we are urging them to pursue.

CONSTRUCTING A THESIS STATEMENT

Preview. *The thesis statement grows from your specific purpose. It is a clear, declarative statement that embodies the principal idea of your speech. It should be focused without being cluttered with too much detail.*

After you have determined your specific purpose, you need to formulate a declarative statement that sums up the thesis of your speech, sometimes called the central idea or **thesis statement** of the speech. You should think of this as your speech in a nutshell. A well-formulated thesis statement will help you focus your research and plan your speech. If you are successful, the thesis statement is what listeners will carry away with them—what they will remember as the heart of your speech.

Guidelines for Constructing a Thesis Statement

There are three basic guidelines to keep in mind when constructing a thesis statement.

THE THESIS STATEMENT IS A SINGLE, COMPLETE DECLARATIVE SENTENCE THAT EMBODIES THE IDEA THAT YOU WANT THE AUDIENCE TO UNDERSTAND OR ACCEPT IN ORDER TO ACCOMPLISH YOUR SPECIFIC PURPOSE It is important to emphasize that the thesis is a *declarative* sentence—an idea you want to convey to your audience—not a question or a phrase that simply announces the topic. *How can we improve our public schools?* is *not* a good thesis statement. A good thesis would answer that question and specify *how* you propose to improve public schools. For example, your thesis might be *The real key to improving public schools is hiring more qualified teachers.*

The thesis statement grows from your specific purpose. In effect, it answers the question, "What do listeners have to understand or feel or believe or do if I am going to get the response I want?" Consider the following examples of specific purposes and the thesis statements that may grow out of them.

Specific purpose: *I want my audience to understand how one qualifies for unemployment insurance.*

Thesis statement: *Unemployment insurance is available for a limited time period and only for those who meet specific criteria.*

Specific purpose: *I want my audience to agree that the "No Child Left Behind" policy failed to improve American education.*

Thesis statement: *The "No Child Left Behind" policy employed unreliable measures of student progress and teaching effectiveness.*

Specific purpose: *I want my audience to support the administration's plan for a new GI Bill.*

Thesis statement: *The administration's proposed GI Bill will provide service members returning from war with a better chance to afford a college education.*

Specific purpose: *I want my audience to honor the late Dana Reeve's tireless efforts on behalf of individuals suffering from spinal cord injuries.*

Thesis statement: *The late Dana Reeve's work with the Christopher and Dana Reeve Foundation is an inspiration to us all.*

THE THESIS STATEMENT SHOULD BE CLEAR AND SPECIFIC WITHOUT BEING SO DETAILED AS TO INCLUDE ALL YOUR MAIN IDEAS The thesis statement is not a summary of all the main points in a speech. Instead, it should encompass all those ideas in a single thought. Here is an example of a thesis statement for a persuasive speech: *Paying our city employees a living wage is a moral and practical imperative.* Now compare that to a thesis statement that tries to include all the points you hope to make and ends up as a kind of summary of the whole speech. *All city employees deserve a living wage because those who are inadequately compensated are more likely to suffer from stress, develop health problems, live in substandard housing, and have strained relationships that can lead to divorce, neighborhood tensions, and even violence.*

Note also that the thesis statement is *not* a presentation of the specific information you will deliver in your speech. Consider this thesis statement: *A recent survey reported in the* New York Times *revealed that when individuals are inadequately compensated for their work, more than half of them develop problems with depression and low self-esteem.* This is a poor thesis statement because it neglects the driving idea of the speech in favor of providing specific evidence that will be used later in the speech. A better thesis statement would be *Low wages can cause serious psychological damage.*

THE THESIS STATEMENT SHOULD BE FOCUSED AND LIMITED IN SCOPE You want to be sure that you do not try to accomplish too much or too many different things in one speech. If you find yourself including more than one idea in your thesis statement, you are probably trying to do too much in a single speech. Consider, for example, the following thesis statement: *A school voucher system will improve public education and should be coupled with national standardized tests to measure student achievement, as well as with content examinations for teachers.* This statement includes at least three ideas that may be separate speeches. Those separate thesis statements might look like this:

School vouchers will give parents the ability to choose the best schools for their children.
Standardized tests lead to greater accountability in public education.
The school board's plan to require periodic content examinations for teachers will improve the quality of classroom instruction.

Avoiding Common Mistakes

As you develop your own thesis statements, you can avoid the most common mistakes by keeping the following principles in mind. A good thesis statement:

- should *not* be written as a question or a topical phrase
- should *not* be a preview of the speech
- should *not* be too complex and hard to follow
- should *not* present excessively detailed information
- should *not* present too many ideas for a single speech

The *Highlighting the Process* feature that follows reviews and illustrates the process of moving from selecting a topic to devising a thesis statement.

HIGHLIGHTING THE PROCESS

From Topic to Purpose to Thesis

As a way of reviewing the procedure we have been describing, consider the process step by step.

1. *Select possible topics.* Consider the following list of possible topics generated from a self-inventory and through brainstorming public issues.
   - Student financial aid
   - Affordable housing for the working poor
   - Materialism in America
   - Nuclear proliferation
   - U.S. policy toward Iran
2. *Consider situational and audience factors.* Because there had been so many stories in the media lately about nuclear proliferation and the threat of a nuclear war, you decided that would be a timely topic.
3. *Pick your tentative topic.* Lots of possibilities are open to you as you narrow the topic, such as the nuclear proliferation treaty, the dangers of North Korea or Iran getting the bomb, or the threat of terrorists obtaining nuclear weapons. Perhaps you decide that one serious problem does not get the attention that it should: the tension between India and Pakistan, two nuclear powers with a history of mutual hostility. So your tentative topic is the threat of nuclear war between India and Pakistan.
4. *Determine the general purpose.* If your assignment is to give a persuasive speech, you then plan a speech to gain agreement or to support a policy.
5. *Craft a specific purpose statement.* You need to determine exactly what response you want from your audience. After conducting and evaluating an audience survey, you discover that many of your listeners are only mildly aware of the antagonism between India and Pakistan. Because of their lack of awareness, they appear unconcerned about the potential seriousness of the problem. So you develop this specific purpose statement: *I want my audience to agree that the India-Pakistan conflict poses a serious threat to world peace.*
6. *Write a thesis statement.* Your purpose will still be somewhat tentative. You can modify it as you gather and organize material for the speech. However, after you have gone through the process from topic selection to specific purpose to thesis statement carefully and thoughtfully and have a well-crafted purpose statement, you are ready to make a thesis statement. In this case, that thesis statement might be *The conflict between India and Pakistan could result in a nuclear war that would ultimately involve the United States.*

SUMMARY

- Preparing yourself to speak begins with the choice of a topic.
- Doing a self-inventory and/or brainstorming significant public issues when choosing a topic is a helpful first step.
- The next step is to narrow the topic so that it is manageable in the time limit, meets the expectations of the assignment or occasion, and can be made interesting to an audience.
- Because the audience is central to the development of your speech, you will need to pay particular attention to how the topic will reflect the listeners' knowledge and experience.

- In choosing a topic, you also must remember your ethical obligations to be accurate and fair-minded and to exercise good judgment in accommodating the tastes and standards of the audience.
- Speeches aim at getting responses from audiences. The principal kinds of responses that speakers aim for in most cases—in the classroom, in the community, and in professional settings—are the general purposes: informative, persuasive, and ceremonial.
  - The goal of informative speeches is to gain audience understanding.
  - The goal of persuasive speeches is to influence beliefs, opinions, and actions relating to a public controversy.
  - The goal of ceremonial speeches is to reinforce shared values as a vehicle of community building.
- Based on the topic that you have chosen, you will be able to create a specific purpose that states precisely the response you want from your audience in a particular situation. A specific purpose is the foundation on which the thesis statement is built.
- The thesis statement—the guiding idea of the speech that you want your listeners to take away from it—should be carefully crafted to be precise and inclusive without being cluttered with too many details.
- As you go through the process of crafting a specific purpose and thesis, you should be mindful of the effects your ideas will have on the audience. You must consider the ethical implications of what you are trying to do.

QUESTIONS FOR REVIEW AND REFLECTION

1. What are the major things to consider when looking for a speech topic? Give a specific example of how each of these categories may relate to you personally.
2. What are some things you will do to make sure that you are exploring significant topics of public concern? Be specific.
3. Why is focusing and narrowing your topic important?
4. What are some of the ethical considerations involved in selecting a topic?
5. What are the general purposes of public speaking? Define each.
6. What is meant by a specific purpose? Why is it important for every public speaker to have a specific purpose? What are the criteria you ought to use to evaluate your specific purpose?
7. Can a single speech have multiple purposes? Why or why not?
8. What is a thesis statement, and why is it important for a speaker to develop one?
9. Suppose someone decides to give a speech with this specific purpose: *I want my audience to vote to repeal the state law that requires motorcyclists to wear safety helmets.* Using the criteria for evaluating purpose statements discussed in this chapter, is this an effective purpose statement? Why or why not?
10. Following are three thesis statements. Which one is the best and why?
    - *Would you like to do something that is both fun and useful this summer?*
    - *Volunteering to work for Habitat for Humanity this summer will be a rewarding personal experience and will provide a useful public service.*

- *If you volunteer to work for Habitat for Humanity, you will get good physical exercise, learn new skills, meet interesting people, get to work with kids your own age, provide homes for needy and deserving people, and earn the gratitude and respect of the people you help.*

ENDNOTES

1. Researchers in cognitive psychology find that an important element of creativity is to find a task interesting, exciting, or personally challenging. People are more creative when they have this sort of intrinsic motivation. See Mary Ann Collins and Teresa M. Amabile, "Motivation and Creativity," in *Handbook of Creativity*, ed. Robert J. Sternberg (New York: Cambridge University Press, 1999), 297–312.
2. See Richard L. Johannesen, *Ethics in Human Communication*, 5th ed. (Prospect Heights, IL: Waveland Press, 2002).
3. For a special issue devoted to communication ethics, see *Communication Quarterly* 38 (Summer 1990): 208–90.
4. For an account of the functions of ceremonial rhetoric see Celeste Michelle Condit, "The Function of Epideictic: The Boston Massacre Orations as Exemplar," *Communication Quarterly* 33 (1985): 284–98.
5. Raymond Cohen, *Negotiating across Culture: Communication Obstacles in International Diplomacy* (Washington, D.C.: Institute of Peace, 1991).
6. Ronald Reagan, "Tribute to the Challenger Astronauts," January 28, 1986, www.americanrhetoric.com/speeches/rreaganchallenger.htm (accessed May 30, 2009).
7. Barack Obama, "Remarks by the President on Memorial Day," May 25, 2009, www.whitehouse.gov/the_press_office/Remarks-by-the-President-on-Memorial-Day (accessed May 30, 2009).
8. See Kenneth R. Andrews, "Ethics in Practice," *Harvard Business Review* 67 (September–October 1989): 99–109.

CHAPTER

7

Responsible and Productive Research

CHAPTER SURVEY

CHAPTER OBJECTIVES

After studying this chapter, you should be able to

1. Understand the importance of establishing a focus to guide your research.
2. Understand how careful, thoughtful note taking helps you develop insight and draft your speech.

CHAPTER OBJECTIVES (*CONTINUED*)

3. Appreciate the importance of information literacy.
4. Use the World Wide Web more efficiently and productively.
5. Better utilize the library for obtaining materials and assistance.
6. Conduct an interview to gather information.
7. Use e-mail more effectively to gather information.
8. Document your sources accurately and know how and when to cite sources in your speech.

After his 6-year-old son, Adam, was abducted and brutally murdered, John Walsh made it his mission to help other victims of violent crime.[1] He recalls walking into Cornell University's library one morning and saying, "I'm the father of a little boy who was murdered. I don't go to classes here or anything, and I don't have a card, but I was wondering if I could use the library?"[2] They welcomed him and assisted his research. He discovered that more could be done—and done more quickly—to recover a missing racehorse or an automobile than to track down a missing child. Outraged, he became a man on a mission.[3]

When Walsh landed the opportunity to address legislators on Capitol Hill, he did more than recount his family's tragic ordeal; he came equipped with facts and figures. Walsh made a compelling case for "a centralized reporting system" and "a nationwide search system for missing children."[4] Well informed, professional, and articulate, he was someone to be taken seriously.

When the Missing Children Act was finally passed one year later, President Reagan invited Walsh and his wife to the signing ceremony. As he listened to the president commend their work, it dawned on him what they had accomplished—"that a heartbroken couple from Florida with no money and no lobby and no resources and nobody behind them except a bunch of caring, passionate people with no real power had actually helped get a federal bill passed."[5]

The Missing Children Act of 1982 was but the beginning of John Walsh's career as one of America's best known crime fighters. For more than 20 years he has hosted television's *America's Most Wanted*—a program that has, to date, helped reunite hundreds of abducted children with their families and capture more than 1,060 fugitives.[6]

Not only can we be inspired by Walsh's example, his success underscores the importance of informing yourself about your subject if you wish to become an effective advocate. Being knowledgeable allows you to formulate better ideas and have more confidence when you speak. You will also enhance your credibility. As you supply the information that informs your thinking, your audience will find you more believable and trustworthy. They will see that you have met your ethical obligation to be knowledgeable about your topic.

This chapter will help you become well informed. We focus on various possibilities for finding information, including print and electronic media as well as interviewing experts and others who have useful information and experience. First, however, we consider how you can effectively and efficiently conduct your investigation, providing suggestions for taking notes and beginning the construction of your speech. These tips can help make the process more manageable and satisfying. Finally, this chapter discusses the importance of identifying your sources during your presentation and shows you how to do so effectively and properly.

A PRODUCTIVE START

Preview. *You begin building a speech by identifying your purpose in speaking and narrowing your focus. Once you have established your focus, you can quickly survey material to determine its relevance, and you can better formulate the main ideas of your speech.*

As we pointed out in Chapter 6, you begin the process of crafting a speech by formulating a thesis statement—however tentative—to guide your investigation. The thesis at this stage is a **working thesis**, an attempt to articulate the overall idea you are examining. For example, after reading predictions that during a pandemic (such as one that may occur with the H1N1 virus) "50 million Americans who lack any health insurance" would "likely . . . flood hospitals for care, further taxing what will be an overburdened system" and "spreading . . . disease in ways that are completely unpredictable,"[7] Michaela, a pre-med student, decided to explore the matter for a persuasive speech. She crafted the following basic idea (working thesis) to focus her research: *The flaws in our health care system could make a pandemic even more disastrous than it otherwise would be.* Her thesis mirrored her specific purpose—the response she wanted from her listeners: *I want my audience to accept the view that there are flaws in our current health system that would put us all at increased risk during a pandemic.* Michaela would now have a good focus to guide her research.

You may, like Michaela, need some initial investigation to arrive at a purpose and tentative thesis. Some probing may be necessary. For a concise look at how to begin your research, see *Highlighting How to Begin Your Investigation* on page 158.

Finding Relevant Information: A High-Speed Pursuit

Once you have a clear focus, you can proceed quickly. Rather than painstakingly reading every article that has a promising title, skim through them to detect which ones contain relevant information and ideas. If an abstract (a brief summary) is available, use it to determine an article's usefulness. Scan the dropdown menus of a credible Web site and quickly explore (and bookmark) any links that seem on target. Evaluate a potentially relevant book by scanning its table of contents and index, then skimming pages that seem promising. This quick survey will help you locate the most valuable material.

Keep your mind free to focus on what you are skimming. Rather than trying to keep a mental record of which sources are valuable and where you found what information, make quick notes regarding the usefulness of a source. Once you have identified which sources are valuable, you can read them more closely, carefully extracting information and ideas from them.

HIGHLIGHTING HOW TO BEGIN YOUR INVESTIGATION

Your choice of topic will dictate which of the following approaches will work best. Many people may, out of habit, begin with a Web search, but what your library has to offer (accessible from your computer via the Internet) often produces faster, superior results. We especially recommend using your library's reference materials and subscription databases.

- *Visit the reference section of your library.* Various reference materials provide facts, data, and other information about your topic and how it has been discussed recently as well as in the past. Here are a few noteworthy examples of what is available, many in electronic form.
  - *Credo.* This popular database contains more than 400 reference items, many previously available only in print form.[8]
  - *American Decades.* This collection discusses the major issues Americans have grappled with during a particular decade. Because many issues persist (e.g., violence in our public schools), this collection can provide an excellent overview and background information.
  - *Atlas of Contemporary America: Portrait of a Nation.* Maps and text illuminate diversity and other demographics, as well as prevailing attitudes of particular regions in the United States. It also maps/discusses the issues that most affect a region (e.g., water rights).
  - *Contemporary World Issues.* In this series, scholars and nonacademic experts examine international matters of controversy. These book-length works are written for the general public.
  - *Encyclopaedia Britannica.* This award-winning encyclopedia, with peer-reviewed entries by leading authorities, offers excellent background information on historical and contemporary topics and issues. It also provides a list of authoritative works for further reading, making it a good place to launch an investigation.
  - *Facts on File: Issues and Controversies.* This collection offers objective, thorough coverage of the hottest issues of our time. Also consult its counterpart, *World Almanac Reference Database*, for background information and data for historical and contemporary issues and events.
  - *Facts on File: World News Digest.* This compilation provides a week-by-week account of major news events, from 1940 to the present day.
- *Discover what reliable news sources have provided.* Newspapers, newsmagazines, and radio and television news sources often provide background information as well as in-depth reporting. Their archives (often available and searchable on their official Web sites) transport us back in time, providing a good sense of what

THE CREATIVE ENTERPRISE OF BUILDING A SPEECH

Preview. *As you compile material for a speech, you can proceed most productively if you establish a method for gathering, recording, and organizing material. The manner in which you take notes can facilitate the discovery of ideas and aid in the process of constructing your speech.*

From the moment you begin contemplating your topic, you begin formulating ideas for your speech on the basis of what you already know or believe. You begin envisioning the areas you will discuss, material you will include, your purpose and thesis, and how to introduce and conclude your speech. This is not busywork; you have begun the process of preparing the speech and should log these thoughts so that none escape.

happened and how people felt about it. Simply be alert to any bias that may exist, because many news sources have political leanings.[9]

Finding material in newspapers and newsmagazines has never been easier. Several databases index and provide access to major U.S. newspapers, and some also index regional and international newspapers. For example, NewsBank's Access World News provides information and perspectives from more than 600 U.S. and 500 international sources—a mix of newspapers, wire services, and news agencies, with many of the international sources translated into English. Other, similar databases include the following:

ProQuest Newsstand
LexisNexis Academic
InfoTrac Custom Newspapers
National Newspaper Index

- *Explore government publications.* Federal, state, and local agencies collect and report data on every topic imaginable. For example, *The Statistical Abstract of the United States,* published annually since 1878 by the U.S. Census Bureau (in print and online), provides a wealth of information about social, political, and economic conditions. You can learn, for instance, how many households in the United States have one or more computers and whether they have Internet access, and you can compare today's figures with those of previous years. You also can compare your state with other states.
- *See what has been discussed and acted on by policy makers.* Congressional hearings define the policy issue and bring together expert witnesses and other sources of testimony. The *Congressional Universe* database indexes and provides full text of these discussions as well as relevant documents, such as regulations. It also will keep you apprised of the status of a particular bill. You can obtain similar information from *CQ Researcher,* which provides in-depth reports and commentary on the major issues of the day, including various viewpoints. Its publisher, *Congressional Quarterly, Inc.* (www.cq.com/), offers numerous other publications and services that summarize and analyze any bill being considered, and you can even have daily updates e-mailed to you.
- *Consult an opinion series.* Books within these series address contemporary issues. Public and academic libraries likely subscribe to one or more series, such as *Opposing Viewpoints, Current Controversies,* or *At Issue.*
- *Search a subscription database for relevant articles.* For how to do so, see *Highlighting Databases as a Research Tool* on page 172.
- *Conduct an online search for credible Web sites.* Use the strategies and resources we discuss in this chapter for a fruitful, efficient search.

As you investigate, you gather information and ideas from a variety of sources and arrive at new insights of your own. Your speech will consist of each of these elements arranged into a coherent form and made more understandable and appealing through good oral style. Your mind will operate on all these levels as you sift through material and record thoughts and information that ultimately may or may not make it into the final draft of your speech.

While researching your topic, record more than information. You also need to note the idea the information suggests and contemplate where it should appear in your speech. Jot down other thoughts that come to you—possible sources to consult, modifications needed for your thesis, the design of a presentational aid, and so forth.

This process of preparation is crucial. The quality of a speech is directly related to the quality of critical and creative thought that goes into its preparation.

Once you have determined the best sources, take notes methodically to save time and maximize productivity.

The Creative Process

Creative thought cannot be rushed; an early start is essential. Once you have a topic in mind, you will notice anything that is relevant, and these various stimuli will help you formulate ideas for your speech.[10] You will also have time for *reflection*—time to evaluate information, to test ideas, and to begin making sense of all you have found.[11]

If you are like most people, you will have good days when everything seems to make sense and fall into place, and days when you struggle to get anywhere.[12] When your thinking is "stuck," you probably need a "time out."[13] Once you are no longer fixated on the problem, your mind can operate quietly in the background, making associations and generating new ideas.[14] An early start allows time for these breaks.

A break can be time well spent. When you return to the task you may experience a rush of ideas and a new, improved understanding of the subject and your goals for the speech. You do not have to be "on task" for these ideas to emerge. As cognitive psychologists explain, "The classic example of coming up with great ideas while taking a shower may simply reflect the importance of releasing oneself from fixated retrieval processes."[15] When these inspirations appear, jot them down as soon as possible to prevent them from escaping. Your energy can then be directed elsewhere, allowing your mind to continue working creatively.[16]

Along with quiet time, you may also benefit from some intensive thinking. For example, you might write down whatever pops into your head without stopping to analyze or critique it. Afterward, you will have something to review and evaluate.[17] You might try a particular brainstorming technique, such as mind mapping (see Figure 7.1) or concept mapping.[18] Both of these formalized techniques advocate the use of keywords and phrases and hand-drawn pictures

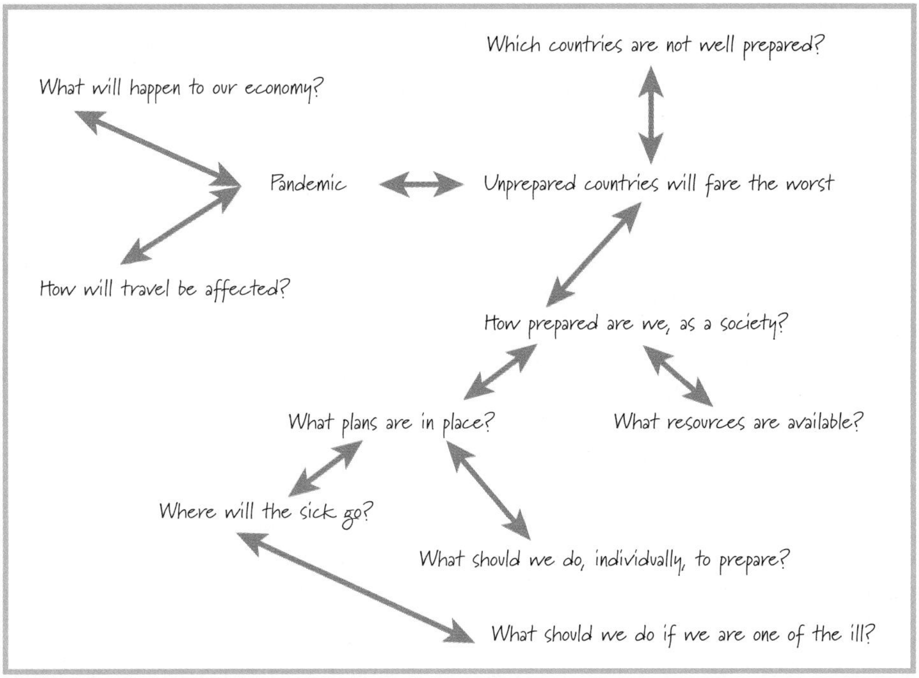

FIGURE 7.1 Mind mapping your thoughts can fuel creativity and assist organization. As with any brainstorming activity, some items will be discarded as you make your way forward.

to capture thoughts and discern relationships. Like other brainstorming strategies, these techniques have specific benefits:

- allowing speedy recording for less restricted flow of thought
- promoting free association (rather than any restrictions a sentence may impose)
- stimulating recall of related information, such as previous learning or experiences
- generating new ideas and perspectives
- promoting understanding of relationships
- assisting organization via grouping/classifying
- unleashing creativity, especially for visual learners

In addition to capturing thoughts on paper, try thinking aloud, perhaps with a friend. You may surprise yourself with the ideas that roll off your tongue[19] and you may also receive valuable feedback from your listener. As with other inspirations, record these immediately!

Along with allowing time for your creative processes to work, you also need time for *incorporation*. Incorporation involves deciding if and where specific information and ideas belong in the speech. You will make these evaluations as you search for materials and continue to fine-tune the focus of your speech.

Productive Note Taking: Drafting as You Investigate Your Topic

To take notes productively, you'll want to keep track of where you got what information as well as how it contributes to your speech. To maximize efficiency and avoid frustration, devise a format for recording source information and for taking notes, and stick to it.

For source information: The format should allow you to find, at a glance, whatever you are looking for—whether it is the page number for a quotation, the title of an article, or the publication date. Keeping good records allows you to cite your sources properly and to save time while taking notes.

- If you are using a library subscription database, use its built-in citation feature to create a bibliography. Once you know you are going to use an article or other item, take a few seconds to grab the already formatted bibliographic entry and paste it into a Works Cited page.
- For nondatabase sources, record source information correctly, using the style guide (*MLA*, *APA*, or *The Chicago Manual of Style*) your instructor has approved for your formal bibliography.
- Record source information completely. Avoid having to retrace your steps to acquire missing information!
- Assign each source a code. The code can be the author's last name (or the last name of the first author listed). Coding each source saves you from having to repeat a full-blown bibliographic entry for each note you make from that source (see Figure 7.2). If you are typing your bibliography as you go, simply type the code you assign in bold at the front of each entry. You can delete the codes later when finalizing your formal bibliography.

For taking notes: A variety of approaches, used alone or in combination, can serve you well.[20] You may enter notes electronically with a computer (perhaps even using a program such as Microsoft's OneNote), by hand on note cards or a pad, or in the margins of material you've printed or photocopied. In any case, you'll want to be able to easily navigate your notes and rearrange them as needed. In addition, you'll want to process material as you go, contemplating how it fits into your speech. Doing so will help spark your creativity.[21]

- Limit each entry to a single idea and the information on which that idea is based (see Figure 7.3). By confining each note to one idea and its basis, you will be able to arrange and rearrange entries and—as a result—easily organize your speech. Entries with more than one idea and bit of information would undermine your ability to arrange and organize.

  If you are typing your notes, restrict each entry to a third of a page to ensure that entries are properly focused—limited to examining a single idea. If you're writing notes by hand, use 4 × 6 index cards or half sheets of paper. If you're writing in the margins of a copy or printout, you'll want to keep a running inventory of those ideas, placed perhaps into a **working outline**—a rough sketch of your speech in progress (see Chapter 10).

FIGURE 7.2
Sample Source Entry
Record source information carefully and completely to avoid backtracking later.

Walsh, B. "How to Prepare for a Pandemic." *Time*, May 18, 2009, 30–33.

[Idea] Numerous uninsured = bigger outbreak

"But truly preparing the country for a pandemic means tackling the basic flaws at the heart of the health care system—starting with the some 50 million . . . who lack any health insurance. They're more likely to flood hospitals for care during a pandemic, further taxing what will be an overburdened system. . . . '[Like] the Typhoid Marys of the last century . . . they'll be spreading this disease in ways that are completely unpredictable.'" [Quoted material]

[Source] Walsh, B., p. 33

FIGURE 7.3
Sample Note Card (Coordinated with the Sample Source Entry)
Think about what you're recording in terms of what it means and where it belongs in your speech.

- Coordinate your notes with your source entries to save time. As noted earlier, the codes you have assigned each source will eliminate what would amount to busywork because they save you from writing comprehensive source information over and over again for each new note from a source. A glance at the code tells you where you got what. (See Figures 7.2 and 7.3 to see an example of a note entry coordinated with a source entry.)
- Format consistently. Whether you're typing entries or writing by hand, use the same format. Record information in what would be the center of an index card, *placing quotation marks around any material you record word for word from the source.* Place the code you have assigned the source and the specific page number or numbers (if it is printed material) in parentheses in a bottom corner. Enter the idea suggested by the information as a heading in the upper right (or left) corner. For notes entered on a printout or photocopy, coordinate entries with a working outline.
- Create a meaningful heading. The heading is more than a descriptor; it should relate the information to the goals of your speech. Rather than write something vague like "health care system," for example, one might enter "numerous uninsured = bigger outbreak," to capture the essence of the information. Obviously, you have some sense of why the information is valuable. Force yourself to write it down, even if you believe that it will be obvious later. Use a concise phrase to articulate the idea suggested by the information. You may often enter the information before writing the idea because you may not have fully determined the meaning and the best wording. Before moving on, though, articulate the idea, even if it is only an approximation. You can revise it later. The point is

that you will want to think about the meaning and relevance of all the information you encounter, especially in terms of how it contributes to your speech.

Think of how inefficient it would be to operate otherwise. Rather than mindlessly taking notes and letting them accumulate into a large collection that you will have to sort through later, make sense of material as you go. Group the entries into categories, noting the areas that emerge. The ideas entered in the headings of your notes may become subpoints in your speech, which you can go ahead and plug into a working outline.

- Make note of your own, original thoughts in similar fashion, so that you can easily find and use them. You might jot down an idea for the introduction, for instance, or the basis for a good, illustrative example or analogy.

As you group and arrange the entries in your notes, create a rough sketch—a working outline—of your speech. Watch it grow and evolve as you continue to sort through your notes and arrange them, reflecting on whether the material belongs in the speech, where it belongs, and its implication for your overall idea—the thesis. You can begin this process at any point during your research, perhaps tackling one area of the speech at a time. For example, you might write about a problem before researching possible solutions.

Once you have created a rough outline, you will be able to evaluate what you have produced—retaining the good, modifying what needs to be rewritten, deleting faulty or extraneous material, and conducting any additional research that may be needed. This activity, called *revision*, is not an "autopsy";[22] it does not merely occur after you have a complete first draft of your speech. Instead it occurs anytime you reassess what you have done, whether it is a word or a sentence or a title. No set formula exists for when and how often revision should occur, but it must occur from time to time throughout the drafting process if you expect to produce a quality message.

The key to good preparation is working through multiple drafts—something professional speechwriters recognize and do. For example, Peggy Noonan—one of President Reagan's speechwriters—would only begin to get comfortable with her progress "on about the fourth draft."[23] Noonan writes, "I'd see that I'd written three or four sentences I liked, and that would relax me . . . [and I'd think] 'there's something of worth here!' "[24] Other presidential speechwriters report similar experiences. Ray Price, one of President Nixon's speechwriters, recalls that, on average, major presidential addresses went through "14 drafts."[25] Nothing has changed; President George W. Bush's 2006 State of the Union Address reportedly went through about "two dozen drafts."[26]

President Obama also recognizes the need for careful revision and multiple drafts. In 2004 he "spent months writing the convention speech that would catapult him onto the national stage."[27] In office, he prefers ample lead time for every speech—time to gather and refine his thoughts. According to *Time*, President Obama does some of his "best writing . . . late at night when he's all alone, scribbling on yellow legal pads. He then logs these thoughts into his laptop, editing as he goes along."[28] At other times he thinks aloud, running his thoughts by his small team of advisers and writers. At some point he involves them in the writing—exchanging a series of drafts but "exercising the final say."[29]

Whether you are a professional or a novice, the process is the same. As you contemplate your speech, there is a constant flow between information and ideas

Revision is an important part of the writing process and can occur at any time.

as you check them against each other.[30] Your investigation tests the tentative thesis you have constructed; you will refine your thesis (and main points) in light of what your investigation reveals. You develop and revise your speech as you evaluate content and arrangement, detect and repair weaknesses, recognize the need for more material, and try out the best phrasing for an idea. Preparing a speech, like any complex creative process, involves intense, multidimensional cognitive activity.[31]

Quintilian, an early teacher of speech, emphasized the importance of revision. Quintilian noted that "correction takes the form of addition, excision, and alteration" and that "erasure" is "as important a function of the pen as actual writing."[32] In other words, one has to learn to be critical of one's own work. Critical thinking is essential for evaluating your own work, and it is also essential as you gather materials, a topic to which we now turn.

SEARCHING THE WORLD WIDE WEB

Preview. *Computer applications have simplified the storage and exchange of information. The World Wide Web has become easier to navigate, but the questionable quality of much of what is posted online requires caution. Experts offer guidance for determining the quality of information encountered.*

Most of us take "the Web" for granted, but it is quite a phenomenon when you stop and think about it. Since it came on the scene around the early 1990s, the World Wide Web has grown exponentially and beyond textual form to images, sound, and video.[33] It increasingly influences the way we conduct business and make decisions—personal and political.

Locating Information

Easy-to-use browsing software (such as Firefox and Internet Explorer) and highly refined search technologies allow us to find information on the Web with relative ease. Continued innovations will make searches even simpler.[34]

To locate information, you can proceed in various ways:

- *Keyword search.* Choose any popular search engine (e.g., Google, Yahoo, or Bing) and search by keyword(s), much as you do with a database. (Consult each engine's directions for specific guidance.) Vary the keywords, proceeding through trial and error to determine which word or words yield the best results. For example, launching Google with "smoking and children" will produce results that are too broad if you want to find out how exposure to tobacco smoke affects children differently from adults. "Smoking and children and health" will yield better results; the returns will be more precise and more manageable in number. You may also try an "advanced" search, if the engine offers one.

  Be aware that each search engine uses different criteria for a search and will, as a result, generate a unique list. If you do not find what you want with one engine, try another one. Or try a metasearch engine—such as Dogpile or Mamma—which launches several engines for the search (see Table 7.1).
- *Subject directory.* In some instances you may find it more effective to explore by subject heading. Most search engine sites offer this alternative, providing shortcuts to information sites for various common subjects. For example, Yahoo! News provides direct links to major media outlets. The News option is searchable, and it is also subdivided into categories such as science, technology, health, and politics. A subject directory can also help you establish a focus. If you are interested in alternative energy but are not sure what alternatives exist, a subject directory will provide an inventory and general information about each. You will also discover the key terms to use for a productive search.
- *Traveling direct.* Most Web addresses (*uniform resource locators*, or *URLs*) are kept simple so users can recall an address or easily guess it. The Environmental Protection Agency's site, for example, is at www.epa.gov/. The Web site of the Sierra Club, an environmental group, is at www.sierraclub.org/. To guess more accurately, be aware that the last three

TABLE 7.1

Popular Search Engines

altavista.com	ask.com	bing.com	lycos.com
excite.com	google.com	yahoo.com	alltheweb.com

Popular Metasearch Engines

dogpile.com	metacrawler.com	search.com	mamma.com

letters designate the organization's kind of Internet membership. The most common extensions are as follows:

- .com (commercial companies)
- .edu (educational institutions)
- .gov (government agencies)
- .org (nonprofit organizations)

Regardless of how you get there, when you find a good site, save its URL so you can return directly to it and have the information you need to cite it in your formal bibliography. To determine whether the site *is* a good one requires careful scrutiny, a matter we will now take up.

Evaluating Internet Resources

The Internet can be described as an endless expanse of "unorganized fragments" that are added to daily by "a myriad of cranks, sages, and persons with time on their hands who launch their unfiltered messages into cyberspace."[35] Anyone who has spent any time on the Web recognizes the truth in these words and knows not to take everything found on the Web at face value. Five critical questions can help us evaluate information on the Web.

1. *What is the source of this information?* You would certainly dismiss a story from a supermarket tabloid that told you aliens had landed in Arizona. Although we may readily spot a tabloid as a sensational source, the Web presents a challenge because we do not have as clear an understanding of the source. The extensions offer some insight. As we've noted, sites ending in .edu indicate an educational institution as sponsor, and .gov is government sponsored. Sites ending in .org are usually sponsored by nonprofit organizations, many of them advocacy groups. Sites with .com usually are trying to market goods or services.

   For many sites we have to look beneath the surface to determine authorship. If a group sponsors the page, what do you know about it? Do not be fooled by the name. For example, in the summer of 2000 a group calling itself Citizens for Better Medicare posted "information" on the Web. Their name suggested an admirable goal, but the Web page did not disclose that the group had been formed by the drug industry to lobby against the Clinton administration's proposal to provide drug coverage for the elderly.[36] Conducting an online search of the name of the group may help you determine who they are, or the browser's View menu may have an option to identify an opened page's sponsor.
2. *What is the purpose of the page?* Some Web pages are designed to give information; others advocate certain policies or causes. It is not always easy to tell the difference because advocacy groups frequently try to give the impression that they are just giving you the facts. The purpose of the page is sometimes given as a mission statement or a "Who We Are" or "About Us" link. When considering information provided by an advocacy group, remain aware of the source's agenda and use that information accordingly—checking other sources to verify accuracy. Information on sites sponsored by companies should also be investigated. If advertisements appear on the site, you can suspect that the content may be influenced.

3. *How balanced and accurate is the content?* Careful study of a Web page can illuminate bias. Are a variety of viewpoints acknowledged? Are the claims supported by good arguments and credible evidence? Are credible sources cited? What about the links to other pages—does this page send you to other sites that are credible? Is there any information presented that you know to be inaccurate or misleading? How does the information or claims hold up when considered against what you have learned from reputable sources?

   In short, judge a Web site the same way you would evaluate any attempt to persuade you to do or believe anything. In the chapters that follow, we will be specific about what makes a sound argument, how to detect fallacies, and what kind of evidence is both effective and ethical. You will want to apply all these tests to material you find on the Web. But for now, at least ask yourself if the content that is presented seems fair, if it is convincing to you, and why you find it so.
4. *How current is the site?* Check to see how recently the site was updated. Regular updating indicates that the site is still active. A page that has been left unchanged for a long time should be viewed with suspicion. If a site *is* maintained regularly, the information is more likely to be up-to-date, though one can never be certain what, specifically, has been updated.
5. *When was the site created?* The creation date lets you know the site has been around a while as opposed to having been newly erected. A longer history may suggest some integrity.

If you cannot answer most of these questions after close inspection of the site, that in itself should raise doubts in your mind about the site's credibility. Be skeptical of a source that does not identify itself or its purpose, that makes unsubstantiated claims, or that is out-of-date.

The thing to remember is that the Internet is not a one-stop research source. Information should be cross-checked with other sources. By all means, use the Internet in your research, but do not use it thoughtlessly and do not use it exclusively. Purdue University's Online Writing Lab provides a good summary of the attitude you should take toward Internet research: "Internet sources can be very timely and very useful, but they should not be your sole source of information."[37]

As authors, we certainly follow this advice. As the endnotes to our chapters reveal, we often have used the Web during our quest for information. We have spent most of our time, though, using library resources. Once you get a taste of what the library has to offer, chances are you, too, will see the wisdom of consulting its experts and using its vast array of easily navigated, high-quality materials, perhaps even beginning your search there.

INVESTIGATING LIKE A PROFESSIONAL: USING LIBRARY RESOURCES

Preview. *Knowing how to find and evaluate relevant information has become increasingly important in our personal, professional, and public lives. At your college or public library, you can get instruction and assistance to acquaint you with the best research tools and to help develop your skills in gathering and evaluating information.*

Information Literacy

Among the most important skills we can learn as citizens in a democracy are those associated with locating and gathering reliable information. The same skills we use to research a speech topic will serve us well throughout college, in our careers, and in our role as informed, active citizens. These skills, termed **information literacy**, involve developing the ability to "recognize when information is needed" and to "locate, evaluate, and use effectively the needed information."[38] These abilities have become increasingly important in the information age; we are bombarded with information in "unfiltered formats," making it necessary that we ascertain its "authenticity, validity, and reliability."[39] As the Association of College and Research Libraries has noted, "the uncertain quality and expanding quantity of information pose large challenges for society. The sheer abundance of information will not in itself create a more informed citizenry without a complementary cluster of abilities necessary to use the information effectively."[40]

Let us examine more closely the skills that make up information literacy.

- *Finding information* means knowing where to look for good information.
- Reference sources with peer-reviewed entries by recognized authorities, such as *Encyclopaedia Britannica*, are more trusted than **Wikipedia**, which allows anyone to author or alter an entry.[41]
- Periodicals also vary in type and quality. Cornell University Library provides an excellent overview, distinguishing between scholarly, substantive news, popular, and sensational periodicals.[42]
  - *Scholarly.* This type of periodical reports original research or experimentation by scholars or researchers respected within a particular scholarly community. Authors carefully and properly document all sources. (e.g., *Public Opinion Quarterly; Rhetoric & Public Affairs*)
  - *Substantive news.* In this type of periodical the author's expertise varies, as does the degree to which sources are cited. Articles are written for an "educated audience" of "concerned citizens."[43] (e.g., *Newsweek; The Los Angeles Times*)
  - *Popular.* Articles in this type of periodical are written by staff members or freelance authors, providing "generally little depth" and "rarely, if ever" citing sources. Their principal purpose is "to entertain the reader, to sell products . . . and/or to promote a viewpoint."[44] (e.g., *People; Good Housekeeping*)
  - *Sensational.* Written with simple language and "flashy headlines," this type of publication is "designed to astonish." Its main purpose "seems to be to arouse curiosity and to cater to popular superstitions," assuming "a certain gullibility in their audience."[45] (e.g., *The National Enquirer; The Star*)

  As you may surmise, scholarly sources are generally trustworthy, whereas substantive news sources vary in quality. Popular sources should be scrutinized especially carefully. As for the sensational, need we even say?
- *Government documents and publications* are highly trusted sources. Topics range from *aquaculture* to *zero tillage.* The publications present census data and other statistical information. States, counties, and some cities also create documents, as do foreign governments and international bodies. These items

are now often available online. You'll find the following sites well organized and well maintained.

- *USA.gov* (www.usa.gov/). This site provides links to federal offices and agencies, as well as a number of federally funded entities. It also provides a link to each state or territory's home page.
- *State and local government on the Net* (www.statelocalgov.net/). As the name suggests, you will find links to each state or territory's official pages, as well as to county and city pages. If a town has a Web site, you will be able to find it here.
- *C-SPAN* (www.c-span.org/). You have likely watched the Cable-Satellite Public Affairs Network at some point and know of its mission to provide unfiltered access to legislative activity and various civic meetings and events. Its Web site provides links to governmental and nongovernmental sites, including blogs.

■ *Evaluating information* entails assessing the credibility of a source and the information it offers so you will not be misled or mislead others. Penn State's Libraries advise us to consider the following factors (which we have adapted).[46]

- *Currency.* Does the date of publication meet your needs? Examine a book's copyright page, a periodical's publication date, or the date a Web page was created and/or updated.
- *Authority.* Is the author an expert? Printed works, especially journals and books, provide an author's note that reveals the author's expertise and also commonly lists other works the author has written. Also consult biographical reference sources, such as *Contemporary Authors.* For Web sites, determine who has posted the pages and what the person or group's motivation may be. Also check to see whether it lists experts or professional organizations that endorse the site.
- *Validity/accuracy.* Is evidence provided for claims? Are sources cited? Is the information consistent with that provided by other sources? If the information is dated, is it still accurate?
- *Audience.* Who is the intended audience? Experts? The general public? Is the level of the content and wording appropriate for you and your needs?
- *Point of view (bias).* In light of what you know from other sources, is the information balanced or one-sided? Does it promote a particular viewpoint or seem to have an agenda? Does it acknowledge other viewpoints and represent them fairly? If any sponsor or sponsors are indicated, would they favor a particular view? One sure sign of potential bias or an agenda is advertising. Does the source feature ads for products or services or for a particular social or political cause?

■ *Properly using information.* Information literacy also requires one to use information responsibly. Guidelines for proper use include the following:

- Integrate information from a variety of sources.
- Acknowledge any biases or agenda a source may have.
- Cite sources properly and accurately within a speech and in a bibliography.
- Quote or paraphrase accurately.
- Respect others' intellectual property adhering to all guidelines pertaining to copyrighted material and fair use.

Developing and exercising these abilities for finding, evaluating, and properly using information will serve you well. The same skills that employers find attractive will set you up for lifelong learning and active citizenship. You can begin developing these skills and reaping the rewards in your speech class.

Virtual and Actual Visits to the Library

The college environment provides ample opportunities for developing information literacy. In addition to instruction in classes, professional librarians offer support. Skilled librarians can also be found in many of our public libraries and may offer training in information literacy for the general public.

Once we understand who librarians are, we can begin to understand their value. Professional librarians are schooled in the latest information and communication technologies, and they use this knowledge and skill daily. They are adept at locating and retrieving information and also work cooperatively with other librarians in the academic, public, and private sectors to classify and organize information so that it is well managed and easily retrieved. Citizens, government officials, manufacturers, researchers, and others rely on librarians and their work.[47]

You, too, can benefit from a librarian's expertise. A library's staff of professionals can help you locate and retrieve current, reliable information about your topic. They offer this assistance in person, of course, but they also provide much help online. You will be well served by the combination.

We disadvantage ourselves when we ignore the assistance that librarians can provide. Given the abundance of information available on the Web, many people may think searching via Google or another popular search engine is the best way to locate and gather information for a speech or other assignment. In fact, *Newsweek* reports that "71% of middle and high school students use the Internet as their number one research venue."[48] According to the Online Computer Library Center (OCLC) this trend continues into college.[49] Certainly, a Web search can prove fruitful (as discussed earlier), but a library's online resources can produce superior and even quicker results.

Each library, of course, will vary in terms of its resources and services. Spend a few minutes perusing your library's home page to see what is available. Even though libraries differ, certain features will be pretty much constant.

- *Subscription databases*. Your school's library likely subscribes to several **databases** (e.g., ProQuest Research Library; Wilson OmniFile; EBSCOhost Academic Search Premier)—immense, searchable collections of indexes, abstracts, and full-text materials. Your status as a student allows you access, and you will certainly want to harness their power. As the American Library Association notes, "database searching has become a central tool in modern research."[50] The popularity of databases is understandable in light of the advantages they offer in terms of variety, timeliness, and efficiency.
  - *Variety*. Databases index and include a variety of materials, allowing you to cast a wide net. Some index articles from newspapers and newsmagazines as well as scholarly journals, government documents, chapters in books, and broadcast news and commentary.

HIGHLIGHTING DATABASES AS A RESEARCH TOOL

Most academic and public libraries feature **subscription databases**—often your best and most efficient means of obtaining quality information. These pointers will assist you in your use of library databases.

1. *Determine the best search term(s).* Finding the right search terms made quite a difference when researching television's effects on the cognitive development of very young children. While searching EBSCOhost's Academic Search Premier (similar to its Academic Search Complete or Academic Search Elite), we entered "television" and "children," which yielded more than 6,200 entries, with most not on target. When we conducted the search using "television" and "toddlers," we got 59 entries, with nearly every one containing precisely the information we were seeking.

   Trickier searches include those for which the search terms may not be as obvious. For example, if you wished to research the social benefits of youth involvement in team sports, you would probably have to experiment with various keywords. Once a promising title appears, launch the search again using the search terms under which the item was indexed, or—if available—choose the option to "find other, similar items."
2. *Determine the best database.* Read the database description to see what material it indexes and search the ones most relevant (e.g., EBSCOhost's Health Source Plus: Consumer Edition, if researching the issue of vaccines for the human papillomavirus). If the results are lacking in one database, search another. You can search multiple databases at the same time, though doing so may or may not prove productive. One risk is that you will have too many entries to wade through. It may prove more effective to launch one database at a time, until you find one or two that produce the best results.
3. *Ask an expert.* If you experience problems using a database, visit the library in person and ask a librarian to assist you. Librarians are usually found at the reference desk during regular business hours. They may also be able to assist you through an online chat, instant messaging, or e-mail. Check to see what your library offers.
4. *Select the best full-text option.* If you wish to print out an article and can choose between HTML and PDF, choose PDF. It will provide the most comprehensive printing—including all tables and charts. HTML may also contain typographical errors and other mistakes. In addition, PDF will preserve the original pagination, allowing you to cite your sources more easily.
   - *Catalogs.* A library offers a wide variety of resources, including periodicals, books, and films. The library's online catalog simplifies finding materials, allowing users to search by subject, author, title, or keyword. The catalog will also indicate whether an item is available or on loan. Once you discover a relevant item, the catalog likely will allow you to search for similar items. For instance, you may be able to find books on the same subject as a book you have found by clicking on its call number. The catalog may also feature integrated shelving, allowing you to locate relevant items across media—books, films, government documents, reference books, and other holdings.
   - *Access to other libraries' collections.* If your library has little available for a particular topic, it will still be able to help. Your library provides a gateway to other libraries' catalogs, allowing you to search their collections and easily request an interlibrary loan (especially because many libraries now belong to a consortium of libraries with regular courier service among the members). Your library is also most

likely a member of the OCLC, a group of more than 53,000 libraries from around the world that cooperatively produce and maintain **WorldCat**, a supercatalog available online. WorldCat will help you discover what relevant items exist, sometimes providing an abstract or full text.

- *Assistance searching the World Wide Web.* A library may also provide links to trusted sites on the Web, such as the Internet Public Library (www.ipl.org/), a well-organized, well-maintained directory that indexes thousands of popular and important issues. At the Internet Public Library, experts evaluate Web content and provide links only to sites they deem reliable and trustworthy, saving you from having to wade through lots of questionable sites while searching for information.[51] In addition to the Internet Public Library, librarians also recommend http://www.libraryspot.com/, which provides links to expert-approved reference and library sites on a variety of subjects.
- *Assistance evaluating Web resources.* Libraries often provide pointers for evaluating sources and content found on the World Wide Web (akin to what we provide in this chapter). For example, the Cornell University library provides excellent pointers for evaluating Web content and searching the Web.[52]
- *Reference materials.* The library's site likely provides online access to reference materials, such as almanacs, encyclopedias, yearbooks, and dictionaries.
- *Customized assistance.* Libraries often provide online research guides (also called subject guides), customized for certain disciplines or classes. These, such as the one featured in Figure 7.4 (for public speaking), can greatly assist your research.
- *Personal assistance.* Many libraries allow patrons to e-mail a question to a librarian or to instant-message or chat with a librarian. They may also post the phone number for the reference desk—the area of the library staffed by librarians.

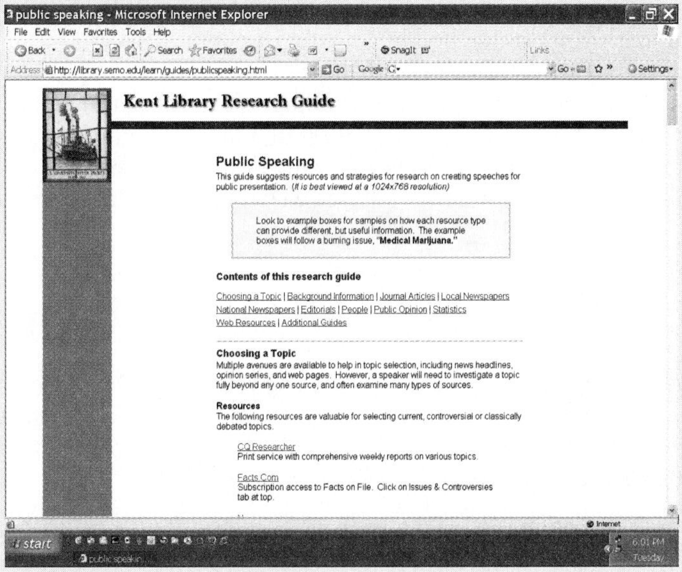

FIGURE 7.4
Research guides, such as this one at Southeast Missouri State University, can help you investigate your topic.

- *Timeliness.* Databases are updated frequently, indexing and providing access to materials recently produced. For example, EBSCOhost and LexisNexis update their database collections continually, as do many other database companies that index and/or provide full-text articles from newspapers and other news sources.
- *Efficiency.* Databases are an efficient way to find relevant articles and other materials. An electronic database allows you to search a span of ten years or more, simultaneously, in multiple indexes, and you can combine two or more keywords to focus the search. Each database will differ in its search procedures. Consult its tips for searching so you can obtain the best results.

Visiting your library in person can also prove beneficial. You can more quickly develop your proficiency at locating and gathering quality information, and you will have access to some materials not available online. Get to know your library's layout and resources. Take a guided tour if one is offered. Knowing what is available and where it is located will allow you to be more efficient and productive. You will spend less time asking questions and more time on research.

When you do have questions, though, librarians can help. They can help you select and use the appropriate index or database for your search for articles, editorials, and other publications or transcripts. Once they understand the type of information you need, they can recommend appropriate resources and help you learn how to use them.

Being at the library also allows you to search its collections thoroughly. Once you have found an item in the catalog that seems relevant, scout the stacks. For example, if you discover a book, scan the spines of neighboring books for titles that seem promising. Even if the book is on loan, you may wish to visit its location on the shelves to scout the area. You may also try a traditional method for locating relevant books—searching by Library of Congress (LC) subject headings. These foot searches can often turn up books that otherwise may be overlooked. A librarian can teach you this method in a matter of minutes.

Your research may take you to more than one library. Some campuses, especially large universities, have specialized libraries for particular disciplines (e.g., journalism) or special collections (e.g., the papers of a famous politician). Remember your local public library, too. It likely has many of the same databases and reference materials that academic libraries offer, as well as librarians to assist you.

GATHERING INFORMATION THROUGH INTERVIEWS

Preview. *Interviewing can provide valuable information for your speech. Determine whether people with expert knowledge or direct experience are available to help you. Prepare carefully by gathering the background information you need and generating good questions. Conduct the interview professionally and efficiently, and follow up appropriately.*

Interviewing for information can yield numerous benefits. Interviews can furnish information and a perspective that otherwise could be lacking—especially for local concerns. In addition to providing valuable information, an interview can lead you to additional resources. The person you interview may provide or suggest other sources of information, perhaps handing you a pamphlet or referring you to an article or Web site. The interviewee may also be able to critique your ideas or your working bibliography, commenting on the quality or credibility of the sources you have consulted and identifying essential sources that are missing. The person may also help you establish a focus for the speech—discussing, for example, an angle you had not considered.

A variety of people can provide valuable information and insights. Once you determine what you need to know, you can determine whom to consult. If you need to know about the history, latest developments, or technical issues related to your topic, you may want to interview an expert. Also consider laypeople who have direct experience with your topic and can recount real-life experiences. They help put a human face on a problem or illustrate the connection to the local community. For many topics you would benefit from interviewing experts *and* laypeople.

Megan knew her speech would benefit from both expert and lay opinions. After reading a *Newsweek* cover story, "The Meth Epidemic," she decided to investigate the problem in her community and propose some solutions. *Newsweek* reported methamphetamine to be a "highly addictive stimulant" that often went undetected until users were hooked.[53] The report rang true for Megan; she had witnessed this firsthand. The husband of one of her best friends had become unpredictable and undependable. The once self-assured young professional grew nervous and made less and less sense when he talked. He had lost weight, had no appetite, and paid scant attention to his wife or their two daughters. He refused his wife's pleas to see a physician. It was only after his business folded and he defaulted on their home loan that she learned he had been using methamphetamine.

Megan wondered how we might detect meth use and what sort of intervention might be best. Her focus suggested assistance from experts, particularly a counselor who helped people overcome addictions and a professor from the criminal justice program on her campus (a member of a local drug task force) who could explain clues that signaled use of methamphetamine. Interviewing these local experts would give her speech greater meaning and authenticity than relying on media reports alone.

To derive the greatest benefit, you will want to prepare for an interview carefully, conduct it efficiently, and report it accurately.

Preparing the Interview

- Determine what you need to know or confirm. What is missing from existing reports/coverage? What needs further confirmation? Generate a set of specific questions that get at your curiosities.
- Determine who might supply the answers—experts? Laypeople? A combination?
- Contact the person to schedule a meeting. Briefly explain how you believe he or she may be able to help you. If the person feels unable to assist, she or he may suggest someone who can.
- Once you have scheduled a time to meet, you might request a fax number or e-mail address so you can provide a brief set of questions in advance so the person can consider his or her responses before talking with you.

- Fine-tune your questions as follows:
    - Keep questions simple and to the point, as well as few in number.
    - Ask a combination of closed and open questions. **Closed questions** ask for a simple yes or no response, whereas **open questions** ask the interviewee to express and explain a belief or opinion.
    - Let the person you are interviewing see that you have done your homework and are sincere and thoughtful in your approach to the topic.
    - Feel free to ask tough questions, but do so respectfully and diplomatically.

Megan followed these guidelines when devising the following questions for the person she knew on the drug task force. (She would alter or change questions for other people she would interview.)

1. According to *Newsweek*, meth users often go undetected by friends and family. Is this true? Why?
2. What are some signs that someone is using meth?
3. Why do users find meth so attractive?
4. What should we do if we suspect a friend or family member is using meth?
5. What explains the high rate of recidivism for meth offenders reported in local news?
6. What measures may make a relapse less likely?

Megan did well crafting her questions. She encouraged elaboration by employing mostly open questions. She was also diplomatic. She did not ask the law enforcement official, "What explains your failure to rehabilitate meth users?" Instead, she posed the question more tactfully, using the term *recidivism*—a concept that law enforcement officials regularly discuss. The questions also revealed that

Interviewing experts and laypersons can provide invaluable information and insights for your speech.

Megan had done her homework. She did not ask basic, factual questions that she could have answered with other sources. Instead, she asked questions that showed she had prepared and that called for the expertise of the person she interviewed.

Conducting the Interview

No matter how well you prepare in terms of initial research and formulating questions, the actual act of conducting the interview will be a crucial point in the information-gathering process. A few simple pointers will help produce good results.

- *Be professional.* Dressing appropriately and arriving on time, for example, create a positive impression, as does thanking the person as you begin and establishing a cordial and respectful tone.
- *Quickly get down to business.* Remind the person of the purpose of your project and how you believe she or he can help you. (e.g., "I'm trying to discover why meth is so attractive to its users and how we might better address a problem *Newsweek* calls an epidemic.") The person can then understand how to assist.
- *Let the person see what you know and don't know.* Mention some of the sources you have consulted and what they suggest. (e.g., "Assistant U.S. Attorney Christopher Casey told *Newsweek* that meth has 'seduced whole families and turned them into zombies.'[54] Does this seem accurate?")
- *Be genuinely involved.* Focus on their responses, providing nonverbal feedback such as nods or smiles, whatever is appropriate. Quick comments, such as "Hmm ... interesting," or "Really?" can convey how you are processing the message. Taking notes, too, signals that you find the remarks valuable or noteworthy.
- *Employ a good system for taking notes.* Enter your questions on one side of a page, reserving the other side for the interviewee's responses and for your reflections about those responses. Also leave plenty of space between questions in case the person pursues an angle you had not considered. Be sure to obtain permission before using an electronic recording device.
- *Be courteous.* Sometimes an interviewee may go off on a tangent. If this happens, politely steer the person back on topic when you get the opportunity.

  Another tactic for keeping the interviewee on track and conducting the interview more efficiently is to make open questions less open. For example, instead of asking "What are the chief motivators that prompt people to try meth?" you might ask, "What is one of the biggest reasons that people decide to try meth?"
- *Be respectful.* Allow the person to have his or her say, even when you disagree with what is being said. You can question specific statements, but do so tactfully.
- *Be accurate.* Accurately record statements made during the interview. Repeat key phrases you wish to quote, for verification, and likewise repeat paraphrased material to check your accuracy. The interviewee will welcome follow-up questions that begin, "If I understand correctly, what you're saying is ..." These questions can also prompt helpful elaboration.

Also make sure you have the person's name and title entered correctly—perhaps request a business card. You will need the information for your bibliography.

- *Conclude on schedule.* If the interviewee wants to keep going, that is another matter.
- *Display your gratitude.* Smile and thank the person for her or his time.

Rather than a face-to-face meeting, you may have to interview the person using some other means, such as telephone or e-mail (which we will discuss shortly). When interviewing by phone, follow the same general guidelines discussed earlier, with these additional pointers.

- *Use a three-part introduction.*
  - Indicate the person you are calling.
  - Identify yourself and your affiliation.
  - Briefly explain why you are calling. For example, you might say, "May I speak with Officer Dunleavy? This is Megan Juarez, a student at Oklahoma State, and I'm seeking information about the methamphetamine problem in our region."
- *Be considerate.* When the person with whom you wish to speak comes on the line, quickly thank the person by name and repeat your purpose for calling. As a courtesy, ask if there is a better time to call.
- *Be brief.* People do not expect to be interviewed for an hour on the phone. Keep the number of questions reasonable so that the interview can be concluded within about ten minutes.
- *Be well prepared.* Follow a set of questions as you would during a face-to-face interview. The questions will keep you on track and will ensure that you cover all you wish to cover.
- *Convey a positive impression with your voice.* Enunciate clearly. Speak fluently, avoiding vocalized pauses and verbal fillers. Also, be as attentive to your facial expressions as you would be if you were face-to-face; your manner will affect the tone of your voice.
- *Bring the conversation to a close.* Begin signaling when you are nearly done asking questions, saying something like, "I have only two more quick questions." End by expressing your gratitude.
- *If you must, leave a recorded message.* If voice mail picks up, use the same three-part introduction you would with a secretary. Request that the person return your call. Provide your number, stating it clearly. As a courtesy, repeat your number. You may also indicate when you are available. Be sure your voice creates a positive impression. Thank the person.

After the Interview

As soon as possible after the interview, review your notes to make sure you accurately recorded the person's statements. You will also be better able to fill in the details for anything that appears sketchy. Send a quick thank-you to the person interviewed to show your gratitude and to help keep open the line of communication.

GATHERING INFORMATION THROUGH E-MAIL AND ONLINE NETWORKING

Preview. *E-mail can be an effective and efficient means to gather information, offering several noteworthy advantages. A few pointers increase the likelihood of getting good results. Online networks may also prove beneficial as we seek relevant information, insights, and opinions.*

E-mail can assist your investigation in several ways. For one thing, you can send source citations and full-text materials to your e-mail account for safe storage and later use, taking full advantage of material already in electronic form. E-mail can also be a good way to request information. An expert on your subject may be too busy to meet you in person but happy to answer questions via e-mail. E-mail can also make long-distance inquiries feasible.

E-mail proved essential to Eva while she investigated her topic. Eva learned from a news report about a nearby city's regulations for barking dogs that addressed the problem 24 hours a day. Owners faced fines that increased incrementally with each disturbance. Eva's hometown addressed the problem only between eleven P.M. and seven A.M. Eva thought her city's policy ignored the rights of people who had to work at night and should be able to sleep, undisturbed, during the day. It also failed to consider the rights of the ill, such as an elderly man she knew who received hospice care in his home. A neighbor's dogs barked continuously throughout the day, only a few yards from the bedroom where he tried to rest. The man's wife asked the neighbor to do something so the man could rest, but the dogs continued to bark.

Eva felt something had to be done. She contacted the nearby city via a link on its Web site and requested details about its new ordinance for barking dogs. Within 24 hours the city e-mailed her a copy of the ordinance, which she appended to the written argument she had drafted for a revised disturbance ordinance. Eva was now ready to attend a city council meeting and request that her city adopt a similar policy.

E-mailing for information can pay off. Be mindful, though, that not all sites allow inquiries or are as prompt or helpful as the city Eva contacted. Continue your search for information elsewhere while awaiting a reply. Also, be sure that any request is not for information you can find with relative ease on that agency's Web pages or elsewhere.

To obtain the best results from e-mail communications, follow these guidelines.

- *Keep inquiries short, simple, and to the point.* Because e-mail is used for convenience, receivers do not want to be burdened by lengthy messages or inquiries that require elaborate responses.
- *Format for a quick read and quick response.* Keep paragraphs short, and leave a blank line between them. Keep sentences short and easy to process—and conversational yet professional. Use a bulleted or numbered list when you are making a series of points or asking a series of questions.
- *Be careful with the subject line.* Craft a subject line that clearly identifies you and your purpose and also reduces the risk of the message being deleted before it is opened (e.g., "citizen re: ordinance for dogs").
- *Disclose your objective in the first line of the message.* Receivers do not want to guess what a message is about. Let them know immediately (e.g., "After

seeing a report about your new ordinance for barking dogs, I hope to have my city adopt a similar policy.").

- *Keep the look simple and professional.* Leave out fancy fonts and colors, and emoticons (such as smiley faces).
- *Remember that what you see may not be what they get.* Be mindful that formatting (e.g., italics, indentations) may appear differently on the recipient's monitor.
- *Critique and proofread before sending.* Check clarity, grammar, spelling, and punctuation. Mistakes can harm your credibility and have a negative impact on the response you will receive.
- *Never say anything in e-mail that you would not want shared in public.* E-mail is not private communication; it can be easily forwarded and shared (intentionally or otherwise) with others.

Like e-mail, online networks, when used with discretion, can yield useful information and insights into your topic. For example, www.academia.edu/ is a social network for academics that can be searched by discipline, person, or school. It provides a direct means to contact experts. Some topic-specific sites also exist, such as the Environmental Communication Network. When seeking information from these networks, keep in mind that the information on such sites has not undergone the rigors of editorial review. You would do well to inquire which publications the person(s) would recommend.

CITING SOURCES OF QUOTED AND PARAPHRASED MATERIAL

Preview. *Once you have gathered information from a variety of sources and have integrated it into your speech, you will want to be sure to reveal those sources to your audience. You may also need to assemble a comprehensive bibliography for your formal outline, formatting it correctly.*

Although you probably have a great interest in your speech topic, you likely are not an expert. Even if you can be regarded as an expert, you still need to seek additional information and opinions, just as most experts do.

Guidelines for Incorporating Material

When you incorporate material into your speech, you may quote the source verbatim, or you may choose to paraphrase. In either instance, you will need to reveal the source *during* your presentation. As we discussed in Chapter 2, plagiarism is a serious matter. Be sure that material taken from another source is properly acknowledged and that the audience understands when you are quoting or paraphrasing material from an outside source.

Deciding whether to quote or paraphrase can be determined in light of a few simple guidelines. Quote information when:

- you wish to bolster your own ethos by associating your ideas with that of a recognized authority
- the information you are presenting is so startling or unusual that the audience will doubt its accuracy unless a respected source is cited

- you support an unpopular position and wish to blunt its unpopularity by citing the opinion of a source whom the audience will respect
- the material is expressed so eloquently that you could not say it more clearly or in a more memorable fashion

Revealing sources during your presentation does more than safeguard against plagiarism; it fulfills one of your most important ethical obligations as a speaker. Ethical speakers openly acknowledge what others have contributed to their thinking.

Revealing sources is not only right, it is smart. As we will see in Chapters 8 and 15, speakers who cite quality sources during a presentation will bolster their ethos, and their audience will more likely accept their message.[55] As Professor William Norwood Brigance observed more than a half century ago, "One is known by the company he [or she] keeps; and when listeners find that you have been keeping company with eminent people of ideas and with expert collectors of information, they are impelled to accept you and your ideas."[56]

In short, by citing reputable sources you will meet your ethical responsibility and you will impress your audience with how well you did your homework. The audience will see that you were well prepared to speak.

Guidelines for Citing Sources during Your Presentation

When you cite sources during your presentation, you need not provide complete bibliographic information. Avoid interrupting the flow of the speech with unnecessary detail. You need not, for instance, specify the page numbers of an article or volume number of a journal. Simply provide enough information to convince the audience of the credibility of the source and allow them to see that the information is up to task. For example, you could say:

> "*Time* magazine reported last month. . . ."
>
> "In a 2005 interview on ABC's *20/20*, former secretary of state Colin Powell stated. . . ."
>
> "The Federal Aviation Administration's Web site currently specifies. . . ."
>
> "Dr. George Edwards, a distinguished professor of political science here at Texas A&M, told me in a recent interview. . . ."

In this last entry, notice how Dr. Edwards's expertise is revealed. Not only is the audience provided with his title, but they are also informed of his area of expertise so they will know why he should be considered credible. If you continue to draw on a particular source, let your listener know. For instance, you might say, "Professor Edwards also told me. . . ." or "In that same interview, Powell made clear. . . ." or "*Time* also identified. . . ."

Establish that the information is current whenever the latest information is needed. When you're providing historical information, the date of publication may not be as important. If, for instance, you are discussing renewed interest in locally produced foods and you discuss their predecessor, the victory gardens of the 1940s, you could rely on sources from that era or any time since.[57] However, when discussing the benefits we'd derive now from local foods, you would need—of course—to discuss the latest thinking and data, such as that provided in *The New York Times Magazine* in October 2008.[58]

Although source information in the speech can be abbreviated, you will need the full citation for every source you use. For one, your instructor will likely require complete bibliographic information in a list of sources at the end of your formal outline. You should also be able to provide complete source information to anyone who may ask about it after your presentation.

To ensure that you cite your sources orally during your presentation, cite them parenthetically in your speaking outline. If, for instance, you were making reference to Colin Powell in the manner described earlier, you might place (Powell, *20/20*) in your speaking outline. In addition to referencing your sources orally during a presentation, you should also identify the source on any PowerPoint slides or other visual aids when the content is taken from a source. For the formal outline that you submit to your instructor, format in-text citations (as well as the bibliography of references/works cited) according to whichever style guide your instructor has approved. *Note*: For examples of *Chicago Manual* style, see the endnotes after each chapter in this text. For information about MLA or APA style, go to Purdue University's Online Writing Lab (http://owl.english.purdue.edu/).

SUMMARY

- Being well informed will allow you to do well in your speeches, and it will also be vital in your career and in your role as a citizen. When you are well informed, you will be better able to:
  - formulate well-founded ideas
  - provide quality support for your ideas
  - have confidence when you speak
  - enhance your credibility
  - meet your ethical responsibility
- A working thesis can help focus your research, allowing you to discern whether information is relevant and which sources will likely prove most valuable.
- Taking notes methodically will provide a good record of where you got what information and will also help you think about your speech and begin writing it.
- Evaluating all that you encounter is part of using information responsibly and becoming a responsible speaker.
- Using various resources can help you become well informed.
  - The World Wide Web, if used judiciously, can provide a wealth of information.
  - Your school's library and many public libraries provide access to many informational resources and professional assistance.
  - Interviews with professionals and laypeople alike can provide good information and insights.
  - E-mail often can substitute for an interview as well as provide a means of efficiently managing information that is available in electronic form.
- Citing sources responsibly not only is ethical but also can enhance credibility.

QUESTIONS FOR REVIEW AND REFLECTION

1. How will a working thesis statement help you formulate ideas and find relevant material?
2. Identify the various creative processes that are involved in crafting a speech.
3. What are the important do's and don'ts in recording information?
4. Why is revision so important in speech preparation?
5. How would you go about finding information using the World Wide Web?
6. How would you evaluate the integrity of a Web site?
7. What is information literacy? Why is it especially important today?
8. Describe at least three important library resources and explain how they could be helpful to you in preparing a speech.
9. What is the role of interviewing in speech preparation?
   a. How would you prepare for an interview?
   b. What are the guidelines for conducting an interview?
   c. How would you follow up an interview?
10. How can e-mail be useful to you when preparing a speech?
11. Under what circumstances should you quote material in your speech?
12. How should you cite sources as you deliver a speech, and why is it important to do so?

ENDNOTES

1. John Walsh and Susan Schindehette, *Tears of Rage: From Grieving Father to Crusader for Justice: The Untold Story of the Adam Walsh Case* (New York: Pocket Star Books, 1997), 53–143.
2. Ibid., 158.
3. Ibid., 158–60.
4. Ibid., 169.
5. Ibid., 191.
6. America's Most Wanted, "Captures," www.amw.com/captures/ (accessed June 1, 2009).
7. Bryan Walsh, "How to Prepare for a Pandemic," *Time*, May 18, 2009, 30–33.
8. For information about CREDO, go to http://corp.credoreference.com/.
9. For example, major newspapers often endorse a particular candidate. For a listing of papers and whom they endorse, go to http://wheretodoresearch.com/Political.htm.
10. Stephen K. Reed, *Cognition, Theory and Application*, 3rd ed. (Pacific Grove, CA: Brooks/Cole, 1992), 223.
11. Ilan Yaniv and David E. Meyer, "Activation and Metacognition of Inaccessible Stored Information: Potential Bases for Incubation Effects in Problem Solving," *Journal of Experimental Psychology: Learning, Memory, and Cognition* 13 (1987): 187–205. Also see Peggy Milam, "The Power of Reflection in the Research Process," *School Library Media Activities Monthly* 21 (February 2005): 26–29.
12. Renate Nummela Caine et al., *12 Brain/Mind Learning Principles in Action: The Fieldbook for Making Connections, Teaching, and the Human Brain* (Thousand Oaks, CA: Corwin Press, 2005).
13. Ronald A. Finke et al., *Creative Cognition: Theory, Research, and Applications* (Cambridge, MA: MIT Press, 1992), 149–50. Also see Steven M. Smith, "Getting Into and Out of Mental Ruts: A Theory of Fixation, Incubation, and Insight," in *The Nature of Insight*, ed. R. J. Sternberg and J. E. Davidson (Cambridge, MA: MIT Press, 1995), 229–51.
14. John B. Best, *Cognitive Psychology*, 5th ed. (Belmont, CA: Brooks/Cole Wadsworth, 1999), 420–23.
15. Finke et al., *Creative Cognition*, 166. Also see David N. Perkins, *The Eureka Effect: The Art and Logic of Breakthrough Thinking* (New York: Norton, 2001); and Mihaly Csikszentmihalyi, *Creativity: Flow and the Psychology of Discovery and Invention* (New York: HarperCollins, 1996).
16. Steven Pressfield, *The War of Art: Break through the Block and Win Your Inner Creative Battles* (New York: Warner Books, 2002).
17. Peter Elbow, *Writing with Power: Techniques for Mastering the Writing Process* (New York: Oxford University Press, 1981).
18. See Tony Buzan and Barry Buzan, *The Mind Map Book: How to Use Radiant Thinking to Maximize Your Brain's Untapped Potential* (New York: Penguin Books, 1993). For concept mapping,

see Joseph D. Novak and D. Bob Gowin, *Learning How to Learn* (New York: Cambridge University Press, 2002). We also recommend doing an advanced search on Google, specifying .edu extensions only as the search parameters for either of these types.

19. R. Keith Sawyer, *Explaining Creativity: The Science of Human Innovation* (New York: Oxford University Press, 2006). Sawyer also emphasizes the importance of an early start and the other strategies we have discussed.
20. For concise advice about taking notes while researching, see Dorothy U. Seyler, *Read, Reason, Write: An Argument Text and Reader*, 8th ed. (Boston: McGraw-Hill, 2008).
21. Linda Flower and John R. Hayes, "A Cognitive Process Theory of Writing," *College Composition and Communication* 32 (1981): 380–81.
22. Jean Wyrick, *Steps to Writing Well: A Concise Guide to Composition*, 6th ed. (New York: Harcourt, Brace, 1996), 103.
23. Peggy Noonan, *What I Saw at the Revolution: A Political Life in the Reagan Era* (New York: Ivy Books, 1990), 77. To learn more about how a president's speeches are written, go to http://millercenter.org/academic/americanpresident.
24. Ibid.
25. Public Broadcasting Service, "Forum Featuring Presidential Speechwriters," www.pbs.org/newshour/inauguration/speech3.html (accessed June 10, 2009).
26. David Greene, "Bush Prepares to Deliver State of Union Address," National Public Radio, 2006, www.npr.org/templates/story/story.php?storyId=5179164&ft=1&f=1001 (accessed June 10, 2009).
27. Jay Newton-Small, "How Obama Writes His Speeches," *Time*, August 28, 2008, www.time.com/time/politics/article/0,8599,1837368,00.html (accessed June 3, 2009).
28. Ibid.
29. Carrie Budoff Brown, "A Peek at Obama's Inaugural Plan," *Politico.com*, January 16, 2009, www.politico.com/news/stories/0109/17515.html (accessed June 3, 2009).
30. Sondra Perl, "Understanding Composing," *College Composition and Communication* 31 (1980): 363–69.
31. Flower and Hayes, "A Cognitive Process Theory of Writing," 365–87.
32. Quintilian, *The Institutio Oratoria of Quintilian*, trans. H. E. Butler (New York: Putnam, 1992), 109–11.
33. Lee Rainie, "Internet Librarians Own the Future," *Information Today* 22 (January 2005): 42.
34. Steven Levy, "All Eyes on Google," *Newsweek*, March 29, 2004, 54.
35. Michael Gorman, "The Corruption of Cataloging," *Library Journal* 120 (September 15, 1995): 34.
36. John M. Broder, "Clinton's Drug Plan Attacked by Industry," *New York Times*, June 28, 2000, A22.
37. Purdue University Online Writing Lab, "Evaluating Internet Sources," http://owl.english.purdue.edu/handouts/print/research/r_evalsource4.html (accessed June 7, 2009).
38. American Library Association, *Information Literacy Competency Standards for Higher Education* (Chicago: Association of College and Research Libraries, 2000), 2–3.
39. Ibid.
40. Ibid.
41. Jon Udell, "Wikipedia's Future," *InfoWorld* 28 (January 9, 2006): 30.
42. Cornell University Library, "Introduction to Research: Distinguishing Scholarly from Non-Scholarly Periodicals: (articles and papers)," www.library.cornell.edu/resrch/intro#2Findingbooks,articles,andothermater (accessed June 4, 2009).
43. Ibid.
44. Ibid.
45. Ibid.
46. Penn State University Libraries, "How to Evaluate the Information," www.libraries.psu.edu/instruction/infolit/andyou/mod7/eval_i.htm (accessed June 4, 2009).
47. Sandy Whitely, ed., *The American Library Association Guide to Information Access: A Complete Research Handbook and Directory* (New York: Random House, 1994), xvii.
48. Levy, "All Eyes on Google."
49. A study by the OCLC found that less than 35 percent of college students reported that they had used online databases, whereas 82 percent responded that they had used search engines (13). See Online Library Computer Center, "Libraries and Information Sources—Use, Familiarity, Favorability," in *Perceptions of Libraries and Information Resources* (Part I), www.oclc.org/

reports/pdfs/Percept_pt1.pdf (accessed June 7, 2009).

50. Whitely, *The American Library Association Guide to Information Access*, 34.
51. For a discussion of alternatives to popular search engines and their advantages, see Brad Stone, "Little Engines That Can," *Newsweek*, March 29, 2004, 59.
52. Go to www.library.cornell.edu/resrch/intro#2Findingbooks,articles,andothermater.
53. David J. Jefferson, "America's Most Dangerous Drug," *Newsweek*, August 8, 2005, 42.
54. Ibid., 47.
55. John C. Reinard, "The Empirical Study of the Persuasive Effects of Evidence: The Status after Fifty Years of Research," *Human Communication Research* 15 (1988): 3–59.
56. William Norwood Brigance, *Speech: Its Techniques and Disciplines in a Free Society*, 2nd ed. (New York: Appleton-Century-Crofts, 1952), 211.
57. See, for example, Char Miller, "In the Sweat of Our Brow: Citizenship in American Domestic Practice during WWII—Victory Gardens," *Journal of American Culture* 26 (2003): 395–409.
58. See Michael Pollan, "Farmer in Chief," *New York Times Magazine*, October 9, 2008, www.nytimes.com/2008/10/12/magazine/12policy-t.html?pagewanted=1&_r=1 (accessed June 10, 2009).

CHAPTER

8

Supporting Your Ideas with Evidence

CHAPTER SURVEY

CHAPTER OBJECTIVES

After studying this chapter, you should be able to

1. Understand the importance of making ideas understandable and believable.
2. Identify the principal types of evidence used to support ideas: facts, definitions, examples, statistics, testimony, and comparison and contrast.
3. Apply tests to determine the quality of different kinds of evidence.
4. Choose evidence carefully to support your ideas.

In daily conversations, we often assert our views while providing little, if any, evidence. We may refer to an article we read or a Web site we visited. We may cite an occasional statistic. But we rarely feel the need to support our assertions or opinions with extensive evidence. By contrast, when we prepare to make some *public* statement about an important issue, the expectations and norms change. As speakers we should back up our statements with evidence from reputable sources. And as listeners we should expect speakers to substantiate their opinions with **supporting material.**

The need to use evidence to support ideas varies with the situation, the audience (and our relationship to them), and the complexity of the idea. If you and your listeners agree on a topic, for example, you will not need much supporting material to make your ideas understandable and believable. Suppose, for example, that you are asking a group of listeners to vote for a political candidate who is running on a platform of educational reform. If your listeners already favor the reforms your candidate supports, then you may not need to use a great deal of supporting material to sway them. However, if you are asking for the support of a different group of listeners—a group that is worried about the cost and effectiveness of your candidate's reform platform—then you will have to come armed with statistics, comparisons, and other forms of evidence. In short, the nature and amount of proof you need to convince one audience may not be enough for another.

Of course, not all supporting material is of equal quality. One speaker may point out, "Police report that the problem of theft is growing on our campus—with more than 20 robberies reported this year so far. That is nearly *twice* as many as last year—and the school year is far from over!" A speaker talking about the problem of domestic violence may share this statistic: "According to the Middle Way House Web site, one woman is beaten every 15 seconds in this country."[1] Still another speaker may try to make his statistics more meaningful with a comparison like this: "According to Dr. Richard A. DeVaul at Texas A&M University's College of Medicine, 100,000 people die annually in the United States from adverse drug reactions. This is the same as if a 727 airliner crashed every day, killing all aboard—approximately 274 individuals per day."[2] Yet another may use a less literal comparison, like the speaker who argued that so-called white-collar criminals can begin by stretching ethical limits until they step over the line into criminal activity. They "seldom set out with the deliberate intent of breaking the law," he said. "They are drawn into it, almost as a boa constrictor defeats its prey."[3]

As listeners, what should we make of the supporting material used by these speakers? Does it strengthen or undermine the speakers' arguments? Does it enhance or hinder each one's credibility? What critical standards should we use to assess the quality of supporting material used by speakers in the classroom or the community?

In this chapter we are concerned with *both* the nature and quality of supporting materials. First, we discuss the various types of supporting materials and how you might incorporate them into your speeches. Then, we will consider criteria for critically examining or "testing" your evidence. Whether you are considering using a particular piece of evidence in your own speech or you are evaluating the evidence presented by another speaker, it is important that you develop a critical attitude toward supporting material and consider both the quality and the ethical implications of different sorts of supporting material.

SUPPORTING IDEAS WITH EVIDENCE

Preview. *Good evidence can make ideas and arguments more understandable and convincing. Good speakers use a variety of evidence, including facts, definitions, examples, statistics, testimony, and comparison and contrast.*

Suppose you hoped to convince your fellow students in your public speaking class of the following assertion: "The minority recruitment program here at our university has been a complete failure." On the basis of that assertion alone, your audience would not know what to believe. You have not described the program, compared its success rate to other programs, or offered any other evidence of its failures. To strengthen your argument, you need to support it with **evidence**. Evidence is the body of fact and opinion that you present in support of your claims.

The kinds of evidence you use will depend on the purpose and topic of your speech. Some speeches, such as technical reports, rely heavily on statistical evidence, perhaps reinforced with charts or graphs. Other speeches may make more use of examples, comparison and contrast, or the opinions of experts. Whatever kind of speech you deliver, it will be more interesting and convincing if you use a variety of good, credible evidence. And don't forget to cite the sources of your evidence; it is important that your audience knows that your evidence came from credible sources (see the guidelines for citing sources in Chapter 7).

Facts

Nearly every speaker will use **facts** as evidence. Facts are data that can be verified by observation. As facts are repeatedly verified by experts and other observers, they come to be thought of as "established" facts. Generally we judge factual information as simply true or false, correct or incorrect, verified or unverified. So, for example, a speaker may share the following facts:

- According to the U.S. Census Bureau, as of 2008, the population of the United States exceeded 304,000,000 people.
- In the state of Indiana, voter registration closes 30 days before the day of the election.
- Article XIII of the U.S. Constitution abolished slavery and involuntary servitude in the United States, except as punishment for certain crimes.

In each of these cases, we could verify the fact—in theory, at least—through observation. In the case of the population count, of course, we rely on the Census Bureau to do the observing for us!

Speakers often take facts and interpret them or try to color their meaning. A student who tried unsuccessfully to vote in Indiana, for example, might label the *fact* that voter registration closes 30 days before the election "unfair" or "discriminatory." Using this kind of interpretive language does not change the fact; it suggests a larger argument about the policy that would need to be supported with other forms of evidence. How, for example, do the voting rules in Indiana compare with those in other states? Are particular groups of people, such as college students, disadvantaged by this rule? How might a change in the rules affect voter turnout? What do voting experts say about the fairness or effects of the 30-day rule?

The language used to describe facts is often interpretive or even "loaded," so it's important that you critically evaluate *how* certain facts are labeled or described. It is an accepted fact, for example, that some alleged terrorists held at the U.S. detention facility at Guantanamo Bay, Cuba, were subjected to a procedure known as "waterboarding," in which interrogators simulate the experience of drowning in an effort to gain information from prisoners. Describing waterboarding as an "enhanced interrogation technique," of course, casts it in a much more positive light than labeling it "torture."

To make sure your facts are sound, validate them by consulting multiple, credible sources. If you find inconsistencies, keep reading. Pay particular attention to the credibility of your sources. You should accept as fact only the observations of those who are genuinely trustworthy. With contemporary topics, make sure your sources are up-to-date. What looks like a factual discrepancy at first glance may simply reflect differences in when the data were collected or reported.

Definitions

Sometimes speakers need to define a word or concept used in their speeches. It is important to ensure a common understanding of key concepts, especially if a word or term can be understood in different ways. In general, you should provide **definitions** for any terms that may be unfamiliar, especially technical terms. A speaker explaining various options to a group of soon-to-be-retired workers commented that "after 10 years, your retirement funds are fully vested." Aware that some in his audience might not know the meaning of "vested," he went on to say, "That is, your retirement funds belong to you, and they cannot be taken away." Similarly, you should define any **acronyms** which may be unfamiliar. Not everyone may know that CORE is short for the Congress of Racial Equality or that NASCAR stands for the National Association for Stock Car Auto Racing.

Definitions can be persuasive as well as informative. A persuasive definition reflects your way of looking at a controversial subject. Others may define the same term or concept quite differently, but *yours* is the definition you want the audience to reflect on, and hopefully accept. Pulitzer Prize–winning author David Shipler uses this approach in defining *poverty* and *the poor* in his book *The Working Poor.* He writes, "'Poverty' is an unsatisfying term, for poverty is not a category that can be delineated by the government's dollar limits or annual income. In real life, it is an unmarked area along a continuum, a broader region of hardship than society usually recognizes. More people than those officially designated as 'poor' are, in fact, weighed down with the troubles associated with poverty. Therefore, I use 'poor' not as a statistician would. I use it imprecisely as it should be used, to suggest the lowest stratum of economic attainment, with all of its accompanying problems."[4]

Definitions, then, can be straightforward—meant only to clarify and provide uncontroversial information—or they can challenge the audience to think in new or creative ways. When new definitions are embraced, listeners may see problems in a different light or be inspired to think or act in different ways.

Examples

One of the most difficult challenges you face as a public speaker is trying to make general principles or abstract notions interesting and meaningful to your audience. One way to do this is by using good examples. Examples provide concrete evidence and can interject life and meaning into the ideas you are communicating.

When carefully selected, examples can function as compelling evidence. In a speech on genocide, for example, you may cite statistics on the number of people killed, but the true horrors of genocide are communicated best through specific examples. That is what makes books like Elie Wiesel's *Night* or films like *Hotel Rwanda* so powerful: their characters are people with whom we can identify; they provide concrete examples that make the statistics both more terrible and more real.

There are two principal kinds of examples that a speaker can use to support ideas: **actual examples** and **hypothetical examples**. Each kind may be brief or developed as a more extended narrative.

ACTUAL EXAMPLES An actual example deals with a real case; it is something that actually happened. Even a brief example, if well chosen, can make your point more vivid and memorable. In a speech delivered at Yale University, for example, J. Edward Hill, president of the American Medical Association, noted that "at any one time, six in ten Americans are overweight and about one in three are considered obese." After sharing this and related statistics suggesting that obesity had become a significant problem in America, he offered this concrete example: "Perhaps more telling [than the statistics] is a newspaper item I read last week, about the Batesville Casket Company, which last year launched its 'Dimensions' line of super-sized coffins. Think about that for a second."[5]

Actual examples not only give your audience a more concrete understanding of some problem, but also can help them imagine a solution—perhaps grasping, for the first time, the actual form that an abstract concept may take. In a speech at Georgetown University, President Clinton discussed responsible citizenship and the ways in which all Americans can work together to promote the good of all. He urged everyone to become involved and cited specific examples of organizations that work to improve their communities.

> More of our citizens have got to say, "What should I do in my community?" You know, it's not just enough to bemoan the rising crime rate or how kids are behaving and whatever—that's just not enough. It is not enough. Not when you have example after example from this LEAP Program, the "I Have a Dream" Program, to the world-famous Habitat for Humanity Program, to all these local initiatives,

support corporations, that are now going around the country, revolutionizing slum housing and giving poor, working people decent places to live; to the work of the Catholic social missions in Washington, D.C., and other places.[6]

NARRATIVES AS ACTUAL EXAMPLES More extended examples may come from your research or your own experiences. The following excerpt from a student speech illustrates the use of a **narrative example** based on the student's personal experience.

> Did your parents go to college? How about your brothers and sisters, or your cousins? Did you just assume that you would attend college from the time you were a child? I didn't. No one in my family had attended college—not even for a year or two. No one in my family even *talked* to me about the possibility of attending college. I think they just thought that I'd work on the farm like everyone else in the family. But when I was in high school, I had a wonderful English teacher who took an interest in my writing. She told me she thought I had some real ability. No one had ever talked to me like that before. She encouraged me to enter a writing contest during my junior year. When I actually *won* the contest, she started giving me college brochures and urging me to check out some Web sites. Before I knew it, I had applied to three colleges and been accepted by all of them with financial aid packages. Without the kindness, support, and encouragement of this *one* teacher, I might never have even *applied* to any college. It is even less likely that I would be about to graduate from one of the best colleges in the state this coming May.

This student went on to talk about the vital role that adults can play in mentoring, encouraging, and serving as role models for youth. She invited her fellow classmates, nearly all graduating seniors, to become role models for other young people in their own communities.

Vivid, engaging examples are usually well received by listeners. During a Remembrance Day ceremony in the Rotunda of the Capitol in April 2009, Fred S. Zeidman, chairman of the United States Holocaust Memorial Council, used a vivid example to make the point that we *can* make a difference, even when the challenges we face seem overwhelming:

> We can see the sheer scale of slaughter and surrender to our own feelings of futility. Or we can choose to see the Six Million ... as individual faces, and say: I might not be able to save them all. But it is within my power to save one. Or two, perhaps dozens, even hundreds. And what is within our power is also our responsibility. What we do matters.
>
> Therein lies a story—a story of heroism of the truest sort. It began on an infamous ship called the *St. Louis*, whose Jewish passengers fled Nazi Germany 70 years ago in May 1939, seeking safety in the United States by way of Cuba. Most of you know the shameful result: First Cuba, then our country, turned them away. The story might have ended there. Because people concluded they could not make a difference. That the forces involved were too powerful, the number of individuals too vast, the dangers too distant.
>
> But two individuals, Lawrence Berenson and Morris Troper, who worked for the American Jewish Joint Distribution Committee, felt otherwise. They knew that

> returning these passengers to Hitler's Germany would doom them. So they ... arranged for the passengers to be accepted in ... four safe European countries.
>
> The following year, the continent was consumed by war, but the JDC clung to the belief that they could still make a difference for the passengers on the *St. Louis.* They tracked them one by one as they spread across Europe.... Of course, they did not save them all. But they saved some. By the scale of the Holocaust, one might say they saved "few." But the ethic these individuals lived by is the same ethic we celebrate today. What you do matters.

Zeidman's account helped make his point that even ordinary people could make a difference.[7]

Hypothetical Examples On some occasions you may choose to use hypothetical rather than real examples to illustrate your point. A hypothetical example is one that plausibly *could* be real, yet it is not an actual, true, or empirically verifiable account. Although it is "made up," a hypothetical example should not be grossly exaggerated or unimaginable; it must be at least realistically believable to be effective.

In a speech to the European Aviation Association, James C. May, CEO of the Air Transport Association of America, used hypothetical examples to illustrate the importance of air cargo. His examples did not refer to actual cases in which critical cargo arrived by air, but they did point to realistic possibilities:

> There's an excellent reason why the cargo carried by air is 89 times more valuable per unit of weight than cargo carried by truck or train. Air cargo fills all kinds of critical needs. If there were no cargo-carrying planes, most of the people waiting in hospitals for organs—hearts, kidneys, livers and lungs—would be out of luck,

In a Remembrance Day ceremony in the Rotunda of the U.S. Capitol, speakers used vivid narrative examples to draw out the lessons of the Holocaust.

> because live organs are normally delivered by commercial air. If there were no planes, you might think that there would be no interruption in the flow of oil, but even if oil moves by ship, it takes skilled workers to get it out of the ground. Think of how people in the oil field services industry would be affected if they were suddenly unable to get urgently needed tools and replacement parts. And think of the just-in-time inventory systems made possible by worldwide supply chains. Do we want these productivity-enhancing supply chains to collapse?[8]

Narratives as Hypothetical Examples Some speakers may choose to use proverbs, stories, or folktales to illustrate an idea or make a compelling point. When used in this way, narratives rely on the audience's imagination or cultural symbols to convey a moral or life "lesson" instead of describing actual people or events. For instance, in a speech to the 96th Annual Convention of the NAACP, national board member Roslyn Brock shared an African folktale about a band of elephants to make a point about helping others:

> As they were traveling across the terrain, they came upon a river. The big elephants did not have a problem stepping into the rough ... waters. However, there were some very small elephants in the group who were afraid to step in the water. Somebody in the middle of the river shouted to the front of the line to those who had crossed over and said, "Brother leaders, we have some folks still standing on the banks of the river who haven't made it into the water to cross over."
>
> Viewing the situation, the larger elephants turned around, got back in the water and stood shoulder to shoulder, allowing their bodies to create a dam that parted the waters to allow those little elephants to cross over on dry ground.
>
> The moral of the story is: once you make it and get to the other side, don't forget ... to turn around ... and get back in the water and help someone else cross over.[9]

After stating the moral of the story, Brock concluded with a powerful call to action, defining the NAACP as the "conscience of the nation" and urging the group to keep fighting for AIDS education, better urban schools, and prison reform.

Because examples are related to our everyday experiences, they can be a powerful tool for supporting your ideas. Still, some examples are better than others, and you need to choose your examples carefully.

Thinking Critically about Examples Several criteria should be used in assessing the quality of examples.

Perhaps the best test of an example is its *typicality.* If a speaker supports a claim with examples, we should ask whether those examples are representative of other examples, or whether they represent the normal course of events. If a speaker were to cite just one example of a homeless person arrested for shoplifting, for instance, we should be skeptical of any sweeping claims about homeless people being responsible for the high costs of retail theft. Similarly, we would not conclude that all professors are reckless drivers because we heard about one professor who was arrested in a hit-and-run accident. Both the homeless shoplifter and the hit-and-run professor may be isolated examples; neither seems a *typical* example.

HIGHLIGHTING SPECIFIC EXAMPLES

Martin Baron, *America Needs Newspapers*

In a speech to the Clinton School of Public Service at the University of Arkansas, Martin Baron, editor of the Boston Globe, *stressed the ways in which newspapers serve the public interest and gave the following example.*

Last year, in South Boston, a 14-year-old girl named Acia Johnson and her 3-year-old sister were killed in an early morning fire.... the girls were trapped on the third floor.... They perished in a fire that was believed to be arson. These tragedies make the evening news. People who watch say, "What a shame." Journalists say, "What really happened here? And why?" And then they do the hard work to find out.

Troubling details emerged from the deaths of 14-year-old Acia Johnson and her 3-year-old sister. The mother was a drug addict with a long criminal record. Acia's father was in jail.... By state order, she wasn't supposed to be living in the house where she died. Two of our reporters sought to answer the lingering question: How did so many fail Acia?... The reporters went to the county prison and met with Acia's father. They interviewed other relatives. They went to... offices of state agencies that were supposed to be monitoring and helping Acia, but failed. This was a story of neglect at every stage...

The story elicited sympathy, ... but fortunately there was more than that.... The child welfare agency instituted reforms that would affect the placement and monitoring of about 500 children a year.... the state's child advocate ... issued a report describing fundamental failures by the state and calling for better training for social workers, improved information-sharing with law enforcement, and more comprehensive documentation of neglect and abuse. The governor pledged to follow through. And we will watch to see that he does follow through.... because that is our job as a newspaper.

The *importance* of an example must also be considered. An example may rarely occur yet still warrant our attention. Several years ago, for example, a speaker criticized the Food and Drug Administration for failing to adequately monitor our food supply. She recalled a specific example of a boy who had died from *E. coli*–related illnesses after consuming some prewashed, bagged spinach—a product sold in grocery stores around the nation. In this case, the example was not typical; thousands of other people had consumed this spinach with no ill effects. Yet given the seriousness of the threat, the one example got people's attention, and the speaker was able to strengthen her argument by noting that more than 100 other people had become sick from the bagged spinach, Again, the typical consumer may not have gotten ill from the product, but there were enough examples of serious, even fatal food-poisoning to warrant concern.

Although examples often provide a "human interest" angle on our topic, they are most compelling when used in tandem with other forms of evidence, such as statistics.

Statistics

Speakers commonly use **statistics** as supporting material. As they attempt to show that a policy or program has had a real impact, for example, speakers may offer statistics to demonstrate how many people signed up for the program or were affected by the policy. They may also use statistics to make predictions about the future. When the executive director of a soup kitchen tells listeners, "We served more than 60,000 meals last year—an increase of 16 percent over the year before," he means to impress them with the growing need for funds. Statistics provide a numerical method of handling large numbers of cases. When used appropriately, they provide some of the most compelling information available to public speakers.

Understanding Statistical Support Statistics offer a way of showing how some things are related to others. They may tell us about the typicality of an occurrence and thus validate our examples. In a speech addressing the problem of prison reform, for instance, a speaker noted the example of a young man who had been in and out of jail 63 times over the course of his life! This actual example was coupled with statistical information demonstrating the general problem of repeat offenders, or *recidivism*, which statistically has been on the rise.[10]

Statistics also may be used to show cause-and-effect relationships, or at least correlations between certain phenomena. One student, in a speech addressing the problem of ozone depletion, used statistical information to argue that the thinning of the ozone layer corresponds to significant increases in skin cancer and cataracts.

Statistical information can be helpful in pointing out trends over time. For example, we can better appreciate how quickly and significantly unemployment has increased if we can see the rise over the last few years. If you wanted to argue that crime is becoming a more serious problem in suburban and rural areas, you need to produce the figures for the crime rate.

Finally, statistics can highlight or reinforce an important point you wish to make. This may be done by using a presentational aid to depict visually the most important figures. But when delivered effectively by the speaker, excellent statistics can have considerable impact on their own. In a speech on national security in December 2008, for example, Mark Gerencser, vice president of Booz Allen Hamilton, a technology consulting firm, reported the striking results from a survey of more than 250 business executives and senior officials from government, private firms, and nonprofit organizations:

> Seventy-seven percent of respondents said their organizations had experienced some form of cyber attack in the past year, and 65 percent expect to be hit again in the next 12 months. Of the US government managers' response, only two percent of respondents have not seen attacks on their systems, and eight out of ten expect an intrusion over the next year. Ninety percent of all respondents believe that we need to be working together on cyber. Yet, the evidence and actions on all our parts is to the contrary.[11]

Statistics, then, are one important way of making ideas more understandable and believable. They should, however, be used responsibly by the speaker and viewed critically by the listener. You should never assume that a statistic always "proves" something conclusively. It is part of the total structure of evidence and should be considered in light of other supporting material.

USING AVERAGES RELIABLY Statistics can sometimes be misleading. *Average*, for example, is a notoriously vague measure, even though it seems to give an air of statistical weight when it is used. Many people just assume that the words *mean* and *average* are synonymous, but they are not.

Averages can be computed in different ways, such as by adding up a list of figures and dividing by the number of figures (the **mean**), by choosing the figure that occurs most often (the **mode**), or by choosing the figure that is the midpoint between the two extreme figures (the **median**). These three methods of computing an average may lead to quite different conclusions. The mean is the arithmetic average, but it is not necessarily the best or the preferred average to quote. If there are extreme scores in the distribution of numbers, the mean will reflect a greatly distorted version of the real central tendency.

Consider this example. A city council was holding an open meeting for public comment on the budget. An item in the budget was the salary for a new city manager. A survey of seven nearby communities with city managers showed a range of salaries paid. One member of the council thought that an average salary would be appropriate and suggested the post be budgeted at $60,280. Another member thought this too low because he calculated the average at $65,000. When the discussion was opened for comment, one member of the audience complained that both council members' figures were much too high. The "real" average, he asserted was $50,000. Technically, all of them were right because "average" is such an ambiguous term. Table 8.1 shows how each average was determined.

Considering the difference in the two salaries at either extreme, the median may be the most sensible "average" in this case. But what is important when using an "average" figure is that the speaker and listener both understand how such an average was determined and what the implications of different "averages" may be.

DESCRIPTIVE VERSUS INFERENTIAL STATISTICS Still other issues should be considered when using statistics or listening to speakers using statistics. First, most statistics

TABLE 8.1

DIFFERENCES AMONG AVERAGES

Individual Salaries	$ 74,000; 70,000; 67,000; 65,000; 50,000; 50,000; 46,000
Total of all salaries:	$ 422,000
Mean as "Average" (Total divided by 7)	$ 60,280
Median as "Average" (The salary in the middle)	$ 65,000
Mode as "Average" (Occurs most frequently)	$ 50,000

quoted in speeches are inferential rather than descriptive; that is, they deal with probabilities rather than with observable facts. In **inferential statistics**, one generalizes from a small group or **sample** to some larger population. For example, polls taken during an election campaign draw inferences about which candidates are leading particular races based on the opinions of a representative sample of voters. When the votes actually come in and are counted on Election Day, the fact that one candidate got 51 percent of the vote and the other got 49 percent is a **descriptive statistic**—it describes how the entire population actually voted.

Many times, speakers turn to inferential statistics because it is inconvenient or impossible to obtain descriptive data. Using inferential statistics is quite acceptable, so long as you recognize that whenever you generalize from a sample to a larger population, there is always some **margin of error**. That margin may be quite small, perhaps three or four percentage points. But the potential for error is always there, and it may be magnified by a poorly designed sample or badly worded survey questions. Whether an inferential statistic is sound depends not only on the size and representativeness of the sample, but also on the techniques of measurement and other factors.

If you wanted to know how students at your college felt about a particular issue, you would need to gather the opinions of a cross section of the entire college, including first-year and senior students, women and men, different ethnic and racial groups, and students representing different majors. In addition, if there were 10,000 students on your campus, you would need a sample size in the hundreds, not just the opinions of five or ten of your friends. That is why most inferential statistics are collected as part of formal surveys or large-scale research projects. Inferential statistics *can* be a powerful form of evidence, but it is critical that your statistics come from reputable sources using sound sampling and measurement techniques.

If you just wanted to survey your own public speaking class, of course, you could easily get a representative sample or even give a questionnaire to the entire class. In Chapter 5, we explained how you might design such a survey. If *everyone* in your class responded to your audience survey, you would obtain a descriptive statistic.

THINKING CRITICALLY ABOUT STATISTICS Sometimes speakers use statistics in ways that are confusing to listeners. The figures may be accurate, but interpretations of statistics can differ radically.

Statistics by themselves don't necessarily "prove" anything. Take, for example, tax legislation passed in May 2006. The Democratic National Committee called the $70 billion in cuts a "tax break for the wealthy and Wall Street" and used this statistic to support its claim that benefits to middle-class families would be meager: "Middle-income households would receive an average tax cut of $20 from the agreement."[12] Although this may be a valid statistic, it is not at all clear what *average* means in this case. And the label "tax break for the wealthy" is not proven by the statistic. For their part, the Republican National Committee announced that House and Senate Republican negotiators had reached a final

HIGHLIGHTING EXAMPLES AND STATISTICS

Combining statistics with a striking example, Ralph W. Basham, commissioner of the U.S. Customs and Border Protection Agency, delivered a powerful speech to a symposium on human trafficking in Washington D.C. on September 9, 2008.

[Human] trafficking generates billions of dollars in profit each year and is one of the world's fastest growing criminal activities. The State Department estimates that between 600,000 and 800,000 people are trafficked across borders each year. As many as 17,000 right here in the United States. The majority are female. Most still children. Most—70%—trafficked for sexual purposes. Men, women, and children from Eastern Europe, Latin America, Asia, and Africa, too, are trafficked for forced prostitution, forced labor, and domestic servitude.

Consider Irina's story: Irina is a 16-year-old Russian high school student. She accepted a family friend's offer of $500 to take a quick trip to the Middle East to bring back merchandise to sell. Irina received a passport, a tourist visa, and a plane ticket. When she had her documentation, the story changed. Irina was told she would be a waitress in a local café for $1,000 a month. Her parents were told that if she didn't go, they would owe huge sums of money for the arrangements that had already been made. When she arrived, Irina found that she would not be a waitress, but a prostitute.

Her passport was taken away. She was threatened. Her life became a series of hotel rooms, madams, and clients. She tried to escape, but the madam claimed she had stolen money and the police sent her back. She was resold to another madam ... and saddled with a huge debt for her misbehavior. The good news for Irina is that she was able to escape with the help of the Russian Embassy.

But not all are so lucky...

Source: From W. Ralph Basham, "Keynote Remarks from CBP Commissioner W. Ralph Basham." Published 2008 by CBP.gov

agreement on a five-year, nearly $70 billion tax package that would "extend President Bush's deep cuts to tax rates on dividends and capital gains, while sparing about 15 million middle-income Americans from the alternative minimum tax [AMT]."[13] The GOP statistic emphasized the number of citizens who would be "spared" the minimum tax without even defining *minimum tax*. Thus, the question of who stood to benefit from the tax cuts and their long-range implications remained a matter of debate. Even if the statistics were accurate, their *meaning* was still a matter of interpretation. That is why we must learn to critically evaluate all statistics.

Like other forms of evidence, statistics should be used only when they provide needed support. No speech should be "padded" with statistics simply because they sound impressive. Moreover, too many statistics can overwhelm listeners. When you do use statistics, you may want to present some visual representation or summary of the statistics to help the audience comprehend them.

Also, every attempt should be made to present the statistics clearly and meaningfully. One student speaker, for example, dramatized the need for improved sanitation at a global level when he said, "In human costs internationally, one child dies every 8 seconds from waterborne disease! ... [T]he human and economic costs are staggering."[14]

It is often helpful to translate a statistic into more specific or more personal terms. Instead of saying that a new school will cost $7 million, you may point out that each taxpayer should expect a property tax increase of about $100 per year over a ten-year period. In this way, the audience can understand what the proposal would mean to them personally.

Finally, statistics change rapidly. Although all evidence should be as recent as possible, nothing is more useless than outdated statistics. Always gather statistical information from the most current sources available and cite those sources in your speech.

In short, statistics must be approached cautiously. Both the speaker and the listener should carefully evaluate the place of statistics in the total pattern of evidence.

Testimony

Another way to support your ideas is to offer testimonial evidence. Whereas statistical evidence seems more "factual" or "objective," **testimony** consists of the opinions, interpretations, or judgments of other people. There are three kinds of testimonial evidence: personal testimony, lay testimony, and expert testimony.

PERSONAL TESTIMONY Regardless of the kind of speech you are making, you are likely to offer your own **personal testimony** from time to time. For many topics and in many speaking situations, this is entirely appropriate. We have pointed out in previous chapters that a speaker's ethos or personal appeal can have a significant impact on listeners. However, you should avoid overreliance on your own testimony to the exclusion of other kinds of support. Equally important, you need to ask yourself a fundamental question: To what extent am I perceived by my audience as being a credible source of information on this subject?

If you have high credibility with your listeners, then your personal views may be an extremely convincing source of support. If, for example, you were a campus police officer, you would be a credible source of testimony on the topic of campus safety. Similarly, a nonprofit leader may speak credibly about funding sources for new programs, or a college student may testify personally to the benefits of participating in student organizations. In one classroom speech, a student used her personal experiences to emphasize the need for volunteers to help rebuild the Gulf Coast after Hurricane Katrina:

> This past January, I had the opportunity to travel to New Orleans, along with a group of other students from around the Midwest, to help rebuild homes and buildings that were destroyed or badly damaged by Hurricane Katrina. I'm sure you're familiar with our school's "Learning through Service" program, which takes place at the end of the holiday break. For two weeks, I worked together with about two dozen students to help rebuild homes, schools, and hospitals. We lived in those famous FEMA trailers and spent a lot of time getting to know the New Orleans residents who had been displaced by the hurricane. Many worked side by side with us—whether on their own homes, the homes of strangers or neighbors, or on public buildings that would benefit the common good.
>
> Although I've taken a lot of great courses during my three years of college, this was, by far, my most meaningful learning experience. I learned some basic skills—how to

rebuild foundations, how to install siding, and even how to put on a roof that is unlikely to easily blow away. But far beyond that, I learned about community and caring and the wonderful resilience of the human spirit.

Personal testimony is not something you will use in all of your speeches. As a college student, you may not have direct experience or expertise on many topics that interest you. You may be interested in alternative energy sources, for example, but that does not make you an expert on the subject. In most cases, then, you will need to go beyond your own experiences and expertise and gather other kinds of testimonial evidence.

LAY TESTIMONY Another kind of opinion evidence is **lay testimony**. Like personal testimony, lay testimony is based on firsthand experience—except in this instance, the experience is not your own. Nor is it the experience of an expert. Rather, lay testimony comes from ordinary women and men whose personal experiences make their testimony compelling.

Let us say, for example, that you wanted to encourage your classmates to become involved in the kind of "Learning through Service" program described earlier. While conducting your research, you may have discovered excellent statistics on the popularity of these kinds of programs. You may have learned that students who participate in these programs tend to be better students and that, on graduation, they are more likely to become engaged citizens in their communities. But beyond sharing such facts and statistics, you want to convey to your listeners the sorts of personal experiences they may have and how those experiences may impact their thoughts and feelings. In other words, you want to *humanize* the topic. If you have not participated in such a program yourself, you will need to find lay testimony from other students who *have* direct experience with such programs.

How effective is lay testimony? Like other forms of evidence, it depends on how carefully you choose that testimony. Standing alone, lay testimony may be insufficient as evidence. But when used in tandem with other strong supporting material, it can be quite effective. In speaking about an economic recession, for example, you may quote expert testimony from the chairman of the Federal Reserve, but you also may want to quote lay testimony from unemployed workers struggling to pay their bills. Your sources of lay testimony may not have special education or training that qualifies them to speak, but they should have direct, firsthand experience that gives them a unique perspective on your topic.

EXPERT TESTIMONY One way to make your own speeches more persuasive is to borrow, in effect, the ethos of experts. **Expert testimony** is among the most frequently used types of evidence, particularly in speeches about complicated or highly technical issues. In such cases, we rely on those whom we regard as experts, or those who have some special education, training, or work-related experience with the subject. In a speech on the Obama administration's economic stimulus program, for example, you may quote expert testimony from the chairman of the Federal Reserve, who asserted in a speech to the Economic Club of New York that "Americans can be confident that every resource is being brought to bear to address the current crisis: historical understanding, technical expertise, economic analysis, financial insight, and political leadership." Or you may choose to quote the part of his speech in which he said, "we now have the tools we need to respond with the necessary force to meet these challenges. Although much work remains and more difficulties surely lie ahead, I remain confident that the American economy, with its great intrinsic vitality and aided by the measures now available, will emerge from this period with renewed vigor."[15]

In using expert testimony, you will need to decide whether you want to quote the exact words the expert used, or whether it's enough to simply paraphrase his or her ideas. If you plan to use the expert's *exact* words, you may want to ensure accuracy by writing them out on a note card that you will read while delivering your speech. You will also want to quote the expert's exact words when those words seem especially compelling, eloquent, or memorable. If you wanted to encourage your listeners to get involved in their community, for example, you might want to use a famous quotation from cultural anthropologist Margaret Mead: "Never doubt that a small group of thoughtful, committed people can change the world. Indeed, it is the only thing that ever has."

On other occasions, you may prefer to convey the basic sense of an expert's argument or capture his or her ideas in your own words. In this case, you will name the expert and perhaps say something about his or her credentials, but you will only be paraphrasing the main ideas of the testimony. If you were addressing the issue of generational poverty, for example, you might paraphrase the words of an education expert by saying, "Long-time educator Ruby Payne has written two books that address the issue of generational poverty. In *Bridges Out of Poverty*, she argues that the poor lack access to basic resources such as financial resources, emotional and spiritual resources, and basic support systems. She points out that most of us focus only on the financial aspect, but it is much more complicated than that." You could then go on to offer concrete examples of these resources and explain how lacking such resources can keep people trapped in poverty. In paraphrasing, of course, it is important to fairly and accurately represent the source's views—never exaggerating or distorting.

Good expert testimony is often one of the best ways to demonstrate that you have done your research and know what you're talking about. However, like all forms of evidence, expert testimony must be carefully chosen and critically evaluated.

Thinking Critically about Expert Testimony Both the ethical speaker and the critical listener need to evaluate expert testimony carefully. By raising questions about the source and the nature of testimony, we can determine whether it is worthy of belief.

First, we need to ask whether our audience considers the source a reputable expert. Are your sources even *known* to your listeners? If not, you may need to identify them—and say something about their credentials—during the speech itself. Thus, you may introduce testimony from an expert on Social Security by saying, "Professor Martin Wilson, a distinguished Harvard economist, has argued that Social Security is one generation away from complete failure." On other occasions, your audience may recognize the name of your source but not know much about the person's credentials, expertise, or experience with your topic.

It never hurts to establish the ethos or credibility of your sources by saying something about why their testimony should be believed.

Sometimes speakers provide only vague references to their sources, saying, "Political analysts have noted that ..." or "One member of the New York City police department said that...." In such cases, listeners have a right to be skeptical. "Political analysts" could mean respected political science professors or paid political "spin doctors." The police officer may be the chief of police or some rookie cop. Critical listeners are unlikely to be impressed or persuaded by such ambiguous references.

Another important question that we should ask about testimony is, How timely is it? People's views may change over time; even experts sometimes change their minds as the situation changes. Many members of both political parties, for example, initially supported authorizing President George W. Bush to use military force in Iraq. Over time, however, the costs of the war skyrocketed, international support waned, and the number of casualties grew—and many who at first supported the war changed their minds. Obviously, it is important to understand *when* and under what circumstances the testimony was given.

When using testimony, you should never misrepresent the *context* in which it was given. In an opinion piece in the *New York Times*, the late Reverend Jerry Falwell explained his invitation to Senator John McCain to give a commencement speech at Liberty University: "The next election for president is two years away. Mr. McCain is the front-runner for the nomination and is the kind of conservative candidate whom I would have little trouble supporting." This statement might have been cited as evidence that Falwell endorsed Senator McCain for president. But that would be taking the comment out of context, for Falwell went on to deny that he was, in fact, endorsing McCain. "The senator's speech," Falwell wrote, "does not symbolize an endorsement of an unannounced candidacy on my part, and it does not mark the quest for such an endorsement on his part. Mr. McCain had never sought such an endorsement, and I have not offered one."[16]

Whenever possible, we should take our testimony from those who have *nothing to gain* from their statements. One would expect the president of a pharmaceutical company to oppose policies that would hurt the industry's profits. Similarly, NASA officials could be expected to support increased government spending on space exploration. Although these people may be authorities in their fields, quoting them may not help your cause because they may be viewed as biased.

Finally, it is important to ask whether a source of testimony has relevant credentials. Unfortunately, we have been conditioned by advertising to accept testimony from celebrities with little or no real knowledge about the products they endorse. We also have become accustomed to movie actors, athletes, and famous singers or musicians endorsing candidates for office or particular political causes. That is their right, of course, but that does not mean we should consider them experts. A famous tennis player may be a good source of testimony on the rules or the history of the game, but that does not mean that he or she knows anything about politics or social welfare policies. Although entertainers and sports figures have every right to their opinions, their celebrity does not qualify them as experts on social, political, or economic issues.

Testimony by those whose experience and credentials qualify them as experts can be especially effective in addressing important and complicated issues.

PRESTIGE TESTIMONY AS EVIDENCE Sometimes it may be acceptable, even desirable, to quote from a celebrity with high visibility. They may not be "experts," but **prestige testimony** *can* provide support for our argument if the source of that testimony is perceived as smart, dedicated, well-educated, or inspirational. Angelina Jolie, for example, has served as a Goodwill Ambassador to the United Nations Commissioner for Refugees, using her high public profile to focus more attention on the plight of refugees throughout the world. The Church World Service, in presenting her with a humanitarian award, cited her as one whose "work on behalf of refugees has made her a role model of individual humanitarian action, an inspiration to people around the world, especially the young. She gives a voice to the often forgotten refugees and displaced persons whose lives have been torn by persecution and war. Her active concern brings the promise of hope."[17] Another example is CBS News anchorwoman Katie Couric, who has used the death of her own husband from colon cancer as inspiration for a personal crusade to promote screening for the disease.

Whenever we use testimony, we have an ethical obligation to assure our listeners that we are quoting or paraphrasing accurately, that we are not taking the testimony out of context, and that the source of the testimony has the expertise or experience to speak authoritatively on the subject. Listeners are not always in a position to judge whether the testimony in a speech is sound, but the critical listener *can* look for signs that it is relevant, timely, and attributed to a credible source.

Comparison and Contrast

One of the principal ways we learn is by comparison and contrast. We compare the unknown to the known. We look for similarities and differences between a new experience and an old one. We try to see ways in which new problems are similar to old problems that we have figured out how to solve. Comparison and contrast are not evidence in the strictest sense of the word; technically, they are a form of reasoning focusing on similarities and differences. Using various forms of evidence, however, comparison and contrast can provide strong support for our ideas and enhance the clarity or persuasiveness of our speeches.

TECHNIQUES OF COMPARISON AND CONTRAST One of the most frequently used ways to make ideas more understandable or believable is by comparing or contrasting the old with the new, the known with the unknown, the familiar with the unfamiliar. New programs are better understood if we consider how they resemble or differ from the programs already in effect. New ideas may seem less "radical" if we show how they compare to ideas we've already had. If our audience is already familiar with a comparable policy, they may be less fearful or more comfortable with a new policy if we can show that it's not all that different. In short, it helps people to understand something new or different if we can compare it to something old and familiar. Comparison and contrast can make people more at ease with the idea of change.

Comparisons are often used by speakers who want to make a difficult or abstract concept more concrete and understandable to listeners. For example, we have all experienced traffic control first-hand. It is relatively easy to understand how a police officer at a sporting event controls the flow of traffic. She allows certain cars to make left-hand turns while oncoming traffic is halted. She might then let traffic proceed both ways or allow those in the right lane to merge right, and so forth. In some ways, the management of traffic is like certain functions performed by the brain. By comparing information flow in the brain to traffic management, a speaker might help an audience visualize this much more complicated process.

One of the most striking uses of comparison to simplify a complicated idea occurred in the 1992 presidential campaign. Ross Perot, an independent candidate for president, hoped to refute Bill Clinton's assertion that his success as Governor of Arkansas proved that he would make a great president. Perot countered this with the observation that such a claim was like comparing the successful management of a mom-and-pop grocery store with managing Wal-Mart.[18]

These comparisons take abstract ideas—how the brain functions, how difficult it is to run a country as big and as varied as the United States—and make them more understandable by identifying them with concrete, observable things with which we are familiar.

Whereas comparison focuses on similarities, contrast highlights differences. This can be a compelling form of support when you advocate an alternative to some idea or policy that generally is thought to have failed. Or you may use contrast to distinguish your own credentials or ideas from those of a competitor. During political campaigns, for example, candidates frequently contrast themselves from their rivals for office. Note how the two candidates for president in 2008 contrasted their views on taxes in the closing week of the campaign.

FOCUS ON CIVIC ENGAGEMENT

Candidates' Contrasting Views

The choice in this election isn't between tax cuts and no tax cuts. It's about whether you believe we should only reward wealth, or whether we should also reward the work and workers who create it. I will give a tax break to 95 percent of Americans who work every day and get taxes taken out of their paychecks every week. I'll eliminate income taxes for seniors making under $50,000 and give homeowners and working parents more of a break. And I'll help pay for this by asking the folks who are making more than $250,000 a year to go back to the tax rate they were paying in the 1990s. No matter what Senator McCain may claim, here are the facts—if you make under $250,000, you will not see your taxes increase by a single dime—not your income taxes, not your payroll taxes, not your capital gains taxes. Nothing. Because the last thing we should do in this economy is raise taxes on the middle class.

Source: From Barack Obama, One Week to Go speech in Canton, Ohio, Oct. 27, 2008. Published 2008.

Whether it's Joe the Plumber here in Ohio or the working men and women across this country, we shouldn't be taxing our small businesses more as Senator Obama wants to do, we need to be helping them expand their businesses and create jobs. America didn't become the greatest nation on earth by giving our money to the government to "redistribute." In this country, we believe in spreading opportunity, for those who need jobs and those who create them. And that is exactly what I intend to do as president of the United States. My opponent's massive new tax increase is exactly the wrong approach in an economic slowdown. The answer to a slowing economy is not higher taxes, but that is exactly what is going to happen when the Democrats have total control of Washington. We can't let that happen. We need pro-growth and pro-jobs economic policies, not pro-government spending programs paid for with higher taxes.

Source: From John McCain, One Week to Go speech in Dayton, Ohio, Oct. 27, 2008. Published 2008.

Neither candidate, of course, would see his plan in the way his opponent has described it. Each, however, is struggling to show a dramatic contrast that will make his program more attractive to voters.

Thinking Critically about Comparison and Contrast Although listeners may find comparison and contrast helpful and persuasive, the basis of comparison should be carefully considered.

Speakers and listeners should ask the same question: are the people, events, places, or objects being compared actually comparable in essential ways? Some may be similar in obvious or superficial ways, but comparison on such bases could be misleading. Those who urge an American-style democracy for Iraq are accused of setting up a false comparison because the histories, cultures, and values of the two countries are so different. On the other hand, proponents of the war in Iraq reject comparisons to the "quagmire" of the Vietnam war because the geopolitical contexts of the two wars are not at all comparable. So care must be exercised in using comparisons. Speakers and listeners should try to satisfy themselves that the things being compared are really similar in ways that are essential to the argument.

Sometimes speakers use a colorful analogy as a way of dramatizing a comparison or contrast they hope to emphasize. In addressing health care reform, the CEO of AARP, William Novelli, advanced the following bold comparison:

> We might compare fixing our health-care system to wrestling an octopus: Two arms are hugging you, two arms are trying to strangle you, and God knows what the other four arms are doing. Every time you think you're making headway, another arm reaches out and grabs you and pulls you back.
>
> This octopus that is the American health-care system seems at times to have us by the arms, legs, and throat ... and the pocketbook. One reason that it seems to be an octopus rather than a Clydesdale, steadily pulling the wagon along, is that the system is not really a system at all, as many of you know so well.
>
> As we try to grapple with one part of the octopus—say the affordability of prescription drugs—we find another tentacle threatening us, then another and another.... The lack of health insurance, the need for more geriatric training in medical schools, the problems with long-term care. This octopus has more than eight arms.[19]

The critical listener would likely conclude that this comparison works well, so long as the octopus analogy does not unfairly exaggerate the seriousness of the challenge. If judged as fair and reasonable, the listener would also probably see Novelli's comparison as reinforcing the complexity of the challenge Americans face—making it memorable and compelling.

TESTING EVIDENCE

Preview. *There are several criteria to use when testing the quality of your evidence: accuracy, completeness, recency, source reliability, and appropriateness for your audience. There are also ethical considerations in testing your evidence. All evidence, regardless of type, should be carefully scrutinized.*

Not all evidence is of equal quality. Simply collecting a great deal of information on a subject is not enough. As you read, talk with individuals, and ponder the information you have unearthed, you have the intellectual and ethical responsibility to carefully judge what should be included in your speech and what should be omitted.

Accuracy

Naturally, you want to use evidence that is true and accurate. Accurate information is redundant and verifiable. You should be able to examine several independent sources and discover essentially the same factual or statistical information. For instance, various sources should all pretty much agree on the number of teenage pregnancies in America each year, the amount of money spent on the space program, or the number of crimes committed in major U.S. cities. When

HIGHLIGHTING SOURCE ACCURACY

Beware of Wikipedia

Wikipedia is a free online encyclopedia that started in 2001. Its content is written collaboratively by users around the globe.

- The site is called *wiki*, meaning that anyone with Web access can add to, correct, or amend it by clicking on an edit function.
- The site had 25.6 million visitors in a single month in 2006, making it the eighteenth most popular site on the Internet.
- Because of the nature of the site, a sobering possibility for misinformation and vandalism exists.
- Already, political operatives have covertly rewritten—or defaced—candidates' biographical entries to make their boss look good, or to make the opponent look ridiculous. Altering senators' ages, entering highly personal information, and posting damaging "jokes" are just a few of the problematic practices that have surfaced.
- Experts in communication technology believe that the sheer size of Wikipedia and the huge number of entries make it impossible to monitor or police it in any effective way.

Source: "Wikipedia: An Online Encyclopedia Being Used for Political Tricks," *Bloomington (IN) Herald-Times*, April 30, 2006, D3.

serious inconsistencies occur, you should question the accuracy of your sources and continue your research until you feel confident that you have found the most accurate information available.

Completeness

You should also test your information for completeness. Although you cannot know all there is to know on a subject, the more thorough, complete, and well-rounded your knowledge on your topic, the better your speech will be.

Completeness and accuracy are clearly related. As you check for accuracy, you will consult numerous sources, making your evidence more and more complete. Having complete information will also help you respond to questions after your speech.

Recency

Generally, you should strive to obtain the most recent information possible. If you are speaking about economic trends, consumer spending, the unemployment rate, or the financial stability of banks and insurance companies, you obviously will want to be armed with the most recent information available. The recency of your information may not be so important when you are discussing other topics, such as a notorious historical character or an event that took place many years ago. As a general rule, however, it's a good idea to look for the most recent evidence available; the more recent your evidence, the better.

Advances in technology have made it easier than ever to find the most up-to-date information on almost any topic. And because your listeners also have access to computer databases and other sources of up-to-date information, it is more important than ever that you, as a speaker, have the most recent information available.

Source Reliability

It is also important to assess the reliability of your sources of information. We have already addressed this concern, but we want to stress here that if you find an impressive piece of testimony or a compelling statistic, you must ask yourself about the credibility of the magazine, newspaper, Web site, or other source in which the information appears.

Whenever you test the reliability of a source, you should ask: Is this source known to have some bias on the subject? Are they promoting a particular point-of-view out of prejudice or self-interest? In general, if you have any reason to doubt a source's objectivity, trustworthiness, or competence, it is best to look elsewhere for information.

Audience Appropriateness

Regardless of the quality of your evidence, it should not be used if it may be considered somehow inappropriate for a particular audience or situation. A human interest story or a personal narrative may be perfectly appropriate in a sermon or an after-dinner speech, but it may seem out of place in a technical report. Similarly, humorous anecdotes may be expected in a speech about a famous entertainer but be considered tasteless when addressing a serious topic such as AIDS or child abuse. The type of speech you are giving, your topic, and your audience's characteristics and values should all be considered as you reflect on the appropriateness of your supporting materials.

Ethical Considerations

In a sense, all of the tests of evidence we have discussed raise ethical considerations. If you use evidence that you know to be inaccurate, incomplete, biased, or offensive to your audience, you have violated the ethical trust of your listeners. You have shown them that you do *not* have their best interests at heart. Sometimes speakers simply lose track of their ethical responsibilities. They want, more than anything, to get the audience to respond—to vote a particular way, to contribute to some cause, or to commit to some action. They want these things so badly that they use evidence in ways that they know to be unethical—perhaps quoting expert testimony out of context, distorting statistics, or citing examples that they know are not typical.

Although anyone can make mistakes, you have an ethical obligation to scrutinize your own evidence carefully and to guard against the temptation to "get the job done" even if the audience is misled in the process. Civic responsibility demands a commitment to ethical public speaking.

SUMMARY

- Even if your ideas have merit, they need to be developed and supported if they are to be understandable and believable to your listeners. Using good evidence is critical.
- Depending on the topic, you will want to use several different types of evidence in your speech:
  - Facts that are accurate and verifiable
  - Definitions that are either informative or persuasive
  - Actual or hypothetical examples that are typical, relevant, and important
  - Statistics that accurately show how things are related and what trends have occurred over time
  - Testimony that is timely and authoritative
  - Comparisons and contrasts that relate the unfamiliar to the familiar or simplify difficult concepts
- Regardless of the specific kind of supporting material used, you will want to:
  - Carefully consider its accuracy, completeness, and recency.
  - Make sure it is appropriate to the audience and the situation and meets high ethical standards.

QUESTIONS FOR REVIEW AND REFLECTION

1. Why should public speakers use supporting material?
2. What are the major kinds of evidence that speakers might use? Briefly define each.
3. How will you determine whether factual information is of high quality?
4. Explain the difference between offering an informative definition and a persuasive one. Offer an example of each.
5. Compare and contrast the actual example with the hypothetical example. Which do you think is generally better to use in speech making? Why?
6. Describe how narratives can be especially effective as examples. Think of one narrative you might use with a speech topic of interest to you.
7. Contrast the three different kinds of averages—mean, median, and mode. Under what circumstances might the mode or median be preferable to the mean as a measure of the true average?
8. Whenever you use statistical support in a speech, what criteria will you use to assess its effectiveness?
9. Under what circumstances might you choose to use personal testimony or lay testimony? How will you make sure you do so effectively?
10. If you were going to use expert testimony in a speech, what criteria would you use in choosing this kind of evidence?
11. Under what circumstances would you say prestige testimony is legitimate? When is it misleading or irrelevant?
12. How might comparisons or contrasts be compelling as supporting material?
13. What are some basic tests for evidence? Why are they important?

ENDNOTES

1. "General Information on Domestic Violence and Sexual Assault," http://middlewayhouse.org/violence.html (accessed July 1, 2009).
2. Taken from *Healthwise*, Richard A. DeVaul's weekly radio program, broadcast on Texas A&M's National Public Radio affiliate, KAMU, 90.9 FM, September 12, 1996.
3. A. Thomas Young, "Ethics in Business," *Vital Speeches of the Day* 58 (1992): 726–27.
4. David K. Shipler, *The Working Poor: Invisible in America* (New York: Knopf, 2004), x–xi.
5. J. Edward Hill, "Priorities in Prevention," *Vital Speeches of the Day* 72 (1995): 88.
6. From Bill Clinton, "Remarks by the President on Responsible Citizenship and the American Community, Georgetown University, July 6, 1995." Published 1995 by National Archives.
7. Reprinted by permission from Fred S. Zeidman, "Remembrance Day Ceremony in the Rotunda of the Capital, April 2009." Copyright © 2009 by US Holocaust Memorial Museum.
8. Reprinted by permission from James C. May, "Connecting and Protecting Our Planet" speech. Copyright © 2009 by Air Transport Association.
9. Reprinted by permission from Roslyn Brock, "NAACP: Conscience of a Nation" speech. Copyright © 2005 by Roslyn Brock.
10. For a detailed description of this and related problems, visit www.therapeuticjustice.com, where you will find a description of the "Community Model," based on the writings of Morgan Moss.
11. Reprinted by permission from Mark Gerencser, "Preparing for the Next Game" speech. Copyright © 2009 by Booz Allen Hamilton.
12. "GOP Plan Leaves Middle Class behind," May 10, 2006, http://dnc.org/a/p/gop_tax_plan_leaves_the_middle_class_behind.html (accessed July 1, 2008).
13. "Republicans Put Forth $70 Billion Tax Relief Measure," May 10, 2006, www.gop.com/News/Read.aspx?ID=6308 (accessed May 15, 2006).
14. Steve Loranger, "How Do We Begin to Solve the Problems?" *Vital Speeches of the Day* 71 (2005): 364.
15. Ben Shalom Bernanke, "Speech to the Economic Club of New York," October 15, 2008, http://americanrhetoric.com/speeches/benbernankenewyorkeconomicclub.htm (accessed July 1, 2009).
16. Jerry Falwell, "An Invitation, Not an Endorsement," *New York Times*, Sunday, May 7, 2006, Section 4, 13.
17. "UNHCR Goodwill Ambassador Angelina Jolie Receives CWS Humanitarian Award," August 23, 2002, www.churchworldservice.org/Immigration/archives/2002/08/11.html (accessed May 9, 2006).
18. See, Peter Goldman, et. al, *Quest for the Presidency: 1992*. (College Station, TX: Texas A&M University Press, 1994), 577.
19. Reprinted by permission from William D. Novelli. "Transforming the Healthcare System" speech, from the AFCEA Solution Series. Copyright © 2005 by AARP.

Why We Need Universal Health Insurance

Robert Stone, M.D., Director, Hoosiers for a Commonsense Health Plan, State Coordinator, Indiana Chapter, Physicians for a National Health Program

Dr. Rob Stone is a strong advocate for universal health care. A dedicated activist, Dr. Stone meets with legislators, addresses rallies, and speaks frequently at local and state groups interested in the issue in order to promote the single-payer or "Medicare-for-all" plan. Dr. Stone routinely conducts extensive question-and-answer sessions following his speeches and encourages listeners to get more information at his organization's Web site. The following is a basic version of the many talks he gives, including a presentation at the First United Methodist Church, Bloomington, Indiana, on April 16, 2009.

Everyone has a story to tell, usually a horror story, about themselves or someone they know. About an outrageous medical bill. About not being able to afford health care. About being afraid of financial ruin due to illness or injury. I see it every day when I work in the ER at Bloomington Hospital, where I have worked the past 23 years.

DR. STONE BEGINS BY ESTABLISHING HIS OWN ETHOS: HE IS AN M.D. WHO HAS PRACTICED FOR 23 YEARS, AND AS AN EMERGENCY ROOM PHYSICIAN HE HAS SEEN COUNTLESS CASES OF PEOPLE WITHOUT RESOURCES TO PAY MEDICAL BILLS.

Recently it was a young fellow who had torn his ACL, a knee ligament that doesn't heal without surgery when it's completely torn. Every time he steps wrong on his leg, the knee swells up and hurts for a week or two. The surgery would cost $15,000. He lost his job that had insurance and his new job doesn't offer any coverage. There's no way he can afford the surgery. He wants to have his life back, to be able to play softball, to be able to work, to be free of fear. He looked at me and asked, "What can I do, Doc? Do I have to keep re-injuring it until I'm completely crippled, go on welfare, and then finally get it fixed?" I had no answer for him. Maybe he can figure a way out of his predicament, and maybe he can't. We have no answer in our current system.

THE USE OF A SPECIFIC EXTENDED EXAMPLE HUMANIZES THE PROBLEM.

You have seen the miserable statistics by now: 46 million people in this country, 860,000 in Indiana, and 15,000 just in Monroe County have no health insurance. The Institute of Medicine, part of the National Institutes of Health, estimates that 18,000 people a year die simply because they lack health insurance. That's a September 11th catastrophe every two months, but we don't see it.

HIS USE OF STATISTICS DEMONSTRATES THE TYPICALITY OF THE EXAMPLE HE HAS JUST USED. THE COMPARISON WITH SEPTEMBER 11 DRAMATIZES THE STATISTIC AND MAKES IT MORE CONCRETE.

People without insurance live sicker and die younger. And it's a myth that there is a safety net. In the ER, I work in the safety net. The reason they call it a "net" is because it is full of holes.

HERE HE USES A CLEVER DEFINITION TO CHALLENGE THE WIDESPREAD BELIEF THAT THE "SAFETY NET" REALLY DOES PROVIDE PROTECTION.

Even if you have insurance, it may not be good enough to protect you. If you have Medicaid, it can be hard to find a doctor who will take you. More and more folks find themselves underinsured, with skimpy policies and very high deductibles. To make it worse, insurance companies have a way of canceling policies once you get sick or injured. The cost of insurance is rising much faster than wages or inflation. Small businesses find it harder and harder to cover their employees. The whole system is collapsing.

THIS ASSERTION IS NOT SUPPORTED BY SPECIFIC EVIDENCE HERE. THE GENERAL PREMISE THAT THE HEALTH CARE SYSTEM IS SERIOUSLY FLAWED IS WIDELY ACCEPTED EVEN IF THE SOLUTIONS ARE CONTESTED. IN ADDITION, DR. STONE TYPICALLY ENLARGES ON THIS POINT WITH SPECIFIC EXAMPLES AND STATISTICS WHEN APPROPRIATE IN THE Q&A.

Here in Monroe County we have seen the community come together around a new entity to serve the uninsured, the Volunteers in Medicine Clinic, which will expand upon our current Community Health Access Program Clinic. We are making a significant effort to address the problems of the uninsured at the local level. We have formed a partnership between the hospital, physicians, and the community, with the support of government, business, and individuals that has proven potent and exhilarating. This is something that we can and will accomplish.

But we understand at the same time that there are larger, systemic problems we need to consider.

Hoosiers for a Commonsense Health Plan is an Indiana group of health care workers and other interested people working for universal health insurance in the state and at the national level. We urge citizens to get involved, educate themselves, and spread the word. It will take a grassroots effort and a lot of work. In Canada, their national system started in the province of Saskatchewan and then spread to the entire country. We want to push the Indiana legislature to solve this problem, and our congressional representatives in Washington as well.

THE EXAMPLE POINTS TO A PROGRAM WITH WHICH THE LISTENERS WOULD BE FAMILIAR. HE RAISES IT IN PART TO RECOGNIZE THAT VARIOUS GROUPS CAN WORK TOGETHER, BUT ALSO TO MAKE SURE THE AUDIENCE DOES NOT BELIEVE THAT THIS IS *THE* SOLUTION.

There are so many problems we face that could be solved if we just had enough money. This isn't one of them. We are already spending enough money on health care. In fact, in the U.S. we spend twice as much per capita as the other wealthy democracies, all of which cover everyone in their populations, and they have better heath statistics than we have, better life expectancy, better infant mortality, and so on. Our problem is that we spend too much money on overhead, inefficiency, and profit. Thirty-one percent of our health care dollars go to overhead, mostly to the private insurance companies. Have you heard how profitable WellPoint/Anthem in Indianapolis is? They have been reporting record earnings this year, and last year their CEO made $25 million. Many studies have shown that if we ran our system as efficiently as Medicare, we would have enough money to cover everyone and have money left over. Compare Medicare with for-profit Anthem/WellPoint. Medicare spends about 3.1 percent of the money it collects on overhead, while WellPoint spends closer to 19 percent. It's not even close.

THE STATISTICS USED HERE ARE DESIGNED TO DISPEL THE NOTION THAT IMPROVING HEALTH CARE WILL COST TOO MUCH MONEY. THE SPECIFIC EXAMPLE OF THE CEO MAKING $25 MILLION REINFORCES HIS POINT ABOUT INSURANCE COMPANY OVERHEAD AND IS ALSO MEANT TO SHOCK LISTENERS.

There are those who reject a single-payer system by labeling it "socialized medicine." But it is not. A single-payer system is one where the government collects and distributes the money, but care is delivered in the private marketplace. Medicare is the classic single-payer system. It was "made in America" and will celebrate its 44th birthday July 30. The sticking point is not that Medicare-for-all is "socialized medicine," but that it would essentially do away with the for-profit insurance as we know it. Congress recently heard from Wendell Potter, former head of corporate communications at Cigna.

HERE DR. STONE REFUTES THE ASSERTION THAT HIS PLAN IS "SOCIALIZED MEDICINE" WITH A SHORT DEFINITION OF "SINGLE-PAYER." BECAUSE "SOCIALIZED MEDICINE" IS OFTEN ASSOCIATED WITH AND COMPARED TO EUROPEAN PLANS, DR. STONE DISPELS THAT NOTION WITH HIS DESCRIPTION OF SINGLE-PAYER AS TRULY AMERICAN.

He said: "I know from personal experience that members of Congress and the public have good reason to question the honesty and trustworthiness of the insurance industry. Insurers make promises they have no intention of keeping; they flout regulations designed to protect consumers; and they make it nearly impossible to understand—or even to obtain—information we need."

HERE IS TESTIMONY FROM A SOURCE DIRECTLY ASSOCIATED WITH THE INSURANCE INDUSTRY ITSELF OFFERING CRITICISM OF THE INDUSTRY BASED ON HIS PERSONAL EXPERIENCE.

Single-payer Medicare-for-all is the commonsense solution for our broken health care system. Call it Medicare Part E—E is for Everyone. Health care for all is an idea whose time has come. It is not a Democratic issue or a Republican issue. It is an idea to unite us, not divide us. This is the real national security issue. Go to our Web page, HCHP.info. Contact us, get involved, make your voice heard, make a difference!

THE SPEECH CONCLUDES WITH AN ASSERTION THAT THIS IS NOT A PARTISAN ISSUE, A REITERATION OF THE IMPORTANCE OF THE ISSUE, AND A CALL TO ACTION.

Source: Reprinted by permission from Robert Stone, "Why We Need Universal Health Insurance" speech.

CHAPTER

9

Organizing Your Speech

CHAPTER SURVEY

The Importance of Good Organization

How Patterns of Organization Connect Ideas

Guidelines for Organizing Your Speech

Transitions as Connectives

Introducing Your Speech

Concluding Your Speech

CHAPTER OBJECTIVES

After studying this chapter, you should be able to

1. Discern the importance of sound organization.
2. Evaluate the quality of ideas.
3. Select and apply appropriate organizational patterns and sequences.
4. Recognize basic principles of good organization.
5. Understand how to construct and use good transitions.
6. Construct effective introductions and conclusions.

Some speakers carefully select and focus their topics, have a clear purpose and thesis, seek out good supporting materials, and still fail to deliver a good speech. Part of their failure may be due to how they have organized their materials. This chapter is devoted to helping you understand how to organize your ideas in a way that will help you achieve your purpose.

THE IMPORTANCE OF GOOD ORGANIZATION

Preview. *Nearly everyone recognizes that a speech must have strong content and be delivered effectively. Yet what impact, if any, does the organization of those ideas and supporting materials have on the listeners' response? Research and experience have shown that sound organization can have a significant effect on the audience's willingness and ability to listen and their impressions of the speaker's credibility.*

Effective speakers organize their speeches carefully. They think about what to include and what to leave out. They do not introduce irrelevant or redundant information. The best speakers understand how much background to cover, which issues to address, and how best to allocate their limited time.

Good organization is important for many reasons. Well-organized speakers appear to be competent, focused, and knowledgeable. As a result, listeners perceive them as more credible.[1] A clearly organized presentation also promotes learning and retention.[2] Delivering a well-organized presentation is one of the *best* ways for you to show respect for your listeners. When you take the time and effort to organize your comments clearly and coherently, you show that you care about making yourself understood. No listener should have to struggle to understand a presentation that is disorganized or incoherent.[3]

The quality of your organization depends on the clarity and simplicity of your ideas, as well as their appropriateness to the particular situation and audience. A well-organized speech is clear, straightforward, and easily comprehended by your listeners.

Clarity of Ideas

To be clear, an idea must first be complete. Consider, for example, Amy, who wants to speak on reforming the way appropriations for pet projects (known as *earmarks*) are inserted into legislation by members of Congress. In drafting an outline, she first clarified her specific purpose and thesis statement. These were clearly articulated and reflected the guidelines for such statements in Chapter 6. The draft read like this:

Specific purpose: *I want my audience to agree that we need to reform the process by which earmarks are added to legislation.*

Thesis statement: *Reforming the way earmarks are added to legislation would control irresponsible congressional spending.*

Main Ideas

I. Earmark examples
II. Criticism of earmarks
III. How earmarks waste money
IV. Benefits of earmarks
V. Transparency and accountability

Although Amy's specific purpose and thesis statement were clear, her main points were not. None of her ideas were in the form of a complete sentence; each was undeveloped and unclear. As a result, the main points were not easily distinguished and some even overlapped. The first idea was not a main idea at all, but rather one type of supporting material—examples—that she might use throughout the speech. Amy's second point was too vague; her third point referred to one of several of the criticisms one might make of earmarks. In addition to wasting taxpayer money, Amy wanted to argue that earmarks were undemocratic because they were not subjected to debate, were often motivated by partisan political concerns, and often led to corrupt practices, such as bribery and noncompetitive bidding on government projects. Amy wanted to acknowledge that earmarks sometimes produced good results, providing funding for badly needed local projects. Yet her ultimate goal was to advocate new policies that would control the abuses associated with earmarks. In short, she wanted to advocate change.

Thus, Amy ultimately decided on a problem-solution pattern of organization, identifying several objections to the current system, then spelling out the specifics of her proposed reforms. Her new outline looked like this:

I. There are several problems with the current system of adding earmarks to legislation in the U.S. Congress.
   A. Earmarks often waste taxpayer money.
   B. Earmarks are not subjected to debate and are therefore undemocratic.
   C. Earmarks are often added to legislation for purely political purposes.
   D. Earmarks can lead to political corruption.
II. President Obama's proposal to reform the legislative process will allow needed earmarks while controlling these abuses.
   A. The new policy would require legislators to post their proposed earmarks on the World Wide Web.
   B. There would be public hearings on all proposed earmarks, requiring members of Congress to justify their proposals and their cost to taxpayers.
   C. All proposals for work by private contractors would require a competitive bidding process.

Amy's plan for the speech was now clear, with straightforward main ideas stated in complete sentences. Her subordinate ideas were also clear and coherent, and all that remained was for her to fill in the details with examples, testimony, and other forms of evidence.

Simplicity of Ideas

Audiences must be able to understand your ideas if they are to respond positively. In addition to clarity, the simplicity of your main ideas is important. You want to state your ideas fully and accurately, yet in terms simple enough that your listeners can understand immediately and recall your main ideas pretty much word for word.

To achieve this ideal, ask yourself whether you have stated your ideas in the most basic ways possible. Avoid combining two or three ideas in one main point. Strive for a balance among your main points, so that you allocate approximately the same amount of time to each.

Some speakers try to include too much information or even a whole series of ideas within one main point. Meleia, for example, proposed the following speech:

Specific purpose: *I want my audience to become more actively involved in politics.*
Thesis statement: *Political involvement leads to positive results.*

She stated her first main idea like this:

I. People who take an interest in politics can have a practical impact, help restore idealism to the process, and learn valuable personal skills.

This main point tries to do too much. It is not a single idea. Instead, it is really two, perhaps even three interrelated ideas. Meleia needs to sort out the ideas and focus separately on each. A revised version of this outline might look like this:

I. There are practical benefits to society when more citizens participate in politics.
II. The political system itself also benefits from more citizen participation.
III. Individuals who participate in the political process gain valuable personal skills.

If Meleia can convince her audience that important benefits can be gained from participating in politics, then she will have achieved her purpose. To accomplish this, of course, she will have to take the next step and develop each of her ideas with supporting materials. She will need to enumerate the benefits that come from political participation, show that they are indeed beneficial, and make them real and compelling for her audience.

Simplicity, then, goes hand in hand with clarity as a basic characteristic of a well-stated main point. What seems simple and clear to one audience, however, may not seem that way to a different audience, so it is also important that you consider the situation and audience as you prepare your speech.

Suitability to the Situation

As we emphasized in Chapter 6, a speech is designed for a specific audience. A speech is also influenced by the occasion that prompts it and the setting in which it occurs. Thus, your ideas must not only be clear and simple, but also appropriate for the particular audience and context.

The level of complexity of any idea will be significantly influenced by the audience's relationship to the topic. If, for example, you wanted to address the threat posed by the growing federal deficit, you might choose to introduce ideas that are highly technical, sophisticated, and complex if you were addressing a group of economists at a professional conference. If, on the other hand, you were speaking to your classmates, you would probably want to offer more basic information about the deficit, including background information and definitions of key terms. How technical or complex your discussion should be, then, depends on what the audience brings to the speech in terms of their background, experience, and expectations.

HOW PATTERNS OF ORGANIZATION CONNECT IDEAS

Preview. *To make a set of ideas reasonable and coherent for your audience, you need to put the ideas together so that they relate to one another in some logical fashion. To do this, you will use such basic patterns of organization as chronological or sequential, spatial, categorical, climactic, cause-and-effect, problem-solution, and narrative.*

When you have developed a good idea or series of ideas, you then face the job of arranging them in some order. It is important to recognize that most speeches can be organized in a variety of different ways. *Your* task is to choose the most appropriate organizational pattern for the particular topic and situation in which you are speaking.

There are many organizational patterns from which to choose, some of which we will talk about more in later chapters. Here, however, we introduce several of the most commonly used organizational patterns.

Chronological or Sequential Order

One commonly used pattern of arrangement is chronological order. You begin with a specific point in time and then move forward or backward, depending on the nature of the subject. Chronological order may be useful with a variety of topics, most notably those that deal with a process or a historical event. Thus, the development of the labor movement in the United States, the events that led up to the dissolution of the Soviet Union, or the evolution of the Christian Coalition as a national political force might all be appropriate subjects for chronological arrangement.

Here is how one student, providing an historical account of Nazi Germany, arranged his ideas in a **chronological pattern**:

Specific purpose: *I want my audience to understand how the Nazis came to power in Germany.*

Thesis statement: *Nazism grew out of social and political unrest.*

I. In 1919, the Treaty of Versailles created several serious problems for Germany.

II. Financial crises encouraged the National Socialists to attempt an unsuccessful coup in Bavaria in 1923.

III. By 1930, the National Socialist Party had emerged as a major political party.
IV. The violent election campaign of 1933 brought the Nazi Party to power.

Similar to the chronological pattern is the **sequential pattern**, which you would use if you wanted your audience to understand some step-by-step procedure or process. For instance, if you wanted listeners to understand the process involved in applying for government-subsidized housing, you could begin with the first step that the applicant takes and follow the process in order, step by step. You could similarly use a sequential pattern to help listeners understand how the Asian long-horned beetle attacks and destroys trees, how terrorists make dirty bombs, or the steps involved in adopting a child.

Spatial Order

A second common pattern is spatial arrangement. With this pattern, you use space as your ordering principle. A speech explaining the architectural plans for a new library, a presentation describing major tourist attractions of a big city (as one travels from north to south), or a speech describing the most progressive, reform-oriented prisons in the United States may all be appropriate candidates for spatial organization.

The following is an example of how one student arranged ideas in a **spatial pattern** determined by geography, as he addressed the need for emergency preparedness in the United States.

Specific purpose: *I want my audience to recognize the serious natural disasters that increasingly threaten all of our geographical regions.*
Thesis statement: *Natural disasters pose a growing threat throughout the United States.*
I. Hurricanes threaten our coasts.
II. Wildfires threaten our woodlands.
III. Tornadoes threaten our midwestern regions.
IV. Floods threaten low-lying areas along streams and lakes.

The student then went on to offer specific examples of each of these natural disasters, as well as illustrating how each has increased in frequency.

Categorical Order

Ideas can also be arranged in a pattern that emphasizes distinct topics—a **categorical pattern**. When you arrange your ideas categorically, you address types, forms, qualities, or aspects of the speech subject. For example, if you were giving a speech on the benefits of higher education, you could develop ideas related to the intellectual, social, or economic advantages of education. Similarly, you might discuss teen pregnancy in terms of those most at risk or prison reform in terms of different models that have been tried.

The following example shows how one student arranged her ideas categorically:

Specific purpose: *I want my audience to understand how restrictions on smoking are becoming common in the United States.*
Thesis statement: *Restrictions on smoking are becoming common in the United States.*
I. Businesses are increasingly going smoke-free.
II. Campuses are increasingly going smoke-free.
III. Municipalities are increasingly going smoke-free.
IV. States are increasingly going smoke-free.

Under each category, the speaker then develops her speech by providing a combination of statistical information, specific examples, and testimony. This pattern and the other patterns described so far are especially well suited for organizing informative speeches.

Climactic Order

Another way of arranging ideas is to use a **climactic pattern**, or a sequence that goes from simple to difficult, from least important to most important, or from emotionally neutral to emotionally intense. When the climactic order reflects audience needs and priorities, it can be an especially effective way to arrange ideas if the goal is to gain audience agreement or action. As you assess your ideas or arguments, you would then arrange them to build up to your strongest argument or most compelling idea.

Like a playwright, a speaker may wish to build on the listeners' interests and concerns until a climactic moment is reached. If, for example, you were addressing an audience with a strong concern for ethics, you might talk about a solution to a community problem in terms of its affordability and its benefits to the community, concluding with the moral imperative to act. The following is an example of ideas patterned climactically, from least to most important, with rising emotional intensity:

Specific purpose: *I want my audience to agree that the United States needs a central food inspection agency.*
Thesis statement: *The United States should create a central food inspection agency.*
I. Oversight by a central agency would yield economic advantages.
II. Oversight by a central agency would curb food-borne illnesses.
III. Oversight by a central agency would save lives.

The climactic pattern is most often used in persuasive speeches.

Causal Order

Ideas can be arranged in an order that leads from cause to effect or from effect to cause. This **causal pattern** is useful for speakers who want an audience to understand how an idea or event has unfolded, or for speakers who want to suggest changes in a chain of relationships that will bring more desirable outcomes. If, for example, you wanted your audience to understand why type 2 diabetes is on the rise, you could arrange your ideas so that they would show the relationship between the disease and the contributing factors (unhealthy diet, lack of exercise). You could also use cause-and-effect order to discuss such topics as the causes of ozone depletion, the effects of gang activities on communities, or the economic factors that typically lead to a recession.

The following is an example of ideas arranged in a causal pattern. Here the president of a neighborhood association argued that the lack of traffic lights and signs produced harmful results and urged the city council to take action.

Specific purpose: *I want council members to agree that a better system of traffic lights and signs is needed in this community.*

Thesis statement: *The present system of traffic control is inconvenient and dangerous.*

I. *Effect:* Pedestrians, young and old alike, have been struck and killed at unguarded crossings.

II. *Effect:* At the main mall entrance, several accidents have resulted when oncoming traffic has failed to stop for the red light.

III. *Effect:* Traffic jams causing long delays occur every weekday during rush hours.

IV. *Cause:* The real culprit contributing to this safety hazard is poor traffic control procedures.

This speaker, at a rally protesting a proposed Alaska pipeline, is appealing to the concerns of those who believe that drilling will cause serious harm to the environment.

When using causal arrangement, keep in mind that a chronological relationship does *not* necessarily equal a causal relationship. One event following another may represent chance as easily as cause. In addition, whenever you look at a given effect to seek its causes, you must guard against oversimplification. Identifying a single cause for a complex problem is usually unrealistic. Finally, sometimes cause-and-effect order is incorporated into a problem-solution pattern. Within the structure of a problem-solution speech, you will analyze the problem (effect) in terms of contributing causes, and then go on to propose solutions. The speaker who advances solutions is clearly speaking persuasively, but informative speeches also may occasionally use a causal pattern (see Chapter 14).

Problem-Solution Patterns

The **problem-solution pattern** is most common in persuasive or political speeches. In such a speech, you might identify an important problem, then propose a solution that you hope the audience will endorse. You might use this approach in proposing solutions to such problems as credit card fraud, the rise in eating disorders among college students, or the unregulated selling of drugs over the Internet.

REFLECTIVE THINKING SEQUENCE The traditional problem-solution pattern is based on educational philosopher John **Dewey's Reflective Thinking Sequence**[4] and typically addresses these questions:

1. How shall we define and limit the problem?
2. What are the causes and extent of the problem?
3. What are the effects of the problem? Who has been hurt?
4. What are the criteria by which solutions should be judged?
5. What are the possible solutions and the relative strengths and weaknesses of each?
6. What is the best solution?
7. How can we put it into effect?

Depending on the problem and the audience's prior knowledge, you might spend more or less time discussing the nature of the problem and its contributing causes. In situations where the audience is well versed on the problem, you might only briefly describe it and spend most of your speaking time exploring viable solutions.

The following is an example of ideas from a student speech that employs a problem-solution pattern:

Specific purpose: *I want my audience to join in the effort to stop deforestation.*
Thesis statement: *Deforestation must be stopped before its adverse effects make the world unfit for future generations.*

I. *Problem (causes):* Deforestation has accelerated in recent years for a variety of reasons.
   A. One cause of deforestation is agriculture, which clears forests for farming.
   B. Another cause is cattle ranching, which needs land for grazing.

   C. In developing countries, people still cut down large numbers of trees for shelter and firewood.
   D. In general, overpopulation drives new development that threatens our remaining forests.

II. *Problem (effects):* The effects of deforestation are often devastating.
   A. With more than 50 percent of the world's plants and animals living in 7 percent of the world's forests, most of them are headed for extinction—thus significantly decreasing biodiversity.
   B. Deforestation also leads to serious erosion and flooding.
   C. Some experts argue that perhaps the most serious effect of deforestation is global warming.

III. *Criteria for solutions:* The solutions may be weighed against such criteria as feasibility, affordability, and fairness.

IV. *Possible solutions:* We can take a number of actions to help end deforestation.
   A. We can support *reforestation* legislation, which would prohibit clear-cutting in designated areas and allow trees to grow back naturally.
   B. We can tackle population control—by educating third-world countries concerning birth control and acting responsibly in building our own families.
   C. We can inform others about the problem while setting a good example by not wasting paper and other forest products.

V. *Best course of action:* In this case, all three solutions are interrelated, and all should be pursued. Some actions are personal and immediate; others are more long-range and deal with developing new policies and educational outreach.

THE MOTIVATED SEQUENCE AS A SPECIAL PROBLEM-SOLUTION PATTERN One specific approach to organizing a problem-solution speech is the **motivated sequence.**[5] This pattern is organized around five steps:

1. *Arouse:* capture the audience's attention and focus on the problem.
2. *Dissatisfy:* make listeners understand that this is a serious problem that needs their attention and action.
3. *Gratify:* reveal the solution to the problem, and assure listeners that it is within *their* power to remedy the situation.
4. *Visualize:* show listeners *exactly* how much they can improve the situation.
5. *Move:* appeal to the audience to take a specific action.

The motivated sequence is best suited to topics with emotional as well as logical appeal. It may work best in a speech on the need for safe housing for domestic abuse victims, or on reducing the practice of euthanizing shelter animals, or on creating after-school programs for at-risk teens. The motivated sequence allows you to engage the audience's emotions and urge them to act.

It addresses the problem *and* the solution, but it concludes with an appeal designed to motivate the audience to *act*. Above all, it aims to convince the audience that they have the *power* to act, and it helps them visualize *how* they can address the problem in specific ways. Visualizing the outcomes as you conclude the speech can be especially moving. Your own passion and commitment, an awareness of the audience's needs and values, and a thorough understanding of the details of your solution are central to the effective use of this problem-solution pattern.

Narrative Patterns

Because of cultural background or personal preference, some speakers may prefer to use less direct and more organic patterns of organization.[6] For instance, a speech may be organized around telling one or more stories, using a **narrative pattern.** Rhetorical scholar Walter Fisher points out that the most compelling narratives are coherent, rather than scattered or fragmented.[7] The speaker may begin by introducing a theme, such as the idea that the best government leaders are highly ethical. Then, the speaker would share various stories to illustrate and reinforce the speech's thesis. Or, he or she might pay tribute to a single person by sharing an extended narrative of the person's life. The speech is a continuous narrative with various internal stories drawn out and emphasized. Each would relate to an overarching theme, perhaps by demonstrating how the person being honored lived a courageous life. Narratives should also possess what Fisher calls **fidelity**—that is, they must "ring true" with the stories that listeners know to be true in their own lives.[8] For example, a speaker might explore the meaning of *courage* by sharing a series of stories of courageous acts. While those acts might be admirable and unusual, they also must seem plausible to the audience if they are to "ring true."

If the speaker wants to build in a sense of drama or climax within a narrative pattern, he or she may choose to use a **spiraling narrative**. For instance, the speaker might give a speech of tribute by sharing stories that build in intensity. A person's simple acts of courage might be shared first, moving to more unusual acts, and perhaps culminating with uncommon acts of valor. Again, each would be united by the general theme. When delivered effectively, narrative patterns can contribute to a powerful, engaging presentation.

This list of organizational patterns is not exhaustive, but it does include the principal ways in which you can arrange your ideas. Some patterns of organization work best with informative speeches, whereas others work better with persuasive speeches. And some topics lend themselves to a chronological or a spatial pattern of organization better than others. In the final analysis, however, it is important to recognize that there is never just one "correct" way to organize a given speech. As you prepare your speech, you may experiment with various ways of arranging your ideas until you come upon the organizational pattern that seems to work best.

FOCUS ON CIVIC ENGAGEMENT

Amanda Shares Her Family's Journey Using a Narrative Pattern

On November 2, 2006, Amanda Cunningham spoke at a Habitat for Humanity fund-raising breakfast. In her moving speech, she shares the story of her parents' courage and determination and reveals how they qualified to become Habitat homeowners. Using a narrative pattern, this speech also functions as a tribute to Amanda's parents and offers testimonial evidence of the impact of Habitat for Humanity on the lives of real people.

My name is Amanda Cunningham. I am a student at Ivy Tech. My parents, Mark and Kim Cunningham, and I are a Habitat for Humanity partner family. Let me tell you a little bit about us. My parents were high school sweethearts and have been married for 24 years now. My dad was laid off from Otis Elevator in 1991 and decided to accept a job offer in Florida to support our family. At the age of 29, two years after moving to Florida, my dad was diagnosed with a rare type of cancer in his sinus cavity. The news from the doctors was not good; they gave my dad a small chance of survival.

After months and months of radiation treatments, the tumor had decreased in size. My brother and I were so young that we do not remember our dad being anything but sick. I remember him coming home from his radiation treatments being so tired that he would just fall asleep on the sofa. I watched him have seizures and feed himself through a tube in his nose.

My dad got very sick, but my mom stood beside him, never once giving up. Mom was not only trying to keep her and Dad's spirits up, but she was also trying to raise two small children and work her job. She ended up working long hours, seven days a week. My dad went through treatments for cancer the entire time we were in Florida. After six years there, we decided to move home to Indiana. We did not know whether the cancer was gone or not.

My dad is now 43 years old. The cancer has been in remission for 14 years, and he has completed college. The years of treatments have left him cancer-free, but his health is not perfect.

GUIDELINES FOR ORGANIZING YOUR SPEECH

Preview. *Regardless of the particular pattern of organization you choose, you will want to keep in mind some basic guidelines. It is important to view the choice of an organizational pattern as a strategic decision. At the same time, you will want to consider issues of balance, the number of main ideas to include in your speech, and where to place your strongest, most compelling ideas and information.*

Given the wide variety of organizational patterns from which you can choose, you should keep a few general principles in mind. Select your organizational pattern carefully.

Making the Pattern a Strategic Choice

The way you present your ideas and information should be *strategic*, designed to enhance the chance that you will elicit the audience response you are seeking. If you are talking to an audience about a problem that is quite complicated or one with which they have little knowledge or experience, you will want to devote a good portion of your speech to educating your listeners. A good organizational strategy in this case may be a traditional problem-solution pattern—one in which

The effects from the radiation treatments have been significant. Dad is now speech, hearing and visually impaired, and is fed through a tube in his stomach. His immune system is not as strong as all of ours, and we are not ever sure if or when he will end up sick and in the hospital.

My parents are the strongest people I will ever know. Their strength is not only an inspiration to my brother and me, but has also given us a solid foundation for our lives. There *are* heroes left in this world, and I count my parents among them. Giving up has never been an option for our family. Whenever a door closed on my parents, they continued to search for one that was open.

The trailer we live in is cold. It has no insulation and drafty windows and doors. The roof leaks and we have to be careful where we walk because the floor is giving way. It has been our home for the last seven years, and we have been looking for any opportunity to get into a better situation.

That opportunity was provided by Habitat for Humanity. Our family has never been looking for a handout, but rather a hand up. Habitat for Humanity offered us more than the opportunity for a place to live. It offered us an opportunity to help ourselves. *Finally*, my parents will have a home to call their own. You cannot imagine how it feels to know that my parents are going to have a home again. I speak for everyone in my family when I say that Habitat for Humanity of Monroe County is a blessing.

As blessings go, the best of blessings are those that bless others as well. We know as a family that being part of Habitat for Humanity is being part of a bigger family that offers hope for more families that need a window of opportunity like us. We can't wait to start building our home with Habitat this spring!

Now, I would like to introduce you to my parents: Mark and Kim Cunningham.

you devote substantial time to defining and exploring the problem and its causes and effects *before* moving on to propose possible solutions.

Developing Main Ideas with a Concern for Symmetry

Second, give some thought to **symmetry** or balance. If the idea you are addressing is one of your speech's main points, then you will want to explore it thoroughly and offer a well-developed, substantive treatment. Sometimes you may be discussing an idea that is particularly controversial or complex, and so you may need to devote a bit more time to it. In general, however, you should advance the main ideas of your speech in a balanced way, giving each one the emphasis it deserves so that your listeners will understand, recall, and hopefully be moved by what you are saying.

Determining the Number of Main Ideas

Sometimes speakers have questions about how many main ideas they can convey in a single speech. In doing research on an engaging topic, the speaker may be tempted to cover a long list of key points. But including too many main ideas may result in the inadequate development of each. To some extent, the time allowed for the speech will influence how many main ideas can be fully developed. If you are delivering a 6- to 8-minute speech (as is common in the classroom), you may be hard-pressed to cover more than two or three main points adequately. A 20-minute presentation (perhaps in a community setting) may allow you to advance a larger number of main ideas (usually no more than five). But there are two constraints to keep in mind. First, many listeners cannot absorb a large number of main ideas during a single presentation (refer to Chapter 4 on listening challenges). In addition, a well-formulated specific purpose statement should limit and focus the speech. You can test each idea you are considering by asking whether it advances your speech's specific purpose. If it does not, you will want to eliminate it.

Choosing the Placement of Main Ideas

Finally, be aware of **primacy** and **recency effects**. Although researchers do not agree on whether arguments are more memorable and persuasive if they are placed first (primacy) or last (recency), they *do* agree that those two positions are the most powerful—and that information or arguments embedded in the middle of a message are less likely to be as memorable or have as much impact on listeners.[9] In most instances, then, you will want to lead with and conclude with information and ideas that are especially crucial to the case you are making.

TRANSITIONS AS CONNECTIVES

Preview. *Transitions add clarity and smoothness to a speech. Without strong transitions, even a well-organized speech may strike listeners as confusing or disorganized. When crafted well, transitions can contribute significantly to the impact of the speaker's overall message.*

As a responsible speaker, you need to help the audience see the relationships among your ideas. Once you have drafted your speech, you must consider how you will progress from one idea to another so that listeners can see the connections.

A **transition** is a bridge that connects one idea to another. Listeners cannot be expected to pay complete attention to the speaker, nor can they be expected to understand the sequence of ideas and information as clearly as the speaker does. You must alert your listeners to a new idea about to be introduced and help them see how it relates to your overall message.

As structural elements, transitions are small but mighty. They are, perhaps, the most unappreciated and underused components of effective speech making. A transition links one major idea with another in a speech, showing their relationship to each other. However, a transition does more than show how an idea fits into a speech. It also reinforces an idea that a speaker wishes to share. Transitions often provide a quick glance back at the idea just discussed and then a quick look forward to the next main idea. A transition, then, may function as a miniature review and preview of ideas, reinforcing key ideas in the speech.[10] For example, a speaker identifying factors that have contributed to the rise in rates of type 2 diabetes may make the following two points:

I. Poor dietary choices have contributed to the rise of type 2 diabetes.
II. Sedentary lifestyles have contributed to the rise of type 2 diabetes.

A transition that bridges the two, simultaneously reinforcing the ideas, could be as follows:

Not only does a poor diet make developing type 2 diabetes more likely, so does a lack of exercise.

Sometimes, in longer, more intricately developed speeches, this reviewing and previewing should be done more extensively. When this is the case, the speaker can rely on an internal preview or an internal summary, both of which are extended transitions.

Internal Previews

When moving from one idea to the next, you can give your audience a brief **internal preview** of the point you are about to make to focus listeners' attention on what's to come. For example, suppose a speaker has just discussed this point: "Pollution of air and water in this community has direct consequences for your health." The next main idea he plans to take up is the following: "Pollution effects can drastically alter the standard of living in this country." To transition into this second point, he might combine a simple restatement of the first idea with an internal preview in this way:

> Pollution, then, can cost you (and those you love) your health. But its effects are even more far-reaching. If pollution isn't controlled now, drastic steps will have to be taken that will impact the way we live every day. Let us consider now the ways in which our standard of living is at risk because of pollution.

You may benefit from using an internal preview when you want to set the stage for a particular portion of your speech, perhaps by explaining *why* you will focus on the programs you have chosen. Suppose, for example, you have been addressing the problems with public education in the United States, with a particular focus on young children from low-income families. Now, you want to explore programs in your community that represent "best practices" in after-school programming for these children. To transition into this portion of your speech, you might say:

> Our community is filled with many interesting after-school programs for children. But three in particular have recently won awards for their excellence and creativity: the Boys and Girls Club After-Hours Program, the Girls, Inc. Leadership Program, and the Mother Hubbard's Cupboard Growing Food for Healthy Bodies Program. In the time that remains, I would like to focus on each of these programs and explore how they have truly enriched the lives of our children.

Internal Summaries

Sometimes, getting from one idea to another has to be more elaborate because the material is complex. In these cases, you may use an **internal summary**, briefly going over the information covered so far before moving on to the next point. A speaker explaining the background of the American Revolution, for example, used an internal summary in her transition:

> We've seen how the Stamp Act in 1765 aroused the first successful organized resistance on the part of the colonists to the British government. Then, British attempts to deal with the problems of taxation and defense, coupled with a growing spirit of

independence in the colonies, caused an ever-widening breach between North America and Great Britain. Now let us see how the events in the months preceding the Declaration of Independence led the young colonies to a final break with the mother country.

That kind of transition—a short summary of what has been said—helps keep the audience mentally on track. It also reinforces key ideas.

Sometimes internal summaries can be brief phrases embedded in new ideas. This is how one speaker used transitions to develop her first main idea in a speech on poverty and dental health:

I. Poor people with impaired dental health confront a variety of problems.
   A. Their general health can be at risk (including heart disease).
   B. *Not only can poor dental health lead to other serious health consequences*, it adversely influences the individual's ability to get a job.
   C. *In addition to basic health and employment problems*, those with poor dental health often find it challenging to establish meaningful relationships with others in their daily lives.

These sample transitions illustrate how words and phrases can help listeners process information and ideas as they are advanced by the speaker.

Signposts

In some instances, you may merely want to provide verbal markers to alert your audience to the fact that you are moving from one idea to another by enumerating each point or by signaling the next point to be made. If so, you can rely on what are known as **signposts**. You may, for example, tell your listeners that you have three good reasons for asking them to sign up for the Big Brothers/Big Sisters program. You may simply say: "*The second reason* for you to sign up now is that the need is so urgent in our community." As you move into the third reason, you may go on to say: "*A final reason* for volunteering is that you will derive great satisfaction from knowing you have really made a difference in a child's life."

Other signposts include words such as *next*, *another*, and *finally*. Here are some examples:

"*The next* good reason is . . ."
"*Another* reason you should sign up is . . ."
"*Finally*, you should join now because . . ."

Rhetorical Questions

A speaker can also use **rhetorical questions** to highlight movement and assist flow, with the added benefit of encouraging listeners' involvement. Rhetorical questions stimulate thought and interest without seeking an oral response. Suppose a speaker has been discussing the need for a Volunteers in Medicine clinic in her community. She has described the medical services currently available in the area. As she moves on to address the issue of those who fall through the cracks of the present system, she asks, *But what happens if you have no health insurance? Who will take care of you when you are sick?*

These rhetorical questions should engage listeners' emotions and make them eager to hear what the speaker has to say. They should also encourage movement in the minds of the audience, allowing the speaker to focus their attention on the community's real need for a VIM clinic.

Taken together, these transitional devices help listeners make the right connections and follow the progression of ideas in your speech. In addition, transitions reinforce ideas and encourage listener involvement.

So far, we have discussed organizational principles and approaches that largely apply to the way you will arrange the main ideas in the body of your speech. Now we turn our attention to how you will begin your speech. The effectiveness of your speech's introduction will likely influence the audience's frame of mind as you move into the presentation of your main ideas.

INTRODUCING YOUR SPEECH

Preview. *Although speech introductions may be structured in different ways, the most effective introductions establish common ground with the audience, capture and hold the listeners' attention, stress the relevance of your topic, establish your credibility as a speaker, clarify your purpose, and provide a preview of your ideas.*

No matter which organizational pattern you follow, you will need to introduce your speech in an effective way. It is not enough to say, "Today I am going to talk with you about why the community needs a free health clinic." Hardly any listener will be riveted by that. Instead, the introduction needs to be structured so that audience members *want* to listen to your speech, view you as a credible source, and have some idea of your speech's purpose and main ideas.

Establish Common Ground

Many speakers seek to establish common ground with listeners as they begin to speak. Audiences tend to listen to speakers with whom they share common experiences, problems, or goals. For example, when giving a speech on student loans in a class with several other working students, Yuko began her speech this way:

> When I get to this class at 8:00 A.M., I have had four hours' sleep. I work full-time as a waitress at Nick's and do not get home until about 2:00 A.M. Like many of you, I need to work to support myself while going to school. Some of you have full-time jobs and some are part-timers. Some of you also have families to care for as well as working and going to school. And I know that at least one of you is also a single parent. For us, getting an education and making ends meet is not easy.

In speaking contexts outside the classroom, the speaker may also want to emphasize similarities between himself or herself and the audience. Perhaps the speaker is perceived as someone whose life experiences have differed significantly from those of the audience. In this case, establishing common ground with listeners creates a sense of "we-ness" that invites the audience to listen. In 1993, President Bill Clinton addressed the convention of the Church of God in Christ in Memphis, Tennessee, speaking from the pulpit where Martin Luther King had given his last sermon. This white president used the occasion to connect with the African-American community by stressing their common goals.

> By the grace of God and your help, last year I was elected President of this great country. I never dreamed that I would ever have a chance to come to this hallowed place where Martin Luther King gave his last sermon. I ask you to think today about the purpose for which I ran and the purpose for which so many of you worked to put me in this great office. I have worked hard to keep faith with our common efforts: to restore the economy, to reverse the politics of helping only those at the top of our totem pole and not the hard-working middle class or the poor; to bring our people together across racial and regional and political lines, to make a strength out of our diversity instead of letting it tear us apart; to reward work and family and community and try to move us forward into the 21st century. I have tried to keep faith.[11]

Establishing common ground (together with other devices described next) may also engage the audience's attention and make them want to hear more.

Capture and Maintain the Listeners' Attention

When you first get up to speak, listeners usually give you their full attention. But that attention may be fleeting. Let us consider several approaches to maintaining the audience's attention and how some speakers have used them.

Tell a Story An interesting story—whether it is emotional, humorous, puzzling, or intriguing—commands attention. The story can be real or hypothetical. It can be a personal story that reveals something of your own experience, or it can be something you have read. Speaking to a group of teachers, Carmen Mariano, an assistant superintendent in the Massachusetts public school system, began with this narrative:

> Ernest Hemingway tells the story of a Spanish man who has a bitter argument one morning with his young son, Paco. When he arrived home later that day, the man discovered that Paco's room was empty—he had run away from home.
>
> Overcome with remorse, the man realized that his son was more important to him than anything else. He went to a well-known grocery store in the center of town and posted a large sign that read, "Paco, come home. I love you. Meet me here tomorrow morning. Signed, your father."
>
> The next morning, the man went to the store. There, he found his son and seven other young boys who had also run away from home. They were all answering the call for love, hoping it was their dad inviting them home.[12]

Mariano used this opening to lead into the point that teaching children who come from tension-filled homes where they do not feel loved or wanted is a great challenge for teachers in the public school system.

Use Rhetorical Questions Earlier in the chapter we discussed how rhetorical questions may assist movement in a speech and encourage involvement. Similarly, in an introduction, rhetorical questions can prompt listeners to think about an issue or idea without seeking an immediate response.

Lin began his speech by raising questions that challenged listeners to consider how they might deal with ethical dilemmas:

> This is an honors public speaking class, and, as honors students, we're all used to getting good grades. Grades are very important to us and we can be very competitive. Well, you might not kill for an A—but, what *would* you do for an A? Would you consider peeking at the answers to someone's exam if you had the chance to do so and were sure you wouldn't get caught? Would you tell a professor that he or she made a mistake in grading an exam if it meant that your grade was lowered? Would you let a friend write a short paper for you and turn it in as your own? Can you think of any time when you've done something that you wouldn't like anyone else to know about to get a good grade? If we're perfectly honest with ourselves, we know that these questions are not so easy to answer in a "socially acceptable" way. Maybe you've never cheated or plagiarized or lied to a friend—but, have you never been tempted?

Lin's audience will likely find their thinking stimulated by these rhetorical questions that relate directly to their lives as students.

Begin with a Memorable Quotation No doubt someone has said or written something that captures the thesis of your speech. The idea has been expressed so well, perhaps by a person whom the audience respects and admires, that you know it will get the listeners' interest and attention right away. An esteemed scholar, scientist, or political figure can be quoted. Or you can use the words of a popular entertainer, author, athlete, singer, or other well-known and highly respected figure.

As a concerned citizen, David wanted to persuade his audience to volunteer with a new community initiative called New Leaf, New Life. The program sought to make the local jail a more humane and educational environment and to provide mentors for prisoners who were about to be released. David began his speech by quoting the famous nineteenth-century union organizer and Socialist Party presidential candidate Eugene V. Debs:

> Eugene V. Debs devoted most of his life to seeking justice for the most vulnerable members of society. Debs once said, "While there is a lower class, I am in it; while there is a criminal element, I am of it; and while there is a soul in prison, I am not free."[13]

By quoting Debs, the speaker hoped to move his listeners to seek social justice by participating in what he described as a life-altering program.

Use Humor Some speakers like to begin a speech with a humorous story, but you need to approach humor with caution. No matter how funny a story may be, it must also be relevant to the point you want to make. Just telling a few jokes is not a good way to begin a speech, and a joke that falls flat is embarrassing. Humor should never be disrespectful or aimed at ridiculing someone or something, so you need to be careful. In the following introduction, Richard Lamm, representing the University of Denver's Center for Public Policy and Contemporary Issues, began his speech to the World Future Society with this humorous anecdote:

> A priest was riding in a subway when a man staggered toward him, smelling like a brewery, with lipstick on his collar. He sat in the seat right next to the priest and started reading the newspaper.
>
> After a few minutes, the man turned to the priest and asked. "Excuse me, Father, what causes arthritis?"
>
> The priest, tired of smelling the liquor and saddened by the lifestyle, said roughly, "Loose living, drink, dissipation, contempt for your fellow man and being with cheap and wicked women!"
>
> "That's amazing," said the drunk and returned to his newspaper. A while later, the priest, feeling a bit guilty, turned to the man and asked nicely, "How long have you had arthritis?"
>
> "Oh," said the man, "I don't have arthritis. I was just reading that the pope did."
>
> The parable, of course, is a lesson on assumptions.[14]

Of course, these techniques are not mutually exclusive; you can use several at once. You may, for example, tell an interesting story that also establishes common ground and arouses curiosity. And you will want to deliver the introduction effectively. For example, pausing after telling a compelling story, posing an engaging rhetorical question, or sharing a memorable quotation may help listeners ponder what you are about to say. The key factor is capturing and holding the audience's attention and interest.

Stress Relevance

Either consciously or unconsciously, your listeners will ask themselves why they should care about your topic. Even when we find something interesting, we soon begin to wonder whether it has any relevance to us or any real impact on the lives of those we care about. In the introduction, you should take the time to establish the significance of your topic, answering for your audience such questions as, "What does this have to do with me?" or "How will this course of action make for a better world?"

Sarah, a student speaker, wanted to get her audience to take an active role in the university's new fund-raiser, the Dance Marathon. In her introduction, she emphasized how her classmates could make a real difference in the lives of children, while participating in a wonderful, truly engaging event. She pointed out that dance marathons had been held on campuses around the country, such as Penn State and Indiana University, for quite a few years. This year, however, was to be Southeast Missouri State's first year to host such an event. Here is how she emphasized the importance of her topic:

> Why would anyone force themselves to dance for 48 hours? The student who chaired the Dance Marathon steering committee at Indiana University put it this way: "Dance Marathon is about learning what is a priority in life. . . . A true priority in someone's life should be giving back to others who need your help." As a dancer, you too can discover the incredible experience of knowing you helped save children's lives. One dancer summed up his experience like this: "I love this. My feet hurt, but the feeling in my heart won't go away." When you participate in the Dance Marathon, you are raising money for the Children's Miracle Network. Money from our marathon will be split between St. Louis Children's Research Hospital and Cardinal Glennon Children's Miracle Center in St. Louis. I have known several children who have been patients at these hospitals, and I know you have too.[15]

No one listening to these introductory remarks could fail to see the importance of this cause and how it could positively impact their lives as well as the lives of countless children.

Establish Your Credibility

The audience should know of any special relationship you have with the topic that would enhance your ethos. Of course, credibility is an ongoing issue

Well known for his courageous actions during the civil rights movement, Congressman John Lewis possesses strong credibility on issues of social justice and human rights.

throughout any speech, but the introduction represents an especially critical time for establishing your credentials. For seasoned professionals, this process may be less daunting. We expect doctors to know about medicine, attorneys to know about law, and accountants to be able to answer questions about our taxes. For student speakers, however, establishing ethos can be more challenging.

Yet student speakers can establish their ethos in compelling ways. Let us look at how one student did it. In her speech urging students to volunteer for a summer work project, Kristin began by relating her own experience:

> Last year I took a different kind of summer vacation. I did not go to the beach to try to get a fabulous tan. I did not go to a lake and learn to water-ski. I did not go to a big city to visit museums and see shows. I went to a hot, dry desert. There was no air conditioning anywhere. After a night spent sleeping in a sleeping bag on a bare floor, I got up, had breakfast, got into an old truck with about a dozen other kids and took off over a dusty road to a house that badly needed repair. In the hot sun I helped plug cracks in the wall, learned how to mix and apply plaster, and stripped and painted peeling boards.
>
> I did this for nothing. Well, that isn't right. I did not get paid money, but I did get something a lot more valuable. Working as a volunteer in a remote town in an Indian reservation, I learned so many things about a different culture. I made close friends among the people I worked with. I helped to make a real difference in real people's lives. I came back from this experience a different—and richer—person than I was when I went. I am going to tell you today how you can enrich your life, too.

Having established her credibility, this speaker is well positioned to use her personal experience to convince her listeners that they should get involved as well.

If you lack the kind of direct topic-related experience illustrated in the preceding example, you can still establish your credibility as a student speaker by telling your audience that you have had a long-standing interest in your topic and have become motivated to do further research to learn even more about it. You may briefly explain what sparked your interest and then go on to show listeners that you really *are* knowledgeable, widely read, and able to respond to challenging questions.

Clarify Your Purpose/Advance Your Thesis

A key function of the introduction is to advance your speech's thesis—stating, in a single declarative statement, the central idea of your speech. By articulating your thesis as part of the introduction, you help the audience discern your central theme, overarching point, or principal argument. No speaker wants to move into the body of the speech with the audience still wondering, "What's the point? Where is this going?"

One speaker, Joel, decided to give a persuasive speech about the U.S. prison system.[16] In his introduction, he pointed out that the U.S. prison population has increased dramatically over the past 35 years. He noted that one out of every 200 U.S. residents is incarcerated, resulting in steeply rising prison costs.[17] He then advanced his thesis: *The government needs to reform the U.S. prison system.* He went on to argue for lighter sentences, a reduction in mandatory sentencing, and an increased emphasis on rehabilitation.

Often, the thesis statement is soon followed by a preview of the speaker's main ideas.

Preview Your Main Points

Before moving into the body of your speech, you should provide a preview. The preview introduces your main ideas, offering a road map so that listeners can more easily follow your speech. In previewing, you are also signaling what you feel is most important—those things you want the audience to remember and reflect on long after you have finished speaking. By providing a preview, you increase the likelihood they will.[18] If, after giving your preview, you follow through with your plan, you will have further enhanced your credibility by demonstrating your careful organization and preparation.

Consider, for example, the speech given by the student speaker, Angela, whose thesis was as follows: *Grade inflation is a problem that we can, and must, address.* After establishing common ground with her audience by reminding them that nearly everyone has taken a class because of its reputation for being easy, she pointed out, "You sleep through the class, hardly do any work, and still come out with a GPA-boosting A." She then went on to preview the ideas she would develop:

> Let's first examine what constitutes grade inflation and why it has become increasingly common. Let's then explore the threat it poses for us and the measures we can take to alleviate the harm.[19]

Having forecast what she planned to do in the speech, the speaker's challenge was to deliver on the promise by developing each point she mentioned in the preview.

Final Tips about Introductions

Remember the power of *first impressions.* Part of your first impression as a speaker will be based on the way you introduce your speech. Craft your introduction with care. Most speakers wait until after they have outlined the body of the speech to develop the introduction. For instance, they may experiment with several different attention-getting devices before they settle on the one they feel is most compelling.

The length of the introduction varies with the needs of the speaking situation. Some formal events require the speaker to offer an introduction that refers to the events at hand and acknowledges or thanks several significant persons related to the event. Usually, however, introductions should be brief. We have all heard speakers who ramble on for some time, then say, after ten minutes or so, "What I'd like to talk about today is . . ." This can prompt the frustrated listener to tune out.

Although we have discussed the main components that are typically present in good speech introductions, it is important to remember that each introduction should be tailored to the situation. For example, if the person introducing you fully establishes your credibility, you may have little need of augmenting what has already been said. If the audience is already keenly aware of the significance of the problem you are addressing, you will not need to offer an elaborate justification. Instead, you may simply say, "We are all aware of the urgency of the problem that has brought us here tonight." In short, each introduction should be crafted not according to a formula but based on the demands of the topic, the listeners, and the situation.

If you develop your introduction carefully and deliver it effectively, you will set the stage for the audience to attend to the main ideas that you will develop throughout the rest of your speech. A strong introduction makes the audience want to hear more.

Bringing your speech to an effective conclusion is also important. Sometimes speakers primarily think about how to arrange and present their main ideas, without paying attention to what they will say at the end of their speech. Yet the conclusion is the last thing the audience hears. If it is memorable and compelling, the conclusion can truly enhance the overall impact of the speech.

CONCLUDING YOUR SPEECH

Preview. *Carefully planning your speech's conclusion is an essential part of preparing to speak. By summarizing your main ideas, challenging your audience, appealing to your audience, visualizing the future, using good quotations, or referring to the introduction—or by using a combination of these techniques—you can craft an effective ending for your speech.*

Many speakers do not really conclude their speeches—they simply stop talking. Others may stumble through their concluding remarks, reducing the effectiveness of the presentation. Sometimes speakers say something like, "Well, I guess that's about it. Any questions?" The conclusion is very important. If you construct it properly, you will bring your speech to a strategic close and create a final positive impact.

As you approach the speech's conclusion, you will want to signal to the audience that you are, in fact, concluding. One of the major vehicles for signaling the conclusion is a summary of your main points.

Summarize Your Ideas

Summaries are especially important when the speech is complex or long. The summary reinforces your ideas and reminds the audience of your most important points. When combined with the preview in your introduction and the development of each main idea in the body of your speech (including the transitions that connect them), the summary provides a final chance to reiterate key ideas and help the audience remember them.

Summaries are often used in conjunction with another concluding device. Sherri used the following summary, along with a rhetorical question, to conclude her speech on a local non-profit agency, Mother Hubbard's Cupboard:

> I have tried to give you a sense of the various programs and services offered through Mother Hubbard's Cupboard: the Food Pantry that focuses on wholesome, healthy foods; the Education Program that emphasizes the importance of good nutrition in helping everyone live healthy, happy lives; and the Community Gardening Program that teaches people an economical way to grow healthy food right in their own backyards. In a few weeks, MHC will host their annual Harvest Team fund-raising breakfast—an event that raised over $46,000 last year. Will you consider joining me at this year's breakfast? I cannot think of a local agency that is more worthy of your support!

Sherri then distributed a sign-up sheet, offering details about the breakfast (including time and place) and speaker and agency contact information.[20]

Challenge Your Audience

Most of the time, summaries do not stand alone. Often they are—or should be—accompanied by some other interesting concluding device. One device that can be effective is a challenge to the audience to act on what you have said. This was the strategy used by then-senator Barack Obama in his keynote speech to the 2004 Democratic Convention:

> Hope—Hope in the face of difficulty. Hope in the face of uncertainty. The audacity of hope!
>
> In the end, that is God's greatest gift to us, the bedrock of this nation. A belief in things not seen. A belief that there are better days ahead.
>
> I believe that we can give our middle class relief and provide working families with a road to opportunity.
>
> I believe we can provide jobs to the jobless, homes to the homeless, and reclaim young people in cities across America from violence and despair.
>
> I believe that we have a righteous wind at our backs and that as we stand on the cross-roads of history, we can make the right choices, and meet the challenges that face us.
>
> America! Tonight, if you feel the same energy that I do, if you feel the same urgency that I do, if you feel the same passion that I do, if you feel the same hopefulness that I do—if we do what we must do, then I have no doubt that all across the country, from Florida to Oregon, from Washington to Maine, the people will rise up in November . . . and this country will reclaim its promise, and out of this long political darkness a brighter day will come.[21]

Speakers who feel strongly about their topic will make every effort to challenge their listeners to act.

Appeal to Your Audience

In your conclusion, you can make a final attempt to move your audience to act or believe more strongly about your proposition. Speaking to an audience of representatives of companies honored as *Parents* magazine's "Best Companies for Working Families," Richard Lamm concluded his speech with this appeal:

> I close with a metaphor on the need for cooperation and community.... The metaphor is an Amazon legend which tells of a priest who was speaking with God about heaven and hell.
>
> "I will show you hell," said God.
>
> They went into a room that had a delicious beef stew on the table, around which sat people chained to their benches and who looked desperately famished. They held spoons with long handles that reached into the pot, but were too long to put the stew back into their mouths. Their suffering was terrible.
>
> "Now, I will show you heaven," said God.
>
> They then went into an identical room with the savory stew on the table, around which sat people with identical spoons and handles, but they were well nourished and joyous.
>
> The priest was baffled until God said, "Quite simply, you see, these people have learned to feed each other."[22]

Lamm's appeal is for the audience to recognize their responsibility for taking care of *everyone* who is part of the organizational family.

Visualize the Future

In a speech in which you advocate important changes, visualizing the results of those changes is an especially appropriate and powerful way to conclude. This device (which is built into the motivated sequence) allows you to picture concretely the projected results of your ideas in an appealing way. One of the most famous examples of visualization occurs in Martin Luther King Jr.'s "I Have a Dream" speech. In his conclusion, he offered this picture of the future:

> And when this happens, and when we allow freedom to ring, when we let it ring from every village and hamlet, from every state and city, we will be able to speed up that day when all of God's children—black men and white men, Jews and Gentiles, Catholics and Protestants—will be able to join hands and to sing in the words of the old Negro spiritual, "Free at last, free at last; thank God Almighty, we are free at last."[23]

End with a Quotation

Ending your speech with a good quotation can help reinforce your thesis and restate the major points you made. Poetry, plays, songs, speeches, and literary works can all supply effective quotations. Speaking at the Harvard University Commencement in June 2008, J. K. Rowling concluded her remarks by expressing her hopes for the graduating class. In doing so, she quoted Seneca, a classical scholar:

> I am nearly finished. I have one last hope for you, which is something that I already had at 21. The friends with whom I sat on graduation day have been my friends for life. They are my children's godparents, the people to whom I've been able to turn in times of real trouble; people who have been kind enough not to sue me when I took their names for Death Eaters. At our graduation we were bound by enormous affection, by our shared experience of a time that could never come again....
>
> So today, I wish you nothing better than similar friendships. And tomorrow, I hope that even if you remember not a single word of mine, you remember those of Seneca, another of those old Romans I met when I fled down the Classics corridor, in retreat from career ladders, in search of ancient wisdom:
>
> *As is a tale, so is life:*
> *not how long it is,*
> *but how good it is,*
> *is what matters.*
>
> I wish you all very good lives.[24]

Refer to the Introduction

You can achieve a sense of symmetry and reinforce your major theme by coming back to the introduction in the conclusion of your speech. This commonly happens when a speaker uses both a preview and a summary, but you can find more interesting ways to do this, often by using one of the techniques we have already discussed. For example, you may return to a story, quotation, or rhetorical question that you used in the opening.

Consider the following example from a speech given by Robert C. Purcell, executive director of General Motors Advanced Technology Vehicles, at the 1998 MBA Recognition Ceremony at the Kelly School of Business, Indiana University. He had introduced his speech with a riveting story from May 1961, in which a group of black and white students, riding on a bus together, were attacked by an angry white mob. One young black seminary student, John Lewis, was nearly killed. His life was saved only because a white Alabama public safety officer, Floyd Mann, chased off the crowd by firing shots into the air. Purcell concluded his speech like this:

> There's a postscript to the story I shared with you when I began today. Not long ago, John Lewis, the young seminary student, returned to Alabama, to the site of that historic attack 37 years ago, for the dedication of a civil rights memorial.... By that time, Lewis had a long and distinguished career.
>
> As we waited for the ceremony to begin, an older gentleman, who seemed vaguely familiar, came over to him.
>
> "You're John Lewis, aren't you?" the man said. "I remember you from the Freedom Rides."
>
> It was Floyd Mann—the same Floyd Mann who had waded into that mob with his revolver, more than 35 years before.
>
> Lewis was overcome with emotion. "You saved my life," he said. And then he embraced Floyd Mann. Not sure as he did so, if even then, black men and white men hugged each other in contemporary Alabama.
>
> But Mann hugged him back, and John Lewis began to cry.
>
> And as the two men released each other, Floyd Mann looked at Lewis and said, "You know ... I'm right proud of your career."
>
> And if there is one hope that I hold for each of you today—it is that 10 or 20 or 30 years from now, when you look back on your careers, you'll be just as proud.[25]

Many speakers use a combination of techniques. Sherri combined a summary with a rhetorical question. Reverend King quoted from an old spiritual while visualizing the future. Robert Purcell brought closure to his speech through an extended story that referred to his introduction. These combined approaches are fairly typical and often work more effectively than any one technique used alone.

Final Tips about Conclusions

Just as the introduction of your speech contributes to the audience's first impression of you, the conclusion represents your last chance to reach out to listeners and reinforce your speech's purpose. The conclusion should be *brief*; this is no place to introduce new information or to tack on something you forgot to say earlier.

Speakers sometimes have trouble ending their speeches. A speaker may say, "Let me leave you with this thought," then ramble on for several more minutes. Or the speaker may pepper his or her remarks with signposts such as *finally* or *in conclusion*—but not stop talking. When a speaker uses these verbal markers, listeners take him or her seriously. If the speaker uses them and continues to speak, listeners may become frustrated or bored, and they will probably stop listening. Even a good speech (and a good speaker) can lose considerable ground if the conclusion is poorly crafted and delivered.

You can signal to the audience that you are concluding by your content and your delivery. Offering a summary clearly communicates that you are approaching the end of your speech, as do signposts such as *finally* or *in closing*. You may also move physically closer to the audience and connect with them directly through eye contact and vocal expressiveness as you offer a concluding quotation, help them visualize the future, or call them to action. Your conclusion is your last opportunity to connect with your audience, and it should never be lost.

SUMMARY

- Effective speakers strive to organize their ideas carefully and strategically.
  - Well-organized speakers are usually viewed as competent and knowledgeable—greatly contributing to their perceived credibility.
  - They are also viewed as being invested in their topic and respectful of the audience.
  - The better organized the speaker, the more likely the audience will learn from the speech and be influenced by it.
- The foundation of a well-organized speech is a set of main ideas that are well thought out and clearly formulated.
  - You design ideas with a specific purpose in mind, making sure that they are clear, simple without being oversimplified, and appropriate to the situation.
- Ideas should be organized in a coherent and reasonable fashion. The principal patterns of organization discussed in this chapter are:
  - Chronological or sequential (arranged in a time or step-by-step order)
  - Categorical (a pattern that emphasizes distinct topics)
  - Climactic (arranged according to importance, size, or degree of simplicity)
  - Causal (moving from causes to effects or from effects to causes)

  - Problem-solution (a logical progression that moves from perceived difficulties to an examination of alternatives to a best solution)
  - Narrative (based on a story-telling model)
- Speakers will also want to consider issues of balance, the number of main ideas to include, and idea placement as they move forward in finalizing their choice of an organizational pattern.
- Once you have chosen the basic organizational pattern and worked on good transitions, you are ready to think about how to begin and conclude your comments.
- In general, the speech's introduction should help you do the following:
  - Establish common ground with the audience
  - Capture and hold the audience's attention
  - Show them why your topic is relevant to them
  - Establish your credibility
  - Advance the speech's purpose
  - Preview your main ideas
- Crafting an effective conclusion is also important. Conclusions allow you to:
  - summarize your main ideas.
  - challenge your audience.
  - appeal to listeners.
  - visualize the future.
  - offer a memorable quotation.
  - create balance and closure by referring to the introduction.
- The conclusion is your last opportunity to connect with your audience and realize your specific purpose.

QUESTIONS FOR REVIEW AND REFLECTION

1. Why is good organization important?
2. In what ways does the purpose of your speech influence the main ideas?
3. What makes an idea a good one? Examine the main ideas you advanced in your last speech. How do they measure up in light of these criteria?
4. What are the principal patterns of organization? Why would you choose one pattern over another?
5. How might each of these concepts be important to you as you go about organizing your next speech?
   a. strategic organization
   b. balance/symmetry
   c. the number of main ideas to include
   d. primacy and recency effects
6. What is the function of transitions? What are the different kinds of transitions that you might use? Briefly define each, and describe whatever advantages each may provide.

7. What are the major components of the speech introduction? Why is each important?
8. Give some examples of how you might capture the listeners' attention in your introduction.
9. What should you accomplish in the conclusion to your speech? What are some techniques that will help you do this?

ENDNOTES

1. James C. McCroskey and R. Samuel Mehrley, "The Effects of Disorganization and Nonfluency on Attitude Change and Source Credibility," *Communication Monographs* 36 (1969): 13–21.
2. Studies generally show that organized speeches are better understood than those that are less well-organized. See, for example, Ernest C. Thompson, "An Experimental Investigation of the Relative Effectiveness of Organizational Structure in Oral Communication," *Southern Speech Communication Journal* 26 (1960): 59–69.
3. When listeners are forced to listen to a disorganized presentation, they are unlikely to respond in a way that is consistent with the speaker's specific purpose. See Raymond G. Smith, "An Experimental Study of the Effects of Speech Organization upon Attitudes of College Students," *Communication Monographs* 18 (1951): 292–301.
4. John Dewey, *How We Think* (Boston: Heath, 1910).
5. This pattern was originally introduced by Alan H. Monroe in *Principles and Types of Speech* (New York: Scott, Foresman, 1935) and has been refined in later editions. See, for example, Alan H. Monroe, Bruce E. Gronbeck, and Douglas Ehninger, *Principles and Types of Speech Communication*, 14th ed. (Boston: Addison-Wesley, 2002).
6. See Karen Zediker, "Rediscovering the Tradition: Women's History with a Relational Approach to the Basic Public Speaking Course," paper, Western States Communication Association, Albuquerque, New Mexico, 1993. This paper reviews the work of Christine Jorgensen-Earp, who argues that these patterns are often used by women and ethnic speakers.
7. Walter R. Fisher, "Narration as a Human Communication Paradigm: The Case of Public Moral Argument," *Communication Monographs* 51 (1984): 1–22.
8. Ibid., 8.
9. See James C. McCroskey, *An Introduction to Rhetorical Communication*, 7th ed. (Boston: Allyn & Bacon, 1997), 205–22; and Howard Gilkinson, Stanley F. Paulson, and Donald E. Sikkink, "Effects of Order and Authority in an Argumentative Speech," *Quarterly Journal of Speech* 40 (1954): 183–92.
10. Assuming that recipients find the message relevant, moderate repetition (such as that which transitions, a preview, and a review provide within a speech) prompts listeners to better understand and better recall what is said, as well as process it more deeply. See, for example, Heather M. Claypool, Diane M. Mackie, Teresa Garcia-Marques, Ashley McIntosh, and Ashton Udall, "The Effects of Personal Relevance and Repetition on Persuasive Processing," *Social Cognition* 22 (2004): 310–35. Also see Robert F. Lorch Jr., Elizabeth Pugzles Lorch, and W. Elliot Inman, "Effects of Signaling Topic Structure on Text Recall," *Journal of Educational Psychology* 85 (1993): 281–90.
11. From Bill Clinton, "Memphis Church of God in Christ Convention Address," November 13, 1993. Published 1993 by Bill Clinton.
12. Reprinted by permission from Carmen Mariano, "You as Teachers are Saving the World" speech. Copyright © 2005 by Carmen Mariano.
13. From Eugene Debs, "Statement to the Court," Federal Court of Cleveland, September 18, 1918.
14. Reprinted by permission from Richard Lamm, "Unexamined Assumptions: Destiny, Political Institutions, Democracy and Population" speech. Copyright © 1998 by Richard Lamm.
15. Reprinted by permission from Sarah Snyder. Published 2007 by SC 105 Speakers Showcase.
16. Joel Grass, SC 105, Fundamentals of Oral Communication, "When Prisons Suffer We All Suffer," December 10, 2008, http://cstl-cla.semo.edu/williams/sc105/samples.htm (accessed March 15, 2009).
17. See, for example, Michael Jacobson, *Downsizing Prisons* (New York: New York University Press, 2005).

18. See Claypool et al., "The Effects of Personal Relevance and Repetition on Persuasive Processing"; and Lorch et al., "Effects of Signaling Topic Structure on Text Recall."
19. Angela Spinzig, SC 105 Speakers Showcase, "Speech to Influence," Spring 2009, http://cstl-cla.semo.edu/williams/shwcase/Sp09.htm (accessed March 11, 2009).
20. For additional information about Mother Hubbard's Cupboard, go to www.mhcfoodpantry.org.
21. From Barack Obama, "Keynote Address to the 2004 Democratic National Convention," July 26, 2004. Published 2004 by BarakObama.com.
22. Reprinted by permission from Richard Lamm, "Family Friendly Institutions." Copyright © 2005 by Richard Lamm.
23. Martin Luther King Jr., "I Have a Dream," in *Contemporary American Speeches*, 8th ed., ed. Richard L. Johannesen, Ron R. Allen, Wilmer A. Linkugel, and J. Bryan Ferald (Dubuque, IA: Kendall/Hunt, 1997), 369.
24. Reprinted by permission from J. K. Rowling, "Commencement Address at Harvard University." Copyright © 2008 by J. K. Rowling.
25. Reprinted by permission from Robert C. Purcell, "Values for Value: Integrity and Stewardship" speech. Copyright © 1998 by Robert C. Purcell.

CHAPTER 10

Outlining Your Speech

CHAPTER SURVEY

CHAPTER OBJECTIVES

After studying this chapter, you should be able to

1. Describe the different types of outlines and the purposes served by each.
2. Explain the basic principles of outlining.
3. Develop outlines as you work on a forthcoming speech.

It is easy to view outlining as an academic exercise—something that is required by the instructor but serves no useful purpose. Yet by outlining, you can correct many mistakes in organizational strategy and the use of supporting material *before* you deliver your speech. Outlines can help you sort through ideas to determine which ones work well together. Outlines can also help you determine whether you need to conduct additional research. And outlines can enhance the effectiveness of your delivery.

The outline is something that you should develop continuously as you prepare your speech. Most speakers construct a rough outline early, representing their initial thinking and ideas. Later, as they read widely and begin to choose some strategy of organization, the outline grows, changes, and is refined. The outline, then, *evolves* as your ideas emerge and you gather new information. Sometimes it is rearranged; often it is expanded to include more detail or support. The final formal outline will reflect all that has gone into the preparation of your speech.

TYPES OF OUTLINES

Preview. *An outline emerges from careful preparation. Working outlines include your first thoughts; formal, full-sentence outlines contain fully developed ideas and support; and keyword outlines serve as notes for speakers.*

Although we have spoken of *the* outline, the reality is that you will use several different kinds of outlines as you prepare to speak. Although no two people prepare a speech in exactly the same way, outlining is always a valuable tool. Through outlining, you can record your early thoughts, experiment with different organizational strategies, consider whether evidence "fits" by observing the relationship between ideas and supporting material, and improve the delivery of your speech.

Working Outlines

First, there is the **working outline**. This is the outline that you develop as you brainstorm ideas, investigate your chosen topic, and reflect on your emerging views. You may change the working outline many times, inserting new information and revising and rearranging main ideas and supporting points. By examining your working outline, you can see if you have given each main idea the appropriate emphasis. You can also note whether you have developed your arguments with sufficient supporting material. In short, this outline is a kind of *diagnostic tool* that helps you see where you've been and where you are going. You may choose to jot down your working outline(s) in longhand, or, if you prefer, enter your thoughts on your computer. Working outlines are for you to use as you see fit.

Formal Outlines

When you have completed your research and are moving toward the delivery of your speech, your instructor may ask you to prepare a **formal outline**. This full-sentence representation of your speech will also include the bibliography of sources you consulted while preparing your speech. The formal outline displays your ideas and arguments as they are fully developed, complete with supporting material. It is a blueprint of the speech you will give.

When your instructor examines your formal outline, he or she can assess whether you have done the following:

- chosen an effective organizational strategy
- achieved proper structure with coordinated thesis, main points, and transitions
- consulted sufficient sources
- developed your main ideas well

The formal outline serves as a tangible symbol of the time, effort, and thought you have put into your speech.

Whenever the formal outline is prepared sufficiently far in advance and submitted to critical scrutiny (by either you, a classmate, or your instructor), it can be altered and strengthened until you must submit it and deliver the speech. When you learn to use the outline to diagnose your own work, you will see your writing improve.

We provide two sample formal outlines later in the chapter. One appears in the *Focus on Civic Engagement* feature on pages 252–254, and the other appears at the end of the chapter.

Keyword Outlines

You will typically use a **keyword outline** when you deliver your speech. A keyword outline is an abbreviated version of your formal outline, designed to remind you of the ideas you want to convey. You still might want to write out a few things completely, such as important transitions, key statistics, or exact quotations—to make sure you quote your sources accurately. When well constructed, a keyword outline enables you to deliver your speech effectively in an extemporaneous style.

Some speakers make the mistake of carefully preparing a formal outline, then throwing together a keyword outline at the last minute. They fail to allow sufficient time for practicing with their keyword outline, which is crucial for a relaxed, conversational style of delivery. Practicing with your keyword outline also allows you to revise and refine your speaking notes until you feel confident about delivering the speech. Many speakers also transfer their keyword outline to note cards for easier handling during delivery. A good example of a keyword outline appears in the *Focus on Civic Engagement* on pages 256–257.

BASIC PRINCIPLES OF OUTLINING

Preview. *A basic system of rules governs outlining. These principles identify the key components to be included in each formal outline and the use of consistent labeling through a system of universal symbols. They mandate focusing on one idea at a time in the speech's* *body and coherently developing ideas with supporting material. The keyword outline has guidelines of its own, such as using words sparingly, writing out key portions, and producing legible notes.*

Although nearly all of us have drafted an outline at some point in our lives, many remain confused about the proper way to develop a formal, full-sentence outline. Following a few simple principles will help.

Guidelines for Developing the Formal Outline

The principles that follow are not trivial. Rather, each one is aimed at getting you to think clearly about how your ideas are related, to examine the nature and extent of your supporting material, and to make sure that your ideas are coherently developed.

INCLUDE THE KEY ELEMENTS The sample formal outline on pages 252–254 offers an illustration of an outline broken into distinct parts. Most formal outlines should include the following components, with each clearly labeled:

- ***Speech title.*** If you are preparing a classroom speech, your instructor may or may not be interested in having you list a title at the top of your outline. Outside the classroom, speakers are often asked to give the program planner a speech title. This title should be placed at the top of your formal outline.
- ***Specific purpose and thesis statement.*** Both the specific purpose and the thesis statement should be listed at the top of the outline. Articulating your central idea and specific purpose at the beginning allows anyone who reads your outline to discern whether your thesis is supported and your specific purpose advanced by the *way* you have organized and developed your speech. You will also want to include and label your thesis statement as part of your introduction, perhaps highlighting it with italics or bold print.
- ***Introduction, body, and conclusion.*** These major elements should be labeled and included in the outline. As we noted in Chapter 9, introductions and conclusions need to be carefully planned in advance. By clearly labeling them on the outline, you will be sure that they are present and well developed. It is also helpful to label the specific components of each, such as the attention-getting device, credibility, thesis, and so forth. (Your instructor may insist that you do so.)
- ***Transitions.*** Transitions hold the speech together and show the progression of ideas, as well as their relationship to one another. They help listeners follow the speech and see how the ideas advanced form a coherent whole. Entering and labeling transitions on your formal outline will ensure that you *have* included them and given them the attention they deserve. You may also want to italicize them, so that they stand out from the rest of the text.

- ***Bibliography***. Normally a list of sources or works consulted is required at the end of a formal outline. Various forms of bibliographic citations are available for you to use. Your instructor may suggest that you use a specific guide, such as the *Chicago Manual of Style* or the style manuals of the Modern Language Association (MLA) or the American Psychological Association (APA). Bibliographic formats change over time. Once you have selected the format you plan to use, you will want to follow it consistently. For assistance with locating different bibliographic formats visit the Web, where you will find links to the most current formats available. The formal outline presented on pages 252–254 includes a sample bibliography that follows the *Chicago Manual of Style*, whereas the formal outline that appears at the end of the chapter illustrates the MLA bibliographic format.

USE A CONSISTENT SYSTEM Use a consistent system of symbols and indentations. Learning a system will help you fix in your mind the relationships between ideas and supporting material that the outline represents and is important in organizing your speech into a coherent structure. These symbols also designate the various components of your speech for your instructor or others you might ask for feedback on your speech. Figure 10.1 illustrates how the system looks when outlining the body of the speech. As with most speeches, some ideas are more fully developed than others, reflecting the speaker's assumptions about the relative importance of each idea and the extent to which each needs to be explained or illustrated.

FIGURE 10.1

Outline Form for the Body of the Speech

I. MAIN IDEA
    A. First main subpoint
        1. Support for this subpoint
            a. First piece of specific information
            b. Second piece of specific information
        2. Additional support for this subpoint
    B. Second main subpoint
        1. First supporting statement
        2. Second supporting statement
            a. Specific information
            b. More specific information
                (1) Very detailed support
                (2) More detailed support
            c. More specific information
    C. Third main subpoint
        1. First supporting statement
        2. Second supporting statement
II. SECOND MAIN IDEA
    A. First main subpoint
        1. First supporting statement
        2. Second supporting statement
    B. Second main subpoint
        1. Support for this subpoint
            a. First piece of specific information
            b. Second piece of specific information
        2. Second supporting statement
III. THIRD MAIN IDEA
And so forth . . .

Focus on a Single Idea in Each Main Point Each main point in the body of your outline should contain only one idea. Here is an example of a poorly worded main idea:

I. Becoming media literate is important because so much information is communicated through the news; yet we have many excuses for not watching the news.

This example contains several different ideas in a single statement. Here is an improved version, focusing on one idea at a time:

I. Many of us avoid watching the news.
   A. Viewership of TV news has declined dramatically.
   B. Young people, in particular, have "tuned out."
II. People give a number of reasons for avoiding the news.
   A. Many people feel that the news is too negative.
   B. Others argue that there's simply too much information to take in—and they feel overwhelmed by it.
   C. Still others are cynical—believing that much of the news has been "managed" or "manipulated" in some way.

Notice the clarity and simplicity that results as we focus on a single idea in each part of the outline. This simplification will assist you as you draft your speech, and it will also assist your listeners, helping them to better process and retain your message.

Coherently Develop Ideas and Supporting Material Your outline should accurately reflect relationships between ideas and supporting material. The main ideas are listed with roman numerals, the subpoints that support those ideas with capital letters, the material that develops the subpoints with arabic numbers, the support for these with lowercase letters, and the most specific supporting materials with numbers in parentheses. See Figure 10.1 for a skeletal illustration of proper outlining form.

The outline thus becomes a *visual representation* of the supporting relationships between ideas and evidence. By examining your outline carefully, you should be able to discern whether the supporting material actually develops, supports, or elaborates your main ideas. Consider the following example, which *fails* to coherently represent the relationship among ideas:

I. Negativity and cynicism stand in our way of becoming media literate.
   A. There is a difference between an "informed" citizen and an "informational" citizen.
   B. Media gatekeepers make it challenging for anyone to become media literate.
   C. Much of the information we must process from the media is cognitive, based on facts.
   D. There are several steps we can take to improve our media literacy.

Any one of these ideas might be explored on its own. But they clearly do not fit together, nor do the subpoints all advance the main point (that negativity and skepticism stand in the way of media literacy). Subpoint A offers a definition of an informed citizen, whereas subpoint B explores one of the challenges to media literacy. Subpoint C introduces a model of media literacy, and the final subpoint proposes actions to improve media literacy.

Here is a better approach to this outline:

I. Becoming media literate requires us to develop our ability to think critically.
   A. According to scholar James Potter, we must be able to evaluate facts—separating false information from that which is valid and reliable—using our *cognitive* ability.
   B. Potter argues that we must also understand the *emotional impact* that visual images and moving language can have on our ability to think critically.
   C. Finally, Potter insists that we must strive to separate "art from artificiality"—becoming more capable of dealing with the *aesthetic dimension* of information.[1]

II. Media scholar Carla Johnson outlines several specific steps we can take to enhance our media literacy.
   A. First, we can develop an *awareness* of how media may be influencing us.
   B. Next, we must exercise our "critical reading/viewing" skills.
   C. We must also reflect on the political, social, economic, and cultural *context* in which information is presented.
   D. Finally, we can engage in media advocacy by demanding that the media meet higher standards.[2]

In this outline, as you can see, the subordinate points illuminate the main ideas. Thus, each of the main ideas is coherently developed. In a complete formal outline, of course, each of these subpoints might be further developed through concise explanations, examples, expert testimony, and other sorts of supporting material.

The *Focus on Civic Engagement* on pages 252–254 presents a fully developed formal outline that illustrates these principles.

The Keyword Outline: Some Special Considerations

Some speakers make the mistake of trying to deliver their speech from their formal outline. But delivering your speech from such a detailed outline may tempt you to read the speech word-for-word. That prevents you from interacting more directly with your listeners.

There is nothing magical about transferring your outline onto note cards. Some speakers try to put their entire formal outline onto small note cards, using cramped writing or even using both sides of the cards. This typically does not

FOCUS ON CIVIC ENGAGEMENT

Job Training for the Poor: A Speech of Advocacy

Culinary Arts for Shalom: Based on a Presentation Prepared for a Competitive Grant

Note: The Shalom Community Center is a daytime shelter and resource center for people who are experiencing poverty and homelessness in Bloomington, Indiana. The Shalom Center also operates a hunger relief program—serving breakfast and lunch five days each week. In a typical month, Shalom provides more than 6,500 meals.

SPECIFIC PURPOSE: I want my audience to award Shalom the funding needed to establish a culinary arts job training program.

THESIS: Creating a program that offers certification in the culinary arts will lead to job opportunities for many.

Introduction

ATTENTION-GETTING DEVICE

I recently met a man named Sam who was homeless for five years. He slept in his car until it was towed away. After that, he slept under a bridge. Sam's life turned around when a friend took him in and helped him find a job cooking at a small café. Sam had always liked to cook, and he soon became famous for his cakes and pies. After working in the café for a couple of years, Sam went back to school and studied the culinary arts. Now, he has a job as head chef in an upscale restaurant.

You may wonder if Sam's situation is unusual. Will training in the culinary arts actually lead to good jobs?

CREDIBILITY

I believe so, and I speak from experience. I am a member of the Shalom board, where I chair the Operations Committee. For four years, I have also worked as a volunteer in the Shalom kitchen and as a job counselor in the Job Links employment program.

JUSTIFICATION

One of our greatest challenges is helping our guests find decent jobs—jobs that pay a living wage (see Ehrenreich's *Nickel and Dimed*). Our guests often lack education, training, or certification—and this poses a huge barrier to employment. If we could provide training in an industry in which jobs are *growing*, we believe that we could make many of our guests employable. Because the restaurant industry is growing all over the country—and our community is no exception—we think it wise to begin there.

THESIS

We are convinced that creating a culinary arts job training program at Shalom will lead to job opportunities for many.

PREVIEW

I'd like to begin by telling you why I think a culinary arts job training program is right for Shalom. Then I'll describe the model we will use to develop our program and explain how we will use the grant money.

Body

I. The restaurant industry is growing—with numerous job opportunities.
   A. Food service jobs are among the most commonly advertised in our community—in restaurants, hospitals, hotels, and schools.
      1. This past week alone, over 20 food-service ads appeared in the *Bloomington Herald Times.*
      2. Nearly 60 percent of these jobs were in traditional restaurants (i.e., *not* fast-food).
   B. In 2006, the National Restaurant Association and the Bureau of Labor Statistics predicted that employment opportunities in the restaurant industry will increase by more than two million job openings over the next seven years.

Transition: Clearly restaurants need a trained workforce, and at Shalom we can help meet that need.

II. The Shalom Center is a logical place to offer training in the culinary arts.
   A. Our state-of-the-art commercial kitchen is sufficiently large and versatile to provide an effective training arena.
   B. We have partners who are interested in helping us develop and offer this kind of program.
      1. We already have an ongoing alliance with Ivy Tech Community College.
      2. The Bloomington Cooking School has agreed to offer classes.
      3. A number of local chefs have also signed on to serve as instructors and mentors.
   C. Many Shalom guests have had diverse experiences working in restaurants—as line and prep cooks, servers, and dishwashers.

Transition: The training we provide will infuse our community with a high-quality workforce.

III. Our program will be available to anyone who qualifies.
   A. Candidates must be unemployed or underemployed.
      1. They may have lost their jobs or been recently released from jail.
      2. They may be working part-time, or doing work that is well beneath their skill level (such as the part-time custodian who once worked full-time in a factory).
   B. They must pass a basic physical examination.
      1. One component of this exam is a drug screening test.
      2. They must also be able to stand for extended periods of time, tolerate heat, move quickly, bend easily, demonstrate good eye-hand coordination, and lift at least 30 pounds.
   C. They must pass a basic skills test.
      1. Each will be tested for basic literacy (ensuring that they can read recipes and cooking directions).
      2. They will also be tested for fundamental math skills (allowing them to make accurate measurements, double recipes as needed, and so forth).
   D. They must pass a screening interview.
      1. This interview will explore such basic issues as employment history, drug treatment programs, and educational background.
      2. Candidates will also be judged in terms of their attitudes and personal characteristics, such as communication skills, motivation, work ethic, and appearance.

Transition: The training they receive will be first-rate.

IV. Our program will build on a successful job training model while creating several *new* components of our own.
   A. A foundational portion of our program will be modeled after the Second Helpings job training program in Indianapolis.
      1. Second Helpings has placed 90 percent of its graduates, and more than 70 percent of those remain employed six months later.
      2. Like Second Helpings, we will offer a food handler course that will meet the new Indiana law requirements for manager certification in the food service industry.
         a. The law requires that each establishment will employ at least one individual who is trained and certified in food safety.
         b. Our Basic Food Handler course will be co-taught by our own culinary instructor and personnel from Ivy Tech.

(*continues*)

FOCUS ON CIVIC ENGAGEMENT (*continued*)

B. In addition to the Food Handler's Certification, we anticipate that the Shalom Culinary Arts Certification Program will contain a number of *new* components.
   1. A Cooking Fundamentals Component will feature special workshops led by local chefs and the Bloomington Cooking School.
   2. A Workforce Readiness Component will be offered by personnel from Work One and our own Job Links program.
   3. An Apprenticeship Component will enable those who are recently certified to receive further training in local restaurants.
   4. A Service Component will require everyone in the program to plan, prepare, and serve at least five meals to those experiencing hunger, poverty, and homelessness.

C. The handouts we distributed show you our proposed budget and tentative timetable for developing the program.
   1. As you can see, we have already begun collaborating with our partners.
   2. With the funds we receive from your foundation, we hope to establish a new administrative culinary arts position.
      a. We will hire someone who will work with our partners to develop and refine the new program.
      b. He or she will also be responsible for administering all aspects of the program, such as advertising, admissions, and testing.
   3. The first students will enter the program in the summer, move through the requirements, be tested, and receive certification by the early fall.
   4. After completing brief apprenticeships, graduates will be placed in area restaurants.
   5. All graduates will be eligible to receive three credits toward Ivy Tech's Hospitality Administration degree program—thus encouraging them to pursue additional education.

Conclusion

SUMMARY

The program we are proposing is easily within our grasp. We have the partners, the facility, and the basic program model in place. With this program, we will be able to offer valuable job training that will lead to employment opportunities and better lives for a number of the guests we serve.

APPEAL

Remember the story of Sam that I shared in the beginning? No longer homeless, Sam glows with pride when he talks about his job and home. He is filled with hope and optimism! It is our dream that Sam's story will become a story shared by many others here in our community. With your foundation's support, we can make it so.

Bibliography

Ehrenreich, Barbara. *Nickel and Dimed: On (Not) Getting By in America.* New York: Holt, 2001.

Ivy Tech Community College, www.ivytech.edu/schools/public-social/hospitality-admin/ (accessed February 23, 2009).

Kilty, Keith M., and Elizabeth A. Segal, eds. *Rediscovering the Other America: The Continuing Crisis of Poverty and Inequality in the United States.* Binghamton, NY: Haworth Press, 2003.

Leonhardt, David. "U.S. Poverty Rate Was Up Last Year," *New York Times*, August 8, 2005, A1, A14.

Second Helpings, www.secondhelpings.org (accessed March 10, 2009).

Friends of Boston's Homeless, http://fobh.org/job-training (accessed February 24, 2009).

Shalom Community Center, www.shalomcommunitycenter.org (accessed April 8, 2009).

produce a useful set of speaking notes. Instead, try following these simple guidelines for developing a keyword outline:

Use Words Sparingly When you create your speaking notes, you should try to write out as *little* as possible so that you will not be tempted to read your notes and risk losing contact with your listeners. While it makes sense to write out and read direct quotations and specific statistical information, you will stay more focused on the audience if you have practiced enough to deliver the speech without relying on your notes too much.

Write Out Key Portions of the Speech Even though you want to use notes sparingly, you may want to write out transitions and other key portions of your speech completely to ensure accuracy. When delivering a speech, you are most likely to forget what comes next after completing your discussion of a main idea. Writing out transitions can serve as a memory prompt and will help you emphasize *how* your ideas are connected. You may also wish to write out *parts* of your introduction and conclusion, such as a preview or summary, as well as specific statistics and quotations appearing anywhere in the speech. In fact, when you read statistics or directly quoted material from a note card, you demonstrate to your audience that you are concerned about conveying that information precisely and accurately.

Strive for Legible Notes You will want to make sure that you can easily read your notes. Keep handwritten entries readable and sufficiently sized. If you type your notes, use a large font and emphasize important words in bold. In either case, leave adequate space between entries. Follow the basic format of your formal outline.

Avoid cramming too much onto any one card. You may want to use 4 × 6 rather than 3 × 5 note cards, so that you can put more notes on each card. Write only on one side of the card to avoid confusion. Number your cards and, of course, practice several times until you are comfortable with your speaking notes. Refer to Chapter 12 for more specific guidelines on how to practice with and use speaking notes.

Give Yourself Delivery Hints When presenting your speech, it is easy to get caught up in following your notes and end up forgetting to deliver your remarks as effectively as possible. During practice, you will probably realize that you need to guard against certain tendencies, such as speaking too rapidly, forgetting to move or use gestures, or failing to look around the room to include all your listeners. In the margins of your notes, then, you may want to jot down delivery reminders, such as "Pause Here" or "Slow Down!!"

Consider Your Options Some speakers prefer to use a sheet of paper instead of note cards for their keyword outline. When using note cards, you can easily carry them with you as you speak, gesturing and moving with ease. However, you *do* have to coordinate moving from card to card. If you use a sheet of paper, you can see the entire outline at a glance, but you will probably need to place the outline on a table or podium because carrying it around while you speak may look awkward and be distracting to your audience. Practice with each method to see which you prefer.

Good speaking notes allow you to feel confident and stay on track while remaining connected to your listeners.

FOCUS ON CIVIC ENGAGEMENT

A Keyword Outline for a Speech of Advocacy

Introduction

SHARE STORY OF SAM—leads to question, "Will training in the culinary arts actually lead to a good job?"

SHARE PERSONAL BACKGROUND—at Shalom, working with Job Links

Eye contact!

JUSTIFY TOPIC—need to find jobs that pay a living wage in a growing industry (refer to Ehrenreich's *Nickel and Dimed*).

Thesis

We are convinced that creating a culinary arts job training program at Shalom will lead to job opportunities for many.

Preview

- I'll explain that this job training program is right for Shalom
- Describe what the model will look like
- Explain how we will use the grant money

Slow down here!

Body

I. Restaurant industry is growing—with lots of job opportunities.
   - 20 food service job ads in *HT* during past week
   - 60 percent in traditional restaurants, schools, hospitals, etc.—not fast-food
   - National Restaurant Assoc. and Bureau of Labor stats—two million jobs predicted over seven years

TRANSITION: Clearly, restaurants need a trained workforce, and at Shalom, we can help meet that need.

Might move here

II. Shalom Center—logical place to meet the need
   - Has state-of-the-art commercial kitchen
   - Partnerships already formed—Ivy Tech, Cooking School, local chefs
   - Shalom guests—cooking backgrounds common

TRANSITION: The training we provide will infuse our community with a high-quality workforce.

USE SPEAKING NOTES OPENLY Unless you have been asked to deliver your speech from memory (which is a rare occurrence), feel free to consult your keyword outline openly as you speak. Hold your cards comfortably or place your full sheet of notes on the podium. Look at your notes as needed, and read from them whenever you are trying to quote precisely. Avoid staring at your notes, however. You should *never* use your speaking notes as a crutch to avoid interacting with your audience. The reason you prepare a keyword outline is so that you can interact *more* with your listeners.

The *Focus on Civic Engagement* below presents a keyword outline, based on the formal outline on pages 252–254.

Taken together, these outlining tools will assist you throughout the process of preparing and delivering your speech. The working outline will help you brainstorm ideas, conduct research, and think through how best to approach the subject. The formal outline reveals the final product—showing how well each main idea is articulated, developed, and supported—as well as how ideas are arranged and balanced. Finally, the keyword outline provides an aid to delivery, helping to boost your confidence and keeping you on track. When the audience perceives your speech as well planned and structured, they will be more likely to view you, the speaker, as a credible source of information and a person whose ideas and proposals are worthy of serious consideration.

III. Program available to anyone who qualifies:
- Unemployed or underemployed
- Passes basic skills test
- Passes screening interview

TRANSITION: The training they receive will be first-rate.

IV. Our program built on successful Second Helpings model in Indy
- Program places 90 percent of grads, with high retention rate (over 70 percent)
- Like SH, we will offer a food handler course **Watch speed!**
- New Indiana requirement
- Course co-taught by Ivy Tech faculty, plus our own instructor
- New components in our program!
  - Cooking Fundamentals
  - Workforce Readiness
  - Apprenticeship
  - Service
- See handouts for budget and timetable for program development
- Collaboration with partners ongoing
- With grant money, will hire new administrator/teacher
- Early summer through late fall, then apprenticeships and placement
- Grads receive three credits toward Ivy Tech program

Conclusion

SUMMARY
- Program within our grasp—have partners, facility, and model in place
- Can offer valuable job training—enriching lives of guests and benefiting the greater community **Eye contact!**

APPEAL
- Refer to Sam's story—no longer homeless, filled with hope!
- Others can share this story—with your foundation's support!

SUMMARY

- As you prepare yourself to speak, an outline will begin to emerge.
- Outlining is important as a diagnostic tool, as well as a visual representation of your speech.
- You will use different types of outlines:
  - Working outlines incorporate preliminary thoughts.
  - Formal, full-sentence outlines contain fully developed ideas and support.
  - Keyword outlines serve as speaking notes.
- As you craft your formal outline, you should:
  - include and label key elements (such as the introduction, body, and conclusion, transitions, and bibliography)
  - use a consistent set of symbols and indentations
  - make sure that each point contains only one idea
  - coherently develop ideas and supporting material
- A keyword outline is used in delivering your speech. It should:
  - usually be written on note cards
  - use words sparingly
  - include a few extended quotations and statistics
  - be written legibly
  - include delivery prompts
  - be used openly
- When listeners perceive your speech as well planned and structured, they will be more likely to view you as a credible speaker whose ideas are worthy of their serious consideration.

QUESTIONS FOR REVIEW AND REFLECTION

1. What are the different kinds of outlines, and what purposes do each serve?
2. What are the main components that need to be labeled and included in a formal outline? Why is each important?
3. Why is it important to restrict each point in the outline to a single idea?
4. How does the outline reflect relationships between ideas and supporting material?
5. How does the use of a consistent system of outlining symbols and indentation help make these relationships clear?
6. What are the most important guidelines to remember when preparing speaking notes?

ENDNOTES

1. See W. James Potter, *Media Literacy*, 3rd ed. (Thousand Oaks, CA: Sage, 2005).
2. See Carla Johnson, *Screened Out: How the Media Control Us and What We Can Do about It* (Armonk, NY: Sharpe, 2000).

Autism: Why Are the Rates Rising?

Kaitlin Rapone

Note: This outline is based on a speech that was delivered in a public speaking class at Southeast Missouri State University in 2008.

Specific purpose: I want my audience to understand some possible explanations for the dramatic increases in the number of children diagnosed with autism.

Thesis: Researchers have offered a variety of different, sometimes competing explanations for the dramatic increase in the number of children diagnosed with autism.

Introduction

Attention-Getting Device

Not long ago, my cousin Susan came to visit our family. She brought her 17-year-old son, Michael, with her. Michael does not behave like other teenagers. He rocks back and forth, rarely looks directly at anyone, and will only eat a few different foods, like chicken nuggets and Cheerios. Michael is autistic. Although he has made incredible progress over the years, Susan is worried about his future.

Credibility

I have known Michael for most of my life and have watched his parents agonize over how to help him communicate and learn the skills he needs to live independently. Because of this personal experience, I have been doing research to better understand the causes of this disorder.

Justification and Background

Autism is becoming increasingly prevalent in our society. *Every day* 60 children in our country are diagnosed as autistic. In a recent article in *U.S. News & World Report*, Dr. Bernadine Healy reported that autism now affects *one in every 150 children* in the U.S. Yet most people know very little about this disorder that the Autism Society of America (ASA) describes as a "complex developmental disability."

There is no simple medical test for detecting autism. Instead, children are diagnosed during the first three years of life through careful observation of their communication, their actions, and their interactions. Signs of the disorder include impaired communication, a lack of emotional and physical contact, and social withdrawal. These behaviors cannot be cured or outgrown, but many autistic children do benefit from education and therapy.

Thesis

Researchers have attributed the increased rates of autism among children to a variety of factors.

Enumerated Preview

Today, I'd like to examine three possible explanations for the rise in autism rates: hereditary factors, environmental factors, and changing definitions of the disorder.

In order to get listeners' attention and show the relevance of her topic, Kaitlin shares a compelling story about someone in her family. She then emphasizes the large number of children who are diagnosed with autism.

To help the audience understand the nature of the disorder, Kaitlin enumerates the general behaviors associated with autism.

After advancing her thesis, the speaker sets the stage for her speech by offering a preview of her main points and transitioning into her speech's first main idea—the theory of heredity.

Body

I. Some experts believe that heredity plays a major role in the development of autism.
   A. Genetics is one of the most obvious and common explanations for why certain children are autistic.
      1. Some researchers believe that certain children are born with a "vulnerability" to the disorder.
      2. These experts believe that children with a family history of autism or similar disabilities have a greater chance of being autistic.
      3. In addition, the ASA notes that children born with certain abnormalities in their brain or nervous system have a higher chance of being autistic.
   B. According to the ASA, many experts believe that when a child is born with a genetic susceptibility to autism, then other external factors may serve as triggers.

KAITLIN SUPPORTS HER FIRST MAIN IDEA WITH RESEARCH ON GENETIC VULNERABILITY, BRAIN ABNORMALITIES, AND SUSCEPTIBILITY TO EXTERNAL FACTORS.

TRANSITION: Along with genetics, our environment could be contributing to increased rates of autism.

II. Some researchers believe that environmental factors could trigger autism.
   A. The ASA explains that complications during pregnancy caused by harmful substances entering the body may cause an unborn child to become more vulnerable to autism.
   B. After birth, exposure to toxins and pollutants, such as lead and pesticides, might also interfere with healthy brain development.
      1. One expert, Dan Orzech, observes: "In the last half-century or so, more than 85,000 industrial chemicals have been registered in the United States, and many of them have found their way into our environment—and our bodies. Children, with their smaller and still-developing bodies, may be the ones most vulnerable to their effects."
      2. The sheer quantity of these harmful substances and the ease with which they find their way into our bodies is of special interest to researchers who believe they might contribute to the rising rates of autism.
   C. Finally, some experts believe that childhood vaccinations might have played a significant role in the rising rates of autism.
      1. Until 2002, childhood vaccines for measles, mumps, and rubella contained a mercury-based preservative, Thimerosal.
      2. However, because cases of autism have continued to rise *after* Thimerosal was removed from vaccines, other experts, including those at the Centers for Disease Control, no longer believe that vaccines should be a cause of concern.
      3. Thimerosal remains suspect, though, due to its presence elsewhere, particularly in flu shots, which can be passed from pregnant women to their babies in utero.

TO SUPPORT HER POINT ABOUT ENVIRONMENTAL INFLUENCES, KAITLIN USES EXPERT TESTIMONY AND STATISTICS ON THE NUMBER OF INDUSTRIAL CHEMICALS THAT HAVE BEEN REGISTERED IN THE UNITED STATES, MANY OF WHICH, THE EXPERT ARGUES, HAVE ENTERED OUR ENVIRONMENT AND OUR BODIES, ESPECIALLY THOSE OF CHILDREN.

IN THIS PORTION OF HER SPEECH, KAITLIN EXPLORES THE CONTROVERSIAL THEORY THAT CHILDHOOD VACCINES MIGHT HAVE TRIGGERED AUTISM IN SOME CHILDREN. SHE NOTES THAT A MERCURY-BASED PRESERVATIVE, THIMEROSAL, HAS BEEN IDENTIFIED AS A POSSIBLE CULPRIT.

TRANSITION: Heredity and environmental factors may well help explain the increase in autism rates, but another explanation has been offered as well, one that focuses on *how* we define and diagnose the disorder.

III. Some experts have argued that the rising number of autism cases may be attributable to nothing more than changes in how we define and diagnose the disorder.
   A. In recent years, as the Centers for Disease Control and Prevention has observed, the definition of autism has broadened significantly.
   B. And because there is no single medical test but rather a growing number of signs or symptoms associated with the disorder, doctors and other health care providers may be stretching the definition further by applying the criteria loosely.
   C. These wide-ranging boundaries for diagnosing autism, as Dr. Janice Hopkins recently pointed out in the *British Journal of Medicine*, could by themselves account for why "the prevalence of autism increased eightfold in the United States" between the early 1980s and the late 1990s.
      1. A good example of how autism may be too readily assumed comes from a study by Susan Bryson, published in *The Canadian Journal of Psychiatry*, which noted that within one group of individuals with various intellectual disabilities, 28 percent were diagnosed with autism.
      2. According to the *Economist*, a similar study by Dorothy Bishop tested 38 individuals who had been diagnosed with language disorders early in their lives and found that twelve of those would have been diagnosed as autistic by today's standards.

IN THIS PART OF HER SPEECH, KAITLIN EXPLORES THE EXPANDED DEFINITION OF AUTISM BY QUOTING THE CENTERS FOR DISEASE CONTROL AND PREVENTION.

KAITLIN CITES AN ARTICLE IN A REPUTABLE PROFESSIONAL JOURNAL TO EMPHASIZE THAT DIAGNOSTIC PRACTICES ALONE MIGHT EXPLAIN THE RISE IN AUTISM.

IN CONCLUDING HER LAST MAIN POINT, KAITLIN SUMMARIZES TWO STUDIES THAT DOCUMENT THE EXPANDED DEFINITION OF AUTISM.

TRANSITION: Whatever is responsible, autism rates may well continue to rise. The disorder has no simple cure and the spectrum of disorders diagnosed as autism is broad.

THIS QUICK SUMMARY SERVES AS A TRANSITION AS KAITLIN MOVES TOWARD HER CONCLUSION.

Conclusion

REFER TO INTRODUCTION

There are days when my cousin, Susan, nearly loses hope. She has had to educate herself about autism—and sometimes she has even had to educate her son's teachers. She has battled with his doctors. She often asks, "How did this happen to my child?" At the time she became pregnant, she had never known anyone with an autistic child.

AS SHE BEGINS HER CONCLUSION, KAITLIN REMINDS HER LISTENERS OF THE DAILY STRUGGLES OF PARENTS WITH AUTISTIC CHILDREN—REFERRING BACK TO THE PERSONAL STORY THAT SHE SHARED IN THE INTRODUCTION.

APPEAL

Today, we are learning more about autism each day. Most of you know at least one autistic person. Maybe you even have someone with autism in your family.

The causes of autism are not fully understood, but the implications are clear for those of us who plan to start a family someday. As future parents, we must be knowledgeable about our family histories. If disorders like autism are prevalent, anyone who becomes pregnant must take extra precautions. Every pregnant woman should talk to her doctor about what she can do to avoid exposing herself and her baby to dangerous toxins that could adversely affect her child.

We also must support researchers who continue to work to more clearly define autism and strive to create reliable tools for its diagnosis and treatment.

FINALLY, THE SPEAKER ARTICULATES THE ISSUES THAT LISTENERS WILL WANT TO REMEMBER AS THEY THINK ABOUT HAVING THEIR OWN FAMILIES. SHE ALSO REMINDS THEM OF THE IMPORTANCE OF SUPPORTING RESEARCHERS AS THEY STRIVE TO IMPROVE OUR UNDERSTANDING OF AUTISM.

Bibliography

"Autism Society: Improving the Lives of Those Affected by Autism." 20 Feb. 2010. Autism Society of America. 22 Feb. 2010 <www.autism-society.org/site/PageServer>.

"Autism Spectrum Disorders (ASDs)." 17 Aug. 2009. Centers for Disease Control and Prevention. 20 Feb. 2010 <www.cdc.gov/ncbddd/autism/topics.html>.

Bryson, Susan. "Prevalence of Autism among Adolescents With Intellectual Disabilities." *Canadian Journal of Psychiatry* 53 (July 2008): 449–59. Academic Search Premier. Ebscohost. SEMO Lib., Cape Girardeau, MO. 15 Feb. 2010 <http://ebscohost.com>.

Healy, Bernadine. "Fighting the Autism-Vaccine War." *U.S. News & World Report* 144 (21 Apr. 2008): 73. Academic Search Premier. Ebscohost. SEMO Lib., Cape Girardeau, MO. 15 Feb. 2010 <http://web.ebscohost.com>.

Hopkins, Janice. "Increase in Autism Due to Change in Definition, Not MMR Vaccine." *British Medical Journal* 330 (15 Jan. 2005): 132 <www.bmj.com/cgi.content>.

"Morbidity and Mortality Weekly Report." 18 Feb. 2010. Centers for Disease Control & Prevention. 21 Feb. 2010 <www.cdc.gov/mmwr>.

"Not More, Just Different." *Economist* 387 (12 April 2008): 89. Academic Search Premier. Ebscohost. SEMO Lib., Cape Girardeau, MO. 10 Feb. 2010 <http://web.ebscohost.com>.

Orzech, Dan. "Environmental Toxins and Child Development." *Social Work Today* 7 (Mar./Apr. 2007): 37 <www.socialworktoday.com>.

CHAPTER

11

Using Language Effectively

CHAPTER SURVEY

CHAPTER OBJECTIVES

After studying this chapter, you should be able to

1. Discuss the symbolic nature of language.
2. Make more effective language choices.
3. Use language that is interesting and engaging for listeners.
4. Choose language that is ethical and appropriate to the situation.
5. Explain how *style* can influence listeners' responses.

Style is a difficult term to define, partly because we use it in so many different ways. If we say a person has style, we may mean that the person dresses well, sings in a unique voice, or plays basketball with a special flair. In those situations, the context of our remark will clarify what we mean when we say that a person has style. When we talk about a speaker's style, however, we mean something different. We still may mean that, in a general sense, the person has a pleasing style of speaking—that is, he or she projects a good image; uses language, movement, and gestures well; or relates to the audience effectively. **Style**, in the ancient tradition of rhetorical theory, has a more specific meaning: it refers to how we use language in oral presentations.

This chapter focuses on this more specific meaning of style: how you choose the language for your speech and the effects of those choices on your overall success as a speaker. We will begin by discussing the connections between language and meaning, keeping in mind that the speaker who wants to use clear language must begin with clear thinking. If you first develop a clear grasp of the ideas you hope to communicate, it will be much easier for you to find the right language to get your message across. Then we will discuss how to choose language that is clear, interesting, effective, and appropriate to the particular situation. By the end of the chapter, you should have a better sense of the importance of style and what you can do to improve your style as a public speaker.

LANGUAGE AND MEANING

Preview. *Style is fundamentally concerned with how the speaker uses language. When crafting a speech, it is critical to choose appropriate language. The language you choose has the potential to influence listeners through its symbolic power and its explicit and implicit meanings. Your choices can help you connect with listeners or can create barriers and misunderstandings.*

Speakers and listeners do not always speak exactly the same language. All of us may speak English, but we do not choose and use language in the same ways. We may come from different backgrounds that provide us with different vocabularies or different meanings for words. Regional uses of English, ethnic uses of language, and generational variations in language can be confusing to those outside a particular linguistic group. Phrases or abbreviations that are commonplace on Facebook or Twitter, for example, may need to be translated for those who do not participate in online social networks. In a sense, we all speak different "languages," and those differences influence how our listeners respond to our speeches.

The words we choose reflect our values, our perceptions, or our attitudes. Depending on our point of view, members of a rebel organization might be labeled *terrorists* or *freedom fighters*. Likewise, an army labeled *invaders* by some might be considered *liberators* by others. During the recent health care debate in America, what some described as needed *reform* was denounced by others as *socialized medicine*.[1] As you prepare to speak, it is important to keep in mind that language is symbolic and allows for a variety of meanings.

The Symbolic Nature of Language

Words are symbols. They are abstractions that allow us to talk about people, places, things, actions, and ideas without providing every detail. The more abstract our words, the more details we omit. Abstract language makes it possible for us to talk about our feelings and values. It permits us to talk about the past and the future, and things that we can only imagine. We conceptualize ideas—such as love, honor, and beauty—through abstract language. Yet using too many abstract words can also cause problems in communication.

As we speak more abstractly, ideas can become more and more difficult to grasp, and the chances of misunderstandings increase. If you were to describe a course of action as "the patriotic thing to do," for example, how your audience will respond depends on what *patriotism* means to them. For some, patriotism might demand that they support the War in Afghanistan; others may feel they have a patriotic duty to protest the war. Similarly, some may assume that *supporting our troops* means sending them care packages or letters of encouragement, whereas others may feel that the best way to support our troops would be to bring them home.

Abstractions are a powerful source of personal identity. We live in a diverse country, made up of people of many different cultural and social backgrounds. The word *American*, for example, can apply to all of us, but it is also an abstraction that can be variously interpreted. Consider how listeners might have responded differently when former secretary of state Colin Powell used the word *American* in a speech to the National Volunteer Summit. Urging his listeners to work toward the day when everyone would live the "American Dream," Powell appealed to the widespread belief that America was especially blessed by a "Divine Providence." He also invoked the principle that we must all be "good stewards" of each other:

> Let us make sure that no child in America is left behind, no child in America has their dream deferred or denied. We can do it. We can do it because we are Americans. We are Americans who draw our strength from this place. We are Americans who believe to the depth of our hearts that this is not a land that was placed here by historic accident, it is a land that was put here by Divine Providence who told us to be good stewards of our land, but especially to be good stewards of each other. Divine Providence gave us this land, blessed it and told us always to be proud to call it America. And so we go forward. Let us go save our children.[2]

Powell's use of abstractions was broad enough so that many people with different specific convictions could agree with his statement. Yet people with different backgrounds may have had different views of what it meant to be an "American," and people of differing religious beliefs may have reacted differently to his reference to "Divine Providence."

Sometimes speakers exploit abstract terms to trick listeners into accepting their ideas without seriously thinking about them. Most of us favor "family values," for example, but Republicans and Democrats often disagree over which policies best promote those values. Similarly, we may all agree that accountability in government is good, or that we should all be responsible citizens. But what it means to be accountable or responsible may vary from person to person.

When a speaker uses such abstract words, details are lost and differences may be glossed over.

Suppose, for example, that a political candidate claims that we need a "safety net" to protect the poorest and most disadvantaged among us. Does that mean that we need more government spending on social services? Or is the candidate advocating that private charities be counted on to provide a safety net for the disadvantaged? In the sample speech following Chapter 8, one health care expert referred to a "safety net" that was "full of holes." In short, the abstract term *safety net* can be used in a wide variety of ways. The careful listener looks for clues as to how a speaker translates abstract terms into specific ideas or policies.

Denotative and Connotative Meaning

Although meaning may vary according to the understanding we bring to abstract words, many words have commonly understood meanings; if this were not so, we could not communicate at all. The meanings of words can be divided into two groups: denotative and connotative meanings. **Denotative meaning** refers to the literal, objective meaning of words stripped of any emotional baggage they may carry. These meanings tend to be more objective and less susceptible to a wide variety of interpretations. For example, the denotative meaning of *pencil* is "a writing implement consisting of a thin rod of graphite or similar substance encased in wood or held in a plastic or metal mechanical device." Its meaning is relatively objective; there are not a lot of personal interpretations and feelings attached to the word *pencil*. When we hear the word, few of us are confused or feel fear, joy, or anger.

Connotative meanings, by contrast, derive from the emotional implications of words and suggest a range of subjective and personal interpretations. Many words in our culture carry strong connotations because of their association with historic events or political controversies. For many U.S. citizens, words such as *terrorist, traitor*, or *un-American* carry strong connotations because they automatically provoke feelings of fear, hostility, or even hatred. Words such as *patriot* or *hero*, on the other hand, invoke more positive feelings and emotions.

Connotative meaning is infused into language by the context in which words appear and by the perceptions of the listener. Nonetheless, in our society, some words seem to be more emotionally charged than others: *honor, free enterprise, racist*, and *neo-Nazi* are just a few examples. All of these words are likely to conjure up intense personal feelings, positive or negative.

During a congressional campaign, pollsters for a political action group conducted focus groups to determine connotative responses to certain words. They issued a pamphlet suggesting "good" words for candidates to use in their campaigns when talking about themselves, and "bad" words to use when discussing their opponents. Figure 11.1 lists some of the "optimistic" words candidates were urged to use in letters, speeches, and ads. The "bad" words, labeled "contrasting," were to be used when referring to an opponent's "record, proposals and party."[3] If you examine these words closely, you'll see that the "optimistic" words all evoke positive feelings and associations, while the "contrasting" words are meant to raise fears, anxieties, disapproval, or discomfort.

FIGURE 11.1

Optimistic		Contrasting	
common sense	passionate	anti-child	greed
courage	pioneer	anti-flag	hypocrisy
dream	pride	betray	incompetent
duty	principle(d)	cheat	lie
empowerment	pro-environment	collapse	radical
fair	prosperity	corruption	self-serving
family	reform	crisis	shallow
freedom	rights	decay	steal
hard work	strength	destroy	taxes
liberty	truth	devour	traitors
moral	"workfare"	failure	welfare

Source: "Language: A Key Mechanism of Control," from, *Power Persuasion: Moving An Ancient Art into the Media*, by Cooper and Williams. © 1992 by Educational Video Group. Used by permission.

In another example of how seriously political strategists take word connotations, Frank Lutz, a Republican consultant, sent the Senate Republican policy committee suggestions for phrasing their objections to President Obama's proposals for health care reform. He recommended one claim that was designed to exploit both fears of losing control over one's own health care and widespread hostility toward the federal government: "A committee of Washington bureaucrats will establish the standard of care for all Americans." He also proposed that the plan be attacked with the claim that it would "deny people treatments they need and make them wait to get the treatments they are allowed to receive." Suggesting that "Washington bureaucrats" would make health care decisions for Americans—instead of their own doctors—and "allow" some treatments was hardly an accurate description of Obama's plan, but it did tap into the negative feelings many Americans have toward the federal government.[4]

Thoughtful speakers and listeners understand the power of words with strong positive or negative connotations, and they look beyond their immediate, surface reactions to the deeper meanings of such words. As speakers, we have an obligation to be sensitive to the emotional power of language. We also need to realize that our language does not automatically mean the same thing to every listener. Your goal as a speaker should be to make yourself as clear as possible, not obscure your real meaning or stir up emotions with highly connotative language.

USING LANGUAGE THAT IS CLEAR AND ACCURATE

Preview. *The most profound idea, clever remark, or astute observation will have little impact if your listeners cannot grasp it. Clear speakers use language familiar to their audience. They also speak with specificity, concreteness, precision, and clarity. Finally, they avoid the use of* *clichés, empty words, and distracting language, and they construct their sentences with a concern for good oral style.*

As you consider the ways in which language choices help you connect with your audience, keep in mind that **oral style** and written style are not the same. In most situations, you will use less formal, more conversational language in speeches than you do in written manuscripts. A good oral style is more informal, simpler, and more repetitious than a written style. Also—and this is important—oral style is more spontaneous. It allows you the flexibility to adapt your language as you speak. In this chapter, we encourage you to make careful and effective language choices. But if you plan to deliver your speech extemporaneously, you probably will not write out every single word of your speech in advance. Rather, you will need to choose appropriate language as you speak.

Also keep in mind that a speech delivered orally is received differently from a written presentation. If you are reading a page and come across difficult or unfamiliar words, you can always reread the passage and try to figure out the meaning of the word from the context, or you can consult a dictionary. Indeed, a good book often challenges readers to learn new words and expand their knowledge of the language. But a speech is a different matter. When you are giving a speech, your listeners cannot stop you and ask you to repeat an unfamiliar word. Nor can they whip out the dictionary and look up a word that they did not understand.

Oral language may be described as "written for the ear." It is language that sounds more informal and is less complex. It usually employs shorter sentences and more contractions than written language. It generally is not as economical either. Although your sentences may be shorter, it may take more sentences—and thus more words—to express an idea. We will address this more fully in Chapter 12 when we discuss delivery, but consider this example of two ideas, one as it might be written, the other as it might be spoken:

- *Written:* Several complex, interrelated factors work together to produce an almost insoluble problem given the political, economic, and social context.
- *Spoken:* This problem doesn't have just one cause. There are many factors that contribute to the difficult situation we're facing now. And because there are many causes of our problem, there are no simple solutions.

As speakers, we need to be sensitive to the differences between oral and written communication and do all we can to achieve clarity and understanding. If our speaking is to be meaningful, we must make sure that what we say is *instantly* intelligible.

Familiar Language

It is important that you use words familiar to your audience. Most of the great speakers in our history did not use big, pompous, important-sounding words. Rather, they used simple, direct language that listeners could easily grasp. In one of Abraham Lincoln's greatest speeches, given when he was nominated for the U.S. Senate in 1858, for example, he put his suspicions of the power of the slaveholders and their allies into clear, unequivocal words. He began with a simple and familiar biblical phrase:

> "A house divided against itself cannot stand." I believe this government can not endure permanently half slave and half free. I do not expect the Union to be dissolved—I do not expect the house to fall—but I do expect it will cease to be divided. It will become all one thing or all the other. Either the opponents of slavery will arrest the further spread of it, and place it where the public mind shall rest in the belief that it is in the course of ultimate extinction; or its advocates will push it forward till it shall become alike lawful in all the states, old as well as new—North as well as South.[5]

Nothing in the language of this passage would have been puzzling to listeners. Every single word was familiar to Lincoln's audience. The same is true of the next example. A senior student gave a speech to incoming freshmen at her university with the purpose of encouraging them to become active in significant projects and activities outside the classroom. In her introduction, she used familiar language to get her audience to look at an ordinary phrase in a different way, then led into her suggestions for getting the most out of their college experience:

> "Multitasking" is something that all of us know a lot about. If you were like me when I was in high school, you could listen to music and do your homework at the same time. You could listen to your mom or dad while texting a friend. Well, you can keep on multitasking now that you're in college, but if you're going to get the most out of your four years here, you're going to have to think about what "tasking" means. If it means playing computer games far into the night while blasting your favorite tunes into your headset and then sleeping through your morning class, your stay here might be one year and not four. Today, I want to talk about a different kind of "multitasking" that you can do at this university by exploring how you can better prepare yourself to be a productive, useful contributor to your community and—and this is a very important *and*—and a happy, satisfied person.

Because the familiarity of your words is important to the clarity of your speech, it is important that you learn as much as you can about your audience's education and vocabulary. Then you will be able to better choose the language most suitable to them.

Technical Language

You need to remember that listeners may not know the meaning of technical words. It is perfectly appropriate to use **technical language** in a speech to a specialized audience who will understand it. But in a speech addressed to a general audience, you should avoid using language that excludes people who lack technical expertise. If you *must* employ technical terms, it is your job to define them for listeners who may not have the knowledge or training to understand their precise meaning. Chemistry majors will know what a *reagent* is, and an accounting major understands what is meant by a *trial balance*. Less specialized audiences, however, will need to have the terms defined.

A student speaking about the challenges of passing a health care reform in the U.S. Senate needed to explain two technical terms: *filibuster* and *cloture*. A filibuster occurs when opponents of a bill use extended debate to prevent the legislation from coming to a vote. Cloture is a motion to end the debate, but under Senate rules a motion for cloture requires a three-fifths majority, or 60 votes. When opponents of reform threatened a filibuster, supporters of reform thus needed to line up not just the simple majority needed to pass the bill, but rather the 60 votes necessary to end a filibuster.

ABBREVIATIONS AND ACRONYMS The same is true, of course, of technical or specialized abbreviations or substitutions for longer words or titles. The best example of this is the *acronym*, which is a series of letters that stand for some longer name or title. Few may know that *RFID* stands for *radio frequency identification*, a technology used in tracking drugs to ensure that they are not tampered with. But even more common acronyms may need a quick explanation. Anyone who is interested in broadcasting will know that *FCC* stands for *Federal Communications Commission*, but others in your audience may not be familiar with this acronym. College students all know what a GPA is, but people not associated with the university may not know this shorthand for *grade-point average*. As speakers, we need to be conscious of the fact that our language grows out of our experience and knowledge and sometimes needs to be translated for listeners.

Concreteness and Specificity

Words chosen for their concreteness and specificity increase clarity. Compare the following two brief passages from student speeches given on related topics.

> *Student #1*: The tragedy of civil war falls heavily on women and children. They are displaced from their homes and suffer so many hardships from disease and injuries. They have the most primitive medical care in the large refugee camps and are attacked by lawless militias. It is hard to imagine the hardships they must endure.

> *Student #2*: Women and children are the innocent victims of civil wars raging in Africa. Life in the refugee camps is a constant struggle to get enough food to survive. Lack of clean water and proper sanitation means that diseases like cholera spread rapidly, and diarrhea is rampant. Those who stray just a few feet outside the camp may be attacked by militiamen wielding machetes. It is not uncommon to see children lying, glassy-eyed, on makeshift beds, with missing limbs and flies swarming over the wounds.

The second passage is clearly more moving. "Hardships" are specified; the results of the "attacks" are made real through the choice of concrete language that helps listeners visualize the enormity of the situation.

Precise Language

Mark Twain once observed that there is no such thing as a synonym; he admonished writers to seek the right word, not its "second cousin." Twain's advice is also good for public speakers. Precise words are important because they allow us to communicate our meaning as accurately as possible.

If you wanted to describe someone walking down the street, how would you do it? Specifically, what verbs would you choose? This would depend entirely on the kind of image you wanted to create. If you wanted to portray the person as being in a hurry, you might use verbs such as *raced, hustled*, or *hurried.* But each of these is different. Which is faster? Which is more informal? To take a different example, suppose you wanted to describe a negative feeling about something. You might say you *disliked* it, but if you felt more strongly, you might choose a verb such as *hated, detested*, or *loathed.* Which conveys the most accurate description of your feeling? In general, you will be more effective with your language if you use words that convey your meaning precisely.

Consider these sentences from student speeches as originally given and as revised to convey more precisely the point the speaker wishes to make:

Original: Many troops have been hurt by these homemade bombs.
Revised: Young American men and women serving in Iraq have been killed or maimed by roadside bombs.
Original: Homeless people increasingly run the risk of random violence.
Revised: People who live in the street have been subjected to beatings with baseball bats; they've been kicked, stabbed, punched, and even killed for no reason other than they're easy targets, and their assailants like to beat up "bums."

Not only do carefully chosen words enhance meaning and promote clarity, they also contribute to the kind of specificity we discussed earlier, thus heightening the impact of your message.

Avoiding Clichés, Empty Words, and Distracting Language

Effective public speakers avoid using **clichés**—trite, overused expressions. At one time, these expressions were probably fresh and interesting. *The bottom line* conveys a clear enough meaning, but the phrase has been used so much that it does not show any originality and may have lost its precise meaning: the total cost of something. Because of overuse, clichés are tired and lifeless, and they are less likely to engage listeners' thoughts and hold their interest.

Avoid empty words—those that add nothing but length to your sentences. For instance, why say *a number of*, when you can say *several* or *many*? You might say *because* instead of *due to the fact that, after* instead of *subsequent to, about* rather than *in connection with*, and *I must* instead of *it will be necessary for me to.*

Even though we may think of a speaking situation as an enlarged conversation, there *are* stylistic differences between the two. A conversation is more interactive. We don't always finish sentences, we may be interrupted from time to time, or others in the conversation may verbalize reactions. Casual conversations are often littered with unnecessary language that may be acceptable in that setting but not in a formal speech. You may say to a friend that "he was, like, very tall and, you know, well built." But "like" and "you know" only clutter a public speech and should be avoided.

If you can avoid empty words, clichés, and distracting language in your speaking, you will say more, say it more efficiently, and speak more clearly. And your audience will benefit through greater knowledge and understanding.

Constructing Sentences to Promote Clarity

Individual words must be clear, and so should sentences. Construct sentences with well-chosen words, but arrange those words so that the sentences they form are direct and easy to follow.

For good oral style, craft sentences so that the subject and the verb are close together. This makes the sentence easier to understand, and it sounds more natural. Consider the following sentence, in which the subject and verb have been separated: "This new program, which has been tried at other colleges similar to our own and has been enormously popular, is worthy of your support." Note how the sentence would be more understandable if reworked to say: "This program is worthy of your support. Other colleges like our own have tried it, and it has been enormously popular."

REPETITION AND RESTATEMENT Speakers may have to repeat certain words, phrases, or ideas to make them stick in listeners' minds. **Repetition** is especially effective when the speaker wants the audience to remember specific, vivid, or especially meaningful words or phrases. You may wish to use **restatement** if you want to emphasize or clarify an idea by discussing it in several different ways. Of course, speakers should not overuse these devices. When used carefully, however, they can reinforce your main ideas and make important expressions memorable.

Perhaps one of the most famous uses of repetition was in a speech given by Winston Churchill in the early days of World War II. In refusing to negotiate with the enemy, Churchill told the House of Commons, "We shall defend our island, whatever the cost may be. We shall fight on the beaches. We shall fight on the landing grounds. We shall fight in the fields and in the streets, and we shall fight in the hills. We shall never surrender."[6]

Through the simple device of repeating a phrase at the end of each example, one student speaker reinforced his contention that all of us are contributing money to large corporations for foolish or wasteful projects:

> Let's take a look at someone like Lockheed Martin, a defense manufacturer. They received only a paltry $25,000 in a tax write-off in 1996. But what did the tax write-off come for? Entertainment expenses that included $20,000 worth of golf balls. That's your tax money at work! Then we have the Walt Disney Corporation, a company whose profits are over $1 billion per year. They received a $300,000 federal subsidy in order to research bigger and better fireworks for their theme parks. That's your tax money at work! But probably the biggest and most insulting federal subsidy of all that I came across happened between 1990 and 1994, when

General Motors received $110.6 million in federal technological subsidies under the auspices of a jobs program. During that time period, their profits skyrocketed. And what happened? They laid off 104,000 of their workers—25 percent of their U.S. workforce. That's your tax money at work!

SHORT, CONCISE SENTENCES In an oral style, you also should keep sentences relatively short. Shorter sentences are easier for listeners to follow. Also avoid needless repetition, unnecessary modifiers, and circumlocutions, such as, "The reason why I think this plan will work is because . . ." Instead, say "This plan will work because . . ." One way to eliminate unnecessary words is to use the active voice. Consider the following examples:

"Great frustration with the lack of progress in enacting a health care reform bill in Congress has been expressed by health care advocates." (*passive voice, too wordy*)
"Advocates for health care reform have expressed frustration over the lack of progress in passing legislation." (*active voice*)
"It has been argued by some advocates of the 'cash for clunkers' program that of all the government programs that have been proposed or put in place that this one should be supported because it is very popular with the public and seems to be working as it was intended." (*passive voice, too wordy*)
"Even many critics of government programs argue that the 'cash for clunkers' program works and should be extended." (*active voice*)

MODIFIERS It is best to use only necessary modifiers. There are two kinds of modifiers: those that comment and those that define. **Commenting modifiers** include *very, most*, and *definitely*. These modifiers add little; instead they boost the force of the words they modify. Yet, if you select your words precisely, they should be able to stand alone without the assistance of such modifiers. Saying that the president is *very seriously worried* about the future of health care adds little to the statement that the president is *seriously worried*.

By contrast, **defining modifiers** provide information that the noun standing alone cannot convey. They tell us something we need to know. It is informative to know that a policy is supported by a *narrow majority* of voters, or that the government has a *contingency plan* to deal with H1N1 flu. Modifiers also are used to color audience perceptions; depending on whether an idea is described as innovative, brilliant, outdated, or preposterous, listeners will respond to it quite differently.

Simplicity

Simple and precise words and sentences contribute to active speech. Consider, for example, the way President Lyndon Johnson urged members of Congress to support him in passing the Voting Rights Act of 1965. When Johnson delivered this speech at a joint session of Congress, the nation was engulfed in racial turmoil. In Alabama, there were bloody confrontations between police and civil rights protesters. Across the country, there was a sense of great tension and urgency. In the following passage from LBJ's speech, there are no exceptional or unusual words and no particularly striking sentence constructions, but the clarity and forcefulness of the language suggest action.

> The bill I am presenting to you will be known as a civil rights bill.
>
> But in a larger sense, most of the program I am recommending is a civil rights program. Its object is to open the city of hope to all people of all races, because all Americans just must have the right to vote, and we are going to give them that right.
>
> All Americans must have the privileges of citizenship, regardless of race, and they are going to have those privileges of citizenship regardless of race.
>
> But I would like to caution you and remind you that to exercise these privileges takes much more than just legal right. It requires a trained mind and a healthy body. It requires a decent home and the chance to find a job and the opportunity to escape from the clutches of poverty.
>
> Of course people cannot contribute to the nation if they are never taught to read or write; if their bodies are stunted from hunger; if their sickness goes untended; if their life is spent in hopeless poverty, just drawing a welfare check.
>
> So we want to open the gates to opportunity. But we're also going to give all our people, black and white, the help that they need to walk through those gates."[7]

Apart from the ideas that are discussed, language can have a force of its own. When used to promote interest, it can help make a speech more persuasive and effective.

In urging passage of the Voting Rights Act of 1965, President Johnson used simple, direct, and forceful language to demand justice for African Americans.

USING LANGUAGE THAT IS INTERESTING

Preview. *As speakers, we can keep listeners interested by using active language—language that is lively and vivid—and figures of speech. We can also use rhetorical questions and parallelism to promote audience interest and identification with the topic.*

Even if your language is clear—so that listeners understand your main ideas or arguments—you may fail to move them unless it is also compelling. Gaining and maintaining listeners' interest is essential if you hope to achieve your desired response. When you use language that stimulates the listeners' imagination, offers memorable images, and is pleasing to the ear, you will have a better chance of also engaging their minds and hearts.

Using Active, Vivid Language

Action holds interest and commands attention. The way we choose language and the way we put it together can create a sense of action for our listeners. We can create the illusion of action and help listeners understand more precisely what we have in mind by using active, vivid language.

Language promotes a feeling of action when it is lively. Language that gives a realistic and specific description of events, people, and ideas is the liveliest. Further, listeners' emotions are often engaged through the use of vivid descriptions of pleasant or unpleasant situations. In Chapter 8, we noted that telling a story about real people tends to promote identification between the audience and the subject. The simple narrative can make us feel ashamed or angry or experience a host of other emotions.

Montel, a public speaking student, began a speech by describing an automobile accident in vivid detail. He explained how the victims of the accident were rushed to the nearest hospital and how one of the victims was hastily examined, then put on a stretcher and left in a hallway unattended. He described the patient's deteriorating condition as the hours passed, and how doctors and nurses hurried by, some occasionally stopping for a quick look and then going on. As he told the story, the sense of frustration, surprise, and anger in the audience was apparent. Everyone wondered why on earth something wasn't being done for that patient. Montel concluded his story by explaining that the accident, which took place several years ago, involved a black woman who had been taken to a hospital in a predominantly white neighborhood. The example was so vivid and the emotions so real that the speaker had little more to do to finish his speech on the evils of racism.

In using vivid language, speakers often try to appeal to listeners' senses. Through **sensory appeals**, audience members are encouraged to see, hear, or feel something. Two famous speeches from our history illustrate the power of vivid language to evoke strong feeling.

The first is by the African-American abolitionist, Frederick Douglass, who vividly depicted the inhumanity of slavery: "What, am I to argue that it is wrong to make men brutes, to rob them of their liberty, to work them without wages, to keep them ignorant of their relations to their fellow men, to beat them with sticks, to flay their flesh with the lash, to load their limbs with irons, to hunt them with dogs, to sell them at auction, to sunder their families, to knock out their teeth, to burn their flesh, to starve them into obedience and submission to their masters?"[8]

The second is a speech by Chief Joseph of the Nez Perce tribe, who surrendered after a long and desperate 1100-mile flight from pursuing U.S. cavalry. Here is his description of his people's plight:

> I am tired of fighting. Our chiefs are killed. Looking Glass is dead. Toohulhulsote is dead. The old men are all dead. It is the young men who say yes or no. He who led the young men is dead.
>
> It is cold and we have no blankets. The little children are freezing to death. My people, some of them, have run away to the hills and have no blankets, no food. No one knows where they are—perhaps freezing to death. I want to have time to look for my children and see how many I can find. Maybe I shall find them among the dead.
>
> Hear me, my chiefs. I am tired. My heart is sick and sad. From where the sun now stands, I will fight no more forever.[9]

Listeners exposed to such vivid and detailed narratives have a strong likelihood of identifying with them. With the bulk of the appeal resting on visual images, the result is a more persuasive presentation.

Lively, vivid language is important, but much still depends on your ability to marshal excellent arguments and your listeners' openness to new and alternative viewpoints. Lively, vivid language alone cannot make up for weak ideas.

Using Figures of Speech

Language that is striking or impressive can create interest and contribute to understanding. For centuries, students of rhetoric have studied what are called **figures of speech**; these are special ways of using language to heighten the beauty of expression, or the clarity of ideas, or the emotional impact of speeches. It is not important for the beginning student of public speaking to understand and identify all the technical names for the different figures of speech. But both listeners and speakers should be aware of some common ways of using language effectively.

SIMILE Language can be used to compare things. A direct comparison can be made between things that an audience may not see as being similar. This kind of comparison, a **simile**, is typically introduced by the word *like* or *as*. When President Bush appointed Tony Snow as his new press secretary in May 2006, one reporter used similes to describe the situation Mr. Snow faced: "Any press secretary taking over the podium for the first time comes off *as a substitute teacher trying to take control of a restless high school class*. With the president's standing in the opinion polls this low, *Mr. Snow was more like a stepfather meeting his wife's children for the first time*."[10]

"A day in the life of the college student," one student began her speech, "is like a day at an amusement park. You have ups and downs; you can get spun around; you can do new things you've never done before; you can have a lot of fun; and you can end by throwing up." More eloquently, John F. Kennedy, in a speech on civil rights, used a simile to express his conviction that denying rights to African Americans was "primarily a moral issue. It is as old as the scriptures and is as clear as the American Constitution." Later in the speech he used another simile to salute the courage of civil rights workers: "Like our soldiers in all parts of the world they are meeting freedom's challenge on the firing line, . . ."[11]

METAPHOR Like a simile, a **metaphor** compares objects that the audience may think of as quite dissimilar. In a metaphor, however, the comparison is not so direct and does not use the words *like* or *as*. For example, a freshman college student, about to join a group heading to the Gulf region to help with cleanup after the Katrina disaster, described her feelings using a swimming metaphor: "I think I understand the principles of swimming, but I'm about to find out by jumping into the deep end of the pool; I just hope I can swim to the other end." And, in a moving tribute to the murdered Mahatma Gandhi, Indian prime minister Jawaharlal Nehru expressed the sadness felt by his fellow Indians by comparing Gandhi to the sun: "A glory has departed and the sun that warmed and brightened our lives has set and we shiver in the dark."[12]

These images create a certain feeling or mood in the audience. In this way, they make an important contribution to the audience's total appreciation of a speech.

ANTITHESIS Language can be used to make contrasts between words or ideas. The special device known as **antithesis** is a way of putting together two things that have sharply different meanings. Through antithesis, ideas can be reinforced and compelling contrasts in thought can be suggested. A definition of *classics*, for example, is that they "are examples of *how* to think, not *what* to think."[13] In a speech criticizing those who polluted the environment in the pursuit of profits, one student speaker used this antithesis: "On this campus we're engaged in an important struggle. We must not support the forces of death and personal profit, but, instead, we must choose the forces of life and personal responsibility." The antithesis pitted life against death, effectively associating those who would put money first with the latter.

IRONY Other stylistic devices can be used to make ideas more believable or understandable. Through **irony**, a speaker can strongly imply a meaning that is opposite that which is stated. Mary Church Terrell was a graduate of Oberlin College, a teacher, the first president of the National Association of Colored Women, and a professional lecturer who spoke out against racism at the beginning of the twentieth century. In a speech given in Washington in 1906 she used irony skillfully to point out the contradictions of racial discrimination evident in the trip from Washington, D.C., to George Washington's tomb at Mount Vernon. In a speech before the United Women's Club she said:

> As a colored woman I cannot visit the tomb of the Father of this country, which owes its very existence to the love of freedom in the human heart and which stands

Mary Church Terrell actively attacked racism in America in the early twentieth century. She pointed to the irony of an American of color being forced to sit in a segregated section of a trolley car when traveling from the nation's capital to George Washington's tomb at Mount Vernon.

for equal opportunity for all, without being forced to sit in the Jim Crow section of an electric car which starts from the very heart of the city—midway between the Capitol and the White House. If I refuse thus to be humiliated, I am cast into jail and forced to pay a fine for violating the Virginia laws.[14]

Irony can be a potent way of pointing out the discrepancies between professed values and real actions.

ALLITERATION A speaker who uses a repetitive pattern of initial sounds that can hold the audience's attention and reinforce the idea is using **alliteration.** One returning student, proud of her new U.S. citizenship, said that becoming an American was "more than just a passport to plenty," it was "a doorway to democracy." In a speech to the NAACP in July 2009, President Obama also used alliteration when speaking of the great civil rights leaders of the past: "They knew that the stain of slavery and the sin of segregation had to be lifted in the courtroom, and in the legislature, and in the hearts and the minds of Americans."[15]

Poets commonly use alliteration and other figures of speech. Edgar Allan Poe wrote of the "silken, sad, uncertain rustling of each purple curtain"[16] to capture the sound of wind blowing through an open window. Whether used in a poem or a speech, alliteration—if not forced or overdone—can be memorable and pleasing to the ear.

PERSONIFICATION The speaker who uses **personification** gives the characteristics of human beings to nonhuman forms or things. One common form of personification is a phrase we hear almost every day; it is a variation of the phrase *The White House says* … or *The White House reacted to the debate in Congress*. … A student speaker observed that "This city can be a very hostile place. It can ignore you, it can frighten you, and it can punish you very severely if you ignore its unwritten rules." This student then went on to talk about such urban problems as loneliness, homelessness, and crime.

Personification adds interest and may also enhance emotional appeal.

OXYMORON In an **oxymoron,** a speaker can combine seemingly contradictory expressions, such as *thunderous silence* or *cheerful pessimist*, using such contradictions to emphasize the contrast between two things. Oxymorons give an unexpected twist of meaning that can be amusing—such as *found missing* or *negative increase*—whereas others are arresting and thought-provoking and can reinforce opinion in a memorable way. For example, those who are frustrated by official bureaucracy and red tape will find *government organization* an oxymoron. Popular films have been given oxymoronic titles such as *Back to the Future* and *Eyes Wide Shut.* Bob Dole, commenting on his political opponent Bill Clinton in the 1996 presidential race, said that "he talks right and runs left."

Although some terms we use, such as *virtual reality*, have become such a part of our language that we no longer even recognize their contradictory quality, oxymorons are often memorable and usually capture listeners' interest and attention.[17]

Memorizing the definitions of these figures of speech is not nearly as important as recognizing this basic principle: choosing language that is effective in promoting your meaning and conveying your feelings helps better connect you with your audience.

RHETORICAL QUESTIONS Speakers sometimes ask listeners questions. When they do so, they are usually not actually looking for an answer from the audience. Instead, they are posing **rhetorical questions**, which pique the audience's curiosity and stimulate thinking. As we noted in Chapter 9, rhetorical questions may be used to gain the audience's attention at the start of a speech, or they may be used as transitions. But they can also be effective stylistic devices when used in other places in a speech.

When a speaker poses a rhetorical question, we are encouraged to think. In most contexts, when we are asked questions, we are being invited to participate. Questions trigger guesses, speculation, and other forms of thought. In short, questions activate our brains.

As with all stylistic devices, rhetorical questions should be chosen carefully. If the question is unimaginative or simplistic, it will not have the desired effect. "Why should you wear your seat belt?" "Why is smoking bad for you?" The answers to these rhetorical questions are probably too obvious to inspire much thought.

The effectiveness of any rhetorical question depends on its wording, its timing, and the way you develop the response to the question. Having posed the question, you are, of course, obliged to answer it. For example, one speaker, who wanted audience members to understand the urgency of supporting a local day shelter and hunger relief program, posed this question: "What does the face of hunger look like in our community?" After pausing to let the audience contemplate the question, she then offered these examples:

> A young couple living in their car with their two young children. Unable to afford child care, the mother stays with the children while the father goes to work.
>
> A Vietnam veteran, who lives in a tent in a wooded area west of town. War injuries have made it impossible for him to maintain steady employment.
>
> A young mother, on work release from jail, struggles to rebuild her life while doing volunteer work for a church and working part-time for a local cleaning company.
>
> A 60-year-old woman—a former nurse's aide, working most of her life in nearby hospitals and nursing homes—is diagnosed with leukemia. Too weak to work, she stays at a local emergency shelter.

Is this how *you* pictured poverty and hunger in our community?

These are only a few of the *real* women, men, and children who take their meals at the Shalom Community Center each day.

As a way of getting listeners to think and to engage issues, rhetorical questions can prove effective.

PARALLELISM When used effectively, **parallelism** can bring force, clarity, rhythm, and interest to a speech. Using parallel sentences or phrases of about equal length can also add emphasis to particular ideas. In speaking about the Great Depression, for example, Franklin Roosevelt emphasized the seriousness and widespread nature of the economic problems facing the nation with a series of parallel sentences:

> I see millions of families trying to live on incomes so meager that the pall of family disaster hangs over them day by day.
>
> I see millions whose daily lives in city and on farm continue under conditions labeled indecent by a so-called polite society half a century ago.
>
> I see millions denied education, recreation and the opportunity to better their lot and the lot of their children.

HIGHLIGHTING LANGUAGE: JOHN McCAIN ACCEPTS THE REPUBLICAN NOMINATION

Senator John McCain used active, vivid language, along with antithesis and parallelism in his speech accepting the Republican presidential nomination in 2009.

I fight to restore the pride and principles of our party. We were elected to change Washington, and we let Washington change us.

We lost the trust of the American people when some Republicans gave in to the temptations of corruption. We lost their trust when rather than reform government, both parties made it bigger.

We lost their trust when instead of freeing ourselves from a dangerous dependence on foreign oil, both parties—and Sen. Obama—passed another corporate welfare bill for oil companies. We lost their trust when we valued our power over our principles.

We're going to change that. We're going to recover the people's trust by standing up again to the values Americans admire. The party of Lincoln, Roosevelt and Reagan is going to get back to basics.

In this country, we believe everyone has something to contribute and deserves the opportunity to reach their God-given potential, from the boy whose descendents arrived on the Mayflower to the Latina daughter of migrant workers. We're all God's children, and we're all Americans.

We believe in low taxes, spending discipline, and open markets. We believe in rewarding hard work and risk-takers and letting people keep the fruits of their labor.

We believe in a strong defense, work, faith, service, a culture of life, personal responsibility, the rule of law, and judges who dispense justice impartially and don't legislate from the bench.

We believe in the values of families, neighborhoods, and communities. We believe in a government that unleashes the creativity and initiative of Americans, government that doesn't make your choices for you, but works to make sure you have more choices to make for yourself.

Source: From John McCain, "Republican Presidential Nomination Acceptance Address, St. Paul, Minnesota, Sept. 4, 2008." Published 2008 by American Presidency Project.

> I see millions lacking the means to buy the products of farm and factory and by their poverty denying work and productiveness to many other millions.
>
> I see one-third of a nation ill-housed, ill-clad, ill-nourished.[18]

As Roosevelt demonstrated, the language a speaker chooses can make a big difference. Becoming familiar with various stylistic devices and learning to use them effectively will help you become a better speaker. It is important to remember, however, that the stylistic choices you make must be appropriate to the situation in which you are speaking.

USING APPROPRIATE AND ETHICAL LANGUAGE

Preview. *Depending on the situation, you may find yourself employing a formal or a more conversational style of speaking. When choosing your language for any speech, however, you should strive for a style that is appropriate to the situation, gender-inclusive, and consistent with your audience's expectations and ethical standards.*

Your choice of language in a public speech should reflect careful thought about the formality or informality of the speaking situation and the characteristics and expectations of your audience. You should always strive to use language that is appropriate, nonsexist, and consistent with the expectations of your audience. You also should use language consistent with your audience's ethical standards.

Appropriateness

One of the most dramatic examples of contrasting uses of language was demonstrated by the release of the famous Watergate tapes. These recorded conversations illustrated the startling differences between the public and private language of President Richard Nixon and many of his advisers.[19] What shocked people was not so much the use of vulgar words, but the fact that those words were used by the president of the United States in the Oval Office of the White House. Most people had surely heard such words before and perhaps even used some of them themselves, but they seemed especially inappropriate when spoken in the White House.

Your choice of language should be influenced by the context in which you speak. In general, you probably think about language choices and choose your language more carefully in a public speech than in a private conversation. The language you choose to introduce your city's mayor at a public forum, for example, should be more formal than the language you use when talking to a friend.

At the same time, a good speaker never "fakes" language to sound like someone else. For example, it would be inappropriate for a well-educated speaker to use poor grammar or coarse language intentionally to establish common ground with a less-educated audience. Not only would that be unethical, but it might be interpreted as condescending and insulting. It likewise would be unwise for a speaker to use the slang or the technical language of a particular audience if that language did not come naturally to that speaker.

The opening of Martin Luther King Jr.'s famous "Dream" speech was made even more dramatic by the fact that it was delivered from the steps of the memorial dedicated to "the Great Emancipator," Abraham Lincoln.

Certain aspects of a situation—the audience, the topic of the speech, and the occasion or setting in which the speech takes place—also have an impact on language choice. Martin Luther King Jr.'s "I Have a Dream" speech is perhaps the best example of adapting language to the situation. His first words were, "Five score years ago a great American in whose symbolic shadow we stand today signed the Emancipation Proclamation."[20] King said this standing on the steps of the Lincoln Memorial. It was well calculated to remind the audience of Lincoln, his Gettysburg Address, and the long and bloody struggle for racial justice that began with the Civil War and culminated in the March on Washington in 1963.

Gender-Inclusive Language

As we have pointed out, language is a powerful force in shaping our perceptions and beliefs. Research has shown that **gendered language**, typically language that excludes women, has negative effects on those excluded.[21] Consider the implications of this statement: "If a student expects to get into medical school, he will have to work hard to get excellent grades." This, of course, implies that only men should aspire to become doctors. Speakers often use gendered language thoughtlessly, without thinking about acceptable, gender-neutral alternatives.

The list in Figure 11.2, adapted from a Web site on gender-sensitive language, offers some common examples of gendered language, as well as some possible alternatives. Also, you may consult several guides to nongendered language, such as the International Association of Business Communication's

FIGURE 11.2

Gendered	Gender-neutral
man	person, individual
mankind	people, human beings, humanity
man-made	machine-made, synthetic
the common man	the average (or ordinary) person
to man	to operate, to cover, to staff
mailman	mail carrier, letter carrier, postal worker
policeman	police officer
congressman	congressperson, legislator, representative

Source: Reprinted by permission from Writing Center at the University of NC at Chapel Hill, "Gender Sensitive Language." Copyright © n.d. by Writing Center. www.unc.edu/depts/wcweb/handouts/gender.html

Without Bias: A Guidebook for Nondiscriminatory Communication (Wiley, 1982) or *The Dictionary of Bias-Free Usage: A Guide to Nondiscriminatory Language* (Oryx, 1991).

Typically, your audience will be made up of both men and women, and nowadays most audiences expect the use of gender-inclusive or gender-neutral language.

Audience Expectations

Whenever you prepare to speak in public, you consider what your audience is already likely to know and think about your topic. In choosing language for your speech, you also need to consider your audience—their level of linguistic sophistication and their stylistic expectations. You should consider not only how formal or casual the setting may be, but also the nature of the forum, the audience's background and education, and any other factors that could influence their expectations for the kind of language you use.

The wise speaker thinks carefully about audience expectations and makes reasonable and appropriate adjustments. This does not mean that you should change your natural style of speaking in order to pander to your audience. It does mean, however, that you may want to make some different language choices depending on the situation. For one audience, for example, *best guess* may be better than *informed speculation.* You want to remain true to your own voice, but you also want to take your audience's expectations into account and respect their linguistic values.

Ethical Language

When we think of speaking appropriately, we may think only about adapting to the situation and audience. But we also have an obligation to speak ethically, choosing language that promotes mutual respect and avoids offending others. Using language that the audience considers offensive or tasteless is not just ineffective; it communicates a lack of respect for their values. Mutual respect, as we've noted throughout this book, is the hallmark of ethical public speaking in a democratic society.[22] You have an *ethical* obligation to choose language that communicates respect for your listeners.

As a speaker, you expect your audience to treat you respectfully. You expect them to make you feel welcome, to not interrupt you while you speak, and to reserve their own questions or comments for the question-and-answer period. If somebody does wish to challenge your views after the speech, you also have a right to expect that they will do so respectfully and without resorting to personal attacks.

These expectations go both ways, of course. If you, as a speaker, do not show respect for your listeners, you should not be surprised if they respond in kind. As partners in the communication process, both speakers and listeners have an obligation to display mutual respect, civility, good taste, and sensitivity to the feelings of others. This obligation extends even to the specific words you choose to use in your speech.

Ethical speakers guard against the use of language that demeans a particular gender, race, religion, or culture. We are not just talking about being "politically correct." We are talking about showing respect for your listeners and others in society. Most of us know that grown women do not want to be referred to as *girls* or *chicks*. Hispanics do not tolerate the label *spic*, and homosexuals rightly take offense at being called *fags* or *dykes*. There are, of course, dozens of other slurs that one may use to insult or demean people of particular groups. It should go without saying that the use of such slurs is unethical, particularly when they substitute for substantive argument or are intentionally designed to silence or intimidate members of minority groups.

Of course, offensive language is not only unethical; it is ineffective as well. Listeners who are offended by a speaker are not likely to continue listening, much less be persuaded to embrace that speaker's point of view.

RESPONDING CRITICALLY TO A SPEAKER'S STYLE

Preview. *When a speaker has good style, listeners are likely to be moved. Critical listeners are aware that style in language can have an impact. They look for sound arguments, good evidence, and substance of thought—regardless of the speaker's style. They avoid overreacting to style in either a positive or a negative sense.*

It should be apparent by now that style can have a strong impact on listeners—almost apart from the ideas being expressed. That is, the *way* in which ideas are expressed can be as important as the ideas themselves in influencing the listeners' reactions. A clear and appropriate speaking style can enhance a speaker's ethos, whereas an otherwise good speech can be undermined by poor stylistic choices.

Using Emotional Language Ethically

The ethical public speaker never uses language to whip the audience into an emotional frenzy. As we have made clear, emotional appeals are often appropriate and necessary to move an audience to action. Most people do not respond to reasoned arguments alone if they do not also feel emotionally engaged. Ethical emotional appeals, however, are backed up with strong evidence and sound reasoning. The ethical speaker *wants* the audience to think critically and constructively, and he or she does nothing to thwart their ability to do so.

Style Substituted for Argument

Speakers have been known to dismiss an idea not by dissecting it, analyzing it, or examining its weaknesses or strengths, but simply by labeling it. For example, a speaker may simply declare that an idea is too "simplistic," too "radical," or perhaps too "reactionary." Such a speaker is substituting style for argument. Here's one example: instead of pointing to the shortcomings of a plan, one speaker simply said, "This is another one of those ultraconservative ideas; it's just what you would expect from right-wingers, and it hardly merits our consideration." What should you do when you hear such an argument? Good critical listeners ask, On what basis will I respond? What does the speaker mean by "ultraconservative ideas"? What are the implications of that label? Is there evidence that this *is* an ultraconservative idea, and if so does that automatically mean it's a bad idea? Asking these kinds of questions will help you avoid falling prey to an attempt to substitute style for argument.

In Chapter 8, we discussed the importance of supporting your ideas with evidence. You should keep the same principle in mind when you listen to others use language to persuade you. Be wary of highly emotional language and labeling. Always look for evidence backing up the speaker's claims. Good speakers anticipate an audience of smart, critical listeners, and they know they must provide support for their ideas.

SUMMARY

- To make a prepared speech truly effective you must choose language that is appropriate for the topic and the audience.
- The purpose of having a good speaking style is to promote the audience's understanding and acceptance through the use of effective language.
  - At the foundation of good language use is clarity. In general, using language that is familiar to listeners, as well as concrete, specific, and precise, will help you achieve a good speaking style.
  - It is also important to avoid crowding sentences with clichés and empty words. Also avoid constructing sentences that are overly complex and hard for listeners to follow.
- Language should be interesting to the audience.
  - Listeners find active language more engaging than passive language.
  - Figures of speech, such as metaphors, antithesis, and alliteration, make language more interesting.
- Language should be appropriate to the situation—well adapted to the setting, the listeners' expectations and levels of understanding, and the constraints of the occasion.

- Using language ethically entails showing respect for the audience, striving not to offend them, using good judgment and good taste, and encouraging listeners to respond thoughtfully rather than impulsively.
- The critical listener guards against being swayed by style alone.
  - The critical listener does not respond to emotionally charged words without considering the evidence and reasoning supporting the argument.
  - The critical listener is not persuaded by a speech that substitutes style for substance.

QUESTIONS FOR REVIEW AND REFLECTION

1. What is meant by *style* in public speaking? How does it differ from other notions of style?
2. Can you identify denotative and connotative language in messages you hear or read? How might emotionally charged language affect your response?
3. What are some ways that a speaker can strive to make his or her language clearer?
4. What is wrong with using expressions such as *it goes without saying*, *last but not least*, and *due to the fact that* when you speak?
5. Why is active language more interesting to listeners than passive language?
6. Provide a good example of each of the following and explain how it makes an idea more effective:
   a. simile
   b. metaphor
   c. antithesis
   d. irony
   e. alliteration
   f. personification
   g. oxymoron
   h. parallelism
   i. rhetorical question
7. To be effective, a speaker must speak appropriately. What are three key guidelines for using language appropriately in a public speech?
8. What is the relationship between using language appropriately and using it ethically?
9. What language do you find offensive and how would you react to a speaker who uses such language?

ENDNOTES

1. For more on how language choices affect the way we think and view the world, see James R. Andrews, *A Choice of Worlds: The Practice and Criticism of Public Discourse* (New York: Harper & Row, 1973); George Lakoff and Mark Johnson, *Metaphors We Live By* (Chicago: University of Chicago Press, 1980); and Gilles Fauconnier and Mark Turner, *The Way We Think* (New York: Basic Books, 2002).
2. Reprinted by permission from Colin Powell, "Sharing the American Dream." Copyright © 1997 by Colin Powell.
3. Reprinted by permission from Cooper and Williams, *Power Persuasion: Moving an Ancient Art into the Media*. Copyright © 1992 by Educational Video Group.
4. "Senate GOP Plans Attack on Health Care Bill," *Bloomington (IN) Herald-Times*, May 8, 2009, E2.
5. From Abraham Lincoln, "A House Divided." Published 1858.
6. Cited in Roy Jenkins, *Churchill: A Biography* (New York: Farrar, Straus and Giroux, 2001), 610.
7. From Lyndon B. Johnson, "The Voting Rights Act of 1965." Published 1965 by U.S. Government.

8. From Frederick Douglass, "What to the Slave in the Fourth of July, July 5, 1852." Published 1852 by Lee, Mann & Co.
9. From Chief Joseph of the Nez Perce, "Surrender Speech, November 5, 1877." Published n.d. by Mary Lou McCloskey, Mindspring.com
10. Alessandra Stanley, "At White House Briefing, Polish Replaces Testiness," *New York Times*, May 17, 2006, A19.
11. From John F. Kennedy, "Civil Rights Message, June 11, 1963." Published 1963 by John F. Kennedy.
12. Qtd. in Jane Blankenship, *A Sense of Style: An Introduction to Style for the Public Speaker* (Belmont, CA: Dickenson, 1968), 70.
13. Eugene E. Brussell, ed., *Webster's New World Dictionary of Quotable Definitions* (New York: Prentice Hall, 1988): 91.
14. From Mary Church Terrell, "What it Means to be Colored in the Capital of the United States," to United Women's Club in Washington DC. Published 1908.
15. Remarks of Barack Obama at the NAACP 100th Anniversary Convention, New York, New York, July 16, 2009, www.presidentialrhetoric.com/speeches/07.16.09.html (accessed July 30, 2009).
16. Edgar Allan Poe, "The Raven," in *The Viking Book of Poetry of the English Speaking World*, ed, Richard Aldington vol. 2 (New York: Viking Press, 1959), 866.
17. Many of these examples, plus others, can be found at Oxymorons.info, www.oxymorons.info/reference/oxymorons/oxymoron-quotes.asp (accessed August 10, 2009).
18. From Franklin Roosevelt, "Second Inaugural Address, January 20, 1937." Published 1989 by U.S. G.P.O.
19. See Dennis S. Gouran, "Communicative Influences on Decisions Related to the Watergate Coverup: The Failure of Collective Judgment," *Central States Speech Journal* 34 (1984): 260–68.
20. Martin Luther King Jr., "I Had a Dream," in Rohler and Cook, *Great Speeches for Criticism and Analysis*, 325.
21. See, for example, Julia Wood, *Gendered Lives: Communication, Gender, and Culture*, 4th ed. (Belmont, CA: Wadsworth, 2001).
22. See Richard L. Johannesen, "The Emerging Concept of Communication as Dialogue," *Quarterly Journal of Speech* 57 (1971): 373–82; and Maurice S. Friedman, *Dialogue and the Human Image: Beyond Humanistic Psychology* (Newbury Park, CA: Sage, 1992).

New Horizons for Women

Mrs. Lyndon Baines (Lady Bird) Johnson, Former First Lady, United States of America

The 1960s were a time of turbulence and change. John Kennedy was assassinated in November 1963, and Lyndon Johnson became president. The new president announced ambitious domestic reforms—"the Great Society"—and signed two civil rights bills in the summer of 1964. In 1963, Betty Friedan wrote The Feminine Mystique, *in which she urged women to break free of traditional prescribed roles, setting the stage for the establishment of the National Organization of Women, which she founded in 1965. Between those two events, in 1964, Lady Bird Johnson gave this speech. The First Lady, in addressing this audience of home economists—teachers and county agents, all of whom were women—stressed the need for women to become involved at a time when they were beginning to strive for the fulfillment of their rights as citizens.*

Address to the National Convention of American Home Economics Association in Detroit, Michigan, on June 24, 1964

While we meet here on an evening in June, the horizons of women all over the world are widening from home to humanity—from our private families to the family of man.

A quiet revolution of emancipation has been taking place in the lives of women everywhere—from Detroit to Delhi. Millions of women have achieved the right to vote, to own property, to be educated. Technological marvels now can free women from the total bondage of home chores. You, as home economists, have helped to make it so. You have taught American women to master the intricacies of push-button washer-dryers, automatic ranges, and convenience foods. More and more, you will be exporting this know-how to other parts of the world.

With these newly won rights and with a rising standard of living, women can move beyond the struggle for equal status and for material goods to the challenges and opportunities of citizenship. Increasingly, we are going to be concerned with what my husband calls "the Great Society"—the quality of goals and the achievement of goals which will mean a better life for all.

As American women, we hold a tremendous potential of strength for good. I do not refer to the sense of power that comes from flicking a switch or turning an ignition key. But to the force we exert when we mark a ballot, teach our children, or work for a better community.

The question is: How can we best mobilize this potential? How can the individual woman practice citizenship to the fullest extent, both at home and abroad?

Ernest Hemingway once said, "Talk and write about what you know." One sees change in terms of one's own experiences.

As a girl, my home was in East Texas. It was a place where Spanish moss was draped from age-old cypresses, where alligators slithered down muddy banks into dark, enchanted bayous. While we fished through the long summer days, we enjoyed the illusion that time was standing still. But time never stands still. I grew up, went to college and married a tall Texan. My horizons have been broadening and my involvement getting deeper ever since.

AS SHE BEGINS HER SPEECH, JOHNSON CHOOSES FIGURATIVE LANGUAGE THAT ANNOUNCES HER THEME. IN USING THE PHRASES *FROM HOME TO HUMANITY* AND *FROM OUR PRIVATE FAMILIES TO THE FAMILY OF MAN*, SHE SUGGESTS THAT HER MESSAGE TO WOMEN IS TO MOVE FROM PERSONAL PREOCCUPATIONS TO INVOLVEMENT IN LARGER ISSUES.

NOTE THE MANY WORDS THE SPEAKER CHOOSES THROUGHOUT THE SPEECH THAT HAVE POSITIVE CONNOTATIONS, SUCH AS *CHALLENGES*, *OPPORTUNITIES*, *POTENTIAL*, *STRENGTH*, *COMMUNITY*. ALL OF THESE SUGGEST BOLD, POSITIVE ACTION.

In the past few years, my own participation has included travel with my husband to all corners of our own land, to Thailand and India, to Senegal and Iceland, and a score of other countries.

This spring, I have been traveling some myself. I have been to areas of serious unemployment and limited opportunities, such as Wilkes-Barre, Pennsylvania, and Breathitt County, Kentucky. For me, it helps me see in human terms the objectives of the war on poverty.

Once in a while I ask myself, "What am I doing here?" Perhaps when I visit, it helps draw the curtain open a little more. Perhaps it gives national attention to a local problem. Perhaps it exposes us to ourselves and says, "This is the other side of America. Look! And act!"

I am only 1 of 65 million American women. Almost all of us are involved, one way or another, in being the best citizens we know how to be. Actually, none of us just sat down and said, "I'm going to get involved." It happens gradually, inspired by husband and family, sometimes triggered by crisis, always influenced by circumstances and opportunity.

For example, let me tell you about one woman who has made a mark on her community and on the lives of many people around her. I went to college with her at the University of Texas. She was—and is—a beautiful girl, gay, filled with character and grace. Then, after she married, she was hit by one of life's hardest blows: her second child was born with cerebral palsy.

THROUGHOUT THE SPEECH JOHNSON USES SIMPLE BUT APPROPRIATE LANGUAGE. IN RELATING SPECIFIC EXAMPLES, SHE DESCRIBES THE EXPERIENCES OF WOMEN WITH LANGUAGE CHOSEN TO BE BOTH CLEAR AND INTERESTING.

After two or three years of fighting this fact, and carrying her child to many, many doctors, she accepted it. She discovered that there were different degrees of this illness, and that in many cases, the victims could be helped. So she went to work.

Largely through her untiring persuasion, she brought together local organizations and city fathers. We now have a clinic in Austin where hundreds of children come from hundreds of miles around for treatment and training. Behind every achievement or success is one dauntless person who keeps gathering together the strength that makes the web of success.

Tonight we met a high school home economics teacher with four children who, I understand, has a daughter born with a physical handicap and a sister-in-law who suffered loss of an arm recently.

Far from restricting her activities because of these family problems, this home economist has gone beyond the call of duty to organize a place of worship for her religious denomination in the community, to initiate and lead a 4-H group, to introduce the National Honor Society in her high school and to serve as the faculty adviser for the student council and the yearbook. And, she is volunteering as bookkeeper for her husband who has just opened his own business! These are just two examples among thousands.

All of us are acquainted with many women working at citizenship. You, yourselves are doing it each day of your lives—bringing home economics know-how to girls and women who have or will have a home of their own.

That has been your role since your association was founded 55 years ago. I like what your founder, Ellen Richards, the first woman graduate from Massachusetts Institute of

Technology, said. It is as applicable today as it was in 1909; to apply principles of science to the home so we may have—and these are her words—"Freedom of the home from the dominance of things."

What better formula with which to develop the full potential of the home as a springboard to citizenship!

For, as someone once said, "When you teach a man, you teach an individual; when you teach a woman, you teach a family." And in this age, I would add to that—You also teach a nation and a world."

For me, your work has a very personal meaning. In Texas, our county home demonstration agents have helped homemakers to live better, to make wiser choices, to tackle problems more intelligently within the family and the community. At the ranch, we have always been delighted to see her coming. We know that when she leaves, we shall have learned much in a few hours.

Over the past fifteen years, as Americans moved to town, the home economist has followed them.

I do not need to tell you that the cities reach out for you—to help people in the public housing units and the crowded slum areas who do not know how to cope with the new and unaccustomed conditions of city life.

Indeed, as I consider your profession, there are so many ways in which the nation needs your help in the unfinished business of America.

You have long been alert to the fact that poverty's roots are deepest in the family structure. Now I am delighted you are stepping up your activities for the low-income family.

An education program geared to the family without modern equipment, the family that can read, perhaps not well or not in English, may offer these people the lifeline they need.

Your president, Florence Lowe, tells me of the El Paso Project in which a bilingual set of instructions about Food for Fitness was mailed out to Mexican-American families. It brought tremendous results.

One reason was that the mail got top attention because these families received so little mail.

The all-out war on poverty needs home economists in the front brigade. And I commend all you are doing to be a full participant in this force.

THE WAR ON POVERTY WAS ONE ASPECT OF PRESIDENT JOHNSON'S GREAT SOCIETY. JOHNSON EMPLOYS THIS METAPHOR TO DIRECTLY INVOLVE HER AUDIENCE, DESCRIBING THEM AS THE "FRONT BRIGADE."

New thinking and teaching is needed if we are to communicate fully to the low-income family. We must reexamine the college curriculum which produces the home economists. As in other professions, this curriculum may be geared too much to the values of the middle-income family.

Our state departments of welfare are realizing, more and more, how important it is to have the home economist to reinforce the case worker. Family problems often stem from a lack of knowledge of wise buying habits. Seventeen states now have full-time home economists on their staffs.

One of the most exciting new horizons for the home economist is helping solve the problems that daily face ten million homemakers in this country who are permanently or temporarily disabled.

The blind woman with the baby needs advice on how to care for it in her own home.

The woman with only one arm needs a little extra attention to learn how to manage her home and bathe the baby.

A mother paralyzed by polio was asked several months ago what she wished she had known when she returned home from the hospital.

"I wish someone had told me to buy a different type of carpet, one that would be right for my wheelchair," she said.

Help from an expert can make life more comfortable and productive.

I trust your professional efforts on behalf of women and families in the developing countries will receive a big push in the coming years. The fact that over 300 home economists are in the Peace Corps—some of them women who came out of retirement to volunteer for service in Sierra Leone and Peru—is an indication of your concern for your fellow man around the world.

One of the great joys of your work is that you can see the results. My husband has often told me that the years which gave him the most intense personal satisfaction were those in which he served under President Roosevelt as a state director of the National Youth Administration. Boys were taken from boxcars and given back their self-respect along with part-time jobs which enabled them to stay in school. To watch this happening, to have a part in its happening, was an experience we shall never forget.

For me, it was the beginning of seeing how politics can bring tangible results. I always hope that the very best of our people will go into politics, and I am sure that some of our best are women. It was for this reason that the President began his effort last winter to bring more women into government.

You home economists are examples of women who manage several lives successfully. Most of you have both a home and a professional career. Many of you, like several of the award winners tonight, also have children. You have much to share.

So, I say: "Don't hold back. Don't be shy. Step forward in every way you can to plan boldly, to speak clearly, to offer the leadership which the world needs."

HERE, JOHNSON USES SIMPLE, DIRECT LANGUAGE TO CHALLENGE HER AUDIENCE—HER IMMEDIATE AUDIENCE OF HOME ECONOMISTS AS WELL AS THE MILLIONS OF AMERICAN WOMEN SHE HOPES TO ENCOURAGE TO PLAY AN ACTIVE ROLE IN CIVIC AFFAIRS.

For me, and probably for most women, the attempt to become an involved, practicing citizen has been a matter of evolution rather than choice. Actually, if given a choice between lying in a hammock under an apple tree with a book of poetry and watching the blossoms float down or standing on a platform before thousands of people, I don't have to tell you what I would have chosen 25 years ago. But 25 years and the invention of the nuclear bomb have left us no choice. The hammocks and apple trees are happy memories except for a few short, cherished moments.

Edmund Burke said, almost 200 years ago, "The only thing necessary for the triumph of evil is for good men to do nothing." I hope he would forgive me if I modernize and amend his statement to say, "The only thing necessary for the triumph of evil is for good men *and good women to do nothing.*"

I am sure that will not be.

SHE ENDS HER SPEECH BY TAKING A FAMOUS QUOTATION AND ADDING TO IT THE WORDS *AND GOOD WOMEN*, REINFORCING HER PLEA FOR WOMEN TO GET INVOLVED IN CIVIC AFFAIRS. HER SIMPLE FINAL SENTENCE IS BOTH AN AFFIRMATION OF HER OWN CONVICTION AND A CALL TO ACTION.

Source: From Mrs. Lyndon B. Johnson, "New Horizons by Women" Address to the National Convention of American Home Association in Detroit, MI. Published 1964.

CHAPTER

12

Delivering Your Speech Effectively

CHAPTER SURVEY

Sounding Good versus Being Sound

Principles of Good Delivery

Speaking Extemporaneously

Alternative Styles of Delivery

Responding to Audience Questions

CHAPTER OBJECTIVES

After studying this chapter, you should be able to

1. Discuss the ethical issues involved in delivering your speech.
2. Describe and apply the basic characteristics of good delivery.
3. Deliver an effective extemporaneous speech using a keyword outline.
4. Compare and contrast different styles of delivery, describing the strengths and weaknesses of each.
5. Anticipate audience questions and various ways of responding to them.

In 1847 a young woman graduated from Oberlin College and began a career as a reformer, lecturing throughout the country. She first spoke in support of the abolition of slavery and then took up the cause of women's suffrage. In a time when women who dared to speak in public were often subjected to ridicule and abuse, it took conviction, courage, and a commanding presence to appear before such hostile audiences. Her supporters, however, frequently praised her logic and command of the facts. According to one listener, her message was "wholly irresistible to every person who cares for reason or justice." Yet she probably would have failed without a powerful delivery—and that Lucy Stone had. She was, one observer wrote, "small in stature but large of soul ... her bearing modest and dignified, her face radiant with feeling, and speaking all over, as it were, in eloquent accord with her earnest voice."[1]

You are not likely to confront the kind of challenges faced by Lucy Stone, and most of us would have a hard time standing up to such challenges. But whenever you speak in public—in the classroom, in a business meeting, or at a town hall meeting—your delivery will play a significant part in your success. Delivery is one of the most obvious aspects of public speaking, and it shapes your listeners' first impressions of your skills as a speaker. Yet you should never count on an engaging delivery to compensate for a speech that is poorly structured or lacking in substance.

SOUNDING GOOD VERSUS BEING SOUND

Preview. *One of your ethical obligations as a speaker is to present a message of substance. Good delivery, though important, is no substitute for sound ideas. Having an ethical and effective delivery means remaining audience-centered, avoiding behaviors that distract from the message, and promoting the listeners' understanding.*

Sometimes you may find yourself thinking that a speaker sounded good but did not have anything important to say. On another occasion, a speaker's delivery may be so dramatic that it actually distracts from the content of the speech. Whether intentional or not, a distracting delivery is not good delivery.

Beyond Delivery: Listening to the Message

We sometimes give too much weight to how a speech is delivered. A speaker who is poised and articulate, has a good voice, and appears confident and friendly may impress us. However, such a speaker might be merely facile—he or she can speak easily but may not have much to say. It is important to distinguish between a speaker who *is* sound and a speaker who just *sounds* good.

A sound speaker's ideas pass the tests of evidence and reasoning discussed in Chapters 8 and 16. As much as we might admire the ease and grace of some speakers, we need to be on our guard against the slick, superficial speaker who tries to manipulate or deceive us rather than engage us in a discussion of important ideas.

The Foundation of Ethical Delivery

Ethical delivery grows out of a collaborative, transactional model of communication (as described in Chapter 3). It means communicating with respect for your listeners, never seeking to manipulate them, but aiming instead for a mutually beneficial outcome. The ethical speaker does not put on an "act," but speaks sincerely and authentically—always mindful of the needs, values, and priorities of those assembled to listen.

Ethical delivery does not distract from the content or meaning of the speech. It is appropriate to the situation, including the size and makeup of the audience. By contrast, an unethical speaker may intentionally use overly dramatic gestures, striking movement, or exaggerated vocal patterns to distract the audience from the speech's content. Not only is this kind of delivery ethically questionable, it also can backfire. Effective and ethical delivery should *reinforce* rather than distract attention from the speaker's ideas.

Finally, ethical delivery promotes the listeners' trust and comprehension. When you make a speech, your body, voice, and gestures must be in tune with the mood and nature of your message. Never forget that your audience will form impressions of you and your ideas based, in some measure, on how you deliver your speech. A speaker may have some compelling ideas, but if that speaker seems dull and lifeless—if the speaker does not seem to care—the message may be lost.

PRINCIPLES OF GOOD DELIVERY

Preview. *Certain basic principles of effective delivery apply to a wide variety of public speaking situations. You will want to adapt your delivery to the specific situation and to audience expectations. In general, effective delivery is associated with proper attire, good eye contact, appropriate gestures and movement, and facial expressions that reinforce your message. A good delivery also means a dynamic yet conversational speaking voice.*

Most of us recognize the importance of delivery, yet we may become apprehensive at the thought of standing in front of a group of people and delivering a speech.[2] As you prepare to deliver a speech, you will confront many questions: Should I use a podium? Should I move around during my speech? Will everybody be able to hear me? There are no absolute answers to any of these questions. You will need to adjust your style of delivery to the demands of each situation.

The person who invited you to speak should be able to offer you guidance concerning the formality of the occasion and the expectations of the audience. It is wise to find out as much as you can about the situation before you begin planning your speech. Above all, you need to think about what sort of delivery style will best help you connect with your audience.

Understand the Situation and Audience Expectations

What is appropriate in one speaking situation may be inappropriate in another. The more you learn about audience members' needs, norms, and preferences, the more likely you will deliver your speech effectively. Do these listeners expect a formal presentation, or do they like to sit in a circle and have the speaker "chat" with them? Is this an after-dinner speech, to be delivered in a hotel conference room equipped with a podium and technological support? If so, will the listeners expect you to speak from behind the podium and make use of that technology?

How you dress when you deliver a speech can also be important. Your appearance can influence how your audience judges your ethos or credibility. Although there are no fixed rules for attire, listeners generally expect an invited speaker to be well groomed and nicely dressed.[3] How the audience itself will be dressed may provide one clue. You do not want to be wearing jeans and a T-shirt if your audience will be dressed in suits and ties.

In your public speaking class, casual attire may be appropriate, but you still want to feel confident and comfortable with the way you look. Avoid shoes that are too tight or clothes that are too snug. Also avoid any attire that detracts from your speech, such as a flamboyant blouse, a T-shirt with written or visual content, or a baseball cap.

Establish Eye Contact

Have you ever talked with someone who did not look you in the eye? Did you feel that the person was uncomfortable? Nervous? Ashamed? Preoccupied? Dishonest? In most cultures, a communicator who does not look us in the eye makes us suspicious.[4] The same is true in formal public speaking. As listeners, we respond more positively to speakers who make eye contact with us.

Of course, there are cultural variations in practices and reactions to eye contact. For instance, Puerto Ricans consider it disrespectful to make prolonged eye contact with those of higher social status.[5] In Japan, participants in meetings often look down or close their eyes while others are talking. By doing so, they show that they are paying attention or even agreeing with the speaker.[6]

Whatever our cultural differences, our eyes can be very expressive. As we squint, smile, laugh, frown, or scowl, we communicate many emotions: concern, commitment, joy, or anger. When we fail to establish eye contact, we must rely solely on our words, voice, gestures, or facial expressions to convey emotions. In U.S. culture, we clearly place ourselves at a disadvantage if we do not use our eyes to communicate.[7]

Good eye contact also conveys sincerity. We are more likely to believe a speaker who looks us in the eye while speaking.[8] When we establish eye contact with our listeners, we come across as more truthful, candid, open, and trustworthy.

Finally, looking at the members of the audience gives us a chance to observe their reactions to our speech. How can we clarify what we are saying if we have not even noticed that our listeners look confused? How can we benefit from appreciative smiles and nods of encouragement if we are not looking? With the exception of comments or questions after the speech, the feedback you get from your audience will consist of nonverbal signs, such as nods, smiles, or expressions of excitement or boredom. If you "close your eyes" to such feedback, you will miss out on an important chance to adjust your speech and to engage in more of a dialogue with your audience. When you *do* respond to audience reactions, you show sensitivity and respect.

As you establish eye contact with your audience, remember to share your attention with everyone. Avoid focusing on only a few friendly faces or your speech instructor. Try to include all sections of the room, and avoid staring at particular audience members as if in a trance. Also avoid darting your eyes or looking up and down from your notes too much. Of all the principles of effective delivery, maintaining good eye contact with your listeners is among the most important.

Reinforce Ideas through Gestures, Movement, and Facial Expressions

Most of us use a number of physical gestures in ordinary conversation. We wave our hands, point, or pound on the table to emphasize a point. How we hold or move our bodies can also communicate information to others, intentionally or unintentionally.[9] If we pace or slouch in our chair, we may imply we are nervous or disinterested. We might move closer to someone to express affection or intimacy, or we might move farther away to create distance or convey aloofness. We communicate a great deal with our faces too.[10] We might smile broadly, scowl, raise an eyebrow, or clench our teeth to communicate our determination, anger, or stubbornness. Through facial expressions, we can "say" a lot.

Our words and physical actions should be mutually reinforcing.[11] If you were talking to a friend about something that really mattered to you, you might say, "I *really* want you to consider doing this!" At the same time, you might lean forward, look into her or his eyes, and nod your head. In public speaking, you can use similar nonverbal signals to reinforce your message, perhaps gesturing to emphasize a point or moving laterally to reinforce a transition. If, on the other hand, you contradict your words with your nonverbal actions—say, you smile when discussing a serious matter or appear uninterested when claiming to be excited—your audience is likely to give more weight to your nonverbal cues.[12]

Perhaps you are uncertain about whether your movement, gestures, and facial expressions are appropriate. If so, you might ask someone to watch you practice your speech and give you feedback. Here are some questions you may want to consider:

- Does my movement seem to reinforce the flow of the speech?
- Are my gestures distracting in any way?
- Do I rely too much on any one gesture?
- Does my face seem to convey sincerity and reinforce the meaning of my speech?
- Are there different gestures, movements, or facial expressions that might better communicate my intended meaning?
- Does my nonverbal communication consistently convey a respectful attitude toward the audience?[13]

Although you may plan a few basic gestures and movements in advance, *most* should occur spontaneously as you interact with your audience. Your nonverbal delivery will vary as you give your speech at different times, in different rooms, and to different audiences. For instance, the same gestures that you use in ordinary conversation may work well if you are speaking to an audience of 25 or fewer. But if you are speaking to 150 people assembled in an auditorium, you may want to enlarge your gestures so that they can be seen by everyone.

Finally, you should work at avoiding nonverbal behaviors that may come across as nervous or distracting. Some speakers pace nervously. Others play with their earrings, stroke their hair, grip the podium, or tap with a pencil. Still others use such exaggerated gestures that they look foolish or melodramatic. Whenever a gesture calls attention to itself, it can distract from the message you hope to convey.

Strive for an Effective Speaking Voice

One of the most obvious aspects of your delivery is your voice. Have you ever listened to a speaker whose voice really bothered you? Perhaps she or he spoke in a monotone, stumbled over words, or inserted *you know* at every pause. Or maybe the speaker's voice sounded too high and squeaky or too low and unvarying. Clearly, our voices can get us into trouble as public speakers. But they can also be used effectively to enhance our messages. When you use your voice effectively, you can add extra emphasis to key ideas, display a variety of emotions, demonstrate your commitment, and enhance your credibility.

How can you improve the vocal aspects of your delivery? You might try speaking into an audio recorder and playing it back to see what your voice sounds like to others. Obtaining feedback from friends also can be helpful. You can modify some features of your voice by recognizing their importance, paying attention to them as you practice your speech out loud, and monitoring them as you speak. The features that you can control and perhaps improve include volume, rate, pitch, and clarity.

Volume If listeners cannot hear your voice, they obviously cannot benefit from your message. Nor will they be able to concentrate on your message if you speak so loudly that they feel uncomfortable.

The volume of your delivery should be determined by the setting in which you speak. Naturally, a small room calls for a quieter voice than does a large lecture hall or an outdoor setting. If you are concerned that you cannot be heard, you could simply ask your audience as you begin to speak. Doing so shows your respect for your listeners, and they will be glad to give you feedback.

In some situations, you may need a microphone to amplify your voice. Some microphones clip to your clothing, while others are handheld or attached to a podium. If you use a microphone, make sure it is working properly before you start your speech. If the microphone is attached to a podium, you may need to adjust its height so that you can speak directly into it.

Rate It is not uncommon for a beginning speaker to sit down after giving a speech, look at the clock, and be amazed to find that the planned ten-minute speech took only seven or eight minutes. Several miscalculations could account for this, but often the problem is that the speaker rushed through the speech. Keep in mind that your audience needs time to absorb and process your speech—especially if you are addressing a complex or thought-provoking issue.

The needs of the listeners should be paramount. Just as they cannot keep up with a speaker who is talking too quickly, they may lose interest in one who speaks too slowly. In most speaking situations, about 125–150 words per minute is considered an appropriate rate of speaking,[14] but you may choose to speak more quickly or slowly, depending on the complexity and novelty of the information you are presenting. Some research suggests that listeners may perceive speakers who speak quickly (though not *too* fast) as more knowledgeable,[15] but you should speak at a rate that fits your own personal style and that allows the audience to process the information you present.

Finally, your speaking rate can be used to emphasize key ideas. The effective use of pauses can give your audience the opportunity to absorb information and ideas. Some speakers even use pauses or silence to reinforce a compelling statistic, quotation, or narrative, in effect saying, "Let's stop to think about this for a moment. This is important." Similarly, you may slow down or use repetition to emphasize an important idea. When you *vary* your rate—by pausing, slowing down, or using restatement or repetition at critical and strategic moments—you enhance your chances of getting your message across.

PITCH Sometimes a speaker's voice is simply unpleasant to listen to. It may be squeaky or raspy, or it may be pitched so low that you can hardly distinguish one word from the next. *Pitch* refers to the highness or lowness of your voice on a musical scale. It is the voice's upward or downward inflection. A speaker's vocal pitch can be too high, too low, or too unvarying. When the pitch is too high, listeners tend to cringe. When the pitch is too low, listeners may be unable to hear what the speaker is saying. An unvarying pitch is called a **monotone**—a vocal quality guaranteed to put your audience to sleep.

Rightly or wrongly, listeners often draw conclusions about speakers whose pitch seems inappropriate. A high pitch may be associated with immaturity, inexperience, tension, or excitability. A low pitch or a monotone may cause listeners to view the speaker as bored or disengaged. By contrast, a richer pitch, one with depth and variety, can communicate a sense of authority and competence.[16]

What can you do about the pitch of your voice? Start by audio-recording your voice and listening to what you sound like. If you are not satisfied, you may want to use some vocal exercises to improve your pitch. In extreme cases, you may want to seek assistance from someone trained in voice therapy. Here are a few pointers to keep in mind:

- Your pitch will vary throughout your life. It will be higher when you are younger and lower later in life. Working with the pitch of your voice is an ongoing process.
- If you are tense, your pitch tends to rise. Use the relaxation techniques outlined in Chapter 3 to help you manage communication apprehension.

- Strive for variety in your pitch. Avoid repetitive pitch patterns, such as *uptalking* (in which your pitch rises as you seem to question the statement you have just made).[17] You want your voice to be interesting, and you want to use all aspects of your voice to emphasize your most important points.

CLARITY To be effective as a speaker, you must be understood. Although speaking at an appropriate speed can help you to communicate more clearly, vocal clarity is also important. A clear vocal style depends on the following:

First, strive for distinctness in *articulation.* Dropping the endings off words, slurring sounds, and running words together can interfere with the clarity of your message. For example, if you say "locked out" but you sound like you said "lucked out," you did not articulate clearly. Articulation especially becomes a problem when a speaker rushes through a speech, failing to take the time to articulate each word carefully.

Second, strive for correct pronunciation of the words you use. Whereas *articulation* refers to the clarity with which we say words, pronunciation involves saying words correctly. If you are unsure of the correct pronunciation of an uncommon or unfamiliar word, look it up in a dictionary. Practice aloud so that you are comfortable saying the words you are using, and especially check the pronunciation of words used in quoted material.

Finally, avoid *vocal mannerisms.* It is pointless and distracting to keep saying *you know* every time you pause during speaking. Some speakers also have a habit of concluding almost every statement with the unnecessary question, "Right?" Also, there are regional mannerisms that clutter speech and thus reduce clarity, such as "Ya know?" Other speakers seem to end every sentence with an *at*, as in "He didn't know where I was *at.*" These vocal mannerisms may be distracting to listeners.[18]

HIGHLIGHTING THE IMPORTANCE OF A GOOD VOICE

The Practices of Demosthenes

One of the greatest orators of ancient Greece was Demosthenes. According to historians, Demosthenes had difficulties speaking clearly, but he recognized the importance of good articulation, so he did all he could to improve. Plutarch writes this:

His inarticulate and stammering pronunciation he overcame and rendered more distinct by speaking with pebbles in his mouth; his voice he disciplined by declaiming and reciting speeches or verses when he was out of breath, while running or going up steep places; and in his house he had a large looking-glass, before which he would stand and go through his exercises.

It is told that someone once came to request assistance as a pleader, and related how he had been assaulted and beaten. "Certainly" said Demosthenes, "nothing of the kind can have happened to you." Upon which the other, raising his voice, exclaimed loudly, "What, Demosthenes, nothing has been done to me?" "Ah," replied Demosthenes, "now I hear the voice of one that has been injured and beaten." Of so great consequence towards the gaining of belief did he esteem the tone and action of the speaker.

Source: From Plutarch,"The Practices of Demothenes" *Plutarch's Lives, vol. 12.* Published 1909 by P.F. Collier & Son.

Remain Flexible

No matter how carefully you plan and practice in advance, some speaking situations will surprise you. Flexibility is the key to responding successfully to these situations. You might find that the podium is missing or the microphone not working. You might be told at the last minute that you have less time to speak than originally planned, and that you will have to cut your speech short. Or, imagine that you expected to deliver a formal speech to a large audience, but when you arrived, only five or six people were present. Rather than standing behind a podium and speaking formally, you might want to adapt to the situation by sitting on the edge of a table and informally "chatting" with the group.

The foundation of flexibility is spontaneity and open-mindedness—a willingness to recognize that there are many different ways to deliver a good speech and an ability to discover a "better" way whenever a situation seems to demand it. Speakers need not always stand or use a podium, and they *can* engage the audience in dialogue if doing so seems fitting and consistent with the audience's norms and expectations.

HIGHLIGHTING FLEXIBILITY

A Dramatic Example

Perhaps the most extraordinary—and certainly unique—example of adapting to the situation came during the presidential campaign of 1912. Former president Theodore Roosevelt, who had failed to secure his own party's nomination, was running for president as a candidate of a third party, the Progressive or "Bull Moose" Party. With scarcely three weeks to go before the election, Roosevelt's campaign pulled into Milwaukee, where he was scheduled to speak before a huge rally of supporters. As Roosevelt left his hotel, a man stepped up to him and fired a gun at point-blank range. The bullet passed through the copy of Roosevelt's speech, which was 50 pages, folded over—long speeches were typical in those days—and his glasses case before lodging in the candidate's chest. Feeling as if he had been "kicked by a mule" but determined to continue, TR refused to go to a hospital, insisting instead that he go on and give his speech. Usually a dynamic speaker with a robust, energetic style, Roosevelt quieted the cheering crowd that greeted him. Raising his arm, he said quietly, "I shall ask you to be as quiet as possible. I don't know whether you fully understand that I have just been shot; but it takes more than that to kill a bull moose." Opening his coat, revealing the bloodstained shirt, Roosevelt showed the crowd the speech text with the bullet hole. Because "the bullet is in me now," Roosevelt explained, he would not give a very long speech. "But," he said, "I will try my best." Speaking without the bullet-torn manuscript, Roosevelt spoke extemporaneously for a very painful hour and a half before his anxious aides were able to get him off the platform and to a hospital.

This example is, of course, dramatic and makes the loss of a note card or facing a larger audience than you anticipated seem like a small thing. You may never experience such an extreme challenge, but you *will* have times when you will have to deliver your speech under difficult circumstances and you will need to be flexible.

Sources: See H. W. Brands, *TR: The Last Romantic* (New York: Basic Books, 1997), 720–22; and Nathan Miller, *Theodore Roosevelt: A Life* (New York: Morrow, 1992), 530–31.

Practice Your Speech

Sometimes speakers think that once they have carefully researched their topic, organized their thoughts, and prepared their outline, all they need to do is read through the outline silently a few times—and they will be ready to go. Nothing could be further from the truth. If you have not practiced your speech aloud several times, chances are you are not prepared to speak.[19]

Here are a few guidelines for practicing your speech:

- Practice delivering your speech aloud with your keyword outline. But first read through your notes silently several times until you feel ready to begin.
- Practice your speech all the way through—noting sections that are rough, rereading and revising your notes, and then practicing again.
- Break the speech into parts and practice major sections, such as the introduction, several times in a row.
- Always take breaks. Avoid practicing so much at one time that you begin to lose your energy, voice, or concentration.
- Practice in front of friends and ask for their constructive feedback. Over a period of time, practice your speech again several times, all the way through, but do not try to memorize your speech.
- Incorporate your visual aids into your practice sessions. If possible, visit the room where you will speak and practice using the equipment there. If you are going to deliver your speech using computer support, such as PowerPoint slides, prepare those slides in advance and incorporate them into your practice sessions. Remember that when you deliver the speech, you want to avoid talking to the screen, standing where you might block any projected image, or reading every word appearing on each slide. At the same time, you will want to point to key features of maps or other visuals to direct the audience's attention to key elements of your speech. See Chapter 13 for a detailed discussion of the preparation and presentation of computer-generated graphics (including a feature that addresses how *not* to use PowerPoint).
- Time yourself several times. If your speech is too long, make appropriate cuts. For instance, you may cut a section that is less important, use fewer examples, or edit long quotations. It is important to remember that practicing your speech is something you do *before* the beginning of class or *before* you are seated in front of your audience. Sometimes speakers read through their notes while others are speaking. Do not fall into this trap. Practice sufficiently beforehand, so that you will be able to listen to other speakers. Not only do they deserve your respectful attention, but you might even learn something that you can refer to in your own speech.

Seek Out Opportunities to Speak

As you gain experience and confidence as a speaker, you will naturally deliver your speeches more effectively. This is especially true if you ask for listener feedback and strive to improve by addressing whatever weaknesses they identify. In addition, you will speak with more confidence and credibility if you speak about topics that genuinely concern you. When you deliver your remarks with

Speakers with deep personal conviction tend to deliver their speeches more effectively.

personal conviction, you tend to speak with more force, clarity, directness, and spontaneity—all hallmarks of effective delivery.

Look for opportunities to speak inside *and* outside the classroom. You may join your college's student speakers bureau, run for political office on campus, or volunteer with a local service or nonprofit organization and join *their* speakers bureau. You can also use your volunteer work as a foundation for bringing your life's passions into the classroom. When you take courses with an emphasis on service learning or civic engagement, you will have more opportunities to make these kinds of connections between your life experiences and the classroom.

SPEAKING EXTEMPORANEOUSLY

Preview. *Extemporaneous speaking requires careful preparation. Using this delivery style and speaking from a keyword outline allows you to be completely involved in your speech. At the same time, you can maintain the flexibility you need to adapt to differing situations.*

Depending on the occasion, listener expectations, and other demands of the situation, speakers may choose to use different styles of delivery. Some of these styles are more informal and spontaneous, whereas others are more formal and scripted. In *most* speaking situations, however, you will probably want to deliver your speech in an *extemporaneous* style.

Extemporaneous speaking should not be confused with *impromptu* speaking, or speaking with no preparation at all. Extemporaneous speaking still requires careful preparation. In preparing an extemporaneous speech, you will thoroughly research your topic, decide how to best organize your ideas, carefully prepare your outline, and practice delivering the speech from notes. An extemporaneous speech is not memorized word for word. Yet neither is it completely spontaneous or delivered "off the cuff."

When delivering a speech extemporaneously, you may commit some key ideas to memory, but your specific words, phrases, and examples may vary both as you practice the speech and during its final delivery. With the extemporaneous style of delivery, you have the advantage of being well prepared, yet you also can adapt to changing circumstances if necessary.

Advantages of Speaking from a Keyword Outline

When you deliver a speech extemporaneously, you will typically use speaking notes with a keyword outline, as described in Chapter 10. This outline keeps you on track and reminds you of your main ideas, but it does not lay out the speech word for word. A keyword outline is not something you can use as a crutch. It will keep you on track, reminding you of your main points and perhaps some of your key examples, statistics, or other forms of evidence. But you will still need to think on your feet and interact with your audience. When delivering your speech extemporaneously, you can speak more directly with your audience, watching for their responses and making any changes in the content or delivery of your speech that may seem necessary.

On occasion, circumstances before your speech may dictate last-minute changes in your own presentation. In your speech class, for example, another student may speak before you and refer to an event or a piece of information that you had planned to discuss. Would you go ahead as planned and just pretend that the other speaker had not already mentioned the matter? Or would you have the flexibility to build on what the other speaker said without just repeating the same information? When you deliver your speech from a keyword outline, you have the flexibility to adapt to changing circumstances. Of course, to take advantage of that flexibility, you need to listen closely to those other speakers and quickly come up with ideas for building on their remarks.

Whenever you do some last-minute fine-tuning on your speech, you demonstrate respect for your fellow speakers and your audience. You show that you have been paying attention to what others have said, and you demonstrate a commitment to dialogue, not just to having your say. In doing so, you help build a sense of community among speakers and listeners. Delivering your speech extemporaneously will not guarantee that it will be a success, but it will give you that flexibility you need to adapt to changing circumstances. In the *Focus on Civic Engagement* on the following page, we provide a sample of a keyword outline that a speaker might use to deliver a speech about Habitat for Humanity.

Keep in mind that there are no hard-and-fast rules for constructing your keyword outline. You may choose to record only a few main ideas to jog your memory, or you may elect to write out the speech in more detail, recording both main ideas and more detailed information, such as statistics, quotations, or particular phrasings that you want to use. In either case, practicing with your notes (as well as revising and refining them as you practice) is essential.

FOCUS ON CIVIC ENGAGEMENT

A Keyword Outline for a Speech about Habitat for Humanity

Introduction

I. Story of single-parent domestic abuse survivor
II. Personal participation in Habitat builds
III. Show relevance—helping others—college is a good time to start
IV. Thesis: Becoming actively involved with Habitat is an excellent way of making a difference in others' lives.
V. Preview—define Habitat, look at where it operates, explain how the system works, and describe how to get involved

Body

I. Habitat is a terrific organization, with many distinguished accomplishments.
  A. Nonprofit Christian housing ministry (according to the Habitat Web site)
  B. Started in the U.S. in 1976 by Millard Fuller
  C. Eliminating substandard housing worldwide
  D. Makes adequate housing a matter of conscience and action
II. HH has gained a large following in its 33 years.
  A. All 50 states in the U.S. (*Habitat World*, January 2006)
  B. Nearly 100 other countries
  C. More than 2,200 total affiliates
  D. Local Habitat building 90th house (*Habitat News*, May 2009)
III. Habitat has developed a model system that is both fair and efficient.
  A. Selection criteria for homeowners (local Habitat director, Thomson)
    1. Need
    2. Ability to repay no-interest mortgage
    3. Willingness to put in "sweat equity" hours
  B. Builds modest homes
    1. About 1,100 square feet
    2. Low mortgage payments—less than $300 per month
  C. Money reverts to a "Fund for Humanity"—supports future projects
IV. Getting involved in HH is easy.
  A. Find local affiliate
  B. Gifts from the heart (financial and food donations)
  C. Global village—Habitat volunteer vacation
  D. Women's Build
  E. Campus chapters and programs
  F. Jimmy Carter's Work Project (distribute handouts)

Conclusion

I. Revisit personal story—working with great people, community building.
II. Summarize—we've looked closely at Habitat—what it is, where it operates, how it works, and how you can get involved.
III. Appeal for action—offer immediate opportunity to join local chapter and end with moving quote from homeowner: "This is the first time my three children have had a real home. They will be able to attend the same school and live in a safe neighborhood. Without HH, this *never* would have been possible."

Why Use Extemporaneous Delivery?

With an extemporaneous delivery, you can more easily adapt to the audience and the situation. You can make changes, clarify or elaborate with examples or illustrations, omit a minor point if time is running short, and more effectively involve the audience in your speech.

HIGHLIGHTING EXTEMPORANEOUS DELIVERY

President Clinton Connects with His Audience

Remember how Bill Clinton electrified a joint session of Congress in 1993 by brandishing a prototype of a national health care card and calling for "health care that can never be taken away, health care that is always there"?

That speech still stands as one of the most impressive formal addresses of his Presidency. And perhaps it was no accident that Mr. Clinton could hold that Congress in his sway even though he was winging it for seven minutes as the wrong text scrolled across the teleprompter. . . .

For Mr. Clinton has a curious split personality when it comes to oratory. Speaking extemporaneously, he can be arresting, eloquent, and amusing. . . . His turns of phrase twang with a delicious backwoodsiness. During the campaign, he said of the Republican budget proposal: "It is their dog. And it was a mangy old dog, and that's why I vetoed that dog." And at the pulpit of a church, Mr. Clinton can burn with a preacher's passion . . .

But put this president in the most stately settings of government with a written text and a teleprompter and his eloquence sometimes fades. Connectedness is the key to his best oratory, his aides say. Mr. Clinton needs the synergy of the crowd; he needs to feel people's enthusiasm or their pain.

Source: From the *New York Times* © February 2, 1997 *The New York Times*. All Rights Reserved.

Extemporaneous speaking, however, demands focused concentration. When delivering a speech extemporaneously, you cannot just read from a manuscript or rely on a detailed outline if you lose your train of thought. You cannot just "zone out" or "wing it." Speaking extemporaneously demands careful preparation, good notes, and a clear mind as you speak.

An extemporaneous style works best when you have a genuine passion for your topic. As you speak extemporaneously, you can interject spontaneous comments or include personal observations that reflect your own interests and experiences. If *you* are intellectually and emotionally engaged, you are better able to speak in the moment and communicate the conviction and passion that you feel to your audience. When well done, an extemporaneous style also contributes to your ethos as a committed and effective advocate.[20] Former president Bill Clinton, who was well-known for connecting personally with his audiences, was at his best when speaking extemporaneously. In the *Highlighting Extemporaneous Delivery* feature above, a reporter for the *New York Times* describes how Clinton actually seemed to do better when speaking *without* a prepared text.

ALTERNATIVE STYLES OF DELIVERY

Preview. *Besides the extemporaneous style of delivery, speakers can choose from several other presentation styles that range from very informal to quite formal. The style you choose will depend on your preference, the demands of the speaking situation, and audience expectations.*

Successful speakers develop the ability to use a variety of different styles of delivery because different topics and occasions may call for different approaches to presenting your speech. You would not want to speak to a large, formal meeting with a casual, off-the-cuff style; nor would you want to speak to your classmates about getting involved in student government by writing out and reading a speech word for word. It is important to fit the delivery style to the situation.

In addition to the extemporaneous style, you may want to consider three other styles of delivery: impromptu, manuscript, and memorized speaking. Although the extemporaneous style is appropriate in most situations, one of these alternative approaches may be called for on certain occasions.

The Impromptu Speech

Impromptu speaking is off-the-cuff and casual, delivered with little or no preparation. In general, you should never choose to make an impromptu speech if you have time to prepare in advance. There may be occasions, however, when you find yourself in a situation where impromptu speaking is the only option.

Imagine that you are attending a community forum on heath care, for example, and you feel the need to respond to what some of the speakers have said. Perhaps you want to share a hair-raising experience you once had in the local hospital's emergency room, or maybe you want to argue for a new health care facility for low-income citizens. At your place of work, you may be called on to articulate your point of view, make a brief report, or explain some rule or procedure. Requests for these spontaneous "speeches" are more common than you may think in business and professional settings. As a student, you may be called on to make brief, impromptu speeches during discussions or debates in your classes. It is important to learn how to respond effectively to these demanding situations, even if you have little or no time to prepare.

If your instructor assigns an impromptu speech in your speech class, take advantage of this opportunity to get accustomed to standing up and speaking in front of your classmates without advance preparation. Your impromptu speech does not have to be perfect. Your instructor and classmates will understand that you had no time to prepare, and they won't expect the same polished performance they might expect in a formal speech. So relax! You may even enjoy this opportunity to "think on your feet" and fashion a speech "off the top of your head."

GUIDELINES FOR GIVING IMPROMPTU SPEECHES When giving an impromptu speech, you have limited time to organize your thoughts. Even so, here are a few things you can do to succeed:

- *Anticipate the possibility that you may be called on to speak and be thinking about what you might say.* If you are taking a class and the instructor knows that you have knowledge or experience relating to the topic being discussed, you may be called on to speak. What will you say? What specific aspects of the topic will be most relevant to the discussion? Jot down a few notes and have them ready if, in fact, you are called on. Similarly, when you plan to go to a meeting or community forum, examine the agenda or the speakers' topic to get some sense of the issues that may be discussed. Even if you have not been invited to speak, you may find yourself wanting to share your views. And it can't hurt to think about what you might say in advance.

- *Practice active listening.* In a meeting, it is critical that you follow the flow of the discussion. You don't want to be daydreaming and then suddenly hear someone say, "Kevin, does this plan make sense to you?" In that situation, you would be hard-pressed to say anything coherent, much less offer a reasoned opinion. If you are listening to formal speeches by others, you likewise will want to listen actively. We offer more guidelines for engaged and active listening in Chapter 4.
- *Increase your feelings of confidence by reminding yourself that no one expects perfection from impromptu remarks.* Listener expectations are always higher when the speaker is delivering a planned presentation. In impromptu speaking, however, listeners expect some small mistakes, more repetition, and perhaps a few more pauses as you gather your thoughts and think about what you want to say.
- *Use even limited preparation time to your advantage.* At community forums or in professional conferences, you can take notes while listening to a panel or symposium. These notes will help you recall more accurately what others have said and can serve as the foundation for your own impromptu remarks.
- *Use basic principles of speech organization.* Even an impromptu speech should have an introduction, a body, and a conclusion. Within the body, you can still organize your main points in some basic strategic order, such as the chronological, spatial, or categorical patterns discussed in Chapter 9. Your organizational pattern may not be as carefully considered or as elaborate as it would be in a formal speech. Yet you may still introduce your remarks, make two or three main points, and summarize those points at the end, as you would in a more formal speech. However limited the time you have to prepare, it is always a good idea to sketch out at least a rough outline of the main points you want to cover.
- *Speak briefly and concisely.* Regardless of the situation, impromptu speeches should not consume too much time. When people gather—for a class, a conference, a business meeting, or a community forum—there is usually a planned agenda. Nobody appreciates a speaker who tries to dominate that agenda. When you are invited to make impromptu comments, keep your comments brief and allow time for others to speak as well.
- *Think of impromptu speaking as an opportunity to practice and improve your delivery skills.* When you speak without notes or with limited notes, you have an opportunity to focus even more on your vocal and physical delivery. Take advantage of that to practice and more closely observe how listeners react to your style of speaking.

The Manuscript Speech

At the other end of the continuum is **manuscript speaking.** Manuscript speeches are carefully prepared formal speeches. They are speeches designed to be delivered exactly as written, such as a speech on a controversial issue that might be covered by the news media, or a ceremonial address with language carefully crafted to sound eloquent or even poetic. In these situations, the manuscript not only allows you to say precisely what you planned to say, but also provides a written transcript of your remarks.

Senator John McCain often delivers his speeches from manuscript, yet he remains animated and connected to his audience.

Some settings may call for manuscript speeches because of their formal nature. The president of the United States delivers many important speeches from manuscript, such as the State of the Union address. Commencement addresses are also typically delivered from manuscript. If you were called on to make formal remarks upon the installation of new officers at a civic or fraternal organization, a manuscript speech again may be most appropriate. Using a manuscript allows you to exercise complete control. You can time your speech precisely, choose your words carefully, and decide exactly how to phrase your most important ideas. The underlying principles of good public speaking still apply to the manuscript speech: even though you may be reading from a manuscript, you should pay attention to audience reactions and be responsive to feedback. And it's important that you prepare a copy of the manuscript that you can read easily while speaking. You also should practice delivering the speech from that manuscript.[21] When speaking from manuscript, you are less likely to diverge from the content of the speech as originally written, but you can still make adjustments in your delivery or even in the content of the speech if you sense that your audience may be confused or bored by your speech.

GUIDELINES FOR GIVING MANUSCRIPT SPEECHES Delivering a manuscript speech presents special challenges relating to eye contact, movement, the use of your voice, and flexibility. Here are some guidelines to follow:

- *Use a manuscript for the right reasons.* Use a manuscript when it is important to choose your words carefully and say exactly what you mean. Do not use it as a crutch to hide behind or as a way to manage your anxieties.
- *Use good oral style.* Even though you are speaking from a manuscript, you should still use language that is appropriate for oral presentation. This means that you will choose words and construct your sentences in ways that are easily spoken and more readily understood by listeners.
- *Practice extensively.* You need to know the speech well enough to look at the audience and get back to the manuscript without losing your place. If you're going to deliver the speech from a written manuscript, prepare a clean, double-spaced copy printed in an easily readable font (14, 16, or even 18 points). If you use a more advanced technology to deliver your manuscript speech, such as a laptop computer or a teleprompter, be sure to practice your speech using that technology. And it's always a good idea to prepare a backup manuscript in case the technology fails.

- *Look for opportunities to move and gesture.* When you speak from a manuscript, you will normally be speaking from behind a podium. As a result, you may feel compelled to stand in one place. You may even feel tempted to lean on the podium or to grasp it as if you were trying to anchor yourself in a strong wind. Resist these temptations. With planning and practice, you can deliver a manuscript speech and still move around, use appropriate gestures, and engage your audience with eye contact and facial expressions.
- *Use your voice effectively.* Some speakers sound artificial or flat when delivering a manuscript speech. Their inflection may be less animated than normal, or they may sound monotonous or singsong, as if they were doing a poor job reading a poem. To speak effectively, concentrate on adding variety, color, and emphasis to your voice—just as you do when speaking extemporaneously. You may want to write delivery reminders on the manuscript itself, such as *Slow down*, *Pause for emphasis*, or *Repeat this*. You can also underline or boldface key words or phrases in the manuscript that you want to emphasize with your voice.
- *Maintain flexibility.* Rather than adapting to the moment or reacting to audience feedback, some speakers feel compelled to read from their manuscript word for word, never deviating, no matter what. Yet your manuscript need not be a straitjacket. Although the idea behind speaking from a manuscript may be to deliver the speech exactly as written, that does not mean you should *never* change a single word or improvise in response to audience reactions. A manuscript speech *can* be changed if circumstances warrant it. You *can* add another example. You *can* (and often should) elaborate on a point with some spontaneous remarks. When you speak from manuscript, you *can* be flexible, remain connected to your listeners, and respond to their feedback.

The Memorized Speech

You will rarely find yourself in a situation where you will want to give a **memorized speech**. Some students participate in speaking contests, such as the American Legion Oratorical Contest, where they deliver memorized speeches. Some formal or ceremonial occasions also may call for a short memorized speech, such as a wedding toast or a brief tribute to a colleague at a retirement dinner. In extemporaneous speaking, you may want to memorize key parts of a longer speech, such as the introductory device, the concluding remarks, or an especially important quotation or passage from a literary work. Generally, however, memorized speeches are a thing of the past—a form of delivery quite common 100 or 150 years ago but increasingly rare today.

GUIDELINES FOR GIVING MEMORIZED SPEECHES If you *do* find yourself in a situation where you want to speak from memory, keep these pointers in mind:

- *Stay focused on your specific purpose and the key ideas you want to convey.* When you memorize, you may be tempted to focus on the specific language you want to use. You may try to memorize your speech word for word, but don't forget that it's more important to remember your basic ideas than your exact phrasing.

- *Speak in the moment.* Sometimes when speakers deliver a speech from memory, they go on "automatic pilot." They appear to forget that they are speaking to an audience and simply recite the words that they have drummed into their head—all the while staring blankly at a wall in the back of the room. When this happens, the speech becomes a ritualistic performance rather than a communicative exchange with an audience. Remember: even if speaking from memory, you should stay focused on your listeners and remember your purpose: to *communicate* with your listeners. If you lose yourself in your own thoughts and fail to speak in the moment, you may say all the words you planned but you will not really be *communicating.*
- *Practice, practice, practice.* To be effective, all speakers must practice, regardless of their method of delivery. The memorized speech, however, may require even more practice—especially if the memorization is part of a speaking

TABLE 12.1

COMPARING STYLES OF DELIVERY

Extemporaneous

- Carefully prepared with thorough research, strategic organization of ideas, and practiced delivery.
- Delivered from speaking notes, typically using a keyword outline.
- Offers the opportunity to deliver the speech with flexibility, spontaneity, and directness.
- Encourages audience adaptation.
- Works best when the speaker cares deeply about the topic and can speak with passion and commitment.

Impromptu

- Off-the-cuff, casual style that deemphasizes preparation.
- Often called for in business, community, and classroom settings.
- Informally jotting down notes as impromptu occasions arise can help with delivery and organization.
- Should be seen as an opportunity to practice and improve delivery skills.

Manuscript

- Carefully prepared formal speeches, usually delivered precisely as written.
- Sometimes delivered using a teleprompter, and often delivered from behind a lectern.
- Typically used in important political speeches or on ceremonial occasions.
- Allows for precise, eloquent language and control of speaking time.
- Requires easily readable manuscript and extensive practice for a more natural style of speaking.

Memorized

- Delivered from memory without the aid of speaking notes or manuscript.
- Sometimes used by students in speaking contests or by citizens delivering toasts or other short tributes.
- Requires extensive practice and concentration on key ideas.
- May be partially incorporated into other styles of delivery, as when a speaker memorizes key quotations or passages within an extemporaneous speech.
- Speakers run risk of "performing" rather than communicating with their audience.

contest and the speaker must memorize a fairly long text. In that situation, you may want to read through the text several times and then practice it in sections before trying to memorize the entire speech. Practice sessions should be spaced out over time rather than crammed into a few hours. That makes it more likely that you will commit the speech to your long-term memory.

Each method of delivery, as we have noted, has its benefits and potential liabilities. Table 12.1 compares the attributes and relative advantages of the four styles of delivery.

Over time you will discover your own preferences, and you may even develop a style of delivery that is uniquely your own. Experiment with different speaking styles. Discover the techniques that make you most comfortable and allow you to speak with confidence and conviction. Whatever style you choose, remember that the purpose of public speaking is to communicate with an audience. So however you deliver your speech, it's crucial that you remain connected to your listeners.

RESPONDING TO AUDIENCE QUESTIONS

Preview. *After you speak, you may be expected to entertain questions. The question-and-answer period is important because it allows you to interact informally with the audience, to provide additional information, to enhance your credibility, and to participate in a mutually beneficial dialogue.*

Some speakers give little thought to the question-and-answer period that often follows a formal address. Instead, they focus all their attention on the preparation and delivery of the speech itself. Yet if you don't respond effectively to questions, you can damage your credibility and undermine the success of your speech. You don't want to give a good speech and then appear defensive, ignorant about related issues, or insensitive to your audience's concerns or questions about your speech.

The question-and-answer period is a potentially decisive moment in the audience's ultimate judgment of your speech. It gives your listeners a chance to ask for clarification or elaboration of the points that most interested them. As such, it provides a good barometer of how well your speech came across, as well as one last opportunity to address any confusion or skepticism left by the speech itself. You should listen carefully to the questions posed by your audience and strive to engage your listeners in a genuine dialogue.

Preparing for the Question-and-Answer Period

Although you cannot anticipate everything listeners may ask, you certainly can make some educated guesses about their potential questions and concerns. You should expect questions about any controversial issues you may bring up during your speech, and you should give some thought in advance to how you might respond to questions about those matters. Try to anticipate arguments that listeners may use to challenge your ideas, and make sure you have a good command of your sources. A questioner may well ask you to provide additional information or evidence for your claims, and you should be prepared to do so. Consider which parts of your speech may prove most difficult to understand and be prepared to elaborate on those matters. Try to have additional examples, statistics, and other sorts of evidence "in reserve," ready to use in response to audience questions. When it seems that you *could* have said much more about your topic, you come across as more credible. The more you know about your topic, of course, the better prepared you will be to deal with questions.

Show Respect for Your Listeners In addition to anticipating questions about the content of your speech, you should think about the sort of attitude you convey as you respond to questions. Will you seem defensive and closed-minded? Or will you strike your listeners as somebody who genuinely respects their opinions and wants to engage in a productive dialogue? Listeners occasionally will challenge or openly disagree with you. Sometimes they may even do so in ways that you consider disrespectful, abrasive, or even rude. Although being challenged in this way can be unpleasant, you should keep your cool! Always try to respond with class and civility. As the speaker, *you* have a lot of control over the tone of the exchange, and you can refuse to respond in kind to a rude or disrespectful questioner. Should you get a hostile question, it is often best to respond only briefly, and then move on to the next question.

The question-and-answer period following a speech is a time for respectful and mutually influential dialogue.

Conducting the Question-and-Answer Period

Decide where you will stand as you receive audience questions. One option is to remain behind the podium. This conveys a sense of formality, maintaining some distance between you and the audience. Another option is to stand at the side or in front of the podium, where you can interact more directly with the audience. Finally, in informal settings, you may sit on a table or a stool and engage in more of a "chat" with your audience. Any of these options may work well, depending on the situation, the audience's expectations, and your own preferences.

The following guidelines will help you conduct the question-and-answer period more effectively.

- *Listen carefully to each question.* If you can't hear a question very well, ask the questioner to stand and repeat it. Or move away from the podium and stand closer to the audience. As you listen, provide a few nonverbal cues, such as nodding your head, to let the questioner know that you understand the question. Generally, you should avoid interrupting audience members while they are asking their questions. Occasionally, however, an audience member will abuse the right to ask a question by making a long, perhaps even belligerent statement. In that case, you may intervene in the interest of allowing others to ask questions.

- *If appropriate, repeat each question so that everyone can hear it and keep track of what is happening.* In repeating the question, you may want to rephrase it because audience members sometimes ask poorly phrased or rambling questions.
- *Do not allow one person to dominate.* If many people raise their hands at once, make sure you call on people who have not already spoken. If someone who already asked a question raises his or her hand again, you might ask, "Is there anyone else who has a question?" Occasionally a persistent questioner may try to engage you for an extended period of time. If that happens, you may invite that person to speak with you later, and then move on to the next question.
- *Do not try to fake your way through a response.* If you do not know the answer to a question or are not familiar with some topic raised by a questioner, it is best to admit it. Perhaps a questioner will ask if you have read a particular book, or whether you know about some incident or event. Admitting that you do not know everything will not hurt your credibility. Indeed, we tend to be more suspicious of speakers who pretend to "know it all"!

  If a listener poses a difficult question that you can't answer, you can always offer to investigate the matter and get back to the person. It is easy to get a listener's e-mail address following your talk—then do your research and follow through with a thoughtful response. When you do this, you are showing respect for the listener. At the same time, you are learning more about your topic—and will be better prepared to answer questions next time you speak.
- *Respect time limits.* Question-and-answer periods should not go on forever. Like speeches, they have time constraints. Sometimes you will be asked to speak briefly and leave plenty of time for audience questions. Other times you will have only a little time left for interaction with the audience. Ask in advance what the audience expects or desires, then follow through, limiting the question-and-answer period to the agreed-upon time.[22]
- *Anticipate the possibility of no audience questions.* On occasion, you may conclude your speech and ask for questions but get no response from the audience. If you have used most of the time available for speaking and responding to questions, you may choose simply to thank them and take your seat. However, if time permits, you may also consider sharing some additional information or experiences that you didn't have the chance to address during your speech. Sometimes listeners need extra time to formulate good questions. By talking just a bit longer (but not too long), you give them the time to think. As a result, they may offer more thoughtful or interesting questions.

SUMMARY

- Ethical delivery grows from a collaborative, transactional approach to public speaking.
  - Good speakers try never to distract the audience with their delivery.
  - They do all they can to promote audience comprehension and understanding.

- They know that good, ethical delivery not only sounds good, it grows from a solid foundation—a carefully constructed, thoughtfully reasoned, and well-supported speech.

- There are many different ways to deliver a speech, ranging from the formal manuscript presentation to the very informal impromptu speech.
- For most public speaking situations, you will likely want to use the extemporaneous style, which involves meticulous preparation and is typically delivered from a keyword outline.
  - When you speak extemporaneously, you are encouraged to speak with flexibility, adapting to audience expectations and to the context.
  - As you speak, you are able to establish eye contact with audience members, use appropriate gestures, and make effective use of your voice.
  - Extemporaneous delivery also encourages you to speak with passion and conviction.
  - Practicing your speech aloud and seeking out opportunities to speak can help you develop an effective extemporaneous style of delivery.
- Other styles of delivery may be appropriate on certain occasions, but each presents some special challenges.
  - Even impromptu speaking requires some preparation and organization.
  - Manuscript speaking demands a special focus on using good oral style, incorporating gestures and movement, and using your voice effectively.
  - Speaking from memory requires extensive practice; it challenges you to speak "in the moment" and to stay focused on the ideas you are conveying.
- The question-and-answer period is an important part of most formal speeches.
  - As you respond to audience questions, you have the chance to show listeners how well informed you are and how quickly you can think on your feet.
  - You can also demonstrate how carefully you listen, how open you are to others' ideas, and how honest you are in responding to difficult questions.
- Anticipate and prepare for possible questions from your audience, and do all you can to establish a climate of respectful and mutually beneficial dialogue.

QUESTIONS FOR REVIEW AND REFLECTION

1. Describe the difference between "sounding good" and "being sound."
2. Your friend has to make an important presentation at a fund-raising event for the local Boys and Girls Club. He comes to you and asks you for advice on how to deliver his speech. What three things would you stress? Why are they important?
3. To what extent may cultural differences influence the way listeners respond to a speaker's delivery?
4. You have heard many people give speeches (classroom speeches, lectures, political speeches, after-dinner speeches, speeches at memorial services). Given your experience as an audience member, what are the things that most annoy you about some speakers' delivery habits or styles? What are some delivery characteristics you especially admire?

5. Define each of the following styles of delivering a speech:
   a. extemporaneous
   b. impromptu
   c. manuscript
   d. memorized
   Compare and contrast the advantages and disadvantages of each delivery style.
6. Why is a keyword outline useful in delivering a speech? Can you think of any potential disadvantages to using such an outline? What might you do to minimize any potential disadvantages?
7. You have given a speech, and now it is time for audience questions. How would you deal with each of these situations?
   a. An audience member is hostile.
   b. An audience member asks three questions in a row.
   c. Someone asks you a question you do not know the answer to.
   d. No one asks you a question.

ENDNOTES

1. Doris G. Yoakam, "Women's Introduction to the American Platform," *History and Criticism of American Public Address*, vol. 1, ed. William Norwood Brigance (New York: McGraw-Hill, 1943), 74–76.
2. See, as examples, Joe Ayres, "Speech Preparation Processes and Speech Apprehension," *Communication Education* 45 (1996): 228–35; Joe Ayres and Tim Hopf, *Coping with Speech Anxiety* (Norwood, NJ: Ablex, 1993); Ralph R. Behnke and Chris R. Sawyer, "Anticipatory Anxiety Patterns for Male and Female Speakers," *Communication Education* 49 (2000): 187–95; and Thomas Robinson II, "Communication Apprehension and the Basic Public Speaking Course: A National Survey of In-Class Treatment Techniques," *Communication Education* 46 (1997): 188–97.
3. See John T. Molloy, *Dress for Success* (New York: Warner Books, 1975), one of the first books to address the importance of appearance in the professional world. For a more recent work, see Molloy's *New Women's Dress for Success* (New York: Warner Books, 1996).
4. For a classic work on nonverbal communication, see Edward T. Hall, *The Silent Language* (Garden City, NY: Doubleday, 1959). More recent works include Edward T. Hall, *The Dance of Life* (New York: Doubleday, 1983); and Mark Knapp and Judith Hall, *Nonverbal Communication in Human Interaction* (Philadelphia: Harcourt Brace Jovanovich, 1997).
5. See, for example, Edward T. Hall and Mildred R. Hall, *Understanding Cultural Differences* (Yarmouth, ME: Intercultural Press, 1990); and Richard D. Lewis, *When Cultures Collide*, rev. ed. (London: Brealey, 2000).
6. Carolyn Calloway-Thomas, Pamela J. Cooper, and Cecil Blake, *Intercultural Communication: Roots and Routes* (Boston: Allyn & Bacon, 1999); Virginia P. Richmond et al., *Nonverbal Communication: The Unspoken Dialogue* (New York: Harper & Row, 1989); Michelle Le Baron, *Bridging Cultural Conflicts: A New Approach for a Changing World* (San Francisco: Jossey-Bass, 2003).
7. You can learn more about these differences by enrolling in a course in intercultural communication.
8. Virginia P. Richmond and James C. McCroskey, *Nonverbal Behavior in Interpersonal Relations*, 3rd ed. (Boston: Allyn & Bacon, 1995).
9. Nathan Bierma, "Hand Gestures May Expand, Express Unspoken Thoughts," *Chicago Tribune*, August 5, 2004, sec. 5, 2.
10. Paul Ekman, *Emotions Revealed: Recognizing Faces and Feelings to Improve Communications and Emotional Life* (New York: Holt, 2004), 84–112.
11. Knapp and Hall, *Nonverbal Communication in Human Interaction, 58–74.*
12. Albert Mehrabian, *Silent Messages: Implicit Communication of Emotions and Attitudes*, 2nd ed. (Belmont, CA: Wadsworth, 1982); Paul

Ekman and Erika Rosenberg, *What the Face Reveals* (New York: Oxford University Press, 1998).

13. For an excellent collection of readings on all aspects of nonverbal communication, see Laura K. Guerrero, Joseph A. DeVito, and Michael L. Hecht, eds., *The Nonverbal Communication Reader: Classic and Contemporary Readings*, 2nd ed. (Prospect Heights, IL: Waveland Press, 1999).
14. PBS Home Programs, www.pbs.org/standarddeviantstv/transcript_public.html#rate (accessed June 22, 2009).
15. Richmond and McCroskey, *Nonverbal Behavior in Interpersonal Relations*, 68–70.
16. "A Powerful Tool: Your Voice," *Costa Connection*, June 2004, 9.
17. See, for example, Deborah Tannen, *You Just Don't Understand: Men and Women in Conversation* (New York: Quill, 2001). Tannen and other linguists have noted that men and women often exhibit different speech patterns, with women more inclined to use inflectional patterns that appear to seek validation from listeners. When using a rising inflection at the end of a statement (as in, "We really have to find a permanent home for the new shelter, don't you think?"), the speaker suggests an attitude of uncertainty. Especially if used often, this kind of vocal pattern can undermine a speaker's credibility.
18. For an extensive guide on vocal communication, see Jeffrey C. Hahner, Martin A. Sokoloff, and Sandra L. Salisch, *Speaking Clearly: Improving Voice and Diction*, 5th ed. (New York: McGraw-Hill, 1996).
19. John O. Greene, Marianne S. Sassi, Terri L. Malek-Madani, and Christopher N. Edwards, "Adult Acquisition of Message-Production Skills," *Communication Monographs* 64 (1997): 181–200. This article emphasizes the importance of practicing speech delivery.
20. See Herbert W. Hildebrandt and Walter W. Stevens, "Manuscript and Extemporaneous Modes of Delivery in Communicating Information," *Communication Monographs* 30 (1963): 369–72.
21. For one of the best guides on the techniques of manuscript speaking, see James C. Humes, *Talk Your Way to the Top* (New York: McGraw-Hill, 1980), 125–35.
22. For additional advice on managing question-and-answer sessions, see Thomas K. Mira, *Speak Smart* (New York: Random House, 1997), 115–23.

CHAPTER

13

Supporting Your Ideas Visually

CHAPTER SURVEY

Functions of Presentational Aids

Options for Presentational Aids

Guidelines for Preparing Presentational Aids

Guidelines for Using Presentational Aids

CHAPTER OBJECTIVES

After studying this chapter, you should be able to

1. Understand the diverse ways that presentational aids can help you as a speaker.
2. Describe the types of presentational aids commonly available to speakers.
3. Follow basic guidelines for creating presentational aids.
4. Follow basic guidelines for using presentational aids.

Visual material has a powerful impact on how we react to information. Photographs from inside the Abu Ghraib prison, capturing the mistreatment of detainees by American military personnel, generated outrage in the United States and abroad and fueled the insurgency in Iraq.[1] Live shots of the tsunami coming ashore in Indonesia and Thailand in 2004—sweeping away all in its path—shocked television viewers around the world, as did media coverage of both Hurricane Katrina's fury as it pummeled New Orleans in 2005 and the earthquake that devastated Haiti in 2010. These shots, and the diagrams and charts that experts created, reminded us of how destructive natural disasters can be and prompted calls for improved early-warning systems and better-coordinated evacuation and relief.[2] In January 2009, pictures of a U.S. Airways jetliner, downed by birds and ditched in the Hudson River, captivated viewers from around the world as the passengers stood atop the wings, calmly awaiting rescue. Onlookers readily pronounced what they saw as "the miracle on the Hudson," praising the pilot and crew for their quick thinking and heroism.[3]

These, of course, are dramatic examples. But visual images can generate quite an impact in less spectacular situations—such as in a classroom or a civic meeting. **Presentational aids** are an important communication tool, especially in our visually oriented society.

Presentational aids must be used carefully, however. Using visual and audio aids effectively calls for careful thinking, strategic planning, and rehearsal. There is nothing magical about presentational aids. They assist us *only* if they function as intended and if we incorporate them effectively.

FUNCTIONS OF PRESENTATIONAL AIDS

Preview. *Presentational aids can help audience members follow, retain, and be moved by the speaker's ideas. They can also help a speaker be perceived as credible and well prepared. Given these possible benefits, a speaker will do well to learn to develop and use presentational aids skillfully.*

Both speakers and listeners can benefit from the effective use of presentational aids. Let's examine some specific ways presentational aids will be important to you as a speaker and a listener.

Promoting Clarity

Effective presentational aids provide clarity. Researchers have found that "human brains extract valuable information from audiovisuals more quickly and more easily than from purely verbal information" and do so with "a more error-free grasp of information."[4] For this reason, as explained in *Highlighting Visual Perception and Thinking*, a speaker will do well to use the visual medium. A simple table depicting a budget provides more clarity than merely describing it in words. Photographs of urban areas in decay provide a clearer understanding of problems confronting American cities than

HIGHLIGHTING VISUAL PERCEPTION AND THINKING

Graphic icons populate our dashboard and every lever in our car. Road signs often feature images, not words. Our smartphone's menu is a series of icons. We have increasingly replaced words with images.

We obtain much of our information these days through graphic images. In fact, Marty Shelton suggests that visual perceptions actually provide an astonishing 99 percent of our knowledge about the world around us. This emphasis is quite natural, Shelton adds, because "we are a visual species."

We "don't think much in words *per se*," he contends, but "do most of our thinking in terms of graphic images—visuals such as pictures, icons, and facsimiles."

When we view news broadcasts, read illustrated books, or experience multimedia presentations, visual or graphic images become our "primary medium of thought." Fruitful, practical thought would be nearly unattainable were it not for such "visual stimuli."

Source: From Marty Shelton, "Special Issue: Visual Communication: Introduction." Copyrighted © 1993 by Technical Communication.

words alone. And listeners who see a statistical trend via a graph are more likely to understand it—and more immediately—than if left to chart it mentally on their own.[5]

It is easy to understand the popularity of graphs and charts; they make quantitative information easy to understand.[6] Speakers who fail to use them appear remiss. When you use statistical support that's the least bit complex, you should provide visual reinforcement to assist comprehension.

Assisting Retention

Presentational aids make information more understandable *and* more memorable. Research indicates that effective presentational aids can make recall easier, faster, and more accurate than "memories of purely verbal messages."[7] One study even found that people remembered 43 percent more information when visuals were used than when they were not.[8] In short, if you want to bolster understanding and leave a lasting impression, use good presentational aids.[9]

Providing Emphasis

A visual aid can help a speaker underscore what is most important. Even a simple list (such as in Figure 13.1)[10] can highlight key ideas as well as help listeners recall them.[11] If you are using a list, consider using **graphical icons**—such as a dollar sign to designate "money saved." Graphical icons can be even more striking and memorable than a list of keywords.[12]

FIGURE 13.1 A list can help your audience follow your speech and remember its main ideas.

Clean Energy Economy

- Restores Economic Competitiveness
- Lessens Dependence on Fossil Fuels
- Avoids Funding Our Enemies
- Lessens International Conflict
- Assists Environmental Recovery

— Source: *Time*, 16 Feb. 2009

Hurricane Landfalls in 2008

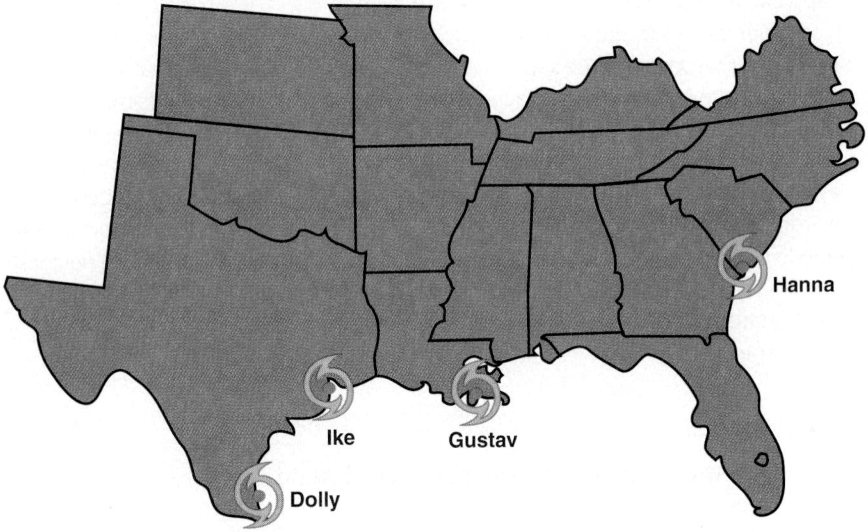

Source: National Oceanic and Atmospheric Administration, 2009.

FIGURE 13.2
A visual aid can communicate efficiently and powerfully.

Providing Support

Presentational aids can also function as evidence to support your ideas. For example, a speaker might argue that hurricane readiness should be a top priority for key coastal regions of the United States. Displaying a map that documents direct hits by hurricanes (see Figure 13.2) allows listeners to see for themselves the number of hurricanes as well as the widespread extent of the threat.[13] Basing the map (or any other visual aid) on information from a reputable source also lends support by adding credibility to your ideas. To derive this benefit, as well as meet your ethical obligations, enter the source on your display *and* cite it orally.

To support ideas, speakers often use graphs, and they are wise to do so. Graphs make statistical information more vivid and show relationships. The most familiar and useful kinds of graphs are line graphs, bar graphs, pictographs, and pie graphs. The type of graph used will depend on the type of information to be conveyed.[14]

- *Line graphs*. **Line graphs** are especially well suited to showing comparative relationships through time. For example, a hospital administrator might use a line graph to show how emergency room visits increase over time among populations who lack access to primary health care. The graph allows us to see the tendency.

  It is possible to place more than one line on a single graph, but it may be at the expense of clarity. If you plan to use multiple lines or curves, try to use strikingly different colors and restrict yourself to two or three lines. It is also important to guard against distorting a trend by compressing or elongating

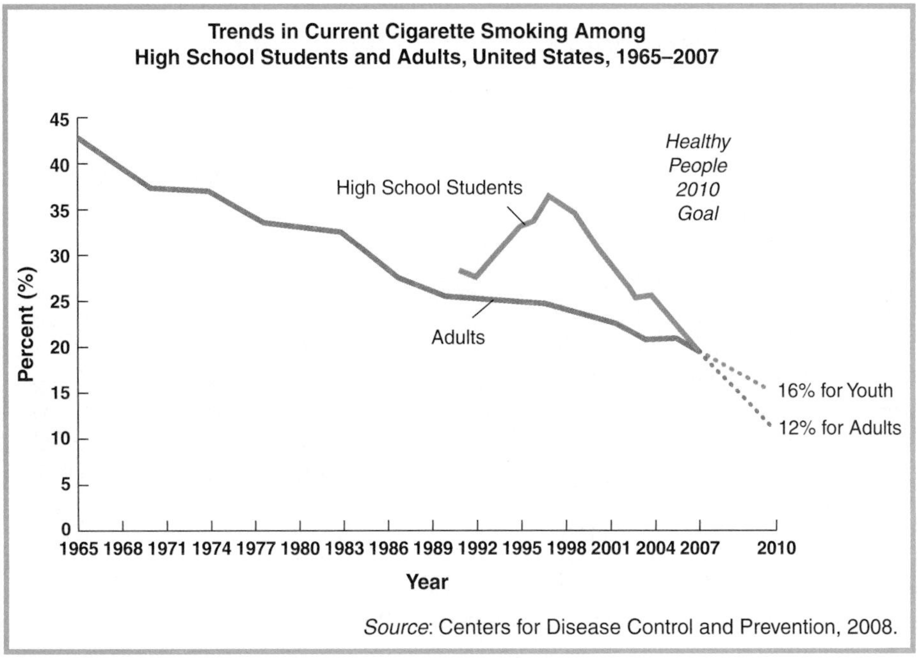

FIGURE 13.3
Line graphs help to reveal trends.

the space allotted to time periods while keeping the other dimension of the graph constant. Whenever you selectively focus on a particular segment of data, be sure to label the graph so that your audience can fully understand what you have elected to show them.[15]

Figure 13.3 provides an example of a line graph. Using this graph helped underscore the downward trend in cigarette smoking in the United States since the late 1990s.[16]

- *Bar graphs.* A **bar graph** can be used to show comparisons and contrasts between two or more items or groups. Even if listeners have little background in reading graphs, the bar graph is easy to understand. In addition, these graphs have a dramatic visual impact. As with line graphs, whenever you focus on a particular segment of data, be sure to label the graph so that your audience can fully understand what you have elected to show them.[17]

  Figure 13.4 compares the estimated percentage of overweight boys and girls from several countries. The speaker using this bar graph quoted Dr. Philip James, chairman of the International Obesity Task Force, in arguing that we have "a truly global epidemic" and detailing its impact on health care systems around the world.[18]
- *Pictographs.* Listeners often find **pictographs** particularly interesting. In a pictograph, a graphical icon is used to form lines or patterns to convey information in the same way other graphs do. Figure 13.5 shows how a pictograph can communicate information in an interesting and meaningful way. A student speaker used this pictograph to support his argument that students who drink

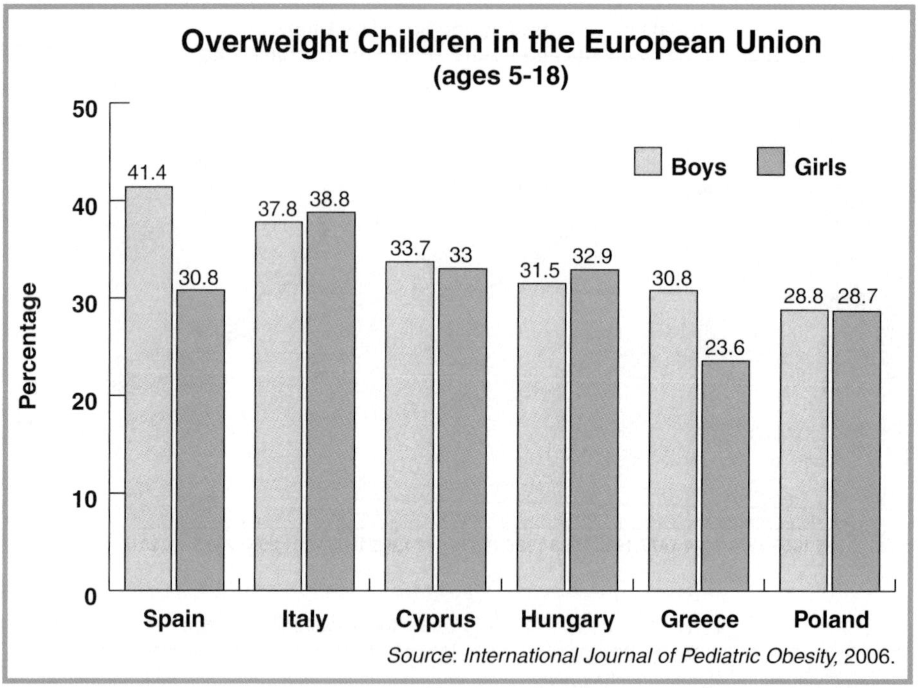

FIGURE 13.4
Bar graphs help to compare and contrast.

excessively suffer from impaired academic performance in college. Pictographs (such as this one created with Photoshop) are more challenging to construct than traditional graphs. They require more creativity and original labor.

- *Pie graphs.* The final type of graph is the **pie graph**, most often used to show numerical distribution patterns. When you need to show how a total figure breaks down into different parts, you will probably want to use a pie graph. Suppose, for example, you're noting the relative amount of our federal dollars spent on defense, Social Security, health care, and various other programs. A pie graph, like the one depicted in Figure 13.6, could efficiently convey that information. Because of their simplicity, pie graphs are easily understood by an audience.

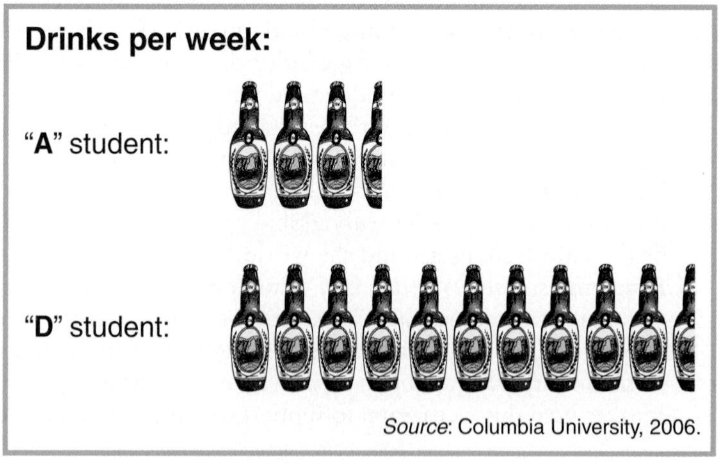

FIGURE 13.5
Pictographs can be powerful and memorable.

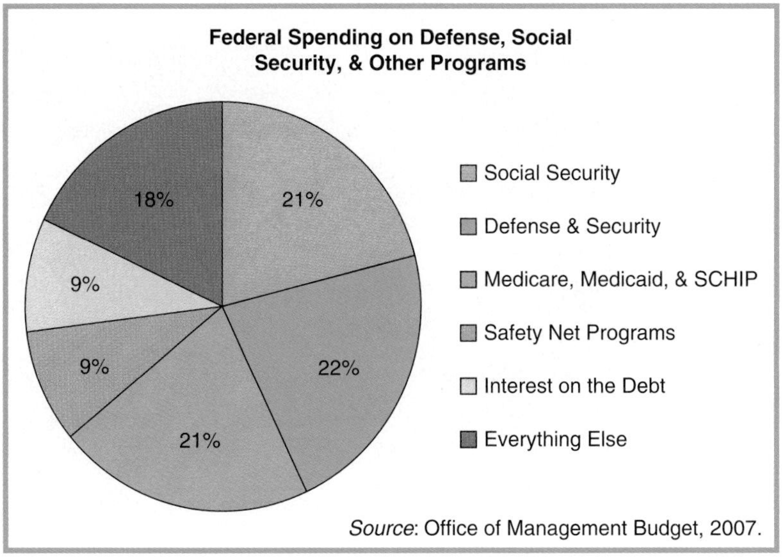

FIGURE 13.6
Pie graphs efficiently convey distribution.

When constructing a pie graph, observe two central guidelines. First, create a two-dimensional, rather than a three-dimensional, pie. As Joel Best, author of *More Damned Lies and Statistics*, explains, "Showing the edge of a tilted pie chart to the viewer (so that it seems to be a three-dimensional disk) ... exaggerates the visual importance of those slices that can be viewed edge-on."[19] In addition, use a bold or bright color to set off the sector you hope to highlight or emphasize. For added emphasis, it can be pulled out slightly from the rest of the pie.[20]

You may use several different kinds of graphs in a single presentation. When carefully constructed and used strategically, they can help you depict statistical information in ways that listeners will likely find understandable, interesting, informative, and convincing.

Creating graphs has become increasingly easy because of software like PowerPoint. However, some design options allow a speaker to easily distort data—intentionally or unwittingly. The author of *How to Lie with Charts*, Gerald Everett Jones, provides some basic pointers for communicating accurately and ethically when presenting data in graphs. See *Highlighting Using Graphs to Communicate Data* on pages 324–325.

To provide support, speakers often use photographs to "document" some phenomenon or otherwise provide "proof." The proliferation of visual imagery requires that speakers and listeners alike develop **visual literacy**, or the ability to think discerningly about visual images—a matter we take up in *Highlighting Visual Literacy* on page 326.[22]

Encouraging Emotional Involvement

A speaker can use pictures that will elicit greater emotional involvement than if the audience were left to conjure up their own images.[23] During the war in Vietnam, a widely published photograph of Vietnamese children fleeing their village after a

This photo of 9-year-old Kim Phuc, badly burned and fleeing her village during a napalm attack, ignited strong antiwar sentiment during the Vietnam war. The journalist, Nick Ut, helped the children to safety, and his photo won a Pulitzer Prize.

HIGHLIGHTING USING GRAPHS TO COMMUNICATE DATA

Some Practical and Ethical Guidelines

- ***Use each type of graph properly.*** Pie graphs depict relationships in terms of percentages or ratios. Line graphs emphasize trends, whereas bar graphs emphasize results at each division of a particular point in time. Pictographs compare basic amounts.
- ***Adhere to traditional formats.*** Line graphs and bar graphs consist of a ***y* axis** and an ***x* axis**. As Jones explains, "Quantity goes up and down on the vertical axis—the *y axis*. Time progresses from left to right along the horizontal axis—the *x axis*."[21] Departing from this conventional arrangement (as many software packages may allow one to do) will impede understanding and/or distort the data. For example, a program may allow you to turn a conventional vertical bar graph on its side, but Jones advises against it. Pictographs, on the other hand, can show increasing magnitude along either axis; each depicted unit of measure can be stacked or can build from left to right, as modeled in Figure 13.5.
- ***Be sensitive to the implications of range.*** Graphs should always begin with zero on the *y axis*. Notice, too, that expanding or compressing the range of either axis (*y* or *x*) can distort the data and suggest different interpretations of the data. For example, Figure 13.7 takes a long view of homicide rates. If a speaker chose to use only the portion of the graph from 1980–1983, though, such data might suggest a 'great decline' in homicides. That interpretation, though, would be misleading; in terms of the long view, the number of homicides would still be high. It may make sense to violate the rule of beginning with zero, so that differences can be better detected when one zooms in to a particular segment. When doing so, just be sure all is labeled clearly, as well as noted aloud for your audience.
- ***Label every element.*** Numbers alone will not suffice. Explain their meaning via a simple label. For instance, each sector of a pie graph should be labeled in terms of its category and percentage, as should the meaning of the whole pie.
- ***Make labels easily readable.*** Employ a simple, easy-to-read style—and a large size—for fonts.
- ***Avoid overwhelming the audience.*** Pies should be confined to five or six slices—never more

napalm attack was credited with igniting strong antiwar sentiment.[24] Pictures of human suffering following the 2004 tsunami in Indonesia, the hurricanes that devastated the Gulf Coast in 2005, and the earthquake in Haiti in 2010 prompted people from all over the world to get involved in the recovery efforts that continue to this day. Images can prompt increased attention to political problems as well. During the recent economic recession, for example, tent cities sprang up across the country, dramatizing the effects of a rash of housing foreclosures.

Stimulating Interest

As we have noted, presentational aids can make a speech easier to follow and understand. They also stimulate interest. When you think of the challenges of listening (discussed in Chapter 4), you will quickly recognize the value of presentational aids. By engaging multiple senses, presentational aids can help keep

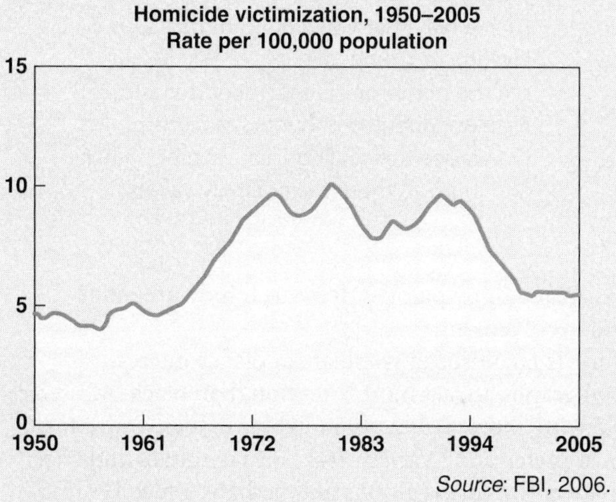

FIGURE 13.7
What does this graph suggest about murders in the United States? How might that interpretation change if the source showed data only from 1994 through 2005? Although technically correct, the impression would be different than when more years are considered.

than eight. Line graphs should have no more than two or three lines—each easily distinguished. Bar graphs should feature six or fewer bars (though each bar can be clustered into two or three vertical sectors).

- ***Avoid "stacked" bars.*** Bars with layered strata of data are harder to read and can obscure relationships.
- ***Proofread.*** Be careful with spelling, usage, correctness, and so on.
- ***Choose colors carefully.*** Use colors that yield good contrast so each element depicted is easily distinguished. Make sure, too, that the color scheme can be seen in the lighting conditions under which you will be making your presentation. Be mindful that what appears on your monitor will likely be much more vivid than what is projected on a screen.
- ***Reveal your sources.*** Cite the source(s) of all information at the bottom of the chart or graph. Also include the date (e.g., Bureau of Labor Statistics, June 2010).

Source: Gerald Everett Jones, *How to Lie with Charts* (San Jose, CA: Authors Choice Press, 2000).

HIGHLIGHTING VISUAL LITERACY

The Visual Dimension of Critical Thinking

Veteran journalist Gregg Hoffmann argues that visual literacy is a "requirement for clear thinking in the 21st century." Hoffman makes his case using a major international news story about an uncle's failed attempt to gain custody and citizenship of his six-year-old Cuban nephew, rescued at sea after the boy's mother died trying to reach Miami by boat and gain refuge for herself and her son, Elian, in the United States. The father, still in Cuba and content to stay there, insisted that his son be returned. He won the legal battle, which ensued for five months. The uncle and other relatives defied the court order to surrender Elian to authorities. The ordeal finally ended with a predawn raid when federal agents removed the boy from a relative's household. Hoffmann writes:

> Two photos likely will become symbolic of the Elian Gonzalez story. First is the Associated Press photo of the federal marshal, dressed in riot gear, demanding the boy be turned over. Second is the photo of the boy smiling at his father. People on both sides of the issue point to those photos to support their contentions.
>
> You can see "what happened" in a photo or video, most people would argue. "A picture is worth a thousand words" is a widely accepted statement. Words are another person's abstraction of what happened, but a photo captures reality.
>
> But does it? Is a photo or video simply a mirror of reality, or is it a product of certain premises and processes that then make it susceptible to manipulation? A photo or video grows from a point of view, or a set of premises. The photographer will select his subject, to a large degree, to represent his or her own world view, or to meet what is perceived as the preferences of an audience.
>
> A skilled photographer can capture your senses and then craft the photo or video in such a way that you leap from that sensory level to very high, abstract levels. So, we see the photo of the federal officer and Elian and jump to thoughts of fascism. Or, we see the smiling Elian with his father and jump to thoughts of family values.

listeners from feeling bored, distracted, or passive. Research indicates that visual aids bolster interest and involvement.[25]

Color, a common element in visual aids, can stimulate audience interest.[26] Colorful poster boards and vivid graphs attract more attention than black-and-white images.[27] In addition, vivid colors are more striking than lighter shades, with blue, red, and green among those most preferred.[28] Variety also helps maintain audience interest. A presentation accompanied by varied graphs and perhaps a few illustrative pictures will be more interesting than one in which the speaker projects list after list.

Enhancing Your Credibility

Using good presentational aids can enhance your credibility. When you use well-constructed aids, you show the audience that you care enough about your presentation to prepare carefully. A well-constructed graph, for example, shows listeners that you took pains with your preparation, and it also shows your concern for their understanding. A speaker who does not use presentational aids may be seen as less organized and less interested in audience understanding.[29]

These two very different photos illustrating the Elian Gonzalez story evoke contrasting reactions. They show how visual depiction can neutralize logical analysis to capture viewers' emotions and direct their thoughts.

In political propaganda, advertising, and other media products, we see these attempts to foster such leaps all the time. The intent is *not* to have the viewer logically analyze or think about the image. The intent is to capture the viewer's senses and then evoke certain emotions and thoughts.

Source: Reprinted with permission of the author and the Institute of General Semantics, publishers of *ETC: A Review of General Semantics*. n.d.

You also demonstrate your trustworthiness when you use presentational aids. Rather than ask your listeners to rely exclusively on your judgment, you let them "see for themselves" when you share an illustrative photo or chart the numbers.[30] As a result, listeners may see you as more open and honest, more willing to let them share in determining the true meaning of the data. Being seen as trustworthy and fair-minded boosts your **ethos**—a matter we explore further in Chapter 15.

Facilitating Extemporaneous Delivery

Presentational aids can assist delivery by serving as speaking notes. Speakers often use **bulleted lists** to help frame their message for the audience. As each item appears on the screen, it functions as a speaking outline, reminding the speaker of what he or she wishes to address next. Some speakers also find that these prompts alleviate communication apprehension.[31]

Of course, you should be aware of the risks of using bulleted lists. For one, a speaker can use too many lists. Constantly displaying and quickly removing list after list can confuse the audience, just as leaving one up long after it is useful can bore or otherwise distract them. A speaker also should avoid visuals that feature too many words, or that simply duplicate his or her oral presentation. If you put your whole outline on a transparency, listeners will concentrate on the display instead of on you.[32] At the other extreme, simply posting key words and failing to supply a needed graph, chart, or other aid may diminish your effectiveness and tarnish your image.

OPTIONS FOR PRESENTATIONAL AIDS

Preview. *Presentational support can range from the low-tech chalkboard to sophisticated computer-generated graphics. A variety of options can reinforce your speech visually or through sound.*

What kind of presentational aids should you use? The answer to this question depends on many factors—such as listeners' expectations, available equipment, and whether the room lends itself to the kind of aid you have in mind. If a room cannot be adequately darkened, for instance, you would be hard-pressed to use slides effectively. In short, consider what options will work best in the setting, for the particular audience and occasion, and for the content of the speech.

Computer-Generated Slide Shows

The classic movie *Star Wars* (1977) provides one of the best illustrations of the power of computer-generated slide shows. Near the film's end, Luke Skywalker and his fellow pilots receive instructions on how to destroy the Death Star. The military strategist projects computer-generated graphics to provide an overview of the enemy's massive battleship, close-ups of its surface, and diagrams of its infrastructure. The visual display—complete with movement—allows the speaker to provide this information to Luke and his squadron with clarity, impact, and efficiency.

What was once confined to science fiction has become commonplace. We regularly view full-motion weather maps, graphical depictions of what has happened on Wall Street, and computer-generated models of what likely occurred during a tragic accident or natural disaster.

Software such as PowerPoint puts this same power in our hands. We can easily create slides and integrate images, sound, and video clips. We can enter data and select the type of graph, chart, or other device that is best suited for conveying the information. Digital images we have taken, scanned, or found online (if eligible for **fair use**, as discussed at www.copyright.gov/) allow us to easily insert them into a slide show. We can even design our own graphics, such as the pictograph in Figure 13.5. In addition, a presentational aid created via computer can easily be modified or updated by simply editing or adding data, even during a live presentation.

Meeting rooms and classrooms often allow this option. If not, you might use the computer indirectly. Simply print out any graph, table, or other visual display that you have created using PowerPoint or even a basic word-processing program. Use it as a handout, print it on transparency stock for use with an overhead projector, or have a copy shop—such as Kinko's—print a poster-sized version.

In any case, you'll want to recognize the strengths of this technology and learn to use it competently and comfortably, following the guidelines we provide in this chapter. Also review the lighthearted cautionary notes in *Highlighting How* Not *to Use PowerPoint*. Because so many people use presentational software poorly (prompting many detractors), you will want to study the guidelines carefully.[33]

HIGHLIGHTING HOW *NOT* TO USE POWERPOINT

We have synthesized various authors' advice—some empirically based—to offer these surefire ways to irritate, insult, and otherwise alienate an audience when using PowerPoint (or any other slideware). We hope you enjoy this tongue-in-cheek look at some of the more common infractions. (And we bet you've seen many of them!)

1. Use a lot of slides. The more the better! Always have something posted onscreen.
2. Read your slides to your audience (and preferably with your back to them, facing the screen).
3. Give them a handout, before your speech, that duplicates the same slides you will read to them.
4. Write out what you intend to say, completely, with full sentences, filling up each slide as much as possible.
5. If you use bullets, post them all at once, rather than bring them up individually.
6. For textual content, use a font that is itsy-bitsy or otherwise difficult to read.
7. Avoid charts, graphs, and graphical icons. Stick to text-based content.
8. If you must use charts, graphs, or graphical icons, do not fret over their substance, such as whether they actually convey or clarify information central to the meaning of your speech.
9. Do not fret over explaining any chart, graph, or depiction. Let the audience figure it out on their own, while you are plodding ahead.
10. When using any graph, chart, or other visual content, simply flash it onto the screen, giving the audience only a millisecond or two to process it.
11. Use auto-timing features to advance your slides—never mind that you may have to speed up or slow down or even stop from time to time to keep pace with your slide show.
12. Present multiple ideas on a single slide, and do not bother explaining their connection or lack thereof.
13. Do not obsess over spelling, grammatical correctness, and the like.
14. Use lots of special effects. Always have something spinning or pulsating on screen. Accompany visual effects with sound effects—squealing and rat-a-tat-tats and the like!
15. Do not worry about a backup plan in case the slide show cannot be used. Simply insist on rescheduling your speech.
16. Remember: The screen is king! Serve the screen!

Selected Sources

Keith Barker et al., "To Read or Not to Read PowerPoint Slides," *Teaching Professor* 18 (November 2004): 4.

Jean-Luc Doumont, "The Cognitive Style of PowerPoint: Slides Are Not All Evil," *Technical Communication* 52 (February 2005): 64–70.

T. Trent Gegax, "Not Another PowerPoint Presentation!" *Newsweek*, May 9, 2005, E29.

Peter Norvig, "PowerPoint: Shot with Its Own Bullets," *Lancet* 362 (August 2, 2003): 343–44.

Geoffrey Nunberg, "The Trouble with PowerPoint," *Fortune*, December 20, 1999, 330–31.

Thomas A. Stewart, "Ban It Now! Friends Don't Let Friends Use PowerPoint," *Fortune*, February 5, 2001, 4.

Chalkboard or Whiteboard

The chalkboard (now commonly replaced by a whiteboard) remains a useful device for speakers who have no other option or who wish to compile a list while working cooperatively with an audience. The chalkboard allows the speaker to highlight information visually and put terms, diagrams, or sketches on the board as an explanation unfolds or a list develops. In addition, moving to and from the board allows the speaker to be active in communicating his or her ideas and can also help the speaker channel nervous energy.

Of course, the chalkboard has its limitations. Because it is so familiar to most audiences, it may seem less interesting or original than other types of visual aids. Poor handwriting and a tendency to look at the board rather than at the audience can also diminish a speaker's effectiveness. In most cases, it is wise to choose a different vehicle for visually enhancing your presentation.

Flip Charts

A **flip chart** is essentially an oversized writing tablet, offering the same advantages and disadvantages as chalkboards. Flip charts are commonly used in business, conference, and workshop settings. In these settings, speakers often use flip charts to record ideas generated during discussions or brainstorming sessions. If you use a flip chart, remember that you will need a tripod for displaying it.

Poster Board Drawings and Displays

Poster board drawings and displays can be constructed well in advance and can be either simple or sophisticated. They can also be colorful and engaging. The advantages end there, however. Aside from the time, effort, and artistic ability necessary to construct content for posters, they are clumsy to transport and handle. You must also make sure that you will be able to display them. For example, will a tripod be available? Will thumbtacks be necessary? If you decide to use poster boards, make sure to investigate the speech setting and prepare adequately.

Handouts

Handouts are helpful when listeners need to be able to recall information accurately for use at a later time, but they can distract when made available during a speech. Consider selecting another means of visual assistance *during* your presentation. For example, you might present a budget on screen and tell listeners you will be distributing a handout containing the budget at the end of your speech. If you distribute multiple handouts, you may want to use a different color for each handout, to better distinguish them.

Handouts can also help promote action. If you urge listeners to voice their opinion about a particular issue, you can provide a handout with specific contact information. By simplifying the task for listeners, you'll increase the chances that they will follow through.[34]

Objects

Sometimes an object is suitable as a presentational aid. For example, when raising awareness about methamphetamine, law-enforcement officers often display some of the common items used to manufacture the drug. Presenting the actual items makes the information more concrete, vivid, and memorable.

Avoid small items that need to be passed around. Circulating something while you are talking can present problems. First, only one person will have the object while you are describing it; other listeners will be in the dark. Moreover, the act of passing something around will distract your listeners, taking their attention away from your speech.

Models

Some speeches call for a model as a visual aid. When informing classmates about "green" architectural design, one student brought in a simple model she had constructed to illustrate how a wide overhang, positioned to work with the angle of the sun in winter versus summer months, can reduce energy consumption. Holding a flashlight at different angles, representative of the different seasons, she showed how the overhang allowed direct light in the windows during the winter months but shaded the windows in the summer, allowing only indirect light to enter.

Obviously, constructing a three-dimensional model requires skill and effort. Many times our students have been able to borrow models, thus simplifying the task.

Transparencies and Overhead Projectors

Overhead projectors, particularly those used to display transparencies, remain common in many meeting rooms. When computer projection is not available, they are the next best thing. They allow a speaker to project lists, figures, charts, graphs, and other information onto a large screen in supersize form. Transparencies are also easy to transport, allowing a speaker to use several in a single presentation. If your printer will not accept transparency stock, check with a local copy shop to see if they can assist. (*Note*: If you're lucky, the overhead projector may work with a regular, paper printout. Many classrooms have these next-generation projectors available.)

Audio and Video Materials

Some topics cannot be explained by using only words and still images. The quickness with which a particular crime can be perpetrated, the force and fury of a hurricane, and the precision and lightning speed of a Hellfire missile are but a few examples. In addition, in an increasingly media-oriented society, many listeners have grown accustomed to audio and video support. These sensory experiences, as we have noted earlier, help generate interest and involvement. Using them successfully, though, requires careful planning and preparation. In general, the more heavily your presentation depends on any form of technology, the more time and effort you must devote to creating your materials and making sure the appropriate equipment will be available and in working order. Also, the room in which you will be speaking must lend itself to using these aids effectively.

A speech that uses audio or video technology well can be extremely interesting and powerful. But if things go wrong—if pertinent clips cannot be located or the equipment malfunctions—the speaker may find it difficult to recover and achieve his or her purpose. Fortunately, most presentational software allows insertion of an audio or video clip, making for a more seamless and trouble-free multimedia presentation.

Be mindful that clips should be short because they are used to illustrate a single idea. Showing a clip that takes up most of your speaking time is not using a presentational aid; it is substituting an audiovisual presentation for a major portion of your speech. Be sure to consult your instructor if you contemplate using a clip. He or she will likely have particular guidelines regarding their use.

The force, speed, and destruction of a tsunami, as it rushes onshore, cannot be captured adequately with a single picture. A short video clip may be necessary.

In short, whenever you choose presentational aids, do so with the audience, setting, and occasion in mind. Find out which presentational options are available and expected in a particular setting—including your classroom. Once you know your options, you can select which one(s) will best serve your needs. Whatever the option, you will want to prepare your presentational aids for maximum impact.

GUIDELINES FOR PREPARING PRESENTATIONAL AIDS

Preview. *Presentational aids must be carefully planned and prepared for maximum impact. In this section, we offer some basic guidelines for constructing presentational materials, including practical tips and ethical considerations.*

Over the years we have seen speakers, in the classroom and in the community, use a variety of presentational aids. We have seen aids that were thoughtfully devised, those that made no real contribution to the speech, and some that actually detracted from the speech. In these latter instances, what was *supposed* to be an aid became a hindrance. A few guidelines can help ensure that you will prepare presentational aids that genuinely contribute to your presentation.

- ***Make sure the presentational aid you are planning to use is truly an aid.*** As you contemplate your speech, note places where a presentational aid would help. Keep in mind that an aid achieves one or more of the following:
  - adds clarity/promotes understanding
  - encourages interest or emotional involvement
  - helps the audience remember what you have said

  If a presentational aid does not fulfill one of these functions, it will not contribute to your speech; it may only distract the audience.

  There are exceptions, of course. A **prop** can sometimes add a healthy element to a speech. A prop is any visual or audio material that enlivens a presentation but is not integral to its success. For example, a student who advocated gardening as a means of rehabilitation for troubled teens had a flat of plants, a watering can, and a hand trowel arranged on a table, simply to set the mood. A prop may be appropriate if it does not distract listeners' attention from the content of the speech.
- ***Design your aid for quick processing.*** Your listeners should be able to grasp the meaning of the aid with minimal effort. When you are preparing *visual aids*, follow these guidelines:
  - *Make them large enough to be seen.* Your audience should never have to strain to see.
  - *Be smart with fonts.* Choose a font that is easy to read. **Sans serif** fonts, such as Arial and Helvetica, are excellent choices. Be sure the font style you select is supported by the computer you will use during your presentation. Otherwise, the text will be garbled. Size the characters so that they can be

read. In most font styles you will need to use at least an 18-point size, but you may need a 40- or 44-point font, depending on the size of the room. Experiment with bold versus plain characters to see which provides the most clarity.

- *Employ good contrast.* Contrast promotes clarity.[35] Start with a fairly light or fairly dark background color and choose an opposite (dark or light) color for the text (see Figure 13.8).[36] For computer-generated color slides, a dark blue background with white content works best.[37] Use the opposite scheme for black-and-white transparencies: dark content on a white/clear background. The contrast between dark and light helps prevent problems with **washout** of a projector's beam so you can leave the lights up a bit. When using colors, be mindful that they are less vivid when projected than they appear on a computer monitor or printout.
- *Consider using fill patterns (for example, dots or stripes) for sectors of a pie graph or bar graph.* Doing so will assist anyone who has trouble distinguishing colors.
- *Keep everything simple.* Use as few words as possible for labels and listings. Your audience should be able to process what is on the screen with a glance. Feature only those terms or expressions that categorize or highlight what you want to emphasize and discuss. Ignore rules, such as "limit each bullet point to six words, with no more than five bullets per slide."[38] Concentrate, instead, on using as few words as possible, rarely if ever exceeding one line per bulleted entry.[39] For other visuals, avoid complicated details; show only the essentials and illustrate only one idea in each chart, graph, or diagram.[40] The idea suggested by the content should be stated at the top.
- *Handwriting (as in the case of using a flip chart) should be large, legible, neat, and—if appropriate—color coded for clarity.*

When you prepare *audiovisual aids*, keep these guidelines in mind:

- *Sound and video recordings should offer sufficient quality for easy viewing or listening.*
- *Limit sound and video recordings to a brief clip that illustrates a single idea.*
- *Inquire about the feasibility of using audiovisual material.* Find out whether using this kind of aid is possible in the classroom or community setting in which you will speak.
- *Avoid razzle-dazzle.* Presentational aids are there to support, emphasize, and clarify key points and information. They are not a show unto themselves. They should not compete with (or merely duplicate) what you are saying. They should *support* your presentation, not *become* your presentation. Avoid too much distracting detail or too many effects, such as having a new element come

FIGURE 13.8
When creating a slide, keep things simple and use good contrast.

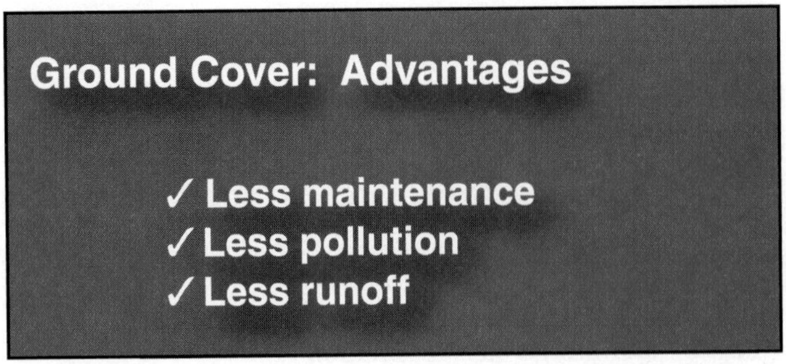
Ground Cover: Advantages
✓ Less maintenance
✓ Less pollution
✓ Less runoff

flying and spinning in, accompanied by a dramatic sound. Effects can be distracting, as well as annoying. Likewise, use moderation with any background or border for your slide. Your visual displays should not upstage you as the speaker.[41]

- ***Strive for professional quality.*** The best results can be achieved by computer. If you must rely on a poster, or some similar option, take great pains to make it of superior quality.
- ***Employ "silence."*** Avoid using too many visual displays or sounds. Display blank slides when you want listeners focused on your spoken words rather than on something on the screen. These can be your most important slides in a presentation, even helping to accentuate subsequent slides containing visual content; when a slide with content appears, the audience will be even more attracted to it.
- ***Anticipate problems.*** Much can go wrong, especially when technology and electricity are involved. It pays to have a backup plan, such as a handout of an all-important graph. In this way you can safeguard against potential disaster if the computer malfunctions or you encounter software incompatibility.

GUIDELINES FOR USING PRESENTATIONAL AIDS

Preview. *Presentational aids must be used properly for maximum impact. In this section, we offer some basic guidelines for using presentational materials, including practical tips and ethical considerations.*

Even when presentational aids are well designed, speakers sometimes fail to *use* them effectively. We have endless examples we could provide, such as presenters unintentionally blocking a projector's beam and others who placed transparencies upside down on a projector. You likely have witnessed similar mishaps. We offer the following guidelines to help you avoid embarrassment.

- *Practice!* Many speakers practice their speeches aloud several times, yet fail to practice using their presentational aids. Perhaps it never occurs to them, or they think it is not necessary. Maybe they just do not want to take the trouble. Practicing with those aids, though, allows one to present more smoothly and confidently. It also safeguards against unwelcome surprises (such as transparencies sticking together, which—by the way—can be eliminated by placing a sheet of paper between each one in the stack).
- *Preview in the venue.* Check out the actual setting ahead of time, if possible, to become familiar with any equipment you will use. Test for sight and sound—from different areas of the room. Audience members who must squint to see the print on a transparency or strain to hear the words on a recording can easily become frustrated and simply tune out the speaker. Too loud a volume, of course, can be annoying and disruptive. If you are using a projector on a rolling stand, you may need to move it farther away from or

closer to the screen for an appropriately sized image. Also note where you should stand to avoid blocking the audience's view or interfering with the beam. It is easy to unwittingly cast a large shadow on the screen. Determine, too, how well you will be able to see your speaking notes under the specific lighting conditions.

- *Have everything set to go.* For example, have presentational software positioned on the first slide (a blank slide, so not to interfere with your introduction) and audiovisuals cued to the proper spot with the proper volume and/or focus. Have transparencies stacked in the proper order. If using a marker, make sure it has ink. With all ready to go, you can relax and get off to a good start.
- *Use only when needed.* Any visual aid must be displayed long enough for the audience to process the information and make sense of it, then put away when it is no longer relevant to the point being made. Visual images attract attention and can easily upstage a speaker. Keep them out of sight until you are ready to refer to them. Remove or cover them when they are no longer needed. Doing so will help you maintain control of the audience's attention. (*Note*: If you are using presentational software, accomplish this by inserting blank slides between content slides, and at the beginning and end of the slide show.)
- *Help listeners focus.* The effective public speaker uses presentational aids so that the audience knows what to focus on, and the speaker helps them process the aids. If, for example, your visual aid has more than one part, direct the audience's attention to the part being discussed by pointing to it with your finger, a pencil, or a laser pointer. Rather than project an entire bar graph, you might display and discuss it one bar at a time to help the audience process the information. Presentational software (such as PowerPoint) may allow you to bring up one element at a time. Otherwise, you can duplicate

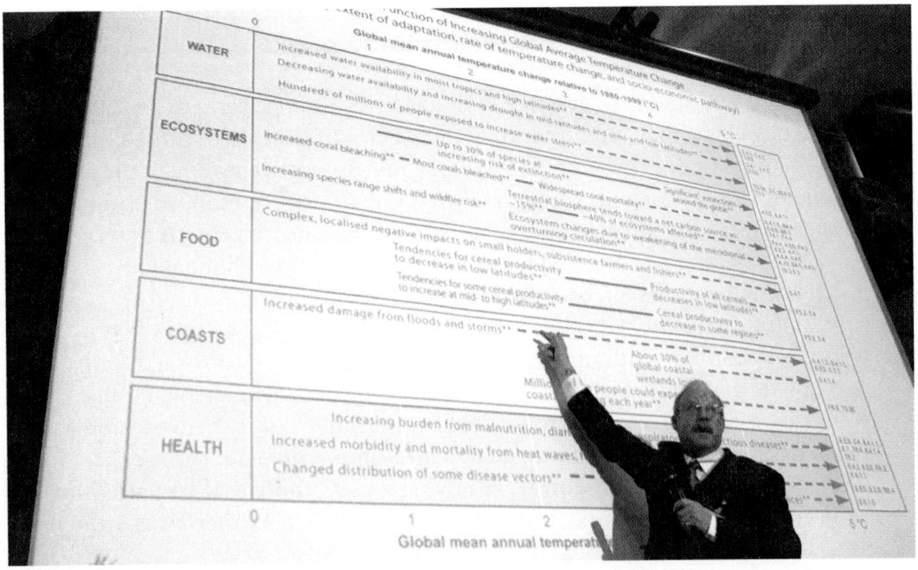

Many speakers do not use visual aids effectively.

a slide several times and then work backward, deleting one element at a time so that during your presentation a click forward results in an added element. If you are using transparencies, you can either produce ones that become progressively more complete and layer one on top of the other as you proceed, or create one complete transparency and use a cover sheet to expose its elements one at a time.

- *Stay connected with your listeners.* As you direct the audience's attention to your visual aid, monitor your bodily movement. Talk to your audience, not to the aid. Avoid turning away from them and facing the screen, for example. Be mindful, too, that even though a room may be darkened, the audience will be able to see you, especially after their eyes have adjusted to the dim lighting. It is important to maintain eye contact with the audience and to gesture and speak with them directly.
- *Use presentational aids ethically.* Speakers often create their own visuals. You might create, for instance, a simple graph to illustrate a statistical trend. Remember that you will need to reveal the source of the data—orally and with a written acknowledgment on the visual aid for the audience to see. Reveal the source on the bottom of the display, simply by noting, for instance, "*Source: Newsweek*, March 2, 2009." (Notice how the sample presentational aids presented throughout this chapter consistently cite their sources.)

HIGHLIGHTING PRESENTATIONAL AIDS AND ETHICS

- ***Recognize and respect the power of visual symbols.*** Media scholars such as James Potter have pointed out that visual symbols function as powerful means of influencing our ideas and behavior. Visuals can attract and sustain attention, enhance emotional appeals, and even function as proof. Using them judiciously, fairly, and along with other substantiating evidence, then, becomes paramount.
- ***Use presentational aids to promote understanding—never seeking to distract or mislead the audience.*** Listeners can be overwhelmed by too many handouts, too many or too fast-moving images, or by "aids" that cannot be easily viewed or heard with clarity.
- ***Select visuals that fairly represent the data you are presenting.*** Avoid using graphs that exaggerate trends, for example.
- ***Recognize that presentational aids function as a form of evidence, and follow the criteria for using evidence presented in Chapter 8.*** Openly reveal information sources, and always strive to present accurate, recent, and complete information.
- ***Openly acknowledge visual manipulation.*** If, for example, you "enhance" a picture to dramatize an effect or encourage an emotional reaction, you should alert listeners to whatever changes you have made. Changing colors, for example, can change the tone and feeling of an image, as when *Time* magazine electronically manipulated a cover photograph of O. J. Simpson to "achieve a brooding, menacing quality."[42]
- ***Make sure your speech can stand on its own—never substituting visual representations for sound argument.*** Although presentational aids can greatly enhance your speech, the substance of your speech should remain strong, even if technology were to fail you.

Source: W. James Potter, *Media Literacy*, 3rd ed. (Thousand Oaks, CA: Sage Publications, 2005).

Sometimes a speaker discovers an existing visual, such as a graph in *USA Today* or another publication. In most settings, it is permissible to use this material (blown up and transferred onto a transparency, for example), but you must acknowledge the source orally *and* on the visual. Before using existing visual material, be sure to ask your instructor whether it is permissible to use it in the classroom; she or he may want you to design your own.

In any case, remember that citing the sources you have drawn upon for creating presentational materials is part of being an ethical public speaker.

SUMMARY

- Most public speakers use presentational aids. In an increasingly visual society, using aids helps engage listeners' senses.
- From the speaker's perspective, using carefully prepared presentational aids is an excellent way to enhance a speech. By using presentational aids, the speaker can:
  - clarify and support main ideas.
  - facilitate understanding.
  - engage listener emotions.
  - deliver the speech effectively.
  - enhance his or her credibility.
- From the listeners' perspective, presentational aids can:
  - focus their attention on what is especially important in the presentation.
  - make the presentation more interesting and engaging.
  - aid in comprehension and retention.
- Almost any speech can benefit from the use of presentational aids. Diverse options abound, such as the chalkboard and computer-generated slide shows.
- Each aid should be carefully chosen and/or constructed, with the audience, the speech, and the setting in mind. In many speaking contexts, including the community and the classroom, listeners *expect* speakers to use presentational aids.
- In developing effective presentational aids, keep these guidelines in mind:
  - Make sure that each aid truly assists the presentation.
  - Design all aids for quick processing by listeners.
  - Strive for professional quality.
  - Learn to employ "silence" (i.e., avoid using too many visuals or sound displays).
  - Anticipate potential problems by always having backups.

- As you use presentational aids, follow these guidelines:
  - Practice your speech *with* the aids.
  - Preview the speaking venue, if possible.
  - Have everything set up, tested, and ready to go before listeners arrive.
  - Reveal presentational aids for as long as needed, but only for as long as needed.
  - Direct the audience's attention to the part of the aid you are discussing and explain/clarify as you move through the presentation.
  - Remain connected with the audience—avoid talking to the aid.
  - Use all presentational aids (graphs and images alike) with a concern for accuracy and integrity.

QUESTIONS FOR REVIEW AND REFLECTION

1. What are some of the ways that using presentational aids can help speakers?
2. How do presentational aids assist audience members as they try to listen attentively to a speech?
3. Can you think of any topic for which no presentational support would be needed? Explain.
4. What are some ways that graphs can be used to clarify and illuminate ideas and information?
5. What are the major presentational aids available to most public speakers? What are the potential advantages and disadvantages of each?
6. How might audience expectations influence your choice of presentational aids?
7. How will you go about developing your presentational aids to maximize the chances that they will enhance the effectiveness of your presentation?
8. What are the key principles you will want to remember as you are setting up and using your presentational aids?
9. In what ways might the motto "Less is more" be advisable for the speaker planning to frame her or his presentation with bulleted lists?

ENDNOTES

1. See, for example, Stephen Kinzer and Jim Rutenberg, "Grim Images Seem to Deepen Nation's Polarization on Iraq," *New York Times*, May 13, 2004, A11; "Abu Ghraib—An Indelible Stain on U.S.," *Christian Science Monitor*, May 7, 2004, 9; Charles Krauthammer, "Abu Ghraib as Symbol," *Washington Post*, May 7, 2004, A33; and Michael M. Phillips, "The Abu Ghraib Fallout: Marines in Iraq See Prison Photos Creating Enemies," *Wall Street Journal*, May 10, 2004, A10.
2. See *Newsweek*'s special report: "After the Tsunami," *Newsweek*, January 10, 2005, 22–45; and *Time* magazine's special report on Hurricane Katrina: "An American Tragedy," *Time*, September 12, 2005, 28–85. See *Time*'s special report: "Haiti's Tragedy," *Time*, January 25, 2010, 30–37.
3. See Robert D. McFadden, "Pilot Is Hailed after Jetliner's Icy Plunge," *New York Times*, January 15, 2009, www.nytimes.com (accessed January 23, 2010).
4. Doris A. Graber, "Say It with Pictures," *Annals of the American Academy of Political and Social Science* 546 (1996): 85–96.

5. Shu-Ling Lai, "Influence of Audio-Visual Presentations on Learning Abstract Concepts," *International Journal of Instructional Media* 27 (2000): 199–207.
6. Priti Shah and James Hoeffner, "Review of Graph Comprehension Research: Implications for Instruction," *Educational Psychology Review* 14 (2002): 47–51.
7. Graber, "Say It with Pictures," 86. Also see Carol L. Hodes, "Processing Visual Information: Implications of the Dual Code Theory," *Journal of Instructional Psychology* 21 (1994): 36–43.
8. Claire Morrison and William Jimmerson, "Business Presentations for the 1990s," *Video Manager* (July 1989), 18.
9. Lih-Juan Chanlin, "The Effects of Verbal Elaboration and Visual Elaboration on Student Learning," *International Journal of Instructional Media* 24 (1997): 333–39.
10. See, for example, Michael Grunwald, "How to Spend the Stimulus," *Time*, February 16, 2009, 20–22.
11. Michael P. Verdi and Janet T. Johnson, "Organized Spatial Displays and Texts: Effects of Presentational Order and Display Type on Learning Outcomes," *Journal of Experimental Education* 65 (Summer 1997): 303–17.
12. Ibid., 303–05.
13. Maria L. Berg and James G. May, "Parallel Processing in Visual Perception and Memory: What Goes Where and When?" *Current Psychology* 16 (1998): 247–83. Also see Lih-Juan Chanlin, "Visual Treatment for Different Prior Knowledge," *International Journal of Instructional Media* 26 (1999): 213–19.
14. Ibid., 253–54.
15. Joel Best, *More Damned Lies and Statistics: How Numbers Confuse Public Issues* (Berkeley: University of California Press, 2004), 45–46.
16. Berg and May, "Parallel Processing in Visual Perception and Memory," 254–62.
17. Best, *More Damned Lies and Statistics*, 45–46.
18. "Study Predicts Number of Fat Children Will Rise," *Bloomington (IN) Herald-Times*, March 6, 2006, C7.
19. Best, *More Damned Lies and Statistics*, 49. Also see Gerald Everett Jones, *How to Lie with Charts* (San Jose, CA: Authors Choice Press, 2000), 30.
20. Jones, *How to Lie with Charts*, 28–29.
21. Ibid., 48.
22. B. A. Chauvin, "Visual or Media Literacy?" *Journal of Media Literacy* 23 (2003): 119–28.
23. Graber, "Say It with Pictures," 90–93.
24. Read about Kim Phuc and the iconic photograph at www.nydailynews.com/news/national/2007/07/16/2007-07-16_napalm_victim_i_know_the_value_of_peace-2.html (accessed January 23, 2010).
25. Hodes, "Processing Visual Information," 36–40.
26. Elizabeth Keyes, "Typography, Color, and Information Structure," *Technical Communication* 40 (November 1993): 638–54.
27. It is important to remember that some listeners may be unable to distinguish among colors. In addition to the correctives we offer, there are other ways of dealing with this issue. See William Horton, *Illustrating Computer Documentation* (New York: Wiley, 1991), 219–44.
28. There is considerable research on effective color combinations that consider hue, value, and saturation. See Edward Tufte, *Envisioning Information* (Cheshire, CT: Graphics Press, 1990).
29. A study conducted at Indiana University found that an instructor received much better course evaluations when she projected keywords to outline her lecture's main points than when she gave the identical lecture without using visuals.
30. It is important to recognize that speakers *do* exercise judgment in choosing photographs, deciding how to display data, and so forth. The ethical speaker chooses never to knowingly distort information. Likewise, the ethical speaker is mindful of the *potential* for bias when using visual images to present information and offers support for arguments.
31. Joe Ayres, "Using Visual Aids to Reduce Speech Anxiety," *Communication Research Reports* 8 (1991): 73–79.
32. Chanlin, "The Effects of Verbal Elaboration and Visual Elaboration on Student Learning," 333–39.
33. Cornelius B. Pratt, "The Misuse of PowerPoint," *Public Relations Quarterly* 48 (2003): 20–26.
34. James Price Dillard, ed., *Seeking Compliance: The Production of Interpersonal Influence Messages* (Scottsdale, AZ: Gorsuch Scarisbrick, 1990).
35. Tufte, *Envisioning Information*, 26–64.
36. Amy C. Bradshaw, "Effects of Presentation Interference in Learning with Visuals," *Journal of Visual Literacy* 23 (2003): 41–68.

37. We have found this color scheme to be the best—even in rooms with minimal dimming—and it's also recommended by Jones, *How to Lie with Charts*, 215.
38. Jeremy Caplan, "Tips on Talks," *Time*, November 15, 2005, 93.
39. Jean-Luc Doumont, "The Cognitive Style of PowerPoint: Slides Are Not All Evil," *Technical Communication* 52 (2005): 64–70.
40. Chanlin, "Visual Treatment for Different Prior Knowledge," 213–19.
41. See, for example, L. Rieber, "Animation as a Distractor to Learning," *International Journal of Instructional Media* 23 (1996): 53–57.
42. Arthur Goldsmith, "Digitally Altered Photography: The New Image Makers," *Britannica Book of the Year: 1995* (Chicago: Encyclopedia Britannica, 1995), 135.

CHAPTER

14

Speaking to Inform

CHAPTER SURVEY

Functions of Informative Speeches

Types of Informative Speeches

Organizing the Informative Speech

How Audiences Learn from Informative Speeches

CHAPTER OBJECTIVES

After studying this chapter, you should be able to

1. Understand the different functions of informative presentations.
2. Compare and contrast the different types of informative speeches.
3. Use appropriate strategies to organize your informative presentations.
4. Describe the different ways that speakers can make information interesting and memorable to an audience.

CHAPTER OBJECTIVES (*CONTINUED*)

5. Organize and deliver an informative speech, following the guidelines for effective preparation and presentation.
6. Understand the ethical issues surrounding informative speaking.

As a professional and as a citizen, you frequently will be called on to deliver informative speeches. In informative speeches, you aim to educate or enlighten rather than persuade. You act as a teacher, not an advocate, providing facts and other information but not taking a stand on controversial issues. Thus, for example, an attorney may enlighten a group of concerned citizens about new laws governing the release of convicted child molesters. The leader of a task force may explain how his organization will generate and administer aid to newly arrived citizens displaced by a natural disaster. A security expert may brief the Parent-Teacher Association on new security measures for their school. A senior student may explain to a group of first-semester students the different ways of becoming involved with student government. You, too, will inevitably be called on to give informative presentations throughout your life—in professional, classroom, and community settings. You may speak in workshops, orientation and training sessions, business meetings, board meetings, and community forums.

Some informative speeches may be preliminary to persuasion. You may transmit information to build a common ground of understanding before urging the audience to support a given point of view or to act in a certain way. In these cases, providing information might become the foundation for persuasion. Nevertheless, when we speak of **informative speaking** in this chapter, we are thinking of a speech whose ultimate purpose is to help the audience gain some understanding of a theory, concept, process, program, procedure, or other phenomenon. Informative speakers do not advocate for any particular position in a public controversy, but rather seek to educate, enlighten, or inform audiences about matters they will find interesting or useful.

Listeners should be skeptical about speakers who attempt to disguise persuasive speeches as "merely" informative. A political candidate who just wants to "explain" her plan for improving Social Security really wants to *convince* you that her plan should be accepted. A builder who says he only wants to "inform" you of how a tract of land could be best developed probably wants to persuade you to accept his scheme for using the land. Speakers who disguise a persuasive message as informative by claiming to be "objective" are acting in an unethical manner. Furthermore, if an audience sees through the speaker's deception, that speaker's **ethos** is destroyed.

FUNCTIONS OF INFORMATIVE SPEECHES

Preview. *All informative speeches seek to foster audience understanding. Yet they may function in different ways. Different types of informative speeches may describe, demonstrate, explain, or report on some process or phenomenon of interest.*

When you give an informative speech, you often will be imparting new information—helping listeners understand something for the first time. On other occasions, you may present a new or different way of thinking about a familiar topic. Although informative speeches function in a variety of ways, they all impart ideas and information. Your goal as an informative speaker is to help your audiences gain understanding.

Sharing Ideas and Information

Perhaps the most common function of an informative speech is to provide information or to share ideas. The speaker may decide that the audience needs to be briefed, taught, or informed about some data, program, issue, or problem. He or she aims to stimulate learning and understanding.

For instance, one student decided to give an informative speech about biometric scanners. He was not trying to get everyone in the class to purchase one of these scanners. Rather, he wanted to make them aware of what a biometric scanner is, how the technology works, and the purposes it serves.[1] He described its history as an outgrowth of fingerprinting—a tool used in law enforcement since the early 1900s. In the final section of his speech, he discussed the ways in which this new technology has been adapted for use by civilians and businesses (such as allowing employees to clock in and out of work or for monitoring access to high-security areas).

Raising Awareness

We are surrounded by a dazzling array of information—from the Internet, television, newspapers, and lectures. It is impossible to take it all in. We have our own interests and information sources, and we tend to limit ourselves as we strive to become well versed on a manageable number of subjects. Inevitably, we overlook many important issues.

Sometimes you may wish to call an audience's attention to something worthy of their consideration. When you do that, you are saying, "Here is something worth knowing. This could prove helpful, enriching, or worthy of further exploration." One speaker may talk about twenty-first-century careers in health care made possible by advances in technology. Another might teach us about the history of New Harmony, Indiana, the site of two of America's most famous utopian communities in the nineteenth century.[2] Still another might describe the principles of feng shui, the Chinese science and art of creating harmony between inhabitants and their environment.[3] In these situations, the speaker's purpose is to raise your awareness, to arouse your interest and curiosity, and to educate or enlighten you. The goal, again, is to promote understanding, not change listeners' opinions about controversial issues.

Articulating Alternatives

Most complex issues can be addressed in a variety of ways. Often we are not aware of our options, or we may know of only a few possibilities when in fact many others exist. Sometimes a speaker will give a presentation aimed at helping listeners grasp the number, variety, and quality of alternatives available to them. A pharmacist may speak to a group of soon-to-be senior citizens about the alternatives among the new Medicare prescription drug benefit plans. An academic adviser may speak to a group of college students about the latest alternatives for completing a semester abroad while simultaneously completing the university's requirements for a service learning certificate.

In articulating alternatives in an informative speech, the speaker must be certain that he or she presents the information in a fair and unbiased manner. The speaker who secretly favors one program or plan but feigns objectivity with listeners commits a serious ethical breach. Trustworthy speakers should be able to set aside their own biases in the interest of helping listeners make good choices from among the available alternatives.

TYPES OF INFORMATIVE SPEECHES

Preview. *Speakers may be called on to present several different types of informative speeches. They may prepare and deliver informative speeches that describe, demonstrate, explain, or report on some process or phenomenon of interest.*

As noted earlier, the major purpose of any informative speech is to share knowledge and ideas with the hope of promoting the audience's understanding or competence. Even so, several different types of informative speeches exist. Understanding their differences can help you prepare and deliver each type more effectively.

The Speech of Description

Sometimes speakers want to describe a place, an event, or a person. By giving a **speech of description**, they hope to help the audience get a clear picture of their subject. Topics that may work well for this kind of speech include green spaces in urban planning, life on an Indian reservation, public transportation options in major metropolitan areas, the wetlands of North America, or experiences while serving in the army in Afghanistan.

If you decide to give a descriptive speech, you will want to take great pains with your language. Precision, color, and clarity are essential. You also might use presentational aids. A computer-generated slide show, for example, may be useful in showing the beauty of nearly extinct birds in North America, the grandeur of old homes in your community, or the ravages of war. However, avoid being overly reliant on visuals. Do the best you can to describe the subject of your speech without them, then add the visuals to clarify certain points or to help explain ideas too complex or difficult to communicate in words alone.

The Speech of Demonstration

If you aim to teach an audience how something works or how to do something, you might give a **speech of demonstration**. A lawn care expert, for example, might demonstrate how listeners can care for their lawns and gardens in environmentally friendly ways. An exercise science major might demonstrate fitness routines that can reduce stress and lower our health care costs. The leader of a Habitat for Humanity crew might demonstrate to a group of volunteers how to build a backyard storage shed. In each case, the speaker is demonstrating some sort of process.

The speech of demonstration may focus on application along with understanding. In some cases, the speaker wants the audience to apply certain principles or steps—to learn how to do something during the course of the speech. The exercise science major would want her audience to understand each step in the fitness program she advocates. The Habitat for Humanity crew leader expects that the volunteers who listened to her presentation will actually be able to build that shed by following the procedures and specifications she described.

On other occasions, the speaker may be describing a more complicated process, simply hoping that the audience will grasp that process, not necessarily perform it. For instance, a nurse in a hospital's cardiovascular unit might use a dummy to teach a group of heart patients about the preparations for their surgery, the surgery itself, and their subsequent recuperation. She wants her listeners to understand what to expect, not necessarily to do anything themselves.

Most speeches of demonstration involve the use of visuals to show, clarify, and make the information more memorable. Many use a sequential pattern of organization. To make sure the audience clearly understands the demonstration, you should allow ample time after your speech for questions from your audience.

This speaker is describing the complicated process by which uncontrollable wildfires develop. Understanding the process is necessary before changes in policy can be effected.

The Speech of Explanation

A speaker who wants to help the audience understand concepts that are complicated, abstract, or unfamiliar will give a **speech of explanation.** The explanatory speech demands that the speaker be knowledgeable about the topic and be able to explain it clearly to the audience.

A professor's lecture may be considered a speech designed to explain abstract or difficult concepts to students. Skilled teachers carefully define concepts being introduced, explain their importance or relevance, offer good clarifying examples, and give students the chance to show what they have learned through some kind of application exercise.

If you are giving a speech of explanation, you typically will define the key terms or concepts in the speech, explain their significance, and offer examples that illustrate them. One student speaker gave a speech whose purpose was to help his classmates understand the meaning of *Learning Disabled (LD).*[4] He began with the legal definition of LD, gave examples of some of the most common kinds of learning disabilities, explained how LD students were typically put in special education classes in the past, and concluded by examining how various types of disability influenced the student's ability to learn in different classroom environments.

When you illuminate a concept that your listeners previously did not understand, you can make a real contribution to their learning. Because explanations of unfamiliar or difficult concepts can be challenging, you again will want to allow plenty of time for audience questions after your speech.

The Informative Oral Report

In business, professional, and community settings, people are often called on to present an **informative oral report.** In some cases, these reports are given informally (perhaps even to one or two listeners) and may be quite brief. On other occasions, the speaker may be asked to prepare a more formal presentation, often technical in nature, to inform others in the organization of recent events, discoveries, or other vital information.

The need to give an informative oral report can arise in business and professional contexts, but are not limited to these settings.[5] For instance, one of this book's authors volunteers with a homeless shelter and recently attended a conference on "supported employment."[6] Upon her return, she was asked to present an oral report to the shelter's employment task force concerning the various forms of supported employment that were being used successfully by similar agencies around the state. Or, in a different context, a student was elected to the student senate and was later asked to represent the senate at an important meeting of the university's board of trustees. At this particular meeting, the trustees were considering several different plans for substantially increasing student tuition—a possibility that had attracted the concern of students and parents alike. The next time the senate met, the student was asked to present an oral report detailing the main features of each of the options the trustees were considering. To clarify the options, she prepared some handouts to accompany her presentation.

Informative reports often provide background that a group will use in making decisions or solving problems. For example, the report on "supported employment"resulted in the homeless shelter hiring a new caseworker to specialize in employment issues. Following a report (or even a series of reports), a group may go ahead with other business.

Although the primary purpose of a speech may be to report, explain, demonstrate, or describe, any speech can include a combination of these goals. For example, a speaker reporting on an innovative product would almost certainly devote part of that speech to describing the product or perhaps even demonstrating how it works. The various types of informative speeches are not always distinct, but they all share a common goal: increasing audience understanding.

ORGANIZING THE INFORMATIVE SPEECH

Preview. *Several different organizational patterns are particularly well suited for organizing informative speeches. You will want to select one of these patterns, and some examples provided in this section will help illustrate how those patterns may work with different informative topics.*

The basic principles of organization that we discussed in Chapter 9 should guide your efforts as you begin to organize your informative presentation. In that chapter, we presented a number of different organizational patterns, some of which work particularly well with informative speeches. These include chronological/sequential, spatial, categorical, and causal patterns. Table 14.1 presents guidelines for choosing an organizational pattern for an informative speech, along with some sample speech topics.

Here are some examples of how each pattern may work with a particular informative topic.

A Chronological Illustration

Suppose you are a history buff, with a particular interest in the role of women in U.S. history. For your informative speech, you decide to help your classmates gain an understanding of the women's suffrage movement that culminated in ratification of the Nineteenth Amendment. You choose to organize your remarks chronologically as you trace the women's suffrage movement over 72 years.

Thesis: *The passage of the Nineteenth Amendment was the conclusion of a long and difficult struggle.*

I. The fight for women's right to vote experienced high and low points during its first phase, in the mid-nineteenth century.
   A. The suffrage movement began at a women's rights convention held in Seneca Falls, New York, on July 19–20, 1848.
      1. This was the first large gathering of women to discuss women's suffrage.
      2. Elizabeth Cady Stanton's famous *Declaration of Sentiments* was introduced at the convention.

TABLE 14.1

GUIDELINES FOR CHOOSING AN ORGANIZATIONAL PATTERN

Pattern	Use When ...	Possible Topics
Chronological/ Sequential	You want to discuss an event, phenomenon, or concept over time *or* you want to show a step-by-step progression	■ Trends in public schooling from the twentieth century to the present ■ The changing demographics of the United States ■ How our voting procedures have evolved from paper-and-pencil to machine voting ■ How to organize a successful town hall meeting
Spatial	You want to help the audience visualize something you are describing *and/or* you want to describe something by moving from point to point through space	■ The spread of AIDS in Africa ■ Introducing the new, affordable health care clinic ■ Homeland security expenditures: regional differences ■ Options for bike trails in our community
Categorical	You want to emphasize the significance of the categories or divisions in some way *or* you are interested in a flexible approach to organization	■ Bringing education to prison: innovative programs ■ Health care options for low-income families ■ Environmentally friendly vehicles ■ New drugs for treating HIV ■ Award-winning service-learning programs
Causal	You want your audience to understand the factors (causes) that have contributed to some outcome (effects) *or* you want your audience to understand the impact (effects) of some problem or phenomenon	■ Factors that influence civic engagement ■ Media influences on women's body image ■ The decline of math scores in the United States ■ Academic misconduct on our campus

3. Although the convention was widely ridiculed in the press, women across America began talking openly about suffrage.

B. When the Civil War started in 1861, movement leaders Stanton and Susan B. Anthony had to make a tough decision—whether to continue to fight for suffrage or support the Union effort to abolish slavery.
   1. After much debate, the women decided to assist in the war effort.
   2. Women played diverse roles—serving as nurses, scouts, and spies for the army, and as seamstresses making uniforms and sewing bandages.
   3. They anticipated that their service would earn them suffrage at the end of the war.

C. After the War, Anthony and other movement leaders felt "betrayed" by the government.
   1. In 1870, the Fifteenth Amendment was passed, giving black men the right to vote.
   2. Anthony saw this amendment as simply expanding male suffrage—leaving women behind.
   3. Movement leaders did not agree among themselves about the next step, leading to a split in leadership.
      a. Lucy Stone, who wanted to work for suffrage through the individual states, separated from Anthony and Stanton, who wanted to fight for a constitutional amendment.
      b. The two groups of suffrage advocates led separate, unsuccessful campaigns over the next 20 years.

D. It was not until 1890 that the three women reunited to form the National American Woman Suffrage Association (NAWSA).

Transition: *After many turbulent years, the debate over women's rights finally reached Congress during the so-called Progressive Era.*

II. The fight for women's suffrage concluded with prolonged struggles in Congress and in state legislatures.

A. America's entrance into World War I in 1917 initially delayed the debate over suffrage.

B. In 1917, the House of Representatives began to debate the bill and finally passed the suffrage amendment in January 1918.

C. As the amendment moved to the Senate, suffrage leader Carrie Catt pleaded with senators to approve it, but they were too distracted by the war.
   1. A brutal flu outbreak in 1918 killed some senators opposed to the amendment and they were replaced by senators more sympathetic to the cause.
   2. In September 1918, however, the Senate finally voted on the amendment and it was narrowly defeated.

D. At President Woodrow Wilson's urging, a new Congress finally passed the amendment in 1919, some 71 years after the beginning of the suffrage movement.

E. Yet it was not yet the law of the land.
   1. For the Nineteenth Amendment to become law, at least 36 states had to ratify it.
   2. After a tough battle, Tennessee became the last state needed to win ratification.
   3. On August 26, 1920, the Nineteenth Amendment was finally signed into law.
   4. The women who had fought so long and so hard for the right to vote could finally celebrate a new amendment to the U.S. Constitution: "The right of the citizens of the United States

to vote shall not be denied or abridged by the United States or by any State on account of sex" (see Linda Monk's *The Words We Live By*).

By using this sort of chronological pattern, you would be able to dramatize the long and difficult struggle of the women who finally made it legal for females to vote.

A Spatial Illustration

At the Shalom Community Center in Bloomington, Indiana (a daytime shelter and resource center for those experiencing homelessness and poverty),[7] the volunteer coordinator often provides tours to prospective volunteers to familiarize them with the two buildings that house the center's programs. Each program is described in relationship to its spatial location, with the coordinator walking with the volunteers from place to place.

Thesis: *The Shalom Community Center addresses the immediate and long-term needs of people experiencing poverty and homelessness.*

I. The centerpiece of the Shalom Center is the hunger relief program and day shelter—located here, in the basement of the First United Methodist Church.
   A. Most volunteers work in the hunger relief program—preparing, cooking, and serving nearly 400 meals each day.
      1. In 2009, Shalom served nearly 80,000 meals, an increase of 21 percent over 2008.
      2. You can volunteer for the breakfast or lunch shifts.
   B. In the kitchen, you may have several different assignments.
      1. You might work here, at the food prep island in the middle of the room, where you will chop vegetables, assemble salads and casseroles, and prepare desserts.
      2. You also might be asked to cook, using the large commercial stove over here to fry hash browns, boil pasta, or roast meat.
      3. Or you could wash dishes, using the heavy-duty, fast-paced, industrial dishwasher located at one end of the kitchen.
   C. Some volunteers also work out in the dining hall, where there are several options for involvement.
      1. In the dining room, you might be asked to help serve food during one of the meals—standing behind the heated food server and putting food onto plates.
      2. Or you might go through the line and sit at one of the dining tables—eating and chatting with our guests.
      3. Some volunteers are also asked to help greet guests, answer their questions, and perhaps sign them up to use the washer and dryer located nearby.

Transition: *The Shalom Center not only offers nutritious meals and a safe daytime space for guests, it also connects them with other agencies and offers an array of personal services.*

II. A block down the street, in the basement of the First Christian Church, is Shalom's resource center and family program.
  A. One option for working in this part of the center is the Job Links program—a program run from a large computer-equipped room at the back of the building.
    1. At Job Links, you will gather information about our guests' backgrounds and employment needs.
    2. You will also help guests identify potential jobs in the area by conducting online searches.
    3. You can even help guests fill out job application forms, draft letters of application, and create résumés.
  B. Another possibility is working at the hospitality desk, located right inside the front door.
    1. In this reception and hospitality area, you will greet guests and help them connect with caseworkers and other resource persons.
    2. You will take and convey phone messages—with the utmost concern for confidentiality.
    3. You will sort and "deliver" mail to guests' mail slots.
    4. You will also sign guests in and out of the shower room and monitor the towel supply.
  C. Finally, you may want to work with the children and family programs, located at the bottom of the stairway—in an area separate from the hospitality and jobs areas.
    1. Here you might interact with children—playing games or reading to them.
    2. You might also talk with parents, offering a comforting ear and referring them to staff resources, as needed.

If the volunteer coordinator were to give this presentation away from the Shalom facilities, of course, she might organize her remarks differently, perhaps discussing volunteer opportunities in terms of types or categories of service. On site, however, she is wise to take advantage of the opportunity to tour the various areas and to organize her remarks spatially, explaining the particular program or service associated with each space visited.

A Categorical Illustration

A student speaker who was volunteering at a local food pantry, Mother Hubbard's Cupboard, decided to speak about the pantry in her public speaking class. After briefly tracing the history of the organization, she went on to use a categorical pattern of organization to discuss the agency's three major programs: the food pantry, nutrition education, and community gardening.

Community gardens allow low-income people to grow their own healthy foods.

Thesis: *Mother Hubbard's Cupboard provides healthful, wholesome food to people in need while educating them about nutrition and developing useful new skills.*

I. Mother Hubbard's Cupboard is perhaps best known for its food pantry, which emphasizes healthful, wholesome food.
   A. The pantry offers a welcoming and positive environment.
   B. On a typical day, MHC patrons take home bags full of fresh produce, organic dairy products, tofu, and locally baked breads.
      1. More traditional foods, such as canned goods, snack foods, and meats are also available.
      2. In 2008, MHC provided 86,758 bags of groceries to low-income people of our community (up 16 percent from 2007, according to *The Harvest Report*, March 2009).
         a. Seventy-two *new clients* were served each week—many asking for help for the first time.
         b. More than *one-third* of those served were children.
   C. Patrons at MHC enjoy free choice of food items.
      1. Each family gets one visit per week without a cutoff period.
      2. Each family can fill one grocery bag per visit.
      3. Every patron signs in but is *not* asked to justify their need.
      4. More than 85 percent of the volunteers at MHC are also patrons who wish to "give back" to the program by helping others.

Transition: *One major food source for the food pantry is another MHC program, the Community Gardens.*

II. The Community Gardening Program promotes self-reliance by teaching people how to grow their own healthy foods.
   A. In this innovative program, MHC teaches low-income patrons the life skill of organic gardening.
      1. Patrons plant, tend, and harvest produce that goes directly to the MHC food pantry and to their own kitchens.
      2. Over the eight years of this program, the MHC staff and volunteers have raised more than 12,000 pounds of organic produce for the MHC food pantry.
      3. In 2009, MHC will tend gardens at four different locations around the community and hold garden education workshops at these sites.

Transition: *Not all MHC educational programs focus on gardening. Their third major program emphasizes nutritional education.*

III. MHC's nutritional education program aims to help patrons with the knowledge needed to make positive, healthy food and lifestyle choices for themselves.
   A. The program includes workshops for patrons on such topics as Tomato Canning, Bread Baking, and Food as Medicine: Making Medicinal Soup.
   B. Seminars are also offered on such subjects as Natural Nutrition, Emotional Eating, and Healthful Weight Loss.
      1. Fourteen classes were offered in 2008.
      2. These classes attracted more than 160 participants.
   C. The program also features an in-store library on nutrition and health and offers recipes and handouts on nutritional issues for patrons to take home.
   D. The store also offers displays and labels to educate patrons about the foods on the pantry shelves, as well as a sample table to expose them to new foods.

After providing her classmates with an excellent overview of the MHC programs, this student speaker distributed copies of the most recent agency newsletter and responded to questions about her volunteer experiences and upcoming events.[8]

A Causal Illustration

Suppose you are a student at a university where there is no service-learning requirement. You have considered taking a service-learning course (in which performing community service is part of the class requirements),[9] but you are uncertain whether you have the time, or even if you would find taking it all that valuable. You decide to do some research on the topic and share your findings with your public speaking class.

Thesis: *Most students who take service-learning courses benefit greatly from the experience.*

This student describes his group's project at the Eighteenth Service Learning Annual Conference at the Albuquerque Convention Center on March 28, 2007.

I. Students benefit in a variety of ways from taking service-learning (SL) courses.
   A. An extensive study of more than 22,000 students by the Higher Education Research Institute at UCLA reported an impressive array of positive student outcomes.
      1. Students' academic performance was enhanced (measured in terms of GPA, writing skills, and critical-thinking skills).
      2. Positive values were also promoted, including stronger commitments to civic engagement and social justice.
   B. Other studies have reported that SL students learn more of the course content than those who take standard versions of the same class.
      1. These studies examined all kinds of courses, including political science, criminal justice, communication, environmental studies, business, anthropology, and sociology.
      2. This learning is further enhanced if students are asked to share their experiences with fellow students and reflect on their service experience through papers or personal journals.
   C. SL students also report that they intend to participate in service or volunteer activities after college.
      1. A 2005 study of hundreds of alumni suggests that these students' intentions are lived out after graduation, as most SL alums reported a high degree of involvement with service in their communities.[10]
      2. This post-graduation involvement seemed to depend on whether the SL course emphasized the theme of civic engagement.
   D. Finally, SL students are more likely than others to choose a career in service—in some cases switching majors in order to do so.

Transition: *Although all of these SL outcomes are positive, a couple of caveats are in order.*

II. Students benefit *most* from SL courses that are thoughtful and well designed.
   A. First, those courses must be grounded in realistic expectations.
      1. The typical SL class requires students to volunteer for two or three hours each week (at a minimum).
      2. SL classes typically have a few extra requirements, including reflection papers and journals.

B. It is also important to anticipate logistical challenges.
   1. SL students may have to coordinate their schedules with other students if the class is organized around group work.
   2. Some students may have transportation problems because some nonprofit agencies are off bus routes or far from campus.

C. Finally, approaching SL classes with genuine discipline and commitment is a must.
   1. Distribute service-learning hours throughout the semester.
      a. If students don't get started with their service early in the semester, they may have difficulty completing all their class assignments.
      b. It is tough to catch up once you fall behind in SL classes.
   2. Recognize, too, that the hours your instructor requires you to volunteer are actually a *minimum*.
      a. The more time you spend working with your agency, the more you will learn and the better you will perform in the class.
      b. Genuinely giving something back to the agency may require you to go the extra mile.

You might then conclude your speech by pointing out that when students approach service-learning courses with a real sense of commitment, both they *and* their agencies reap many benefits. At the same time, you might warn students who cannot make this kind of commitment that a SL course may not be right for them.

In choosing your organizational pattern, you should let your specific purpose be your guide. What pattern is most likely to produce the response you hope to get from your audience? What strategy is most likely to assist in raising their awareness and understanding?

HOW AUDIENCES LEARN FROM INFORMATIVE SPEECHES

Preview. *Listeners who are motivated to learn make the speaker's job much easier. Often, however, listeners are not as motivated as the speaker may hope, challenging the speaker to find ways to capture and maintain their interest and attention.*

Speakers need to understand the strategies available for heightening listener interest and helping them learn and retain information.[11] A good place to start is by thinking about the extent to which listeners are motivated to listen.

The Role of Listener Motivation

Perhaps you have heard the old saying: "You can lead a horse to water, but you can't make it drink." Any teacher will tell you that the learning process works like that: you can give people information, but you cannot make them learn. In informative speaking, much depends on the listeners and the understanding, beliefs, and attitudes they bring to the speaking situation. The ideal listener, as we discussed in Chapter 4, is the motivated listener, who is intrinsically interested in the topic, willing to work at listening, and eager to gain some new understanding. When listeners are motivated to listen and learn, the speaker's job is much easier.

Unfortunately, listening sometimes takes place under less than ideal circumstances. Sometimes audience members do not have the background they need to be truly prepared to listen. Sometimes they resent having to listen to a presentation. At other times, they are simply bored. Under these circumstances, trying to impart information can be challenging.

Usually when we are called on to make informative presentations, audience members are a mixed bag. Some are eager, some knowledgeable, and others less than motivated. Fortunately, there are things you can do to heighten listeners' interest and overcome, or at least reduce, initial inertia and apathy.

Capturing and Maintaining the Audience's Attention

A good place to begin is with thinking about how to interest listeners in what you are saying. Interest motivates learning.[12] In general, audience members respond with interest to ideas and information that are relevant, novel, and varied.[13]

RELEVANCE In Chapter 6, we discussed the importance of choosing a topic that the audience will perceive as relevant. You will want to address the matter of relevance right away, during the introduction of your speech. Why should your listeners want to hear about hybrid cars or the proposed community public transit system? One student speaker established her topic's relevance by pointing this out:

> Sometimes, as students, we get so busy that we don't pay attention to what experts are saying that might directly affect our lives. I know this happens to me sometimes. Do you ever imagine yourself being the victim of some kind of natural disaster—such as an earthquake, flood, wildfire, or tsunami? How about being the victim of a terrorist attack? After the September 11 attacks, many of us *did* harbor such fears, but over time, we tend to become less concerned. Recently, however, leaders of FEMA and the American Red Cross have argued that every household *should* have an emergency supplies kit. And this is especially so if we live in an area that is particularly vulnerable to disasters—natural or otherwise. As you know, our college is located in an area where wildfires are quite common. So, knowing what items to collect for this kind of emergency kit ought to be a real priority for us.

Of course, the issue of relevance needs to be addressed throughout the speech, not just during the introduction. If your listeners begin to think: "Wait a minute! What does this have to do with me?" they are probably not learning much.

NOVELTY Listeners are often interested in things they find startling, unusual, or new. Novelty gains attention. By contrast, overly familiar or trite topics are often perceived as boring or unimaginative. Of course, topics that lack novelty for some audiences may be fine for others. For example, a speaker who explains how to organize a town hall meeting to an audience of seasoned community leaders would likely find her listeners bored by what for them is an overly familiar subject. However, the same topic may be seen as novel and engaging by an audience of listeners who want to organize such a meeting but have had no experience doing so.

Whether information is seen as novel, then, will depend on the audience and what they already know. If listeners know little about urban sprawl, how to protect themselves from identity theft, or recognizing Internet scams, such topics may generate interest. With any topic, some initial audience interest must exist—a readiness to learn or at least openness to becoming interested. If a topic is seen as bizarre or irrelevant, the fact that it is also seen as new or unusual may not help much.

Sometimes a speaker can approach a topic in a novel or unusual manner and immediately gain the audience's interest. In general, when a speaker has personal, direct experience with a topic, he or she brings a fresh perspective that audience members may find interesting. During National Homelessness and Hunger Awareness Week in 2008, several citizens in a small Indiana community agreed to live on the budget of a federal food stamp recipient—$21.00 for the entire week. At the end of the week, they participated in a community forum, where they addressed the challenges they had faced and the feelings they had experienced. The speakers included the publisher of the local newspaper, the city's mayor, a county judge, a prominent real estate agent, and a woman living in poverty. By far, the most interesting and engaging presentation was given by the woman who had had actual, long-term experience with homelessness and poverty. As she spoke about her and her family's months of homelessness, her quest for a job that paid a living wage, and her ongoing struggles to provide nutritious food for her two children, the audience sat riveted. Because of her direct and extensive experience, she provided a unique perspective on the topic—one the audience found illuminating and memorable.

VARIETY Most of us have had the experience of being bored during others' presentations. Speakers can be predictable, overly repetitious, or dull. Longer presentations entail special challenges in this regard, because listener attention spans are often far too short.[14]

Speakers can help sustain the audience's interest by introducing some variety into their presentations. Variety is not so much about the topic chosen for a speech as it is about the *way* the speaker presents it. Variety can come in many forms. Speakers may mix humor with more serious speech segments. They may use presentational aids in imaginative ways to create visual variety. Speakers may deliver a speech with varied movement, voice, and facial expressions. In almost all cases, they will want to use a variety of supporting material, such as testimony, statistics, comparison, and narrative. These are just a few of the options available to help sustain listener attention. With variety comes unpredictability—a certain level of suspense and increased interest.

An effective speaker will use the attention-capturing factors just discussed in combination and in varying ways throughout his or her speech. For instance, a novel topic may be of little interest to the audience unless the speaker can show its importance. And even the most relevant topic may seem uninteresting if the speaker presents it in a less than engaging way. Establishing and maintaining the audience's attention should be an ongoing concern for every speaker.

Helping Listeners Learn

In Chapter 4, we discussed the audience's listening challenges, including ways to help them better attend to messages. If you are to give a successful informative speech, you have to present information that is, among other things, new to your listeners. However, new information can also be overwhelming if it is not presented effectively. You will want to pace yourself carefully, provide clarifying visual reinforcement as needed, and use language that is well adapted to the audience's knowledge level and background.

We have discussed other ways to promote listener attentiveness and learning throughout the book. You can help listeners learn when you limit the number of main points you address (as discussed in Chapter 9). You can also avoid presenting excessive details, and you should translate statistics into terms that listeners can understand (see Chapter 8). Ask yourself, "What is essential for my audience to understand, recall, and perhaps use?" When you decide that something is really important, you will want to emphasize it—perhaps by using restatement or repetition (Chapter 11), or by altering your delivery to signal its significance (Chapter 12). You will also want to take the time to respond to audience questions. For an extended discussion of the question-and-answer period, refer to Chapter 12.

Cognitive experts agree that people learn far more when they are actively involved in the learning process than when they remain passive, as we addressed in Chapter 4.[15] Do all you can to engage your audience. Choose a topic that allows you to share relevant, important, or novel information that you hope the audience will find intrinsically interesting. Beyond that, you may pose provocative rhetorical questions, quiz listeners with a few select questions that simultaneously review and reinforce what you covered, or ask them to write down their own questions.

With a longer presentation, such as a workshop, you may build in all sorts of activities, such as small discussion groups or exercises. You may present a concept, illustrate it with a brief video example, and then follow up with an audience discussion. You may provide breaks, which allow time for informal chitchat. Be creative in thinking of ways to get the audience involved. A student speaker recently gave an informative presentation on the barriers faced by disabled students at the university. As part of her presentation, she asked listeners to try to exit the room in a wheelchair, to climb a stairway with a leg brace, and to brush their teeth using only one arm.

Ethical Considerations

When you give an informative speech, be certain of the accuracy of the information you present. Invite the audience to investigate on their own, encourage them to listen to you critically and constructively, and give them sufficient time to raise questions and clear up misunderstandings. When they do ask questions, respond honestly, indicating when you are uncertain or when you need to do further research.

Of primary importance is the point we made earlier in the chapter: it is inherently unethical to camouflage a persuasive purpose by portraying it as informative. To reinforce the value of ethical communication, you may want to think of yourself as a teacher. Ask yourself, "What have I learned from good teachers?" You know that good teachers have your best interests at heart. They go to great pains to make sure that you understand. They strive to be clear as they make abstract concepts concrete through excellent examples. They watch for your confusion and respond to it. They ask you questions to make sure you are following. They encourage you to apply what you are learning, and they give you plenty of chances to ask them questions. Striving for this degree of integrity lies at the heart of effective and ethical informative speaking.

SUMMARY

- Informative speeches are commonly delivered in diverse business, professional, classroom, and community settings. The informative speaker aims to help listeners gain understanding.
  - Some speakers do this by sharing ideas and information, others through shaping listeners' perceptions, and still others by articulating alternatives.
  - Informative speeches may describe, demonstrate, explain, or report on some process, problem, or phenomenon of interest.
  - Informative speeches should *not* be given when the speaker's aim is really persuasive, as is the case with most issues of public controversy.
- Various organizational strategies are available for arranging informative speeches. Among the organizational patterns commonly used for informative speaking are the following:
  - chronological/sequential
  - spatial
  - categorical
  - causal
- Like other speeches, informative speeches can be approached in a variety of ways, depending on the speaker's specific purpose.
- Every informative speaker must be concerned with how listeners learn.
  - Unfortunately, not all listeners are intrinsically motivated to learn.
  - If listeners are resentful, bored, or simply not convinced that they need to know what is being discussed, they can present real challenges for the speaker.
- Listeners pay more attention if the speaker can show how ideas are relevant, useful, and novel.

- The informative speaker should think about the learning process and strive to help listeners acquire information with a concern for ethical communication.
  - Learning is more likely to take place if the speaker limits main points and details, provides emphasis, responds to audience questions, and actively engages the audience.
  - The ethical informative speaker avoids giving a persuasive speech under the guise of an informative one; uses reliable, accurate sources; openly acknowledges any existing bias; and presents alternatives in a fair-minded manner.

QUESTIONS FOR REVIEW AND REFLECTION

1. What is the overarching purpose of an informative speech? What are the three functions of informative speeches discussed in this chapter? Describe special issues and challenges associated with each.
2. What are some topics that may be appropriate for a speech of description? How important are visual aids to this kind of speech?
3. What are some of the key points you will probably want to address in giving a speech of explanation?
4. Think of one context in which a student may be called on to give an informative oral report. What would be the keys to effectiveness in this situation?
5. In what ways are the patterns discussed in this chapter (chronological/sequential, spatial, categorical, and causal) particularly well suited to informative speaking?
6. Describe the role of listener motivation in informative speaking.
7. What are some ways that speakers can make their ideas and information interesting to listeners? Which are the most important and why? Can you think of other ways of capturing the audience's attention?
8. The informative speaker's challenge is to help listeners learn. Think of your most effective teachers. What do they do to facilitate your learning in the classroom? How can you apply what they do to your own informative presentations?
9. When you listen to someone make an informative presentation, how do you determine whether he or she is communicating ethically? How will you ensure that *you* communicate ethically?

ENDNOTES

1. Paul Korzeniowski, "Fingerprinting Plays a Key Role in Biometrics Boom," *TechNewsWorld*, January 18, 2005, www.technewsworld.com/story/39467.html (accessed March 12, 2010).
2. See, for example, William E. Wilson, *The Angel and the Serpent: The Story of New Harmony* (Bloomington: Indiana University Press, 1984).
3. See, for example, Simon Brown, *Practical Feng Shui* (London: Ward Lock, 1997).
4. Lois Burke et al., *A Cornucopia of Strategies for Working with LD and ADD Students* (Columbus: Ohio State University Office for Disability Services, 1999).
5. Laura J. Gurak, *Oral Presentations for Technical Communication* (Boston: Allyn & Bacon, 2000).
6. "Supported employment" refers to providing employment and advancement opportunities for people with disabilities. See the Web site of the Association for Persons in Supported Employment (APSE), www.aspe.org/ (accessed March 12, 2010).
7. For more information about Shalom's mission, values, and programs, visit the Shalom Web site at www.shalomcommunitycenter.org (accessed September 12, 2009).

8. For additional information about Mother Hubbard's Cupboard, visit their Web site at www.mhcfoodpantry.org (accessed October 21, 2009).
9. See, for example, Wisconsin Department of Public Instruction, "Service-Learning: Definition and Philosophy," http://dpi.wi.gov/fscp/sldppage.html (accessed March 17, 2009). Service learning is often defined as a form of experiential learning where students apply academic knowledge and critical-thinking skills to address genuine community needs.
10. See, for example, Yan Wang and Robert Rodgers, "Impact of Service-Learning and Social Justice Education on College Students' Cognitive Development," *NASPA Journal* 43, no. 2 (2006): article 7; and various articles in the *Michigan Journal of Community Service-Learning*, www.umich.edu/~mjcsl/ (accessed March 18, 2009).
11. For a discussion of retention, see Robert L. Greene, *Human Memory: Paradigms and Paradoxes* (Hillsdale, NJ: Erlbaum, 1992).
12. Abraham Maslow, *Motivation and Personality* (New York: Harper & Row, 1954).
13. See Jane Blankenship, *A Sense of Style: An Introduction to Style for the Public Speaker* (Belmont, CA: Dickenson, 1968); Pamela J. Cooper, *Communication for the Classroom Teacher*, 5th ed. (Scottsdale, AZ: Gorsuch Scarisbrick, 1995); and James C. McCroskey, *An Introduction to Rhetorical Communication*, 7th ed. (Boston: Allyn & Bacon, 1997).
14. See, for example, Joan Middendorf and Alan Kalish, "The 'Change-up' Lectures," *National Teaching and Learning Forum* 5 (1996): 1–4.
15. See William J. McKeachie, *Teaching Tips: Strategies, Research, and Theory for College and University Teachers* (Boston: Houghton Mifflin, 1999), 209–15; and Martha Petrone, "Teaching and Learning as a Transactional Process," in *Teaching and Learning in College: A Resource for Educators*, 4th ed., ed. Gary S. Wheeler (Elyria, OH: Info-Tec, 2002), 143–76.

CHAPTER

15

Persuasive Speaking in a Democratic Society

CHAPTER SURVEY

The Anatomy of Public Controversy

Questions of Fact, Value, and Policy

Ethical Proof in Persuasive Speaking

Appealing to Audience Emotions

CHAPTER OBJECTIVES

After reading this chapter, you should be able to

1. Define *public controversy.*
2. Discuss what it means to *deliberate in good faith.*
3. Distinguish among the different types of persuasive issues.
4. Define *ethos* and discuss what contributes to strong credibility.
5. Discuss the techniques and ethics of appealing to an audience's emotions.

A student urges his fellow students to boycott a speech by a controversial public figure. A public health nurse urges the distribution of condoms in the local high schools. A lawyer argues against imposing limits on the amount of money juries can award in medical malpractice cases. The president of the United States goes before a national television audience to urge public support for his economic stimulus plan.

Every day all sorts of people—from ordinary citizens to world leaders—try to persuade other people. That is, they seek to influence the beliefs, values, or actions of others or "make the case" for a new policy or program. Sometimes we seek to persuade others about trivial or purely personal matters. We may persuade a friend to go to a movie, for example, or to take up yoga. In a democracy, however, persuasion takes on greater significance. Persuasion is the chief mechanism through which we select our leaders, determine our civic priorities, resolve controversies and disputes, and choose among various policies. Indeed, the reliance on persuasion rather than force is what most clearly distinguishes a democracy from a dictatorship.

Perhaps you have studied persuasion in an earlier public speaking class. Or you may have studied persuasion in psychology, sociology, or public relations and advertising. In all of these fields, persuasion is important, because to understand persuasion is to understand human behavior. In this chapter, however, we are concerned with the role of persuasion in our democratic society. We will consider, first, how public controversies invite persuasion and the sorts of issues we debate as citizens in a democracy. Then we will reflect on some of the means of persuasion and the ethical constraints on persuasive speaking in a democracy.

THE ANATOMY OF PUBLIC CONTROVERSY

Preview. *Persuasion is rooted in controversy. We deal with personal controversies every day, yet not all controversies involve matters of public importance. When you speak about a public controversy, you have a responsibility to do more than simply express your opinion. As a citizen, you have an obligation to back up your opinions with arguments and evidence and to "test" those opinions in the give-and-take of public debate.*

Prayer in the schools. The future of Social Security. Illegal immigration. Affirmative action. Medical malpractice. Gay marriage. All of these issues spark controversy because people have strong yet conflicting opinions. They are *public* controversies because they affect large numbers of people—and because they require that we make decisions about new laws, how to spend our tax dollars, or what programs and policies to adopt. Not every difference of opinion leads to a public controversy, of course. You may have disagreed with your parents over which college you should attend, or perhaps you have debated with your friends over where to go on spring break. These issues may be important to you personally, but they are not *public* controversies. **Public controversies** involve the choices we must make as *citizens*; they affect the whole community, perhaps even the nation or the world.

Some public controversies literally involve matters of life or death. When we debate whether the government should restrict stem cell research, for example, our decision could affect tens of thousands who potentially may benefit from such research. So, too, do people's lives hang in the balance when we debate whether to send more troops to Afghanistan or whether to intervene to stop the genocide in Darfur, Sudan. Obviously, not all public controversies have such grave implications. Sometimes we may address little-known controversies or try to call attention to problems that are only beginning to emerge or that we believe have been ignored or neglected. In just the past few years, for example, we have begun to hear warnings about the environmental hazards posed by "e-waste,"[1] and we also have heard predictions of an "acute shortage" of nurses and other health care professionals.[2] Every day new controversies arise over our nation's economic, social, and political problems and policies. As citizens in a democracy, we need to participate in public discussions of these important issues. Indeed, that's what it *means* to be a citizen in a democracy: participating in the process of governing ourselves.

Let us begin by reflecting on one recent controversy and what that controversy can teach us about the anatomy—that is, the shape, structure, and parts—of a public controversy. Since at least 2004, there has been an ongoing debate over the use of so-called enhanced interrogation techniques by U.S. military and intelligence personnel in the war against terrorism. Inspired by allegations of torture and prisoner abuse, this debate has pitted former members of the Bush administration against a variety of critics, including Bush's successor as president, Barack Obama. In one of his first major foreign policy addresses, Obama denounced "so-called enhanced interrogation techniques" as both ineffective and immoral. "I know some have argued that brutal methods like waterboarding were necessary to keep us safe," he stated. "I could not disagree more." In Obama's view, such methods not only were ineffective, they also undermined the "rule of law," alienated our allies, and served as a "recruitment tool for terrorists." They also risked the lives of American troops by making it less likely that enemy combatants would surrender and more likely that captured Americans would be tortured. Those who defended such techniques were simply "on the wrong side of the debate, and the wrong side of history," Obama concluded. "We must leave these methods where they belong—in the past. They are not who we are. They are not America."[3]

On the other side of the debate, former vice president Dick Cheney defended enhanced interrogation techniques as both lawful and effective. According to Cheney, the legal authority for such methods was drawn from the Constitution and from a congressional resolution authorizing the administration to use "all necessary and appropriate force" to protect the American people after the 9/11 attacks. Calling the interrogations "legal, essential, justified, successful, and the right thing to do," Cheney insisted that such methods were used only on "hardened terrorists" after "other efforts failed," and he claimed that the information gathered had prevented the "violent death of thousands, if not hundreds of thousands, of innocent people." From the start, Cheney explained, "there was only one focused and all-important purpose" for the interrogations, and that was to obtain "specific information on terrorist plans." That purpose was fulfilled and terrorist plots were "averted." To rule out such techniques in the future, Cheney concluded, would be "recklessness" and "make the American people less safe."[4]

Like most complex public controversies, the debate over enhanced interrogation techniques raised a number of factual questions: What sorts of interrogation techniques were actually employed by U.S. agents, and what exactly did waterboarding and other such methods entail? How many alleged terrorists were subjected to such techniques, and what information was obtained from them? How, if at all, did that information help the U.S. avert terrorist attacks? Was President Obama right that such methods hurt America's reputation around the world and helped to recruit new terrorists? Or was Dick Cheney right that such methods are necessary to save innocent lives? Beyond these questions, the whole controversy raised larger, more difficult questions about the legal and ethical justifications for such actions. Did the Bush administration have the legal authority to authorize such techniques? What rights, if any, do alleged terrorists have? In time of war, are such methods really necessary to protect our national security? Are they morally justifiable? These are just a few of the larger and more difficult questions raised by the debate.

In today's political climate, some people inevitably try to exploit such controversies for personal or political gain. On talk radio and TV debate shows, politicians and representatives of various special interests put their own spin on the controversy, eager to score points. For most Americans, however, the debate over enhanced interrogation methods was not about who might gain the political advantage. Rather, it was about finding the truth and striking the right balance between equally worthy goals—upholding our ideals and protecting our national security. Unfortunately, answers to the factual, legal, and political questions raised by the controversy were neither simple nor obvious. Historians will someday judge whether the Bush administration acted properly in authorizing such methods. But the larger issue will always be with us: how far are we willing to go to protect our national security?

As citizens in a democracy, we have a right to our opinions on such controversial issues. If we express those opinions in public, however, we assume a greater responsibility—the responsibility to back up our opinions with *arguments*. By speaking out in public, we also invite those who disagree to speak out as well. As citizens, we have an ethical obligation to treat those who accept that invitation with civility and respect. The success of our democracy depends on our willingness to subject our ideas to the scrutiny of public debate—and to be open-minded and respectful toward those who disagree.

Deliberating in Good Faith

In Chapter 2, we introduced the phrase **deliberating "in good faith."** Among other things, we noted that deliberating in good faith means making *arguments* in support of your opinions. But what is a good argument? What does deliberating in good faith mean in terms of your responsibilities as a speaker?

First, it means telling the truth, at least as you see it. Your beliefs and opinions may not always turn out to be right. Yet speakers who *deliberately* misrepresent the facts, or speakers who publicly advocate ideas that they do not *sincerely* believe, are not merely mistaken; they are unethical. They deserve to be condemned by all who value free and open debate.

Second, deliberating in good faith means backing up your personal opinions with evidence and reasoning. In public debate, you have an obligation not only to be honest but also to *prove* your claims. Proving one's claim does *not* mean presenting conclusive or irrefutable evidence; it does *not* mean settling an issue once and for all. It *does* mean presenting a *reasonable* argument—one at least worthy of serious consideration and further debate.

Third, deliberating in good faith means accepting your **burden of proof**, or your responsibility to meet a certain standard of proof in a particular context. Perhaps you have heard the phrase *burden of proof* in a legal context. In a courtroom, the burden of proof refers to the level of proof necessary for the prosecution to win the case. Depending on the type of case, that burden of proof may range from a *preponderance of the evidence*—the standard typical in a civil case—to the much higher standard required in criminal cases: *beyond a reasonable doubt*. In public debate, the burden of proof is not so clearly defined, yet we expect some advocates to meet a higher standard of proof than others. As in the courtroom, those who accuse others of wrongdoing carry a heavier burden of proof than those who speak in self-defense. Likewise, those who advocate new policies carry a heavier burden of proof than those who defend well-established or existing policies. After all, the existing policy at least has a track record, and there is always some risk to trying something new. In public debate, of course, there will be no judge to instruct you on your burden of proof or to enforce the rules of debate. Nevertheless, it is important that you understand the expectations and standards of proof in public debate.

The "rules" of democratic deliberation often break down on TV talk shows, where participants often seem more interested in "scoring points" than in finding common ground.

We will return to the practical implications of meeting your burden of proof in Chapter 16. For now, it is enough to understand that public deliberations, like courtroom debates, are governed by *rules*, and that you have an obligation to live up to those rules—however irresponsible or unconstrained other speakers may seem. No doubt you have seen speakers attack their political opponents, cite dubious evidence, or stir up ugly emotions. That does not mean that you should resort to the same tactics. The fact that other speakers may be irresponsible is all the more reason for you to uphold higher standards. By following the rules yourself, you can set a good example and contribute to more constructive public discussions.

QUESTIONS OF FACT, VALUE, AND POLICY

Preview. *Persuasive issues revolve around questions of fact (what is true), value (what is good or bad), and policy (what should be done in the future). As you prepare to speak about a particular topic, you need to identify the types of issues surrounding that topic and focus your efforts on unresolved controversies.*

Is That the Truth?

Normally we use the word *fact* to describe something that is already established as true. We think of a fact as something that we can just look up in a reference book, or that we can establish by using the appropriate measurement device. Thus, we may say that it is a fact that Peru is in Latin America, or that the thermometer shows that it is currently 80 degrees. These are not the sorts of facts that are disputed or debated. In ordinary usage, a fact is something that we all agree is true.

On many occasions, however, we disagree over the facts relating to a particular subject, and we discuss and debate what may or may not be "true." Does the Loch Ness Monster really exist? How many people are currently unemployed in this country? Do artificial sweeteners cause cancer or other health problems? What might account for the rash of hurricanes in recent years? These are the sorts of issues where the "facts" themselves are in dispute. Many public controversies, such as the debate over Social Security and disagreements over the causes of global warming, rest on unresolved or debatable questions of fact.

A **question of fact** typically involves issues of existence, scope, or causality. We would address a controversy over *existence* if, for example, we tried to persuade our audience that the ivory-billed woodpecker, a bird once thought extinct, still survives in remote forests of the American Southeast. Issues of *scope* may emerge in debates over the extent of the AIDS or swine flu epidemics, whereas we debate *causality* when we disagree over the causes of juvenile delinquency or the epidemic of obesity in the United States. In addition to involving different sorts of questions, some factual controversies may revolve around questions about the past (How many people have died from breast cancer in the past decade?), whereas others may involve predictions about the future (Will the Obama administration's economic stimulus plan really "save or create about 3.5 million jobs,"[5] as the president predicted?).

Whatever the specific focus, issues of fact invite empirical proof: real examples, statistics, and testimony from experts. In addition, we typically try to resolve questions of fact *before* we debate questions of value or policy. If, for example, we cannot agree about the existence or causes of global warming, it makes little sense to discuss possible solutions. Similarly, before we debate how best to control illegal immigration, we should first answer some factual questions: How many immigrants enter America illegally each year? Where and how do they enter the country? And what motivates them to enter our country? Again, an analogy to courtroom debates may help clarify how controversies evolve. In a criminal trial, lawyers must first establish the *facts of the case*. Only then do they debate which laws may have been violated. And only after the court has decided which laws have been broken do the lawyers debate the appropriate sentence. In public controversies, the rules are less clearly defined, but the process is essentially the same: only after we have resolved major factual controversies does it make sense to debate how to *evaluate* those facts or how to *act* in response.

Is This Good or Bad?

A **question of value** focuses on what we consider good or bad, right or wrong, just or unjust, and moral or immoral. Questions of value focus not just on what we believe to be true but what we consider appropriate, legal, ethical, or moral. Advocates of animal rights try to persuade us that medical experiments on animals are morally wrong, for example, whereas their opponents deem them necessary to save human lives. Opponents of affirmative action contend that racial preferences violate our commitment to equal treatment under the law, whereas those who favor such preferences deem them necessary to "level the playing field." In both of these debates, it is not so much the facts that are in dispute as the differing *values* applied to those facts by the advocates involved. That is what debates over questions of value are all about: determining how we should *evaluate* specific facts, ideas, or actions.

In the courtroom, the law itself provides the general principles we use to evaluate facts. Yet it is not always clear which laws ought to apply in a particular case, and the meaning of the law itself is sometimes in dispute. Once they have determined the facts of the case, for example, lawyers in a murder trial still might debate whether the facts warrant a verdict of first- or second-degree murder. Outside the courtroom, the general principles or criteria that we use to evaluate ideas and actions are even more diverse and unsettled—and hence more "debatable." During the civil rights debates of the 1960s, for example, some people condemned civil rights protestors for deliberately breaking local laws that segregated the races in the South, whereas the activists themselves invoked "higher laws"—the Constitution's guarantee of equal rights under the law, for example, or even "God's law" that all people are created equal.

How do we choose and define the general principles that we employ in value-level argument? In some cases, we may find such principles written down, in a law book or in a professional code of ethics. In other cases, we might rely on reputable authorities to suggest the appropriate principles or criteria of judgment. If we wish to judge the constitutionality of a particular action, for example, we may consult with experts in constitutional law. If we wish to render a moral judgment, we should consult whomever our audience considers a credible moral authority—a religious leader, perhaps, or maybe a well-known philosopher or ethicist. In many cases, the best source of the standards or criteria we employ in our arguments will be the audience itself, because such arguments work best when they are grounded in our listeners' own value system. Only after we have convinced our audience that a problem exists or that some wrong has been done does it make sense to move on to the highest level of controversy: issues of policy.

What Are We Going to Do?

A **question of policy** has to do with our actions in the future: there is something wrong in our world, and we need to correct it; we have a problem that needs to be solved. Yet even when we agree that we have a problem, we still may not agree about how best to solve it. In our complex society, we inevitably have a variety of options for addressing various problems. And in considering each option, we must weigh not only its effectiveness in solving the problem, but also its costs, its feasibility, and any advantages or disadvantages that it might have.

We may all agree that health care for the poor and the elderly in the United States is a serious problem. Yet we continue to debate how best to respond to that challenge, with some arguing for universal health care coverage and others emphasizing "market solutions." Likewise, everybody seems to agree that our current income tax system should be reformed. Still, we debate a wide variety of policy alternatives, ranging from minor changes in the existing tax code to a "flat tax" or even a national sales tax that would eliminate income taxes altogether.

Even when we all agree on a particular approach to some problem, we may find ourselves debating the details of implementation, financing, or administration. We may agree that wealthy nations should do more to fight the spread of AIDS in developing nations. But exactly how much should the United States contribute to that effort? And where should our aid go? People worried about the effects of television on children likewise seem to agree that there are problems with children's programming. But does that mean we need more government regulations? What should those regulations say, and how would they be enforced? And how, if at all, do we balance the protection of children with the rights of those who produce and advertise on children's television?

Whatever issues you address in your speeches, it is important that those choices be grounded in thorough research and analysis of both your topic and your audience. Controversies evolve, and what were once hotly contested issues may no longer be seriously debated. At one time, for example, there was a vigorous debate over whether cigarette smoking caused cancer—a question of fact. That debate has largely been settled now, of course, and the debate over smoking now revolves around questions of policy: Should smoking be banned in public places? Should tobacco companies be held liable for the health costs of smoking? In some persuasive speeches, your sole purpose may be to establish a disputed fact, whereas in other speeches your audience may already agree that there is a

HIGHLIGHTING THE CHALLENGE OF PERSUADING OTHERS

Will You Give Blood?

In a study of people's willingness to donate blood, a group of people reluctant to donate were asked to listen to a powerfully emotional speech, delivered by a young hemophiliac. Immediately following the speech, a questionnaire revealed an impressive change in attitudes. More than 70 percent of those who previously had refused to give blood now indicated that they *would* donate blood if given the opportunity! Yet when presented with official Red Cross blood donation sign-up cards, nearly 80 percent of those with "changed" attitudes *still* declined to commit themselves to the *action* of donating blood. The authors concluded from this study that it is one thing to change minds, but motivating people to *act* is an even greater challenge.

Source: Patricia Hayes Andrews and John E. Baird Jr., *Communication for Business and the Professions*, 6th ed. (Madison, WI: Brown & Benchmark, 1995), 359–60.

serious problem. In that case you can focus on policy issues. Whatever your purpose, it should reflect the current status of the public controversy surrounding your topic and the existing beliefs and opinions of your audience.

It is important that you make your persuasive purpose clear when you speak. Given the nature of the issue and the existing attitudes of your audience, do you hope merely to stimulate their thinking—that is, to get a previously apathetic or indifferent audience thinking about some issue? Or do you aspire to change minds, persuading listeners to reconsider their opinions? Do you hope to inspire your audience to *act* in some way, perhaps by sending money to some organization or volunteering their time? As you might imagine, getting people to *do* something is harder than getting them merely to *think* about it.

ETHICAL PROOF IN PERSUASIVE SPEAKING

Preview. *Since ancient times, theorists of persuasion have recognized three broad categories or "modes" of proof: ethos, pathos, and logos. We begin our examination of the modes of proof with ethos, or ethical proof, which refers to the audience's perception of the credibility of the speaker and his or her sources. The constituents of strong ethos are trustworthiness, competence, open-mindedness, and dynamism. Your ethos as a speaker is shaped by the content, structure, and clarity of your speech, as well as by how you deliver it.*

Have you ever responded negatively to a speech, only to realize later that it was not the content of the speech that bothered you so much as the person delivering it? Perhaps the speaker's voice irritated you. Or maybe the speaker belonged to a group or political organization that you have always distrusted. On the other hand, you also may have followed someone's advice not so much because he or she gave you good reasons, but because that person seemed knowledgeable and trustworthy. For good or ill, we all react to messages on the basis not only of what is said but of who says it. The perception we have of a speaker—whether that perception is positive or negative—constitutes that person's **ethos**.

Students of public speaking have long recognized the importance of ethos. More than 2,000 years ago, the Greek rhetorician and philosopher Aristotle identified the speaker's character, intelligence, and goodwill as the most important dimensions of ethos.[6] Later theorists have refined and modified Aristotle's original concept. Modern researchers have stressed that ethos depends on what an audience *thinks* about the speaker, and they have noted that people sometimes have very different *perceptions* of the same speaker. In other words, ethos refers to *how the audience sees a speaker*, not to the *actual intelligence or character* of that person.

Ethos is not the same thing as *ethics*, but the two concepts are closely related. A person who is perceived as ethical has a good reputation—a positive ethos—even before he or she speaks. If, on the other hand, a speaker is perceived as unethical, we may find his or her arguments less convincing. Whatever the speaker's true ethical commitments, what is important, again, is our *perception* of the speaker.

Scholars have identified a number of specific qualities that influence our perceptions of a speaker.[7] From their research, we can identify four major qualities that contribute to a positive ethos:

- Trustworthiness
- Competence
- Open-mindedness
- Dynamism

Trustworthiness

Not surprisingly, we are more likely to listen to and act on the advice of people who we think are honest and concerned about our best interests. Integrity and sincerity are qualities that inspire trust. Suppose, for example, you were trying to decide what to do after you graduate from college. An older friend whom you trust—a teacher, a counselor, or a family friend—suggests that you join Teach for America, a program in which college graduates spend two years teaching in public schools in economically depressed areas. You are more likely to take this advice if you believe this person not only is knowledgeable about the program but also has your best interests at heart.

Public figures rely heavily on perceptions of their trustworthiness to persuade listeners. In 1986, for example, President Ronald Reagan survived the biggest scandal of his career by assuring Americans that he had *tried* to do the right thing in trading arms for American hostages being held in Iran. In his 1987 State of the Union address, Reagan admitted his mistakes but asked Americans to *trust* that his intentions were good:

> I have one major regret. I took a risk with regard to our action in Iran. It did not work, and for that I assume full responsibility. The goals were worthy. I do not believe it was wrong to try to establish contacts with a country of strategic importance or try to save lives. And certainly it was not wrong to try to secure freedom for our citizens held in barbaric captivity. But we did not achieve what we wished and serious mistakes were made trying to do so.[8]

Reagan survived the so-called Iran-Contra affair because of his strong personal ethos.

In contrast to Reagan, former Illinois governor Rod Blagojevich inspired only skepticism and ridicule when he denied any wrongdoing following his arrest on federal corruption charges on December 9, 2008. Accused of trying to "sell" the U.S. Senate seat vacated by Barack Obama, Blagojevich was impeached and removed from office by the Illinois Senate, despite more than a dozen TV appearances and a 47-minute "closing argument" before the senators themselves. In proclaiming his innocence, Blagojevich insisted that he "never, ever intended to violate the law" and that there was "no evidence, zero" that he had done so. Yet not a single senator rose to his defense, and he was impeached by a unanimous vote, with senators calling him a "devious, cynical, crass, and corrupt politician" and an "unusually good liar."[9] In *Time* magazine, commentator James Poniewozik compared Blagojevich to one of those "bad auditioners" on *American Idol*: "Does he really have no idea how he sounds to other people? It's gotta be an act, right?"[10] Obviously, Blagojevich had lost the *trust* of his fellow politicians; his personal ethos had been destroyed.

"Oh, he's jolly enough, but he lacks credibility."

Source: Reprinted by permission from www.cartoonstock.com.

Competence

Listeners tend to be persuaded more easily by speakers they view as intelligent, well informed, or personally competent. Whether it comes from native intelligence, education and training, or firsthand experience, the perceived competence of a speaker is a crucial part of his or her ethos. Indeed, competence is often *the* issue in a political campaign, especially when candidates have similar views on policy questions. During the 2008 Democratic primaries, for example, Senator Hillary Clinton frequently reminded voters that she would not need "on-the-job training" if elected president; she would be "ready on day one." Insisting that the country needed "someone the world knows, looks up to, and has confidence in," she ridiculed rival Barack Obama's suggestion that living in Indonesia as a child had given him special insight: "Now voters will judge whether living in a foreign country at the age of 10 prepares one to face the big, complex international challenges the next president will face.... I think we need a president with more experience than that."[11] Later in the race, Clinton again emphasized "the experience gap," comparing Obama's lack of foreign policy experience to that of George W. Bush. "We've seen the tragic result of having a president who had neither the experience nor the wisdom to manage our foreign policy and safeguard our national security," she told an audience at George Washington University. Sharing the stage with a half dozen retired military officers who had endorsed her, she concluded: "We can't let that happen again."[12]

Obama eventually won the Democratic nomination, of course, but Senator Clinton made a close race of it by emphasizing her more extensive experience. Concerns about Obama's youth and lack of experience—his *competence* to assume perhaps the most challenging job in the world—was also the chief reason many voters supported his rival, Senator John McCain, in the fall presidential election.

Open-Mindedness

A speaker's ethos is also influenced by the impressions listeners have of his or her open-mindedness. Nobody is perfectly objective. But audiences value speakers who seem willing to enter into a dialogue with them, consider various points of view, and search for common ground. Of course, open-mindedness is not the same thing as empty-headedness; a speaker has the right to take sides in a controversy. Yet that does not mean you should distort, exaggerate, or otherwise misrepresent the facts in order to "win" a debate. Nor does it give you the right to dismiss the arguments, values, or feelings of those who disagree with you. To say that you are open-minded is not to say that you are wishy-washy. Rather, it means that you are willing to listen to others, treat their ideas fairly, and remain open to changing your own mind.

In many situations, a speaker's objectivity may be in doubt because of his or her position or reputation or because of the setting in which the speech takes place. In one of the most celebrated political speeches in history, for example, an African-American congresswoman from Texas, Barbara Jordan, rose above partisanship and displayed a broader vision of America's promise at the 1976 Democratic National Convention. Jordan had become famous for denouncing President Richard Nixon during the Watergate scandal, and some of her fellow Democrats might have expected a hard-hitting attack on the Republicans. Instead, Jordan talked about our common dreams and the need for all Americans to come together. Perhaps that's why we still remember the speech as one of the great keynote addresses in U.S. history:

> I could easily spend this time praising the accomplishments of this party and attacking the Republicans but I don't choose to do that.
>
> I could list the many problems Americans have. I could list the problems which cause people to feel cynical, angry, frustrated; ... I could recite these problems and then I could sit down and offer no solutions. But I don't choose to do that either.
>
> The citizens of America expect more. They deserve and they want more than a recital of problems.
>
> We are a people in a quandary about the present. We are a people in search of our future. We are a people in search of a national community.
>
> We are a people trying to solve the problems of the present ... but we are attempting on a larger scale to fulfill the promise of America. We are attempting to fulfill our national purpose; to create and sustain a society in which all of us are equal.[13]

Jordan was hardly an objective observer. But by rising above partisanship, she earned a positive ethos and delivered a memorable speech.

Dynamism

Finally, audiences look positively on speakers who are energetic and enthusiastic—in other words, speakers who are dynamic. Dynamism does *not* mean ranting and raving; it means achieving the right balance of enthusiasm and self-control. It means setting the right tone for the occasion. On the one hand, we want to avoid appearing as if we're just "going through the motions," talking in a colorless monotone or focusing more on our notes than our listeners. On the other hand, we do not want to scream at our audience, engage in distracting physical gyrations, or appear so intense that our audience thinks we're crazy! A dynamic speaker takes the middle ground, enthusiastically engaging the audience but not getting "in their face." Dynamic speakers talk *with* us rather than *at* us, communicating their personal enthusiasm but remaining "tuned in" to our reactions.

Perhaps the best way to summarize ethos is to consider the constituents of ethos as a kind of filter: everything you say is filtered through the *perception* your audience has of your trustworthiness, competence, open-mindedness, and dynamism. What an audience thinks of a speaker—a speaker's ethos—may sometimes be determined by his or her past reputation. Still, every speech you give should be viewed as an opportunity to improve your ethos by demonstrating that *you* have the qualities we admire in a speaker.

Contextual Factors Influencing Ethos

Although ethos is always important, the characteristics that we admire in speakers may vary from situation to situation. If we attend a public briefing on a new sewage treatment plant, we may not care whether the engineers explaining the system are dynamic or open minded. We are more concerned with whether they can explain technical aspects of the plant clearly—whether they have the *competence* to answer our questions about how the plant would work. Conversely, we do not expect everybody at a town hall meeting to be an "expert" on every issue. Not everybody understands the tax laws or the best way to build a bridge. In that situation, we may be more concerned with the speaker's sincerity and open-mindedness, or we may be impressed by how passionately a speaker feels about some issue.

The context in which we speak thus determines what characteristics—or combination of characteristics—will affect our ethos. As speakers, we should reflect on which of the constituents of ethos may be most important to our audience in particular situations. As citizens, we should ask whether other speakers have *earned* the right to be trusted. Do they have the experience or knowledge necessary to speak convincingly about that issue?

In today's society, we are often tempted to judge the credibility of speakers by standards that have little to do with their background or training. Many advertisers, for example, pay celebrities to endorse their products. Perhaps it makes sense for a basketball player to endorse Nike shoes or a nutritional supplement. But even before his recent troubles, should we have believed golfer Tiger Woods when he said he drove a Buick? Is stock car driver Mark Martin really a good source of information about the prescription drug Viagra? Should we believe Jessica Simpson when she tells us that Proactiv cured her acne? Does anybody really believe that Paris Hilton eats at Hardee's? Perhaps these celebrities have at least *tried* some of the products they endorse. But it would be naïve to think that their endorsements have *nothing* to do with the millions of dollars they get from advertisers.

Sometimes factors beyond our control influence our ethos. When Barbara Bush was invited to deliver a commencement address at Wellesley College in 1990, some students objected that she had done nothing to earn that honor—besides marrying the president of the United States! To her credit, Bush won over her audience by establishing her *own* ethos during the course of the speech. Reflecting on the challenges of balancing life as a mother with her role as First Lady, Bush concluded on a humorous note: "And who knows? Somewhere out in this audience may even be someone who will one day follow in my footsteps, and preside over the White House as the president's spouse. And I wish *him* well!" Disarming her critics with humor, Mrs. Bush also communicated that she shared the ideals of her listeners at this progressive women's college.

Depending on the context, the same individual may have both a highly negative and a highly positive personal ethos. Indeed, many public figures who might be described as *controversial* or *polarizing* provoke widely differing audience responses, depending on the situation. On February 28, 2009, for example, talk show host Rush Limbaugh received an "immense ovation" when he delivered the keynote address at the Conservative Political Action Conference (CPAC) in Washington, D.C. Given his frequent criticisms of "feminazis" and "environmental wackos," however, he likely would have been greeted differently at a conference of the National Organization of Women (NOW) or the Sierra Club. Similarly, the Reverend Jesse Jackson Sr., a longtime civil rights activist, received a warm reception when he addressed an NAACP fund-raising dinner in Detroit on May 3, 2009. Had he been speaking instead to the American Jewish Committee, the reception might have been cooler. Among many in that group, resentment still lingers over Jackson's 1984 reference to Jews as "Hymies" and New York City as "Hymietown."[14]

At this point in your life, you probably do not have to worry about how past indiscretions or media coverage of your life might affect your ethos. Each time you speak, however, people will form impressions of you, so it is important to keep the components of ethos in mind. Even in your speech class, your listeners will draw conclusions about your trustworthiness, competence, open-mindedness, and dynamism. It is never too early to begin building a positive ethos—a reputation that will help you succeed as a public speaker.

So what can you do to enhance your ethos? There is no simple answer, because everything you do affects how listeners perceive you: the content of your speech, how you organize and deliver it, and how you come across in general. But here are some specific things you can do to strengthen your ethos.

Show Your Audience That You Share Their Experiences and Concerns Showing your audience that you have something in common with them can strengthen your ethos. We feel a natural attraction to people we perceive to be like ourselves;

HIGHLIGHTING CREDIBILITY

Credibility is an essential quality for any politician. Following are excerpts from former presidential candidate Mike Huckabee's speech to the Republican National Convention in September 2008. Notice how, even in defeat, Huckabee worked to build a positive ethos. By recalling the civil rights movement and expressing "great respect" for Barack Obama, he demonstrated his goodwill, open-mindedness, and devotion to the good of the country. In recalling his childhood, he reminded his audience of his humble background and displayed his sense of humor. At the same time, he countered negative images of Republicans as a party of the rich.

> I grew up at a time and in a place where the civil rights movement was fought. I witnessed firsthand the shameful evil of racism. I saw how ignorance and prejudice caused people to do the unthinkable to people of color not so many years ago.
>
> So I say with sincerity that I have great respect for Senator Obama's historic achievement to become his party's nominee—not because of his color, but with indifference to it. Party or politics aside, we celebrate this milestone because it elevates our country. . . .
>
> I really tire of hearing how the Democrats care about the working guy as if all Republicans grew up with silk stockings and silver spoons. In my little hometown of Hope, Arkansas, the three sacred heroes were Jesus, Elvis, and FDR, not necessarily in that order.
>
> My own father held down two jobs, barely affording the little rented house I grew up in. My dad worked hard, lifted heavy things, and got his hands dirty. The only soap we had at my house was Lava.
>
> Heck, I was in college before I found out it wasn't supposed to hurt to take a shower.
>
> I'm not a Republican because I grew up rich, but because I didn't want to spend the rest of my life poor, waiting for the government to rescue me.

Source: Reprinted by permission from Associated Press, Mike Huckabee's Speech.

we assume they face the same challenges and understand our values and priorities. In a speech advocating tougher penalties for academic cheating, for example, one student recalled the pressures he faced from his parents and others to get into a top college. At one point, he even admitted that he had been tempted to cheat in order to get better grades. The students listening to the speech not only appreciated the fact that he had chosen a topic relevant to their lives, but also that he shared their aspirations and understood the pressures they faced. He was honest enough to admit that he had been tempted to cheat, yet in the end he realized he would only be cheating himself.

Bolster Your Own Ethos with the Ethos of Reputable Experts When you give speeches on highly complex or technical issues, you need information from experts. Your own lack of expertise on such topics need not undermine your ethos. When your remarks are supported by acknowledged experts, your audience can still have confidence in what you say. In Chapter 8, we explored the use of expert testimony in detail, but it is worth repeating here that you can bolster your own ethos by using testimony from highly reputable sources.

Suppose, for example, that you wish to speak about the effects of global warming on weather patterns or our forest ecosystems. You may have read many newspaper articles on the subject, and perhaps you have seen several reports on TV about global warming. But does that make you an expert? Of course not. You are a concerned citizen, and perhaps you know more about the topic than the average citizen. Yet if you hope to be persuasive, you will still need testimony from reputable experts who have studied the problem, such as meteorologists, climatologists, and ecologists.

If you are genuinely open-minded, you might modify your own opinion as you read what leading experts have to say. But once you have settled on a firm opinion, the challenge is to communicate not only your conclusions but also the support for those conclusions among credible experts. Remember, a speech is not like a term paper, where you can just footnote your sources. Rather, you need to identify and establish the credibility of your expert sources *in the speech itself*. That means both naming your sources and saying something about their credentials. If you were to cite Paul Krugman in a speech on the economy, for example, you might identify him as an economist from Princeton University who won the 2008 Nobel Prize in Economics. By offering support from such renowned experts, you can improve your own ethos and make a more convincing argument.

Strengthen Your Ethos with Personal Experiences You are more likely to be seen as trustworthy and competent when you have had some personal experiences related to your topic. A student aiming to help her audience understand the plight of Native Americans, for example, established her special qualifications to speak on this topic by recalling how she had spent three weeks on an Indian reservation, helping to repair homes and paint schools. Of course, you will not always have firsthand experience with the issues you speak about. But when you do, you can strengthen your ethos by talking about those experiences during your speech.

Strive to Be Clear and Interesting Listeners appreciate speakers who make their ideas understandable and who make an effort to keep the audience interested. Unfortunately, some speakers try to impress their audiences with "big words." Other speakers make little effort to organize their speeches so they're easy to follow. Still others may come across as not genuinely interested in their topic. We have all sat through dull and uninteresting speeches—speeches that hardly provide any "news" at all. Typically, it is not the topic itself that is the problem, but the failure of the speaker to consider ways to make the speech relevant and interesting to the audience.

You should try to gain the audience's attention and interest from the outset of the speech—in your introduction. Doing so will create a positive first impression and improve your ethos throughout the speech. You also can maintain interest by citing examples that are familiar and relevant to the audience and by speaking directly *to* your listeners rather than staring down at your notes or reading from a manuscript. Sometimes little things make all the difference in whether your audience develops a positive view of your ethos. For example, some speakers hurt their ethos simply by talking too long. By showing respect for your audience's comfort and expectations, you can enhance your ethos as a speaker.

Show Your Audience That You Have Considered Different Points of View If you can show that you have considered other people's opinions, you will demonstrate that you are both well informed and open minded. For example, when the Indiana Department of Natural Resources proposed to allow a two-day hunt to thin the deer population in Brown County State Park, both experts and ordinary citizens disagreed passionately over the idea. A student who favored the hunt began by showing that she initially shared some of the emotions felt by its opponents. She then explained how she changed her mind after carefully researching the topic and discovering all the problems caused by overpopulation, including disease and starvation in the deer herd. Recalling her interviews with both activists opposed to the hunt and DNR officials who favored it, she showed that she was open minded and had considered both sides of the controversy.

Develop a Dynamic, Audience-Centered Delivery How you deliver your speech can dramatically affect your ethos. One student with a well-prepared speech about crime and personal safety on campus failed to persuade her audience simply because listeners had trouble hearing her. Sitting in the back of the room and straining to hear what she said, some listeners became irritated and concluded that the speaker did not care about her topic or her audience. Likewise, speakers who use lots of vocalized pauses—*um, you know*, and *like*, for example—often irritate listeners and come across as inarticulate or even unintelligent. Finally, speakers who read rapidly through written manuscripts, without looking up or otherwise engaging listeners, may damage their own ethos.

Jesse Jackson's dynamic delivery contributes to his ethos as a sincere, passionate, and committed advocate for the poor and disadvantaged.

Dynamic speakers remain continuously in touch with their audiences. Speakers who seem bored or detached cannot expect their audiences to respond any differently, and they may even be perceived as less knowledgeable, competent, or sincere. As we suggested in Chapter 12, you can do many things to improve your presentational skills. Vocal variation, gestures, facial expressions, and eye contract can all have a significant effect on your ethos. Delivery may not be the only thing affecting your ethos, but it *can* make a difference.

Your audience's perceptions of your intelligence, character, and sincerity can affect the success of your speech. You can bolster your ethos by establishing common ground with your audience, by showing that you share common concerns, by citing reputable experts, and by mentioning personal experiences that qualify you to speak on your topic. Making an effort to be clear and interesting also can help your ethos, as can showing your audience that you have considered other points of view.

FOCUS ON CIVIC ENGAGEMENT

Former Presidents Bury the Political Hatchet

Former presidents George H. W. Bush and Bill Clinton were bitter political rivals. During the 1992 presidential campaign, Bush attacked the challenger Clinton as a "tax-and-spend liberal" and, in a moment of uncharacteristic enthusiasm, even called him a "bozo." For his part, Clinton portrayed Bush as an agent of "privileged private interests" who had betrayed his promise of a "kindler, gentler" America. In his speech accepting the Democratic nomination in 1992, Clinton accused Bush of talking a "good game" but having "no game plan to rebuild America."[15]

Imagine people's surprise, then, when the two former presidents joined hands to lead the U.S. relief effort following the devastating tsunami in the Indian Ocean in 2004. Traveling to the region and raising millions of dollars to help rebuild homes and lives ravaged by the disaster, they used their ethos as former presidents and political rivals to make an important point: that even in an era of deep partisan divisions, people can work together for the common good. Following Hurricane Katrina, the two again joined forces to raise more than $120 million for rebuilding colleges and churches devastated by the storm. Since they joined forces, the pair have raised more than $1 billion for disaster relief. The "Odd Couple," as Barbara Bush has characterized them, not only did a lot of good but became close personal friends. Perhaps most important, they took advantage of their return to the public spotlight—and their unique ethos as former presidential rivals—to call for more civility and cooperation in American politics. "Politics doesn't have to be uncivil and nasty," Clinton said when asked about his relationship with Bush. "Where we can find common ground and do something for the future of the country and for the future of our children and grandchildren, I think we ought to do it."

Sources: Michael Duffy, "Bill Clinton and George H. W. Bush," *Time*, April 30, 2006, www.time.com/time/magazine/printout/0,8816,1187350,00.html (accessed June 5, 2009); ABC News, "People of the Year: Bill Clinton and George H. W. Bush," *World News Tonight*, December 27, 2005, http://abcnews.go.com/WNT/print?id=1446477 (accessed June 5, 2009).

Finally, you can enhance your ethos by delivering your speech effectively. By engaging your audience and delivering your speech with enthusiasm, you can show your listeners that you care about them and your topic.

APPEALING TO AUDIENCE EMOTIONS

Preview. *If you hope to persuade your audience, you need to engage their emotions. You can engage your audience's emotions by using strong, affective language; appealing to shared social values; providing specific, vivid details; helping listeners visualize what you are talking about; and comparing the unfamiliar to the familiar. Emotional appeals, however, can be deceptive and manipulative and should never substitute for reasoned arguments.*

Listeners who have little or no emotional involvement in a speech are unlikely to be persuaded. Appealing to an audience's emotions is fundamental to motivating them to act. You may even need to engage their emotions to get them to listen in the first place. If people are not emotionally involved in a topic, they are not likely to be persuaded.

Former president Ronald Reagan, the Great Communicator, used emotional appeals to build support for dramatic increases in military spending.

Fear, pride, anger, reverence, hatred, compassion, and love—all are strong emotions and can be powerful motivators. Successful speakers know that listeners can be motivated by appeals to such emotions. Notice how former president Ronald Reagan, the Great Communicator, used emotional appeals to build support for dramatic increases in military spending. Instead of reviewing the "long list of numbers" in his proposed defense budget, Reagan tapped into some of his audience's most basic emotions: their fear of nuclear war, their sense of "duty" as citizens, and their concern for protecting their children and their "free way of life":

> The subject I want to discuss with you, peace and national security, is both timely and important.... This subject involves the most basic duty that any president and any people share, the duty to protect and strengthen the peace.
>
> At the beginning of this year, I submitted to the Congress a defense budget which reflects my best judgment of the best understanding of the experts and specialists who advise me about what we and our allies must do to protect our people in the years ahead. That budget is much more than a long list of numbers, for behind all the numbers lies America's ability to prevent the greatest of human tragedies and preserve our free way of life in a sometimes dangerous world.[16]

Appeals to your audience's emotions should never substitute for logical arguments backed by the best available evidence. Yet neither can we ignore the role of emotions in human behavior, especially if we hope to motivate our audience to act. A speech that fails to engage the audience's emotions is dull, boring, and lifeless—and, in the end, probably ineffective. The techniques that you might use to engage your audience emotionally include using affective language, identifying shared values, using vivid detail, using visualization, and comparing the familiar with the unfamiliar.

Use Affective Language

Affective language is strong language that plays on emotions or feelings. Consider the emotional impact of this series of statements:

"I see things differently from Bob."
"I think Bob's statement is not quite accurate."
"What Bob is saying seems misleading."
"Bob is a liar."

To call Bob "a liar" is to use strong, affective language. As a persuader, you must choose your language carefully, taking into account both the ideas you hope to convey and the emotional connotations of the words you choose.

Eugene Debs, a four-time Socialist candidate for president of the United States, passionately opposed American involvement in World War I. Yet in the pro-war climate of the time, Congress passed laws that limited the right to criticize the government's war policies. Along with other antiwar speakers, Debs was arrested, tried, and convicted under one of these laws, the Sedition Act of 1917. At his sentencing, however, Debs refused to tone down his rhetoric. Instead, he spoke out against social injustice in emotionally powerful language:

> Your Honor, years ago I recognized my kinship with all living beings, and I made up my mind that I was not one bit better than the meanest on earth. I said then, and I say now, that while there is a lower class, I am in it, while there is a criminal element, I am of it, and while there is a soul in prison, I am not free....
>
> I am thinking this morning of the men in the mills and the factories; of the men in the mines and on the railroads. I am thinking of the women who for a paltry wage are compelled to work out their barren lives; of the little children who in this system are robbed of their childhood ... and forced into the industrial dungeons, there to feed the monster machines while they themselves are being starved and stunted, body and soul. I see them dwarfed and diseased and their little lives broken and blasted because ... money is still so much more important than the flesh and blood of childhood....
>
> Your Honor, I ask no mercy and I plead for no immunity.... I never so clearly comprehended as now the great struggle between the powers of greed and exploitation on one hand and upon the other the rising hosts of industrial freedom and social justice.
>
> I can see the dawn of a better day for humanity. The people are awakening. In due time they will and must come to their own.[17]

By today's standards, Debs's language may seem excessive, with its references to children "robbed" of their childhood, "dwarfed and diseased," their "little lives broken and blasted." But nearly 70 years later, César Chavez used equally powerful language to describe the plight of migrant farm workers in America. In a speech before the Commonwealth Club of California on November 9, 1984, Chavez began by describing what motivated him to fight for the rights of migrant workers:

> Today, thousands of farm workers live under savage conditions, beneath trees and amid garbage and human excrement near tomato fields in San Diego County.... Vicious rats gnaw at them as they sleep. They walk miles to buy food at inflated prices and they carry in water from irrigation ditches.
>
> Child labor is still common in many farm areas. As much as 30 percent of Northern California's garlic harvesters are underaged children.... Some 800,000 underaged children work with their families harvesting crops across America. Babies born to migrant workers suffer 25 percent higher infant mortality rates than the rest of the population. Malnutrition among migrant workers' children is 10 times higher than

> the national rate. Farm workers' average life expectancy is still 49 years, compared to 73 years for the average American. All my life, I have been driven by one dream, one goal, one vision: to overthrow a farm labor system in this nation that treats farm workers as if they were not important human beings. Farm workers are not agricultural implements; they are not beasts of burden to be used and discarded.[18]

Chavez, of course, had statistics to back up his argument, but it was his affective language—his references to "savage conditions," living amid "garbage and human excrement," sleeping among "vicious rats," and so on—that gave his speech its emotional power.

Identify Shared Values

Listeners are more likely to be emotionally engaged when their own values are involved. You should aim to identify values that you and your audience hold in common and show how your ideas or proposals relate to those values.

After Barack Obama's election in November 2008, the new president used a series of weekly "transition" addresses to rally the country behind his election, reminding Americans of their shared values and urging them to work together. In his first address just a week after the election, he observed that "in America we can compete vigorously in elections and challenge each other's ideas, yet come together in service of a common purpose once the voting is done." America faced "the most serious challenges of our lifetime," he reminded his listeners, but America was "a strong and resilient country," and he expressed confidence that those challenges could be overcome if we could just "put aside partisanship and work together as one nation." A week later, he again suggested that we would "rise or fall as one nation, as one people" and argued that the difficult challenges of our time would "require not just new policies but a new spirit of service and sacrifice, where each of us resolves to pitch in and work harder and look after not only ourselves, but each other." Finally, in his third transition address, he put the burden of success or failure squarely on the people, calling on every citizen to recapture that spirit of service and devotion to the common good that historically had made America great:

> The survival of the American Dream for over two centuries is not only a testament to its enduring power, but to the great effort, sacrifice, and courage of the American people. It has thrived because in our darkest hours we have risen above the smallness of our divisions to forge a path toward a new and brighter day. We've acted boldly, bravely, and above all, together. That is the chance our new beginning now offers us, and that is the challenge we must rise to in the days to come. It is time to act.[19]

Not everybody embraced Obama's vision of a "new beginning," of course. But many did respond to his call to service, especially young people. On the official White House Web site, hundreds of people posted their personal stories of volunteer service on a page titled "How Are You Delivering on Change?" In Boise, Idaho, a young man named Samuel served as a junior volunteer in a local medical center. In California, a full-time college student, Samantha, helped children with special needs and learning disabilities. In Pennsylvania, a high school student named Vanessa helped organize blood drives, visited nursing homes, worked at a soup kitchen, and rang bells for the Salvation Army.[20] These and many other stories appeal to our emotions because they invoke shared values: sympathy for the less fortunate, devotion to the common good, and even personal sacrifice and courage.

Use Vivid Detail

Using vivid detail can help your audience relate to your topic emotionally. Listeners respond more positively to concrete examples and stories than they do to abstractions. Charities that raise money to help sick children, for example, often choose a "poster child" who represents thousands of other children afflicted with disease. The "poster child" gives potential donors somebody they can relate to emotionally—a real person whose suffering they can help relieve.

Persuasive speakers engage audiences' feelings by reinforcing their ideas with vivid details. Before the Civil War, for example, the great abolitionist speaker Frederick Douglass painted a vivid portrait of slavery that enhanced the emotional power of his most famous speech, "What to the Slave is the Fourth of July?" Highlighting the irony of slavery in a nation founded on liberty and freedom, Douglass argued logically that slavery violated America's most sacred ideals. At the same time, however, he made a powerful emotional appeal by vividly describing the scene with a slavemaster, "armed with pistol, whip and bowie-knife," drove a group of a hundred men, women, and children "from the Potomac to the slave market at New Orleans." "Mark the sad procession," Douglass continued, "as it moves wearily along," with an "inhuman wretch" barking out orders. "Hear his savage yells and his blood-chilling oaths, as he hurries on his affrighted captives!" Describing the sights and sounds of the scene in vibrant detail, Douglass encouraged his listeners to "see the old man, with locks thinned and gray," and the young mother, "shoulders . . . bare to the scorching sun, her briny tears falling on the brow of the babe in her arms." He also urged his listeners to "see" a girl of thirteen, "weeping, yes, weeping, as she thinks of the mother from whom she has been torn!" As the march continues, "heat and sorrow" finally overcome the slaves, and "suddenly you hear a quick snap, like the discharge of a rifle; the fetters clank, and the chain rattles simultaneously; your ears are saluted with a scream, that seems to have torn its way to the center of your soul!" That "crack," Douglass explained, "was the sound of the slave-whip; the scream you heard, was from the woman you saw with the babe." Douglass concluded with still more vivid images of the auction itself, where the men were "examined like horses" and the women "rudely and brutally exposed to the shocking gaze of . . . slave-buyers." As the slaves were "sold and scattered forever," Douglass helped his listeners to "hear" the "deep, sad sobs" of the "scattered multitude."[21]

Use Visualization

In an effort to make messages more concrete, speakers often employ **visualization,** or techniques that allow their audience to "see" what they are talking about. By helping your listeners visualize some problem or crisis, you can stir their emotions, get them thinking more deeply about your topic, and clarify information that otherwise may be vague or unclear.

The most obvious way to help your audience visualize a problem is, of course, to show them a picture. Perhaps you have heard the old saying "Pictures don't lie." In an age of digitally altered photos, of course, pictures *can* lie. But used responsibly, they can communicate information that may be difficult to communicate in words. Pictures also can have a strong emotional impact on your audience. "A picture is worth a thousand words," goes another old saying, and that is especially true for pictures that surprise, shock, scare, or otherwise engage our emotions.

Dramatic visual images of the 9/11 terrorist attacks have a powerful effect on our emotions, provoking shock, horror, and anger toward those responsible.

Sometimes pictures can provide powerful, irrefutable evidence for a speaker's claims. During the Cuban Missile Crisis in 1962, for example, the American ambassador to the United Nations, Adlai Stevenson, confronted the Russian ambassador with high-altitude reconnaissance photos that dramatically disproved Russia's denial that nuclear missiles had been stationed in Cuba. On other occasions, photos may be used simply to increase the emotional impact of an argument. Mothers Against Drunk Driving, for example, personalize their statistics with photos of young victims of alcohol-related crashes. Similarly, supporters of a strong defense invoke images of those two hijacked planes crashing into the Twin Towers of the World Trade Center. By rekindling the feelings of horror and anger many Americans felt on that day, they hope to build support for a more aggressive war against terrorism.

Visualization is not just something you do by showing pictures to your audience. By painting "word pictures," you can use language to help your audience visualize a problem, "see" an abstract idea, or grasp an otherwise incomprehensible statistic. During the building of the Panama Canal, for example, journalists helped their audiences back home visualize the magnitude of the project with mind-boggling comparisons. One wrote of how the dirt removed from the canal route would build 63 pyramids the size of the Great Pyramid of Egypt. Others compared the canal to digging a tunnel 14 feet in diameter "through the very heart of the earth," or building a longer version of the Great Wall of China—"from San Francisco to New York." One account even reported that the soil excavated for the canal would fill a train long enough to encircle the earth four times—a train that could be pulled only by a string of locomotives stretching from "New York to Honolulu."[22]

Visualization also can be used to contrast a troubling present with a brighter future. In his famous "I Have a Dream" speech, for example, Martin Luther King Jr. imagined a racially integrated America, where "little black boys and black girls" would "join hands with little white boys and white girls as sisters and brothers."[23] Similarly, former New York governor Mario Cuomo asked his audience at the 1992 Democratic National Convention to visualize a parade like those we stage to honor military heroes. This time, however, the parade would celebrate safe communities, affordable housing, adequate health care, and economic security. Like parades celebrating the safe return of our soldiers, this parade would be spirited and jubilant. The people would sing "proud songs, happy songs," and the parade would include blue collar workers "who have a real stake in their company's success," parents glad to be living in safe neighborhoods "where children can be children," and young people who have the opportunity to attend college and someday own their own homes. At the end of the parade, there would be fireworks and still more celebration, with the citizens giving thanks for the nation's strong economy and for our success at "outproducing and outselling our overseas competitors."[24] Of course, after twelve years of Republican leadership, we could only imagine such a parade, Cuomo told his audience as if waking them from a dream. Regrettably, we had witnessed parades honoring soldiers returning from the Persian Gulf, but we had no victories worth celebrating in education, housing, health care, or the economy. By allowing his audience to "see" such a parade, at least in their mind's eye, Cuomo helped them imagine how things might be different under a Democratic administration.

Compare the Unfamiliar to the Familiar

Speakers often relate new ideas, plans, or proposals to familiar things, not so much to prove their value but to help listeners *feel* more comfortable with something new. By this means, complicated and even controversial ideas can be made to seem more familiar and "everyday"—and hence more acceptable. Before America entered World War II, for example, Franklin Delano Roosevelt defended his controversial plan to supply ships and other war materials to the British—his "lend-lease" plan—by comparing it to how you might help a neighbor whose house was on fire. Logically, perhaps, the two situations were not really comparable. Yet FDR's illustration helped many Americans *feel* that his lend-lease plan was a good idea—the "neighborly" thing to do:

> Well, let me give you an illustration: Suppose my neighbor's home catches fire, and I have got a length of garden hose four or five hundred feet away; but, by Heaven, if he can take my garden hose and connect it up with his hydrant, I may help him to put out his fire. Now what do I do? I don't say to him before the operation, "Neighbor, my garden hose cost me $15; you have got to pay me $15 for it." ... I don't want $15—I want my garden hose back after the fire is over. All right. If it goes through the fire all right, intact, without any damage to it, he gives it back to me and thanks me very much for the use of it. But suppose it gets smashed

> up—holes in it—during the fire.... I say to him, "I was glad to lend you that hose; I see I can't use it anymore, it's all smashed up." He says, "How many feet of it were there?" I tell him, "There were 150 feet of it." He says, "All right, I will replace it." Now, if I get a nice garden hose back, I am in pretty good shape. In other words, if you lend certain munitions and get the munitions back at the end of the war, if they are intact—haven't been hurt—you are all right; if they have been damaged or deteriorated or lost completely, ... you have them replaced by the fellow that you have lent them to.[25]

By comparing a complicated governmental policy to the familiar act of helping the folks next door, FDR made his lend-lease policy *feel* like the neighborly thing to do.

The Ethics of Emotional Appeals

In advertising, we are constantly bombarded with emotional appeals. Yogurt commercials feature an elderly man and his even older mother, implying that if we eat yogurt, we, too, can live to a ripe old age. Ads for athletic shoes exploit the dreams and ambitions of young people, suggesting that if they wear the same shoes as their heroes, they, too, can be superstars. Political ads show candidates sympathizing with the sick or the elderly, or they try to frighten us into thinking that the other candidate may take away our Social Security or blow up the world. Advertisers know that successful marketing often depends on an audience's emotional reactions. Thus, they persuade us by associating their products with personal success, physical or economic security, or love and "family values."

Emotional appeals, however, can be deceptive and manipulative. More than 2,000 years ago, the rhetorician Aristotle warned that emotional appeals could warp an audience's judgment, producing hasty, ill-considered decisions.[26] When feelings such as fear, anger, love, rage, and guilt are stirred, the results can be powerful and unpredictable. Ethical public speakers respect the power of emotions. They never use emotional appeals to distract, disorient, or manipulate their listeners.

In speaking persuasively, you should never short-circuit the reasoning process or provoke an emotional overreaction on the part of your listeners. Vivid stories about brutal crimes, the suffering of victims of natural disaster, or the horrors of war may sometimes be appropriate, depending on the situation and the audience. However, we all have heard speakers who go too far. In striving to stir audience emotions, some speakers use crude or tasteless language and images, justifying such tactics as necessary to get people "fired up." Apart from the possibility that such tactics may backfire, the ethical speaker avoids overwhelming listeners with emotions so strong that they can hardly think. Appeals to emotion should supplement and complement well-reasoned arguments, not undermine reasoned deliberation or provoke hasty, violent actions.

When in doubt, ask yourself this question: Underneath the emotional appeal, do I have a sound argument—a substructure of evidence and reasoning—that can withstand critical scrutiny? You do not want your audience members to respond unthinkingly. Rather, you want to appeal to their minds while recognizing that emotions play an important role in human behavior.

SUMMARY

- Persuasion is rooted in public controversy, or disagreements over matters of political or social significance.
- As citizens in a democracy, we have an obligation to deliberate "in good faith," respecting our fellow citizens and backing up our opinions with good reasons and evidence.
- Public controversies typically revolve around questions of fact, value, or policy.
  - Questions of fact involve controversies over existence, scope, or causality.
  - Questions of value revolve around how ideas and actions should be evaluated or judged.
  - Questions of policy involve choices among future courses of action.
- Ethical proof, or *ethos*, refers to the audience's perceptions of the credibility of the speaker and his or her sources.
  - The constituents of ethos are trustworthiness, competence, open-mindedness, and dynamism.
  - Your ethos will be influenced by the context or situation in which you speak.
  - You can enhance your ethos by showing your audience that you share their concerns, citing reputable sources, relating personal experiences, striving to be clear, considering different points of view, and delivering your speech effectively.
- Emotional appeals can be powerful motivators.
  - You can engage the emotions of your audience by using affective language, identifying shared values, using vivid detail, using visualization, or comparing the unfamiliar to the familiar.
  - Emotional appeals should never be used to deceive or manipulate, or to *replace* well-reasoned arguments.

QUESTIONS FOR REVIEW AND REFLECTION

1. Define *public controversy* and identify two or three public controversies that you think are important today. Do you believe that public debate over those controversies has helped clarify the issues involved or the options for resolving those controversies?
2. What does it mean to deliberate "in good faith"? Do you think most politicians today deliberate in good faith? What about the political commentators and representatives of interest groups and "think tanks" that you hear on radio or TV talk shows? Do they deliberate in good faith?

3. What are the differences between questions of fact, value, and policy? Can you think of a major public controversy today that revolves mostly around questions of fact? Can you identify other controversies that focus more on questions of value or policy?
4. The following is a list of well-known public figures. How would you describe the ethos of each, and what do you think have been the most important influences shaping their ethos?
   - Barack Obama
   - Dick Cheney
   - Bono
   - Oprah Winfrey
   - Rush Limbaugh
   - Angelina Jolie
   - Tiger Woods
5. What, in your opinion, determines whether appeals to emotion are ethical? Are there certain types of emotional appeals—or appeals to certain emotions, such as fear or hatred—that are inherently unethical? Does a speaker's purpose influence your assessment of whether his or her emotional appeals are ethical?

ENDNOTES

1. Brad Stone, "Tech Trash, E-Waste: By Any Name, It's an Issue," *Newsweek*, December 12, 2005, 11.
2. Anne Underwood, "Diagnosis: Not Enough Nurses," *Newsweek*, December 12, 2005, 80.
3. Barack Obama, "Remarks by the President on National Security," National Archives, Washington, D.C., The White House, Office of the Press Secretary, news release, May 21, 2009, www.whitehouse.gov/the_press_office/Remarks-by-the-President-On-National-Security-5-21-09/ (accessed May 26, 2009).
4. Dick Cheney, "Text of Cheney's Speech on National Security," *Washington Post*, May 21, 2009, www.washingtonpost.com/wp-dyn/content/article/2009/05/21/AR2009052104387.html (accessed May 26, 2009).
5. See "Economy" under the "Issues" tab on the White House Web site, www.whitehouse.gov/issues/economy/ (accessed May 16, 2009).
6. *The Rhetoric of Aristotle*, trans. George Kennedy (New York: Oxford University Press, 1991).
7. Gary Cronkhite and Jo Liska, "A Critique of Factor Analytic Approaches to the Study of Credibility," *Communication Monographs* 43 (1976): 91–107; James C. McCroskey and Thomas J. Young, "Ethos and Credibility: The Construct and Its Measurement after Three Decades," *Central States Speech Journal* 32 (1981): 24–34; Jack L. Whitehead, "Factors of Source Credibility," *Quarterly Journal of Speech* 54 (1968): 59–63.
8. Ronald Reagan, "State of the Union Address," in *Three Centuries of American Rhetorical Discourse*, ed. Ronald F. Reid (Prospect Heights, IL: Waveland Press, 1988), 743.
9. Ray Long and Rick Pearson, "Impeached Gov. Blagojevich Has Been Removed from Office," *Chicago Tribune*, January 30, 2009, www.chicagotribune.com/news/local/chi-blagojevich-impeachment-removal,0,5791846.story (accessed May 22, 2009).
10. James Poniewozik, "Blago Talks! (And Talks ...)," *Time*, January 29, 2009.
11. Russell Berman, "Clinton Criticizes Obama's Foreign Experience," *New York Sun*, November 21, 2009, www.nysun.com/national/clinton-criticizes-obamas-foreign-experience/66787/?print=0091003421 (accessed May 25, 2009).
12. Patrick Healy and Julie Bosman, "Clinton Campaign Starts 5-Point Attack on Obama," *New York Times*, February 26, 2008, www.nytimes.com/2008/02/26/us/politics/26clinton.html?_r=1 (accessed May 25, 2009).
13. From Barbara Jordan, "Keynote Address to the Democratic Convention," Published 1976 by Democratic National Committee.
14. Larry J. Sabato, *Feeding Frenzy: How Attack Journalism Has Transformed American Politics* (New York: Free Press, 1993), 12.

15. William Jefferson Clinton, "1992 Democratic National Convention Acceptance Address," *American Rhetoric*, www.americanrhetoric.com/speeches/wjclinton1992dnc.htm (accessed June 17, 2009).
16. From Ronald Reagan, "Address to the Nation on Defense and National Security." Published March 23, 1983 by U.S. Government.
17. From Eugene Debs, "Statement to the Court," Cleveland, Ohio, 1918. Published 1918.
18. From Cesar Chavez, "What the Future Holds for Farmworkers and Hispanics," address to the Commonwealth Club, Nov. 9, 1984, Copyright © 1984 by Cesar Chavez Foundation.
19. From Barack Obama, Democratic Radio Address, Friday, November 21, 2008. Published 2008 by BarackObama.com.
20. See "How are You Delivering on Change?," www.whitehouse.gov/change/ (accessed May 28, 2009).
21. From Frederick Douglass, "What to the Slave in the Fourth of July, July 5, 1852." Published 1852 by Lee, Mann & Co.
22. J. Michael Hogan, *The Panama Canal in American Politics* (Carbondale: Southern Illinois University Press, 1986), 49.
23. Martin Luther King Jr., "I Have a Dream," in *Great Speeches for Criticism and Analysis*, 4th ed., ed. Lloyd Rohler and Roger Cook (Greenwood, IN: Alistair Press, 2001), 352.
24. From Mario Cuomo, "Nominating Address of Clinton for the Presidency," Democratic National Convention. Copyright © 1992 by Mario Cuomo.
25. From Franklin D. Roosevelt, Press Conference, December 17, 1940. Published 1940 by FDR Library.
26. *Rhetoric of Aristotle*, 235.

CHAPTER

16

Arguing Persuasively

CHAPTER SURVEY

Persuasion and Demagoguery in a Free Society

Constructing a Reasonable Argument

The Forms of Reasoning

Fallacies of Reasoning and Evidence

CHAPTER OBJECTIVES

After studying this chapter, you should be able to

1. Distinguish between persuasion and demagoguery.
2. Define *argument* and identify the components of a complete argument.
3. Understand what it means to make a reasonable argument.
4. Identify and critique different *types* of reasoning.
5. Recognize and describe some common fallacies of reasoning and evidence.

Democracies are fragile things. They require committed, honest leaders, and they depend on ordinary citizens to assume the responsibility of governing themselves. That means that citizens must participate in public deliberations and learn to distinguish between good and bad arguments. They must be committed to deliberating in good faith, and they must be willing to put the common good ahead of their own selfish interests. In a diverse democratic society, it is sometimes difficult to reconcile all the competing interests in a major public controversy. That is all the more reason that we must learn *how* to deliberate. If our democracy is to thrive, we must learn to discuss and debate public issues with intelligence, civility, and respect for our fellow citizens.

Historically, America has not always lived up to this ideal. In the 1950s, for example, a reckless demagogue named Joseph McCarthy rose to power by exploiting the fears and uncertainty of the Cold War era. Claiming that "card-carrying" communists had infiltrated the government, McCarthy inspired anti-communist "witch hunts" across the nation, throwing our political system into chaos and destroying innocent lives. At another time, McCarthy's outrageous accusations might have been ignored. In an era of fear, uncertainty, and political complacency, however, he caused a national sensation and became the most feared man in America.[1]

Today we live in another era of widespread apathy and uncertainty. Pointing to low voter turnout and declining involvement in civic affairs, some worry that another great demagogue might rise to power and throw the nation into political chaos. Could a modern-day Joseph McCarthy exploit today's economic problems or our fears of terrorism to advance a dangerously reactionary political agenda? Are we so ill-informed and complacent that we would fall for such tactics again? Or have we learned the lesson of the McCarthy era: that as citizens in a democracy, we must guard against those who seek to manipulate and deceive the public. In this chapter, we pick up where we left off in the previous chapter, exploring in greater depth the role of persuasion in our democratic society. Specifically, we will distinguish between persuasion and demagoguery, defining persuasion as "reason-giving argument" and contrasting it with the deceptions and manipulations of the demagogue. Then we will reflect more practically on what it means to construct a *reasonable* argument, examining the components of a complete argument and identifying some of the most common fallacies or errors in reasoning and evidence. Contrary to what one might conclude from watching political talk shows, arguing about civic affairs does *not* have to mean attacking your political enemies or stirring up public passions. To the contrary, it *should* mean *engaging* your fellow citizens in a constructive dialogue about issues of mutual concern.

PERSUASION AND DEMAGOGUERY IN A FREE SOCIETY

Preview. *Persuasion is an essential tool of democratic governance. Indeed, reliance on persuasion to resolve conflicts and induce social cooperation is the main difference between a democracy and a totalitarian or authoritarian state. Yet precisely because they depend so much on persuasion, democracies are especially vulnerable to demagoguery, or deceptive and manipulative speech. With advances in technology, demagoguery has become an even greater threat. If we hope to sustain our democratic way of life, we must understand the differences between persuasion and demagoguery and demand high ethical standards from all who speak in public.*

Persuasion, as we have emphasized throughout this book, is an essential tool of democratic citizenship. The earliest treatises on persuasion, such as Aristotle's *Rhetoric*,[2] prepared citizens to participate in the judicial and legislative assemblies of the Greek city-state. Passed down over centuries, this classical tradition evolved in response to changing social and political conditions, but its essential purpose remained the same: to educate people for citizenship. As part of that education, citizens were taught to distinguish between good and bad arguments, between the legitimate techniques of democratic persuasion and the tricks of the sophist or the demagogue.

America's founders were well schooled in this classical rhetorical tradition. Taught to view **demagoguery** as "the peculiar vice to which democracies were susceptible," they designed our constitutional system to guard against what Alexander Hamilton described as the "temporary delusions" of a public misled by those who might "flatter their prejudices to betray their interests." As James Madison observed, there would be times in any democracy when the public might be "misled by the artful misrepresentations of interested men." In those "critical moments," Madison looked to the Senate—the legislative branch more insulated from public opinion—to moderate public passions until the people regained their "cool and deliberate" judgment.[3]

More than a hundred years later, a young scholar named Woodrow Wilson echoed the founders' concerns. As a student of oratory and politics, Wilson wrote at length about protecting our democracy against demagoguery by properly educating both our leaders and our citizens. Like the ancient rhetoricians, Wilson drew a clear, *ethical* distinction between the responsible, civic-minded orator—a leader he dubbed the **orator-statesman**—and those "artful dialecticians" who manipulated public opinion through "subtle word-play," "dialectic dexterity," or "passionate declamation." As an educator, Wilson taught that "high and noble thoughts" were the hallmarks of the orator-statesman, and he professed faith in the ability of ordinary citizens to "exercise intelligent discretion."[4] As Wilson wrote early in his career, "A charlatan cannot long play the statesman successfully while the whole country is looking critically on."[5]

Today, some doubt the public's ability to "exercise intelligent discretion." Many Americans lack even the most basic understanding of our nation's institutions and traditions,[6] and advances in communication technologies have created new possibilities for the manipulation of public opinion. So how, in the modern world, might we protect ourselves against demagoguery? In an age of global propaganda and the politics of spin, does the ancient distinction between persuasion and demagoguery still have meaning?

We believe that it does, for regardless of the political context or the technologies of communication, we can still distinguish between good and bad **arguments**. The ancient Greeks lived in very different times, but their basic lesson remains relevant: if democracy is to thrive, every citizen must learn to distinguish between

FOCUS ON CIVIC ENGAGEMENT

The Politics of Outrageousness

In her 2006 book *Godless: The Church of Liberalism*, political commentator Ann Coulter took her reputation for making outrageous statements a step further by accusing four women who had lost their husbands in the September 11 terrorist attacks—the so-called Jersey Girls—of exploiting their personal loss for political purposes. "These broads are millionaires, lionized on TV and in articles about them, reveling in their status as celebrities and stalked by grief-arrazies," Coulter wrote. "I've never seen people enjoying their husbands' deaths so much." And just for good measure, Coulter added: "And by the way, how do we know their husbands weren't planning to divorce these harpies?"

Broads? Harpies? Had Coulter "gone off the deep end," as some observers suggested? Or were her remarks simply a marketing ploy, an effort to "rise above the din" of the 24-hour news cycle and to stand out in the "blogosphere," where such rhetorical excess has become common?

At one level, perhaps, Coulter made a reasonable argument: that simply because they lost loved ones in the 9/11 attacks, the Jersey Girls should not be given a free pass to criticize the Bush administration or to make partisan speeches without backing up their claims. At another level, however, Coulter was obviously trying to provoke people, as she deliberately used offensive language. Whatever her point, Coulter crossed the line of propriety and civility. Not only did Senator Hillary Clinton protest the remarks as "vicious" and "mean-spirited," but New York's Republican Governor George Pataki and even Fox News commentator Bill O'Reilly criticized her as well.

Of course, Coulter is not the only practitioner of the politics of outrageousness. Radio talk show

sound and unsound arguments. Today, as in ancient times, *reasoned* arguments are the substance of democratic deliberation, while demagoguery relies on personal and emotional appeals. Claiming a monopoly on truth, demagogues cultivate a charismatic ethos, setting themselves apart from ordinary citizens and demanding deference to their supposedly "supernatural, superhuman, or at least specifically exceptional powers or qualities."[7] Appealing to our fears and prejudices, demagogues use *pathos* as a distraction, substituting passion for argument and concocting various scapegoats and "enemies." Demagogues do *not* appeal to what Abraham Lincoln called the "better angels of our nature."[8] To the contrary, they exploit the envy, resentment, hatred, or fears of their audiences.[9]

As rhetorical scholar James Darsey has reminded us, the agitator, the political *provocateur*, even the zealot has a role to play in our democratic system. Occasionally, we *need* speakers to shake things up, shattering our complacency and motivating us to act. Radical speakers *can* be a source of democratic inspiration and renewal, reminding us of our revolutionary heritage and demanding that we live up to our ideals.[10] But in the day-to-day business of democratic governance, we still must guard against rhetorical excess and extremism. The hard work of self-governance cannot be done by a divided and polarized citizenry.

As we discuss what it means to *argue persuasively*, our emphasis will be on the constituents of a *reasonable* argument. We will first examine the various components of an argument and the major types of reasoning. Then we will discuss some of the most common errors or *fallacies* of reasoning and evidence. As we shall see, arguing persuasively is not about getting your own way or manipulating hosts have perfected the form, and public figures on both the left and the right have become known for offensive or outrageous remarks. In our media-saturated culture, the politics of outrageousness may be one way to rise above the din and attract attention to one's self. But as concerned citizens, we ought to be asking other questions: Does such rhetoric contribute anything constructive to the public dialogue? Does it help us understand or resolve important public controversies? Does such talk encourage citizens to participate in politics and civic affairs? In short, does the politics of outrageousness serve the public good?

Ann Coulter and the other practitioners of the politics of outrageousness have a right to their opinions—and even to their confrontational and polarizing ways of expressing those opinions. But as citizens, we do *not* have to listen, much less take them seriously. Calling Coulter a "hater," at least one newspaper editor, Bob Unger of the *Centre Daily Times* in State College, Pennsylvania, quit carrying her syndicated column, provoking cries of censorship from her admirers. But does refusing to publish hateful rhetoric constitute censorship? Do media "gatekeepers" have a right to decide who gets to be heard? Should newspapers banish columnists on both the right and the left whom they consider hateful? In principle, Unger has a point: Coulter and others like her poison the public dialogue. Yet who gets to decide who will be censored or silenced? Ultimately, it is up to us—as citizens—to decide who has crossed the line of acceptable public debate. Coulter and others like her may have a right to talk, but we also have the right *not* to listen.

Source: Jocelyn Noveck, "Outrageousness an Art Form for Top Practitioners," *Centre Daily Times*, June 14, 2006, A2.

an audience. Rather, it is about coming together with your fellow citizens to discuss and debate the issues of the day.

CONSTRUCTING A REASONABLE ARGUMENT

Preview. *A good argument is not one that echoes our own views, nor is a good argument simply one that "works." To the contrary, a good argument is one that adheres to certain rules of evidence and reasoning. A good argument may not always win the day. Indeed, the best argument may be one that forces us to reconsider our own opinions. Good arguments engage our listeners' emotions and draw strength from our ethos. But in the final analysis, a good argument is one that meets certain tests of reasoning and evidence and fulfills its burden of proof.*

We all know that there are good and bad arguments. But what do we mean when we make that judgment? Unfortunately, many of us seem to think that a good argument is one that confirms what we already believe—an argument that has us shaking our head in agreement. Others take a more pragmatic view: a "good" argument is one that "works"—one that persuades other people. That too seems a bit shortsighted. As we have noted, a demagogue's arguments may "work," but they have *ethical* shortcomings—they twist the truth, or they appeal to ugly emotions. Obviously, we do not want to praise a speaker for being an effective liar.

Like any artistic creation, an argument can be judged not only in terms of how it is received, but also by certain theoretical and ethical principles. We already have

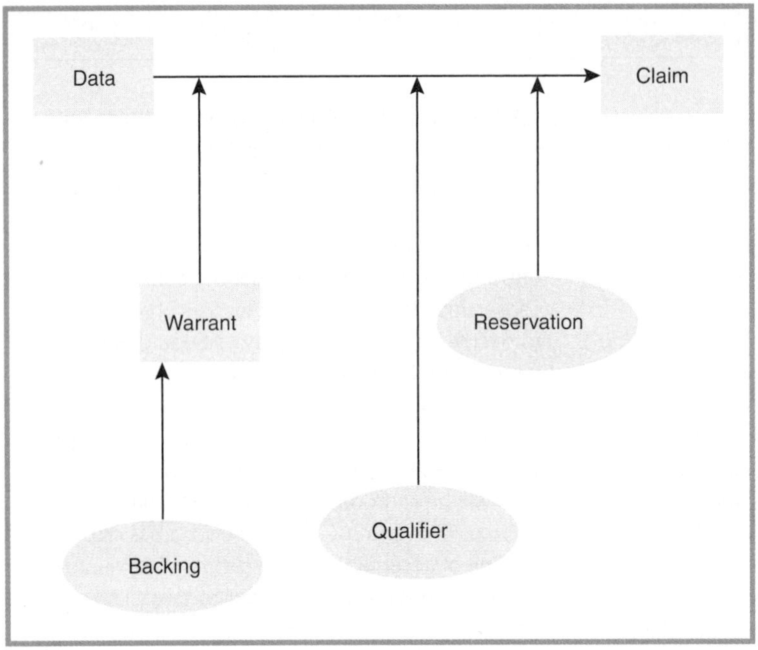

FIGURE 16.1
The Toulmin Model of Argument

suggested some of those principles: truth, for example, and a commitment to the common good. Those are ethical standards we already have discussed. But what does it mean to say that an argument is *theoretically* sound? What, in theory, defines a "good" argument, and how do we go about evaluating an argument?

Unfortunately, there is no simple list of rules defining a "good" argument. The whole tradition of rhetorical studies, dating back more than 2,000 years, may be seen as a search for such rules. Today, some even reject the need for rules altogether, arguing that any such rules reflect cultural biases or "silence" some voices.[11] Yet most who study speech would still agree on a couple of points. First, a good argument must be complete; that is, it must have all the basic components of the so-called Toulmin model of argument (see Figure 16.1): a claim, evidence to back it up, and a *warrant* (or general principle) that links the evidence to the claim.[12] Second, a good argument must be *reasonable*—that is, it must be worthy of serious consideration by a hypothetical listener who is reasonably intelligent, well informed, and fair minded. Perhaps you have heard of the *reasonable person* test in a court of law.[13] Something like that test can help us distinguish between reasonable and unreasonable arguments in public debate.

Claims

Claims are the debatable assertions put forward by a speaker. They are the contested positions you want your audience to accept, such as the claim that illegal immigration poses a threat to our national security, or the claim that capital punishment deters crime. When you make a claim, you do not expect your listeners to automatically nod their heads in agreement. By definition, a claim takes sides on a controversial matter and invites debate. If you hope to prevail in that debate, you still need to *prove* your claims.

Claims take many different forms, mostly arising out of the types of persuasive issues or controversies discussed in Chapter 15. If you are debating whether something exists, what *caused* something to happen, or the *scope* or *magnitude* of some phenomenon, you are debating *claims of fact*. If you are debating whether something is good or bad, you are making *claims of value*. Value claims assume a variety of forms, including claims about what's effective or ineffective, just or unjust, moral or immoral, legal or illegal, and beneficial or harmful. In debates over what we should do—debates over future courses of action—we make *claims of policy*. These are, by their very nature, the hardest to prove, because they involve, in effect, predicting the future.

Precisely because they are the hardest to prove, policy claims tend to come more heavily qualified than other sorts of claims. **Qualifiers** are words that indicate our level of confidence in our claims—words such as *possibly*, *probably*, or *beyond any doubt*. So, for example, we may qualify a factual claim if our evidence is not conclusive: "The major cause of increased levels of mercury in fish is *probably* emissions from coal-fired power plants." If we overqualify our claims, of course, we sound unsure or wishy-washy, but if we do not qualify our claim at all, we may overstate our case. A reasonable argument is qualified at a level appropriate to the strength of the reasoning and evidence behind it.

Reservations are exceptions to our claim, or stipulated conditions under which we no longer hold to our claim. Thus, for example, the chairman of the Federal Reserve might argue that a proposed increase in interest rates will be sufficient to control inflation—*unless* energy prices continue to escalate. As with qualifiers, reservations can be overdone, leaving virtually no conditions under which you still hold to your claim ("I predict that inflation will remain low *unless* prices for food, shelter, clothing, and energy go up!"). By identifying one or two major reservations, however, you can assert your claim more confidently ("Inflation will *almost certainly* remain low, *unless* energy prices go up.") and still make a reasonable argument.

Whatever sorts of claims you make, you will be expected to back them up with evidence. Evidence, as we discussed in Chapter 8, may include statistics, testimony, examples, or comparison/contrast. But whatever types of evidence you choose, you need to use it properly and make sure that it meets certain tests of quantitative and qualitative sufficiency.

Evidence

When attempting to persuade an audience to accept a factual claim, you might use statistics, specific examples, testimony by experts, and other sorts of evidence. When long-distance telephone companies sought approval from the public utilities commission for a reduction in the fees they paid to local phone companies, for example, one student used a variety of evidence to convince his audience that consumers would save little, if any, under the plan. The factual claim and supporting material he used looked like this:

The proposed reduction in fees will not result in lower costs for consumers.

A. According to the *New York Times*, documents filed by AT&T indicate that basic rates on One Rate plans would increase by 66 percent. *(statistic)*
B. According to a spokesperson for the Consumers Union, new per-minute fees would go up every day except Sunday, resulting in higher bills for low-volume callers. *(testimony)*
C. A customer who made 45 minutes of long-distance calls on Saturday would pay $4.95 under the old plan and $13.05 under the new plan. *(statistics/contrast)*
D. Even if the companies changed to a flat 5-cents-per-minute rate, the cost to consumers would still go up an average of $8.55. *(example/statistics)*

In proving claims of value—claims about good and bad, right and wrong—you need more than just factual evidence. Not only must you cite examples, statistics, and other empirical evidence, but you also must consider the *criteria* or *standards* that support your *evaluations* of those facts. In a murder case, for example, it is one thing to prove that that the accused pulled the trigger, resulting in the death of the victim. It is quite another to convince a jury that the defendant committed premeditated, first-degree murder. Depending on the circumstances, the same action—shooting another person dead—might be considered first-degree murder, or it may be reckless homicide or even self-defense. In this sort of case, the facts alone do not determine the verdict. The facts must be considered *in light of the law*.

In public policy debates, the standards of judgment are rarely as clear as they are in a court of law. Still, it is important that we reflect on the rules, principles, or standards we employ in making our judgments. In a speech on medical malpractice, for example, one student cited the example of her uncle, who had undergone what was supposed to be a routine operation but ended up seriously disabled. She also cited other examples of people hurt by medical errors. Yet in order to convince her listeners that medical malpractice was a "very serious problem" in America, she needed some broader basis for her judgment. She was able to establish that basis with statistics on the leading causes of death and through comparisons to other, more familiar health threats such as car accidents and AIDS. With this evidence she was able to show that medical malpractice posed as "serious" a threat as these other, more familiar dangers.

Policy arguments pose the greatest challenge because they involve choices about what we *should* do in the future. Because we cannot present *direct* evidence of a proposed policy's feasibility, costs, or effects, we typically must rely on comparisons to similar policies, or we may use testimony from experts in the field. If we wish to propose a new program for recycling high-tech waste, for example, we might look for evidence of how similar programs have worked in other communities. Or we might turn to experts in waste management for testimony on the value, cost, feasibility, and benefits of such programs. In the final analysis, however, we really cannot say for sure how a policy that has worked well in the past will work under different circumstances in the future.

Whatever sort of evidence you use, it needs to be sufficient, both quantitatively and qualitatively, to convince a "reasonable person" that your claims are worthy of serious consideration. There are three basic tests of the adequacy of your evidence.

First, the quality of the evidence should justify the audience's acceptance. As we discussed in Chapter 8, certain questions should always be asked about particular types of evidence, such as the following:

- Are the examples representative?
- Are the statistics reliable?
- Is the testimony authoritative?
- Are the comparisons sound—that is, are the objects or ideas being compared really comparable?

Beyond these questions, there are some general "tests" of evidence that we should always apply: Is the evidence accurate, recent, and complete? Is the source of the evidence credible?

Second, the evidence must be relevant to the claim. Evidence can be accurate and truthful and still not prove the claim. Consider, for example, Meagan's argument in favor of voting for Josh as student government president:

> What we need most in a president is strong leadership. Josh has been my friend since we arrived here at the university. He has always been there for me, often putting aside his own problems or needs to help me when I needed help.
>
> Everyone likes Josh. He has a great sense of humor. When things got tense in our study group, Josh always found something funny to say to break the tension.

Everything that Meagan said about her friend may be true; Josh is no doubt a nice guy. But is that relevant to Meagan's claim? Does the fact that Josh has been a good friend to Megan, or the fact that he makes people laugh, prove that he would be a strong leader?

Third, the amount of evidence used must be sufficient to support the claim. Your evidence must not only be true and relevant, but also quantitatively sufficient. Of course, what constitutes a sufficient *amount* of evidence depends on your topic and your audience. If you are addressing a highly controversial issue or an especially skeptical audience, you will need to present more evidence. If your topic is relatively uncontroversial and your audience is open minded, less evidence may be required.

Consider, for example, what would be "sufficient" evidence to refute claims made by former player Jose Canseco that steroid use is widespread in Major League Baseball (MLB). To fans of sluggers Barry Bonds and Sammy Sosa, the players' denials that they used performance-enhancing drugs might be sufficient. When the scandal reached Congress in March 2005, however, members of the House Government Reform Committee demanded more proof. Sosa, Rafael Palmeiro, and Mark McGwire all denied—or at least refused to admit—that they had used illegal substances. Yet when MLB executives appeared before the committee, the legislators "all but scorned" their denials that baseball had a drug problem. Despite more than eleven hours of testimony, the committee remained unconvinced. "I have not been reassured one bit," Representative Steven Lynch of Massachusetts concluded.[14] Obviously, the baseball executives failed to provide *sufficient* evidence to overcome the committee's doubts.

Major League Baseball players Sammy Sosa (sitting next to his translator, Patricia Rosell), Mark McGwire, Rafael Palmeiro, and Curt Schilling appear before a congressional committee investigating steroid use in baseball. The committee appeared unconvinced by the testimony at the hearings.

There are, of course, no set rules to determine what constitutes sufficient evidence. In the final analysis, that depends on your audience—their existing knowledge and beliefs, their attitude toward the topic and the speaker, and their willingness to take the evidence you present at face value. That is one more reason to always analyze your audience carefully.

Warrants

Warrants are the general assumptions, principles, or rules that connect our evidence to our claims. Suppose, for example, that a politician claims that his opponent in the election is "unfit for office." And suppose further that he bases that claim on the fact that his opponent never served in the military. In this debate, the evidence may not be in dispute; the candidate's service record is a matter of public record. But does fitness for office *require* military service? Is the claim that the candidate is unfit for office *warranted* by the fact that she did not serve in the military? In this case, the argument turns not on the evidence but on a general principle: that politicians who have not served in the military are unfit for office. For most Americans, of course, that would be a dubious assumption. Military service may *contribute* to one's fitness for office, but few would agree that military service is a *necessary* qualification.

Some warrants may already be accepted by your audience and may go unstated in your argument. In the United States, for instance, most listeners would agree that under our Constitution, everyone is entitled to fair and equal treatment under the law. Thus, we may use that warrant to link evidence about a particular policy—say, racial profiling by police—to the claim that the policy is unconstitutional. In that argument, there would be little need to back up or even state the warrant; most Americans agree that our Constitution entitles us to fair and equal treatment. Our main burden, then, would be to prove that racial profiling does exist, and that it violates the principle of "fair and equal treatment" under the law.

When we invoke general rules or principles that are themselves controversial, we may need to provide **backing** for those warrants. Returning to our earlier example, suppose that our hypothetical candidate claimed that his opponent was unfit for office because she was divorced or because she was gay. Does either of these characteristics warrant the argument that she is unfit for office? Fifty or sixty years ago, many people *did* view divorce as a moral failing that disqualified people from high political office. Today, some people still think one's sexual preference is a relevant political credential. Yet in an age of greater social tolerance, divorced candidates are now routinely elected to political office, and in many communities homosexuality is no longer a political liability. The point, of course, is that warrants themselves are sometimes controversial, and that you may need to back them up with additional support.

The Burden of Proof

There is no such thing as an argument that is "reasonable" under any and all circumstances. What qualifies as a reasonable argument in one situation may not seem so reasonable in another, depending on the audience and the situation. One way to anticipate what might be considered a reasonable argument is to reflect on your burden of proof. Although meeting your burden of proof does not guarantee that you will "win" a debate, it does mean that you have made an argument that is at least reasonable enough to warrant serious consideration and further debate.

As we noted in the previous chapter, the theory of **presumption** and **burden of proof** is most familiar in the legal context. We have all heard how, in a court of law, we are *presumed* innocent until *proven* guilty. That means that a defendant has the *presumption* of innocence; the prosecution has the burden of proof. In civil cases, that burden of proof means that the prosecution must prove the defendant guilty by a *preponderance of evidence*, whereas in criminal cases the burden of proof is greater: *beyond a reasonable doubt*. Because more is at stake in a criminal trial, it makes sense that our system demands a higher burden of proof.

In public debates, the burden of proof is not so clearly defined, but there are certain expectations about what constitutes a *reasonable* case. In debates over public policy, for example, advocates of change have the burden of proof because change involves risk—because it means abandoning the known for the unknown. Advocates of new policies are therefore expected to establish, first, that there is some *need* for change. Then we expect them to present a specific *plan*, not only describing their proposed policy or program, but also explaining how it is to be implemented, funded, and enforced or administered. Finally, we expect policy advocates to prove that their plan is *workable*—that is, that it is feasible, will solve some problem, and perhaps even produce some benefits or advantages over other possible solutions. In sum, a reasonable argument for a policy change answers these questions: Why do we need a new policy? What would that new policy entail? How would the plan be implemented? Would it be workable and solve the problem? And why should we prefer that plan over other alternatives?

A reasonable argument does not end but begins the discussion. If you make an argument that is, on its first face, reasonable (in Latin, a *prima facie* case), you have a right to expect that your listeners will take it seriously. At the same time, you should be willing to defend your position in debate, perhaps responding to questions or even offering additional arguments and evidence. Part of making a reasonable argument is remaining open to further discussion. Democratic deliberation is an ongoing conversation, and you should never expect to have the "final word."

THE FORMS OF REASONING

Preview. *The process of reaching a sound conclusion involves reasoning, or the process of drawing inferences from known facts. Reasoning always involves some mental leap from the known to the unknown. There are four common types of reasoning: inductive, deductive, causal, and analogical. Understanding these types of reasoning and how they work can help you build solid, well-reasoned persuasive speeches.*

Rarely do the facts speak for themselves. More commonly, we must *reason* from facts to conclusions, asking our audience to accept certain *inferences* we make. Thus, for example, we may know that 1,200 respondents to a poll said they planned to vote for the incumbent in an upcoming election—by a margin, say, of 55 to 45 percent. But to predict the outcome of the election based on that evidence involves several assumptions and inferential leaps. First, of course, we assume that the respondents did not lie to the pollster. More important, we trust that those 1,200 respondents are *representative* of the larger population. Finally, we assume that no major events will change voters' minds between the time the survey was taken and election day. In short, we assume *a lot* when we reason from a poll to a prediction of how an election will turn out. All that we *really* know is how 1,200 people said they *planned* to vote. To predict the outcome of the election from that evidence requires an inferential leap.

The process of making inferential leaps is called **reasoning**, and it commonly assumes one of four forms: (1) *inductive reasoning*, in which we reason from specific instances to a more general conclusion; (2) *deductive reasoning*, or reasoning from an accepted generalization to a conclusion about a particular case; (3) *causal reasoning*, which means reasoning from cause to effect or effect to cause; and (4) *analogical reasoning*, in which we reason that what is true of one case will be true of a similar case. Each of these types of reasoning involves inferences; none leads to conclusions that are absolute or certain. All lead to *probable* conclusions, with the strength of those conclusions dependent on the quality of our evidence and reasoning.

Inductive Reasoning

Inductive reasoning involves reasoning from a set of specific examples or a series of observations to a general conclusion. So, for example, we may investigate ten medical malpractice cases in order to draw a more general conclusion about the typical case—and whether such cases tend to be justified or frivolous. Polls and surveys also rely on inductive reasoning, of course, when they generalize from a small but representative sample to some larger population. So, too, do many other kinds of scientific research: the forester reasons inductively about the threat posed by pine beetles based on an examination of a sample of trees; the sociologist interviews a sample of juvenile delinquents before drawing conclusions about what, in general, motivates such bad behavior; and the communication researcher tests reactions to violent images on a small group of experimental subjects before drawing larger conclusions about the effects of media violence.

The strength of inductive reasoning rests on the number of cases examined and the representativeness of those cases. The first questions one should ask about inductive reasoning are thus obvious: How many examples support the generalization? And is that a sufficient number to warrant the generalization? Representativeness is a trickier matter, because it requires us to make assumptions about the characteristics that may be most relevant to the generalization. When designing election surveys, for example, pollsters go to great lengths to design samples that reflect all the characteristics that may affect how one votes: age, gender, race, education, income, occupation, party affiliation, and so on. Similarly, it would be crucial to ask, when generalizing about the problem of medical malpractice, whether the cases examined were *typical* of malpractice suits. Did the cases involve errors *commonly* made by doctors? Or were they the sort of "freak accidents" that make headlines but do not commonly occur?

When reasoning inductively, you should qualify your claims carefully, avoiding sweeping generalizations based on just one or two examples. You also might attach reservations to your claim, identifying conditions under which your generalization may not hold true. Thus, for example, a pollster might conclude that the incumbent president will win reelection—*unless* there is a major crisis or an economic downturn before election day.

Finally, inductive reasoning can be strengthened by testimony and/or statistics that establish the reliability or representativeness of your examples. Are experts willing to testify that your examples are typical of those they have encountered in their research? Do statistics show that the examples you cite are common or widespread? In inductive reasoning, it is important not only that you have *enough* examples, but also that your examples are both true and typical.

Deductive Reasoning

Deductive reasoning is the process of drawing conclusions about specific cases based on inferences from a generally accepted premise or principle. A classic example of deductive reasoning, called a *syllogism*, looks like this:

A. All Democrats are liberal. *(major premise)*
B. My neighbor Tim is a Democrat. *(minor premise)*
C. Therefore, we may conclude that Tim is liberal. *(conclusion)*

Most of us do not think or talk this formally, of course, and it is rare in the world of practical affairs to reason from universal premises like "All Democrats are liberal." In the real world, we more commonly reason from *qualified* premises ("Most Democrats are liberal") to *probable* conclusions ("My neighbor Tim is probably liberal").

Suppose, for example, that you were trying to persuade an audience that we cannot win the war in Afghanistan because we are fighting an indigenous, or "homegrown," religious insurgency. Your claim is that we cannot win; perhaps you have evidence that the insurgency is indigenous and motivated by religious beliefs. What's missing, of course, is what we earlier called the *warrant*: the assumption that, in general, indigenous religious insurgencies are difficult to defeat. Of course, history may show that it is not *always* true that indigenous religious insurgencies prevail militarily, and you also may discover evidence that some of the Afghan insurgents are neither homegrown nor religiously motivated. Thus, you would want to *qualify* your argument: "It will be *difficult* to win the war in Afghanistan because *many* of the insurgents are indigenous and motivated by strong religious beliefs."

Often speakers do not even state their premises because they are already accepted by their audience. That is, they assume that the audience will supply the missing premise from their own store of beliefs and values. Thus, for example, we might assume that our audience already believes that "politicians who have lied in the past will lie in the future." If we can prove that a particular politician has lied in the past, our audience will probably accept the conclusion that he or she is likely to lie again. This sort of reasoning is called a *rhetorical syllogism*, or

enthymeme. It reflects how we typically construct deductive arguments in everyday talk. If our audience does, in fact, already accept our general premises, these arguments can be persuasive.

If your audience is likely to be skeptical of your premises, you should not only state them but provide evidence to back them up. Suppose, for example, that you want to argue for a ban on selling carbonated soft drinks in school vending machines. Your deductive reasoning may look something like this:

> **Major premise:** Sugary carbonated sodas are the major cause of an epidemic of obesity and related health problems in America.
> **Minor premise:** School vending machines are the chief source of carbonated sodas for millions of young people.
> **Conclusion:** Therefore, banning the sale of carbonated sodas in school vending machines is the best way to combat the epidemic of obesity and related health problems.

As with all deductive reasoning, the persuasiveness of this argument depends, in part, on whether you can prove that school vending machines are the "chief source" of carbonated sodas consumed by young people. But it also depends on whether your audience is willing to accept the major premise: "Sugary carbonated sodas are a major cause of an epidemic of obesity and related health problems in America." Thus, just to be sure, you might provide backing for that warrant, quoting something like the following statement from the Center for Science in the Public Interest:

> More than two-thirds of Americans are overweight or obese, and soft drinks are the only food or beverage that has been shown to increase the risk of . . . obesity. Obesity costs $95 billion a year in medical expenditures. . . . Obesity also causes numerous other problems, including reduced self-esteem and lower productivity. . . .
>
> Several scientific studies have shown that soft drinks are directly related to weight gain. Weight gain is a prime risk factor for type 2 diabetes, heart attacks, strokes, and cancer. Frequent consumption of soft drinks is also linked to osteoporosis, tooth decay, and dental erosion.[15]

Causal Reasoning

Another everyday form of inference is **causal reasoning**—reasoning from effect to cause, or from cause to effect. Suppose, for example, that we notice a significant increase in crime or a decrease in the number of traffic deaths across the nation. We naturally want to know about the causes of these trends. By the same token, we often want to know what effects might result from some change in policy. What impact will a proposed welfare reform policy have on the number of people on welfare? Would allowing social security recipients to invest in private accounts help solve the system's financial crisis or provide more secure retirements for the elderly? These sorts of questions invite causal reasoning.

Causal reasoning is at the heart of all scientific investigation. In trying to solve the mysteries of the world, researchers routinely reason from cause to effect and effect to cause. What causes some volcanoes to violently explode, while others lay dormant for centuries? What caused the great chestnut forests of the eastern United States to disappear? What are the causes of a recent increase in the number of high school dropouts?[16] Why do some people become sexual predators, preying on innocent children? These are just a few of the questions scientists and social scientists are trying to answer through causal reasoning.

Scientists know just how difficult it can be to establish causation. In the natural world, causation is often complex, involving multiple causes or chains of causation. What is *the* cause of declining songbird populations? The answer is that there *is* no single cause. Some ornithologists point to climatic change, acid rain, or disappearing habitat as the primary culprits. Others emphasize the destruction of nesting habitats resulting from the planting of nonnative shrubs, competition or parasitism among different species of birds, or the proliferation of such predators as domestic cats, gray squirrels, and raptors. No doubt still more causes will be discovered as the research continues. The decline in songbird populations is a complex problem with multiple and dynamic causes. It is impossible to point the finger at any single cause.

Imagine how much more difficult it can be to prove what causes humans to do some of the things they do! What causes the anorexic literally to starve herself to death, or the bulimic to binge and purge? What leads people to a life of crime, or to a life of violence against others? Why do some people become obsessive about their work, neglecting their families and all of the pleasures of life just to "get ahead"? Again, these are complex questions with no simple answers. Even more than the natural world, human behavior involves systems of multiple and interrelated causes that even the best experts have difficulty sorting out.

In short, establishing causation is rarely simple. The responsible public advocate recognizes the difficulty of proving causation and seeks out the best information and evidence available from reputable sources. The responsible advocate also *qualifies* his or her causal claims, acknowledging that we can rarely assert causal claims with absolute certainty or talk about any single factor as *the* cause of a complex problem.

Analogical Reasoning

Consider the following two arguments, both of which you have probably heard before in one form or another:

1. The current economic crisis is another Great Depression. We must act boldly to shore up the banking industry, stimulate the economy, and create new jobs before our entire financial system collapses, as it did in the 1930s.
2. Politics is like a horse race. It doesn't matter who's first out of the gate, and even the best horses occasionally stumble. True champions have stamina, perseverance, and the courage to let others take the early lead. But as the race heats up, true champions emerge out of the pack, charging to the front with the race on the line. They have a nose for the finish line.

Both of these arguments are based on comparisons. Both illustrate **analogical reasoning**, in which we conclude that what is true of one case will also be true of the other. Yet are the two arguments equally reasonable? Of course not. In the

WHITE HOUSE
25000
NEW YORK LEDGER
THE GREAT POLITICAL RACE!
STAKES, $25,000 A YEAR!
The LINCOLN Horse is ahead, free and unencumbered, while the others are in the back-ground loaded down with their favorite riders.

FIGURE 16.2

Political cartoonists historically have compared the presidential election to a horse race. In this cartoon from 1860, Abraham Lincoln is depicted as the lead horse in the race for the White House, while his chief competitors are slowed by riders representing slavery, the Dred Scott decision, and a newspaper that obstructs the rider's vision

first example we are comparing one economic crisis to another. This is what we call a literal analogy, comparing two similar examples. In the second, we are comparing electoral politics to a horse race. That is a *figurative* analogy, like the metaphors discussed in Chapter 11. Figurative analogies may be useful for illustrating a point or giving a speech stylistic color. But they rarely *prove* anything. If we hope to make serious, logically compelling analogical arguments, we should rely upon *literal* analogies.

The explanation for this is simple: the logical strength of analogical reasoning rests on the degree of similarity between the cases being compared. So, for example, if we really hoped to convince people that the current economic crisis is "another Great Depression," it would be important to establish as many similarities as possible between today's economic conditions and those of the 1930s. Similarly, if we advocated a new recycling program for our city, it would be important to establish that such a program has worked well in a similar city—a city with the same population, perhaps, or one that has similar waste management problems. In short, the more similar the cases, the stronger the analogical argument. That is why figurative analogies carry little persuasive weight.

Analogical reasoning is most frequently used in policy arguments. When proposing a new policy, you should investigate whether similar policies have been tried elsewhere. Then you may draw your evidence from places where the policy has already worked. During the late 1990s, for example, welfare reform swept the nation, with state after state setting tougher eligibility requirements and adopting a variety of new policies to encourage aid recipients to find work. Overall, these reforms reduced the welfare rolls nationwide by more than half. Yet what worked in one state did not necessarily work in another, even though all the policies reflected the Clinton administration's goal of "ending welfare as we know it."[17]

Like all forms of reasoning, analogical reasoning involves a leap from the known to the unknown. In policy arguments, we may know that a particular program has worked in the past. But we never know for certain what the future will bring, nor can we identify all the circumstances that may affect how well a particular policy might work. Thus, analogical arguments, like all arguments, should be *qualified* at the appropriate level of certainty. Based on the fact that a policy has worked in the past, we can conclude that it *may* or even *probably will* work in the future. But we can never say that with certainty; the future is always, to some extent, unknown.

FALLACIES OF REASONING AND EVIDENCE

Preview. *Arguments are unsound when they have flaws of reasoning or evidence, called fallacies. Common fallacies occur when speakers draw irrelevant conclusions, employ faulty reasoning, provide insufficient evidence, or indulge in personal attacks.*

As we have pointed out, any claim is only as good as the reasoning and evidence that support it. Many things can go wrong during the reasoning process, leading one to draw a faulty conclusion. Following are some common **fallacies** of reasoning and evidence that ought to be avoided by speakers—and rejected by listeners. Also sometimes known by the Latin names given to them centuries ago, the fallacies may be categorized as follows:

- fallacies of relevance
- fallacies of faulty reasoning
- fallacies of inadequate evidence
- fallacies of personal attack

Fallacies of Relevance

Fallacies of relevance occur when a speaker, in effect, changes the subject, talking about matters that are simply not relevant to the issue at hand. Fallacies of relevance are sometimes deliberately employed to distract audiences and divert attention away from the real issues.

Appeal to Ignorance (*Ad Ignorantiam*) Speakers sometimes try to convince us that because something has not been proven wrong, it must be right! If a friend told you that it has never been proven that aliens from other planets have *not* visited earth, would that persuade you that we *have* been visited by aliens? Of course not! Yet we hear similar arguments every day from people who do not really have any evidence to prove their claims. A legislator, for example, might offer the following argument:

> I am convinced that my bill to require teachers to lead schoolchildren in reciting the pledge of allegiance each day will increase patriotism among young people. So far, no one has proven that I'm wrong about this. Why would anyone oppose teaching our kids to be more patriotic?

True, nobody can prove that reciting the pledge will *not* make children more patriotic. Yet neither does this legislator cite any evidence that it *would* increase patriotism.

The *ad ignorantiam* fallacy may assume the opposite form as well: just because something has *not* been proven true does not mean that it is false. In the following example, a student committed the *ad ignorantiam* fallacy in an argument about television's effects on children:

> So we've seen that while there are instances of some children acting violently after watching television—and while some studies indicate that television violence can desensitize children to violent acts—no one has been able to establish a direct link between TV and violence. We can only conclude that television is not to blame for violent behavior among children.

This student may be right that nobody has established a "direct link" between TV and violence. But his own evidence suggests the *possibility* of such a link, and the fact that nobody has proven that connection conclusively does not prove that there is *no* link between TV and violence.

Appeal to Popular Beliefs (*Ad Populum*) Sometimes known as a ***bandwagon appeal***, this fallacy occurs when a speaker urges listeners to accept something simply because so many others accept it. Many of us are tempted to "follow the crowd," and public speakers sometimes take advantage of this by urging us to do something because "everybody is doing it." Knowing that other people support an idea or a policy is certainly one piece of information that you may want to take into account. But that fact alone should not be persuasive.

In a democracy, the majority rules, of course, so the fact that 63 percent of Americans support some plan may be *one* reason for adopting it. But majority support does not prove that it is a *good* policy—that it will solve some problem or serve the national interest. In American history, the majority has proven wrong on more than one occasion, and over time minority views sometimes *become* the majority view. In the following excerpt, for example, we hear a line of argument commonly used to silence debate over controversial wars. It was an argument heard during the Vietnam War, which most Americans initially supported but *later* came to oppose:

> The polls are clear, the people have spoken: the vast majority of Americans supports this war. The time for dissent has passed, and now is the time to support our men and women in uniform, no matter how we feel about the war.

There may well be good reasons for supporting our troops regardless of how we feel about a war. And in a democracy, majority opinion must be respected. Yet in a free society, we should never allow an appeal to popular beliefs to silence debate over the merits of an idea or policy.

THE NON SEQUITUR ***Non sequitur*** is Latin for "it does not follow." In other words, this fallacy occurs when a conclusion does not follow logically from the arguments and evidence that precede it. In a sense, all logical fallacies are more specific types of non sequiturs. But when the problem with an argument is that, in general, the evidence is simply not relevant to the claim, we say that the speaker has committed a *non sequitur*.

To continue with our previous example, suppose now that our pro-war speaker began the same way: "The polls are clear ... the vast majority of Americans supports this war." Instead of concluding that we should stop criticizing the war because a majority supports it, however, suppose that our speaker then said the following: "So, as we can see, the president's decision to go to war was constitutional under his powers as commander in chief." Here the problem is not that the speaker is asking us to jump on the bandwagon, but that public support for the war simply has nothing to do with whether the president's actions were legal under the Constitution. That is a question for experts in constitutional law, not a matter to be resolved by public opinion.

APPEAL TO TRADITION (*AD VERECUNDIAM*) You have probably heard this fallacy expressed this way: "We've never done it that way before." Or perhaps you have heard it expressed another way: "This is the way we've always done it." People get set in their ways, and speakers sometimes exploit this fact to argue against change. An advocate of change *does* have the burden of proof in a policy debate, but that does not mean that those who oppose change can simply respond, "We've always done it this way." Tradition is not, in itself, a good reason for sticking with the status quo.

Appeals to tradition are often heard in contexts where the ideas or policies being challenged have a long history. So, for example, the Virginia Military Institute (VMI) appealed to tradition for many years to justify excluding women from its programs. In 1996, however, the Supreme Court, in *United States v. Virginia et al.*, ruled that women had a right to attend VMI under the equal protection clause of the Constitution.[18] Similarly, students at Texas A&M University resisted for many years efforts to end a 90-year tradition of building "the world's largest bonfire" on the eve of their annual football rivalry with the University of Texas. Yet after the 59-foot-high structure collapsed in 1999, killing 12 students and injuring 27 others, arguments about safety and liability finally prevailed over appeals to tradition.[19]

At Texas A&M University, it took a terrible tragedy to overcome appeals to tradition, as a log structure built for the "world's largest bonfire" collapsed, killing twelve students. Rescue workers are shown here responding to the tragedy.

Tradition can be a good thing, of course, but it is unreasonable to use it as a shield against compelling arguments for change. Change involves risk, and advocates of change must meet their burden of proof. But if they meet that burden, they have a right to a real debate, not a deflection of their arguments by appeals to tradition.

THE RED HERRING FALLACY The term **red herring** comes from an old practice of using the strong odor of smoked herring to throw hunting dogs off the track of a fox, either as a training exercise or to keep them out of farmers' fields. In argumentation theory, a red herring is an attempt to throw an audience off track by raising an irrelevant, often highly emotional issue that prevents critical examination of an argument. In a debate over whether prayer ought to be allowed in the public schools, for example, an advocate may divert attention from the real issues by declaring, "The issue here is whether we are going to allow atheists to determine what happens in our schools." Many who oppose prayer in schools, of course, are not atheists at all, but are simply concerned about the separation of church and state. The real issue is not the threat posed by atheists, but whether school prayer violates the Constitution.

Consider another example of how a red herring might distract attention from the real issue at stake. Imagine a defense lawyer saying the following:

> My client is a fine, upstanding citizen who has spent his life in community service. He was a Boy Scout leader, sang in his church choir, and coached Little League. This man has lived in this town all his life and never has been charged with a crime. Would such a man embezzle money from his employer?

Perhaps it is hard to imagine such a man embezzling money, but his attorney has avoided the real issue here. The man's guilt or innocence must be established by the evidence, not by a recitation of his personal virtues. The introduction of his exemplary life is a red herring, designed to distract attention from the real issue at hand.

THE STRAW MAN FALLACY In the **straw man fallacy**, a speaker attributes a flimsy, easy-to-refute argument to his opponent, and then proceeds to demolish it. In the process, of course, the speaker misrepresents the opponent's real position. In some cases, the speaker may even try to make the opponent look silly for making such a ridiculous argument. So, for example, an environmentalist might portray a so-called wise use advocate—one who supports *some* logging or mining on public lands—as favoring "the sale of our national forests to the highest bidder." That exaggerates the position of the wise use advocate, creating a straw man that is easy to attack.

Straw men have been prominent in debates over welfare reform in the United States. The following example is hypothetical, but it sounds like some of the arguments actually heard during the welfare debates of the late 1990s:

> We need to find ways to reform the welfare system so that our tax dollars are not wasted on those who just want a free handout. Opponents of reform believe that anyone who doesn't want to work shouldn't have to. They argue that if a woman wants to have children out of wedlock, well, that's her right, and the state should take care of those children. I, for one, disagree with those who think that taxpayers' money ought to be used to encourage people not to work, not to get married, or to have more children out of wedlock. My opponents want to continue this culture of welfare dependency that has cost taxpayers billions of dollars. I say the time has come for a new approach.

Opponents of welfare reform never made such arguments, of course. Almost everybody agreed about the need for reform. The real debate was over what *sorts* of policies might get people off welfare and end the "culture of dependency." The welfare advocate who *favored* "free handouts" and *wanted* to see more children born out of wedlock was a straw man.

These fallacies—appeal to ignorance, appeal to popular beliefs, the *non sequitur*, appeal to tradition, the red herring, and the straw man—all produce conclusions that do not follow logically from the evidence. They are all ways to distract attention from the real issues at stake. When employed intentionally, they violate the spirit of deliberating in good faith.

Fallacies of Faulty Reasoning

Fallacies of reasoning are errors in analogical or causal arguments, or they may involve "arguing in circles" or creating false choices. Like fallacies of relevance, fallacies of faulty reasoning may be unintentional, reflecting only fuzzy thinking on the part of an advocate. Or they may be used deliberately as propaganda techniques.

THE FALSE DILEMMA The **false dilemma** is a fallacy that occurs when a speaker suggests that we have only two alternatives, when in fact more than two alternatives exist. Typically this takes the form of an either/or proposition: "Either we fight to win in Afghanistan, or we 'cut and run' as we did in Vietnam." This reasoning is faulty, of course, because there are a number of policy options between the extremes of all-out escalation and total retreat.

The false dilemma is routinely evident in budget debates. Consider, for example, the following passage:

> The budget deficit has once again become a serious threat to our economy and to the future welfare of our children. The only way to make sure that the budget deficit doesn't continue to grow out of hand is to cut social programs. Some people may be hurt by this, but we have no choice—either we cut these programs, or we run the risk of huge budget deficits that will stop our economic growth and create a huge burden for the next generation of American taxpayers.

The problem here, of course, is that other choices are possible. One choice is to do nothing and see whether an improving economy takes care of the budget deficit. Another is to raise taxes to bring down the deficit. Still another is to combine cuts in social programs with tax increases. Perhaps radical cuts in social programs really are needed, but that remains to be proven. To say that we must *either* make drastic cuts *or* suffer huge budget deficits is a false dilemma.

The false dilemma may assume more complex forms, of course, proposing three or more false alternatives. Thus, for example, an advocate may say that we *must* do one of three or four things—or face horrible consequences. Again, what determines whether such reasoning is fallacious is not the number of alternatives per se, but whether the advocate has listed *all* the realistic alternatives. In dealing with complex issues, we typically have many options, so we should always be suspicious of those who say that we have only one or two choices.

BEGGING THE QUESTION **Begging the question** occurs when a speaker makes a claim that *assumes* the very thing he or she hopes to prove. This typically takes the form of circular reasoning, in which the speaker offers no support for a claim, but instead simply restates the claim itself in different words. Thus, for example, a speaker may claim that "illegal immigrants are a drain on our nation's economy." When asked for evidence, the response may be: "Well, we all know that illegal immigrants use expensive social services yet pay no taxes." Here the speaker has not offered any evidence for the original assertion, but has simply restated the original claim in different, more specific terms. In effect, the speaker is offering one unsupported assertion as support for the other.

Speakers often attempt to disguise efforts to beg the question with words such as *obviously*, *of course*, or *as we all know*. So, for example, a speaker may say the following:

> As we all know, capital punishment deters crime. Obviously, potential criminals will think twice before committing a crime if they know they will be executed if they are caught. With capital punishment reinstated in every state, we would, of course, see a dramatic reduction in the murder rate.

This speaker claims that capital punishment deters crime. But what is her evidence? When forced to support her contention, she simply restated the same claim in another way, speculating that criminals "obviously" would "think twice" if they faced execution.

THE FAULTY ANALOGY As we noted earlier, the strength of analogical reasoning depends on the similarity of the two things being compared. When speakers compare things that are not, in fact, similar, they commit the fallacy of **faulty analogy**. There are no specific rules for when an analogy becomes "faulty," but *figurative* analogies—almost by definition—are logically faulty. Literal analogies *may* provide support for an argument, but the legitimacy of such comparisons is always open to debate. Suppose, for example, that an opponent of stricter gun control made the following argument:

> Gun control is not a new idea. In Nazi Germany, guns were confiscated to prevent any groups from taking actions that might have undermined Hitler. In Cuba, Castro made sure that no one but his own Communist followers had guns. Whenever dictators want to stifle opposition, they take away people's guns. Now we have men and women in Washington who want to pass new gun control legislation and take away your guns.

Is the speaker's comparison of gun control advocates in America to Hitler and Castro legitimate? Are the similarities between the United States and Nazi Germany—or between the United States and Cuba—sufficient to warrant such comparisons? The analogies used by this speaker certainly add pathos to the argument, but scaring listeners is not the same as arguing logically. From a logical point of view, this may well be a faulty analogy, ignoring important political and cultural differences between the nations being compared. In addition, the analogy wrongly equates all gun control measures with the *confiscation* of guns. Not only is this argument based on a faulty analogy, but it also creates a straw man.

THE SLIPPERY SLOPE The fallacy of the **slippery slope** occurs when a speaker claims that some cause will *inevitably* lead to undesirable effects, ultimately resulting in some worst-case scenario. If you take the first step down the slippery slope, or so the reasoning goes, you will quickly slide all the way to the bottom. Again, opponents of gun control are probably guilty of this fallacy when they insist that any gun control legislation inevitably will lead to the confiscation of all guns. The slippery slope also can be heard in debates over rising tuition costs, as in this passage from a student speech:

> The Board of Trustees is once again considering raising tuition next year. This is a dangerous action and threatens to undermine the very foundation of public education. A state university is supposed to serve the interests of the citizens of the state; if this tuition increase is implemented, it will be the first step in an ever-increasing spiral of rising costs for students. Eventually, only the rich will be able to attend our state universities and have the opportunity to get a college education.

Of course, it is not necessarily fallacious to argue that some action will lead to bad consequences down the road. We reason like that every day—for example, in arguing that bad eating habits will lead to health problems. The slippery slope, however, treats *probable* or *possible* causal links as certain and inevitable, and it preys on fears of the worst-case scenario.

These fallacies—false alternatives, begging the question, the faulty analogy, and the slippery slope—are all perversions of otherwise legitimate forms of reasoning. It is not the form of reasoning *per se* that leads to fallacious arguments, but rather faulty assumptions and unwarranted inferential leaps in otherwise legitimate forms of reasoning.

Fallacies of Inadequate Evidence

Fallacies of inadequate evidence occur when a speaker simply does not have sufficient evidence to back up his or her claim. Generally, speakers who commit these errors have some but not enough evidence to prove their claims.

FALSE CAUSE (*POST HOC, ERGO PROPTER HOC*) The **false cause** fallacy occurs when a speaker confuses a chronological relationship with a causal one. It is often known by its Latin name, *post hoc, ergo propter hoc*—"after this, therefore because of this." Simply because one event precedes another, of course, does not mean that it *caused* it. Crime may decline after a new gun control law is passed, but that does not prove that the legislation *caused* the decline. The economy may improve in the wake of tax cuts, but that does not mean that tax cuts *caused* the improvement. As we noted earlier, most political, economic, and social trends have complex, often multiple causes that may be difficult to sort out. In their effort to simplify explanations, advocates sometimes *oversimplify* causation, and that often takes the form of the *post hoc* fallacy.

THE HASTY GENERALIZATION The **hasty generalization** fallacy occurs when a speaker generalizes from too few examples. Perhaps the speaker observed but a handful of students at one university before concluding that all college students are binge drinkers. Or maybe she talked to just three senior citizens before generalizing that all seniors suffer from depression. In either case, the speaker committed a hasty generalization. He or she drew a sweeping generalization based on too few examples.

HIGHLIGHTING THE *POST HOC* FALLACY

The Gun Control Debate

As is often the case in long-running, highly emotional public debates, *both* sides in the gun control debate have been guilty of logical fallacies. Indeed, one can often find the same logical fallacies committed by advocates both for and against gun control. Consider, for example, the following two arguments:

1. "The only policy that effectively reduces public shootings is right-to-carry laws. Allowing citizens to carry concealed handguns reduces violent crime. In the 31 states that have passed right-to-carry laws since the mid-1980s, the number of multiple-victim public shootings and other violent crimes has dropped dramatically. Murders fell by 7.65%, rapes by 5.2%, aggravated assaults by 7%, and robberies by 3%."
2. "[E]vidence shows that even state and local handgun control laws work. For example, in 1974 Massachusetts passed the Bartley-Fox Law, which requires a special license to carry a handgun outside the home or business. The law is supported by a mandatory prison sentence. Studies by Glenn Pierce and William Bowers of Northeastern University documented that after the law was passed handgun homicides in Massachusetts fell 50% and the number of armed robberies dropped 35%."

Both of these examples commit the *post hoc* fallacy, reasoning that because a drop in crime occurred *after* new legislation was passed, the legislation must have *caused* the drop. In the first example, from the *Phyllis Schlafly Report*, an advocate opposed to gun control claims that "right-to-carry" laws "effectively reduce[d]" public shootings and violent crime. This claim is supported by statistics on falling crime rates since the mid-1980s in states that have passed such laws. In the second example, from an organization called Handgun Control, Inc., an advocate of stricter state and local gun control laws claims that such laws "work" to lower handgun crime—another causal claim. Again, the claim is supported by statistics on falling crime rates.

Violent crime fell generally in the United States in the late 1980s and 1990s, and a number of factors may have contributed to that trend. Moreover, neither Schlafly nor Handgun Control, Inc. provides us with the *comparative* data necessary to prove that declining crime rates can be attributed to the passage of new legislation. Schlafly provides no data from states that did *not* pass "right to carry" laws, so we have no way of knowing whether crime declined any faster in states that passed such laws than in those that did not. Likewise, the pro-gun-control argument provides no basis for comparison to other states. In addition, it doesn't even make clear *when* Massachusetts's drop in crime occurred, except that it occurred "after"—*post hoc*—passage of the new handgun control law. Gary N. Curtis, author of *The Fallacy Files*, concludes, "The very fact that comparative information is *not* supplied in each argument is suspicious, since it suggests that it would have weakened the case."

Source: "Post Hoc," *The Fallacy Files*, www.fallacyfiles.org/posthocf.html (accessed July 20, 2009).

Consider the following argument from a student speech about funding for public schools in poor neighborhoods. Drawing on his personal experience, the student made the following argument:

> Last spring I spent three weeks as an observer in one of these poor schools. What I saw was lazy teachers and lazy students. Everyone seemed to be going through the motions. Students weren't motivated to learn and teachers were just too tired

> and frustrated to try to get anything out of these kids. I don't believe that pouring money into these poor schools will help them much. People just won't do things they don't want to do.

In this case, of course, the student probably did not actually observe "everyone" in the school. Moreover, all of the teachers and students he observed were from just this one school. To generalize about *all* "poor schools" based on this limited experience would be to commit a hasty generalization. Most reasonable people would agree that generalizing from just one school is unwarranted and fallacious.

These two fallacies—the false cause (*post hoc*) and the hasty generalization—occur when conclusions are drawn without sufficient evidence to support them. Evidence that one thing occurred after another does not prove causation, and sound inductive reasoning requires more than just one or two examples.

Fallacies of Personal Attack

Personal attacks are perhaps the most troubling fallacies, because they contribute to the negative tone of our politics and "turn off" many citizens. Fallacies of personal attack are sometimes used deliberately to shift attention away from the real issues at hand. They substitute name-calling or character assassination for engagement of other people's arguments.

THE *AD HOMINEM* FALLACY Unfortunately, the ***ad hominem*** fallacy has become increasingly familiar in our political campaigns. Although the character, integrity, or even intelligence of a political candidate may be a legitimate "issue" in some elections, too often attacks on the person are substituted for arguments about a candidate's ideas or proposals.

Here is an example of an *ad hominem* fallacy that may sound vaguely familiar:

> The congressman's criticism of the president is hypocrisy of the worst sort. The congressman has, for many years, had an extramarital affair. Who is he to attack the president for moral indiscretions? The congressman himself has behaved immorally, displaying his own lack of commitment to "family values."

Now it may be true that the congressman is a hypocrite. If he attacked the president for his personal misconduct, perhaps it is only fair that he be subjected to the same sort of criticism. Still, this argument commits the *ad hominem* fallacy because it sidesteps the accusations against the president. The response does not deny the charges against the president, nor does it defend the president's actions. Instead, it attacks the person who raised the issue, in effect changing the subject.

GUILT BY ASSOCIATION The guilt-by-association fallacy arises when we judge an idea, person, or programs solely on the basis of their association with other ideas, persons, or programs. If you view yourself as a political liberal, for example, you may be tempted to dismiss any idea or proposal that comes from the likes of Newt Gingrich or Rush Limbaugh. If you consider yourself conservative, you may be equally likely to dismiss—without serious thought or analysis—the ideas of liberals such as Howard Dean or Nancy Pelosi. Research shows that many people rate an idea, an essay, a speech, or even a painting higher if they are told that it came from a person they respect.[20] This, of course, illustrates the power of ethos. Put in more negative terms, however, it also suggests how we may discredit an otherwise good idea simply by associating it with an unpopular source.

Guilt by association refers to attacking the worth of people or their ideas solely on the basis of their associations. Rather than assessing the quality of an idea or argument, guilt by association dismisses it by connecting it to something already discredited in the minds of the audience. Consider, for example, the following hypothetical argument:

> How can we believe that this proposal is made with our best interests in mind? Mr. Morgan says it will save us a lot of money. But Mr. Morgan once belonged to an investment club in which many of the investors lost everything. One member of that club was actually indicted for fraud, while others pulled out just in time to make a lot of money at the expense of their fellow members.

Mr. Morgan was not the one indicted for fraud, nor was he likely one of the members who pulled out "just in time." If he had been guilty of either of those things, his critic probably would have mentioned it. Indeed, Mr. Morgan may have been one of the victims himself. But bent on discrediting Morgan's proposal, the speaker suggests that his plan is suspect simply because of his former associations. This is fallacious because it diverts attention from the real issue at hand—whether the proposal is a good idea—by discrediting the source.

Arguments that are based on personal attacks—the *ad hominem* attack and guilt by association—are flawed because they sidestep the real issues. More than that, they debase the quality of our public discourse, undermining the politics of ideas with what former president Bill Clinton once called "the politics of personal destruction."

The fallacies we have discussed are not the only forms of faulty reasoning. Scholars of argumentation have identified hundreds of fallacies and propaganda devices, all of which can detract from the quality of our public deliberations. As responsible citizens, we should avoid committing fallacies in our own speeches, and we should learn to recognize and speak out against the fallacious arguments of others. Fallacies are among the techniques that demagogues and propagandists use to deceive and mislead the public. As citizens in a democracy, we need to recognize and resist such techniques and speak out against those who use them.

SUMMARY

- Persuasion is a legitimate, essential tool of democratic deliberation, whereas demagoguery subverts reasoned deliberation with charismatic and emotional appeals.
- A good argument is not one that confirms our existing beliefs or "works" to persuade an audience, but one that is complete, reasonable, and meets certain tests of reasoning and evidence.
- *Claims* are debatable assertions about fact, value, or policy that we put forward in a persuasive speech.

- *Evidence* provides support for our claims and should meet certain tests of quantitative and qualitative sufficiency.
- *Warrants* are general assumptions, principles, or rules that connect our evidence to our claims.
- The burden of proof is the level of proof necessary to warrant serious consideration of an argument.
- The process of drawing inferences from known facts is called *reasoning*.
- There are four common types of reasoning: inductive, deductive, causal, and analogical.
  - Inductive reasoning draws a general conclusion from a set of specific examples.
  - Deductive reasoning draws conclusions about specific cases from a generally accepted premise or principle.
  - Causal reasoning makes inferences from cause to effect or effect to cause.
  - Analogical reasoning infers that what is true of some known case is or will be true of a similar case.
- Fallacies are errors or flaws of reasoning and evidence.
- There are four major categories of fallacies: fallacies of relevance, fallacies of reasoning, fallacies of inadequate evidence, and fallacies of personal attack.
  - Fallacies of relevance include the appeal to ignorance, the appeal to popular beliefs, the disconnected conclusion (or non sequitur), the appeal to tradition, the red herring, and the straw man.
  - Fallacies of faulty reasoning include the false dilemma, begging the question, the faulty analogy, and the slippery slope.
  - Fallacies of inadequate evidence include the false cause (*post hoc*) and the hasty generalization.
  - Fallacies of personal attack include the attack against the person (*ad hominem*) and guilt by association.

QUESTIONS FOR REVIEW AND REFLECTION

1. How would you distinguish between persuasion and demagoguery? Can you identify one or two public figures today whom you would consider demagogues? *Why* do you think they deserve that label?
2. What makes for a good argument? Is a good argument always *persuasive*? Is there such a thing as a *reasonable* argument that people do not find *persuasive*? What, exactly, does it mean to say that an argument is *reasonable*, and what sorts of standards or tests might we use in judging arguments?
3. Distinguish among the different types of *claims* discussed in this chapter, and think of one example of each type of claim. Can you think of a major public controversy that still revolves around claims of fact? What about claims of value and policy?
4. What is meant by *burden of proof*, and who would have the burden of proof in debates over (a) an allegation of wrongdoing by a public official and (b) a proposal for a new tax policy? If you meet your burden of proof, what does that mean? Does that mean you "win" the debate?

5. Distinguish among the four types of reasoning discussed in this chapter and discuss what makes for strong inductive, deductive, causal, and analogical reasoning. Besides the examples given in the book, can you think of one more example of each type of reasoning that you have heard in a speech or public debate?
6. Which of the *fallacies of relevance* discussed in this chapter do you think are most common in today's political environment? In other words, do we hear more red herrings than straw man fallacies? More appeals to popular belief than appeals to tradition?
7. Are the fallacies discussed in this book *always* errors in reasoning? Are they *always* "illogical"? Is there ever a time, for example, when an appeal to popular beliefs is reasonable? Is an appeal to tradition ever legitimate? Is it ever reasonable to attack the person or to discredit the source of an argument because of the people or groups they associate with ("guilt by association")?

ENDNOTES

1. See Albert Fried, *McCarthyism: The Great American Red Scare: A Documentary History* (New York: Oxford University Press, 1997).
2. Aristotle, *Rhetoric*, trans. W. Rhys Roberts (Chicago: University of Chicago Press, 1952).
3. See Jeffrey K. Tulis, *The Rhetorical Presidency* (Princeton, NJ: Princeton University Press, 1987), 27–39.
4. See J. Michael Hogan, *Woodrow Wilson's Western Tour: Rhetoric, Public Opinion, and the League of Nations* (College Station: Texas A&M University Press, 2006), 27–41.
5. Woodrow Wilson, "Congressional Government," in *The Papers of Woodrow Wilson*, ed. Arthur S. Link et al., 69 vols. (Princeton, NJ: Princeton University Press, 1966–1994), 1: 565–66.
6. In a survey sponsored by the McCormick Tribune Freedom Museum, for example, it was found that only about one in a thousand Americans could identify all five rights protected by the First Amendment: freedom of speech, freedom of religion, freedom of the press, freedom of assembly, and the right to petition the government for redress of grievances. About two-thirds of the sample were able to name freedom of speech as a First Amendment right, but fewer than a quarter (23 percent) named freedom of religion and only 10 percent identified freedom of the press as First Amendment rights. Interestingly, a number of respondents attributed other rights to the First Amendment that are not guaranteed by the Constitution at all, including the right to drive a car (17 percent) and the right to own pets (21 percent). Also, the study revealed that the characters in the television show *The Simpsons* were more familiar to most Americans than their First Amendment rights. See "Characters from 'The Simpsons' More Well Known to Americans Than Their First Amendment Freedoms, Survey Finds," McCormick Tribune Freedom Museum, news release, March 1, 2006, www.freedommuseum.us/files/pdf/museum.survey_release.pdf (accessed July 20, 2009).
7. Max Weber, *The Theory of Social and Economic Organization*, trans. A. M. Henderson and Talcott Parsons (New York: Oxford University Press, 1947), 358.
8. Abraham Lincoln, "First Inaugural Address (1861)," in *American Voices: Significant Speeches in American History, 1640–1945*, ed. James R. Andrews and David Zarefsky (New York: Longman, 1989), 290.
9. For more on the rhetorical techniques of demagogues, see J. Justin Gustainis, "Demagoguery and Political Rhetoric: A Review of the Literature," *Rhetoric Society Quarterly* 20 (1990): 155–61.
10. James Darsey, *The Prophetic Tradition and Radical Rhetoric in America* (New York: New York University Press, 1997).
11. See J. Michael Hogan and Dave Tell, "Demagoguery and Democratic Deliberation: The Search for Rules of Discursive Engagement," *Rhetoric and Public Affairs* 9 (Fall 2006), 479–87.

12. See Stephen E. Toulmin, *The Uses of Argument* (Cambridge, UK: Cambridge University Press, 1958). Also see Wayne Brockriede and Douglas Ehninger, "Toulmin on Argument: An Interpretation and Application," *Quarterly Journal of Speech* 46 (1960): 44–53.
13. In law, the "reasonable person" is a "legal fiction" used primarily in negligence and contract law cases. Under this test, the court imagines how a "reasonable person"—a hypothetical person who is intelligent, informed, aware of the law, and fair minded—might react to arguments before the court. So, for example, a negligence case might raise the question of whether a defendant took the necessary precautions to avoid an accident—with those "necessary precautions" defined, of course, by the "reasonable person" test. Would the reasonable person have anticipated the circumstances that led to the accident? What kinds of precautions would the "reasonable person" have taken? What would the "reasonable person" have recognized as his or her legal rights and obligations in the aftermath of the accident?
14. David Thigpen, "Hall of Shame," *Time*, March 20, 2005, www.time.com/time/magazine/article/0,9171,1039703-1,00.html (accessed July 17, 2009).
15. Reprinted by permission from "Why Tax Soft Drinks?" *Liquid Candy: How Soft Drinks are Harming America's Health*. Copyright © n.d. by Center for Science in the Public Interest.
16. See Nathan Thornburgh, "Dropout Nation," *Time*, April 17, 2006, 31–40.
17. See R. Kent Weaver and Thomas Gais, "State Policy Choices under Welfare Reform," CCF Policy Briefs Number 21, Brookings Institution, April 2002, www.brookings.edu/papers/2002/04welfare_gais.aspx (accessed July 20, 2009).
18. See Legal Information Institute, Cornell School of Law, "*United States v. Virginia et al.* (94–1941), 518 U.S. 515 (1996)," *Supreme Court Collection*, www.law.cornell.edu/supct/html/94-1941.ZO.html (accessed July 20, 2009).
19. See "Texas A&M University Bonfire Memorial," www.tamu.edu/bonfirememorial/ (accessed July 20, 2009).
20. Jack L. Whitehead, "Factors of Source Credibility," *Quarterly Journal of Speech* 54 (1968): 59–63.

Global Climate Change

Kathryn Gromowski

In this speech delivered at a public speaking contest in 2008, Penn State student Kathryn Gromowski urged her listeners to support legislation to combat global warming. Although the bill she advocated did not become law, similar legislation is still being debated in Congress, and many of her arguments remain relevant to the ongoing debate over climate change. Kathryn uses causal reasoning, statistical evidence and expert testimony, and a simple problem-solution organization to meet her burden of proof and make a reasonable argument for the legislation. She reinforces the logical reasoning of the speech with credible sources (ethos) and mild but effective emotional appeals (pathos) grounded in fears of a climatic disaster.

We have all seen these pictures. Ice caps shrinking. Cities going underwater. People displaced with nowhere to go due to storms and expanding oceans. They are terrifying, but to many of us, they are just images. Soon, however, they may become realities if we continue to stand by and do nothing about global climate change. According to David Elliot Cohen, author of a best-selling book about climate change, those scary pictures may "someday be the iconic images of our decade . . . because they presage the images we will spend this century viewing—on our screens, and out our windows." If we are to prevent this from becoming a reality, we need to start by finally doing something to curb global warming, and that means tackling carbon emissions more aggressively. A bill currently before Congress, the Sanders-Boxer Global Warming Pollution Reduction Act, is America's best hope for preventing further damage from global warming. Today, I will discuss the problem we face, describe the provisions of the Sanders-Boxer Act, and explain why it is the best horse to bet on in the race for our planet's survival.

KATHRYN BEGINS WITH A CONCISE INTRODUCTION, GRABBING HER AUDIENCE'S ATTENTION BY REFERRING TO FAMILIAR IMAGES BUT THEN GETTING RIGHT TO THE POINT: SHE WANTS HER AUDIENCE TO SUPPORT A BILL IN CONGRESS THAT WOULD "AGGRESSIVELY" COMBAT GLOBAL WARMING.

Although climate change might refer to any number of natural or human-caused environmental changes, the greatest danger we face is global warming. Global warming is caused by atmospheric gases through a phenomenon known as the greenhouse effect. According to the Environmental Protection Agency, or EPA, "The greenhouse effect is a natural phenomenon that helps regulate the Earth's temperature. Greenhouse gases . . . act like an insulating blanket, trapping solar energy that would otherwise escape into space." Over the last century or so, human activities have dramatically increased the natural greenhouse effect, causing the earth's average temperature to rise.

The primary greenhouse gases are carbon dioxide, methane, and nitrous oxide, but the real killer is carbon dioxide. According to the Carbon Dioxide Information Analysis Center, the concentration of CO_2 as of September 2008 is 383.9 parts per million, which may not seem like much, but over the entire surface of the earth that amount of CO_2 causes a warming effect equivalent to roughly 141 billion 60-watt lightbulbs. In fact, a *New York Times* article from February 6, 2007, stated that, "if greenhouse gas emissions continue unabated, they will most likely warm the earth by about 3 to 7 degrees Fahrenheit by the end of this century," with an even greater effect of up to 12 degrees possible. Also, the EPA indicates that this atmospheric buildup of CO_2 and other greenhouse gases is, and I quote, "largely the result of human activities such as the burning of fossil fuels."

KATHRYN DESCRIBES SOME FAIRLY TECHNICAL MATTERS IN TERMS HER AUDIENCE CAN EASILY UNDERSTAND, COMPARING THE "GREENHOUSE EFFECT" TO AN "INSULATING BLANKET" AND THE INCREASE IN TEMPERATURE TO THE HEAT PRODUCED BY 141 BILLION LIGHTBULBS!

This buildup of greenhouse gases could have serious repercussions. As you can see from this graph from the Pew Center on Global Climate Change [Figure 16.3], the earth's

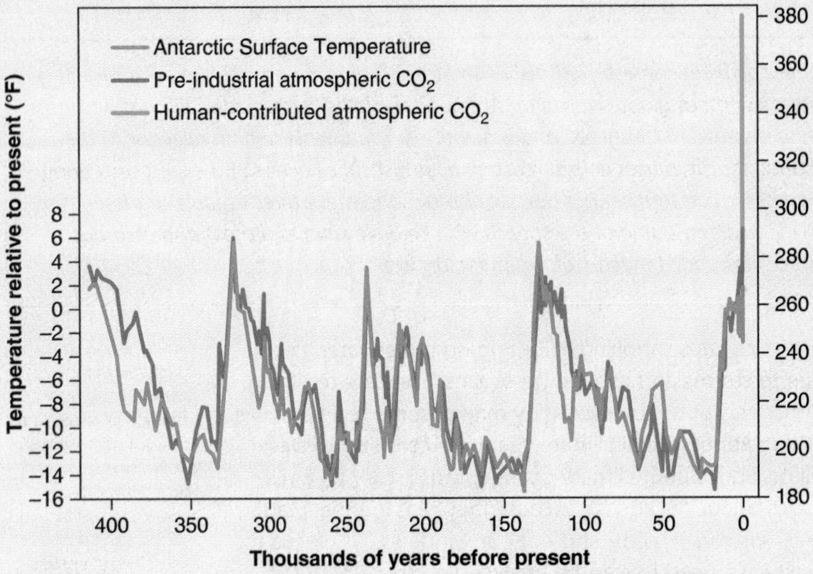

Reprinted by permission from "Climate Change 101: Science and Impacts." Copyright © 2009 by PEW Center on Global Climate Change. *Sources*: Surface temperature: Brohan, P., J. J. Kennedy, S. F. B. Tett, and P. D. Jones. "Uncertainty estimates in regional and global observed temparature changes: A new dataset from 1850." *Journal of Geophysical Research* 111, no. D12106 (2006): doi: 20.2092/2005JD006548. Ocean heat: Domingues, C. M., J. A. Church, N. J. White, P. J. Gleckler, S. E. Wijffels, P. M. Barker and J. R. Dunn. 2008. "Improved estimates of upper ocean warming and multi-decadal sea-level rise." *Nature* 453: 1090–1093.

FIGURE 16.3

temperature over the last 400,000 years, shown in orange, has closely tracked the amount of CO_2 in the atmosphere, shown in blue. Those CO_2 levels have now reached unprecedented heights, due to the human-contributed CO_2 shown in green toward the right of the graph. If we don't act quickly to reduce these levels of greenhouse gases, we could soon see temperatures rise to correspondingly high levels. These temperature increases could have catastrophic effects. The Pew Center has noted that global warming already appears to be causing more frequent and more severe hurricanes, changes in precipitation that cause flooding in some areas and droughts in others, and widespread melting of the polar ice caps, which in turn is causing sea levels to rise. The Pew Center has predicted that sea levels could rise by as much as one meter by 2100, which would cause many low-lying areas around the world to be flooded.

KATHRYN MAKES A CAUSAL ARGUMENT BACKED UP WITH STATISTICAL DATA ABOUT THE RELATIONSHIP BETWEEN GREENHOUSE GASES AND GLOBAL TEMPERATURES. SHE RELAYS EXPERT OPINION ABOUT THE POTENTIAL EFFECTS OF GLOBAL WARMING AND PROVIDES A DRAMATIC EXAMPLE OF HOW AN ISLAND NATION LIKE THE MALDIVES MAY BE AFFECTED.

A *New York Times* article from November 2008 indicates just how real this threat is for some people in the world. In the Maldives, for example, the president-elect has promised to establish an investment fund for buying up new lands for the people who now live in the 1,200 islands that make up this nation. Many in the Maldives now live less than three feet above sea level and will be displaced if global warming raises the sea level of the Indian Ocean.

Stephan Schneider, a climate scientist at Stanford University, summed things up nicely in a September 2008 article in *USA Today*, stating that if the trend of increased greenhouse emissions continues over the next century, we'd be "luckier than hell for it to just be bad, as opposed to catastrophic." Obviously, we face a serious problem. What can be done about this threat? What are the best ways to reduce global warming? A good start would be passage of the so-called Sanders-Boxer Act, which is the most comprehensive of several climate change bills now being considered in Congress.

The Sanders-Boxer Act has the potential to significantly reduce CO_2 levels across the planet. How can it do that by restricting carbon dioxide emissions only in the U.S.? The answer is simple. According to a *New York Times* article from February 3, 2007, "The United States, with about 5 percent of the world's population, contributes about a quarter of greenhouse gas emissions, more than any other country." While a good portion of the industrialized world falls under the blanket of the Kyoto Protocol, which was ratified in February 2005 and caps emissions in 39 other industrialized countries, the U.S. refused to ratify the agreement. Now, the Kyoto Protocol is due to expire in 2012, and by that time we might be able to renegotiate the treaty to include not only the U.S. but also rapidly industrializing countries, such as China and India. In the meantime, however, we need the Sanders-Boxer Act. We cannot afford to wait another four years before cutting back on the amount of greenhouse emissions in the United States.

The Sanders-Boxer Act is the right combination of aggressive and flexible measures. As you can see from this second chart from the Pew Center on Global Climate Change [Figure 16.4], there are a number of proposals before Congress for addressing the problem. The orange line on the graph represents how carbon emissions will continue to increase if we choose to do nothing. The blue line, which represents the projected effects of the Sanders-Boxer Act, shows the most dramatic *decrease* in emissions over the next half century. The Sanders-Boxer Act aims for an overall reduction in emissions of 80 percent by 2050. The projected effects of another popular bill in Congress, the Boxer-Lieberman-Warner Climate Security Act, is represented by this green line on the graph. This bill is popular with industry because it demands little action by polluters until the

KATHRYN INTRODUCES THE SPECIFIC LEGISLATION SHE ENDORSES AND EXPLAINS IN GENERAL WHY SUCH LEGISLATION IS NEEDED. THEN SHE TURNS IMMEDIATELY TO STATISTICAL PROJECTIONS, AGAIN PRESENTED VISUALLY WITH A LINE GRAPH, CONTRASTING THE LEGISLATION SHE FAVORS WITH OTHER BILLS BEFORE CONGRESS.

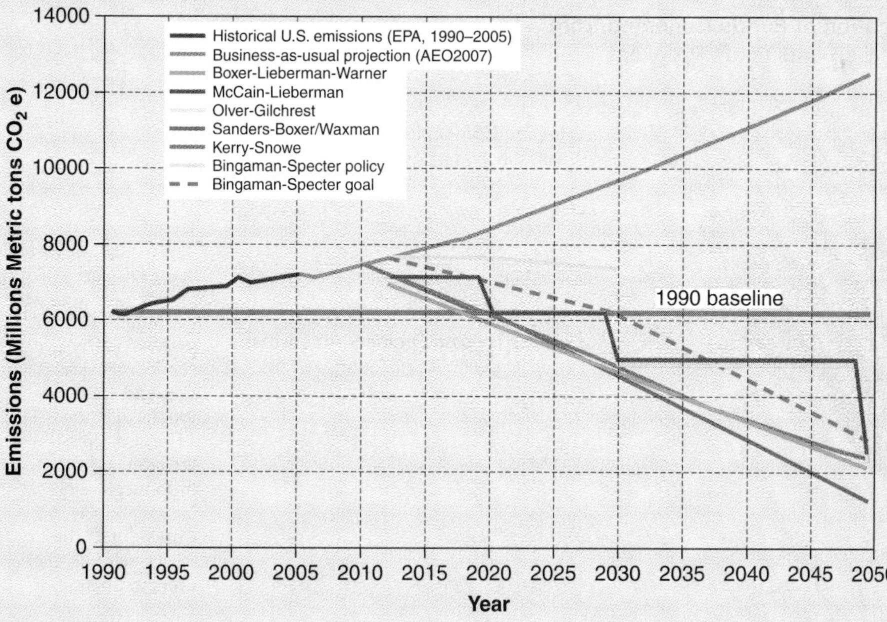

Reprinted by permission from "Climate Change 101: Science and Impacts." Copyright © 2009 by PEW Center on Global Climate Change.

FIGURE 16.4

year 2036 and it sets a less-dramatic goal of reducing emissions by 71 percent by the year 2050. Some argue that bill would allow the economy time to adapt, but according to the Sierra Club and other environmental groups, it simply doesn't go far enough.

The Sanders-Boxer Act will achieve its more dramatic results through a variety of methods. First, it would regulate all greenhouse gases rather than just those covered by cap-and-trade provisions, which pertain only to certain industries, according to the Pew Center. It does this at the national level, relying heavily on the EPA to measure and enforce limitations on how much carbon dioxide can be produced. Secondly, it imposes limits on vehicle emissions that must be met by 2016, according to the Library of Congress. It also directs that all gasoline sold in the U.S. contain a certain percentage of renewable fuel. Lastly, it includes a cap-and-trade program for dealing with problem industries, much like the one utilized effectively in the 1990 Clean Air Act.

According to the Center for American Progress, a cap-and-trade program essentially allows companies to buy from the government the right to emit a certain number of carbon "units." This would provide a steady source of revenue of up to $300 billion a year. This money in turn would be allocated as shown in this graph [Figure 16.5], with most of the money going to research and development of new clean air technologies and aid to American consumers coping with higher energy costs. Companies that buy more carbon units than they need would be free to resell them to companies that underestimated their emissions. An article in the *New York Times* in January 2007 indicates that "such a market, already in effect in Europe," would "stimulate innovation in technologies that would reduce emissions or produce goods or power without the same high

HAVING DEMONSTRATED THE BILL'S MORE DRAMATIC EFFECTS, KATHRYN AGAIN REASONS CAUSALLY BY EXPLAINING THOSE EFFECTS IN TERMS OF THE LEGISLATION'S PROVISIONS. SHE ALSO USES STATISTICS AND A PIE GRAPH TO EXPLAIN THE FINANCIAL BENEFITS OF A CAP-AND-TRADE PROVISION IN THE BILL.

Allocation of Funds Collected from Cap-and-Trade Program

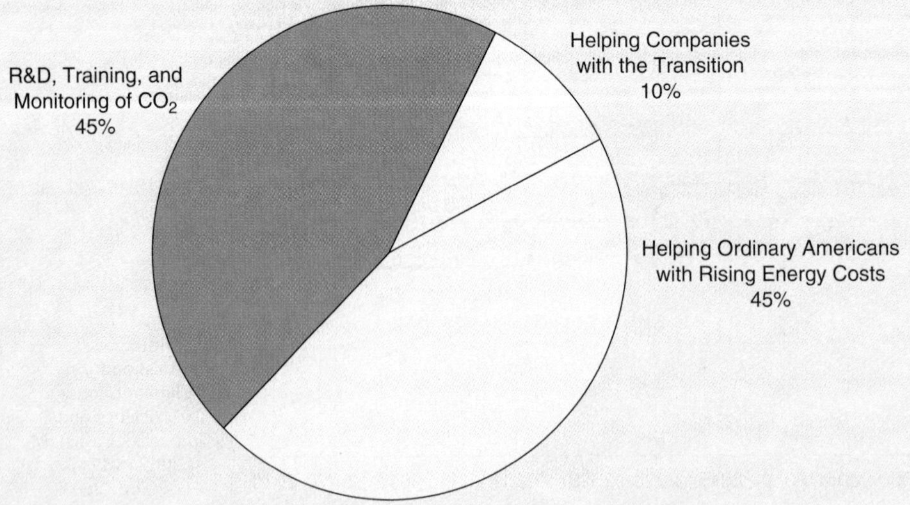

FIGURE 16.5

emissions common today." So why is the Sanders-Boxer Act the best option among the several bills now being debated in Congress?

The Sanders-Boxer Act is the best choice because it addresses all the sources of carbon emissions, not just some of them. As I mentioned earlier, its chief competition in Congress is the Climate Security Act, sponsored by Senators Boxer, Lieberman, and Warner. According to the National Resources Defense Council, the Climate Security Act would regulate only 86 percent of the total carbon emissions because it only applies only to capped industry emissions. Also, the Climate Security Act simply isn't aggressive enough. Although the 9 percent difference between the two bills in the projected emission reductions might not seem like much, it could make a huge difference in the long run. In a report on CNN in 2007, world-renowned climatologist James Hansen stated that we have only "eight more years to reverse the flow of carbon into the atmosphere" before we suffer serious and perhaps irreversible harms. The Climate Security Act has a great deal of political support, but it simply does not do as much as the Sanders-Boxer Act to reverse the dangerous trend toward ever-increasing emissions.

The Sanders-Boxer Act has the potential to pull the world out of its predicament. It addresses all of the carbon being emitted by our economy, in both the industrial and the transportation sectors. It is also the most aggressive bill proposed. According to Senator Bernie Sanders, one of the two authors of the bill, "simply raising our fuel-efficiency standards to forty miles per gallon would save roughly the same amount of oil as we import from Saudi Arabia." The Sanders-Boxer Act also would use an organization already in place, the EPA, to regulate emissions, and it would allow for a market-based system so that companies that need extra time to comply with the new emission standards will literally be able to buy it. Lastly, the Sanders-Boxer Act is politically realistic. President-Elect Obama, Vice-President-Elect Joe Biden, and Senator Hillary Clinton have all pledged to support it, and the bill already has 16 co-sponsors in the Senate. At the moment, the Climate Security Act has broader political support, but it simply is not as good a bill as the Sanders-Boxer Act.

KATHRYN PROVIDES A CONCISE SUMMARY OF THE COMPARATIVE ADVANTAGES OF THE BILL AND PROCLAIMS IT POLITICALLY FEASIBLE.

In conclusion, I have discussed the problem of global warming, how the Sanders-Boxer Act will address the problem of carbon emissions, and why the Sanders-Boxer Act is the best of several bills now before Congress. The root problem we face today is global warming, which is caused by greenhouse gases, and specifically, carbon dioxide. The Sanders-Boxer Act proposes to use a variety of methods to reduce carbon emissions in the U.S. It seeks to do this in a more comprehensive and aggressive manner than the rival Climate Security Act. With our atmospheric carbon levels rising every second, now is not the time to be timid. As David Elliot Cohen says, "the next few years are a kind of final exam for the human species. Does that big brain really work or not? It gave us the power to build coal-fired power plants and SUVs . . . but does it give us the power . . . to build a world that isn't bent on destruction?" Unfortunately, only time will tell. But one thing is certain: if we do nothing, the world as we know it will one day cease to exist.

KATHRYN CLOSES BY QUOTING FROM THE BOOK ON CLIMATE CHANGE THAT SHE MENTIONED AT THE START OF THE SPEECH. HER SPEECH CONCLUDES WITH AN OMINOUS WARNING ABOUT WHAT MAY HAPPEN "IF WE DO NOTHING."

CHAPTER

17

Speaking on Special Occasions

CHAPTER SURVEY

Ceremonial Speaking in a Free Society

Social Values in Ceremonial Speaking

The Forms of Ceremonial Speech

Style and Delivery in Ceremonial Speaking

CHAPTER OBJECTIVES

After studying this chapter, you should be able to

1. Discuss the role of ceremonial speaking in a free society.
2. Explain how ceremonial speeches define and reinforce social values.
3. Identify and describe different types of ceremonial speeches.
4. Define *eloquence* and discuss the importance of style and delivery in ceremonial speaking

At some point in your life, you will be called on to deliver a ceremonial speech—the type of speech that the ancient Greeks called **epideictic**. This is the sort of speech you deliver when you pay tribute to someone, present or accept an award, or mark some special occasion or event. Ceremonial speeches are often associated with culturally significant occasions: weddings, funerals, graduations, awards banquets, conferences and conventions, or major political events. We also deliver ceremonial speeches to mark important dates in our history, such as Memorial Day or the Fourth of July.

Traditionally, ceremonial speeches were considered less "serious" than informative or persuasive speeches. In Aristotle's *Rhetoric*, for example, epideictic speeches were treated as mere "display," a sort of "poetic" speech in which speakers showed off their speaking skills but did not say anything of great political or social significance. According to Aristotle, epideictic speakers engaged in "praise and blame," and they focused on the present rather than the past or the future. Some have interpreted this to mean that the audiences for such speeches act as mere "observers," appreciating the "skill of the orator" but not making important judgments or collective decisions. In this view of epideictic speech, the speaker aims not to elicit action but only to influence "the general attitude of the audience toward a particular person or behavior."[1]

Today, we recognize that ceremonial speaking plays a crucial role in defining and sustaining our civic culture. More than a mere display of the speaker's skill, ceremonial speeches shape our collective identity, remind us of our history and traditions, and imagine the world "as it ought to be rather than as it is."[2] Epideictic speeches bring us together as members of a community, and they remind us of our responsibilities as citizens. Honoring our heroes and commemorating important events, ceremonial speeches articulate and reinforce important social values and strengthen the bonds that unite us. In short, ceremonial speeches help sustain our civic culture.

We begin this chapter by reflecting further on the role of ceremonial speaking in a free society. Identifying four important functions of ceremonial speaking, we examine how epideictic speeches remind us of our heritage, celebrate our heroes, identify important social values, and give us inspiration and encouragement. Then we will consider in more detail the role of ceremonial speeches in articulating and reinforcing social values. In the third section of the chapter, we will review the wide variety of epideictic speeches we encounter in everyday life, ranging from brief speeches of introduction to historic inaugural and keynote addresses. Finally, we will discuss the importance of language and delivery in ceremonial speaking, reflecting on what it means to be *eloquent* and offering some tips for writing and delivering ceremonial speeches.

CEREMONIAL SPEAKING IN A FREE SOCIETY

Preview. *Ceremonial speeches are often presented on formal occasions and may be associated with important cultural rituals. Through ceremonial speeches, we remember the past, honor our heroes, celebrate shared beliefs and values, and offer inspiration and encouragement.*

Speeches given on ceremonial occasions are rich in symbolic content. They help define who we are as a people and bind us together as members of a group, community, or nation. As we honor our heroes, pay tribute to those we love or have lost, or celebrate our accomplishments, we remind ourselves of our shared history and traditions. We articulate and reinforce our shared beliefs and values and find inspiration and encouragement to take on new challenges. Ceremonial speeches comfort us, inspire us, and reinforce our faith in ourselves and in one another. Ceremonial speeches may be ritualistic and symbolic, but in some ways that makes them even more important than other types of speeches.

Remembering the Past

In 1863, Abraham Lincoln pledged in his Gettysburg Address that the world would "never forget" the soldiers who "gave the last full measure of devotion" to assure that "government of the people, by the people, for the people" would not "perish from the earth." A century and a half later, New York mayor Rudy Giuliani, in an address to the 2004 Republican National Convention in New York, recalled that sunny September morning when he looked up and saw smoke pouring out of the World Trade Center—and realized that the world had changed forever. Giuliani mourned those who had died in the "worst attack in our history," and he pledged to never forget the scene he had witnessed on that fateful day: the twin towers engulfed in "the flames of hell" as people jumped to their deaths. In just those few seconds, Giuliani recognized that we were "facing something that we had never, ever faced before": a new "creed of terrorism" aimed not only at killing Americans but at destroying our culture and way of life.[3] Like Lincoln in his Gettysburg address, Giuliani helped his listeners understand the historical significance of the moment, as well as its implications for the future. Never before had something like this happened, he suggested, and we had a duty to make sure that it never happened again.

Remembering historic events is more than "mere ritual." When we remember the past, we come to a clearer understanding of ourselves and the challenges we face. We also look to the past for "lessons of history." In a variety of settings, ceremonial speakers recall past events to help define who we are, what we stand for, and where we are headed in the future.

Consider how just one historical event, the American Revolution, has supplied inspiration and guidance for generations of Americans. For the first generation of Americans, of course, the Revolution was a live memory, and for more than a decade large crowds gathered in Boston to commemorate an incident that took place on March 5, 1770: the so-called Boston Massacre. According to scholars, the Boston "massacre" was little more than a "barroom brawl" between "wharf-side rabble" and a few "surly" British soldiers. Yet between 1771 and 1783, some of the most famous orators in America came to Boston every year to reflect on the "massacre" and its "lessons."[4] Speaking on the fourth anniversary of the incident, for example, John Hancock, one of the signers of the Declaration of Independence, spoke about the threat posed by standing armies in a free

In this famous engraving by Paul Revere, a British commander orders his troops to fire into a crowd of civilians in Boston. Historians doubt the accuracy of the depiction, but Revere's engraving, along with annual speeches commemorating the "massacre," helped inspire the American Revolution.

society and declared: "[L]et our misfortunes teach posterity to guard against such evils for the future."[5]

During the Civil War, Abraham Lincoln also drew inspiration from the Revolution. Lincoln began his famous Gettysburg Address by referring to the founding and reminding his audience of the principles that more than 360,000 union soldiers died for during that bloody conflict: "Fourscore and seven years ago our fathers brought forth on this continent a new nation, conceived in liberty, and dedicated to the proposition that all men are created equal." After the war, a progressive southerner, Henry Grady, also recalled the Revolution but for a different purpose: to urge Northerners to forget the "Old South" and embrace the "New South" of "union and freedom." As Grady reminded his audience, both northerners and southerners "were lost in the storm of the first Revolution," and out of that storm was born the "American citizen," who taught the whole world about the blessings of democracy.[6]

Today, we still invoke the Revolution as the source of our ideals and inspiration. Yet so, too, do we remember a long list of other historical events that have shaped our character and purposes as a nation: the Civil War, the abolition of slavery, the Great Depression, two world wars, the Cuban Missile Crisis, and the assassinations of John F. Kennedy and Martin Luther King Jr., to name just a few. Many of those memories are painful, but they serve as important reminders. When speakers urge us to "Remember the Alamo" or the sacrifices of D-Day, they hope to inspire respect for our men and women in uniform. When they recall building the Panama Canal or landing a man on the moon, they hope to rekindle our "can do" spirit and inspire us to take on new challenges.

For today's generation, of course, the terrorist attacks of September 11, 2001, represent an important public memory. Already that day has been commemorated in countless ceremonial speeches, ranging from eulogies and dedications to keynote and commencement addresses. Whatever the occasion, the events of 9/11 have become a fertile source of "lessons"—both positive and negative—about the principles and ideals that define us as a nation. In the years to come, 9/11 will continue to both sadden and inspire, as speakers invoke memories of that fateful day in a variety of ceremonial settings.

Honoring Heroes

Part of remembering the past is celebrating our heroes. In honoring our heroes, we emphasize themes of *character* and *personal virtue*, hoping to inspire others by holding up role models worth emulating. In praising our heroes, we remind ourselves of the ideals that define the life well lived.

Some of our heroes are "larger than life," others are ordinary people—our parents, teachers, neighbors, or friends. But whomever we count as a hero, we honor their achievements, invite them to share their wisdom with us, and mourn them when they die. Honoring our heroes allows us to speak about the personal characteristics we admire and to reflect on the social values we share as a community. Like remembering the past, honoring our heroes is an educational act, illuminating the "lessons" to be learned from their lives.

Some of the most famous speeches in our history have been eulogies to our national heroes. Campaigning for the Democratic presidential nomination in 1968, for example, Robert F. Kennedy delivered an impromptu eulogy to Dr. Martin Luther King Jr. just moments after learning that King had been assassinated in Memphis, Tennessee. After sharing the news with his predominantly African-American audience, Kennedy summarized, in but a single sentence, the essence of King's "dream": "Martin Luther King dedicated his life to love and to justice between fellow human beings." Next, he elaborated on the "lesson" to be learned from King's life: "What we need in the United States is not division; what we need in the United States is not hatred; what we need in the United States is not violence and lawlessness, but ... love and wisdom, and compassion toward one another, and a feeling of justice toward those who still suffer within our country, whether they be white or whether they be black." Finally, Kennedy urged his audience to rededicate themselves to the ancient ideals King championed: "Let us dedicate ourselves to what the Greeks wrote so many years ago: to tame the savageness of man and make gentle the life of this world. Let us dedicate ourselves to that, and say a prayer for our country and for our people."[7]

Over the course of American history, epideictic speakers have celebrated a remarkable array of heroes: presidents, explorers, military heroes, movie stars, great writers, and popular musicians. We still honor the founders of our nation, of course—George Washington, Thomas Jefferson, and Benjamin Franklin, among others. We also honor some of the presidents who came later: Lincoln, Roosevelt, and Kennedy, to name just a few. Yet ceremonial speakers have also paid tribute to philanthropists such as Andrew Carnegie, great thinkers and writers such as Einstein and Harriet Beecher Stowe, and successful entrepreneurs from Henry Ford to Bill Gates. Mother Teresa has been honored for her charitable work, and aviation pioneer Amelia Earhart for her courage and determination. Even controversial figures have sometimes found redemption in ceremonial speeches. Although she was widely criticized in her own day, for example, we now honor Susan B. Anthony for her tireless efforts to secure the vote for women.

Occasionally, we even elevate ordinary citizens to the status of national heroes. In his 1982 State of the Union address, for example, President Ronald Reagan introduced the nation to a government worker named Lenny Skutnik, who had helped rescue people from a jetliner that crashed into the Potomac River. "We don't have to turn to our history books for heroes," Reagan began. "They're all around us." Reagan then introduced Skutnik, who was sitting in the audience:

> Just two weeks ago, in the midst of a terrible tragedy, we saw again the spirit of American heroism at its finest—the heroism of dedicated rescue workers saving crash victims from icy waters. And we saw the heroism of one of our young government employees, Lenny Skutnik, who, when he saw a woman lose her grip on the helicopter line, dived into the water and dragged her to safety.[8]

On January 15, 2009, another ordinary American became an overnight hero. After his Airbus A320 struck a flock of birds and lost both engines, US Airways pilot Chesley B. "Sully" Sullenberger skillfully landed the disabled jetliner on the Hudson River, then made sure that all 155 people on board made it to rescue boats. New York governor David Paterson proclaimed it the "Miracle on the Hudson," and New York City mayor Michael Bloomberg praised Sullenberger for a "masterful job." Before workers could even lift the 81-ton plane out of the river, Sullenberger "vaulted to fame nationwide and across cyberspace," with more than 10,000 people joining his Facebook fan club in a single day.[9] Later, he was honored with invitations to President Barack Obama's swearing-in ceremony and to the new president's speech before a joint session of Congress on February 24, 2009.[10]

Chesley B. "Sully" Sullenberger and the Airbus A320 jetliner that he crash-landed on the Hudson River in New York City on January 15, 2009.

Honoring our heroes is not just a meaningless ritual. In doing so, we define the personal virtues and social values that we admire as a culture, and we create role models for others, especially our young people. Occasionally, of course, we also recall notorious or infamous figures in history, such as Adolf Hitler or Saddam Hussein. In doing so, however, our mission remains essentially the same: to teach important lessons about personal character and civic virtue.

Celebrating Shared Beliefs and Values

Ceremonial speeches articulate and reinforce common beliefs and values. As you think about delivering an epideictic speech, you should ask: What is the occasion for this speech? What defines the audience as a group? Which of the group's victories or accomplishments inspire the most pride? What do they believe most deeply, and what principles do they cherish? These questions may lead you to an inventory of beliefs and values shared by your audience and, then, to the major themes of your speech. The shared beliefs and values you identify may be philosophical or practical, religious or political, social or economic. But whatever their nature, they reflect the audience's collective understanding of themselves.

In their inaugural addresses, U.S. presidents typically emphasize those beliefs and values that unite *all* Americans, regardless of party. In his celebrated inaugural address, for example, John F. Kennedy identified "freedom" as just such a value and embraced the responsibility of "defending freedom in its hour of maximum danger."[11] Similarly, Dwight D. Eisenhower concluded his second inaugural address by reemphasizing the themes of freedom and peace. Like Kennedy, Eisenhower articulated the ideals that he believed were shared by all Americans: "May the light of freedom, coming to all darkened lands, flame brightly—until at last the darkness is no more. May the turbulence of our age yield to a true time of peace, when men and nations shall share a life that honors the dignity of each, the brotherhood of all."[12]

Other ceremonial speeches revolve around the beliefs and values of smaller groups or subcultures, or they emphasize values associated with a specific occasion. In delivering the keynote address to a conference of newspaper editors, for example, a speaker might celebrate our constitutional guarantee of a free press, whereas commencement addresses invariably stress the value of education. Similarly, it may be appropriate for a minister to praise Jesus in a sermon before an audience of believers. In addressing a religiously diverse audience of civic leaders, however, the same preacher might celebrate the constitutional separation of church and state.

It is important to recognize that the shared beliefs and values of one group may be controversial or rejected altogether within another community. In a keynote address to the National Organization for Women, for example, one might expect to hear a celebration of feminist values, whereas speakers before a more conservative group may praise traditional family values. By the same token, the beliefs and values celebrated in some types of ceremonial speeches may be wholly inappropriate in others. In a humorous after-dinner speech, for example, one might "roast" the honoree by recalling some embarrassing flub or failure. At that same person's funeral, however, it would be in bad taste to recall such an incident.

Offering Inspiration and Encouragement

When speakers present awards, pay tribute to individuals, speak at commencements, or deliver keynote addresses, they offer encouragement and inspiration to their listeners. In effect, they deliver motivational speeches. A life well lived provides an example for all of us. Thus, the speaker accepting an award might suggest to the audience: "You can do this, too! I have confidence in you." Similarly, the commencement speaker does not simply congratulate the graduates, but encourages them to continue striving—to "reach for the stars." Even a eulogy can be inspirational, reminding us that life is short and inspiring us to live life to the fullest. Whatever the specific type of speech, the goal remains the same: to inspire and encourage people to be good citizens, do good work, and "give back" to their communities.

Occasionally, speakers are called on to sustain people's morale through difficult times. That is precisely what British prime minister Winston Churchill did in one of his best-known speeches during World War II, an address to the

House of Commons on June 4, 1940. In this famous speech, Churchill reported on a "colossal military disaster"—the evacuation of Dunkirk, in which French and British forces were driven off the European continent by the advancing German army. Churchill also mourned the loss of 30,000 men and warned of an impending invasion of the British homeland. Yet pledging to "defend to the death" his "native soil," Churchill reassured his fellow citizens that their cause would prevail and promised a vigorous response to the Nazi threat wherever it might appear—whether in France or in Britain, whether on land, in the air, and on the open seas. Projecting complete confidence, Churchill famously declared, "we shall fight on the beaches, we shall fight on the landing grounds, we shall fight in the fields and in the streets, we shall fight in the hills; we shall never surrender. . . .[13] And in Churchill's pledge to "never surrender," the British people not only found the strength to survive but the courage to regroup, rally, and fight on to ultimate victory. Churchill's ringing declaration of his nation's determination and resolve demonstrated the power of words to sustain public morale through even the most trying of times—and to change the course of history.

SOCIAL VALUES IN CEREMONIAL SPEAKING

Preview. *Ceremonial speeches do more than merely entertain us. They perform important educational and cultural functions. Most important, they reinforce the shared social values that define us as a community. Sometimes ceremonial speeches affirm traditional values and work to preserve things as they are. Yet ceremonial speeches can also be powerful agents of change, challenging prevailing values or pointing to contradictions between our ideals and our actions.*

In an informative speech, you hope to teach your audience something new. In a persuasive speech, you aim to change your audience's beliefs or opinions. In a ceremonial speech, however, your purpose typically is to articulate and reinforce *existing* social values. As the speaker on a ceremonial occasion, you aim to give eloquent expression to the beliefs and values *already* held by the audience.

Consider, for example, how a eulogy differs from an informative or persuasive speech. In delivering a eulogy, we may safely assume that the audience knows the deceased; people generally do not attend the funerals of strangers! So there's no need for an informative speech. Nor does the eulogist typically persuade, trying to convince us that the dearly departed was not such a bad fellow after all! Instead, the eulogist's job is to give voice to the shared feelings of love and loss among family and friends. Put another way, the eulogist tries to "put into words" the feelings already held by the audience.

Ceremonial speeches supply the "glue" that holds our communities together. Even in ancient times, when ceremonial speeches were viewed as a kind of artistic performance, it was recognized that they also served important educational and cultural functions. In Greek funeral orations, for example, listeners were called on to imitate the virtues of the deceased.[14] The Roman rhetorician Quintilian viewed teaching itself as a form of epideictic rhetoric.[15] Today, we recognize even more clearly the political, social, and cultural importance of ceremonial speaking. In a wide variety of contexts, ceremonial speakers not only help us celebrate special occasions, but also remind us of the values, traditions, and aspirations we share as a people. They also work to define our collective identities, defining what it means to be an American or a member of some other group with distinct social values. Sometimes they even make implicit political arguments by honoring people associated with particular ideas and policies. In those cases, epideictic speeches become something of a hybrid form, containing characteristics of a deliberative or policy speech as well.

Some argue that ceremonial speeches are inherently conservative because they articulate and reinforce *existing* social values.[16] Historically, however, ceremonial speeches have been powerful agents of change, invoking "shared values as a basis for promoting a vision of what could be."[17] That certainly was true of the most famous ceremonial speech in U.S. history: Martin Luther King Jr.'s "I Have a Dream" speech. It is also true of many other ceremonial speeches, ranging from abolitionist and suffrage speeches in the nineteenth century to contemporary speeches marking Earth Day or Gay Pride Week.

One of the most famous ceremonial speeches in our history was a Fourth of July speech in 1852 by a former slave named Frederick Douglass. Calling slavery "the great sin and shame of America," Douglass chose to mark Independence Day with an ironic speech highlighting the contradictions between our revolutionary ideals and the institution of slavery. Posing a famous question, Douglass called attention to the hypocrisy of a nation founded on the principle of liberty yet built on the labor of slaves:

> What to the American slave is your Fourth of July? I answer, a day that reveals to him . . . the gross injustice and cruelty to which he is the constant victim. To him, your celebration is a sham; your boasted liberty, an unholy license; your national greatness, swelling vanity; your sounds of rejoicing are empty and heartless; your denunciations of tyrants, brass-fronted impudence; your shouts of liberty and equality, hollow mockery; your prayers and hymns, . . . are to him mere bombast, fraud, deception, impiety, and hypocrisy—a thin veil to cover up crimes which would disgrace a nation of savages. There is not a nation on the earth guilty of practices more shocking and bloody than are the people of these United States, at this very hour.[18]

Calling on the nation to live up to its professed ideals, Douglass's speech illustrates how ceremonial speeches can be powerful agents of social change.

On occasion, ceremonial speeches even provide an opportunity for groups or communities to reassess their *own* traditions, beliefs, or social values. In a speech to civil rights activists in 2004, for example, actor Bill Cosby asked African Americans to honor the pioneers of the civil rights movement by facing up to the problems in their own communities. The speech, featured in the *Focus on Civic Engagement* that follows, shows how ceremonial speeches can challenge an audience to reassess their own values even as they celebrate common heroes and a shared history.

FOCUS ON CIVIC ENGAGEMENT

Bill Cosby's "Pound Cake" Speech

On May 17, 2004, actor Bill Cosby accepted an award from the National Association for the Advancement of Colored People (NAACP) for his support of historically black colleges and universities. The occasion was a gala celebration commemorating the 50th anniversary of *Brown v. Board of Education*, the landmark Supreme Court decision desegregating America's public schools. The occasion called for a celebration of the civil rights movement and the progress of African Americans since that landmark decision. For Cosby, however, it also was an occasion for serious reflection on the problems facing the black community in America, particularly in parenting, education, and popular culture.

Proud of both his acting career and his doctorate in education, Cosby thanked the gathered dignitaries for the award and paid tribute to those who had fought for equal educational access 50 years earlier. But that is where the resemblance to a typical ceremonial speech ended. Cosby devoted most of the address to lamenting the high dropout rate among black students, the large number of young black males in jail, and the problem of black women "having children by five, six different men." Blacks could not "blame white people" for these problems, nor could they just keep "asking Jesus" for help. The problem was a lack of parenting, along with a materialistic culture that devalued education. As Cosby put it: "They're buying things for the kid—$500 sneakers—for what? They won't buy or spend $250 on *Hooked on Phonics*."

Cosby criticized those who blamed all their problems on the police or the criminal justice system. "Looking at the incarcerated," he said, "these are not political criminals. These are people going around stealing Coca-Cola. People are getting shot in the back of the head over a piece of pound cake! Then we all run out and are outraged: 'The cops shouldn't have shot him.' What the hell was he doing with the pound cake in his hand?" Cosby also criticized those who put their "clothes on backwards," pants "down around the crack," and took African names like Shaniqua, Shaligua, or Mohammed. "Those people are not Africans," Cosby observed; "they don't know a damned thing about Africa." Pointing to fashion trends as a "sign of something . . . wrong," Cosby concluded by making his point directly: "What's the point of giving them strong names if there is not parenting and values backing it up?"

Recalling those who had sacrificed in the fight for school desegregation, Cosby observed that the early civil rights activists must be "wondering what the hell happened." All these people "marched and were hit in the face with rocks and punched in the face to get an education," and now we have "these knuckleheads" walking around "who don't want to learn."

Not surprisingly, Cosby's speech provoked controversy. The audience reacted with a mixture of "astonishment, laughter, and applause," and none of the speakers who followed, including NAACP president Kweisi Mfume, seemed "amused in the slightest."[19] Later, cultural critic Michael Eric Dyson accused Cosby of blaming poor people rather than white racism or failed policies for problems in the black community.[20] Cosby, however, refused to apologize. Speaking several weeks later in Chicago, he accused his critics of trying to hide the black community's "dirty laundry" and dismissed concerns that white racists might use his comments "against our people." "Let them talk," he said.[21]

Source: Bill Cosby, "Pound Cake Speech," *American Rhetoric*, www.americanrhetoric.com/speeches/billcosbypoundcakespeech.htm (accessed August 12, 2009).

THE FORMS OF CEREMONIAL SPEECH

Preview. *There are many different kinds of ceremonial speeches: introductions, presentation and acceptance speeches, welcome and farewell speeches, commemoration and commencement speeches, tributes and eulogies, inaugural and keynote addresses, after-dinner speeches, and even some sermons. Each type of ceremonial speech is unique, but all share the same basic mission: to reflect on the significance of a special occasion and to give voice to the shared beliefs and values of the audience.*

What does a commencement address have in common with a eulogy? A keynote address with an after-dinner speech? The answer, as we have already suggested, is that they are all ceremonial speeches, or what the ancient Greeks called *epideictic*. They are all speeches delivered on special occasions, when people gather to honor other people or to celebrate some special anniversary or event. Those special occasions vary widely, of course, so there are important differences between, say, an inaugural address and a eulogy. Yet all ceremonial speeches have the same basic mission: to reflect on the larger meaning of the occasion and to "put into words" the shared beliefs and values of the audience.

The Speech of Introduction

The **speech of introduction** sometimes sounds like an informative speech, introducing us to an unknown speaker. More commonly, it celebrates the achievements of a well-known speaker who has been invited to speak on a special occasion.

Many people who introduce other speakers underestimate the importance of their role. They prepare very little, hastily scratching down a few notes or quickly underlining a few points on the speaker's résumé. Some cop out completely, saying, "I'm delighted to welcome our speaker tonight, a person who needs no introduction." Others go to the opposite extreme, giving a lengthy introduction to a person already quite familiar to the audience. When introducing other speakers, keep in mind that your purpose is to *introduce* another speaker, not to steal the spotlight yourself. You should never take away from the principal speaker's time or try to upstage his or her message.

The effective speech of introduction should do three things. First, it should extend a genuinely warm welcome to the speaker. Second, it should reinforce the speaker's ethos by emphasizing key educational or professional accomplishments. Finally, it should provide listeners with any information they may need to understand or process the speech. At the very least, the person introducing the main speaker should mention the topic or title of the speech, and the introductory speaker also might indicate whether the speaker will take questions following the address.

Here are just a few tips for preparing a good speech of introduction:

- *Do your homework*. The speech of introduction should be well researched. Study any materials the speaker has provided, such as a biographical sketch or résumé. Call and chat with the speaker if you lack information, and make sure to ask about the topic or title of the speech.
- *Look for connections between the speaker and the audience.* The speaker you introduce may have accomplished many things. You cannot cover them all.

You will want to highlight information that would be important for your group to know. What does the speaker have in common with this particular audience? What values do they share? If you make these connections, you will help the speaker establish common ground with the audience.

■ *Stay focused on the speaker.* Your purpose should be to introduce the speaker, not focus attention on yourself. Some people end up sharing stories about how they met the speaker or talk about their common experiences. It may be fine to share a brief anecdote, but do not get carried away.

Welcome and Farewell Addresses

Comings and goings do not, under ordinary circumstances, inspire speech making. When you come back from your vacation, you do not expect your neighbor to deliver a speech. When the president of the United States visits another country, however, we *do* expect speeches, both on his arrival and as he prepares to depart. In addition, politicians and other prominent people often give "farewell addresses" at the end of their careers, reflecting on their years of service or giving advice to their successors.

Welcome addresses are not just for world leaders. They are also common at conventions, festivals, trade shows, and other large public gatherings. When a college or university hosts an academic conference, for example, it is common for a dean or even the president of the university to offer a few words of welcome. Similarly, when a city attracts a major business conference or trade show, the mayor or some other local official typically welcomes the group. Generally, the task of the speaker in such situations is simple: on behalf of the hosts, convey a sincere welcome. When welcoming a group, you also might offer tips for making the most out of their visit. The mayor's welcome may mention some local attractions, for example, while a conference organizer might preview some highlights of the upcoming meeting.

Farewell addresses are sometimes short, simple expressions of gratitude. Yet even short farewells can be powerfully moving. On July 4, 1939, for example, one of the greatest players in the history of baseball, Lou Gehrig, delivered a farewell address that was barely 250 words long, but it said everything that needed to be said to the 62,000 fans at Yankee Stadium. Struck down in the prime of his career by amyotrophic lateral sclerosis (ALS), a rare degenerative disease later named *Lou Gehrig's disease*, the all-star player began by mentioning his "bad break"—a reference to the terrible disease that would take his life just two years later. Then proclaiming himself "the luckiest man on the face of the earth," Gehrig shifted the focus to his positive experiences over seventeen years of professional baseball. "Sure I'm lucky," Gehrig repeated as he recalled the "kindness and encouragement" of the fans, all the great players he had known, and even the support of his mother-in-law. Fighting back tears, Gehrig concluded, "So, I close in saying that I might have been given a bad break, but I've got an awful lot to live for." When Gehrig finished, there was "not a dry eye in Yankee Stadium," and the speech remains "one of the most poignant and emotional moments in the history of American sports."[22]

Not nearly so sentimental was Dwight D. Eisenhower's famous "farewell address" on January 17, 1961. Stepping down after two terms as president, Eisenhower took to the airwaves "with a message of leave-taking and farewell," including just a "few final thoughts" about matters of politics and national security. Those "few thoughts" turned into a somber and famous warning about "the acquisition of unwarranted influence" by what he labeled the "military-industrial complex." Urging his fellow citizens to avoid becoming "captive" to the "scientific-technological elite," Eisenhower worried out loud about how the technology of war was outpacing human understanding. He then closed with a hope and a prayer: that "in the goodness of time, all peoples will come to live together in a peace guaranteed by the binding force of mutual respect and love."[23]

Not all welcome and farewell addresses are so historic or philosophical, of course. Many consist of little more than a few brief remarks, thanking a visitor for coming or bidding a fond farewell. Like all ceremonial speeches, however, welcome and farewell addresses should be carefully prepared and adapted to the particular audience and situation in which they are given.

Presentation and Acceptance Speeches

Award ceremonies may or may not be occasions for formal speeches. Nowadays, most **presentation** and **acceptance speeches** consist of a few brief remarks, with presenters announcing the winner of the award and the winner simply thanking the presenter and perhaps a few other people. On a few occasions, however, an award ceremony calls for a longer, more substantive speech. If you someday win the Nobel Peace Prize, for example, you will be expected to deliver a formal speech before a distinguished audience of royalty and Nobel laureates in Oslo, Norway. With the king and queen of Norway and several hundred guests in attendance, you will express your gratitude and reflect on the larger significance of the Nobel Prize.

That is precisely what His Holiness the Dalai Lama did in his Nobel Prize acceptance speech in 1989. Like most acceptance speeches, the Dalai Lama's address began with an expression of gratitude and humility: "I am very happy to be here with you today to receive the Nobel Prize for Peace. I feel honored, humbled and deeply moved that you should give this important prize to a simple monk from Tibet." Then, he interpreted the award itself as "recognition of the true value of altruism, love, compassion and non-violence." Accepting the award "on behalf of the oppressed everywhere," the Dalai Lama spoke of the injustices against his own Tibetan people and his determination, despite their suffering, to see that their "long struggle" remain "non-violent and free of hatred." Transcending that immediate conflict, he then articulated the broader, more universal principles that motivated his efforts to build a more peaceful world:

> I believe all suffering is caused by ignorance. People inflict pain on others in the selfish pursuit of their happiness or satisfaction. Yet true happiness comes from a sense of brotherhood and sisterhood. We need to cultivate a universal responsibility for one another and the planet we share. Although I have found my own Buddhist religion helpful in generating love and compassion, . . . I am convinced that everyone can develop a good heart and a sense of universal responsibility with or without religion.[24]

His Holiness the Dalai Lama, winner of the 1989 Nobel Prize for Peace.

Generally, the formula for *presenting* an award is simple: introduce yourself and your purpose in speaking, say a few words about the significance or history of the award itself, then extol the virtues of the recipient. Sometimes the winner will be known in advance; on other occasions, you may reveal the recipient in your speech. In either case, your goal is to deliver a speech that clearly expresses the values associated with the award and that honors the recipient.

When *accepting* an award, you want to convey a sincere sense of gratitude but also humility, perhaps by acknowledging the support of others who contributed to your success. This does not mean that you should read a long list of names, including everyone who has ever done you a favor. But you do want to thank those most responsible for your moment in the limelight—a teacher or a coach who prepared you for a competition, perhaps, or a partner or spouse who supported you. Finally, you might acknowledge the deeper meaning of the award, using language that fits the dignity of the occasion. Of course, you also want to show that you genuinely appreciate the honor.

Whether presenting or accepting an award, it is important that you do the following:

- *Learn as much as you can about the award.* Knowing about the award—its history and meaning—can help you prepare your speech. If you are the first person to present or receive the award, you may want to note that fact. If other people have received the award previously, you may want to acknowledge one or two of those previous winners.
- *Plan and practice your speech in advance.* A person asked to *present* an award typically prepares a speech in advance, but some people think it is wrong or

even "bad luck" to prepare to *accept* an award. That may explain why we hear so many bad speeches at the Academy Awards! Generally, however, you will be told in advance if you have won some award and whether you are expected to speak at the awards ceremony. In that case, you definitely should prepare the speech ahead of time. Even if you will not know whether you have won an award until the ceremony itself, you can still sketch out some brief remarks—just in case you *do* win. Then, if you win, you can deliver those remarks extemporaneously, without pulling notes or a manuscript out of your pocket. After all, you do not want to look *too* prepared, as if you fully *expected* to win!

- *Make your tone and language fit the occasion.* Presentation and acceptance speeches are usually delivered in formal settings, and your language should reflect that. Your tone should be dignified and sincere. This is a time to speak formally yet "from the heart."
- *Make your speech brief.* Most presentation and acceptance speeches should be very brief, probably no longer than a minute or two. In many settings where awards are presented, there is other business to conduct, perhaps even a keynote speaker. So a brief yet carefully crafted speech is usually expected and appreciated.

Commemoration and Commencement Speeches

A **commemorative speech** marks an important date or event, whereas a commencement address celebrates one specific type of event: a graduation ceremony. Commemorative speeches are heard on a wide variety of occasions, ranging from national holidays, to dates with special significance for particular groups, to personally significant occasions, such as birthdays or wedding anniversaries. We may hear a commemorative speech on the Fourth of July, or we may hear one marking Black History Month. We still hear speeches commemorating the bombing of Pearl Harbor on December 7, 1941—a "date which will live in infamy," as FDR predicted. We also hear speeches commemorating more positive events, such as the Wright Brothers' first flight at Kitty Hawk or astronaut Neil Armstrong's first step on the moon. Some people reserve formal commemorative speeches for public holidays, while others may view their own birthday or retirement party as an occasion for speech making. People still toast the bride and groom at wedding receptions, although toasts typically consist of a few impromptu remarks rather than prepared speeches.

The **commencement address**, of course, is a special kind of commemorative speech. Delivered at graduation ceremonies, commencement speeches have acquired an unfortunate reputation for being dull, predictable, and lacking in substance. Indeed, graduation speakers often joke about the insignificance of commencement speeches and promise to keep their remarks brief. Speaking to the graduates of Howard University in 1994, for example, former secretary of state Colin Powell cited a make-believe poll on student attitudes toward commencement addresses, then joked about how most people forget their commencement speaker:

> The real challenge ... of being a commencement speaker ... is trying to figure out how long you're gonna talk. If you ask the students, the answer is very, very simple. Talk for about four minutes and then sit down. Polls have been taken that show that

> 10 years after the event, 80 percent of all graduating students don't have a clue who their commencement speaker was. Well, you ain't gonna do that to me. The name is Powell, P-o-w-e-l-l.[25]

Despite their bad reputation, commencement addresses have played an important role in American history. Indeed, some of the most famous speeches in our history have been delivered at graduation ceremonies. With Hitler's armies overrunning Europe in 1940, for example, Franklin Delano Roosevelt used a commencement address at the University of Virginia to condemn the invasion of France by Mussolini's Italian fascists. "On this tenth day of June 1940," the president solemnly intoned, "the hand that held the dagger has stuck it into the back of its neighbor."[26] President John F. Kennedy delivered another historic commencement address at American University on June 10, 1963. Speaking at the height of the Cold War, Kennedy used the occasion to reflect on the horrors of modern war. Kennedy's address had a remarkable effect on world opinion and is still considered one of the greatest speeches in U.S. history. Far from a series of platitudes about the "challenges of life," Kennedy's speech was a thoughtful reflection on the insanity of war in the atomic age:

> I speak of peace because of the new face of war. Total war makes no sense in an age where great powers can maintain large and relatively invulnerable nuclear forces and refuse to surrender without resort to those forces. It makes no sense in an age where a single nuclear weapon contains almost ten times the explosive force delivered by all the allied air forces in the Second World War. It makes no sense in an age when the deadly poisons produced by a nuclear exchange would be carried by wind and water and soil and seed to the far corners of the globe and to generations yet unborn.
>
> Today the expenditure of billions of dollars every year on weapons acquired for the purpose of making sure we never need them is essential to the keeping of peace. But surely the acquisition of such idle stockpiles—which can only destroy and never create—is not the only, much less the most efficient, means of assuring peace. . . . I realize the pursuit of peace is not as dramatic as the pursuit of war, and frequently the words of the pursuers fall on deaf ears. But we have no more urgent task.[27]

Not all commencement speeches address such weighty and serious topics, of course. Most focus on the immediate event—the graduation ceremony—and offer advice on how to find success and happiness in life. Like all commemorative speeches, commencement addresses should reflect on the larger significance of the day and offer inspiration and guidance. But they are also part of a celebration and should, as a rule, be positive and upbeat in tone.

Tributes and Eulogies

We commemorate events, but we pay tribute to *people*. And, of course, there are no more important speeches than those with which we celebrate our heroes and honor our dead. In paying tribute to people—living or dead—we both reinforce our shared social values and define the meaning of *virtue* and *character*. By recognizing the special talents, unique accomplishments, and extraordinary contributions of people we admire, we define the life well lived and create role models for the next generation.

Television star Oprah Winfrey speaking at a memorial service for Rosa Parks in Washington, D.C., on October 31, 2005.

Tributes to living people are delivered on many occasions, such as award ceremonies, birthdays, anniversaries, and retirement celebrations. Whatever the occasion, the purpose remains the same: to highlight the person's unique contributions or talents and to praise him or her as an individual. In a speech honoring composer John Williams at the Kennedy Center for the Performing Arts, for example, filmmaker Steven Spielberg called Williams a "national treasure" and "as American as apple pie."[28] At a White House ceremony, secretary of defense Donald Rumsfeld praised a very different man in similar terms, calling economist Milton S. Friedman "a rare talent—indeed, a talent to be treasured." Praising Friedman for "unleashing the power of human freedom," Rumsfeld marked the 90th birthday of this champion of free markets by crediting him with changing "the course of history."[29]

Funerals are typically private affairs, with eulogists mourning the loss and giving voice to the pain and grief of loved ones. When famous people die, however, eulogists typically say more, proclaiming the deceased an inspiration, perhaps even a national "hero." Speaking at the funeral of civil rights pioneer Rosa Parks, for example, Oprah Winfrey recalled how her father had told her about "this colored woman who had refused to give up her seat," and she imagined that Parks must have been "really big"—"at least a hundred feet tall." When she had the honor of meeting Parks, of course, she was in for a surprise. "Here was this petite, almost delicate lady who was the personification of grace and goodness." At that meeting, Winfrey thanked Parks for all she had done for African Americans, and she thanked her again at her funeral, crediting Parks with all that she had achieved in life: "That day that you refused to give up your seat on the bus, you, Sister Rosa, changed the trajectory of my life and the lives of so many other people in the world."[30]

The death of a president or other political leader likewise tends to inspire **eulogies** that go beyond simple mourning. Typically, eulogies for political leaders urge us to honor their legacy by continuing their work. In a speech to Congress two weeks after the assassination of President Kennedy, for example, Lyndon Johnson mourned Kennedy's death, lamenting that the "greatest leader of our time" had been "struck down by the foulest deed of our time." Giving voice to millions of Americans, he added: "No words are sad enough to express our sense of loss." Yet then Johnson declared "let us continue," repeated the phrase several times, and declared it the "duty" of all Americans to carry on Kennedy's crusade for civil rights and world peace. He concluded by assuring the world that "John F. Kennedy did not live or die in vain."[31]

Inaugural and Keynote Addresses

Inaugural addresses are speeches we give upon assuming a new office or position. Inaugural addresses may be delivered by newly appointed corporate CEOs, incoming officers of private clubs or fraternal associations, or newly elected politicians. The best-known inaugural addresses, of course, are delivered every four years by the newly elected president of the United States. Indeed, a handful of presidential inaugurals—those of Thomas Jefferson, Abraham Lincoln, Franklin Delano Roosevelt, and John F. Kennedy—are counted among the greatest speeches in U.S. history.[32] Like all inaugural addresses, presidential inaugurals perform certain rituals of office taking, such as articulating one's "vision" of the future. Yet presidential inaugurals also perform other political functions, such as reunifying the nation after a divisive campaign and laying the groundwork for the new president's legislative agenda.

The power of an inaugural address to build unity after a divisive election is perhaps best illustrated by Thomas Jefferson's celebrated inaugural address in 1801. During the election of 1800, sharp partisan divisions emerged for the first time in U.S. history. The Federalists, led by John Adams and Alexander Hamilton, favored a strong central government. The Republicans, led by Jefferson, wanted government to play a more limited role. Both parties claimed to be the true heirs to the American Revolution, and both suspected the other of conspiratorial designs, even disloyalty. The campaign was one of the most bitter in all of American history; some doubted that the Federalists would relinquish power peacefully. When he delivered his inaugural address, few expected Jefferson to reach out to the Federalists in a spirit of reconciliation. Yet he did just that, calling the election a mere "contest of opinion" and declaring that, *of course*, all would now "unite in common efforts for the common good." Urging his "fellow citizens" to "unite with one heart and one mind," Jefferson declared that "every difference of opinion is not a difference of principle," then delivered the most famous lines of the address: "We are all Republicans; we are all Federalists. If there be any among us who would wish to dissolve this Union or change its republican form, let them stand undisturbed as monuments of the safety with which error of opinion may be tolerated where reason is left free to combat it."[33]

Other inaugural addresses have been more like deliberative or policy speeches, sketching at least the broad outlines of the new president's agenda. In his first inaugural, for example, Franklin D. Roosevelt proposed no detailed plan for combating the Great Depression, but he did promise "action, and action now." He then articulated the major aims of his New Deal policies: "put people to work," make better use of natural resources, support agriculture, stop foreclosures on homes and small farms, "drastically reduce" the costs of government, unify relief activities, and establish "national planning" and "supervision of all forms of transportation and of communications ... that have a definitely public character."[34] Similarly, John F. Kennedy's inaugural address foreshadowed his administration's aggressive Cold War policies by sounding a metaphorical trumpet and calling his fellow Americans to "a long twilight struggle." Speaking as the voice of a "new generation" of Americans—"born in this century, tempered by war, disciplined by a hard and bitter peace, [and] proud of our ancient heritage"—Kennedy made clear his determination to defend freedom around the world: "Let every nation know, whether it wishes us well or ill, that we shall pay any price, bear any burden, meet any hardship, support any friend, oppose any foe to assure the survival and the success of liberty."[35]

Keynote addresses are featured speeches at meetings, conferences, or other formal gatherings. Keynote addresses typically give expression to the purposes and significance of the group and its gathering. The best-known keynote addresses, of course, are those delivered every four years at the presidential nominating conventions of the two major political parties. Although these keynotes have become increasingly partisan in recent years, they still include some of the most timeless and celebrated speeches in U.S. history.

Among the most memorable keynote addresses is Texas congresswoman Barbara Jordan's speech to the 1976 Democratic National Convention in New York City. As an African-American woman, Jordan began by noting that, in the past, it would have been "most unusual for any national political party to ask a Barbara Jordan to deliver a keynote address." Thus, her very presence on the podium became, for Jordan, "evidence that the American Dream need not forever be deferred." The rest of the speech was a classic keynote address, articulating the ideals of the Democratic Party and celebrating the values shared by all Americans. In the wake of the Watergate scandal, Jordan also acknowledged people's skepticism toward government and called on her fellow politicians to accept responsibility for the problem. "We as public servants must set an example for the rest of the nation," she declared at a time of widespread political cynicism. "More is required ... of public officials than slogans and handshakes and press releases.... We must hold ourselves strictly accountable. We must provide the people with a vision of the future."[36]

You may never be elected president of the United States or address a national political convention, but you can emulate the spirit of the great inaugural and keynote addresses. Whether speaking as the new president of a local civic club or as the keynote speaker at a professional conference, your goal should be the same: to give eloquent expression to the shared beliefs and values of your group or community.

The After-Dinner Speech

Sometimes epideictic speeches are delivered after lunch or dinner, perhaps at a business meeting or conference. Although **after-dinner speeches** are often entertaining, they also may address more serious topics. If Federal Reserve chair Ben Bernanke is asked to deliver an after-dinner speech, for example, people expect him to say something significant about the economy. In other situations, an after-dinner speaker may be asked to pay tribute to a person or to deliver something akin to a keynote address. In these situations, the speaker also is expected to say something substantive yet still be entertaining or perhaps even amusing.

Not surprisingly, after-dinner speeches can pose quite a challenge. Not only have audience members just eaten a meal, but they may have been in meetings all day, with the dinner as their "reward." As a result, the after-dinner speaker must look for ways to enliven the speech, perhaps by telling anecdotes or stories or by delivering the speech in a more spontaneous and energetic style.

Humor, of course, is one way that speakers enliven after-dinner speeches, but humor can be tricky. Some people seem to have a knack for telling amusing stories; others do not. Some seem to have good comic timing; others stumble over punch lines. The point is not that you should avoid humor in an after-dinner speech. But if you do aspire to be funny, you need to think carefully about what your audience may or may not find amusing.

Generally, an after-dinner speech should not be too long, perhaps no more than five or ten minutes. Stay in touch with how the audience is responding during the speech. Build your speech flexibly, so that you can cut some material during the speech if the audience appears to be losing interest. The most common complaint about an after-dinner speech is that it was too long. One rarely hears people complain that an after-dinner speech was too short!

Finally, keep in mind that audiences expect to walk away from an after-dinner speech with something to think about, remember, or talk about with others attending the event. Some after-dinner speeches might even provide the basis for further discussion and action. However much your audience may enjoy themselves, it is important that they also get something meaningful out of the speech. Even a humorous after-dinner speech can be used to communicate a serious message, as when we pay sincere tribute to somebody by "roasting" him or her at a banquet.

Sermons

Sermons and other religious speeches may or may not be epideictic addresses, depending on their purpose and audience. When we seek to convert somebody to our religion, we obviously are trying to persuade. But when we celebrate and reaffirm our audience's existing faith—when we "preach to the choir"—the sermon functions like other ceremonial speeches, reinforcing or strengthening existing beliefs and values.

The line between epideictic and persuasive speaking is sometimes blurred in sermons that urge believers to cleanse themselves of sin. In the early nineteenth century, for example, a revivalist preacher named Lyman Beecher delivered a series of famous sermons on the "evils of intemperance," elaborating on the "deleterious influence" of alcohol on both individuals and the nation. Most of Beecher's followers already agreed with him about the evils of alcohol. Yet tempted by sin, many still drank. So Beecher took it upon himself to warn the nation (in the metaphorical style of epideictic) that "our sun is fast setting" and that "the darkness of an endless night is closing in upon us." At one level, of course, Beecher was trying to persuade his flock not to drink. At another level, however, his sermons were simply reinforcing their existing beliefs, urging them to have the strength of their convictions and resist the temptation to sin.[37]

STYLE AND DELIVERY IN CEREMONIAL SPEAKING

Preview. *Speakers tend to sound more "poetic" on ceremonial occasions, as they strive to give eloquent expression to the significance of the occasion and the shared social values of the audience. This emphasis on "eloquence" focuses more attention on the speaker's language. When preparing a ceremonial speech, you should choose your language carefully, using vivid language and figures of speech to create memorable images and a poetic rhythm and cadence. And because of the emphasis on style, most ceremonial speeches are delivered word-for-word from a manuscript.*

Throughout this chapter, we have emphasized how ceremonial speakers perform important educational and cultural functions, shaping listeners' identity as members of a community and reinforcing shared social values. Yet ceremonial speakers do more than honor our heroes or teach us about our traditions. They also *inspire* us with their eloquence, touching our hearts or motivating us to reaffirm our civic and cultural commitments. In Chapter 11, we discussed the resources of language, including some of the ways that you might make your language more lively and interesting. In the remainder of this chapter, we will revisit that discussion of style, focusing on how you might exploit the resources of language to make your ceremonial speeches more memorable.

Vivid Language and Imagery

The difference between a dull and lifeless ceremonial speech and one that is inspirational and eloquent often boils down to the speaker's choice of words. As we noted in Chapter 11, one way to make your speech more lively and interesting is to strive for *vivid* language, or language that is specific and concrete and appeals to your listeners' physical senses. Specific, concrete words allow your audience to see, hear, smell, taste, or feel what you are talking about, and that sort of language can enhance the emotional impact of your speech. In the following passage, notice how former president Ronald Reagan used vivid, concrete language to recreate the scene on D-Day in 1944 as he commemorated the 40th anniversary of that fateful day in Pointe du Hoc, France:

> We stand on a lonely, windswept point on the northern shore of France. The air is soft, but 40 years ago at this moment, the air was dense with smoke and the cries of men, and the air was filled with the crack of rifle fire and the roar of cannon. At dawn, on the morning of the sixth of June, 1944, 225 Rangers jumped off the British landing craft and ran to the bottom of these cliffs. Their mission was one of the most difficult and daring of the invasion: to climb these sheer and desolate cliffs and take out the enemy guns. . . .
>
> The Rangers looked up and saw the enemy soldiers . . . shooting down at them with machine guns and throwing grenades. And the American Rangers began to climb. They shot rope ladders over the face of these cliffs and began to pull themselves up. When one Ranger fell, another would take his place. When one rope was cut, a Ranger would grab another and begin his climb again. They climbed, shot back, and held their footing. Soon, one by one, the Rangers pulled themselves over the top, and in seizing the firm land at the top of these cliffs, they began to seize back the continent of Europe. Two hundred and twenty-five came here. After two days of fighting, only 90 could still bear arms.[38]

So powerful were Reagan's images—so vivid was his recreation of the scene on D-Day 40 years earlier—that some of the grizzled old veterans in his audience actually broke down in tears during the speech.

President Ronald Reagan used a visually dramatic setting and vivid language and imagery to commemorate the 40th anniversary of D-Day at Point du Hoc, Normandy, in 1984. In his audience were many of the surviving U.S. Army Rangers who stormed the cliffs on that fateful day.

Imagery refers to the "word pictures" that our language creates, and Reagan painted a vivid one. So, too, did Theodore Roosevelt in a famous speech delivered at the dedication of a new federal office building in 1906. In "The Man with the Muck Rake," Roosevelt compared the irresponsible journalists of his day to a famous literary figure from Bunyan's *Pilgrim's Progress*—the man with the muck rake, who "could look no way but down." Refusing to see anything positive or "lofty," he instead fixed his eyes "with solemn intentness only on that which is vile and debasing." To Roosevelt's mind, that perfectly described those journalists who reported nothing but bad news and engaged in "hysterical exaggeration" of America's problems. "Hysterical sensationalism is the poorest weapon wherewith to fight for lasting righteousness," Roosevelt declared in summarizing his point. And the imagery stuck: to this day, we use the term "muckraker" to describe journalists who specialize in sensational exposés.

Ceremonial speakers often use *figurative language* or specific *figures of speech* to create imagery. In his "I Have a Dream" speech, for example, Martin Luther King Jr. used metaphors to contrast the "dark and desolate valley of segregation" with the "sunlit path of racial justice." He began with an extended metaphor, comparing the March on Washington in 1963 to cashing a check:

> In a sense we've come to our nation's capital to cash a check. When the architects of our republic wrote the magnificent words of the Constitution and the Declaration of Independence, they were signing a promissory note .... This note was a promise that all men, yes, black men as well as white men, would be guaranteed the unalienable rights of life, liberty, and the pursuit of happiness.

> It is obvious today that America has defaulted on this promissory note insofar as her citizens of color are concerned. Instead of honoring this sacred obligation, America has given the Negro people a bad check, a check which has come back marked "insufficient funds."

King used metaphors throughout his speech to create vivid imagery and to give more specific meaning to abstract terms, such as *freedom, justice, opportunity*, and *equality*. It would have been one thing for King to announce that blacks were unsatisfied with the progress of the civil rights movement. It was quite another for him to disavow the "tranquilizing drug of gradualism" and to declare, in biblical terms, that he and his followers would "not be satisfied until justice rolls down like waters, and righteousness like a mighty stream."[39]

You may not have King's gift of eloquence. Yet simply by using more specific, concrete words or a striking metaphor or two, you can enhance the imagery and eloquence of your ceremonial speeches. Writing a ceremonial speech is not like writing poetry, yet neither is it the same as writing a persuasive or informative speech. In a ceremonial speech, you should pay closer attention to language and choose your words carefully to achieve a more eloquent tone. Not all epideictic speeches are flowery or poetic, but all should reflect careful attention to language and style.

Rhythm and Cadence

As you prepare your ceremonial speech, pay special attention to its rhythm and cadence. That is, write the speech with a view toward how well it will "flow" when delivered. In general, strive for a smooth, balanced rhythm, paying special attention to the length and structure of the speech's phrases and sentences. You also may employ stylistic devices that contribute to a more "poetic" rhythm, such as antithesis, parallelism, or simple repetition.

When writing an epideictic speech, keep in mind that you are writing for oral delivery. It is crucial that your speech *sound* good when delivered out loud. Generally, this means that you should strive for shorter sentences, perhaps even using phrases or sentence fragments that might be inappropriate in a written essay. You want a speech that you can deliver smoothly, without stumbling over words that are difficult to pronounce or sentences that are awkwardly constructed. It is always a good idea to practice your speech out loud before you deliver it.

We remember some of the most famous ceremonial speeches in history not only for their imagery but for their rhythm and cadence. In his inaugural address, for example, John F. Kennedy made effective use of antithesis, most notably in the best-known line of the address: "Ask not what your country can do for you—ask what you can do for your country." Yet that was not the only example of antithesis in the speech. Kennedy also used a complex, extended antithesis to open the speech: "We observe today not a victory of party but a celebration of freedom—symbolizing an end as well as a beginning—signifying renewal as well as change." Midway through the speech, he employed antithesis again: "Let us never negotiate out of fear. But let us never fear to negotiate." Finally, he concluded by echoing the most famous line of the address, directing a similar antithesis to "citizens of the world": "Ask not what America will do for you, but what together we can do for the freedom of man."[40]

King's "I Have a Dream" speech is also noteworthy for its rhythm and cadence, primarily because of the repetition and parallelism toward the end of the address. Although striking for its metaphorical imagery, the speech is perhaps even better remembered for King's repetition of the phrase that gave the speech its title, "I have a dream today!" King repeated that phrase to punctuate a series of longer statements about his vision of the future—a future when the sons of former slaves and slaveholders would "sit down together at the table of brotherhood" and "not be judged by the color of their skin but by the content of their character." Then, in closing, King used parallelism to build to a dramatic climax, imagining the ultimate triumph of justice and freedom:

> So let freedom ring from the prodigious hilltops of New Hampshire. Let freedom ring from the mighty mountains of New York. Let freedom ring from the heightening Alleghenies of Pennsylvania. Let freedom ring from the snow-capped Rockies of Colorado. Let freedom ring from the curvaceous slopes of California. But not only that. Let freedom ring from Stone Mountain of Georgia. Let freedom ring from Lookout Mountain of Tennessee. Let freedom ring from every hill and molehill of Mississippi, from every mountain side, let freedom ring.[41]

Again, you may not possess King's natural eloquence, and not every ceremonial occasion calls for a speech so poetic in tone. In preparing your own ceremonial speeches, however, you *should* strive for a more eloquent style, and that means paying close attention to the language, rhythm, and cadence of your speech.

Speaking from a Manuscript

On most occasions, you will deliver your ceremonial speech from a manuscript rather than from an outline or brief notes. That is, you will take care to present the speech exactly as written. This is not to say that you should stand before your audience, eyes glued to your manuscript, and simply read the speech. To the contrary, you should have the same concern with delivering your ceremonial speech effectively as you would any other speech.

The reason most ceremonial speeches are delivered from manuscript should be obvious: because of the emphasis on language and style, it is important that we deliver the speech precisely as written. That is not to say that you should never diverge from your manuscript or "ad lib" a few lines. Yet when you invent that memorable turn of phrase or come up with the perfect metaphor—that is, when you carefully craft the language of your speech—you want to deliver those lines exactly as written. In his first inaugural address, Franklin Roosevelt knew exactly what he wanted to say: the "only thing we have to fear is fear itself." Imagine if FDR had delivered that line extemporaneously, concerned only with the idea behind it. Instead of that famous line, he instead might have said: "Let's not be paralyzed by our fears." Or even just: "Don't be scared!"

Unfortunately, delivering a speech from manuscript poses special challenges. Most speakers find it more difficult to maintain eye contact, use physical movement and gestures, sustain the appropriate rate and volume, and react to audience feedback while reading from a manuscript. Delivering a speech from manuscript requires that you write the speech in a good oral style, using words and sentence constructions that you will not stumble over as you speak. It also requires that you make a special effort to maintain a slow, deliberate pace that allows you to stay connected to your audience. In Chapter 12, we offered some other tips for delivering a manuscript speech, including ways to move and gesture and use your voice effectively while speaking from a manuscript. But perhaps the best advice for delivering a manuscript speech is simple: never forget that you are delivering a *speech*, not simply reading out loud.

SUMMARY

- Ceremonial speeches perform important cultural functions in a free society.
  - They help us remember the past.
  - They honor our heroes.
  - They celebrate shared beliefs and values.
  - They provide inspiration and encouragement.
- Ceremonial speeches articulate and reinforce shared social values.
  - Most ceremonial speeches reaffirm existing values and traditions.
  - Some ceremonial speeches promote social reform or encourage groups to reassess their values and priorities.
- There are many different forms of ceremonial speeches, each unique but all with the same basic mission: to celebrate a special person or occasion.
  - Speeches of introduction should be brief and focused on the featured speaker.
  - Speeches of welcome or farewell often offer instruction or guidance.
  - Presentation and acceptance speeches may focus on the virtues of an award recipient or the significance of the award itself.
  - Commemoration and commencement addresses mark special dates or events.
  - Tributes and eulogies honor people and teach us about character and personal virtue.
  - Inaugural and keynote addresses articulate the "vision" of a new leader or the key principles of some group.
  - After-dinner speeches combine entertainment and a serious message.
  - Sermons may be considered *epideictic* speeches when they celebrate and reinforce the faith of believers.
- Ceremonial speeches should be written with careful attention to language and typically are delivered from manuscript.

QUESTIONS FOR REVIEW AND REFLECTION

1. What are some of the main purposes of ceremonial speeches in a free society?
2. Suppose you learn that you are going to receive an award and have to give a brief acceptance speech. Would you talk more about yourself, other people, or the award itself?
3. Do you remember any of the commemorative or commencement speeches you have heard in the past? What made those speeches memorable?

4. Think of an important public figure, celebrity, or other notable person, living or dead, whom you admire. If you were to deliver a tribute or eulogy to that person, what character attributes or personal virtues would you emphasize?
5. What are the major differences between an inaugural address and a keynote address?
6. Do ceremonial addresses always reinforce *traditional* social values? Can you think of speakers who have delivered ceremonial addresses that challenged traditional values?
7. Define *eloquence* and discuss what you think makes some speeches more eloquent than others.
8. What are some of the stylistic devices that contribute to vivid imagery or create a poetic rhythm and cadence in a ceremonial speech?

ENDNOTES

1. Dale L. Sullivan, "A Closer Look at Education as Epideictic Rhetoric," *Rhetoric Society Quarterly* 23 (1993): 71–72.
2. George Kennedy, *The Art of Persuasion in Greece* (Princeton, NJ: Princeton University Press, 1963), 160.
3. From Rudy Giuliani, "2004 Republican National Convention Address." Copyright © 2004 by Rudy Giuliani.
4. See Celeste Michelle Condit, "The Functions of Epideictic: The Boston Massacre Orations as Exemplar," *Communication Quarterly* 33 (1985): 284–99.
5. John Hancock, "Boston Massacre Oration," in *American Rhetorical Discourse*, 3rd ed., ed. Ronald F. Reid and James F. Klumpp (Long Grove, IL: Waveland Press, 2005), 103.
6. Henry W. Grady, "The New South," in *American Rhetorical Discourse*, 494–95.
7. Robert F. Kennedy, "On the Death of Martin Luther King," *The History Place*, www.historyplace.com/speeches/rfk.htm (accessed August 12, 2009).
8. From Ronald Reagan, "State of the Union, 1982." Published 1982 by U.S. Government.
9. Alex Altman, "Chesley B. Sullenberger III," *Time*, January 16, 2009, www.time.com/time/nation/article/0,8599,1872247,00.html (accessed August 10, 2009).
10. Jonathan Martin, "Hero Pilot to Attend Obama Speech," *Politico.com*, February 24, 2009, www.politico.com/news/stories/0209/19229.html (accessed August 12, 2009).
11. John F. Kennedy, "Inaugural Address," in *American Rhetorical Discourse*, 789.
12. Dwight D. Eisenhower, "Second Inaugural Address: The Price of Peace," in *The Presidents Speak*, ed. Davis Newton Lott (New York: Holt, 1994), 310.
13. From Winston Churchill, "We Shall Fight on the Beaches." Copyright © 1940 by British Crown and Churchill Family.
14. See Nicole Loraux, *The Invention of Athens: The Funeral Oration in the Classical City*, trans. Alan Sheridan (Cambridge, MA: Harvard University Press, 1986).
15. Sullivan, "A Closer Look at Education as Epideictic Rhetoric," 76–79.
16. Writing in the late 1950s, for example, scholars Chaim Perelman and Lucie Olbrechts-Tyteca observed that epideictic speeches were typically delivered by "those who, in a society, defend the traditional and accepted values, those which are the object of education, not the new and revolutionary values which stir up controversy and polemics." Chaim Perelman and Lucie Olbrechts-Tyteca, *The New Rhetoric: A Treatise on Argumentation*, trans. John Wilkinson and Purcell Weaver (Notre Dame, IN: University of Notre Dame Press, 1969), 51.
17. Cynthia Miecznikowski Sheard, "The Public Value of Epideictic Rhetoric," *College English* 58 (1996): 755–56.
18. From Frederick Douglass, "What to the Slave in the Fourth of July, July 5, 1982." Published 1852 by Lee, Mann & Co.
19. Jabari Asim, "Did Cosby Cross the Line," *Washington Post*, March 24, 2004, www.washingtonpost.com/wp-dyn/articles/A51273-2004May24.html (accessed August 13, 2009).
20. For Dyson's point-by-point rebuttal of Cosby's speech, see "Talking Points: Bill Cosby vs. Michael Eric Dyson," www.michaelericdyson.com/cosby/points.html (accessed August 13, 2009).
21. Dick Meyer, "Cosby Stands His Ground," *CBS News*, July 2, 2004, www.cbsnews.com/stories/2004/07/02/national/main627156.shtml (accessed August 13, 2009).

22. See *Lou Gehrig: The Official Web Site*, www.lougehrig.com/about/speech.htm (accessed August 13, 2009).
23. Dwight D. Eisenhower, "Farewell Address," in *Great Speeches for Criticism and Analysis*, ed. Lloyd Rohler and Roger Cook (Greenwood, IN: Alistair Press, 1988), 316–19.
24. Reprinted by permission from Dalai Lama, "His Holiness the Dalai Lama's Nobel Prize Acceptance Speech, University Aula, Oslo, December 10, 1989." Copyright © 1989 by Dalailama.com
25. Reprinted by permission from Colin Powell, "Commencement Speech at Howard University, May 1994." Copyright © 1994 by Colin Powell.
26. Franklin D. Roosevelt, "Address at University of Virginia, June 10, 1940," *The American Presidency Project*, www.presidency.ucsb.edu/ws/index.php?pid=15965&st=&st1= (accessed August 13, 2009).
27. From John F. Kennedy, "American University Commencement Address, 1963." Published 1963 by U.S. National Archives.
28. See Tatiana Morales, "A Tribute to 'Rebels': Warren Beatty and Elton John among Kennedy Center Honorees," *The Early Show*, December 6, 2004, www.cbsnews.com/stories/2004/12/06/earlyshow/main659314.shtml (accessed August 13, 2009).
29. Donald H. Rumsfeld, "Lucky Us: A Tribute to Milton Friedman," *National Review Online*, www.nationalreview.com/nrof_document/document073102.asp (accessed August 13, 2009).
30. Oprah Winfrey, "Eulogy for Rosa Parks," *American Rhetoric*, www.americanrhetoric.com/speeches/oprahwinfreyonrosaparks.htm (accessed August 13, 2009).
31. Lyndon Baines Johnson, "Let Us Continue," *American Rhetoric*, www.americanrhetoric.com/speeches/lbjletuscontinue.html (accessed August 12, 2009).
32. In a survey of rhetorical scholars to determine the top 100 speeches of the twentieth century, FDR's first inaugural and Kennedy's inaugural address were ranked third and second, respectively, behind another epideictic speech, Martin Luther King Jr.'s "I Have a Dream." Jefferson and Lincoln's inaugural addresses were not part of the ranking, of course, because they were not delivered in the twentieth century. But they are included in almost all anthologies of great American speeches. See Stephen E. Lucas and Martin J. Medhurst, ed., *Words of a Century: The Top 100 American Speeches, 1900–1999* (New York: Oxford University Press, 2008).
33. Thomas Jefferson, "First Inaugural Address (1801)," in *American Voices: Significant Speeches in American History, 1640–1945*, ed. James R. Andrews and David Zarefsky (New York: Longman, 1989), 115–16.
34. Franklin D. Roosevelt, "First Inaugural Address," in *American Rhetorical Discourse*, 749.
35. John F. Kennedy, "Inaugural Address," in *American Rhetorical Discourse*, 788–90.
36. Barbara Jordan, "Keynote Address," in *Great Speeches for Criticism and Analysis*, 53–55.
37. Lyman Beecher, "The Evils of Intemperance," in *American Rhetorical Discourse*, 278–85.
38. From Ronald Reagan, "On the 40th Anniversary of D-Day." Published 1984 by U.S. Government.
39. Reprinted by arrangement with the Heirs to the Estate of Martin Luther King Jr., c/o Writers House as agent for the proprietor New York, NY. Copyright 1963 Dr. Martin Luther King Jr; copyright renewed 1991 Coretta Scott King.
40. Kennedy, "Inaugural Address," in *American Rhetorical Discourse*, 788.
41. Reprinted by arrangement with the Heirs to the Estate of Martin Luther King Jr., c/o Writers House as agent for the proprietor New York, NY. Copyright 1963 Dr. Martin Luther King Jr; copyright renewed 1991 Coretta Scott King.

Liberty University Commencement Address

John McCain

After labeling the Reverend Jerry Falwell an "agent of intolerance" during the 2000 presidential campaign, Senator John McCain (R-Arizona) accepted an invitation to deliver the 2006 commencement address at Falwell's Liberty University. McCain used the occasion to talk about humility, patriotism, tolerance, respect, and forgiveness. He also celebrated free speech in America and urged his listeners to devote themselves to a cause greater than themselves.

May 13, 2006

Thank you. Thank you. Thank you. Thank you, Dr. Falwell. Thank you, faculty, families and friends, and thank you Liberty University Class of 2006 for your welcome and your kind invitation to give this year's commencement address. I want to join in the chorus of congratulations to the Class of 2006. This is a day to bask in praise. You've earned it. You have succeeded in a demanding course of instruction. Life seems full of promise, as is always the case when a passage in life is marked by significant accomplishment. Today, it might seem as if the world attends you.

McCAIN BEGINS BY THANKING HIS HOSTS AND OFFERING CONGRATULATIONS TO THE GRADUATES AND THEIR PARENTS, AS IS TYPICAL IN A COMMENCEMENT ADDRESS.

But spare a moment for those who have truly attended you so well for so long, and whose pride in your accomplishments is even greater than your own—your parents. When the world was looking elsewhere your parents' attention was one of life's certainties. So, as I commend you, I offer equal praise to your parents for the sacrifices they made for you, for their confidence in you and their love. More than any other influence in your lives they have helped you—make you the success you are today and might become tomorrow.

Thousands of commencement addresses are given every year, many by people with greater eloquence and more original minds than I possess. And it's difficult on such occasions to avoid resorting to clichés. So let me just say that I wish you all well. This is a wonderful time to be young. Life will offer you ways to use your education, industry, and intelligence to achieve personal success in your chosen professions. And it will also offer you chances to know a far more sublime happiness by serving something greater than your self-interest. I hope you make the most of all your opportunities.

IN THIS PARAGRAPH, HE FIRST ESTABLISHES HIS ETHOS BY EXPRESSING HUMILITY, THEN STATES THE CENTRAL THEME OF THE ADDRESS: THAT HAPPINESS COMES FROM "SERVING SOMETHING GREATER THAN YOUR SELF-INTEREST."

When I was in your situation, many, many years ago, an undistinguished graduate—barely—of the Naval Academy, I listened to President Eisenhower deliver the commencement address. I admired President Eisenhower greatly. But I must admit I remember little of his remarks that day, impatient as I was to enjoy the less formal celebration of graduation, and mindful that given my class standing I would not have the privilege of shaking the president's hand. I do recall, vaguely, that he encouraged his audience of new Navy ensigns and Marine lieutenants to become "crusaders for peace."

I became an aviator and, eventually, an instrument of war in Vietnam. I believed, as did many of my friends, we were defending the cause of a just peace. Some Americans believed we were agents of American imperialism who were not overly troubled by the many tragedies of war and the difficult moral dilemmas that constantly confront our soldiers. Ours is a noisy, contentious society, and always has been, for we love our liberties much. And among those liberties we love most, particularly so when we are young, is our right to self-expression. That passion for self-expression sometimes overwhelms our civility, and our presumption that those with whom we may have strong disagreements, wrong as they might be, believe that they, too, are answering the demands of their conscience.

When I was a young man, I was quite infatuated with self-expression, and rightly so because, if memory conveniently serves, I was so much more eloquent, well informed, and wiser than anyone else I knew. It seemed I understood the world and the purpose of life so much more profoundly than most people. I believed that to be especially true with many of my elders, people whose only accomplishment, as far as I could tell, was that they'd been born before me, and, consequently, had suffered some number of years deprived of my insights. I had opinions on everything, and I was always right. I loved to argue, and I could become understandably belligerent with people who lacked the grace and intelligence to agree with me. With my superior qualities so obvious, it was an intolerable hardship to have to suffer fools gladly. So I rarely did. All their resistance to my brilliantly conceived and cogently argued views proved was that they possessed an inferior intellect and a weaker character than God had blessed me with, and I felt it was my clear duty to so inform them. It's a pity that there wasn't a blogosphere then. I would have felt very much at home in that medium.

In this section of the speech, he recounts his personal journey from "undistinguished graduate" of the U.S. Naval Academy to U.S. senator. Using self-deprecating humor, he recalls how, as a young man, he was "infatuated" with his own eloquence and wisdom and belligerent toward those who "lacked the grace and intelligence to agree with" him. This not only reinforces his ethos as a humble and thoughtful man, but also reinforces a major theme of the address: that in our "noisy, contentious society," we should not let our "passion for self-expression" overwhelm our "civility" toward others.

It's funny, now, how less self-assured I feel late in life than I did when I lived in perpetual springtime. Some of my critics allege that age hasn't entirely cost me the conceits of my youth. All I can say to them is, they should have known me then, when I was brave and true and better looking than I am at present. But as the great poet Yeats wrote, "All that's beautiful drifts away, like the waters." I've lost some of the attributes that were the object of a young man's vanity. But there have been compensations, which I have come to hold dear.

We have our disagreements, we Americans. We contend regularly and enthusiastically over many questions: over the size and purposes of our government; over the social responsibilities we accept in accord with the dictates of our consciousness [conscience] and our faithfulness to the God we pray to; over our role in the world and how to defend our security interests and values in places where they are threatened. These are important questions worth arguing about. We should contend over them with one another. It is more than appropriate: it is necessary that even in times of crisis, especially in times of crisis, we fight among ourselves for the things we believe in. It is not just our right, but our civic and moral obligation.

Here, McCain celebrates free speech, calling it our "civic and moral obligation" to speak out on important issues, but also reminding us of our duty to serve the larger good through military service, charitable work, or politics.

Our country doesn't depend on the heroism of every citizen. But all of us should be worthy of the sacrifices made on our behalf. We have to love our freedom, not just for the private opportunities it provides, but for the goodness it makes possible. We have to love it as much, even if not as heroically, as the brave Americans who defend us at the risk and often the cost of their lives. We must love it enough to argue about it, and to serve it, in whatever way our abilities permit and our conscience requires, whether it calls us to arms or to altruism or to politics.

I supported the decision to go to war in Iraq. Many Americans did not. My patriotism and my conscience required me to support it and to engage in the debate over whether and how to fight it. I stand that ground not to chase vainglorious dreams of empire; not for a noxious sense of racial superiority over a subject people; not for cheap oil (we could have purchased oil from the former dictator at a price far less expensive than the blood and treasure we've paid to secure those resources for the people of that nation); not for the allure of chauvinism, to wreck [wreak] destruction in the world in order to feel superior to it; not for a foolishly romantic conception of war. I stand that ground because I believed, rightly or wrongly, that my country's interests and values required it.

In these paragraphs, he tackles a controversial issue: the war in Iraq. He defends his own support for the war, but he also declares war an "awful business" and concludes: "Only a fool or a fraud sentimentalizes war." Finally, he calls for more, not less, debate over the war, declaring it the right and obligation of those opposed to the war to "state their opposition" and "argue for another course."

War is an awful business. The lives of the nation's finest patriots are sacrificed. Innocent people suffer. Commerce is disrupted, economies damaged. Strategic interests shielded by years of statecraft are endangered as the demands of war and diplomacy conflict. Whether the cause was necessary or not, whether it was just or not, we should all shed a tear for all that is lost when war claims its wages from us. However just or false the cause, however proud and noble the service, it is loss—the loss of friendships, the loss of innocent life, the innocence—the loss of innocence; and the veteran feels most keenly forevermore. Only a fool or a fraud sentimentalizes war.

Americans should argue about this war. They should argue about it. It has cost the lives of nearly 2,500 of the best of us. It has taken innocent life. It has imposed an enormous financial burden on our economy. At a minimum, it has complicated our ability to respond to other looming threats. Should we lose this war, our defeat will further destabilize an already volatile and dangerous region, strengthen the threat of terrorism, and unleash furies that will assail us for a very long time. I believe the benefits of success will justify the costs and the risks we have incurred. But if an American feels the decision was unwise, then they should state their opposition, and argue for another course. It is your right and your obligation. I respect you for it. I would not respect you if you chose to ignore such an important responsibility. But I ask that you consider the possibility that I, too, am trying to meet my responsibilities, to follow my conscience, to do my duty as best as I can, as God has given me light to see that duty.

Americans deserve more than tolerance from one another; we deserve each other's respect, whether we think each other right or wrong in our views, as long as our character and our sincerity merit respect, and as long as we share, for all our differences, for all the noisy debates that enliven our politics, a mutual devotion to the sublime idea that this nation was conceived in—that freedom is the inalienable right of mankind, and in accord with the laws of nature and nature's Creator.

McCain urges his listeners not merely to tolerate but to respect those who disagree with their views. At the same time, he insists that there is more that unites than divides us, reminding us of our common enemy in Islamic extremism and citing Rwanda and Darfur as examples of genocide that we all should oppose. There is no "clash of civilizations," McCain insists, but rather a "clash of ideals" between those who abuse human rights and those who champion human freedom.

We have so much more that unites us than divides us. We need only to look to the enemy who now confronts us, and the benighted ideals to which Islamic extremists pledge allegiance—their disdain for the rights of man, their contempt for human life—to appreciate how much unites us.

Take, for example, the awful human catastrophe under way in the Darfur region of the Sudan. If the United States and the West can be criticized for our role in this catastrophe it's because we have waited too long to intervene to protect the multitudes who are suffering, dying because of it.

Twelve years ago, we turned a blind eye to another genocide, in Rwanda. And when that reign of terror finally, mercifully exhausted itself, with over 800,000 Rwandans slaughtered, Americans, our government, and decent people everywhere in the world were shocked and ashamed of our silence and inaction, for ignoring our values, and the demands of our conscience. In shame and renewed allegiance to our ideals, we swore, not for the first time, "never again." But "never" lasted only until the tragedy of Darfur.

Now, belatedly, we have recovered our moral sense of duty, and we are prepared, I hope, to put an end to this genocide. Osama bin Laden and his followers, ready, as always, to sacrifice anything and anyone to their hatred of the West and our ideals, have called on Muslims to rise up against any Westerner who dares intervene to stop the genocide, even though Muslims, hundreds of thousands of Muslims, are its victims. Now that, my friends, is a difference, a cause, worth taking up arms against.

It is not a clash of civilizations. I believe, as I hope all Americans would believe, that no matter where people live, no matter their history or religious beliefs or the size of their GDP, all people share the desire to be free; to make by their own choices and industry better lives for themselves and their children. Human rights exist above the state and beyond history—they are God-given. They cannot be rescinded by one government any more than they can be granted by another. They inhabit the human heart, and from there, though they can be abridged, they can never be wrenched.

This is a clash of ideals, a profound and terrible clash of ideals. It is a fight between right and wrong. Relativism has no place in this confrontation. We're not defending—we're not defending an idea that every human being should eat corn flakes, play baseball, or watch MTV. We're not insisting that all societies be governed by a bicameral legislature and a term-limited chief executive. We're insisting that all people have a right to be free, and that right is not subject to the whims and interests and authority of another person, government, or culture. Relativism, in this context, is most certainly not a sign of our humility or ecumenism; it is a mask for arrogance and selfishness. It is, and I mean this sincerely and with all humility, not worthy of us. We are a better people than that.

We're not a perfect nation. Our history has had its moments of shame and profound regret. But what we have achieved in our brief history is irrefutable proof that a nation conceived in liberty will prove stronger, more decent, and more enduring than any nation ordered to exalt the few at the expense of the many or made from a common race or culture or to preserve traditions that have no greater attribute than longevity.

WHILE CONCEDING THAT WE ARE NOT A "PERFECT" NATION, MCCAIN CELEBRATES AMERICA'S ACHIEVEMENTS AS "IRREFUTABLE PROOF" OF THE STRENGTH AND DECENCY OF A FREE NATION. WARNING AGAINST COMPLACENCY, HE ALSO REMINDS HIS LISTENERS OF THEIR DUTY TO "SACRIFICE FOR A CAUSE GREATER THAN YOURSELF."

As blessed as we are, no nation complacent in its greatness can long sustain it. We, too, must prove, as those who came before us proved, that a people free to act in their own interests will perceive those interests in an enlightened way, will live as one nation, in a kinship of ideals, and make of our power and wealth a civilization for the ages, a civilization in which all people share in the promise and responsibilities of freedom.

Should we claim our rights and leave to others the duty to the ideals that protect them, whatever we gain for ourselves will be of little lasting value. It will build no monuments to virtue, claim no honored place in the memory of posterity, offer no worthy summons to the world. Success, wealth, and celebrity gained and kept for private interest is a small thing. It makes us comfortable, eases the material hardships our children will bear, purchase[s] a fleeting regard for our lives, yet not the self-respect that, in the end, matters most. But sacrifice for a cause greater than yourself, and you invest your life with the eminence of that cause, your self-respect assured.

All lives are a struggle against selfishness. All my life I've stood a little apart from institutions that I willingly joined. It just felt natural to me. But if my life had shared no common purpose, it would not have amounted to much more than eccentricity. There is no honor or happiness in just being strong enough to be left alone. I've spent nearly 50 years in the service of this country and its ideals. I have made many mistakes, and I have many regrets. But I've never lived a day, in good times or bad, that I wasn't grateful for the privilege. That's the benefit of service to a country that is an idea and a cause, a righteous idea and cause. America and her ideals helped spare me from the weaknesses in my own character. And I cannot forget it.

RETURNING TO HIS PERSONAL STORY, MCCAIN RECALLS THE LESSONS HE HAS LEARNED FROM 50 YEARS OF PUBLIC SERVICE. THAT SERVICE "HELPED SPARE" HIM "FROM THE WEAKNESSES IN" HIS "OWN CHARACTER," HE RECALLS, AND TAUGHT HIM THAT THERE WAS MORE TO LIFE THAN "SELF-GLORY."

When I was a young man, I thought glory was the highest attainment, and all glory was self-glory. My parents had tried to teach me otherwise, as did my church, as did the Naval Academy. But I didn't understand the lesson until later in life, when I confronted challenges I never expected to face.

In that confrontation, I discovered that I was dependent on others to a greater extent than I had ever realized, but neither they nor the cause we served made any claims on my identity. On the contrary, they gave me a larger sense of myself than I had had before. And I am a better man for it. I discovered that nothing in life is more liberating than to fight for a cause that encompasses you but is not defined by your existence alone. And that has made all the difference, my friends, all the difference in the world.

Let—let us argue with each other then. By all means, let us argue. Our differences are not petty. They often involve cherished beliefs, and represent our best judgment about what is right for our country and humanity. Let us defend those beliefs. Let's do so sincerely and strenuously. It is our right and duty to do so. And let's not be too dismayed with the tenor and passion of our arguments, even when they wound us. We have fought among ourselves before in our history, over big things and small, with worse vitriol and bitterness than we experience today.

EMPLOYING PARALLEL PHRASES BEGINNING WITH "LET US," MCCAIN REMINDS US OF OUR RESPONSIBILITY TO DEBATE OUR DIFFERENCES WITH CIVILITY AND RESPECT FOR THOSE WHO DISAGREE.

Let us exercise our responsibilities as free people. But let us remember, we are not enemies. We are compatriots defending ourselves from a real enemy. We have nothing to fear from each other. We are arguing over the means to better secure our freedom, promote the general welfare, and defend our ideals. It should remain an argument among friends; each of us struggling to hear our conscience, and heed its demands; each of us, despite our differences, united in our great cause, and respectful of the goodness in each other. I have not always heeded that injunction myself, and I regret it very much.

I had a friend once, who, a long time ago, in the passions and resentments of a tumultuous era in our history, I might have considered my enemy. He had come once to the capitol of the country that held me prisoner, that deprived me and my dearest friends of our most basic rights, and that murdered some of us. He came to that place to denounce our country's involvement in the war that had led us there. His speech was broadcast into our cells. I thought it a grievous wrong then, and I still do.

A few years later, he had moved temporarily to a kibbutz in Israel. He was there during the Yom Kippur War, when he witnessed the support America provided our beleaguered ally. He saw the huge cargo planes bearing the insignia of the United States Air Force rushing emergency supplies into that country. And he had an epiphany. He had believed America had made a tragic mistake by going to Vietnam, and he still did. He had seen what he believed were his country's faults, and he still saw them. But he realized he has—he had let his criticism temporarily blind him to his country's generosity and the goodness that most Americans possess, and he regretted his failing deeply. When he returned to his country he became prominent in Democratic Party politics, and helped [elect] Bill Clinton president of the United States. He criticized his government when he thought it wrong, but he never again lost sight of all that unites us.

McCain uses a long personal anecdote to illustrate his theme that even bitter political enemies can find common ground. The story is about antiwar protestor David Ifshin, who denounced the war in Vietnam over Radio Hanoi while McCain was still being held there as a POW. Later, Ifshin became a campaign aide to President Bill Clinton, and McCain not only became friends with Ifshin but worked with him to promote human rights.

We met some years later. He approached me and asked to apologize for the mistake he believed he had made as a young man. Many years had passed since then, and I bore little animosity for anyone because of what they had done or not done during the Vietnam War. It was an easy thing to accept such a decent act, and we moved beyond our old grievance.

We worked together in an organization dedicated to promoting human rights in the country where he and I had once come for different reasons. I came to admire him for his generosity, his passion for his ideals, and for the largeness of his heart, and I realized he had not been my enemy, but my countryman, my countryman, and later my friend. His friendship honored me. We disagreed over much. Our politics were often opposed, and we argued those disagreements. But we worked together for our shared ideals. We were not always in the right, but we weren't always in the wrong either, and we defended our beliefs as we had each been given the wisdom to defend them.

David [Ifshin] remained my countryman and my friend, until the day of his death, at the age of 47, when he left a loving wife and three beautiful children, and legions of friends behind him. His country was a better place for his service to Her, and I had become a better man for my friendship with him. God bless him.

In conclusion, McCain reinforces the importance of this basic theme—that his listeners have a responsibility to serve humanity.

And may God bless you, Class of 2006. The world does indeed await you, and humanity is impatient for your service. Take good care of that responsibility. Everything depends upon it.

And thank you, very much, for the privilege of sharing this great occasion with you.

Source: From John McCain, "Liberty University Commencement Address, May 13, 2006." Published 2006 by John McCain.

CHAPTER

18

Speaking and Deliberating in Groups

CHAPTER SURVEY

Understanding Public Deliberation

Group Structures That Encourage Dialogue and Deliberation

Factors That Influence Effective Group Deliberation

Group Presentations

Guidelines for Deliberating in Groups

CHAPTER OBJECTIVES

After studying this chapter, you should be able to

1. Explain the role and importance of public deliberation.
2. Describe the fundamental steps in the deliberative process.
3. Provide illustrations of specific group structures that promote deliberation and dialogue.

CHAPTER OBJECTIVES (*CONTINUED*)

4. Describe those factors that influence the effective functioning of deliberative groups.
5. Explain the attitudes and communication behaviors that characterize successful participation in group presentations.
6. Participate effectively in a group deliberation, following the guidelines explored in this chapter.

By speaking out in public, we fulfill one of our most important responsibilities as citizens: to work together with our fellow citizens to build stronger communities and a better world. Most of this book focuses on formal speeches, in which you deliver carefully prepared remarks to an audience of listeners. In many instances, however, your listeners will not be passive receivers but active participants in a discussion. In these group settings, you may still engage in advocacy, but your "speeches" will be less formal and more spontaneous. This process of communicating within a group—with speakers and listeners frequently exchanging roles—is called *deliberation*. In group deliberations, you may still be an advocate for a particular point of view, but your ultimate goal may be consensus building, information sharing, or conflict resolution.

We all participate in a variety of formal and informal group deliberations. Professionally, we may spend many hours attending staff meetings or meeting with clients or customers. In our local community, we may participate in a community forum, attend a school board meeting, or work on a task force appointed to tackle some problem. As you interact in such groups, you will learn from others, form friendships, and contribute knowledge and skills vital to the success of the group's efforts. Deliberating in a group is not the same as talking individually with another person or working alone to solve some problem. A group is both dynamic and complex. Done right, group deliberations may lead to long-term, productive relationships and inspire creative decision making. When they go badly, however, they can cause tension and prevent action. This chapter focuses on ways to promote healthy, productive group deliberations.

The frequency with which you deliberate in groups is itself reason enough to read this chapter carefully. Your effectiveness in any organization or community will be influenced by how well you communicate in groups. As businesses and nonprofit organizations have become increasingly team-oriented, group communication skills have also become more important in the workplace. Knowing how to be a team player, how to interact effectively with others to complete projects, and how to provide group leadership are all highly valued skills in the twenty-first century.[1]

Group communication skills learned in one setting are quite applicable to others. Whether you are deliberating as a board member of a nonprofit agency, as a citizen in a community group, or as member of your work team, you will be more effective if you prepare carefully, thoughtfully analyze the problem, maintain an open and flexible attitude, and listen respectfully. When you communicate effectively in a group, you are likely to exert more influence and rise to a position of leadership. You also will find it easier to maintain a civil and respectful atmosphere as you collaborate with others to solve problems. The more involved you become as a citizen in your community, the more frequently you will work in groups dealing with such issues as education, crime and public safety, or housing and environmental policy. Your ability to contribute constructively to groups will affect your community's ability to solve its problems. For all these reasons, developing the ability to work effectively in groups is vital. We begin by examining the form that group communication typically takes in a civic or community setting: the process known as public deliberation.

UNDERSTANDING PUBLIC DELIBERATION

Preview. *Deliberative forums vary in size and specific purpose, but the same basic principles of effective and responsible deliberation govern them all. Public deliberation differs from debate; it is not a contest with winners and losers, but a process of engaging in dialogue to promote understanding or solve problems. At its best, deliberation can lead to a variety of positive outcomes. When not characterized by a spirit of dialogue, however, deliberation will not have such positive results.*

The concept of **public deliberation** grows out of democratic theory. According to political scientist Simone Chambers, the theory of deliberative democracy focuses on the communicative processes of opinion formation that precede voting.[2] Although the act of voting itself is a personal decision, the process of deliberation is concerned with public "account giving"—how people articulate, explain, and justify their political opinions and policy preferences to their fellow citizens. In other words, the theory of democratic deliberation is talk-focused. In a sense, then, public deliberation is the process through which democracy is enacted.[3]

Communication scholar John Gastil defines public deliberation as "judicious argument, critical listening, and earnest decision making."[4] Gastil echoes educational philosopher John Dewey, who described *full* deliberation as a careful examination of a problem or issue, including the identification of possible solutions, the establishment of evaluative criteria, and the use of those criteria in identifying the best solution.[5] Of course, deliberation in the real world does not always work so neatly. But by striving to deliberate as fully and completely as possible, citizens can improve its process and outcomes.

Public deliberation, then, is discourse among citizens—as they engage in dialogue, explore ideas, and strive to reach common understandings and agreements about community problems or courses of action. Public deliberation is a real measure of civic engagement—as much so as voting, attending meetings, working for a political party, or participating in voluntary organizations. Deliberating with others provides the opportunity for citizens to develop and express their views, learn from the ideas of others, identify shared concerns and preferences, and come to common understandings and judgments about matters of public concern. These exchanges can be a "central way of clarifying and negotiating deep divisions over material interests and moral values."[6] At the same time, they can provide a mechanism for airing disagreements that have *not* been articulated and point the way toward resolving differences within a community.

There are many different forms of public deliberation. Some deliberations take place in large, formal settings, such as a town hall meeting between elected officials and their constituents. Other deliberations take place in homes, schools, churches, libraries, or community centers. Public deliberation can also involve face-to-face exchanges, phone conversations, e-mail exchanges, and Internet forums. It may focus on local issues and problems or matters of national or even international significance.

Engaging in Dialogue

Whether the goal of public deliberation is education, consensus building, conflict resolution, or advocacy,[7] the deliberative process is more likely to be successful if the participants engage one another in a respectful dialogue. As award-winning author Daniel Yankelovich points out, dialogue is most easily understood by contrasting it with the kind of debate in which the goal is to *win* an argument.[8]

Journalist Scott London points out that **deliberative dialogue** differs from other forms of public discourse because its objective is to *think together*, "not so much to reach a conclusion as to discover where a conclusion might lie."[9] Thinking together involves listening deeply and with empathy for other points of view. In many discussions, participants bat ideas back and forth, but they seem

HIGHLIGHTING DIALOGUE

Making Deliberation Work

Debate	Dialogue
Assuming that there is a right answer and you have it	Assuming that many people have pieces of the answer and that together they can craft a solution
Attempting to prove the other side wrong in a combative manner	Working together toward a common understanding in a collaborative manner
Emphasizing winning over finding common ground	Emphasizing discovering common ground over winning
Listening to find flaws and make counterarguments	Listening to understand, to find meaning and agreement
Defending assumptions as truth	Revealing assumptions for reevaluation
Critiquing the other side's position	Reexamining all positions
Defending one's own views against those of others	Admitting that others' thinking can improve one's own
Searching for flaws and weaknesses in others' positions	Searching for strengths and value in others' positions
Seeking a conclusion or vote that ratifies your position	Discovering new options, not seeking to win

Source: Reprinted with the permission of Simon & Schuster, Inc., from *The Magic of Dialogue* by Daniel Yankelovich.

more interested in articulating their *own* views than in truly understanding what others are saying.

When you participate in deliberations, it's important to approach the dialogue in a spirit of equality. As Yankelovich maintains, "In genuine dialogue, there is no arm-twisting, no pulling of rank, no hint of sanctions for holding politically incorrect attitudes, no coercive influences of any sort, whether overt or indirect."[10] In many contexts, of course, differences of status may exist among the participants, making it more difficult to achieve a genuine dialogue. In that case, those of higher rank or status must take the initiative to build trust and make everybody feel comfortable about airing their views.[11] Differences of power or status can make deliberating more challenging, but those differences *can* be overcome.

The deliberative process usually revolves around problem solving, but it also can be used simply to increase knowledge, understanding, or empathy for different perspectives. London notes that the Greeks believed that individuals could uncover the truth for themselves by reasoning with others. He inventories what they envisioned, writing:

> By questioning and probing each other, carefully dissecting and analyzing ideas, finding inconsistencies, never attacking or insulting, but always searching for what they could accept between them, they could gradually attain deeper understanding and insight.[12]

In this spirit, deliberative dialogue aims at establishing a framework for mutual understanding and a common purpose that transcends individual ideas and opinions. Although it may not produce consensus, it *can* produce collective insight and judgment that reflects the thinking of the group as a whole. When the deliberative process works well, it links people's private ideas and interests with public knowledge and **public values**—knowledge and values that are clarified and corroborated through the process of group inquiry.

FOCUS ON CIVIC ENGAGEMENT

The Exchange: A Marketplace of Student Ideas

Nobody is born with the habits and skills of civic engagement. We *learn* how to be good citizens, and the National Constitution Center in Philadelphia has developed an innovative program to help high school students do just that: The Exchange: A Marketplace of Student Ideas. Using Internet-2 videoconferencing technologies, The Exchange brings together students from across the nation for live discussions of some of the most pressing issues of the day, including religion in the public schools, health care reform, immigration, and same-sex marriage. Funded by the Annenberg Foundation and hosted by MTV news correspondent SuChin Pak, The Exchange teaches students the difference between competitive debate and collaborative deliberation, and it cultivates a variety of skills necessary for engaged democratic citizenship, including research, critical listening, public speaking, and group deliberation skills.

For more information and video clips from The Exchange, visit http://studentexchange.ning.com/ or the National Constitution Center, http://constitutioncenter.org/ncc_edu_TheExchange.aspx.

Understanding How Deliberative Dialogue Works While there is no fixed procedure for organizing a deliberative dialogue, certain steps or stages are fairly typical. To begin, a facilitator welcomes participants, invites self-introductions, and quickly reviews the guidelines for dialogue. If participants have questions about the guidelines, the facilitator will address those before proceeding.

Participants then enter into *exploratory dialogue*—a potentially awkward time when some sit back and watch or express their views tentatively, perhaps sizing up others in the group or scrutinizing the procedures. As individuals begin to relate personal stories of their relationship to the issue at hand, a more comfortable group dynamic begins to unfold. Through the exploratory phase, group members may begin to establish trust and cohesiveness. They also grapple with "naming" the issue—a process that may take them in new and perhaps unanticipated directions. They may discover, for example, that the issue they thought they had come to discuss is only a part, or a symptom, of a deeper and more complex issue. So a community group might initially come together because they are concerned about neighborhood crime, but as they deliberate, they may end up focusing on a broader set of concerns, such as poverty or at-risk youth.

Later, the dialogue shifts from inquiry and exploration to *purposeful deliberation*, as the group begins to wrestle with what may look like competing choices. Conflict and disagreement are almost certain as the group seeks to identify core group values that transcend individual differences. Participants help generate productive dialogue when they indicate that their ideas are tentative, not cast in stone, and signal their willingness to listen, to grow, and to change. Participants also advance a spirit of dialogue when they give everybody a chance to speak, so that no one dominates the conversation. Finally, participants show their commitment to dialogue by establishing a supportive environment where mutual respect is the norm.[13]

Deliberative groups come together for different reasons and with different outcomes in mind. Some are content to set an agenda for further study or to arrive at a shared sense of how best to address an issue. Others aim for a collective judgment about the best course of action to pursue. Whatever the goal, the deliberative process ends when the facilitator sums up what has been said (or asks group members to do so), points out areas of agreement and lingering disagreement, articulates the overarching concerns that have been shared, allows for final comments, and identifies the "next steps" for the group.

Based on his studies of a number of deliberative groups, London argues that what distinguishes an ordinary from an extraordinary dialogue is the "presence of some transforming moment, or critical turning point." At this crucial point, participants break out of their own point of view and entertain the possibility of developing a collective understanding of the issue at hand.[14]

Compelling personal narratives may trigger this kind of turning point, making abstract and ideological views more concrete and understandable. When individuals in the group recount their personal struggle with drug addiction, their experience of living on the streets, their battle with mental illness, or their anger and despair at being the target of racist or homophobic remarks, others in the group may be moved, perhaps for the first time. Personal narratives give the problem a human face.[15]

Benefits of Public Deliberation

The potential benefits of public deliberation are many. The following are among the most consistently cited:

- Citizens become more engaged and active in civic affairs.
- Tolerance for opposing points of view increases.
- Citizens improve their understanding of their own preferences and can better justify those preferences with arguments.
- People in conflict set aside their "win-lose" approach as they begin to sense their interdependence.
- Faith in the democratic process is enhanced as citizens feel empowered.
- Political decisions become more considered and informed by relevant reasons and evidence.
- Collective decision making grows in frequency and quality.[16]

Under the right circumstances, public deliberation can produce impressive results. Gastil, for example, has documented numerous real-world deliberative initiatives, such as a community "visioning process" held in Chattanooga, Tennessee. This deliberative process involved 50 community activists and volunteers who met over a 20-week period. Their deliberations produced a list of priorities and solutions, including a shelter for abused women and a riverfront park. The organizers next developed a series of neighborhood associations and new nonprofit organizations. Eight years later, most of the solutions that had emerged from the forums had been implemented.[17]

Participants often emerge "changed" by the process of deliberating. Research on the National Issues Forums has shown that deliberation can produce an array of positive results, including increasing the participants' sense of community, enhancing their interest in politics, and making them more open-minded in their political conversations.[18] An extensive survey of another group of participants in small group deliberations revealed that, as a result of their deliberations, those participants donated money to charitable organizations (57 percent), became more interested in politics or social issues (45 percent), volunteered in the community (43 percent), changed their mind about a political or social issue (40 percent), or participated in a political rally or political campaign (12 percent).[19]

Potential Problems

Public deliberation does not always yield such positive outcomes. Much depends on participants' expectations, the deliberative format used, the facilitator's skill, and whether the groups feel that their deliberations have any real impact. For example, one study reported on the feelings of frustration experienced by members of a deliberative group that had made specific recommendations for health care reform and environmental regulation. When the federal government failed to enact any sort of reform, they felt that their deliberations had been in vain.[20] In general, when participants feel that they are "just talking" and that their talk will not have any real impact on policy making, they will experience post-deliberation frustration.[21]

Participating in deliberative forums may also increase participants' sense of *self*-efficacy while reducing their sense of *group* efficacy. One study found that participants left a challenging forum more confident in their own ability to take effective individual action but more skeptical of the efficacy of group-based political action. However, the reactions of participants seemed to depend on the nature of their experiences in the forums. Those who engaged in relatively successful forums—with well-prepared participants, clear guidelines, effective facilitators, and adequate time devoted to deliberation—reported greater attitude changes and more positive feelings about the group experience.[22] In cases where deliberative forums do not go well, however, participants may end up feeling even more powerless and ineffectual.

Facilitators must be well trained and skilled, capable of providing adequate structure while allowing plenty of room for the exploration of diverse ideas. They also must be able to help group members achieve a sense of closure. Either too much intervention (so that the group members are not freely deliberating) or too little (so that the group rambles out of control) can lead to poor outcomes and dissatisfaction.[23] In addition, facilitators must create a climate in which all participants feel they can express their views without fear of reprisal.

GROUP STRUCTURES THAT ENCOURAGE DIALOGUE AND DELIBERATION

Preview. *A number of foundations and educational groups have developed programs to promote more open, constructive, and engaged public deliberations. These programs provide models for deliberative groups of differing sizes and purposes.*

Although many different types of deliberative groups exist, including citizen juries, roundtables, and public hearings, we focus here on three of the most common models: study circles, town hall meetings, and National Issues Forums.

Study Circles

The Study Circles Resource Center (SCRC) was created by the Topsfield Foundation in 1989 to advance deliberative democracy and improve the quality of public life in the United States. The center was renamed "Everyday Democracy" in 2002. Its goal is to develop communication tools to involve a large number of people, from every background and way of life, in face-to-face dialogue leading to real-world solutions.[24]

A **study circle** typically consists of eight to twelve participants guided by an impartial facilitator. Study circle members are encouraged to consider many perspectives, rather than advocating for a particular point of view. Ground rules set the tone for a respectful, productive discussion. Participants are encouraged to listen attentively to one another and to work at building trusting relationships. A typical study circle meets over multiple sessions, with members initially sharing personal experiences, then examining diverse points of view and seeking common

FOCUS ON CIVIC ENGAGEMENT

A Study Circle Success Story

Indianapolis, Indiana—Started in 2000 with initial funding and support from the Annie E. Casey Foundation and the Indianapolis Foundation, the Indianapolis Neighborhood Resource Center has engaged more than 1,600 residents in dialogue on a variety of issues, including building strong neighborhoods, child development, public safety, creating a community vision, and youth programs. Over the years, the center's dialogue-to-change efforts have led to a number of outcomes:

- A summer arts and urban farming program for elementary and high school students.
- A group working with city officials to address flooding and sewer issues in a neighborhood.
- A reading room with mentoring and tutoring services at a local elementary school to help students improve their reading skills.
- A sign contest that inspired children to create a new community identity for their neighborhood.
- Other action projects included billboards with news about various neighborhoods at bus shelters throughout the city, a newcomer's resource guide to one neighborhood, and a program to bring youth and senior citizens together to get to know each other and share stories of their neighborhood.

Source: "Profiles of Successful Study Circles Programs Strengthening Neighborhoods," www.everyday-democracy.org/en/Article.295.aspx (accessed June 5, 2009).

ground (while respecting individual differences). Ultimately, the goal is to devise creative strategies for action. Facilitators remind group members that they *can* make a difference.

Individual study circles are often part of a community-wide effort in which a number of study circles meet simultaneously to address an issue of common concern. These groups contain men and women of all ethnic backgrounds and income levels. They also involve individuals and organizations from different sectors of the community, such as the Chamber of Commerce, the faith community, the media, local government, the United Way, the police department, the YMCA, the Urban League, and various neighborhood associations. Each brings unique tools, knowledge, and grassroots connections to the partnership.

Community-wide study circles are designed to involve the whole community in public dialogue and problem solving. At the end of the process, members of different study circles assemble in a community-wide meeting in which they learn how others are working to make a difference. They may begin to discern how their contribution might fit into the larger picture. Some groups may decide to join forces and work together, whereas others will choose to remain independent. In either case, everyone has the chance to exchange ideas with public officials and other community members about public policy and discover ways to collaborate.[25]

Town Hall Meetings

Traditionally, a **town hall meeting** is a gathering where the citizens of an entire geographic area are invited to deliberate over administrative, political, or legislative issues. Typically, everyone in the community is invited to attend, voice their concerns and opinions, and hear responses from public figures and elected officials.

The town hall meeting is a kind of democratic forum that has been used in the United States since the 1600s. Early town meetings brought citizens together to discuss and vote on policies and budgets for their community. Today, however, town hall meetings are often forums for people to state their views but are not truly deliberative forums, where ordinary citizens decide on policies. U.S. politicians now commonly hold what they call "town hall meetings" as campaign events. In 2008, Senators John McCain and Barack Obama both staged town hall meetings as part of their presidential campaigns. Following the election, President Obama has continued to conduct these meetings in the United States and around the globe. In some cases, he has used the Internet to engage citizens from around the country—responding to questions from a live audience and also addressing questions submitted by thousands of citizens who "tune in" and cast their votes on the most critical issues facing the nation.[26]

During the summer of 2009, bitter divisions over an overhaul of the health care system resulted in angry confrontations at town hall meetings across the country. Members of Congress were "shouted down, hanged in effigy, and taunted by crowds"[27] as they attempted to engage citizens in dialogue about the proposed reforms. In several cities, noisy demonstrations led to fistfights, arrests, and even injuries. Although a few representatives claimed to enjoy the lively debate, many appeared to agree with the media's portrayals of the protests as "town brawls." When Representative John D. Dingell, a veteran Democrat, was shouted down during a town hall meeting in Michigan, he lashed out against those trying to "demagogue the discussion."[28] Democratic Representative Tim Bishop temporarily suspended his town hall meetings, pointing to the futility of trying to meet with his constituents when "an unruly mob prevents you from

Barack Obama calls on a citizen at one of his many town hall meetings.

having an intelligent conversation."[29] Bishop had held more than 100 town hall meetings since he was elected in 2002.

The issue of health care reform has been hotly contested for years. Yet the magnitude and intensity of the town hall protests took many by surprise. Democrats accused conservative lobbying groups like FreedomWorks of organizing protesters and training them in confrontational, disruptive tactics.[30] Republicans argued that the protests grew naturally from deep opposition to the administration's proposals. Whatever the causes, responsible deliberation could not take place, and the voices of average citizens—those with questions about the proposed reforms but no strong opinion either way—were lost in the shuffle. Representative Frank Kratovil was so overwhelmed by screaming protesters at a town hall meeting that he was unable to point out that he *opposed* the health care reform legislation. Quoting the Maryland Democrat, *New York Times* columnist Sheryl Stolberg wrote:

> And what of the Average Joe, who might want to talk to his elected representative about the kind of mundane matters that do not inspire protesters to yell and scream and get arrested? Mr. Kratovil, the Maryland Democrat, said he feared that such voters would no longer turn out for public meetings. He is making plans to hold office hours to meet them quietly, one on one.[31]

Some have suggested that the traditional town hall format may *not* be the best way for lawmakers to connect with their constituents. James Fishkin, director of the Center for Deliberative Democracy at Stanford University, argues that town hall meetings work better in smaller communities but are less effective for large populations. He points to the "illusion that a district of 650,000 potential voters can be represented by the unscientifically self-selected who decide to show up." He goes on to note that these meetings become unpredictable, "open invitations for interest groups and grass roots campaigns to capture the public dialogue."[32] Fishkin thus recommends the use of *deliberative polls*, in which a survey is used to identify the range of attitudes in a particular district *before* inviting a randomly selected, representative sample of constituents to attend one of the meetings. Trained moderators then guide the discussion so that all voices are heard and participants are asked to deliberate thoughtfully and respectfully. The Center for Deliberative Democracy has conducted more than 50 deliberative polls around the world, with excellent results.[33]

Other organizations that help communities organize and conduct town hall meetings suggest these guidelines for organizing a productive meeting:[34]

- *Assemble an organizing committee.* Make sure that the organizers will be seen as neutral or represent all major shades of opinion. The more points of view the committee encompasses, the more successful the project is likely to be.
- *Define the issue or goals.* The committee will have to agree on exactly what issues to tackle and what the meeting is expected to accomplish.
- *Attract broad participation.* Seek endorsements for the meeting from groups and individuals who have large followings in the community and span a wide range of opinions.

- *Maximize public and media interest.* The meeting will have the greatest impact on the community if it draws a big turnout and is covered by local media. Prepare and distribute a press kit that explains how the meeting could lead to resolving an issue that greatly concerns the community.

When town hall meetings are conducted with a concern for inclusiveness and respectful participation—when citizens become actively involved in working *together* to find solutions to their common problems—they *can* be a source of creative and effective solutions that win widespread public support.

National Issues Forums

National Issues Forums (**NIF**) is a nonpartisan, nationwide network of locally sponsored public forums on important public policy issues. NIF is rooted in the simple notion that people in a democracy need to come together to reason and to talk—to deliberate about common problems.[35] The NIF network has grown to include thousands of civic clubs, religious organizations, libraries, schools, and many other groups who meet to discuss critical public issues. Scholars have described the NIF process as the most pervasive model of small group deliberation in the United States, used yearly by as many as 15,000 groups.[36] Forum participants range from teenagers to retirees, from prison inmates to community leaders, and from community residents to university students.

NIF formats are varied and may include small groups, such as study circles, or large group gatherings similar to town hall meetings. NIF does not advocate specific solutions or points of view. Rather, it provides citizens of diverse views and experiences with the opportunity to carefully study an issue, consider a range of choices (weighing the pros and cons of each), and discuss those options with others. The goal is to identify common concerns and, if possible, to discover areas of agreement about the best course of action.

Although all NIF forums are locally organized, moderated, and financed, the materials they use are produced by the Kettering Foundation and distributed by the National Issues Forums Institute. Prior to a NIF forum, organizers encourage participants to read an "issue book" from the NIF Institute. Each book provides factual information and outlines three or four broad policy choices for addressing an issue. During the forums, trained moderators encourage participants to consider the nature of the problem being discussed, the pros and cons of each approach to solving the problem, and the values underlying each choice. Forum moderators are trained to maintain neutrality and to steer participants away from digressions, logical pitfalls, indecisiveness, or disruptive comments.[37] Recent NIF issue books include the following:

- *Terrorism: What Should We Do Now?*
- *Crime and Punishment: Is Justice Being Served?*
- *Money and Politics: Who Owns Democracy?*
- *The Environment at Risk: Responding to the Growing Dangers*
- *The Health Care Crisis: Containing Costs, Expanding Coverage*
- *Preparing Today's Kids for Tomorrow's Jobs: What Should Our Community Do?*[38]

These issue books all address large national and even international problems, but they also have implications for the local communities where the NIF forums are held.

Whatever form deliberations take, nearly 60 years of group communication research have taught us that specific factors influence whether they have good results.

FACTORS THAT INFLUENCE EFFECTIVE GROUP DELIBERATION

Preview. *As groups work to complete tasks or grapple with difficult problems, they may interact in ways that enhance the quality of their decisions and form strong bonds within the group, or they may deliberate less effectively because they fail to recognize some of the complex dynamics of group communication.*

A variety of factors influence the effectiveness of group deliberations, whatever the context. How groups handle these factors determines whether the deliberations prove empowering and productive for participants, or only increase their frustrations or feelings of powerlessness.

Conflict

Whenever people deliberate about important and controversial issues, conflict is likely to occur. It can emerge over differences in opinions, values, or goals, or it can result from personal incompatibilities, status differences, or cultural misunderstandings. Ultimately, conflict results from deficiencies in information, understanding, and communication.[39]

In public life, conflict is inevitable. It is difficult to imagine any community—especially in a diverse society—where there are no differences of interests or opinion. The freedom to express those differences is fundamental to the process of democratic deliberation. Deliberation is all about finding ways to live with, work through, and resolve our conflicting ideas and interests. The challenge is to find ways to make conflict *productive* rather than polarizing and destructive. Although study circles, town hall meetings, and National Issues Forums are a good start, we need to create still more democratic arenas in which everyday people can productively explore their differences.

Public controversies are often treated as zero-sum games, in which one side must win and the other must lose. Antagonisms among some may overshadow the eagerness of most people to search for common ground and to find solutions to their problems.[40] We may underestimate the ability of the community and society as a whole to come together to solve public problems. The media, of course, often play a role in this, emphasizing stories of seemingly intractable conflict over news of cooperation, compromise, and productive collaboration. The nuances of complex issues and the moderation or ambivalence of most people may be lost in the media's search for a good story.

In situations of conflict, it is up to ordinary citizens to come together and voice their interest in overcoming their differences and finding solutions. By involving large numbers of people in addressing issues of shared concern, communities can balance the voices of those with exceptionally strong opinions with voices of moderation and compromise. It is important that those who feel ambivalent or uncertain *not* be left out of conversations about such critical public issues as education, poverty, jobs, youth issues, and immigration.[41] In the absence of such voices, we may get a distorted view of public opinion, concluding that people appear more angry or more polarized than they really are.

Whether conflict functions in a positive or negative way depends on how it is viewed and managed. Although many of us try to avoid conflict, we must recognize that conflict *can* lead to enhanced creativity, a deeper understanding of complex problems, and better solutions. Conflict is not so much to be avoided or feared as *managed* constructively.[42]

Role Structure

The **norms** that develop in deliberative groups typically suggest (or require) appropriate modes of conduct for all group members. Some groups expect that all participants will have read up on the issue to be discussed and will arrive well-informed and aware of the various perspectives. Other groups establish norms of respectful dialogue or actively encourage participants to remain open-minded. In addition, individual participants in group deliberations often assume particular roles, either formally or informally. Your group or committee may elect a chair, for example, to keep the discussion on track and enforce the rules of engagement. Other members of groups assume their roles more informally, taking it upon themselves to do things necessary for the group to function effectively.

The importance of various roles and deliberative functions varies from group to group. In one group, for example, a member may use humor to relieve tension or to build group cohesiveness. Another may ask questions to elicit necessary information or to introduce the next issue that needs to be discussed. Of course, both humor and questions *can* be used negatively; sarcastic humor is sometimes used to diminish or silence other members of a group, and questions *can* be phrased as a challenge or a put-down ("What would *you* know about working in a minimum-wage job?"). Thus, it is important that you choose to play a *constructive* role in your group, helping it accomplish the task at hand and contributing to its morale and cohesiveness.[43]

Task roles contribute to the group's ability to solve problems, make decisions, exchange information, and resolve conflicts. One man who serves on the board of a nonprofit organization, for example, excels at offering financial data, explaining the budget, and providing clarification for anyone who is confused. Another listens thoughtfully to everyone, probes for additional information and opinions, and then integrates what others have said into a coherent summary. Sometimes, he offers suggestions for new ways of approaching a problem. Both of these men play important roles on the board, keeping it on task and enhancing its ability to make effective decisions.

HIGHLIGHTING THE WRITTEN RECORD

Keeping Meeting Minutes

Many groups designate a person to record the minutes of each meeting. In formal groups, such as a board of directors, a secretary is elected to perform that task, whereas in smaller, more informal groups an elected chair both runs the meeting and records the minutes. Regardless, the minutes should include the following:

- The name of the assembled group and the date, time, and meeting location
- A list of those present, those absent, and the name of the person presiding
- A brief summary of key committee reports
- A list of actions taken by the group (with or without a summary of the discussion surrounding each issue, depending on the customs of the group)
- The vote taken on each action item; for example, a set of minutes might read: "The board voted (9–3) to participate in a collaborative fund-raiser with other local nonprofit agencies."
- A list of announcements
- The time at which the meeting adjourned
- The date, time, and place of the group's next meeting

Other major roles help build and maintain the group—or help develop and sustain the interpersonal relationships within it. Group members who play these roles help others feel positive about their participation and interact harmoniously and respectfully with others. On the same board mentioned previously, one woman excels at mediating conflict and reconciling differences of opinion. She also encourages reticent group members to speak. Another man does an exceptional job of praising others for offering creative or interesting ideas. By performing these group maintenance roles, these board members encourage cooperation among others and help build a spirit of solidarity within the group.

In contrast to the positive roles, of course, some group members occasionally assume negative or destructive roles—roles that promote their own self-interests, or roles that undermine the cohesiveness or productivity of the group. One group member, for example, may dominate the conversation, with little regard for giving others their turn to speak. Another may be overly critical of others' ideas or even engage in personal attacks on others in the group. These self-serving or disruptive roles can get the group seriously off track and lead to tensions.

In general, when positive roles are enacted and shared in deliberative groups and negative roles minimized, groups have more constructive outcomes, including enhanced morale and better decision making.[44] Those who assume such positive roles are often recognized as the leaders of the group and credited with its success in accomplishing its goals.

Tolerance of Dissent

Sometimes we lose patience with the slow processes of democratic deliberation. We may want to make a decision quickly. We may feel that we have been grappling with a problem for a long time, with no agreement on a course of action. Or we become annoyed by a person who raises objections or suggests a different way of viewing things. When an individual or a small minority expresses a dissenting opinion, the majority may react with intolerance. If the majority of the group decides that it's time to move on, they may pressure those who stand in the way to fall in line.

Group pressure for uniformity can be quite powerful. One early study found that if those in the majority within a group simply state their opinions, those in the minority often pretend to agree, even if there is no pressure on them to do so.[45] Giving in to group pressure can be especially tempting for those who really value their group membership or strongly identify with the group.[46]

Situational factors may play a significant role, too.[47] In general, we are more likely to conform to group pressures in situations that are ambiguous or confusing, when other group members are unanimous in their views, or when the group contains people of higher status. We may also feel a lot of pressure when the group appears highly cohesive, or if a crisis or state of emergency exists. Under such circumstances, the group may be under external pressure to come to a quick decision.[48]

Those in the majority may use a variety of tactics to pressure minority members into yielding, ranging from teasing to hostile questioning or ridicule. Often great pressure is put on those who stand in the way of consensus.[49] How a group responds to a dissenter may depend on his or her status in the group. Groups sometimes tolerate more "deviation" from those of higher status.[50]

How should you respond to group pressures? Some people tend to "go with the flow," preferring to fit in with the group rather than risk being perceived as "making waves." Others may come to agree with the group's perceptions—either because they are, in fact, genuinely persuaded, or have begun to question the validity of their own views. Finally, some individuals simply refuse to give in. Challenging the group's authority in this way can result in a variety of outcomes, including rejection or punishment. Organizational communication scholar Phil Tompkins recounts the story of the engineer who unsuccessfully argued against launching the ill-fated space shuttle *Challenger*, which exploded shortly after takeoff in 1986. Even though several other engineers had expressed reservations about the launch, they eventually went along with the management team's decision to proceed with the launch. The lone dissenting engineer lost his job and was socially ostracized.[51]

When we tolerate or even encourage dissent, we bring a broader range of views into the discussion. Those who disagree with the prevailing view may even end up carrying the day. The *way* those in the minority articulate their views can make a huge difference. If they hope for tolerance of their dissenting views, they too have an obligation to be well informed and to debate in a spirit of respectful dialogue.[52]

GROUP COHESIVENESS As citizens deliberate in groups over time, they may develop a strong sense of group loyalty. Although **cohesiveness** *may* function positively, it can also lead to intolerance of dissent and impaired decision making. One of the most extensive investigations of the potentially negative impact of cohesiveness on group decision making was conducted by psychologist Irving Janis.[53] Janis examined the decision-making processes leading to several historic military and political fiascoes, including the decision to escalate the Korean War, the Kennedy administration's invasion of Cuba at the Bay of Pigs, the escalation of the war in Vietnam, and the decisions surrounding the Watergate cover-up. More recently, others have used his framework to examine the U.S. decision to go to war with Iraq.[54]

Janis introduced the term **groupthink** to describe how cohesive groups sometimes make bad decisions. Groupthink is "a model of thinking that people engage in when they are deeply involved in a cohesive in-group, when the members' striving for unanimity overrides their motivation to realistically appraise alternative courses of action."[55] He also pointed out that those caught up in groupthink tend to seek consensus "prematurely," cutting off full and free discussion of alternative courses of action.[56] Janis identified a number of factors that commonly lead to groupthink, including an illusion of invulnerability, an unquestioned belief in the group's inherent morality, a shared illusion of unanimity, self-censorship, and, of course, direct pressure exerted on dissenters.[57]

Fortunately, not all cohesive groups fall prey to groupthink. In fact, participating in a highly cohesive group can be a productive and satisfying experience. Much depends on the group norms that develop—whether everyone is committed to hard work and the constructive and critical examination of everyone's ideas. Later in the chapter, we discuss how the group's leader can play a key role in setting a positive climate for group deliberations.

Status and Power

Although much research on group roles has taken place in laboratory settings, enacting roles in real-life civic or professional settings is more complex. When individuals deliberate in task forces, community groups, study circles, or workplace teams, they bring to such meetings their professional identity as well as their status within the community. For example, one of the authors of this book recently joined a community group, the "social entrepreneurship" committee. The committee's task is to pool community resources and seek ways to help nonprofit organizations become more self-sustaining by starting their own businesses and generating their own revenue. The committee consists of the executive directors of several prominent nonprofits (including two that are already running successful businesses), the director of the United Way, a well-known judge, a member of the city council, a representative of the mayor's office, the president of the Chamber of Commerce, the director of the local university's Center on Social Entrepreneurship, and a few concerned citizens.

In real-life groups like this, members vary in their *status* (the value, importance, or prestige associated with their given position) and *power* (their potential for controlling resources and/or influencing others). In general, members of the social entrepreneurship committee possess high status. Still, there are significant differences. Some bring success stories to the group. Others have labored with social justice issues in the community for more than three decades. Still others bring impressive academic credentials or strong ties to potential sources of financial support. A few are new to their positions or are simply eager to get involved. Who will have the most influence as this group deliberates over time? Who will help the group advance its goals? Will those with less experience or knowledge participate actively? Much will depend on how those with the *greatest* power and status conduct themselves.

The bases of power are many.[58] Some people are powerful because they have the capacity to reward or punish. The United Way director, for example, can influence which nonprofits receive financial support from the United Way. Others—those with compelling success stories—are held up as experts or as role models. Still others have the connections to make things happen because of their positions or their political networks (the judge and the social justice leader, for example). Some have several sources of power. The center director from the university, for example, is charismatic, has resources, is knowledgeable about successful entrepreneurship models throughout the United States, and is politically well connected.

Whenever deliberative groups are composed of people with varying degrees of power and status, group members do not communicate as equals, and this inequality may serve as an obstacle to effective interaction and decision making. When communicating with someone of higher status, those of lower status often communicate cautiously, attempting to win approval by downplaying "bad" news or acting deferentially.[59] In this kind of communication climate, it can be a challenge to find out what people *really* think.

Leadership

Leaders of deliberative groups are in a position to encourage and empower others. They can insist on hearing from everyone. They can ask other group members to help with specific leadership functions (such as attending an important meeting in their place and reporting back to the group). They can listen intently, ask probing questions, insist on hearing dissenting points of view, encourage constructive conflict, and make sure they do not dominate the conversation. They can create a climate of shared leadership, shared problem solving, and shared responsibility for the outcome of the group's deliberations. Although there are many factors to consider when choosing a leadership style, most groups work more effectively when important roles are shared and the climate encourages all to participate without fear of embarrassment or retribution.

When Irving Janis studied group decision making, he looked at groups of individuals who had worked with and advised U.S. presidents. Based on his research, he concluded that leaders need to take some direct actions to make their groups healthy and effective. Specifically, he encouraged leaders to do the following:

- Assign to everyone the role of critical evaluator.
- Avoid stating personal views, particularly at the outset.
- Bring in outsiders representing diverse interests to talk with and listen to the group.
- Play the devil's advocate and ask others to take turns in that role.
- Let the group deliberate without the leader from time to time.
- Hold a "second-chance" meeting after a decision is made, asking each member to express as strongly as possible any residual doubts.[60]

The judicious use of authority to encourage the free expression of ideas and to reward initiative and innovative thinking can go far in eliminating the doubts and skepticism of less powerful group members.

As we have noted throughout this chapter, groups may deliberate in private settings as part of a committee or task force, or they may deliberate in public spaces as part of a community forum. On other occasions, individuals speak in public on behalf of a group, presenting the findings or recommendations of the group.

GROUP PRESENTATIONS

Preview. *When we deliberate as part of a group, we may also be expected to communicate with others outside the group. In doing so, we hope to deepen others' understanding of the issues we view as important. We may not view ourselves as experts. Nevertheless, we may be called upon to speak on behalf of some group that the larger community looks to for advice, guidance, or recommendations.*

Public discussions often bring together representatives from several different groups or organizations, all of whom may have some expertise or differing perspectives on the issue. For example, a recent community forum on hunger and poverty in Bloomington, Indiana, brought together the executive directors of five local agencies: Martha's House (a transitional housing unit for the homeless), Mother Hubbard's Cupboard (a food pantry), the Community Kitchen (an agency that provides free meals to those in need), the Shalom Community Center (a day shelter and resource center for the homeless), and the Hoosier Hills Food Bank (another food pantry). Each director made a brief presentation, followed by an extensive question-and-answer period with the audience.

As you gain knowledge and assume a leadership role within a group, you may be asked to speak on behalf of the group at a panel discussion or symposium. To help prepare you for this role, you should take advantage of opportunities at school to learn about the various forms and functions of group presentations. Although group presentations share some similarities with delivering a speech, there also are some special considerations when speaking as part of a group.

Panel Discussions

Group presentations assume a variety of forms. Panel discussions and symposia are two of the most common. In a **panel discussion**, participants interact directly and often spontaneously under the guidance of a moderator. No one participant delivers a long, formal speech. Instead, each speaks briefly, frequently, and in conversation with others on the panel. Here are some guidelines for preparing for and participating in panel discussions:

- *Know the group.* Find out who the other panel members are and what organizations or positions they represent. Having this information, as well as information about the group's size, will help you tentatively plan what you want to say and how much you will want to talk.
- *Obtain an agenda for the discussion.* The moderator should have some plan for how he or she wishes to organize the panel discussion. Use the agenda as your guide to prepare for the discussion. Make a few notes, although most of your remarks should be spontaneous.

■ *Participate actively but share the floor with others.* The moderator may start the panel discussion with a brief statement or by posing a question. He or she also may ask each participant for any opening remarks they may have. Otherwise, you should feel free to jump in and comment whenever you have something significant to say. Make your comments succinct and to the point. Take turns with other panel members. The best panel discussions are freewheeling, lively, and dynamic, yet also civil and inclusive. All participants should have the opportunity to speak and to get a respectful hearing.

■ *Use good interpersonal communication skills.* Listen to others attentively. If you do need to interrupt, do so politely and tactfully. Build on others' comments, if possible. Establish good eye contact with listeners while also communicating directly with other panelists. Cooperate with the moderator.

Symposium Presentations

A more formal type of group presentation is the **symposium**, in which discussants prepare brief speeches representing their viewpoints. Each group member speaks in turn without interruption or interaction. The symposium leader usually introduces the group members and provides a summary at the end of the discussion. During the actual discussion, however, there should be no need for the moderator to interrupt or intervene in the presentations, except to provide a transition between speakers. Here are some guidelines for participating in a symposium:

■ *Know your assigned role.* Understand what you are expected to talk about, as well as what other members of the symposium will be expected to do. Make sure you do not talk about subjects that others have been assigned to cover. Once you know your topic, prepare your symposium presentation just as you would any other speech.

■ *Respect group norms.* Stay within the time limits you have been given so that everyone will have a fair chance to speak. When you are not speaking, listen attentively to others. You are part of the group but also part of the audience. If possible, adapt your style of delivery to that of others in the group. If others remain seated while speaking (and you are comfortable doing so), remain seated as well. If others step up to a podium in a more formal style, you should follow suit.

■ *Maintain a cooperative attitude.* Being asked to speak as part of a group can raise competitive feelings. You want to come across well to the audience, of course, but you should never try to "show up" others on the panel. Stay focused on communicating as effectively as you can, and commit to doing all you can to make the symposium as a whole a success.

Both the panel discussion and the symposium are almost always followed by a question-and-answer period. During this time, members of the audience will not only ask questions but express their opinions. The forum is generally guided by the moderator, and questions may be directed to individual members or to the group as a whole. In either case, it is important that you anticipate responding to audience questions and that you not become defensive or quarrelsome in response to comments or questions from the audience.

In a symposium, each member of the group speaks in turn without interruption; typically a question-and-answer session follows.

Regardless of the format, certain guidelines will serve you well as you speak or deliberate in groups. In the final section of the chapter, we offer some tips for participating successfully in group deliberations.

GUIDELINES FOR DELIBERATING IN GROUPS

Preview. *Regardless of the context in which you are deliberating—whether you are part of a study circle, participating in a National Issues Forum, or serving as a member of a task force at work or in your community—there are a variety of things you can do to contribute to the success of the group's deliberations.*

A group deliberation is only as good as its participants. Informed, active members contribute to a deeper understanding of the issue or task before the group, and they also enhance the chances that good decisions will be made. Uninformed, uninvolved, or unskilled participants, on the other hand, almost guarantee the group's failure. In this section, we describe some of the ways that you can contribute to more positive group outcomes.

Prepare Carefully for Each Meeting

Every group member needs to be as knowledgeable as possible regarding the subject of the discussion or deliberation.[61] It is probably inevitable that some members of your group will be better informed than others. It is also inevitable that some will understand certain aspects of the topic better than others. But everybody has *some* knowledge or experience worth contributing, and you can always contribute even more by preparing carefully in advance of a meeting. Do your homework. Reflect on the important issues that are likely to arise. And jot down a few notes to yourself in advance of the deliberation.

Often the group's chair distributes an agenda in advance of the deliberations. The agenda sets forth the plan for the meeting—providing a list of issues to be addressed, as well as the order in which they will be discussed. Group leaders should distribute the agenda well before the meeting, allowing ample time for everyone to read and think about the issues the group will discuss. Sometimes a *proposed* agenda is sent to participants, asking if they have any additions or corrections. Examine that agenda carefully, for it can have a powerful effect on the direction and substance of the group's deliberations. If an issue is *not* on the agenda, it probably will not be addressed at all. If an issue appears near the end of a long agenda, there may not be time to discuss it fully; or the issue might even be postponed to a later meeting. Pay attention to the proposed agenda, offer input if you have the chance, and come to the meeting prepared to talk about the issues on the agenda.

Approach the Deliberation with a Collaborative Attitude

We previously noted the importance of approaching group interactions in a spirit of collaboration. Avoid making judgments in advance of the group's deliberations. Allow for judgments and decisions to emerge out of the group as it deliberates over time. Each person shares some responsibility for the success or failure of the entire group. Whenever you allow personal ambitions to overwhelm your commitment to the group, you are undermining the group's success.

Participate Actively

Every group member should take an active part in the discussion and activities of the group. If you sit back silently during group meetings, you contribute nothing to the group or to your own credibility. On the other hand, if you participate actively and make positive contributions, you help the group achieve its goals, improve your own standing within the group, and build a reputation as a valued asset to the community. That reputation may in turn lead to other opportunities to become involved in group deliberations and problem solving.

Keep an Open Mind

When working in groups, it is important that you not only have a collaborative attitude but also keep an open mind. Over the course of a group's deliberations, you may hear a diversity of opinions, some of which you may find misguided or even offensive at first. Rather than trying to "shoot down" such opinions, you should encourage the group to explore a broad diversity of opinions and viewpoints. As the group's deliberations proceed, you might even find yourself rethinking your own point of view. It is a good idea *not* to assert your own opinions too strongly early in the process. An effective group participant is one who remains open to changing his or her own mind as the discussion proceeds.

Pay Attention to Nonverbal Communication

When we work in groups, we tend to focus on what other participants are saying. But it is also important to watch how they are acting.[62] Lack of eye contact may signal disengagement, poor preparation, or interpersonal tensions. Folded arms could suggest dissatisfaction with what others are saying or the course of action being pursued. Of course, differences in cultural norms and practices should be taken into consideration.[63] In general, however, the nonverbal signs that some group members may be uncomfortable or disengaged are easy to read; as a participant devoted to the success of the group, you should take action to ensure that all participants feel valued and engaged in the group's work.

Listen Carefully, Constructively, and Critically

When others are talking, listen carefully and try to understand their points of view. Even if you do not agree, give their opinions fair consideration. Try to offer constructive suggestions that move the discussion forward. At the same time, do not hesitate to question someone who seems vague or who fails to articulate ideas clearly. Research has shown that effective groups are careful and rigorous in the way they explore ideas and evaluate alternatives.[64] Good group members take each other seriously and have a healthy respect for one another, but they are not afraid to challenge each other's ideas.

HIGHLIGHTING DIVERSITY

Recognizing Cultural Differences in Nonverbal Communication

As the groups we work with increasingly include people with diverse cultural backgrounds, it is important that we improve our skills in interpreting nonverbal behaviors. Rather than interpreting others' behavior in terms of our own cultural norms, we should be respectful of cultural differences. Here are a few examples:

- North Americans prefer to maintain a greater personal distance with other parties than do those from the Middle East or Latin America. Many Arabs and Latin Americans see North Americans as distant and cold, whereas North Americans see the others as invading their personal space.
- Americans expect others to look them in the eye as a way of exhibiting trust, openness, and sincerity, while other cultures consider this kind of eye contact impolite or even insulting. Africans, for example, are taught to avoid eye contact when listening to others.
- Arabs tend to use elaborate and ritualized forms of communication, especially during greetings. Wide gestures and animated faces may come across as boisterous, loud, and unprofessional to Americans.
- Although the Japanese are comfortable with silence and may even close their eyes when they are deeply concentrating, others (including Arabs and Americans) may perceive silence as a sign that something is wrong.

Sources: Michelle Le Baron, *Bridging Cultural Conflicts: A New Approach for a Changing World* (San Francisco: Jossey-Bass, 2003); Richard D. Lewis, *When Cultures Collide*, rev. ed. (London: Brealey, 2000).

Play Several Different Roles

Group communication scholars have identified nearly 20 different roles that group members may play, ranging from information giver to harmonizer. It is easy to get into a rut and perform only one or two roles. For instance, a well-informed or dominant participant might provide ideas and information and control the flow of the conversation. That person could develop a more balanced approach, perhaps, by *also* eliciting others' ideas or offering praise for a good plan of action. When roles are shared and participants play several different roles in deliberative groups, everyone benefits.

Focus on Matters of Substance, Not Personalities

Every group member should concentrate on substantive concerns, not personality differences. Every deliberative group has a task to accomplish. The individuals composing the group, however, are human beings who possess personalities that occasionally conflict. Severe personality clashes can damage the group's ability to find common ground and make good decisions.

As a group member, you will inevitably find some of your fellow members insensitive, uninformed, or even lacking in intelligence. Some may seem domineering or rude. Even so, the success of the group depends on *all* members, so you seek ways to overcome conflicts or irritations rooted in personality differences. In a sense, overcoming personality differences is part of your *ethical* responsibility as a member of a group.

HIGHLIGHTING ETHICS

Communicating Ethically in Groups

Embedded in all the other suggestions in this chapter is a concern for the ethics of deliberation. Here are some guidelines:

- Show concern for others' ideas, respect for their feelings, and a willingness to give them time to reflect on new information.
- Develop a collaborative attitude, less concerned with who "wins" the argument than with finding common ground and building consensus.
- Refuse to allow the group to become a platform for special interests or for your own self-interest.
- Remain as eager to listen to and learn from others as you are to offer them your opinions and advice.
- Approach group deliberations in a spirit of dialogue.
- Be willing to take extra time and perhaps put up with extra meetings for the sake of a better, more fully informed decision.
- Develop a sense of responsibility for the good of the group as a whole.
- Demonstrate the maturity to realize that other legitimate groups may have different priorities and perspectives.
- Recognize that no matter how hard your group deliberates or how well it performs, others work hard as well and have legitimate needs to be fulfilled.

In sum, the ethical group member is a good thinker, a good listener, a hard worker, and a responsible member of the community.

SUMMARY

- Deliberating in groups is common in our professional and civic lives. In deliberating, we share information, gain new perspectives, seek common ground, and make decisions.
- Organizations are increasingly team-based, and citizens encounter many opportunities to help solve problems in their communities by deliberating with others in all kinds of groups.
- In community settings, citizens often gather to deliberate about important public issues.
  - Ideally, these deliberations lead to positive outcomes such as increased civic engagement, deeper understanding of the issues, increased tolerance for opposing points of view, and enhanced faith in the democratic process.
  - Whether these positive outcomes are realized depends on such contextual factors as the facilitator's skill, participant expectations and preparation, and whether the group's deliberations have any practical impact.
  - The more citizens interact in a respectful spirit of dialogue, the better their chances of having a successful experience.
- Certain group structures and formats, such as study circles, town hall meetings, and National Issues Forums, encourage informed, cooperative deliberations with a view toward more effective problem solving.
- Many factors influence the effectiveness of a group's deliberations.
  - Learning to manage conflict constructively plays a huge role in any group's comfort levels, creativity, and productivity.
  - In healthy groups, members tend to play a variety of task and maintenance roles, with self-serving behaviors minimized.
  - Welcoming diverse views and tolerating dissent is another key factor. If majority group members pressure those with differing views to "go along with the group," their ability to make judicious decisions may be impaired.
  - Highly cohesive groups whose members are strongly bonded may be vulnerable to groupthink—leading them to seek agreement before fully exploring alternative courses of action and listening to dissenters. Cohesive groups with positive norms, however, can function quite effectively.
  - Power and status differences must be carefully managed. The burden is on those of higher status to establish an environment of trust.
  - Leaders set the tone for the deliberations and have the opportunity to foster an open and empowering communication climate.
- On occasion, you may be called on to make public presentations as part of a group.
  - Some of these group presentations take the form of a panel (complete with spontaneous interaction under the guidance of a moderator); others are organized more formally in the form of a symposium (with each group member making a short speech).
  - After group presentations are made, listeners usually ask questions. The question-and-answer period often leads to extensive sharing of ideas

and information and a great deal of interaction between speakers and members of the audience.

- In all group settings, public or private, small or large, participants should seek to be well prepared, embrace a group orientation, participate actively, maintain an open mind, listen thoughtfully, play different constructive roles, pay attention to nonverbal communication (including cultural variations), focus on matters of substance, and communicate with the highest concern for ethics.

QUESTIONS FOR REVIEW AND REFLECTION

1. Why is it important for you to be knowledgeable about deliberating effectively in groups?
2. Explain your understanding of "public deliberation." Have you ever witnessed or participated in any kind of event or meeting that you would characterize as public deliberation? If so, describe how it worked.
3. What are the benefits and potential pitfalls of public deliberation?
4. What does it mean to communicate in a spirit of dialogue? Be sure to contrast dialogue with debate.
5. Compare and contrast study circles, town hall meetings, and National Issues Forums as group structures that encourage dialogue and deliberation. What are some topics in your community that might be fruitfully explored through one of these formats?
6. How might the following factors influence the effectiveness of any deliberative group? Think of concrete examples from your own group experiences.
   - Conflict
   - Group role structure
   - Intolerance of dissent
   - Group cohesiveness
   - Norms
   - Status and power differences among group members
   - Leadership
7. Compare and contrast a panel discussion with a symposium as particular forms of group presentations. How would you prepare for participating effectively in each of these? If you have ever presented as part of a panel or symposium, describe your experience.
8. This chapter describes a number of guidelines for effective participation in deliberative groups. Which of these do you think are especially important? Why? Can you think of any others that may also matter in particular contexts? If so, explain.
9. Have you ever worked in deliberative groups whose members were culturally diverse? If so, how did cultural differences impact the way you communicated with others and the overall effectiveness of the group?
10. What does ethical group deliberation mean to you? You can use the discussion here as a foundation, and then add your own perspective and experience.

ENDNOTES

1. See David A. Whetten and Kim Cameron, *Developing Management Skills*, 6th ed. (Englewood Cliffs, NJ: Prentice Hall, 2005), 390–450.
2. Simone Chambers, "Deliberative Democratic Theory," *Annual Review of Political Science* 6 (2003): 307–26.
3. Michael X. Delli Carpini, Fay Lomax Cook, and Lawrence R. Jacobs, "Public Deliberation, Discursive Participation, and Citizen Engagement: A Review of the Empirical Literature," *Annual Review of Political Science* 7 (2004): 315–44.
4. John Gastil, *By Popular Demand: Revitalizing Representative Democracy through Deliberative*

Elections (Berkeley and Los Angeles: University of California Press, 2000).

5. See Randy Y. Hirokawa and Kathryn M. Rost, "Effective Group Decision-Making in Organizations," *Management Communication Quarterly* 5 (1992): 267–88.
6. Carpini, Cook, and Jacobs, "Public Deliberation," 319.
7. Mark Button and Kevin Mattson, "Deliberative Democracy in Practice: Challenges and Prospects for Civic Deliberation," *Polity* 31 (1999): 612–13.
8. Reprinted with the permission of Simon & Schuster, Inc., from *The Magic of Dialogue* by Daniel Yankelovich. Copyright © 1999 by Daniel Yankelovich. All rights reserved.
9. Scott London, "Thinking Together: The Power of Deliberative Dialogue," www.scottlondon.com/reports/dialogue.html (accessed July 1, 2009). This essay was adapted from an essay by the same name, published in *Public Thought and Foreign Policy*, ed. Robert J. Kingston (Dayton, OH: Kettering Foundation, 2005).
10. Yankelovich, *The Magic of Dialogue*, 41–46.
11. Some scholars have argued that setting aside status differences is a naïve expectation. See Mary Tonn, "Taking Conversation, Dialogue, and Public Therapy," *Rhetoric and Public Affairs* 8 (2005): 405.
12. London, "Thinking Together."
13. Jack Gibb, "Defensive Communication," *Journal of Communication* 11 (1961): 141–48; Sharon Ellison, *Don't Be So Defensive* (Kansas City, KS: Andrews McMeel, 1998).
14. London, "Thinking Together"; Connie Gersick, "Time and Transition in Work Teams: Toward a New Model of Group Development," in *Small Group Communication: Theory and Practice*, 8th ed., ed. Randy Y. Hirokawa et al. (Los Angeles: Roxbury, 2003), 59–75. Gersick points to the transformative potential and power of "transitional moments" in determining successful or unsuccessful group outcomes.
15. London, "Thinking Together"; David M. Ryfe, "Narrative and Deliberation in Small Group Forums," *Journal of Applied Communication Research* 34 (2006): 72–93.
16. Both Gastil, *By Popular Demand*, and Carpini, Cook, and Jacobs, "Public Deliberation," do an excellent job of summarizing the arguments in favor of public deliberation.
17. See Gastil, *By Popular Demand*, 149–60.
18. Michael K. Briand, *Practical Politics: Five Principles for a Community That Works* (Urbana: University of Illinois Press, 1999); Michael Delli Carpini, "The Impact of the 'Money + Politics' Citizen Assemblies on Assembly Participants," report to the Pew Charitable Trusts, Philadelphia, Pennsylvania, 1997.
19. Robert Wuthnow, *Sharing the Journey: America's New Quest for Community* (New York: Free Press, 1994).
20. Mark Lindeman, "Opinion Quality and Policy Preferences in Deliberative Research," in *Research in Micropolitics: Political Decisionmaking, Deliberation, and Participation*, ed. Michael X. Delli Carpini, Leonie Huddy, and Robert Y. Shapiro (Greenwich, CT: JAI Press, 2002), 195–221.
21. Button and Mattson, "Deliberative Democracy in Practice," 609–37.
22. John Gastil, "The Effects of Deliberation on Political Beliefs and Conversation Behavior," paper, International Communication Association, San Francisco, California, 1999.
23. Ryfe, "Narrative and Deliberation in Small Group Forums," 72–93.
24. Catherine Flavin-McDonald and Martha L. McCoy, "What's So Bad about Conflict? Study Circles Move Public Discourse from Acrimony to Democracy Building," *Dispute Resolution Magazine* 4 (1998): 14–17; also see www.everyday-democracy.org//en/Page.AboutUs.aspx# (accessed July 1, 2009).
25. Martha L. McCoy and Patrick L. Scully, "Deliberative Dialogue to Expand Civic Engagement: What Kind of Talk Does Democracy Need?" *National Civic Review* 91 (2002), www.ncl.org/publications/ncr/91-2/ncr91-2_article.pdf (accessed July 3, 2009).
26. Sheryl Gay Stolberg, "Obama's Interactive Town Hall Meeting," http://thecausus.blogs.nytimes.com/2009/03/26/obamas-interactive-town-hall-meeting/ (accessed June 6, 2009).
27. Ian Urbina, "Beyond Beltway, Health Debate Turns Hostile," *New York Times*, August 8, 2009, sec. A, 1.
28. Ibid., 10.
29. Alex Isenstadt, "Town Halls Gone Wild," *Politico*, July 31, 2009, http://syn.politico.com/printstory.cfm?uuid (accessed August 18, 2009).
30. Urbina, "Beyond Beltway," 1.

31. Sheryl Gay Stolberg, "Where Have You Gone, Joe the Citizen?" *New York Times*, August 9, 2009, Week in Review Section, 2.
32. James Fishkin, "Town Halls by Invitation," *New York Times*, August 16, 2009, Week in Review Section, 9.
33. Ibid.
34. See, for example, AmericaSpeaks: Engaging Citizens in Governance, www.americaspeaks.org/?gclid=CL_J2cWZ9psCFRghDQoduyhr9Q (accessed July 27, 2009).
35. John Gastil, "Adult Civic Education through the National Issues Forums: Developing Democratic Habits and Dispositions through Public Deliberation," *Adult Education Quarterly* 54 (2004): 311; National Issues Forums, www.nifi.org (accessed July 2, 2009).
36. Keith Melville, Taylor Willingham, and John Dedrick, "National Issues Forums: A Network of Communities Promoting Deliberation," in *The Deliberative Democracy Handbook: Strategies for Effective Civic Engagement in the Twenty-First Century*, ed. John Gastil and Peter Levine (San Francisco: Jossey-Bass, 2005), 35–58.
37. See Gastil, *By Popular Demand*, 116–17.
38. See National Issues Forums, "Issue Books," www.nifi.org/issue_books/index.aspx (accessed July 1, 2009).
39. See Whetten and Cameron, *Developing Management Skills*, 390–450.
40. Joseph P. Folger, Marshall Scott Poole, and Randall K. Stutman, *Working through Conflict*, 3rd ed. (New York: Longman, 1997).
41. Several books have addressed the need for communities to handle conflicts constructively. See, as examples, Daniel Yankelovich, *Coming to Public Judgment: Making Democracy Work in a Complex World* (Syracuse, NY: Syracuse University Press, 1991); *Civic Index: Measuring Your Community's Civic Health* (Washington, DC: National Civic League, 2003); and Linda Ellinor and Glenna Gerard, *Dialogue: Rediscover the Transforming Power of Conversation* (New York: Wiley, 1998).
42. Robert R. Blake and Anne A. McCanse, *Leadership Dilemmas—Grid Solutions* (Houston, TX: Gulf, 1991).
43. Kenneth D. Benne and Paul Sheats, "Functional Roles of Group Members," *Journal of Social Issues* 4 (1948): 41–49.
44. Michael E. Mayer, "Behaviors Leading to More Effective Decisions in Small Groups Embedded in Organizations," *Communication Reports* 11 (1998): 123–32.
45. Solomon E. Asch, "Studies of Independence and Conformity: A Minority of One against a Unanimous Majority," *Psychological Monographs* 70 (1956): No. 416.
46. George Cheney, "On the Various and Changing Meanings of Organizational Membership: A Field Study of Organizational Identification," *Communication Monographs* 50 (1983): 342–62.
47. Patricia Hayes Andrews, "Ego-Involvement, Self-Monitoring, and Conformity in Small Groups: A Communicative Analysis," *Central States Speech Journal* 36 (1985): 51–61.
48. For a more extended discussion of social pressure and conformity, see Patricia Hayes Andrews, "Group Conformity," in *Small Group Communication: Theory and Practice*, 7th ed., ed. Robert S. Cathcart, Larry. A. Samovar, and Linda D. Henman (Madison, WI: Brown & Benchmark, 1996), 225–35.
49. Carl L. Thameling and Patricia Hayes Andrews, "Majority Responses to Opinion Deviates: A Communicative Analysis," *Small Group Research* 23 (1992): 475–502.
50. Dennis S. Gouran and Patricia Hayes Andrews, "Determinants of Punitive Responses to Socially Proscribed Behavior: Seriousness, Attribution of Responsibility, and Status of Offender," *Small Group Behavior* 15 (1984): 524–44; Edwin P. Hollander, "Conformity, Status, and Idiosyncrasy Credit," *Psychological Review* 65 (1958): 117–27.
51. Phillip K. Tompkins, *Organizational Communication Imperatives: Lessons of the Space Program* (Los Angeles: Roxbury, 1993). Also see Dennis S. Gouran, Randy Y. Hirokawa, and Amy E. Martz, "A Critical Analysis of Factors Related to Decisional Processes Involved in the *Challenger* Disaster," *Central States Speech Journal* 37 (1986): 119–35.
52. See, for example, Andrews, "Group Conformity," 225–35; and Renee Meyers et al., "Majority-Minority Influence: Identifying Argumentative Patterns and Predicting Argument-Outcome Links," *Journal of Communication* 50 (2000): 3–30.
53. Irving Janis, *Groupthink*, 2nd ed. (Boston: Houghton Mifflin, 1982), 3.

54. See Senate Intelligence Committee Report on Pre-War Intelligence on Iraq, July 9, 2004, http://intelligence.senate.gov/ (accessed: July 19, 2009).
55. Janis, *Groupthink*, 9.
56. Rebecca Cline, "Detecting Groupthink: Methods for Observing the Illusion of Unanimity," *Communication Quarterly* 38 (1990): 112–26.
57. Janis, *Groupthink*, 197–98.
58. John R. P. French and Bernard Raven, "The Social Bases of Power," in *Studies in Social Power*, ed. Dorwin Cartwright (Ann Arbor, MI: Institute for Social Research, 1959), 65–84.
59. Dennis S. Gouran and Randy Y. Hirokawa, "Counteractive Functions of Communication in Effective Group Decision-Making," in *Communication and Group Decision-Making*, ed. Randy Y. Hirokawa and Marshall Scott Poole (Beverly Hills, CA.: Sage, 1986), 81–90.
60. See Cline, "Detecting Groupthink," 120–26; and Irving Janis, "Vigilant Problem Solving," in *Crucial Decisions: Leadership in Policymaking and Crisis Management*, ed. Irving Janis (New York: Free Press, 1989), 89–117.
61. Hirokawa and Rost, "Effective Group Decision-Making in Organizations"; Randy Y. Hirokawa and Robert Pace, "A Descriptive Investigation of the Possible Communication-Based Reasons for Effective and Ineffective Group Decision Making," *Communication Monographs* 50 (1983): 363–79.
62. See, for example, Mark L. Knapp and Judith A. Hall, *Nonverbal Communication in Human Interaction* (Belmont, CA: Wadsworth, 2005).
63. William Gudykunst, *Cross-Cultural and Intercultural Communication* (Thousand Oaks, CA: Sage, 2003).
64. Randy Y. Hirokawa, Larry Erbert, and Anthony Hurst, "Communication and Group Decision-Making Effectiveness," in *Communication and Group Decision-Making*, ed. Randy Y. Hirokawa and Marshall Scott Poole (Beverly Hill, CA: Sage, 1986), 269–300.

GLOSSARY

acceptance speech A type of ceremonial or epideictic speech in which the speaker expresses gratitude for an award or some other recognition and gives credit to those who contributed to his or her success.

active listening Channeling our energies and efforts so that we actively concentrate on the speaker's complete message.

actual example A real-life case or specific instance.

ad hominem The fallacy that occurs when a speaker substitutes an attack on a person for a refutation of that person's arguments.

aerobic exercise Physical activity that increases one's heart rate and respiration and, as a result, lessens tension.

affective language Strong, provocative language that stirs up an audience's emotions.

after-dinner speech A ceremonial speech designed to entertain while still saying something significant.

alliteration A repetitive pattern of initial sounds in a sequence of words, used to gain attention and reinforce an idea.

analogical reasoning Inferring that what is true of one case will be true of another, similar case.

antithesis Placing two images together that have sharply different meanings.

appeal to tradition A fallacy in which a speaker offers past ways of doing things as the only reason for or against doing something now or in the future.

argument A series of ideas, each one supported by evidence, used to advance a particular position about an issue.

attitudes Mental constructs that represent people's positive or negative views or feelings toward other people, places, things, or events.

backing In the Toulmin model, additional support for a disputed or controversial warrant, or general principle, in an argument.

bandwagon appeal The fallacy that occurs when a speaker urges listeners to accept something simply because so many others accept it.

bar graph A graph in which a series of bars depict comparative amounts of certain features or elements.

begging the question The fallacy that occurs when a speaker makes a claim that assumes the very thing he or she hopes to prove, thus arguing in a circle.

beliefs The ideas or assumptions we have about what is true or factual in the world.

brainstorming The process of thinking creatively and imaginatively to come up with new ideas, temporarily suspending critical judgments or analysis of those ideas.

bulleted list A list of key words or phrases, presented one-by-one during a presentation and marked by a typographical symbol such as an arrow, a circle, a square, or a diamond.

burden of proof The standards or expectations that define a "reasonable argument" in a particular situation, or the proof necessary to warrant serious consideration and further debate over an advocate's claims.

captive audience An audience that is required to attend a presentation.

categorical pattern An organizational pattern in which several independent, yet interrelated, categories are used to advance a larger idea.

causal pattern An organizational pattern in which ideas focus on causes or effects, or are arranged to reveal cause-to-effect or effect-to-cause relationships.

causal reasoning Reasoning that aims to prove relationships between effects and causes.

chronological pattern An organizational pattern in which ideas are arranged in a logical, time-based or sequential order.

citizen-critic A citizen educated to critically evaluate the claims, reasoning, and evidence he or she encounters in public deliberations.

civic engagement Actively participating in community or public affairs, not only by voting, but also by keeping up with the news, discussing issues with fellow citizens, and participating in civic and volunteer activities.

civic literacy The historical, political, and cultural knowledge necessary to participate actively as a citizen in a democracy.

civic virtue The attitudes and behaviors of good citizenship in a democracy.

claims The debatable assertions put forward by a speaker.

clichés Trite, overused expressions.

climactic pattern An organizational pattern in which the ideas being advanced in a speech are arranged so that they build in intensity.

closed question A question in an interview or survey that restricts responses to a limited number of options.

cohesiveness A group dynamic that produces unity, agreement, and peer pressure on dissident group members to go along with the majority.

commemorative speech A ceremonial speech marking an important date or event.

commencement address A type of ceremonial speech—more specifically, a type of commemorative speech—celebrating the social values associated with graduation from an educational institution.

commenting modifiers Modifiers that attempt to boost the meaning of a word but reveal nothing new.

communication apprehension The feeling of anxiety that a speaker experiences before and/or during a public presentation. (*Note:* This term is used interchangeably with *communication anxiety* and *speech anxiety*.)

connotative meaning The subjective or emotional meaning associated with a particular word or phrase.

critical listening Listening analytically, carefully evaluating all that is said.

database An immense, searchable collection of materials (indexes, abstracts, and full text) available in electronic form.

decode To interpret the verbal and nonverbal content of a message so as to give it meaning.

deductive reasoning Reasoning from an accepted generalization to a conclusion about a particular case.

deep breathing Expanding the diaphragm to increase one's intake of air, to assist with relaxation and enhance vocal delivery.

defining modifiers Modifiers that provide new, needed information.

definitions Meanings provided for words that are unfamiliar to listeners or technical in nature.

deliberating "in good faith" Debating and discussing controversial issues in a spirit of mutual respect, with a commitment to telling the truth, backing up arguments with sound reasoning and evidence, and remaining open to changing one's mind.

deliberative dialogue A respectful exchange aimed at establishing a framework for mutual understanding and a common purpose that transcends individual ideas and opinions.

demagoguery Deceptive or manipulative speech, often relying upon the charismatic ethos of the demagogue and appealing to "dark" emotions like hatred or fear.

demographics Audience characteristics that shape listeners' beliefs, values, and attitudes.

denotative meaning Meaning that is considered literal, objective, or universally accepted.

descriptive statistic A statistic that quantifies or characterizes a dataset without drawing inferences about some larger population.

Dewey's Reflective Thinking Sequence A problem-solution pattern that takes listeners through a thorough problem exploration before considering possible solutions and arguing for the preferred course of action.

effeminate style A style of speech with stereotypically feminine characteristics, such as storytelling, self-revelation, and emotional appeals.

empathic listening Listening supportively to another with the goal of understanding his or her feelings or point of view.

encode To put ideas or information into a particular format for transmission over a particular channel, as when a speaker chooses the specific language to communicate his or her ideas in a speech.

enthymeme A "rhetorical syllogism," or a form of deductive reasoning in which the speaker draws inferences from a general principle or rule, often unstated, that is already accepted by the audience.

epideictic speech The ancient Greek term for ceremonial speeches, or speeches presented on special occasions.

ethical delivery Speaking authentically, with respect for one's listeners and concern for their well-being.

ethnocentrism The belief that one's own racial or ethnic heritage is superior to all others.

ethos The ancient Greek term for ethical proof, or the audience's perception of the speaker's credibility.

eulogy A ceremonial speech paying tribute to a recently deceased person.

evidence The statistics, examples, testimony, or comparisons that we offer in support of our claims.

expert testimony Testimony based on those whose expertise and experience make them especially trustworthy.

extemporaneous speaking The presentation of a thoroughly prepared speech using an abbreviated set of speaking notes, often in the form of a keyword outline.

facts Data that can be verified by observation.

fair use The doctrine in copyright law that allows for educators, scholars, and students to use limited amounts of copyrighted material for noncommercial purposes without obtaining formal permission.

fallacy A flaw in reasoning or evidence that renders an argument logically unsound.

false cause (*post hoc ergo propter hoc*) The fallacy that occurs when a speaker assumes that because one event precedes another, it must have caused it.

false dilemma The fallacy that occurs when a speaker suggests that we have only two alternatives, when in fact more than two alternatives exist.

farewell address A type of ceremonial or epideictic speech in which the speaker bids a formal farewell to his or her hosts during an extended visit, or to employees, supporters, or constituents after serving for a time in a particular office or position.

faulty analogy The fallacy of analogical reasoning that occurs when speakers compare things that are not, in fact, similar.

fidelity Narratives that seem authentic to listeners because they ring true with their own life experiences.

figures of speech Stylistic devices, such as metaphors or personification, that heighten the beauty of one's language or make that language clearer, more meaningful, or more memorable.

flip chart An oversized writing tablet that speakers can place on a tripod for use during a presentation, interactive workshop, or brainstorming session.

formal outline Outlines in which ideas and their development are articulated completely and precisely, usually using full sentences.

gendered language Language that reinforces or perpetuates gender stereotypes.

gender identity One's sense of sexual identity, of male and female tendencies and characteristics, as shaped by social norms and expectations that vary across cultures and change over time.

general purpose A speaker's ultimate goal in speaking, whether that goal is to gain audience understanding, change minds and win agreement, motivate to action, or simply reinforce existing beliefs and values.

ghostwriting Writing a speech for another person to deliver as his or her own.

glass ceiling An invisible barrier of prejudices and discrimination that hampers one's ability to rise to the top of some organization or profession.

graphical icons A symbol, such as a dollar sign, which is widely understood and used in place of verbal representations.

group pressure for uniformity The pressure exerted by majority group members on those in the minority in an attempt at getting the minority to conform.

groupthink A group mindset that hinders the group's ability to critically appraise ideas and express lingering concerns; seeking agreement on a course of action before the group has thoroughly and thoughtfully analyzed the problem and allowed everyone to express their points of view.

guilt by association The fallacy that occurs when an advocate judges an idea, person, or program solely on the basis of its association with other ideas, people, or programs.

hasty generalization The fallacy that occurs when a speaker generalizes from too few examples.

hate speech Language that demeans or degrades whole classes of people based on their race, ethnicity, religion, or other characteristics.

hypothetical example An example that describes an action or event that could easily or plausibly occur.

impromptu speaking Casual, off-the-cuff delivery used when a speaker has little or no time for preparation.

inaugural address A type of ceremonial address given upon assuming a new office or position.

incorporation Determining if and where specific information and ideas belong in a speech.

inductive reasoning Reasoning from particular instances or examples to a general conclusion.

inferential statistics Statistics that generalize from a small group to a larger population, based on probability.

informational listening Listening in order to learn.

information literacy Understanding when information is needed and knowing how to locate, gather, and evaluate information and use it responsibly.

informative oral report An informative presentation, often technical in nature, intended to assist a group's performance or decision making.

informative speaking Speaking that aims to gain audience understanding of a theory, concept, process, program, procedure, or other phenomenon.

internal preview A quick look ahead at what will be covered under one of the main points or within a particular section of a speech.

internal summary A brief review of what one has presented under a main point or within a particular section of a speech.

internet literacy The knowledge and critical skills needed to find information and to distinguish good from bad information on the World Wide Web.

irony The use of language to imply a meaning that is the total opposite of the literal meaning of a word or expression.

isometric exercise Tensing a muscle and holding it for a short time, followed by complete relaxation of the muscle.

keynote address A ceremonial speech designed to set the tone and sound the key themes of a meeting, conference, or other formal gathering.

keyword outline An abbreviated outline that serves as a speaker's notes during the delivery of a speech.

lay testimony Testimony based on the experiences of ordinary men and women whose direct experiences make their testimony compelling.

line graph A graph in which one or more lines depict a trend or trends over time.

listening Actively attending to and processing the verbal and nonverbal elements of a message.

listening for appreciation Listening with the simple goal of enjoying what is being said.

loaded questions Biased questions, or questions phrased in such a way that they lead respondents to a particular answer.

manuscript speaking Presenting a speech from a prepared text, often in formal ceremonial settings.

margin of error The range of possible error associated with the sampling procedures used in inferential statistics.

Maslow's hierarchy A scale of human needs ranging from very basic physiological needs to higher-order psychological needs, such as the need for self-actualization.

mean The mathematical average.

median The number representing the midpoint between the largest and the smallest numbers within a particular set of numbers.

memorized speech A prepared speech presented from memory, without the assistance of speaking notes.

mental argument Mentally formulating rebuttals to the speaker's ideas and, in the process, losing track of the speaker's message as a whole.

metaphor An implicit comparison in which two dissimilar objects are compared.

mode The most frequently occurring number within a particular set of numbers.

monotone Use of the same vocal pitch without variation.

motivated sequence An organizational pattern for a persuasive speech that is based on psychological studies of what engages people's emotions and motivates them to act.

narrative example An extended example that tells a story, based either on true experiences or on symbolism, perhaps in the form of proverbs.

narrative pattern An indirect, organic organizational pattern that often uses a coherent series of stories to convey the main ideas of the speech.

National Issues Forums (NIF) A nonpartisan, nationwide network of locally sponsored public forums for the consideration of public policy issues.

noise Any interference that distorts or interrupts message flow.

non sequitur A fallacy that occurs when a conclusion simply does not follow logically from the arguments and evidence that precede it.

nonverbal communication Facial expressions, vocal qualities, and physical movements that reinforce or contradict one's verbal messages.

norms A set of assumptions or expectations held by a particular group concerning what is good, appropriate, or acceptable language or behavior.

objectivity The audience's perception of a speaker's honesty or fair-mindedness in considering diverse points of view.

open question A question in an interview or survey that allows for multiple responses and detailed elaboration.

oral style Language that is chosen with a listener in mind, characterized by short, simple, straightforward sentences and familiar word choices and repetition; generally more informal/conversational than a written style.

orator-statesman Woodrow Wilson's term for the ethical, civic-minded public speaker.

oxymoron An expression that presents, in combination, seemingly contradictory terms.

panel discussion A public discussion format in which the participants interact directly and spontaneously under the guidance of a moderator.

parallelism The use of a series of sentences with similar length and structure to signify the equality of ideas.

paraphrasing Summarizing or restating another person's ideas in your own words.

passivity syndrome Denying one's accountability as a listener and assuming that the burden of effective communication resides wholly with the speaker.

personal testimony Testimony based on your own personal experiences and beliefs.

personification A description of an inanimate form or thing as if it were human.

persuasion The chief mechanism through which citizens in a democracy select their leaders, determine their civic priorities, resolve controversies and disputes, and choose among various policies.

persuasive definition A definition that reflects the speaker's way of looking at a controversial subject.

persuasive speech A speech that seeks to influence the beliefs, values, or actions of others or "make the case" for a new policy or program.

pictograph A graph that relies on a set of self-explanatory icons to depict growth or decline over time or between situations.

pie graph A graph, in the shape of a circle, in which segments of the circle (cut into slices, like those of a pie) depict the relative size of particular features or elements within the whole.

plagiarism Taking all or part of your speech from a source without proper attribution.

poster board A type of display board, made of thin cardboard, suitable for drawings or for affixing flat, printed material or small objects.

presentational aids Visual or audiovisual materials that help clarify, support, and/or strengthen the verbal content of a speech.

presentation speech A type of ceremonial or epideictic speech in which the speaker formally announces the winner of some award or other recognition and reminds the audience of why the recipient is worthy of the recognition.

prestige testimony The views of a popular or famous person who, though not an expert, expresses a genuine commitment to the cause.

presumption In a courtroom debate, the idea that the accused is presumed innocent until proven guilty by the prosecution.

preview A glimpse of the major points one will be treating in a speech or in a section of a speech.

primacy effects The presumed impact of placing the most compelling information or arguments first in a speech.

problem-solution pattern An organizational pattern in which a problem is identified and one or more specific solutions are proposed.

promiscuous audience In the nineteenth century, an audience consisting of both men and women.

prop Visual or audio material that enlivens a presentation but is not a necessary element.

public controversy A controversy that affects the whole community or nation and that we debate and decide in our role as citizens in a democracy.

public deliberation The discursive process through which people in a democracy articulate, explain, and justify their political opinions and policy preferences to their fellow citizens.

public values Values that are clarified and corroborated through the process of group inquiry.

qualifiers In the Toulmin model, the words or phrases that indicate the level of confidence we have in our claims.

question of fact A question about existence, scope, or causality.

question of policy A question about what policy or program we should adopt, or what course of action we should take.

question of value A question about whether an idea or action is good or bad, right or wrong, just or unjust, moral or immoral.

racism The denial of the essential humanity of people of a particular race.

reasoning Reaching a conclusion on the basis of supporting evidence.

recency effects The presumed impact of saving the strongest argument or the most important information for near the end of a speech.

red herring A fallacy in which the speaker attempts to throw an audience off track by raising an irrelevant, often highly emotional issue that prevents critical examination of an argument.

repetition Repeating, word for word, key elements presented in a message.

reservations In the Toulmin model, the stated exceptions to our claims, or the conditions under which we no longer hold to our claims.

restatement Rephrasing, in slightly different language or sentence construction, the key elements in a message.

rhetorical question A question posed by a speaker to stimulate audience interest and thought, not to solicit information or answers.

saliency The level of interest or concern that our listeners have in a particular issue or topic.

sample The portion of some larger population that we actually test, interview, or otherwise gather information about in order to draw generalizations about the larger group.

sans serif A style of typeface lettering devoid of any embellishments (such as "feet") that might blur the separation between letters in a word or a line of text. A common type of font in electronic or online texts.

self-actualization needs The desire to achieve to the fullest extent of our capabilities; the highest need level in Maslow's hierarchy.

self-inventory Thinking about what you really know and care about in order to generate possible topics that are both meaningful to you and significant issues for your audience.

sensory appeals Vivid language that attempts to evoke one of our five senses: seeing, hearing, smelling, tasting, or feeling.

sequential pattern An organizational pattern in which the various steps of a process or phenomenon are identified and discussed, one by one.

sermons Religious speeches that may be either persuasive or ceremonial (epideictic), depending on the occasion, purpose, and audience.

signposts Words that alert listeners to where you are in your speech, particularly in relation to the speech's overall organization.

simile A figurative comparison made explicit by using the word *like* or *as*.

slippery slope The fallacy that occurs when a speaker claims that some cause will inevitably lead to undesirable effects, ultimately resulting in some worst-case scenario.

socially constructed The process by which roles and behaviors are judged as appropriate within different cultures with different cultural norms.

spatial pattern An organizational pattern in which ideas are arranged according to their natural spatial relationships.

specific purpose A precise statement of how the speaker wants the audience to respond to his or her message, which serves to direct the research and construction of the speech.

speech of demonstration An informative speech intended to teach an audience how something works or how to do something.

speech of description An informative speech intended to provide a clear picture of a place, event, person, or thing.

speech of explanation An informative speech intended to help an audience understand complicated, abstract, or unfamiliar concepts or subjects.

speech of introduction A type of ceremonial or epideictic speech in which the speaker's purpose is to welcome and introduce another speaker, reinforce that speaker's credibility, and provide any background information necessary for the audience to understand the featured speech.

spiraling narrative A narrative pattern that builds in intensity from the beginning to the end of the speech.

state anxiety Anxiety caused by worrisome factors in a specific speaking situation.

statistics A numerical method of interpreting large numbers of instances to display or suggest such factors as typicality, cause and effect, and trends.

stereotyping Making assumptions about someone based on such factors as race or gender without considering the person's individuality.

straw man fallacy The fallacy that occurs when a speaker attributes a flimsy, easy-to-refute argument to his opponent, then proceeds to demolish it, in the process misrepresenting the opponent's real position.

study circles Diverse, small groups that are guided by an impartial facilitator and that meet over several sessions to tackle community problems and devise creative strategies for action through respectful deliberation.

style A speaker's choice and use of language.

subscription database An immense, searchable collection of indexes, abstracts, or full-text materials compiled by a private vendor (such as EBSCOhost or ProQuest) and made available on the Internet by subscription.

supporting material Information that you present in your speech to substantiate and strengthen your main ideas.

symmetry Using a balanced approach to developing and presenting ideas in a speech, so that each idea is developed with a similar level of elaboration.

symposium A public discussion in which each group member speaks in turn without interruption or interaction, with the moderator providing introductions, transitions, and closure.

target audience Those whom the speaker would most like to influence with the message.

technical language Any language that has precise meaning within a particular field or endeavor.

temporal context Previous, current, and anticipated events that affect what can or should be said and how it might be received.

testimony Opinions, interpretations, or judgments quoted from other people, including personal testimony, lay testimony, and expert testimony.

thesis statement A single, simple, declarative sentence that expresses the principal idea of a speech that the speaker would have the audience understand or accept.

town hall meeting A community-wide meeting that brings together a diverse array of citizens representing different and often conflicting interests in an effort to find common ground or solutions to community problems.

trait anxiety Internal anxiety that an individual brings to the speaking situation; not dependent on the specific situation.

transactional communication The process of constructing shared messages or understandings between two or more individuals.

transitions Words, phrases, or sentences that help the audience perceive the relationship of ideas and the movement from one main idea to another.

tribute A type of ceremonial speech honoring a person, group, event, organization, town, or community.

values Things that we consider good and desirable.

visualization Using language that creates "word pictures" and helps your audience "see" what you are talking about.

visual literacy The ability to think critically and discerningly about visual images and depictions.

warrants In the Toulmin model, the general assumptions, rules, or principles that connect evidence to claims.

washout The reduction in brilliance of an image being projected onto a screen due to interference by light.

welcome address A type of ceremonial or epideictic speech in which the speaker formally welcomes some honored guest or dignitary or some group of participants to a convention, fair, or similar public event.

Wikipedia A free, online encyclopedia to which anyone can contribute information, and whose accuracy cannot be effectively monitored.

working outline Early drafts of your speech outline, representing your work in progress.

working thesis A tentative thesis, formulated to guide one's investigation and writing.

WorldCat An electronic catalog of the holdings for more than 53,000 libraries from around the world.

x axis The horizontal axis of a graph, often depicting the progression of time.

y axis The vertical axis of a graph, typically depicting an amount or quantity.

INDEX

PHOTO CREDITS

Page 1: © Marilyn Humphries/The Image Works; **page 4:** Alberto Tamargo/Getty Images, Inc.; **page 6:** Penn State Dance Marathon Photographers; **page 14:** Jim Cole/AP Wide World; **page 19:** Jose Luis Magana/AP Wide World; **page 26:** AFP PHOTO/Mandel NGAN/Newscom; **page 30:** Eric S. Swist/The Courier/AP Wide World; **page 32:** © Rob Bartee/Alamy; **page 39:** © Luke Frazza/Mai/Mai/Time Life Pictures/Getty Images; **page 41:** AP Wide World Photos; **page 53:** Paul J. Richards/AFP/Getty Images; **page 59:** Time Life Pictures/Pix Inc./Time Life Pictures/Getty Images; **page 68:** Bob Daemmrich/PhotoEdit Inc.; **page 79:** Chris Carlson/AP Wide World; **page 86:** Luke Frazza/Pool/AP Wide World; **page 89:** AP Wide World Photos; **page 99:** Jeff Greeneberg/PhotoEdit Inc.; **page 104:** David Young-Wolff/PhotoEdit Inc.; **page 109:** Manuel Balce Ceneta/AP Wide World; **page 116:** Nell Redmond/AP Wide World; **page 132:** Lon C. Diehl/PhotoEdit Inc.; **page 138:** © Jim West/Alamy; **page 146:** Charles Rex Arbogast/AP Wide World; **page 155:** Spencer Grant/PhotoEdit; **page 160:** Tim Pannell/Corbis Super RF/Alamy; **page 165:** PhotoDisc/Getty Images; **page 176:** Michael Newman/PhotoEdit; **page 186:** Getty Images; **page 192:** Alex Wong/Getty Images; **page 203:** Florida Times-Union, M. Jack Luedke/AP Wide World; **page 213:** Gary Conner/PhotoEdit; **page 220:** Jonathan Nourok/PhotoEdit; **page 233:** Rob Carr/AP Wide World; **page 238:** Monika Graff/The Image Works; **page 245:** Image Source/AGE Fotostock; **page 256:** Tony Freeman/PhotoEdit; **page 263:** Itsuo Inouye/AP Wide World; **page 274:** AP Wide World Photos; **page 278:** Courtesy of the Library of Congress, Prints and Photographs Division [Reproduction number: LC-USZ62-54722 DLC]; **page 282:** AP Wide World Photos; **page 292:** Time & Life Pictures/Getty Images; **page 302:** Scott Cohen/AP Wide World; **page 308:** © Ralf-Finn Hestoft/CORBIS All Rights Reserved; **page 312:** Tony Avelar, Palo Alto Daily News/AP Wide World; **page 317:** Steven Day/AP Wide World; **page 324:** Nick Ut/AP Wide World Photos; **page 327 (left):** Alan Diaz/AP Wide World Photos; **page 327 (right):** Tim Sloan/Agence France Presse/Getty Images; **page 332:** John Russell/AFP/Getty Images; **page 336:** Virginia Mayo/AP Wide World; **page 342:** Getty Images, Inc.; **page 346:** Rich Pedroncelli/AP Wide World; **page 353:** Ariel Skelley/Blend Images/Alamy Images; **page 355:** Bruce Silcox. Copyright © National Youth Leadership Council; **page 363:** David J. Phillip/AP Wide World; **page 367:** William B. Plowman/NBC NewsWire; **page 379:** Chris Pizzello/Reuters/Landov; **page 381:** Diana Walker/Time Life Pictures/Getty Images; **page 385:** Getty Images, Inc.; **page 391:** ERproductions Ltd./Blend Images/Getty Images, Inc-Jupiter Images; **page 399:** Win McNamee/Getty Images, Inc.; **page 410:** Pat Sullivan/AP Wide World; **page 426:** Provided courtesy HarpWeek, LLC; **page 429:** Courtesy of the Library of Congress; **page 432:** AP Wide World; **page 440:** Getty Images, Inc.; **page 443:** Manuel Balce Ceneta/AP Wide World Photos; **page 448:** Getty Images Inc.—Hulton Archive Photos; **page 460:** Tim Sharp/AP Wide World; **page 469:** Bill Haber/AP Wide World; **page 480:** David Young-Wolff/PhotoEdit Inc.